Course	Financial Accounting
Course Number	**ACFI 100**
	Bridgewater State University

http://create.mcgraw-hill.com

ISBN-10: 0697810380   ISBN-13: 9780697810380

Contents

Credits

NOTE FROM THE AUTHORS

This is a concepts-based / user-oriented text that encourages students to *think* rather than memorize. What do we mean by a concepts-based textbook? We mean the text stresses the relationships between business events and financial statements. The primary objective is to develop students who can explain how any given business event affects the income statement, balance sheet, and statement of cash flows. Do assets increase, decrease or remain unchanged? What effect does the event have on liabilities, equity, revenue, expenses, gains, losses, net income, and dividends? Furthermore, how does the event affect cash flows? In summary, *the focus is on learning how business events affect financial statements*.

Analyzing statement effects brings a new perspective to the user oriented approach. Specifically, the text considers *managers* as well as *investors* and *creditors* as key constituents of financial information. Students not only want to know how to evaluate investment and credit opportunities but also how to run a company. Managers frequently ask questions like "how will this deal affect our financials? Learning to think like real world managers stimulates student interest and encourages the development of critical thinking skills.

Implementing the Concepts-Based / User-Oriented Approach Is Surprisingly Easy

Instead of focusing on recording details, teach your students to record accounting events directly into financial statements. To facilitate this teaching approach, the text employs an innovative *horizontal financial statements model*. The model arranges the balance sheet, income statement, and statement of cash flows horizontally across a single line of text as follows:

The text shows students how to record events in the statements model on a transaction by transaction basis. Under the traditional approach students learn to journalize a series of events and to present summarized information in financial statements. They never see how individual transactions affect financial statements. In contrast, when students record transactions into a statements model, they see a direct connection between a specific business event and its effects on the financial statements. Most business people think "if I take this particular action, how will it affect the bottom line," not "if I do these fifteen things how will they be journalized." Accordingly, the statements model approach provides a learning experience that is more intuitive and relevant than the one provided by traditional teaching methodology.

Does it work? The statements model is a unique feature of the market-leading series of textbooks by Edmonds, et al. The existing franchise has been adopted by more than 200 colleges and universities. Since this text is a variation of an already highly successful teaching approach, you can rest assured that your students will have positive learning experience.

**Debits/Credits User
Approach**

Effects of Financial Statements over Multiple Accounting Cycles

The text uses a vertical statements model that shows financial statements from top to bottom on a single page. This model displays financial results for consecutive accounting cycles in adjacent columns, thereby enabling the instructor to show how related events are reported **over multiple accounting cycles.**

DRYDEN ENTERPRISES
Financial Statements

	2008	2009	2010	2011	2012
Income Statements					
Rent revenue	$11,000	$ 7,000	$ 9,000	$ 5,000	$ 0
Depreciation expense	(8,000)	(4,000)	(6,000)	(2,000)	0
Operating income	3,000	3,000	3,000	3,000	0
Gain on sale of van	0	0	0	0	500
Net income	$ 3,000	$ 3,000	$ 3,000	$ 3,000	$ 500
Balance Sheets					
Assets					
Cash	$12,000	$19,000	$28,000	$33,000	$37,500
Van	24,000	24,000	24,000	24,000	0
Accumulated depreciation	(8,000)	(12,000)	(18,000)	(20,000)	0
Total assets	$28,000	$31,000	$34,000	$37,000	$37,500
Stockholders' equity					
Common stock	$25,000	$25,000	$25,000	$25,000	$25,000
Retained earnings	3,000	6,000	9,000	12,000	12,500
Total stockholders' equity	$28,000	$31,000	$34,000	$37,000	$37,500
Statements of Cash Flows					
Operating Activities					
Inflow from customers	$11,000	$ 7,000	$ 9,000	$ 5,000	$ 0
Investing Activities					
Outflow to purchase van	(24,000)				
Inflow from sale of van					4,500
Financing Activities					
Inflow from stock issue	25,000				
Net Change in Cash	12,000	7,000	9,000	5,000	4,500
Beginning cash balance	0	12,000	19,000	28,000	33,000
Ending cash balance	$12,000	$19,000	$28,000	$33,000	$37,500

Unparalleled Coverage of the Statement of Cash Flows

Financial analysts are fully aware that cash flow is less susceptible to manipulation than earnings. Indeed, since the enactment of Sarbanes-Oxley there has been a dramatic increase in the use of the statement of cash flows by financial analyst. While some authors give lip service to an early exposure to the statement of cash flows, serious coverage continues to be relegated to the last chapter of virtually all introductory accounting textbooks.   This text is different. It places the statement of cash flows on parity with the income statement and balance sheet. Coverage begins in the first chapter and continues throughout the text.

In Chapter 1 students learn to classify individual increases and decreases in the cash account as operating, investing, or financing activities. They are then taught to organize these activities into a statement of cash flows. This simple classification approach enables continuous coverage of cash flows. As new accounting events are introduced in subsequent chapters, their effects on all of the financial statements including the statement of cash flows are explained. Therefore, knowledge of the statement of cash flow develops gradually throughout the course instead of being relegated to the final chapter of the text. You will be absolutely amazed at how easy it is to teach cash flow using this method.

Extensive Coverage of Financial Statement Analysis

We provide unparalleled coverage of financial statement analysis. A separate section titled the "Financial Analyst" is included in each chapter of the text. This section introduces simple ratios that pertain to the content discussed in each chapter. We not only show how to calculate financial ratios but also explain how those ratios are used to evaluate businesses. Is a gross margin percentage of 25% good or bad? Clearly, the answer depends on the type of company under consideration. While most textbooks show students how to calculate financial ratios, this text goes a step beyond by providing real-world industry data that facilitates the development of analytical skills. For instructors who desire more comprehensive coverage, the text includes a separate, stand alone chapter that is devoted solely to financial statement analysis.

Exercises, problems, and cases that reference real-world data are incorporated in each chapter. Instructions regarding access to the Edgar data base are provided in Appendix A of the text. Several exercises and cases encourage students to make judgments about companies based on the SEC data contained in Edgar. Target's full scale 10-K report is included in Appendix B of the text. The end-of-chapter materials in every chapter contain specific questions that require students to examine this annual report

Special Analyze, Think, and Communicate Section of End-of-Chapter Materials.

In addition to the normal set of exercises and problems that are typically included in textbooks, every chapter of this text contains real-world cases, financial statement analysis projects, group exercises, writing assignments and ethics cases that are contained in a special section of end-of-chapter materials titled "Think, Analyze, and Communicate." These teaching materials make implementing a user-oriented approach an easy transition.

Debits and credits are isolated in a single chapter located at the end of the text.

Many schools that employ a user-oriented approach use a bridge course to prepare their accounting majors for entry into intermediate accounting. Another option is to identify accounting majors during the last few weeks of class and provide exposure to recording procedures for these students at that time. In this case, non-accounting majors may be given some type of financial statement analysis project at the time the accounting majors are covering the recording procedures. Finally, some user-oriented instructors want all of their students to have some exposure to debit and credits. This text includes coverage of debits /credits and other recording procedures in the final chapter of the text so that the material you need is available regardless of the approach you choose. Indeed, if you choose to eliminate debits / credits from your course entirely, isolating the coverage of recording procedures in the last chapter of the text enables you to easily omit this material from your course entirely.

Established Learning Outcome Assessment Programs

Members of the author team are intimately involved in AACSB learning outcome assessment programs at their schools. We are more than happy to share our experiences with instructors who are involved in assessment programs at their schools.

CONCLUDING REMARKS

We appreciate your taking time to read this note. We encourage your questions or comments. Contact information for members of the author team are as follows:

Tom Edmonds	Frances McNair	Phil Olds
205-934-8875	662-325-1636	804-828-7120
tedmonds@uab.edu	fmcnair@cobilan.msstate.edu	prolds@vcu.edu

HOW DOES THE BOOK

Real-World Examples

The text provides a variety of thought-provoking, real-world examples of financial and managerial accounting as an essential part of the management process. There are descriptions of accounting practices from Coca-Cola, Chevron, Zales, Albertsons, and CBS Corporation. These companies are highlighted in blue in the text.

The Curious Accountant

Each chapter opens with a short vignette that sets the stage and helps pique student interest. These pose a question about a real-world accounting issue related to the topic of the chapter. The answer to the question appears in a separate sidebar a few pages further into the chapter.

Focus on International Issues

These boxed inserts expose students to international issues in accounting.

Chart of Accounts

Account Name	Description
Revenues	
Revenues	Sales of products in the ordinary course of business
ce Revenues	Sales of services in the ordinary course of business
l Revenues	Amounts earned by renting out company property
st Revenues	Amounts earned on savings accounts and certificates of deposit
end Revenues	Dividends earned from investing in other companies
r Revenues	Miscellaneous sources of revenues
Expenses	
of Goods Sold	Cost of products sold in the ordinary course of business
airs & Maintenance	Cost of routine maintenance and upkeep of buildings/equipment
ertising Expense	Cost of advertising services obtained during the period
reciation Expense	Cost of plant and equipment used up during the period
urance Expense	Cost of insurance coverage for the current period
aries & Wages Expense	Cost of employees' salaries and wages for the period
nt Expense	Cost of rent for the period
pplies Expense	Cost of supplies used up during the period
ansportation Expense	Cost of freight to transport goods out to customers
lities Expense	Cost of power, light, heat, internet, and telephone for the period
nortization Expense	Cost of intangible assets used up or expired during the period
terest Expense	Interest charged on outstanding debts owed
come Tax Expense	Taxes charged on reported earnings

Sample Chart of Accounts (Balance Sheet Accounts Only)

	Description
Assets	
	Includes cash in the bank and in the cash register
s Receivable	Amounts owed to your business by customers for sales on credit
Receivable	Interest owed to your business by others
es	Goods on hand that are being held for resale
	Items on hand that will be used to make goods or provide services
xpenses	Rent, insurance, and other expenses paid for future services
eivable	Amounts loaned to others under a formal agreement ("note")
	Cost of land to be used by the business
	Cost of buildings the business will use for operations
	Cost of equipment used to produce goods or provide services
ssets	Trademarks, brand names, goodwill, and other assets that lack a physical presence
Liabilities	
vable	Amounts owed to suppliers for goods or services bought on credit
ole	Amounts owed to others for salaries, wages, and bonuses
lities	Amounts owed to others for advertising, utilities, interest, etc.
enues	Amounts (customer deposits) received in advance of providing goods or services to customers
	Amounts borrowed from lenders, involves signing a promissory note
	Amounts borrowed from lenders, involves issuance of bonds
	A variety of liabilities with smaller balances
Stockholders' Equity	
ital	Amount of cash received for stock issued
s	Amount of accumulated earnings not distributed as dividends

Debits/Credits User
Approach

MOTIVATE STUDENTS?

CHECK *Yourself* 2.1

During 2010, Anwar Company earned $345,000 of revenue on account and collected $320,000 cash from accounts receivable. Anwar paid cash expenses of $300,000 and cash dividends of $12,000. Determine the amount of net income Anwar should report on the 2010 income statement and the amount of cash flow from operating activities Anwar should report on the 2010 statement of cash flows.

Answer Net income is $45,000 ($345,000 revenue − $300,000 expenses). The cash flow from operating activities is $20,000, the amount of revenue collected in cash from customers (accounts receivable) minus the cash paid for expenses ($320,000 − $300,000). Dividend payments are classified as financing activities and do not affect the determination of either net income or cash flow from operating activities.

Check Yourself
These short question/answer features occur at the end of each main topic and ask students to stop and think about the material just covered. The answer follows to provide immediate feedback before students go on to a new topic.

Reality BYTES

"Closed for Inventory Count" is a sign you frequently see on retail stores sometime during the month of January. Even if companies use a perpetual inventory system, the amount of inventory on hand may be unknown because of lost, damaged, or stolen goods. The only way to determine the amount of inventory on hand is to count it. Why count it in January? Christmas shoppers and many after-Christmas sales shoppers are satiated by mid-January, leaving the stores low on both merchandise and customers. Accordingly, stores have less merchandise to count and "lost sales" are minimized during January. Companies that do not depend on seasonal sales (e.g., a plumbing supplies wholesale business) may choose to count inventory at some other time during the year. Counting inventory is not a revenue generating activity; it is a necessary evil that should be conducted when it least disrupts operations.

Reality Bytes
This feature provides examples or expansions of the topics presented by highlighting companies and showing how they use the accounting concepts discussed in the chapter to make business decisions.

THE FINANCIAL ANALYST

This section of each chapter introduces topics related to analyzing real-world financial reports. We focus first on the types of businesses that operate in the real world. We also discuss the annual report that is used to communicate information to stakeholders.

Real-World Financial Reports

As previously indicated, organizations exist in many different forms, including business entities and not-for-profit entities. Business entities are typically service, merchandising...

The Financial Analyst
Financial statement analysis is highlighted in each chapter under this heading.

A Look Forward >>

Chapters 1 and 2 focused on businesses that generate revenue by providing services to their customers. Examples of these types of businesses include consulting, real estate sales, medical services, and legal services. The next chapter introduces accounting practices for businesses that generate revenue by selling goods. Examples of these companies include Wal-Mart, Circuit City, Office Depot, and Lowe's.

A Look Back/A Look Forward
Students need a roadmap to make sense of where the chapter topics fit into the whole picture. A Look Back reviews the chapter material and a Look Forward introduces new material to come in the next chapter.

Debits/Credits User
Approach

HOW ARE CHAPTER

Regardless of the instructional approach, there is no shortcut to learning accounting. Students must practice to master basic accounting concepts. The text includes a prodigious supply of practice materials and exercises and problems.

Self-Study Review Problem

These sections offer problems and solutions of major chapter concepts.

Exercise and Problem Sets

• Check figures

The figures provide a quick reference for students to check on their progress in solving the problem.

• Excel

Many exercises and problems can be solved using the Excel™ spreadsheet templates contained on the text's Online Learning Center. A logo appears in the margins next to these exercises and problems for easy identification.

Debits/Credits User
Approach

CONCEPTS REINFORCED?

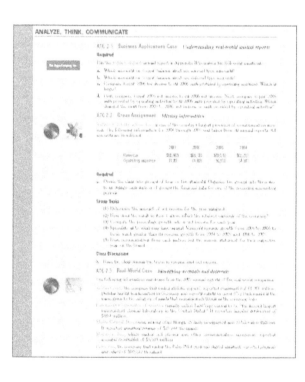

Analyze, Think, Communicate (ATC)

Each chapter includes an innovative section entitled Analyze, Think, Communicate (ATC). This section contains:

* Business application cases related to the annual report for Topps Company

* Writing assignments

* Excel spreadsheet applications

* Group exercises

* Real company examples

* Ethics cases

* Internet assignments

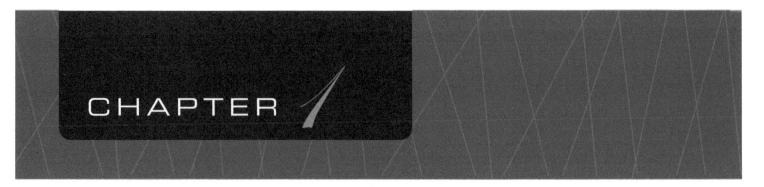

CHAPTER 1

An Introduction *to* Accounting

LEARNING OBJECTIVES

After you have mastered the material in this chapter you will be able to:

1 Identify career opportunities in the accounting profession.

2 Distinguish among the different accounting entities involved in business events.

3 Name and define the major elements of financial statements.

4 Describe the relationships expressed in the accounting equation.

5 Record business events in general ledger accounts organized under an accounting equation.

6 Explain how the historical cost and reliability concepts affect amounts reported in financial statements.

7 Classify business events as asset source, use, or exchange transactions.

8 Use general ledger account information to prepare four financial statements.

9 Record business events using a horizontal financial statements model.

CHAPTER OPENING

Why should you study accounting? You should study accounting because it can help you succeed in business. Businesses use accounting to keep score. Imagine trying to play football without knowing how many points a touchdown is worth. Like sports, business is competitive. If you do not know how to keep score, you are not likely to succeed.

Accounting is an information system that reports on the economic activities and financial condition of a business or other organization. Do not underestimate the importance of accounting information. If you had information that enabled you to predict business success, you could become a very wealthy Wall Street investor. Communicating economic information is so important that accounting is frequently called the language of business.

The *Curious* Accountant

Who owns Coca-Cola? Who owns the American Heart Association (AHA)? In addition to owners, many people and organizations are interested in the operations of Coke and the AHA. These parties are called *stakeholders*. Among others, they include lenders, employees, suppliers, customers, benefactors, research institutions, hospitals, doctors, patients, lawyers, bankers, financial analysts, and government agencies such as the Internal Revenue Service and the Securities and Exchange Commission. Organizations communicate information to stakeholders through *financial reports*.

How do you think the financial reports of Coke differ from those of the AHA? (Answer on page 8.)

CAREERS IN ACCOUNTING

Identify career opportunities in the accounting profession.

An accounting career can take you to the top of the business world. *BusinessWeek* studied the backgrounds of the chief executive officers (CEOs) of the 1,000 largest public corporations. More CEOs had backgrounds in finance and accounting than any other field. Exhibit 1.1 provides additional detail regarding the career paths followed by these executives.

What do accountants do? Accountants identify, record, analyze, and communicate information about the economic events that affect organizations. They may work in either public accounting or private accounting.

Public Accounting

You are probably familiar with the acronym CPA. CPA stands for certified *public* accountant. Public accountants provide services to various clients. They are usually paid a fee that varies depending on the service provided. Services typically offered by public accountants include (1) audit services, (2) tax services, and (3) consulting services.

■ *Audit services* involve examining a company's accounting records in order to issue an opinion about whether the company's financial statements conform to generally accepted accounting principles. The auditor's opinion adds credibility to the statements, which are prepared by the company's management.

■ *Tax services* include both determining the amount of tax due and tax planning to help companies minimize tax expense.

■ *Consulting services* cover a wide range of activities that include everything from installing sophisticated computerized accounting systems to providing personal financial advice.

All public accountants are not certified. Each state government establishes certification requirements applicable in that state. Although the requirements vary from state to state, CPA candidates normally must have a college education, pass a demanding technical examination, and obtain work experience relevant to practicing public accounting.

Private Accounting

Accountants employed in the private sector usually work for a specific company or nonprofit organization. Private sector accountants perform a wide variety of functions for their employers. Their duties include classifying and recording transactions, billing customers and collecting amounts due, ordering merchandise, paying suppliers, preparing and analyzing financial statements, developing budgets, measuring costs, assessing performance, and making decisions.

Private accountants may earn any of several professional certifications. For example, the Institute of Certified Management Accountants issues the *Certified Management Accounting (CMA)* designation. The Institute of Internal Auditors issues the *Certified Internal Auditor (CIA)* designation. These designations are widely recognized indicators of technical competence and integrity on the part of individuals who hold them. All professional accounting certifications call for meeting education requirements, passing a technical examination, and obtaining relevant work experience.

EXHIBIT 1.1

Career Paths of Chief Executive Officers

Finance and accounting **31%**

Engineering and technical **22%**

Other **20%**

Marketing **27%**

MEASUREMENT RULES

Suppose a store sells an MP3 player in December to a customer who agrees to pay for it in January. Should the business *recognize* (report) the sale as a December transaction or as a January transaction? It really does not matter as long as the storeowner discloses the rule the decision is based on and applies it consistently to other transactions. Because businesses may use different reporting rules, however, clear communication also requires full and fair disclosure of the accounting rules chosen.

Communicating business results would be simpler if each type of business activity were reported using only one measurement method. World economies and financial reporting practices, however, have not evolved uniformly. Even in highly sophisticated countries such as the United States, companies exhibit significant diversity in reporting methods. Providers of accounting reports assume that users are educated about accounting practices.

The **Financial Accounting Standards Board (FASB)**[1] is a privately funded organization with the primary authority for establishing accounting standards in the United States. The measurement rules established by the FASB are called **generally accepted accounting principles (GAAP).** Financial reports issued to the public must follow GAAP. This textbook introduces these principles so you will be able to understand business activity reported by companies in the USA.

Companies are not required to follow GAAP when preparing *management accounting* reports. Although there is considerable overlap between financial and managerial accounting, managers are free to construct internal reports in whatever fashion best suits the effective operation of their companies.

Focus On INTERNATIONAL ISSUES

IS THERE GLOBAL GAAP?

As explained in this chapter, financial reporting is a measurement and communication discipline based on rules referred to as *generally accepted accounting principles.* The accounting rules described in this text are based on GAAP used in the United States. Not all economies throughout the world use the same accounting rules. Although there are many similarities among the accounting principles used in different countries, there also are major differences. In recent years, however, there has been a concerted effort to bring the accounting standards of the major industrialized nations into uniformity, or at least, to have less diversity. This process is usually referred to as *harmonization,* but simply put, there is no "global GAAP." Examples of how financial reporting in other countries differs from that in the United States are presented throughout this book.

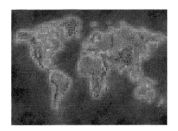

Accounting rules differ among countries for a variety of reasons, including the economic and legal environments in each country and how the GAAP in that country is established. Generally accepted accounting principles in the United States are primarily established by the Financial Accounting Standards Board (FASB). The FASB is a nongovernment rule-making body established by the accounting profession. In some countries, such as Japan for example, the GAAP is established by government bodies. In these countries GAAP is established more like the way federal laws and regulations are established in the United States.

Furthermore, in the United States any connection between GAAP established by the FASB and tax accounting rules established by Congress and the Internal Revenue Service (IRS) is coincidental, not deliberate. In some countries there is a close connection between tax accounting rules and GAAP.

---

[1]The FASB consists of seven full-time members appointed by the supporting organization, the Financial Accounting Foundation (FAF). The FAF membership is intended to represent the broad spectrum of individuals and institutions that have an interest in accounting and financial reporting. FAF members include representatives of the accounting profession, industry, financial institutions, the government, and the investing public.

REPORTING ENTITIES

Distinguish among the different accounting entities involved in business events.

Financial accounting reports disclose the financial activities of particular individuals or organizations described as **reporting entities.** Each entity is a separate reporting unit. For example, a business, the person who owns the business, and a bank that loans money to the business are viewed as three separate reporting entities. Accountants would prepare three separate sets of financial reports to describe the economic activities of each of the three entities.

This text describes accounting from the perspective of a business entity. This point of view may require that you mentally adjust the way you look at business transactions. You likely think from a customer perspective. For example, as a customer you consider a sales discount a great bargain. The view is different, however, from the perspective of the business granting the discount. A sales discount means an item did not sell at the expected price. To move the item, the business had to accept less money than it originally planned to accept. From this perspective, a sales discount is not a good thing. To understand accounting, train yourself to interpret transactions from the perspective of a business rather than a consumer.

CHECK  1.1

In a recent business transaction, land was exchanged for cash. Did the amount of cash increase or decrease?

Answer   The answer depends on the reporting entity to which the question pertains. One entity sold land. The other entity bought land. For the entity that sold land, cash increased. For the entity that bought land, cash decreased.

ELEMENTS OF FINANCIAL STATEMENTS

Name and define the major elements of financial statements.

The individuals and organizations that need information about a business are called **stakeholders.** Stakeholders include owners, lenders, government agencies, employees, news reporters, and others. Businesses communicate information to stakeholders through four financial statements:[2] (1) an income statement, (2) a statement of changes in equity, (3) a balance sheet, and (4) a statement of cash flows.

The information reported in **financial statements** is organized into ten categories known as **elements.** Eight financial statement elements are discussed in this chapter: assets, liabilities, equity, contributed capital, revenue, expenses, distributions, and net income. The other two elements, gains and losses, are discussed in a later chapter. In practice, the business world uses various titles to identify several of the financial statement elements. For example, business people use net income, net *earnings,* and net *profit* interchangeably to describe the same element. Contributed capital may be called *common stock* and equity may be called *stockholders' equity, owner's capital,* and *partners' equity.* Furthermore, the transfer of assets from a business to its owners may be called *distributions, withdrawals,* or *dividends.* Think of accounting as a language. Different

---

[2]In practice these statements have alternate names. For example, the income statement may be called *results of operations* or *statement of earnings.* The balance sheet is sometimes called the *statement of financial position.* The statement of changes in equity might be called *statement of capital* or *statement of stockholders' equity.* Since the Financial Accounting Standards Board (FASB) called for the title *statement of cash flows,* companies do not use alternate names for that statement.

terms can describe the same business event. Detailed definitions of the elements and their placement on financial statements will be discussed in the following sections of the chapter.

Using Accounts to Gather Information

Detailed information about the elements is maintained in records commonly called **accounts.** For example, information regarding the element *assets* may be organized in separate accounts for cash, equipment, buildings, land, and so forth. The types and number of accounts used by a business depends on the information needs of its stakeholders. Some businesses provide very detailed information; others report highly summarized information. The more detail desired, the greater number of accounts needed. Think of accounts like the notebooks students keep for their classes. Some students keep detailed notes about every class they take in a separate notebook. Other students keep only the key points for all of their classes in a single notebook. Similarly, some businesses use more accounts than other businesses.

Diversity also exists regarding the names used for various accounts. For example, employee pay may be called salaries, wages, commissions, and so forth. Do not become frustrated with the diversity of terms used in accounting. Remember, accounting is a language. The same word can have different meanings. Similarly, different words can be used to describe the same phenomenon. The more you study and use accounting, the more familiar it will become to you.

Assets, Income, and Claims on Assets

You may have heard "you have to have money to make money." In fact, you will need more than just money to start and operate a business. You will likely need such resources as materials, equipment, buildings, and land. The resources used to operate a business are called **assets.** A business uses its assets in order to produce greater quantities of other assets. The difference between the assets used and the assets produced is called **income.** For example, suppose a law firm pays one of its employees $400 to create a will for one of its clients. The firm then charges its client $700 for the will. In this case the law firm earned $300 ($700 − $400) of income.

The assets of a business belong to its creditors and investors.

- **Creditors** lend financial resources to businesses. Instead of a share of business income, creditors expect businesses to repay borrowed resources at a future date.

- **Investors** provide financial resources in exchange for ownership interests in businesses. Owners expect businesses to return to them a share of the business income earned.

If a business ceases to operate, its remaining assets are sold and the sale proceeds are returned to the creditors and investors through a process called business **liquidation.** Creditors have a priority claim on assets in business liquidations. After creditor claims are satisfied, any remaining assets are distributed to investors (owners).

To illustrate, suppose a business acquired $100 cash from investors and $200 cash from creditors. Assume the business lost $75 and returned the remaining $225 ($300 − $75) to the resource providers. The creditors would receive $200; the investors (owners) would receive only $25. If the business lost $120, the creditors would receive only $180 ($300 − $120); the investors would receive nothing.

As this illustration suggests, both creditors and investors can lose resources when businesses fail. Creditors, however, are in a more secure position because of their priority claim on resources. In exchange for their more secure position, creditors normally do not share business profits. Instead, they receive a fixed amount of money called **interest.**

Answers to The *Curious* Accountant

Anyone who owns stock in Coke owns a part of the company. Coke has many owners. In contrast, nobody actually owns the American Heart Association (AHA). The AHA has a board of directors that is responsible for overseeing its operations, but the board is not its owner.

Ultimately, the purpose of a business entity is to increase the wealth of its owners. To this end, it "spends money to make money." The expense that Coke incurs for advertising is a cost incurred in the hope that it will generate revenues when it sells soft drinks. The financial statements of a business show, among other things, whether and how the company made a profit during the current year.

The AHA is a not-for-profit entity. It operates to provide services to society at large, not to make a profit. It cannot increase the wealth of its owners, because it has no owners. When the AHA spends money to reduce heart disease, it does not spend this money in the expectation that it will generate revenues. The revenues of the AHA come from contributors who wish to support efforts related to reducing heart disease. Because the AHA does not spend money to make money, it has no reason to prepare an *income statement* like that of Coke.

Not-for-profit entities do prepare financial statements that are similar in appearance to those of commercial enterprises. The financial statements of not-for-profit entities are called the *statement of financial position,* the *statement of activities,* and the *cash flow statement.*

THE ACCOUNTING EQUATION

Describe the relationships expressed in the accounting equation.

The assets of a business and the creditor and investor claims on those assets can be expressed though the **accounting equation.**

$$\text{Assets} = \text{Claims}$$

Creditor **claims** are called **liabilities** and investor claims are called **equity.** Substituting these terms into the accounting equation produces the following expanded form.

$$\overset{\text{Claims}}{\text{Assets} = \overline{\text{Liabilities} + \text{Equity}}}$$

Liabilities can also be viewed as future *obligations of the enterprise.* To settle the obligations, the business will probably either relinquish some of its assets (e.g., pay off its debts with cash), provide services to its creditors (e.g., work off its debts), or accept other obligations (e.g., trade short-term debt for long-term debt).

As indicated by the accounting equation, the amount of total assets is equal to the total of the liabilities plus the equity. To illustrate, assume that Hagan Company has assets of $500, liabilities of $200, and equity of $300. These amounts appear in the accounting equation as follows.

$$\overset{\text{Claims}}{\text{Assets} = \overline{\text{Liabilities} + \text{Equity}}}$$
$$\$500 \;=\; \$200 \;+\; \$300$$

The claims side of the accounting equation (liabilities plus equity) may also be viewed as listing the sources of the assets. For example, when a bank loans assets (money) to a business, it establishes a claim to have those assets returned at some future date. Liabilities can therefore be viewed as sources of assets.

Equity can also be viewed as a source of assets. In fact, equity represents two distinct sources of assets. First, businesses typically acquire assets from their owners (investors). Many businesses issue **common stock** certificates as receipts to acknowledge assets received from owners. The owners of such businesses are often called **stockholders,** and the ownership interest in the business is called **stockholders' equity.**

Second, businesses usually obtain assets through their earnings activities (the business acquires assets by working for them). Assets a business has earned can either be distributed to the owners or kept in the business. The portion of the earned assets that is kept in the business is called **retained earnings.** Since stockholders own the business, they are entitled to assets acquired through its earnings activities. Retained earnings is therefore a component of stockholders' equity. Further expansion of the accounting equation can show the three sources of assets (liabilities, common stock, and retained earnings).

$$\text{Assets} = \text{Liabilities} + \overbrace{\text{Common stock} + \text{Retained earnings}}^{\text{Stockholders' equity}}$$

CHECK *Yourself* 1.2

Gupta Company has $250,000 of assets, $60,000 of liabilities, and $90,000 of common stock. What percentage of the assets was provided by retained earnings?

Answer First, use algebra to determine the dollar amount of retained earnings:
Assets = Liabilities + Common stock + Retained earnings
Retained earnings = Assets − Liabilities − Common stock
Retained earnings = $250,000 − $60,000 − $90,000
Retained earnings = $100,000

Second, determine the percentage:
Percentage of assets provided by retained earnings = Retained earnings/Total assets
Percentage of assets provided by retained earnings = $100,000/$250,000 = 40%

RECORDING BUSINESS EVENTS UNDER THE ACCOUNTING EQUATION

An **accounting event** is an economic occurrence that changes an enterprise's assets, liabilities, or stockholders' equity. A **transaction** is a particular kind of event that involves transferring something of value between two entities. Examples of transactions include acquiring assets from owners, borrowing money from creditors, and purchasing or selling goods and services. The following section of the text explains how several different types of accounting events affect a company's accounting equation.

Record business events in general ledger accounts organized under an accounting equation.

Asset Source Transactions

As previously mentioned, businesses obtain assets (resources) from three sources. They acquire assets from owners (stockholders); they borrow assets from creditors; and they earn assets through profitable operations. Asset source transactions increase total assets and total claims. A more detailed discussion of the effects of asset source transactions is provided below:

EVENT 1   **Rustic Camp Sites (RCS) was formed on January 1, 2010, when it acquired $120,000 cash from issuing common stock.**

When RCS issued stock, it received cash and gave each investor (owner) a stock certificate as a receipt. Since this transaction provided $120,000 of assets (cash) to the business, it is an **asset source transaction.** It increases the business's assets (cash) and its stockholders' equity (common stock).

	Assets		=	Liab.	+	Stockholders' Equity	
	Cash	+ Land	=	N. Pay.	+	Com. Stk.	+ Ret. Earn.
Acquired cash through stock issue	120,000	+ NA	=	NA	+	120,000	+ NA

Notice the elements have been divided into accounts. For example, the element *assets* is divided into a Cash account and a Land account. Do not be concerned if some of these account titles are unfamiliar. They will be explained as new transactions are presented. Recall that the number of accounts a company uses depends on the nature of its business and the level of detail management needs to operate the business. For example, Sears would have an account called Cost of Goods Sold although GEICO Insurance would not. Why? Because Sears sells goods (merchandise) but GEICO does not.

Also, notice that a stock issue transaction affects the accounting equation in two places, both under an asset (cash) and also under the source of that asset (common stock). All transactions affect the accounting equation in at least two places. It is from this practice that the **double-entry bookkeeping** system derives its name.

EVENT 2   **RCS acquired an additional $400,000 of cash by borrowing from a creditor.**

This transaction is also an asset source transaction. It increases assets (cash) and liability claims (notes payable). The account title Notes Payable is used because the borrower (RCS) is required to issue a promissory note to the creditor (a bank). A promissory note describes, among other things, the amount of interest RCS will pay and for how long it will borrow the money.[3] The effect of the borrowing transaction on the accounting equation is indicated below.

	Assets		=	Liab.	+	Stockholders' Equity	
	Cash	+ Land	=	N. Pay.	+	Com. Stk.	+ Ret. Earn.
Beginning balances	120,000	+ NA	=	NA	+	120,000	+ NA
Acquired cash by issuing note	400,000	+ NA	=	400,000	+	NA	+ NA
Ending balances	520,000	+ NA	=	400,000	+	120,000	+ NA

The beginning balances above came from the ending balances produced by the prior transaction. This practice is followed throughout the illustration.

Asset Exchange Transactions

Businesses frequently trade one asset for another asset. In such cases, the amount of one asset decreases and the amount of the other asset increases. Total assets are unaffected by asset exchange transactions. Event 3 is an asset exchange transaction.

[3]For simplicity, the effects of interest are ignored in this chapter. We discuss accounting for interest in future chapters.

EVENT 3   RCS paid $500,000 cash to purchase land.

This asset exchange transaction reduces the asset account Cash and increases the asset account Land. The amount of total assets is not affected. An **asset exchange transaction** simply reflects changes in the composition of assets. In this case, the company traded cash for land. The amount of cash decreased by $500,000 and the amount of land increased by the same amount.

	Assets			=	Liab.	+	Stockholders' Equity		
	Cash	+	Land	=	N. Pay.	+	Com. Stk.	+	Ret. Earn.
Beginning balances	520,000	+	NA	=	400,000	+	120,000	+	NA
Paid cash to buy land	(500,000)	+	500,000	=	NA	+	NA	+	NA
Ending balances	20,000	+	500,000	=	400,000	+	120,000	+	NA

Another Asset Source Transaction

EVENT 4   RCS obtained $85,000 cash by leasing camp sites to customers.

Revenue represents an economic benefit a company obtains by providing customers with goods and services. In this example the economic benefit is an increase in the asset cash. Revenue transactions can therefore be viewed as *asset source transactions*. The asset increase is balanced by an increase in the retained earnings section of stockholders' equity because producing revenue increases the amount of earnings that can be retained in the business.

	Assets			=	Liab.	+	Stockholders' Equity			
	Cash	+	Land	=	N. Pay.	+	Com. Stk.	+	Ret. Earn.	Acct. Title
Beginning balances	20,000	+	500,000	=	400,000	+	120,000	+	NA	
Acquired cash by earning revenue	85,000	+	NA	=	NA	+	NA	+	85,000	Revenue
Ending balances	105,000	+	500,000	=	400,000	+	120,000	+	85,000	

Note carefully that the $85,000 ending balance in the retained earnings column is *not* in the Retained Earnings account. It is in the Revenue account. It will be transferred to the Retained Earnings account at the end of the accounting period. Transferring the Revenue account balance to the Retained Earnings account is part of a process called *closing the accounts.*

Asset Use Transactions

Businesses use assets for a variety of purposes. For example, assets may be used to pay off liabilities or they may be transferred to owners. Assets may also be used in the process of generating earnings. All **asset use transactions** decrease the total amount of assets and the total amount of claims on assets (liabilities or stockholders' equity).

EVENT 5   RCS paid $50,000 cash for operating expenses such as salaries, rent, and interest. (RCS could establish a separate account for each type of expense. However, the management team does not currently desire this level of detail. Remember, the number of accounts a business uses depends on the level of information managers need to make decisions.)

In the normal course of generating revenue, a business consumes various assets and services. The assets and services consumed to generate revenue are called **expenses.**

Revenue results from providing goods and services to customers. In exchange, the business acquires assets from its customers. Since the owners bear the ultimate risk and reap the rewards of operating the business, revenues increase stockholders' equity (retained earnings), and expenses decrease retained earnings. In this case, the asset account, Cash, decreased. This decrease is balanced by a decrease in the retained earnings section of stockholders' equity because expenses decrease the amount of earnings retained in the business.

	Assets			=	Liab.	+			Stockholders' Equity		
	Cash	+	Land	=	N. Pay.	+	Com. Stk.	+	Ret. Earn.	Acct. Title
Beginning balances	105,000	+	500,000	=	400,000	+	120,000	+	85,000	
Used cash to pay expenses	(50,000)	+	NA	=	NA	+	NA	+	(50,000)	Expense
Ending balances	55,000	+	500,000	=	400,000	+	120,000	+	35,000	

Like revenues, expenses are not recorded directly into the Retained Earnings account. The $50,000 of expense is recorded in the Expense account. It will be transferred to the Retained Earnings account at the end of the accounting period as part of the closing process. The $35,000 ending balance in the retained earnings column shows what would be in the Retained Earnings account after the balances in the Revenue and Expense accounts have been closed. The current balance in the Retained Earnings account is zero.

EVENT 6   RCS paid $4,000 in cash dividends to its owners.

To this point the enterprise's total assets and equity have increased by $35,000 ($85,000 of revenue − $50,000 of expense) as a result of its earnings activities. RCS can keep the additional assets in the business or transfer them to the owners. If a business transfers some or all of its earned assets to owners, the transfer is frequently called a **dividend.** Since assets distributed to stockholders are not used for the purpose of generating revenue, *dividends are not expenses.* Furthermore, dividends are a transfer of *earnings,* not a return of the assets acquired from the issue of common stock.

	Assets			=	Liab.	+			Stockholders' Equity		
	Cash	+	Land	=	N. Pay.	+	Com. Stk.	+	Ret. Earn.	Acct. Title
Beginning balances	55,000	+	500,000	=	400,000	+	120,000	+	35,000	
Used cash to pay dividends	(4,000)	+	NA	=	NA	+	NA	+	(4,000)	Dividends
Ending balances	51,000	+	500,000	=	400,000	+	120,000	+	31,000	

Like revenues and expenses, dividends are not recorded directly into the Retained Earnings account. The $4,000 dividend is recorded in the Dividends account. It will be transferred to retained earnings at the end of the accounting period as part of the closing process. The $31,000 ending balance in the retained earnings column shows what would be in the Retained Earnings account after the balances in the Revenue, Expense, and Dividend accounts have been closed. The current balance in the Retained Earnings account is zero.

HISTORICAL COST AND RELIABILITY CONCEPTS

EVENT 7　**The land that RCS paid $500,000 to purchase had an appraised market value of $525,000 on December 31, 2010.**

Although the appraised value of the land is higher than the original cost, RCS will not increase the amount recorded in its accounting records above the land's $500,000 historical cost. In general, accountants do not recognize changes in market value. The **historical cost concept** requires that most assets be reported at the amount paid for them (their historical cost) regardless of increases in market value.

　　Surely investors would rather know what an asset is worth instead of how much it originally cost. So why do accountants maintain records and report financial information based on historical cost? Accountants rely heavily on the **reliability concept.** Information is reliable if it can be independently verified. For example, two people looking at the legal documents associated with RCS's land purchase will both conclude that RCS paid $500,000 for the land. That historical cost is a verifiable fact. The appraised value, in contrast, is an opinion. Even two persons who are experienced appraisers are not likely to come up with the same amount for the land's market value. Accountants do not report market values in financial statements because such values are not reliable.

LO 6

Explain how the historical cost and reliability concepts affect amounts reported in financial statements.

RECAP: TYPES OF TRANSACTIONS

The transactions described above have each been classified into one of three categories: (1) asset source transactions; (2) asset exchange transactions; and (3) asset use transactions. A fourth category, claims exchange transactions, is introduced in a later chapter. In summary

LO 7

Classify business events as asset source, use, or exchange transactions.

■ **Asset source transactions** increase the total amount of assets and increase the total amount of claims. In its first year of operation, RCS acquired assets from three sources: first, from owners (Event 1); next, by borrowing (Event 2); and finally, through earnings activities (Event 4).

■ **Asset exchange transactions** decrease one asset and increase another asset. The total amount of assets is unchanged by asset exchange transactions. RCS experienced one asset exchange transaction; it used cash to purchase land (Event 3).

■ **Asset use transactions** decrease the total amount of assets and the total amount of claims. RCS used assets to pay expenses (Event 5) and to pay dividends (Event 6).

As you proceed through this text, practice classifying transactions into one of the four categories. Businesses engage in thousands of transactions every day. It is far more effective to learn how to classify the transactions into meaningful categories than to attempt to memorize the effects of thousands of transactions.

SUMMARY OF TRANSACTIONS

The complete collection of a company's accounts is called the **general ledger.** The general ledger account information for RCS's 2010 accounting period is shown in Exhibit 1.2. The revenue, expense, and dividend account data appear in the retained earnings column. These account titles are shown immediately to the right of the dollar amounts listed in the retained earnings column. To help you review RCS's general ledger, the business events that the company experienced during 2010 are summarized below.

1.　RCS issued common stock, acquiring $120,000 cash from its owners.
2.　RCS borrowed $400,000 cash.
3.　RCS paid $500,000 cash to purchase land.

EXHIBIT 1.2

General Ledger Accounts Organized Under the Accounting Equation

Event No.	Assets			=	Liabilities	+	Stockholders' Equity			Other Account Titles
	Cash	+	Land	=	Notes Payable	+	Common Stock	+	Retained Earnings	
Beg. bal.	0		0		0		0		0	
1.	120,000						120,000			
2.	400,000				400,000					
3.	(500,000)		500,000							
4.	85,000								85,000	Revenue
5.	(50,000)								(50,000)	Expense
6.	(4,000)								(4,000)	Dividend
7.	NA		NA		NA		NA		NA	
	51,000	+	500,000	=	400,000	+	120,000	+	31,000	

4. RCS received $85,000 cash from earning revenue.
5. RCS paid $50,000 cash for expenses.
6. RCS paid dividends of $4,000 cash to the owners.
7. The land that RCS paid $500,000 to purchase had an appraised market value of $525,000 on December 31, 2010.

As indicated earlier, accounting information is normally presented to external users in four general-purpose financial statements. The information in the ledger accounts is used to prepare these financial statements. The data in the above ledger accounts are color coded to help you understand the source of information in the financial statements. The numbers in *green* are used in the *statement of cash flows*. The numbers in *red* are used to prepare the *balance sheet*. Finally, the numbers in *blue* are used to prepare the *income statement*. The numbers reported in the statement of changes in stockholders' equity have not been color coded because they appear in more than one statement. The next section explains how the information in the accounts is presented in financial statements.

PREPARING FINANCIAL STATEMENTS

Use general ledger account information to prepare four financial statements.

The financial statements for RCS are shown in Exhibit 1.3. The information used to prepare these statements was drawn from the ledger accounts. Information in one statement may relate to information in another statement. For example, the amount of net income reported on the income statement also appears on the statement of changes in stockholders' equity. Accountants use the term **articulation** to describe the interrelationships among the various elements of the financial statements. The key articulated relationships in RCS's financial statements are highlighted with arrows (Exhibit 1.3). A description of each statement follows.

Income Statement and the Matching Concept

Businesses consume assets and services in order to generate revenues, thereby creating greater quantities of other assets. For example, RCS may pay cash (asset use) to an employee who maintains the camp sites. Maintaining the sites is necessary in order to collect cash (obtain assets) from customers. The **income statement** *matches* asset

EXHIBIT 1.3	Financial Statements

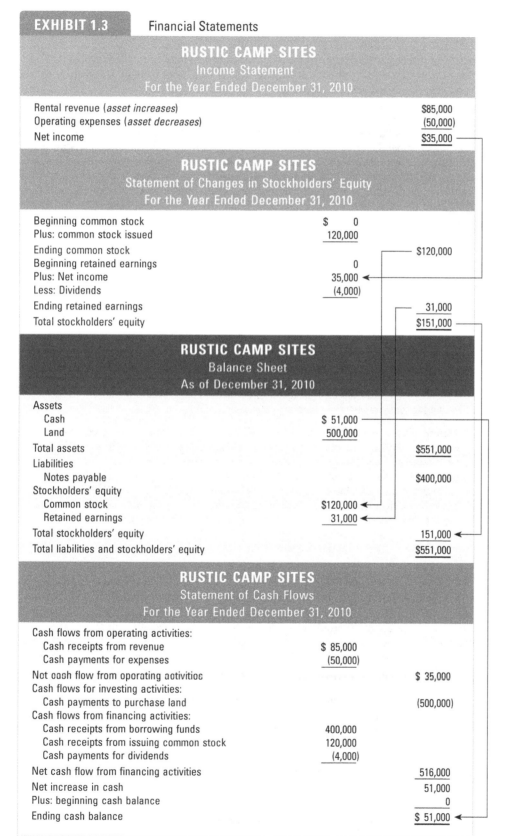

RUSTIC CAMP SITES
Income Statement
For the Year Ended December 31, 2010

Rental revenue (*asset increases*)	$85,000
Operating expenses (*asset decreases*)	(50,000)
Net income	$35,000

RUSTIC CAMP SITES
Statement of Changes in Stockholders' Equity
For the Year Ended December 31, 2010

Beginning common stock	$ 0	
Plus: common stock issued	120,000	
Ending common stock		$120,000
Beginning retained earnings	0	
Plus: Net income	35,000	
Less: Dividends	(4,000)	
Ending retained earnings		31,000
Total stockholders' equity		$151,000

RUSTIC CAMP SITES
Balance Sheet
As of December 31, 2010

Assets		
Cash	$ 51,000	
Land	500,000	
Total assets		$551,000
Liabilities		
Notes payable		$400,000
Stockholders' equity		
Common stock	$120,000	
Retained earnings	31,000	
Total stockholders' equity		151,000
Total liabilities and stockholders' equity		$551,000

RUSTIC CAMP SITES
Statement of Cash Flows
For the Year Ended December 31, 2010

Cash flows from operating activities:		
Cash receipts from revenue	$ 85,000	
Cash payments for expenses	(50,000)	
Net cash flow from operating activities		$ 35,000
Cash flows for investing activities:		
Cash payments to purchase land		(500,000)
Cash flows from financing activities:		
Cash receipts from borrowing funds	400,000	
Cash receipts from issuing common stock	120,000	
Cash payments for dividends	(4,000)	
Net cash flow from financing activities		516,000
Net increase in cash		51,000
Plus: beginning cash balance		0
Ending cash balance		$ 51,000

increases from operating a business with asset decreases from operating the business.[4] Asset increases resulting from providing goods and services to customers in the course of normal operations are called *revenues*. Asset decreases resulting from consuming assets and services for the purpose of generating revenues are called *expenses*. If revenues are greater than expenses, the difference is called **net income.** If expenses exceed revenues, the difference is a **net loss.**

The income statement in Exhibit 1.3 indicates that RCS has earned more assets than it has used. The statement shows that RCS has increased its assets by $35,000 (net income) as a result of operating its business. Observe the phrase *For the Year Ended December 31, 2010* in the heading of the income statement. Income is measured for a span of time called the **accounting period.** While accounting periods of one year are normal for external financial reporting, income can be measured weekly, monthly, quarterly, semiannually, or over any other desired time period. Notice that the cash RCS paid to its stockholders (dividends) is not reported as expense. The decrease in assets for dividend payments is not incurred for the purpose of generating revenue. Instead, dividends are transfers of wealth to the owners of the business. Dividend payments are not reported on the income statement.

CHECK *Yourself* 1.3

Mahoney, Inc., was started when it issued common stock to its owners for $300,000. During its first year of operation Mahoney received $523,000 cash for services provided to customers. Mahoney paid employees $233,000 cash. Advertising costs paid in cash amounted to $102,000. Other cash operating expenses amounted to $124,000. Finally, Mahoney paid a $25,000 cash dividend to its stockholders. What amount of net income would Mahoney report on its earnings statement?

Answer The amount of net income is $64,000 ($523,000 Revenue − $233,000 Salary Expense − $102,000 Advertising Expense − $124,000 Other Operating Expenses). The cash received from issuing stock is not revenue because it was not acquired from earnings activities. In other words, Mahoney did not work (perform services) for this money; it was contributed by owners of the business. The dividends are not expenses because the decrease in cash was not incurred for the purpose of generating revenue. Instead, the dividends represent a transfer of wealth to the owners.

Statement of Changes in Stockholders' Equity

The **statement of changes in stockholders' equity** explains the effects of transactions on stockholders' equity during the accounting period. It starts with the beginning balance in the common stock account. In the case of RCS, the beginning balance in the common stock account is zero because the company did not exist before the 2010 accounting period. The $120,000 of stock issued during the accounting period is added to the beginning balance to determine the ending balance in the common stock account.

In addition to reporting the changes in common stock, the statement describes the changes in retained earnings for the accounting period. RCS had no beginning balance in retained earnings. During the period, the company earned $35,000 and paid $4,000 in dividends to the stockholders, producing an ending retained earning balance of $31,000 ($0 + $35,000 − $4,000). Since equity consists of common stock and retained earnings, the ending total equity balance is $151,000 ($120,000 + $31,000).

---

[4]This description of the income statement is expanded in subsequent chapters as additional relationships among the elements of financial statements are introduced.

This statement is also dated with the phrase *For the Year Ended December 31, 2010,* because it describes what happened to stockholders' equity during 2010.

Balance Sheet

The **balance sheet** draws its name from the accounting equation. Total assets balances with (equals) claims (liabilities and stockholders' equity) on those assets. The balance sheet for RCS is shown in Exhibit 1.3. Note that total claims (liabilities plus stockholders' equity) are equal to total assets ($551,000 = $551,000).

Note the order of the assets in the balance sheet. Cash appears first, followed by land. Assets are displayed in the balance sheet based on their level of **liquidity.** This means that assets are listed in order of how rapidly they will be converted to cash. Finally, note that the balance sheet is dated with the phrase *As of December 31, 2010,* indicating that it describes the company's financial condition on the last day of the accounting period.

CHECK *Yourself* 1.4

To gain a clear understanding of the balance sheet, try to create one that describes your personal financial condition. First list your assets, then your liabilities. Determine the amount of your equity by subtracting your liabilities from your assets.

Answer Answers for this exercise will vary depending on the particular assets and liabilities each student identifies. Common student assets include automobiles, computers, stereos, TVs, phones, CD players, clothes, and textbooks. Common student liabilities include car loans, mortgages, student loans, and credit card debt. The difference between the assets and the liabilities is the equity.

Statement of Cash Flows

The **statement of cash flows** explains how a company obtained and used *cash* during the accounting period. Receipts of cash are called *cash inflows,* and payments are *cash outflows.* The statement classifies cash receipts (inflows) and payments (outflows) into three categories: financing activities, investing activities, and operating activities.

Businesses normally start with an idea. Implementing the idea usually requires cash. For example, suppose you decide to start an apartment rental business. First, you would need cash to finance acquiring the apartments. Acquiring cash to start a business is a financing activity. **Financing activities** include obtaining cash (inflow) from owners or paying cash (outflow) to owners (dividends). Financing activities also include borrowing cash (inflow) from creditors and repaying the principal (outflow) to creditors. Because interest on borrowed money is an expense, however, cash paid to creditors for interest is reported in the operating activities section of the statement of cash flows.

After obtaining cash from financing activities, you would invest the money by building or buying apartments. **Investing activities** involve paying cash (outflow) to purchase productive assets or receiving cash (inflow) from selling productive assets. **Productive assets** are sometimes called long-term assets because businesses normally use them for more than one year. Cash outflows to purchase land or cash inflows from selling a building are examples of investing activities.

After investing in the productive assets (apartments), you would engage in operating activities. **Operating activities** involve receiving cash (inflow) from revenue and paying cash (outflow) for expenses. Note that cash spent to purchase short-term assets such as office supplies is reported in the operating activities section because the office supplies would likely be used (expensed) within a single accounting period.

EXHIBIT 1.4

Classification Scheme for Statement of Cash Flows

Cash flows from operating activities:
  Cash receipts (inflows) from revenue (including interest)
  Cash payments (outflows) for expenses (including interest)

Cash flows from investing activities:
  Cash receipts (inflows) from the sale of long-term assets
  Cash payments (outflows) for the purchase of long-term assets

Cash flows from financing activities:
  Cash receipts (inflows) from borrowing funds
  Cash receipts (inflows) from issuing common stock
  Cash payments (outflows) to repay borrowed funds
  Cash payments (outflows) for dividends

The primary cash inflows and outflows related to the types of business activity introduced in this chapter are summarized in Exhibit 1.4. The exhibit will be expanded as additional types of events are introduced in subsequent chapters.

The statement of cash flows for Rustic Camp Sites in Exhibit 1.3 shows that the amount of cash increased by $51,000 during the year. The beginning balance in the Cash account was zero; adding the $51,000 increase to the beginning balance results in a $51,000 ending balance. Notice that the $51,000 ending cash balance on the statement of cash flows is the same as the amount of cash reported in the asset section on the December 31 year-end balance sheet. Also, note that the statement of cash flows is dated with the phrase *For the Year Ended December 31, 2010,* because it describes what happened to cash over the span of the year.

CHECK *Yourself* 1.5

Classify each of the following cash flows as an operating activity, investing activity, or financing activity.

1. Acquired cash from owners.
2. Borrowed cash from creditors.
3. Paid cash to purchase land.
4. Earned cash revenue.
5. Paid cash for salary expenses.
6. Paid cash dividend.
7. Paid cash for interest.

Answer   (1) financing activity; (2) financing activity; (3) investing activity; (4) operating activity; (5) operating activity; (6) financing activity; (7) operating activity.

The Closing Process

As previously indicated, transaction data are recorded in the Revenue, Expense, and Dividend accounts during the accounting period. At the end of the accounting period the balances in these accounts are transferred to the Retained Earnings account. The process of transferring the balances is called **closing.** Since the Revenue, Expense, and Dividend accounts are closed each period, they are called **temporary accounts.** At the beginning of each new accounting period, the temporary accounts have zero balances. The Retained Earnings account carries forward from one accounting period to the next. Since this account is not closed, it is called a **permanent account.**

CHECK *Yourself* 1.6

After closing on December 31, 2009, Walston Company had $4,600 of assets, $2,000 of liabilities, and $700 of common stock. During January of 2010, Walston earned $750 of revenue and incurred $300 of expense. Walston closes it books each year on December 31.

1. Determine the balance in the Retained Earnings account as of December 31, 2009.
2. Determine the balance in the Retained Earnings account as of January 1, 2010.
3. Determine the balance in the Retained Earnings account as of January 31, 2010.

Answer

1. Assets = Liabilities + Common Stock + Retained Earnings

   $4,600 = $2,000 + $700 + Retained Earnings

   Retained Earnings = $1,900

2. The balance in the Retained Earnings account on January 1, 2010, is the same as it was on December 31, 2009. This year's ending balance becomes next year's beginning balance. Therefore, the balance in the Retained Earnings account on January 1, 2010, is $1,900.

3. The balance in the Retained Earnings account on January 31, 2010, is still $1,900. The revenue earned and expenses incurred during January are not recorded in the Retained Earnings account. Revenue is recorded in a Revenue account and expenses are recorded in an Expense account during the accounting period. The balances in the Revenue and Expense accounts are transferred to the Retained Earnings account during the closing process at the end of the accounting period (December 31, 2010).

THE HORIZONTAL FINANCIAL STATEMENTS MODEL

Financial statements are the scorecard for business activity. If you want to succeed in business, you must know how your business decisions affect your company's financial statements. This text uses a **horizontal statements model** to help you understand how business events affect financial statements. This model shows a set of financial statements horizontally across a single page of paper. The balance sheet is displayed first, adjacent to the income statement, and then the statement of cash flows. Because the effects of equity transactions can be analyzed by referring to certain balance sheet columns, and because of limited space, the statement of changes in stockholders' equity is not shown in the horizontal statements model.

Record business events using a horizontal financial statements model.

The model frequently uses abbreviations. For example, activity classifications in the statement of cash flows are identified using OA for operating activities, IA for investing activities, and FA for financing activities. NC designates the net change in cash. The statements model uses "NA" when an account is not affected by an event. The background of the *balance sheet* is red, that of the *income statement* is blue, and that of the *statement of cash flows* is green. To demonstrate the usefulness of the horizontal statements model, we use it to display the seven accounting events that RCS experienced during its first year of operation (2010).

1. RCS acquired $120,000 cash from the owners.
2. RCS borrowed $400,000 cash.
3. RCS paid $500,000 cash to purchase land.

4. RCS received $85,000 cash from earning revenue.
5. RCS paid $50,000 cash for expenses.
6. RCS paid $4,000 of cash dividends to the owners.
7. The market value of the land owned by RCS was appraised at $525,000 on December 31, 2010.

Event No.	Balance Sheet										Income Statement						Statement of Cash Flows	
	Assets			=	Liab.	+	Stockholders' Equity											
	Cash	+	Land	=	N. Pay.	+	Com. Stk.	+	Ret. Earn.		Rev.	−	Exp.	=	Net Inc.			
Beg. bal.	0	+	0	=	0	+	0	+	0		0	−	0	=	0		NA	
1.	120,000	+	NA	=	NA	+	120,000	+	NA		NA	−	NA	=	NA		120,000	FA
2.	400,000	+	NA	=	400,000	+	NA	+	NA		NA	−	NA	=	NA		400,000	FA
3.	(500,000)	+	500,000	=	NA	+	NA	+	NA		NA	−	NA	=	NA		(500,000)	IA
4.	85,000	+	NA	=	NA	+	NA	+	85,000		85,000	−	NA	=	85,000		85,000	OA
5.	(50,000)	+	NA	=	NA	+	NA	+	(50,000)		NA	−	50,000	=	(50,000)		(50,000)	OA
6.	(4,000)	+	NA	=	NA	+	NA	+	(4,000)		NA	−	NA	=	NA		(4,000)	FA
7.	NA	+	NA	=	NA	+	NA	+	NA		NA	−	NA	=	NA		NA	
Totals	51,000	+	500,000	=	400,000	+	120,000	+	31,000		85,000	−	50,000	=	35,000		51,000	NC

Recognize that statements models are learning tools. Because they are helpful in understanding how accounting events affect financial statements, they are used extensively in this book. However, the models omit many of the details used in published financial statements. For example, the horizontal model shows only a partial set of statements. Also, since the statements are presented in aggregate, the description of dates (e.g., "as of" versus "for the period ended") does not distinguish periodic from cumulative data.

THE FINANCIAL ANALYST

This section of each chapter introduces topics related to analyzing real world financial reports. We focus first on the types of businesses that operate in the real world. We also discuss the annual report that is used to communicate information to stakeholders.

Real-World Financial Reports

As previously indicated, organizations exist in many different forms, including *business* entities and *not-for-profit* entities. Business entities are typically service, merchandising, or manufacturing companies. **Service businesses,** which include doctors, attorneys, accountants, dry cleaners, and maids, provide services to their customers. **Merchandising businesses,** sometimes called *retail* or *wholesale companies,* sell goods to customers that other entities make. **Manufacturing businesses** make the goods that they sell to their customers.

Some business operations include combinations of these three categories. For example, an automotive repair shop might change oil (service function), sell parts such as oil filters (retail function), and rebuild engines (manufacturing function). The nature of the reporting entity affects the form and content of the information reported in an entity's financial statements. For example, not-for-profit entities provide statements of revenues, expenditures, and changes in fund equity while business entities provide income statements. Similarly, income statements of retail companies show an expense item called *cost of goods sold,* but service companies that do not sell goods have no such item in their income statements. You should expect some diversity when reviewing real-world financial statements.

Annual Report for The Topps Company, Inc.

Organizations normally provide information, including financial statements, to *stakeholders* yearly in a document known as an **annual report.** The annual report for Topps is reproduced in Appendix B of this text. This report includes the company's financial statements (see pages 15–19 of the report). Immediately following the statements are footnotes that provide additional details about the items described in the statements (see pages 20–47). The annual report contains the *auditors' report,* which is discussed in Chapter 2. Annual reports also include written commentary describing management's assessment of significant events that affected the company during the reporting period. This commentary is called *management's discussion and analysis* (MD&A).

The U.S. Securities and Exchange Commission (SEC) requires public companies to file an annual report on a document known as a 10-K. The SEC is discussed in more detail later. Even though the annual report is usually flashier (contains more color and pictures) than the 10-K, the 10-K is normally more comprehensive with respect to content. As a result, the 10-K report can substitute for the annual report, but the annual report cannot substitute for the 10-K. In an effort to reduce costs, some companies use the 10-K report as their annual report.

Special Terms in Real-World Reports

The financial statements of real-world companies include numerous items relating to advanced topics that are not covered in introductory accounting textbooks, especially the first chapter of an introductory accounting textbook. Do not, however, be discouraged from browsing through real-world annual reports. You will significantly enhance your learning if you look at many annual reports and attempt to identify as many items as you can. As your accounting knowledge grows, you will likely experience increased interest in real-world financial reports and the businesses they describe.

One thing you will notice about real-world companies' financial statements is that dollar amounts are usually stated in thousands or millions of dollars. This rounding is permitted under the concept of materiality. Financial reporting considers an item to be material only if knowing, versus not knowing, about the item would affect the decision of an average investor. Consider that in 2007 Wal-Mart's revenues were $374,526 million. One million dollars to Wal-Mart is the equivalent of 27 cents to an individual who earned $100,000 in 2007. The fact that Wal-Mart rounded its revenues to the nearest million dollars should not affect investors' decisions.

Reality BYTES

How did Kevin Rose make 60 million dollars in just 18 months? He built a company investors wanted to buy. So how, in just 18 months, did he build a company so big that only a portion of it was worth $60 million? When investors buy a company they are really buying a right to share in the *future* earnings of that company. The existing company does not have to be so large. It is the potential for future earnings that has to be big.

Kevin risked everything to start his business—"all his time, all his cash, and even his girlfriend, who fought with him after he poured his savings into his company instead of a down payment on a house." Kevin's idea was to use information that others would "dig up" on the Web. Kevin's Web site would allow his users to post links to other Web sites they had found containing interesting stories. The "diggers" would then vote for the best links to be placed onto the front page of Digg.com. As more and more users came to the site to find the most interesting stories, they would also become contributors by listing their favorite links. A snowball effect would make Digg.com a very popular Web site, thereby enabling the company to earn mega revenues from advertising.

Kevin and a small cadre of friends and supporters worked feverishly to establish the hardware and software that would enable the realization of Kevin's dream. The big question was "if we build it, will they come?" Roughly 18 months later they had their answer—a resounding yes. By 4 P.M. on launch day Digg.com had signed up more than 13,000 registered users. Growth continued to soar. Shortly thereafter Digg.com was ranked the 24th most popular Web site in the United States.

At this point Digg.com was just breaking even with advertising revenues and operating expenses of approximately $3 million. While net income was virtually zero, investors established a price based on the potential for future profits. Indeed, financial analysts estimated that, given the opportunity, investors would be willing to pay approximately $200 million to buy the company. Kevin's share of the company was worth roughly $60 million.

As this story illustrates, investors frequently use information that is not reported in a company's annual report. The annual report focuses on historical data. This information is important because the past is frequently a strong predictor of what will happen in the future. However, innovative ideas may generate companies that have little or no history but that nevertheless have very promising futures. Also, investors and creditors may be motivated by nonfinancial considerations such as social consciousness, humanitarian ideals, or personal preferences. While accounting information is critically important, it is only one dimension of the information pool that investors and creditors use to make decisions.

We encourage you to look for annual reports in the library or ask your employer for a copy of your company's report. The Internet is another excellent source for obtaining annual reports. Most companies provide links to their annual reports on their home pages. Look for links labeled "about the company" or "investor relations" or other phrases that logically lead to the company's financial reports. The best way to learn accounting is to use it. Accounting is the language of business. Learning the language will serve you well in almost any area of business that you pursue.

<< A Look Back

This chapter introduced the role of accounting in society and business: to provide information helpful to operating and evaluating the performance of organizations. Accounting is a measurement discipline. To communicate effectively, users of accounting must agree on the rules of measurement. *Generally accepted accounting principles (GAAP)* constitute the rules used by the accounting profession in the United States to govern financial reporting. GAAP is a work in progress that continues to evolve.

This chapter has discussed eight elements of financial statements: *assets, liabilities, equity, common stock (contributed capital), revenue, expenses, dividends (distributions),* and *net income.* The elements represent broad classifications reported on financial statements. Four basic financial statements appear in the reports of public companies: the *balance sheet,* the *income statement,* the *statement of changes in stockholders' equity,* and the *statement of cash flows.* The chapter discussed the form and content of each statement as well as the interrelationships among the statements.

  This chapter introduced a *horizontal financial statements model* as a tool to help you understand how business events affect a set of financial statements. This model is used throughout the text. You should carefully study this model before proceeding to Chapter 2.

A Look Forward >>

To keep matters as simple as possible and to focus on the interrelationships among financial statements, this chapter considered only cash events. Obviously, many real-world events do not involve an immediate exchange of cash. For example, customers use telephone service throughout the month without paying for it until the next month. Such phone usage represents an expense in one month with a cash exchange in the following month. Events such as this are called *accruals.* Understanding the effects that accrual events have on the financial statements is included in Chapter 2.

 SELF-STUDY REVIEW PROBLEM

During 2011 Rustic Camp Sites experienced the following transactions.

1. RCS acquired $32,000 cash by issuing common stock.
2. RCS received $116,000 cash for providing services to customers (leasing camp sites).
3. RCS paid $13,000 cash for salaries expense.
4. RCS paid a $9,000 cash dividend to the owners.
5. RCS sold land that had cost $100,000 for $100,000 cash.
6. RCS paid $47,000 cash for other operating expenses.

Required

a. Record the transaction data in a horizontal financial statements model like the following one. In the Cash Flow column, classify the cash flows as operating activities (OA), investing activities (IA), or financing activities (FA). The beginning balances have been recorded as an example. They are the ending balances shown on RCS's December 31, 2010, financial statements illustrated in the chapter. Note that the revenue and expense accounts have a zero beginning balance. Amounts in these accounts apply only to a single accounting period. Revenue and expense account balances are not carried forward from one accounting period to the next.

Event No.	Balance Sheet												Income Statement						Statement of Cash Flows
	Assets			=	Liab.	+	Stockholders' Equity												
	Cash	+	Land	=	N. Pay.	+	Com. Stk.	+	Ret. Earn.				Rev.	−	Exp.	=	Net Inc.		
Beg. bal.	51,000	+	500,000	=	400,000	+	120,000	+	31,000				NA	−	NA	=	NA		NA

b. Explain why there are no beginning balances in the Income Statement columns.
c. What amount of net income will RCS report on the 2011 income statement?
d. What amount of total assets will RCS report on the December 31, 2011, balance sheet?
e. What amount of retained earnings will RCS report on the December 31, 2011, balance sheet?
f. What amount of net cash flow from operating activities will RCS report on the 2011 statement of cash flows?

Solution

a.

Event No.	Balance Sheet										Income Statement						Statement of Cash Flows	
	Assets			=	Liab.	+	Stockholders' Equity											
	Cash	+	Land	=	N. Pay.	+	Com. Stk.	+	Ret. Earn.		Rev.	−	Exp.	=	Net Inc.			
Beg. bal.	51,000	+	500,000	=	400,000	+	120,000	+	31,000		NA	−	NA	=	NA		NA	
1.	32,000	+	NA	=	NA	+	32,000	+	NA		NA	−	NA	=	NA		32,000	FA
2.	116,000	+	NA	=	NA	+	NA	+	116,000		116,000	−	NA	=	116,000		116,000	OA
3.	(13,000)	+	NA	=	NA	+	NA	+	(13,000)		NA	−	13,000	=	(13,000)		(13,000)	OA
4.	(9,000)	+	NA	=	NA	+	NA	+	(9,000)		NA	−	NA	=	NA		(9,000)	FA
5.	100,000	+	(100,000)	=	NA	+	NA	+	NA		NA	−	NA	=	NA		100,000	IA
6.	(47,000)	+	NA	=	NA	+	NA	+	(47,000)		NA	−	47,000	=	(47,000)		(47,000)	OA
Totals	230,000	+	400,000	=	400,000	+	152,000	+	78,000		116,000	−	60,000	=	56,000		179,000	NC*

*The letters NC on the last line of the column designate the net change in cash.

b. The revenue and expense accounts are temporary accounts used to capture data for a single accounting period. They are closed (amounts removed from the accounts) to retained earnings at the end of the accounting period and therefore always have zero balances at the beginning of the accounting cycle.

c. RCS will report net income of $56,000 on the 2011 income statement. Compute this amount by subtracting the expenses from the revenue ($116,000 Revenue − $13,000 Salaries expense − $47,000 Other operating expense).

d. RCS will report total assets of $630,000 on the December 31, 2011, balance sheet. Compute total assets by adding the cash amount to the land amount ($230,000 Cash + $400,000 Land).

e. RCS will report retained earnings of $78,000 on the December 31, 2011, balance sheet. Compute this amount using the following formula: Beginning retained earnings + Net income − Dividends = Ending retained earnings. In this case, $31,000 + $56,000 − $9,000 = $78,000.

f. Net cash flow from operating activities is the difference between the amount of cash collected from revenue and the amount of cash spent for expenses. In this case, $116,000 cash inflow from revenue − $13,000 cash outflow for salaries expense − $47,000 cash outflow for other operating expenses = $56,000 net cash inflow from operating activities.

KEY TERMS

Net loss 18
Operating activities 17
Permanent accounts 19
Productive assets 17
Reliability concept 13

Reporting entities 6
Retained earnings 9
Revenue 11
Service businesses 21
Stakeholders 6

Statement of cash flows 17
Statement of changes in
  stockholders' equity 16
Stockholders 9

Stockholders' equity 9
Temporary accounts 18
Transaction 9

QUESTIONS

1. Compare and contrast public accounting with private accounting.

2. Explain the term *stakeholder*.

3. What type of compensation does an investor expect to receive in exchange for providing financial resources to a business? What type of compensation does a creditor expect from providing financial resources to an organization or business?

4. How do financial and managerial accounting differ?

5. What are the U.S. rules of accounting measurement called?

6. Is there a global GAAP (generally accepted accounting principles)? Explain your answer.

7. What body has the primary responsibility for establishing GAAP in the United States?

8. Distinguish between elements of financial statements and accounts.

9. What is the most basic form of the accounting equation?

10. What role do assets play in business profitability?

11. To whom do the assets of a business belong?

12. Explain the order of priority for asset distributions in a business liquidation.

13. Name the element used to describe the ownership interest in a business.

14. Name the element used to describe creditors' claims on the assets of a business.

15. What is the accounting equation? Describe each of its three components.

16. Who ultimately bears the risk and collects the rewards associated with operating a business?

17. What does *double-entry bookkeeping* mean?

18. Identify the three types of accounting transactions discussed in this chapter. Provide an example of each type of transaction, and explain how it affects the accounting equation.

19. How does acquiring resources from owners affect the accounting equation?

20. Name the two primary components of stockholders' equity.

21. How does earning revenue affect the accounting equation?

22. What are the three primary sources of assets?

23. What is included in retained earnings?

24. How does distributing assets (paying dividends) to owners affect the accounting equation?

25. What are the similarities and differences between dividends and expenses?

26. What four general-purpose financial statements do business enterprises use to communicate information to stakeholders?

27. Which of the general-purpose financial statements provides information about the enterprise at a specific designated date?

28. What causes a net loss?

29. What three categories of cash receipts and cash payments do businesses report on the statement of cash flows? Explain the types of cash flows reported in each category.

30. How are asset accounts usually arranged in the balance sheet?

31. What type of information does a business typically include in its annual report?

EXERCISES

All applicable Exercises are available with McGraw-Hill
Connect Accounting.

Exercise 1-1   *Careers in accounting*   LO 1

Accountants establish careers in either the public or private sectors of the economy.

Required

a. Explain how a career in public accounting differs from a career in private accounting.

b. Name and describe three areas of service provided by public accountants.

c. Identify four typical duties performed by accountants working in the private sector.

LO 2

Exercise 1-2   *Distributions in a business liquidation*

Assume that Brandy Company acquires $1,400 cash from creditors and $1,800 cash from investors (stockholders). The company then has an operating loss of $2,000 cash and goes out of business.

Required

a. Define the term *business liquidation*.
b. What amount of cash will Brandy's creditors receive?
c. What amount of cash will Brandy's investors (stockholders) receive?

LO 2

Exercise 1-3   *Identifying the reporting entities*

Carlos Bueso recently started a business. During the first few days of operation, Mr. Bueso transferred $30,000 from his personal account into a business account for a company he named Bueso Enterprises. Bueso Enterprises borrowed $40,000 from the State Bank of Texas. Mr. Bueso's father-in-law, James Bright, invested $64,000 into the business for which he received a 25 percent ownership interest. Bueso Enterprises purchased a building from Leigh Realty Company. The building cost $120,000 cash. Bueso Enterprises earned $28,000 in revenue from the company's customers and paid its employees $25,000 for salaries expense.

Required

Identify the entities that were mentioned in the scenario and explain what happened to the cash accounts of each entity that you identify.

LO 3, 8

Exercise 1-4   *Titles and accounts appearing on financial statements*

Annual reports normally include an income statement, statement of changes in equity, balance sheet, and statement of cash flows.

Required

Identify the financial statements on which each of the following titles or accounts would appear. If a title or an account appears on more than one statement, list all statements that would include it.

a. Retained Earnings
b. Revenue
c. Common Stock
d. Financing Activities
e. Salaries Expense
f. Land
g. Ending Cash Balance
h. Beginning Cash Balance
i. Notes Payable
j. Dividends

LO 4

Exercise 1-5   *Components of the accounting equation*

Required

The following three requirements are independent of each other.

a. Michael's Motors has assets of $4,550 and net assets of $3,200. What is the amount of liabilities? What is the amount of claims?
b. Sweet Tooth Bakery has liabilities of $4,800 and equity of $5,400. What is the amount of assets? What is the amount of net assets?
c. Pam's Candy Co. has assets of $49,200 and liabilities of $28,200. What is the amount of equity? What is the amount of net assets?

Exercise 1-6 *Effect of events on the accounting equation and careers in accounting*

LO 1, 4

Olive Enterprises experienced the following events during 2010.

1. Acquired cash from the issue of common stock.
2. Paid cash to reduce the principal on a bank note.
3. Sold land for cash at an amount equal to its cost.
4. Provided services to clients for cash.
5. Paid utilities expenses with cash.
6. Paid a cash dividend to the stockholders.

Required

a. Explain how each of the events would affect the accounting equation by writing the letter I for increase, the letter D for decrease, and NA for does not affect under each of the components of the accounting equation. The first event is shown as an example.

				Stockholders' Equity	
Event Number	Assets	= Liabilities	+	Common Stock	+ Retained Earnings
1	I	NA		I	NA

b. Sarah Culver audited Olive Enterprise's financial statements and provided assurances that the statements were prepared in accordance with GAAP. Sarah holds only one professional certification. Which certification to you expect Sarah holds? Explain why you chose this certification.

Exercise 1-7 *Effects of issuing stock*

LO 3, 8

Joseph Company was started in 2009 when it acquired $15,000 cash by issuing common stock. The cash acquisition was the only event that affected the business in 2009.

Required

a. Write an accounting equation, and record the effects of the stock issue under the appropriate general ledger account headings.
b. What is the amount of net income appearing on the income statement?
c. Where would the stock issue be reported on the statement of cash flows?

Exercise 1-8 *Effects of borrowing*

LO 3, 8

East Asia Company was started in 2011 when it issued a note to borrow $6,200 cash.

Required

a. Write an accounting equation, and record the effects of the borrowing transaction under the appropriate general ledger account headings.
b. What is the amount of net income reported on the income statement? (Ignore any effects of interest.)
c. Where would the note issue appear on the statement of cash flows?

Exercise 1-9 *Effects of revenue, expense, and dividend events*

LO 5, 8

Ruff Company was started on January 1, 2009. During 2009, the company experienced the following three accounting events: (1) earned cash revenues of $13,500, (2) paid cash expenses of $9,200, and (3) paid a $500 cash dividend to its stockholders. These were the only events that affected the company during 2009.

Required

a. Write an accounting equation, and record the effects of each accounting event under the appropriate general ledger account headings.

b. Prepare an income statement for the 2009 accounting period and a balance sheet at the end of 2009 for Ruff Company.

LO **3, 8**   **Exercise 1-10**   *Classifying items for the statement of cash flows*

Required

Indicate how each of the following would be classified on the statement of cash flows as operating activities (OA), investing activities (IA), financing activities (FA), or not applicable (NA).

a. Borrowed $8,000 cash from State Bank.

b. Paid $5,000 cash for salary expense.

c. Signed a contract to provide services in the future.

d. Performed services for $25,000 cash.

e. Paid $9,000 cash to purchase land.

f. Paid $1,500 cash for utilities expense.

g. Sold land for $5,000 cash.

h. Paid $4,000 cash on the principal of a bank loan.

i. Paid a $2,000 cash dividend to the stockholders.

j. Received $30,000 cash from the issue of common stock.

LO **5, 8**   **Exercise 1-11**   *Effect of transactions on general ledger accounts*

At the beginning of 2011, T & M Corp.'s accounting records had the following general ledger accounts and balances.

T & M CORP. Accounting Equation							
Event	Assets		=	Liabilities	+	Stockholders' Equity		Acct. Titles for RE
	Cash	Land		Notes Payable		Common Stock	Retained Earnings	
Balance 1/1/2011	10,000	20,000		12,000		7,000	11,000	

T & M Corp. completed the following transactions during 2011.

1. Purchased land for $5,000 cash.

2. Acquired $25,000 cash from the issue of common stock.

3. Received $75,000 cash for providing services to customers.

4. Paid cash operating expenses of $42,000.

5. Borrowed $10,000 cash from the bank.

6. Paid a $5,000 cash dividend to the stockholders.

7. Determined that the market value of the land is $35,000.

Required

a. Record the transactions in the appropriate general ledger accounts. Record the amounts of revenue, expense, and dividends in the Retained Earnings column. Provide the appropriate titles for these accounts in the last column of the table.

b. Determine the amount of net income for the 2011 period.

c. What is the amount of total assets at the end of 2011? What is the amount of stockholders' equity at the end of 2011?

d. What is the balance in the retained earnings account immediately after Transaction 3 is recorded?

Exercise 1-12   *Preparing financial statements*   LO 5, 8

Dakota Company experienced the following events during 2010.

1. Acquired $30,000 cash from the issue of common stock.
2. Paid $12,000 cash to purchase land.
3. Borrowed $10,000 cash.
4. Provided services for $20,000 cash.
5. Paid $1,000 cash for rent expense.
6. Paid $15,000 cash for other operating expenses.
7. Paid a $2,000 cash dividend to the stockholders.
8. Determined that the market value of the land purchased in Event 2 is now $12,700.

Required

a. The January 1, 2010, general ledger account balances are shown in the following accounting equation. Record the eight events in the appropriate general ledger accounts. Record the amounts of revenue, expense, and dividends in the Retained Earnings column. Provide the appropriate titles for these accounts in the last column of the table. The first event is shown as an example.

DAKOTA COMPANY
Accounting Equation

Event	Assets		=	Liabilities	+	Stockholders' Equity		Acct. Titles for RE
	Cash	Land		Notes Payable		Common Stock	Retained Earnings	
Balance 1/1/2010 1.	2,000 30,000	12,000		0		6,000 30,000	8,000	

b. Prepare an income statement, statement of changes in equity, year-end balance sheet, and statement of cash flows for the 2010 accounting period.

c. Determine the percentage of assets that were provided by retained earnings. How much cash is in the retained earnings account?

d. What is the balance in the Service Revenue account on January 1, 2011?

Exercise 1-13   *Classifying events as asset source, use, or exchange*   LO 7

Vera Company experienced the following events during its first year of operations.

1. Acquired $16,000 cash from the issue of common stock.
2. Paid $3,500 cash for salary expenses.
3. Borrowed $10,000 cash from New South Bank.
4. Paid $6,000 cash to purchase land.
5. Provided boarding services for $10,500 cash.
6. Acquired an additional $1,000 cash from the issue of common stock.
7. Paid $2,400 cash for utilities expense.
8. Paid a $1,500 cash dividend to the stockholders.
9. Provided additional services for $6,000 cash.

10. Purchased additional land for $2,500 cash.

11. The market value of the land was determined to be $24,000 at the end of the accounting period.

Required

Classify each event as an asset source, use, or exchange transaction.

LO 3, 4

Exercise 1-14   *Relationship between assets and retained earnings*

West Company was organized when it acquired $2,000 cash from the issue of common stock. During its first accounting period the company earned $800 of cash revenue and incurred $500 of cash expenses. Also, during the accounting period the company paid its owners a $200 cash dividend.

Required

a. Determine the ending amount of the retained earnings account.

b. As of the end of the accounting period, determine what percentage of total assets were provided by earnings.

LO 6

Exercise 1-15   *Historical cost versus market value*

JMD, Inc., purchased land in January 2009 at a cost of $270,000. The estimated market value of the land is $350,000 as of December 31, 2011.

Required

a. Name the December 31, 2011, financial statement(s) on which the land will be shown.

b. At what dollar amount will the land be shown in the financial statement(s)?

c. Name the key concept that will be used in determining the dollar amount that will be reported for land that is shown in the financial statement(s).

LO 2

Exercise 1-16   *Relating accounting events to entities*

Sharp Company was started in 2009 when it acquired $25,000 cash by issuing common stock to Katie Sharp.

Required

a. Was this event an asset source, use, or exchange transaction for Sharp Company?

b. Was this event an asset source, use, or exchange transaction for Katie Sharp?

c. Was the cash flow an operating, investing, or financing activity on Sharp Company's 2009 statement of cash flows?

d. Was the cash flow an operating, investing, or financing activity on Katie Sharp's 2009 statement of cash flows?

LO 4

Exercise 1-17   *Retained earnings and the closing process*

Firwood Company was started on January 1, 2010. During the month of January, Firwood earned $4,600 of revenue and incurred $3,000 of expense. Firwood closes its books on December 31 of each year.

Required

a. Determine the balance in the Retained Earnings account as of January 31, 2010.

b. Comment on whether retained earnings is an element of financial statements or an account.

c. What happens to the Retained Earnings account at the time expenses are recognized?

LO 4

Exercise 1-18   *Missing information in the accounting equation*

As of December 31, 2010, Thomas Company had total assets of $156,000, total liabilities of $85,600, and common stock of $52,400. During 2011 Thomas earned $36,000 of cash revenue, paid $20,000 for cash expenses, and paid a $2,000 cash dividend to the stockholders.

Required

a. Determine the amount of retained earnings as of December 31, 2010, after closing.

b. Determine the amount of net income earned in 2011.

c. Determine the amount of retained earnings as of December 31, 2011, after closing.
d. Determine the amount of cash that is in the retained earnings account as of December 31, 2011.

Exercise 1-19 *Missing information for determining net income*   LO 4, 8

The December 31, 2009, balance sheet for Crow Company showed total stockholders' equity of $82,500. Total stockholders' equity increased by $53,400 between December 31, 2009, and December 31, 2010. During 2010 Crow Company acquired $13,000 cash from the issue of common stock. Crow Company paid an $8,000 cash dividend to the stockholders during 2010.

Required

Determine the amount of net income or loss Crow reported on its 2010 income statement. (*Hint:* Remember that stock issues, net income, and dividends all change total stockholders' equity.)

Exercise 1-20 *Effect of events on a horizontal financial statements model*   LO 9

Tim's Auto Service experienced the following events during 2011.

1. Purchased land for cash.
2. Issued common stock for cash.
3. Collected cash for providing auto repair services to customers.
4. Paid a cash dividend to the stockholders.
5. Paid cash for operating expenses.
6. Paid cash to reduce the principal balance on a liability.
7. Determined that the market value of the land is higher than its historical cost.

Required

Use a horizontal statements model to show how each event affects the balance sheet, income statement, and statement of cash flows. Indicate whether the event increases (I), decreases (D), or does not affect (NA) each element of the financial statements. Also, in the Cash Flows column, classify the cash flows as operating activities (OA), investing activities (IA), or financing activities (FA). The first transaction is shown as an example.

Event No.	Balance Sheet											Income Statement						Statement of Cash Flows
	Cash	+	Land	=	N. Pay	+	C. Stock.	+	Ret. Ear.			Rev.	−	Exp.	=	Net Inc.		
1.	D	+	I	=	NA	+	NA	+	NA			NA	−	NA	=	NA		D IA

Exercise 1-21 *Record events in the horizontal statements model*   LO 8, 9

Arnett Co. was started in 2011. During 2011, the company (1) acquired $11,000 cash from the issue of common stock, (2) earned cash revenue of $18,000, (3) paid cash expenses of $10,500, and (4) paid a $1,000 cash dividend to the stockholders.

Required

a. Record these four events in a horizontal statements model. Also, in the Cash Flows column, classify the cash flows as operating activities (OA), investing activities (IA), or financing activities (FA). The first event is shown as an example.

Event No.	Balance Sheet									Income Statement						Statement of Cash Flows
	Cash	=	N. Pay	+	C. Stock.	+	Ret. Ear.		Rev.	−	Exp.	=	Net Inc.		
1.	11,000	=	NA	+	11,000	+	NA		NA	−	NA	=	NA		11,000 FA

b. What does the income statement tell you about the assets of this business?

LO **8, 9**

Exercise 1-22   *Effect of events on a horizontal statements model*

Holiday, Inc., was started on January 1, 2009. The company experienced the following events during its first year of operation.

1. Acquired $50,000 cash from the issue of common stock.
2. Paid $12,000 cash to purchase land.
3. Received $50,000 cash for providing tax services to customers.
4. Paid $9,500 cash for salary expenses.
5. Acquired $5,000 cash from the issue of additional common stock.
6. Borrowed $10,000 cash from the bank.
7. Purchased additional land for $10,000 cash.
8. Paid $8,000 cash for other operating expenses.
9. Paid a $2,800 cash dividend to the stockholders.
10. Determined that the market value of the land is $25,000.

Required

a. Record these events in a horizontal statements model. Also, in the Cash Flows column, classify the cash flows as operating activities (OA), investing activities (IA), or financing activities (FA). The first event is shown as an example.

Event No.	Balance Sheet										Income Statement						Statement of Cash Flows
	Cash	+	Land	=	N. Pay	+	C. Stock.	+	Ret. Ear.		Rev.	−	Exp.	=	Net Inc.		
1.	50,000	+	NA	=	NA	+	50,000	+	NA		NA	−	NA	=	NA		50,000 FA

b. What is the balance in the Retained Earnings account immediately after Event 3 is recorded?
c. What is the net income earned in 2009?
d. What is the amount of total assets at the end of 2009?
e. What is the net cash flow from operating activities for 2009?
f. What is the net cash flow from investing activities for 2009?
g. What is the net cash flow from financing activities for 2009?
h. What is the cash balance at the end of 2009?
i. As of the end of the year 2009, what percentage of total assets were provided by creditors, investors, and earnings?

LO **7, 9**

Exercise 1-23   *Types of transactions and the horizontal statements model*

Jodi's Pet Store experienced the following events during its first year of operations, 2009.

1. Acquired cash by issuing common stock.
2. Purchased land with cash.
3. Borrowed cash from a bank.
4. Signed a contract to provide services in the future.
5. Paid a cash dividend to the stockholders.
6. Paid cash for operating expenses.
7. Determined that the market value of the land is higher than the historical cost.

Required

a. Indicate whether each event is an asset source, use, or exchange transaction.
b. Use a horizontal statements model to show how each event affects the balance sheet, income statement, and statement of cash flows. Indicate whether the event increases (I), decreases (D), or does not affect (NA) each element of the financial statements. Also, in

the Cash Flows column, classify the cash flows as operating activities (OA), investing activities (IA), or financing activities (FA). The first transaction is shown as an example.

Event No.	Balance Sheet									Income Statement					Statement of Cash Flows
	Cash	+	Land	=	N. Pay.	+	Com. Stk.	+	Ret. Earn.	Rev.	−	Exp.	=	Net Inc.	
1.	I	+	NA	=	NA	+	I	+	NA	NA	−	NA	=	NA	I FA

Exercise 1-24   *Types of business entities*

LO 9

Required

Give an example of each of the following types of business entities.

a. Service business
b. Merchandising business
c. Manufacturing business

PROBLEMS

All applicable Problems are available with McGraw-Hill *Connect Accounting.*

connect
|ACCOUNTING

Problem 1-25   *Accounting entities*

LO 2

The following business scenarios are independent from one another.

1. Mary Poort purchased an automobile from Hayney Bros. Auto Sales for $9,000.
2. John Rodman loaned $15,000 to the business in which he is a stockholder.
3. First State Bank paid interest to Caleb Co. on a certificate of deposit that Caleb Co. has invested at First State Bank.
4. Parkside Restaurant paid the current utility bill of $128 to Gulf Utilities.
5. Gatemore, Inc., borrowed $50,000 from City National Bank and used the funds to purchase land from Morgan Realty.
6. Steven Wong purchased $10,000 of common stock of International Sales Corporation from the corporation.
7. Dan Dow loaned $4,000 cash to his daughter.
8. Mega Service Co. earned $5,000 in cash revenue.
9. McCloud Co. paid $1,500 for salaries to each of its four employees.
10. Shim Inc. paid a cash dividend of $3,000 to its sole shareholder, Marcus Shim.

CHECK FIGURE

a1. Entities mentioned: Mary Poort and Hayney Bros. Auto Sales

Required

a. For each scenario, create a list of all of the entities that are mentioned in the description.
b. Describe what happens to the cash account of each entity that you identified in Requirement *a*.

Problem 1-26   *Relating titles and accounts to financial statements*

LO 3, 8

Required

Identify the financial statements on which each of the following items (titles, date descriptions, and accounts) appears by placing a check mark in the appropriate column. If an item appears on more than one statement, place a check mark in every applicable column. The first item is completed as an example.

Item	Income Statement	Statement of Changes in Stockholders' Equity	Balance Sheet	Statement of Cash Flows
Notes payable			✓	
Beginning common stock				
Service revenue				
Utility expense				
Cash from stock issue				
Operating activities				
For the period ended (date)				
Net income				
Investing activities				
Net loss				
Ending cash balance				
Salary expense				
Consulting revenue				
Dividends				
Financing activities				
Ending common stock				
Interest expense				
As of (date)				
Land				
Beginning cash balance				

LO 1, 3, 4, 5, 8

Problem 1-27 *Preparing financial statements for two complete accounting cycles and careers in accounting*

Susan's Consulting Services experienced the following transactions for 2010, the first year of operations, and 2011. *Assume that all transactions involve the receipt or payment of cash.*

Transactions for 2010

1. Acquired $50,000 by issuing common stock.
2. Received $100,000 for providing services to customers.
3. Borrowed $15,000 cash from creditors.
4. Paid expenses amounting to $60,000.
5. Purchased land for $40,000 cash.

Transactions for 2011

Beginning account balances for 2011 are

Cash	$65,000
Land	40,000
Notes payable	15,000
Common stock	50,000
Retained earnings	40,000

1. Acquired an additional $20,000 from the issue of common stock.
2. Received $130,000 for providing services in 2011.
3. Paid $10,000 to reduce notes payable.
4. Paid expenses amounting to $75,000.
5. Paid a $15,000 dividend to the stockholders.
6. Determined that the market value of the land is $50,000.

Required

a. Write an accounting equation, and record the effects of each accounting event under the appropriate headings for each year. Record the amounts of revenue, expense, and dividends in the Retained Earnings column. Provide appropriate titles for these accounts in the last column of the table.

b. Prepare an income statement, statement of changes in stockholders' equity, year-end balance sheet, and statement of cash flows for each year.

c. Determine the amount of cash that is in the retained earnings account at the end of 2010 and 2011.

d. Compare the information provided by the income statement with the information provided by the statement of cash flows. Point out similarities and differences.

e. Determine the balance in the Retained Earnings account immediately after Event 2 in 2010 and in 2011 are recorded.

f. Would the financial statements for Susan's Consulting Services be prepared by a public or a private accountant? Explain your answer.

Problem 1-28 *Interrelationships among financial statements*

LO **8**

Crawford Enterprises started the 2009 accounting period with $50,000 of assets (all cash), $18,000 of liabilities, and $4,000 of common stock. During the year, Crawford earned cash revenues of $38,000, paid cash expenses of $32,000, and paid a cash dividend to stockholders of $2,000. Crawford also acquired $15,000 of additional cash from the sale of common stock and paid $10,000 cash to reduce the liability owed to a bank.

Required

a. Prepare an income statement, statement of changes in stockholders' equity, period-end balance sheet, and statement of cash flows for the 2009 accounting period. (*Hint:* Determine the amount of beginning retained earnings before considering the effects of the current period events. It also might help to record all events under an accounting equation before preparing the statements.)

b. Determine the percentage of total assets that were provided by creditors, investors, and earnings.

Problem 1-29 *Classifying events as asset source, use, or exchange*

LO **6**

The following unrelated events are typical of those experienced by business entities.

1. Acquire cash by issuing common stock.
2. Borrow cash from the local bank.
3. Pay office supplies expense.
4. Make plans to purchase office equipment.
5. Trade a used car for a computer with the same value.
6. Pay other operating supplies expense.
7. Agree to represent a client in an IRS audit and to receive payment when the audit is complete.
8. Receive cash from customers for services rendered.
9. Pay employee salaries with cash.
10. Pay back a bank loan with cash.
11. Pay interest to a bank with cash.
12. Transfer cash from a checking account to a money market account.

13. Sell land for cash at its original cost.

14. Pay a cash dividend to stockholders.

15. Learn that a financial analyst determined the company's price-earnings ratio to be 26.

Required

Identify each of the events as an asset source, asset use, or asset exchange transaction. If an event would not be recorded under generally accepted accounting principles, identify it as not applicable (NA). Also indicate for each event whether total assets would increase, decrease, or remain unchanged. Organize your answer according to the following table. The first event is shown in the table as an example.

Event No.	Type of Event	Effect on Total Assets
1	Asset source	Increase

LO 9

Problem 1-30   *Recording the effect of events in a horizontal statements model*

Doyer Corporation experienced the following transactions during 2010.

1. Paid a cash dividend to the stockholders.

2. Acquired cash by issuing additional common stock.

3. Signed a contract to perform services in the future.

4. Performed services for cash.

5. Paid cash expenses.

6. Sold land for cash at an amount equal to its cost.

7. Borrowed cash from a bank.

8. Determined that the market value of the land is higher than its historical cost.

Required

Use a horizontal statements model to show how each event affects the balance sheet, income statement, and statement of cash flows. Indicate whether the event increases (I), decreases (D), or does not affect (NA) each element of the financial statements. Also, in the Cash Flows column, classify the cash flows as operating activities (OA), investing activities (IA), or financing activities (FA). The first transaction is shown as an example.

Event No.	Cash	+	Land	=	N. Pay	+	C. Stock.	+	Ret. Ear.	Rev.	−	Exp.	=	Net Inc.	Statement of Cash Flows
					Balance Sheet						**Income Statement**				
1.	D	+	NA	=	NA	+	NA	+	D	NA	−	NA	=	NA	D FA

LO 8, 9

Problem 1-31   *Recording events in a horizontal statements model*

Madden Company was started on January 1, 2011, and experienced the following events during its first year of operation.

1. Acquired $30,000 cash from the issue of common stock.

2. Borrowed $40,000 cash from National Bank.

3. Earned cash revenues of $48,000 for performing services.

4. Paid cash expenses of $45,000.

5. Paid a $1,000 cash dividend to the stockholders.

6. Acquired an additional $20,000 cash from the issue of common stock.
7. Paid $10,000 cash to reduce the principal balance of the bank note.
8. Paid $53,000 cash to purchase land.
9. Determined that the market value of the land is $75,000.

Required

a. Record the preceding transactions in the horizontal statements model. Also, in the Cash Flows column, classify the cash flows as operating activities (OA), investing activities (IA), or financing activities (FA). The first event is shown as an example.

Event No.	Balance Sheet									Income Statement					Statement of Cash Flows
	Cash	+	Land	=	N. Pay	+	C. Stock.	+	Ret. Ear.	Rev.	−	Exp.	=	Net Inc.	
1.	30,000	+	NA	=	NA	+	30,000	+	NA	NA	−	NA	=	NA	30,000 FA

b. Determine the amount of total assets that Madden would report on the December 31, 2011, balance sheet.
c. Identify the sources of the assets that Madden would report on the December 31, 2011, balance sheet. Determine the amount of each of these sources.
d. Determine the net income that Madden would report on the 2011 income statement. Explain why dividends do not appear on the income statement.
e. Determine the net cash flows from operating activities, financing activities, and investing activities that Madden would report on the 2011 statement of cash flows.
f. Determine the percentage of assets that were provided by investors, creditors, and earnings.

Problem 1-32   *Distinguishing revenue from retained earnings and closing*   LO **3, 8**

After closing on December 31, 2010, Direct Delivery Company (DDC) had $9,200 of assets, $4,000 of liabilities, and $1,400 of common stock. During January of 2011 DDC earned $1,500 of revenue and incurred $600 of expense. DDC closes it books each year on December 31.

Required

a. Determine the balance in the Retained Earnings account as of December 31, 2010.
b. Determine the balance in the Retained Earnings account as of January 1, 2011.
c. Determine the balance in the Retained Earnings account as of January 31, 2011.

ANALYZE, THINK, COMMUNICATE

ATC 1-1   Business Applications Case   *Understanding real world annual reports*

Required

Use the Topps Company's annual report in Appendix B to answer the following questions.

The Topps Company, Inc.

a. What was Topps' net income for 2006?
b. Did Topps' net income increase or decrease from 2005 to 2006, and by how much?
c. What was Topps' accounting equation for 2006?
d. Which of the following had the largest percentage increase from 2005 to 2006: net sales, cost of sales, or selling, general, and administrative expenses? Show all computations.

ATC 1-2   Group Assignment   *Missing information*

The following selected financial information is available for ROC, Inc. Amounts are in millions of dollars.

Income Statements	2009	2008	2007	2006
Revenue	$ 860	$1,520	$ (a)	$1,200
Cost and expenses	(a)	(a)	(2,400)	(860)
Income from continuing operations	(b)	450	320	(a)
Unusual items	-0-	175	(b)	(b)
Net income	$ 20	$ (b)	$ 175	$ 300
Balance Sheets				
Assets				
Cash and marketable securities	$ 350	$1,720	$ (c)	$ 940
Other assets	1,900	(c)	2,500	(c)
Total assets	2,250	$2,900	$ (d)	$3,500
Liabilities	$ (c)	$ (d)	$1,001	$ (d)
Stockholders' equity				
Common stock	600	720	(e)	800
Retained earnings	(d)	(e)	800	(e)
Total stockholders' equity	1,520	1,345	(f)	2,200
Total liabilities and stockholders' equity	$2,250	$ (f)	$3,250	$3,500

a. Divide the class into groups of four or five students each. Organize the groups into four sections. Assign Task 1 to the first section of groups, Task 2 to the second section, Task 3 to the third section, and Task 4 to the fourth section.

Group Tasks

(1) Fill in the missing information for 2006.
(2) Fill in the missing information for 2007.
(3) Fill in the missing information for 2008.
(4) Fill in the missing information for 2009.

b. Each section should select two representatives. One representative is to put the financial statements assigned to that section on the board, underlining the missing amounts. The second representative is to explain to the class how the missing amounts were determined.

ATC 1-3   Real-World Case   *Classifying cash flow activities at five companies*

The following events occurred at five real-world companies.

On March 17, 2008, H&R Block, Inc., announced that it had signed an agreement to sell the mortgage loan servicing business that is a part of its Option One Mortgage Corporation subsidiary for approximately $1 billion. Assume this sale was completed.

On March 19, 2008, Visa, Inc., issued approximately 450 million shares of stock for almost $20 billion.

On February 19, 2008, Chrysler, LLC, announced that it planned to significantly expand existing engineering operations in countries outside the United States. These plans include adding new development centers outside the country. Assume these plans were accomplished.

During 2007, Target Corporation borrowed $6.75 billion using notes payable that were due to be repaid between 2013 and 2038.

During 2007, Levi Strauss & Co. had cash sales of approximately $4.25 billion.

Required

Determine if each of the transactions above should be classified as an *operating, investing,* or *financing* activity. Also, identify each cash flow as an *inflow* or *outflow.*

ATC 1-4   Business Applications Case   *Use of real-world numbers for forecasting*

The following information was drawn from the annual report of Machine Import Company (MIC):

	For the Years	
	2009	2010
Income Statements		
Revenue	$800,000	$920,000
Operating Expenses	720,000	820,000
Income from Continuing Operations	80,000	100,000
Extraordinary Item—Lottery Win		20,000
Net Income	$ 80,000	$120,000
Balance Sheets		
Assets	$700,000	$720,000
Liabilities	$300,000	$200,000
Stockholders' Equity		
Common Stock	150,000	150,000
Retained Earnings	250,000	370,000
Total Liabilities and Stockholders' Equity	$700,000	$720,000

Required

a. Compute the percentage of growth in net income from 2009 to 2010. Can stockholders expect a similar increase between 2010 and 2011?

b. Assuming that MIC collected $120,000 cash from earnings (net income), explain how this money was spent in 2010.

c. Assuming that MIC experiences the same percentage of growth from 2010 to 2011 as it did from 2009 to 2010, determine the amount of income from continuing operations that the owners can expect to see on the 2011 income statement.

d. During 2011, MIC experienced a $15,000 loss due to storm damage (note that this would be shown as an extraordinary loss on the income statement). Liabilities and common stock were unchanged from 2010 to 2011. Use the information that you computed in Part *c* plus the additional information provided in the previous two sentences to calculate net income for 2011 and prepare a balance sheet as of December 31, 2011.

ATC 1-5   Writing Assignment   *Elements of financial statements defined*

Bob and his sister Marsha both attend the state university. As a reward for their successful completion of the past year (Bob had a 3.2 GPA in business, and Marsha had a 3.7 GPA in art), their father gave each of them 100 shares of The Walt Disney Company stock. They have just received their first annual report. Marsha does not understand what the information means and has asked Bob to explain it to her. Bob is currently taking an accounting course, and she knows he will understand the financial statements.

Required

Assume that you are Bob. Write Marsha a memo explaining the following financial statement items to her. In your explanation, describe each of the two financial statements and explain the financial information each contains. Also define each of the elements listed for each financial statement and explain what it means.

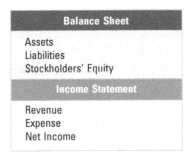

Balance Sheet
Assets
Liabilities
Stockholders' Equity

Income Statement
Revenue
Expense
Net Income

ATC 1-6 Ethical Dilemma *Loyalty versus the bottom line*

Assume that Jones has been working for you for five years. He has had an excellent work history and has received generous pay raises in response. The raises have been so generous that Jones is quite overpaid for the job he is required to perform. Unfortunately, he is not qualified to take on other, more responsible jobs available within the company. A recent job applicant is willing to accept a salary $5,000 per year less than the amount currently being paid to Jones. The applicant is well qualified to take over Jones's duties and has a very positive attitude. The following financial statements were reported by your company at the close of its most recent accounting period.

Financial Statements

Income Statement

Revenue	$57,000
Expense	(45,000)
Net Income	$12,000

Statement of Changes in Stockholders' Equity

Beginning Common Stock	$20,000	
Plus: Stock Issued	5,000	
Ending Common Stock		$25,000
Beginning Retained Earnings	50,000	
Net Income	12,000	
Dividends	(2,000)	
Ending Retained Earnings		60,000
Total Stockholders' Equity		$85,000

Balance Sheet

Assets	
Cash	$85,000
Stockholders' Equity	
Common Stock	$25,000
Retained Earnings	60,000
Total Stockholders' Equity	$85,000

Statement of Cash Flows

Operating Activities		
Inflow from Customers	$57,000	
Outflow for Expenses	(45,000)	
Net Inflow from Operating Activities		$12,000
Investing Activities		0
Financing Activities		
Inflow from Stock Issue	5,000	
Outflow for Dividends	(2,000)	
Net Inflow from Financing Activities		3,000
Net Change in Cash		15,000
Plus: Beginning Cash Balance		70,000
Ending Cash Balance		$85,000

Required

a. Reconstruct the financial statements, assuming that Jones was replaced at the beginning of the most recent accounting period. Both Jones and his replacement are paid in cash. No other changes are to be considered.

b. Would a public or private accountant be more likely to face this type of dilemma?

ATC 1-7 Research Assignment *Finding real-world accounting information*

The Curious Accountant story at the beginning of this chapter referred to the Coca-Cola Company and discussed who its stakeholders are. This chapter has introduced the basic structure of the four financial statements used by companies to annually keep their stakeholders informed as to their accomplishments and financial situation. Complete the requirements below using the most recent (20xx) financial statements available on xx Coke's website. Like many companies, Coke uses the Form 10-K that it files with the Securities and Exchange Commission (SEC) as its annual report. Obtain the statements on the Internet by following the steps below. (The formatting of the company's website may have changed since these instructions were written.)

■ Go to www.thecoca-colacompany.com.

■ Click on the "Investors" link at the top of the page.

■ Click on the "Financial Information" link at the left side of the page.

■ Under the "Financial Information" heading, click on xx "Annual & Other Reports."

■ Click on "20xx Annual Report on Form 10-K."

■ Use the Table of Contents at the beginning of the Form 10-K to locate the company's "Financial Statements and Supplementary Data" section. Go to the company's financial statements and complete the requirements below.

Required

a. What was the company's net income in each of the last three years?

b. What amount of total assets did the company have at the end of the most recent year?

c. How much retained earnings did the company have at the end of the most recent year? *Note:* Coke uses the name *reinvested earnings* rather than retained earnings.

d. For the most recent year, what was the company's cash flow from operating activities, cash flow from investing activities, and cash flow from financing activities?

CHAPTER 2

Accounting *for* Accruals *and* Deferrals

LEARNING OBJECTIVES

After you have mastered the material in this chapter you will be able to:

1 Record basic accrual and deferral events in a horizontal financial statements model.

2 Organize general ledger accounts under an accounting equation.

3 Prepare financial statements based on accrual accounting.

4 Describe the closing process, the accounting cycle, and the matching concept.

5 Prepare a vertical financial statements model.

6 Explain how business events affect financial statements over multiple accounting cycles.

7 Identify the primary components of corporate governance.

8 Classify accounting events into one of four categories:

   a. asset source transactions.

   b. asset use transactions.

   c. asset exchange transactions.

   d. claims exchange transactions.

CHAPTER OPENING

Users of financial statements must distinguish between the terms *recognition* and *realization*. **Recognition** means formally *reporting* an economic item or event in the financial statements. **Realization** refers to collecting money, generally from the sale of products or services. Companies may recognize (report) revenue in the income statement in a different accounting period from the period in which they collect the cash related to the revenue. Furthermore, companies frequently make cash payments for expenses in accounting periods other than the periods in which the expenses are recognized in the income statement.

To illustrate, assume Johnson Company provides services to customers in 2010 but collects cash for those services in 2011. In this case, realization occurs in 2011. When should Johnson recognize the services revenue?

Users of *cash basis* accounting recognize (report) revenues and expenses in the period in which cash is collected or paid. Under cash basis accounting Johnson would recognize the revenue in 2011 when it collects the cash. In contrast, users of **accrual accounting** recognize revenues and expenses in the period in which they occur, regardless of when cash is collected or paid. Under accrual accounting Johnson would recognize the revenue in 2010 (the period in which it performed the services) even though it does not collect (realize) the cash until 2011.

Accrual accounting is required by generally accepted accounting principles. Virtually all major companies operating in the United States use it. Its two distinguishing features are called *accruals* and *deferrals.*

- The term **accrual** describes an earnings event that is recognized **before** cash is exchanged. Johnson's recognition of revenue in 2010 related to cash realized in 2011 is an example of an accrual.
- The term **deferral** describes an earnings event that is recognized **after** cash has been exchanged. Suppose Johnson pays cash in 2010 to purchase office supplies it uses in 2011. In this case the cash payment occurs in 2010 although supplies expense is recognized in 2011. This example is a deferral.

The *Curious* Accountant

Suppose Sarah Greenwood wishes to purchase a subscription to *American Baby* for her sister who is scheduled to give birth to her first child in early September 2010. She pays $12 for a one-year subscription to the Meredith Corporation, the company that publishes *American Baby, Better Homes and Gardens, The Ladies Home Journal*, and several other magazines. It also owns 13 television stations. Her sister will receive her first issue of the magazine in September.

How should Meredith Corporation account for the receipt of this cash? How would this event be reported on its December 31, 2010, financial statements? (Answer on page 59.)

ACCRUAL ACCOUNTING

Record basic accrual and deferral events in a horizontal financial statements model.

The next section of the text describes seven events experienced by Cato Consultants, a training services company that uses accrual accounting.

EVENT 1   Cato Consultants was started on January 1, 2010, when it acquired $5,000 cash by issuing common stock.

The issue of stock for cash is an **asset source transaction.** It increases the company's assets (cash) and its equity (common stock). The transaction does not affect the income statement. The cash inflow is classified as a financing activity (acquisition from owners). These effects are shown in the following financial statements model:

Assets	=	Liab.	+	Stockholders' Equity			Rev.	−	Exp.	=	Net Inc.	Cash Flow
Cash	=			Com. Stk.	+	Ret. Earn.	Rev.	−	Exp.	=	Net Inc.	Cash Flow
5,000	=	NA	+	5,000	+	NA	NA	−	NA	=	NA	5,000 FA

Accounting for Accounts Receivable

EVENT 2   During 2010 Cato Consultants provided $84,000 of consulting services to its clients. The business has completed the work and sent bills to the clients, but not yet collected any cash. This type of transaction is frequently described as providing services *on account*.

Accrual accounting requires companies to recognize revenue in the period in which the work is done regardless of when cash is collected. In this case, revenue is recognized in 2010 even though cash has not been realized (collected). Recall that revenue represents the economic benefit that results in an increase in assets from providing goods and services to customers. The specific asset that increases is called **Accounts Receivable.** The balance in Accounts Receivable represents the amount of cash the company expects to collect in the future. Since the revenue recognition causes assets (accounts receivable) to increase, it is classified as an asset source transaction. Its effect on the financial statements follows.

Assets			=	Liab.	+	Stockholders' Equity			Rev.	−	Exp.	=	Net Inc.	Cash Flow
Cash	+	Accts. Rec.	=			Com. Stk.	+	Ret. Earn.	Rev.	−	Exp.	=	Net Inc.	Cash Flow
NA	+	84,000	=	NA	+	NA	+	84,000	84,000	−	NA	=	84,000	NA

Notice that the event affects the income statement but not the statement of cash flows. The statement of cash flows will be affected in the future when cash is collected.

EVENT 3   Cato collected $60,000 cash from customers in partial settlement of its accounts receivable.

The collection of an account receivable is an **asset exchange transaction.** One asset account (Cash) increases and another asset account (Accounts Receivable) decreases. The amount of total assets is unchanged. The effect of the $60,000 collection of receivables on the financial statements is as follows.

Assets			=	Liab.	+	Stockholders' Equity			Rev.	−	Exp.	=	Net Inc.	Cash Flow
Cash	+	Accts. Rec.	=			Com. Stk.	+	Ret. Earn.	Rev.	−	Exp.	=	Net Inc.	Cash Flow
60,000	+	(60,000)	=	NA	+	NA	+	NA	NA	−	NA	=	NA	60,000 OA

Notice that collecting the cash did not affect the income statement. The revenue was recognized when the work was done (see Event 2). Revenue would be double counted if it were recognized again when the cash is collected. The statement of cash flows reflects a cash inflow from operating activities.

Other Events

EVENT 4   **Cato paid the instructor $10,000 for teaching training courses (salary expense).**

Cash payment for salary expense is an **asset use transaction.** Both the asset account Cash and the equity account Retained Earnings decrease by $10,000. Recognizing the expense decreases net income on the income statement. Since Cato paid cash for the expense, the statement of cash flows reflects a cash outflow from operating activities. These effects on the financial statements follow.

Assets		=	Liab.	+	Stockholders' Equity							
Cash	+	Accts. Rec.	=		Com. Stk.	+	Ret. Earn.	Rev.	−	Exp.	=	Net Inc.	Cash Flow
(10,000)	+	NA	=	NA	+	NA	+	(10,000)	NA	−	10,000	=	(10,000)	(10,000) OA

EVENT 5   **Cato paid $2,000 cash for advertising costs. The advertisements appeared in 2010.**

Cash payments for advertising expenses are asset use transactions. Both the asset account Cash and the equity account Retained Earnings decrease by $2,000. Recognizing the expense decreases net income on the income statement. Since the expense was paid with cash, the statement of cash flows reflects a cash outflow from operating activities. These effects on the financial statements follow.

Assets		=	Liab.	+	Stockholders' Equity							
Cash	+	Accts. Rec.	=		Com. Stk.	+	Ret. Earn.	Rev.	−	Exp.	=	Net Inc.	Cash Flow
(2,000)	+	NA	=	NA	+	NA	+	(2,000)	NA	−	2,000	=	(2,000)	(2,000) OA

EVENT 6   **Cato signed contracts for $42,000 of consulting services to be performed in 2011.**

The $42,000 for consulting services to be performed in 2011 is not recognized in the 2010 financial statements. Revenue is recognized for work actually completed, *not* work expected to be completed. This event does not affect any of the financial statements.

Assets		=	Liab.	+	Stockholders' Equity							
Cash	+	Accts. Rec.	=		Com. Stk.	+	Ret. Earn.	Rev.	−	Exp.	=	Net Inc.	Cash Flow
NA	+	NA	=	NA	+	NA	+	NA	NA	−	NA	=	NA	NA

Accounting for Accrued Salary Expense (Adjusting Entry)

It is impractical to record many business events as they occur. For example, Cato incurs salary expense continually as the instructor teaches courses. Imagine the impossibility of trying to record salary expense second by second! Companies normally record transactions when it is most convenient. The most convenient time to record many expenses is when they are paid. Often, however, a single business transaction pertains to more than one accounting period. To provide accurate financial reports in such cases, companies may need to recognize some expenses before paying cash for them. Expenses that are recognized before cash is paid are called **accrued expenses.** The accounting for Event 7 illustrates the effect of recognizing accrued salary expense.

EVENT 7   At the end of 2010 Cato recorded accrued salary expense of $6,000 (the salary expense is for courses the instructor taught in 2008 that Cato will pay him for in 2011).

Accrual accounting requires that companies recognize expenses in the period in which they are incurred regardless of when cash is paid. Cato must recognize all salary expense in the period in which the instructor worked (2010) even though Cato will not pay the instructor again until 2011. Cato must also recognize the obligation (liability) it has to pay the instructor. To accurately report all 2010 salary expense and year-end obligations, Cato must record the unpaid salary expense and salary liability before preparing its financial statements. The entry to recognize the accrued salary expense is called an **adjusting entry.** Like all adjusting entries, it is only to update the accounting records; it does not affect cash.

This adjusting entry decreases stockholders' equity (retained earnings) and increases a liability account called **Salaries Payable.** The balance in the Salaries Payable account represents the amount of cash the company is obligated to pay the instructor in the future. The effect of the expense recognition on the financial statements follows.

Assets			=	Liab.	+	Stockholders' Equity							
Cash	+	Accts. Rec.	=	Sal. Pay.	+	Com. Stk.	+	Ret. Earn.	Rev.	−	Exp.	=	Net Inc.	Cash Flow
NA	+	NA	=	6,000	+	NA	+	(6,000)	NA	−	6,000	=	(6,000)	NA

This event is a **claims exchange transaction.** The claims of creditors (liabilities) increase and the claims of stockholders (retained earnings) decrease. Total claims remain unchanged. The salary expense is reported on the income statement. The statement of cash flows is not affected.

Be careful not to confuse liabilities with expenses. Although liabilities may increase when a company recognizes expenses, liabilities are not expenses. Liabilities are obligations. They can arise from acquiring assets as well as recognizing expenses. For example, when a business borrows money from a bank, it recognizes an increase in assets (cash) and liabilities (notes payable). The borrowing transaction does not affect expenses.

CHECK *Yourself* 2.1

During 2010, Anwar Company earned $345,000 of revenue on account and collected $320,000 cash from accounts receivable. Anwar paid cash expenses of $300,000 and cash dividends of $12,000. Determine the amount of net income Anwar should report on the 2010 income statement and the amount of cash flow from operating activities Anwar should report on the 2010 statement of cash flows.

Answer   Net income is $45,000 ($345,000 revenue − $300,000 expenses). The cash flow from operating activities is $20,000, the amount of revenue collected in cash from customers (accounts receivable) minus the cash paid for expenses ($320,000 − $300,000). Dividend payments are classified as financing activities and do not affect the determination of either net income or cash flow from operating activities.

Summary of Events

The previous section of this chapter described seven events Cato Consultants experienced during the 2010 accounting period. These events are summarized below for your convenience.

Event 1 Cato Consultants acquired $5,000 cash by issuing common stock.

Event 2 Cato provided $84,000 of consulting services on account.

Event 3 Cato collected $60,000 cash from customers in partial settlement of its accounts receivable.

Event 4 Cato paid $10,000 cash for salary expense.

Event 5 Cato paid $2,000 cash for 2010 advertising costs.

Event 6 Cato signed contracts for $42,000 of consulting services to be performed in 2011.

Event 7 Cato recognized $6,000 of accrued salary expense.

The General Ledger

Exhibit 2.1 shows the 2010 transaction data recorded in general ledger accounts. The information in these accounts is used to prepare the financial statements. The revenue and expense items appear in the Retained Earnings column with their account titles immediately to the right of the dollar amounts. The amounts are color coded to help you trace the data to the financial statements. Data in red appear on the balance sheet, data in blue on the income statement, and data in green on the statement of cash flows. Before reading further, trace each transaction in the summary of events into Exhibit 2.1.

Organize general ledger accounts under an accounting equation.

EXHIBIT 2.1   Transaction Data for 2010 Recorded in General Ledger Accounts

	Assets			=	Liabilities	+	Stockholders' Equity			
Event No.	Cash	+	Accounts Receivable	=	Salaries Payable	+	Common Stock	+	Retained Earnings	Other Account Titles
Beg. bal.	0		0		0		0		0	
1	5,000						5,000			
2			84,000						84,000	Consulting revenue
3	60,000		(60,000)							
4	(10,000)								(10,000)	Salary expense
5	(2,000)								(2,000)	Advertising expense
6										
7					6,000				(6,000)	Salary Expense
End bal.	53,000	+	24,000	=	6,000	+	5,000	+	66,000	

Vertical Statements Model

The financial statements for Cato Consultants' 2010 accounting period are represented in a vertical statements model in Exhibit 2.2. A vertical statements model arranges a set of financial statement information vertically on a single page. Like horizontal statements models, vertical statements models are learning tools. They illustrate interrelationships among financial statements. The models do not, however, portray the full, formal presentation formats companies use in published financial statements. For example, statements models may use summarized formats with abbreviated titles and dates. As you read the following explanations of each financial statement, trace the color coded financial data from Exhibit 2.1 to Exhibit 2.2.

Prepare financial statements based on accrual accounting.

Prepare a vertical financial
statements model.

EXHIBIT 2.2	Vertical Statements Model

CATO CONSULTANTS
Financial Statements*
Income Statement
For the Year Ended December 31, 2010

Consulting revenue	$84,000
Salary expense	(16,000)
Advertising expense	(2,000)
Net income	$66,000

Statement of Changes in Stockholders' Equity
For the Year Ended December 31, 2010

Beginning common stock	$ 0	
Plus: Common stock issued	5,000	
Ending common stock		$ 5,000
Beginning retained earnings	0	
Plus: Net income	66,000	
Less: Dividends	0	
Ending retained earnings		66,000
Total stockholders' equity		$71,000

Balance Sheet
As of December 31, 2010

Assets		
Cash	$53,000	
Accounts receivable	24,000	
Total assets		$77,000
Liabilities		
Salaries payable		$ 6,000
Stockholders' equity		
Common stock	$ 5,000	
Retained earnings	66,000	
Total stockholders' equity		71,000
Total liabilities and stockholders' equity		$77,000

Statement of Cash Flows
For the Year Ended December 31, 2010

Cash flows from operating activities		
Cash receipts from customers	$60,000	
Cash payments for salary expense	(10,000)	
Cash payments for advertising expenses	(2,000)	
Net cash flow from operating activities		$48,000
Cash flow from investing activities		0
Cash flows from financing activities		
Cash receipt from issuing common stock	5,000	
Net cash flow from financing activities		5,000
Net change in cash		53,000
Plus: Beginning cash balance		0
Ending cash balance		$53,000

*In real-world annual reports, financial statements are normally presented separately with appropriate
descriptions of the date to indicate whether the statement applies to the entire accounting period or a specific
point in time.

Income Statement

The income statement reflects accrual accounting. Consulting revenue represents the price Cato charged for all the services it performed in 2010, even though Cato had not by the end of the year received cash for some of the services performed. Expenses include all costs incurred to produce revenue, whether paid for by year-end or not. We can now expand the definition of expenses introduced in Chapter 1. Expenses were previously defined as assets consumed in the process of generating revenue. Cato's adjusting entry to recognize accrued salaries expense did not reflect consuming assets. Instead of a decrease in assets, Cato recorded an increase in liabilities (salaries payable). An **expense** can therefore be more precisely defined as *a decrease in assets or an increase in liabilities resulting from operating activities undertaken to generate revenue.*

Statement of Changes in Stockholders' Equity

The statement of changes in stockholders' equity reports the effects on equity of issuing common stock, earning net income, and paying dividends to stockholders. It identifies how an entity's equity increased and decreased during the period as a result of transactions with stockholders and operating the business. In the Cato case, the statement shows that equity increased when the business acquired $5,000 cash by issuing common stock. The statement also reports that equity increased by $66,000 from earning income and that none of the $66,000 of net earnings was distributed to owners (no dividends were paid). Equity at the end of the year is $71,000 ($5,000 + $66,000).

Balance Sheet

The balance sheet discloses an entity's assets, liabilities, and stockholders' equity at a particular point in time. Cato Consultants had two assets at the end of the 2010 accounting period: cash of $53,000 and accounts receivable of $24,000. These assets are listed on the balance sheet in order of liquidity. Of the $77,000 in total assets, creditors have a $6,000 claim, leaving stockholders with a $71,000 claim.

Statement of Cash Flows

The statement of cash flows explains the change in cash from the beginning to the end of the accounting period. It can be prepared by analyzing the Cash account. Since Cato Consultants was established in 2010, its beginning cash balance was zero. By the end of the year, the cash balance was $53,000. The statement of cash flows explains this increase. The Cash account increased because Cato collected $60,000 from customers and decreased because Cato paid $12,000 for expenses. As a result, Cato's net cash inflow from operating activities was $48,000. Also, the business acquired $5,000 cash through the financing activity of issuing common stock, for a cumulative cash increase of $53,000 ($48,000 + $5,000) during 2010.

Comparing Cash Flow from Operating Activities with Net Income

The amount of net income measured using accrual accounting differs from the amount of cash flow from operating activities. For Cato Consulting in 2010, the differences are summarized below.

	Accrual Accounting	Cash Flow
Consulting revenue	$84,000	$60,000
Salary expense	(16,000)	(10,000)
Advertising expense	(2,000)	(2,000)
Net income	$66,000	$48,000

Many students begin their first accounting class with the misconception that revenue and expense items are cash equivalents. The Cato illustration demonstrates that a company may recognize a revenue or expense without a corresponding cash collection or payment in the same accounting period.

The Closing Process

Describe the closing process, the accounting cycle, and the matching concept.

Recall that the temporary accounts (revenue, expense, and dividend) are closed prior to the start of the next accounting cycle. The closing process transfers the amount in each of these accounts to the Retained Earnings account, leaving each temporary account with a zero balance.

Exhibit 2.3 shows the general ledger accounts for Cato Consultants after the revenue and expense accounts have been closed to retained earnings. The closing entry labeled Cl.1 transfers the balance in the Consulting Revenue account to the Retained Earnings account. Closing entries Cl.2 and Cl.3 transfer the balances in the expense accounts to retained earnings.

EXHIBIT 2.3

General Ledger Accounts for Cato Consultants

Assets		=	Liabilities		+	Stockholders' Equity	
Cash			**Salaries Payable**			**Common Stock**	
(1)	5,000		(7)	6,000		(1)	5,000
(3)	60,000		Bal.	6,000			
(4)	(10,000)					**Retained Earnings**	
(5)	(2,000)						
Bal.	53,000					Cl.1	84,000
						Cl.2	(16,000)
						Cl.3	(2,000)
Accounts Receivable						Bal.	66,000
(2)	84,000						
(3)	(60,000)					**Consulting Revenue**	
Bal.	24,000						
						(2)	84,000
						Cl.1	(84,000)
						Bal.	0
						Salary Expense	
						(4)	(10,000)
						(7)	(6,000)
						Cl.2	16,000
						Bal.	0
						Advertising Expense	
						(5)	(2,000)
						Cl.3	2,000
						Bal.	0

Steps in an Accounting Cycle

An accounting cycle, which is represented graphically in Exhibit 2.4, involves several steps. The four steps identified to this point are (1) recording transactions; (2) adjusting the accounts; (3) preparing financial statements; and (4) closing the temporary accounts. The first step occurs continually throughout the accounting period. Steps 2, 3, and 4 normally occur at the end of the accounting period.

The Matching Concept

Cash basis accounting can distort reported net income because it sometimes fails to match expenses with the revenues they produce. To illustrate, consider the $6,000 of accrued salary expense that Cato Consultants recognized at the end of 2010. The instructor's teaching produced revenue in 2010. If Cato waited until 2011 (when it paid the instructor) to recognize $6,000 of the total $16,000 salary expense, then $6,000 of the expense would not be matched with the revenue it generated. By using accrual accounting, Cato recognized all the salary expense in the same accounting period in which the consulting revenue was recognized. A primary goal of accrual accounting is to appropriately match expenses with revenues, the **matching concept.**

Appropriately matching expenses with revenues can be difficult even when using accrual accounting. For example, consider Cato's advertising expense. Money spent on advertising may generate revenue in future accounting periods as well as in the current period. A prospective customer could save an advertising brochure for several years before calling Cato for training services. It is difficult to know when and to what extent advertising produces revenue. When the connection between an expense and the corresponding revenue is vague, accountants commonly match the expense with the period in which it is incurred. Cato matched (recognized) the entire $2,000 of advertising cost with the 2010 accounting period even though some of that cost might generate revenue in future accounting periods. Expenses that are matched with the period in which they are incurred are frequently called **period costs.**

Matching is not perfect. Although it would be more accurate to match expenses with revenues than with periods, there is sometimes no obvious direct connection between expenses and revenue. Accountants must exercise judgment to select the accounting period in which to recognize revenues and expenses. The concept of conservatism influences such judgment calls.

EXHIBIT 2.4

The Accounting Cycle

1 Record transactions

2 Adjust accounts

3 Prepare statements

4 Close temporary accounts

The Conservatism Principle

When faced with a recognition dilemma, **conservatism** guides accountants to select the alternative that produces the lowest amount of net income. In uncertain circumstances, accountants tend to delay revenue recognition and accelerate expense recognition. The conservatism principle holds that it is better to understate net income than to overstate it. If subsequent developments suggest that net income should have been higher, investors will respond more favorably than if they learn it was really lower. This practice explains why Cato recognized all of the advertising cost as expense in 2010 even though some of that cost may generate revenue in future accounting periods.

SECOND ACCOUNTING CYCLE

The effects of Cato Consultants' 2011 events are as follows:

EVENT 1 Cato paid $6,000 to the instructor to settle the salaries payable obligation.

Cash payments to creditors are *asset use transactions.* When Cato pays the instructor, both the asset account Cash and the liability account Salaries Payable decrease. The

LO 1

Record basic accrual and deferral events in a horizontal financial statements model.

cash payment does not affect the income statement. The salary expense was recognized in 2010 when the instructor taught the classes. The statement of cash flows reflects a cash outflow from operating activities. The effects of this transaction on the financial statements are shown here.

Assets	=	Liab.	+	Stk. Equity		Rev.	−	Exp.	=	Net Inc.	Cash Flow
Cash	=	Sal. Pay.				Rev.	−	Exp.	=	Net Inc.	Cash Flow
(6,000)	=	(6,000)	+	NA		NA	−	NA	=	NA	(6,000) OA

Prepaid Items (Cost versus Expense)

EVENT 2   On March 1, 2011, Cato signed a one-year lease agreement and paid $12,000 cash in advance to rent office space. The one-year lease term began on March 1.

Accrual accounting draws a distinction between the terms *cost* and *expense*. *A* **cost** *might be either an asset or an expense.* If a company has already consumed a purchased resource in the process of earning revenue, the cost of the resource is an *expense.* For example, companies normally pay for electricity the month after using it. The cost of electric utilities is therefore usually recorded as an expense. In contrast, if a company purchases a resource it will use in the future to generate revenue, the cost of the resource represents an *asset.* Accountants record such a cost in an asset account and **defer** recognizing an expense until the resource is used to produce revenue. Deferring the expense recognition provides more accurate **matching** of revenues and expenses. Exhibit 2.5 illustrates the relationship between costs, assets, and expenses.

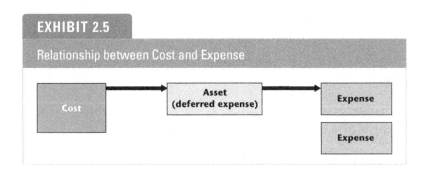

EXHIBIT 2.5

Relationship between Cost and Expense

The cost of the office space Cato leased in Event 2 is an asset. It is recorded in the asset account *Prepaid Rent.* Cato expects to benefit from incurring this cost for the next twelve months. Expense recognition is deferred until Cato uses the office space to help generate revenue. Other common deferred expenses include *prepaid insurance* and *prepaid taxes.* As these titles imply, deferred expenses are frequently called **prepaid items.**

Purchasing prepaid rent is an asset exchange transaction. The asset account Cash decreases and the asset account Prepaid Rent increases. The amount of total assets is unaffected. The income statement is unaffected. Expense recognition is deferred until the office space is used. The statement of cash flows reflects a cash outflow from operating activities. The effects of this transaction on the financial statements are shown here.

Assets			=	Liab.	+	Stk. Equity		Rev.	–	Exp.	=	Net Inc.	Cash Flow	
Cash	+	Prep. Rent						Rev.	–	Exp.	=	Net Inc.	Cash Flow	
(12,000)	+	12,000	=	NA	+	NA		NA	–	NA	=	NA	(12,000)	OA

Accounting for Receipt of Unearned Revenue

EVENT 3   Cato received $18,000 cash in advance from Westberry Company for consulting services Cato agreed to perform over a one-year period beginning June 1, 2011.

Cato must defer (delay) recognizing any revenue until it performs (does the work) the consulting services for Westberry. From Cato's point of view, the deferred revenue is a liability because Cato is obligated to perform services in the future. The liability is called **unearned revenue.** The cash receipt is an *asset source transaction.* The asset account Cash and the liability account Unearned Revenue both increase. Collecting the cash has no effect on the income statement. The revenue will be reported on the income statement after Cato performs the services. The statement of cash flows reflects a cash inflow from operating activities. The effects of this transaction on the financial statements are shown here.

Assets	=	Liab.	+	Stk. Equity		Rev.	–	Exp.	=	Net Inc.	Cash Flow	
Cash	=	Unearn. Rev.				Rev.	–	Exp.	=	Net Inc.	Cash Flow	
18,000	=	18,000	+	NA		NA	–	NA	=	NA	18,000	OA

Accounting for Supplies Purchase

EVENT 4   Cato purchased $800 of supplies on account.

The purchase of supplies on account is an *asset source transaction.* The asset account Supplies and the liability account Accounts Payable increase. The income statement is unaffected. Expense recognition is deferred until the supplies are used. The statement of cash flows is not affected. The effects of this transaction on the financial statements are shown here.

Assets	=	Liab.	+	Stk. Equity		Rev.	–	Exp.	=	Net Inc.	Cash Flow
Supplies	=	Accts. Pay.				Rev.	–	Exp.	=	Net Inc.	Cash Flow
800	=	800	+	NA		NA	–	NA	=	NA	NA

Other 2011 Events

EVENT 5   Cato provided $96,400 of consulting services on account.

Providing services on account is an *asset source transaction.* The asset account Accounts Receivable and the stockholders' equity account Retained Earnings increase.

Revenue and net income increase. The statement of cash flows is not affected. The effects of this transaction on the financial statements are shown here.

Assets	=	Liab.	+	Stk. Equity		Rev.	−	Exp.	=	Net Inc.	Cash Flow
Accts. Rec.	=			Ret. Earn.		Rev.	−	Exp.	=	Net Inc.	Cash Flow
96,400	=	NA	+	96,400		96,400	−	NA	=	96,400	NA

EVENT 6   Cato collected $105,000 cash from customers as partial settlement of accounts receivable.

Collecting money from customers who are paying accounts receivable is an *asset exchange transaction.* One asset account (Cash) increases and another asset account (Accounts Receivable) decreases. The amount of total assets is unchanged. The income statement is not affected. The statement of cash flows reports a cash inflow from operating activities. The effects of this transaction on the financial statements are shown here.

Assets			=	Liab.	+	Stk. Equity		Rev.	−	Exp.	=	Net Inc.	Cash Flow
Cash	+	Accts. Rec.						Rev.	−	Exp.	=	Net Inc.	Cash Flow
105,000	+	(105,000)	=	NA	+	NA		NA	−	NA	=	NA	105,000 OA

EVENT 7   Cato paid $32,000 cash for salary expense.

Cash payments for salary expense are *asset use transactions.* Both the asset account Cash and the equity account Retained Earnings decrease by $32,000. Recognizing the expense decreases net income on the income statement. The statement of cash flows reflects a cash outflow from operating activities. The effects of this transaction on the financial statements are shown here.

Assets	=	Liab.	+	Stk. Equity		Rev.	−	Exp.	=	Net Inc.	Cash Flow
Cash	=			Ret. Earn.		Rev.	−	Exp.	=	Net Inc.	Cash Flow
(32,000)	=	NA	+	(32,000)		NA	−	32,000	=	(32,000)	(32,000) OA

EVENT 8   Cato incurred $21,000 of other operating expenses on account.

Recognizing expenses incurred on account are *claims exchange transactions.* One claims account (Accounts Payable) increases and another claims account (Retained Earnings) decreases. The amount of total claims is not affected. Recognizing the expenses decreases net income. The statement of cash flows is not affected. The effects of this transaction on the financial statements are shown here.

Assets	=	Liab.	+	Stk. Equity		Rev.	−	Exp.	=	Net Inc.	Cash Flow
		Accts. Pay.	+	Ret. Earn.		Rev.	−	Exp.	=	Net Inc.	Cash Flow
NA	=	21,000	+	(21,000)		NA	−	21,000	=	(21,000)	NA

EVENT 9   Cato paid $18,200 in partial settlement of accounts payable.

Paying accounts payable is an *asset use transaction.* The asset account Cash and the liability account Accounts Payable decrease. The statement of cash flows reports a cash outflow for operating activities. The income statement is not affected. The effects of this transaction on the financial statements are shown here.

Assets	=	Liab.	+	Stk. Equity		Rev.	–	Exp.	=	Net Inc.		Cash Flow	
Cash	=	Accts. Pay.				Rev.	–	Exp.	=	Net Inc.		Cash Flow	
(18,200)	=	(18,200)	+	NA		NA	–	NA	=	NA		(18,200)	OA

EVENT 10   Cato paid $79,500 to purchase land it planned to use in the future as a building site for its home office.

Purchasing land with cash is an *asset exchange transaction.* One asset account, Cash, decreases and another asset account, Land, increases. The amount of total assets is unchanged. The income statement is not affected. The statement of cash flows reports a cash outflow for investing activities. The effects of this transaction on the financial statements are shown here.

Assets			=	Liab.	+	Stk. Equity		Rev.	–	Exp.	=	Net Inc.		Cash Flow	
Cash	+	Land						Rev.	–	Exp.	=	Net Inc.		Cash Flow	
(79,500)	+	79,500	=	NA	+	NA		NA	–	NA	=	NA		(79,500)	IA

EVENT 11   Cato paid $21,000 in cash dividends to its stockholders.

Cash payments for dividends are *asset use transactions.* Both the asset account Cash and the equity account Retained Earnings decrease. Recall that dividends are wealth transfers from the business to the stockholders, not expenses. They are not incurred in the process of generating revenue. They do not affect the income statement. The statement of cash flows reflects a cash outflow from financing activities. The effects of this transaction on the financial statements are shown here.

Assets	=	Liab.	+	Stk. Equity		Rev.	–	Exp.	=	Net Inc.		Cash Flow	
Cash	=			Ret. Earn.		Rev.	–	Exp.	=	Net Inc.		Cash Flow	
(21,000)	=	NA	+	(21,000)		NA	–	NA	=	NA		(21,000)	FA

EVENT 12   Cato acquired $2,000 cash from issuing additional shares of common stock.

Issuing common stock is an *asset source transaction.* The asset account Cash and the stockholders' equity account Common Stock increase. The income statement is unaffected. The statement of cash flows reports a cash inflow from financing activities. The effects of this transaction on the financial statements are shown here.

Assets	=	Liab.	+	Stk. Equity		Rev.	–	Exp.	=	Net Inc.		Cash Flow	
Cash	=			Com. Stk.		Rev.	–	Exp.	=	Net Inc.		Cash Flow	
2,000	=	NA	+	2,000		NA	–	NA	=	NA		2,000	FA

Adjusting Entries

Recall that companies make adjusting entries at the end of an accounting period to update the account balances before preparing the financial statements. Adjusting entries ensure that companies report revenues and expenses in the appropriate accounting period; adjusting entries never affect the Cash account.

Accounting for Supplies (Adjusting Entry)

EVENT 13   After determining through a physical count that it had $150 of unused supplies on hand as of December 31, Cato recognized supplies expense.

Companies would find the cost of recording supplies expense each time a pencil, piece of paper, envelope, or other supply item is used to far outweigh the benefit derived from such tedious recordkeeping. Instead, accountants transfer to expense the total cost of all supplies used during the entire accounting period in a single year-end adjusting entry. The cost of supplies used is determined as follows.

$$\frac{\text{Beginning}}{\text{supplies balance}} + \frac{\text{Supplies}}{\text{purchased}} = \frac{\text{Supplies}}{\text{available for use}} - \frac{\text{Ending}}{\text{supplies balance}} = \frac{\text{Supplies}}{\text{used}}$$

Companies determine the ending supplies balance by physically counting the supplies on hand at the end of the period. Cato used $650 of supplies during the year (zero beginning balance + $800 supplies purchase = $800 available for use − $150 ending balance). Recognizing Cato's supplies expense is an *asset use transaction*. The asset account Supplies and the stockholders' equity account Retained Earnings decrease. Recognizing supplies expense reduces net income. The statement of cash flows is not affected. The effects of this transaction on the financial statements are shown here.

Assets	=	Liab.	+	Stk. Equity		Rev.	−	Exp.	=	Net Inc.	Cash Flow
Supplies	=			Ret. Earn.		Rev.	−	Exp.	=	Net Inc.	Cash Flow
(650)	=	NA	+	(650)		NA	−	650	=	(650)	NA

Accounting for Prepaid Rent (Adjusting Entry)

EVENT 14   Cato recognized rent expense for the office space used during the accounting period.

Recall that Cato paid $12,000 on March 1, 2011, to rent office space for one year (see Event 2). The portion of the lease cost that represents using office space from March 1 through December 31 is computed as follows.

Cost of annual lease ÷ 12 = Cost per month × Months used = Rent expense

$12,000 cost of policy ÷ 12 = $1,000 per month × 10 months = $10,000 Rent expense

Recognizing the rent expense decreases the asset account Prepaid Rent and the stockholders' equity account Retained Earnings. Recognizing rent expense reduces net income. The statement of cash flows is not affected. The cash flow effect was recorded in the March 1 event. These effects on the financial statements follow.

Assets	=	Liab.	+	Stk. Equity		Rev.	−	Exp.	=	Net Inc.	Cash Flow
Prep. Rent	=			Ret. Earn.		Rev.	−	Exp.	=	Net Inc.	Cash Flow
(10,000)	=	NA	+	(10,000)		NA	−	10,000	=	(10,000)	NA

CHECK *Yourself* 2.2

Rujoub Inc. paid $18,000 cash for one year of insurance coverage that began on November 1, 2010. Based on this information alone, determine the cash flow from operating activities that Rujoub would report on the 2010 and 2011 statements of cash flows. Also, determine the amount of insurance expense Rujoub would report on the 2010 income statement and the amount of prepaid insurance (an asset) that Rujoub would report on the December 31, 2010, balance sheet.

Answer Since Rujoub paid all of the cash in 2010, the 2010 statement of cash flows would report an $18,000 cash outflow from operating activities. The 2011 statement of cash flows would report zero cash flow from operating activities. The expense would be recognized in the periods in which the insurance is used. In this case, insurance expense is recognized at the rate of $1,500 per month ($18,000 ÷ 12 months). Rujoub used two months of insurance coverage in 2010 and therefore would report $3,000 (2 months × $1,500) of insurance expense on the 2010 income statement. Rujoub would report a $15,000 (10 months × $1,500) asset, prepaid insurance, on the December 31, 2010, balance sheet. The $15,000 of prepaid insurance would be recognized as insurance expense in 2011 when the insurance coverage is used.

Accounting for Unearned Revenue (Adjusting Entry)

EVENT 15 **Cato recognized the portion of the unearned revenue it earned during the accounting period.**

Recall that Cato received an $18,000 cash advance from Westberry Company to provide consulting services from June 1, 2011, to May 31, 2012 (see Event 3). By December 31, Cato had earned 7 months (June 1 through December 31) of the revenue related to this contract. Rather than recording the revenue continuously as it performed the consulting services, Cato can simply recognize the amount earned in a single adjustment to the accounting records at the end of the accounting period. The amount of the adjustment is computed as follows.

$18,000 ÷ 12 months = $1,500 revenue earned per month

$1,500 × 7 months = $10,500 revenue to be recognized in 2011

The adjusting entry moves $10,500 from the Unearned Revenue account to the Consulting Revenue account. This entry is a *claims exchange transaction.* The liability account Unearned Revenue decreases and the equity account Retained Earnings increases. The effects of this transaction on the financial statements are shown here.

Assets	=	Liab.	+	Stk. Equity						
		Unearn. Rev.	+	Ret. Earn.	Rev.	−	Exp.	=	Net Inc.	Cash Flow
NA	=	(10,500)	+	10,500	10,500	−	NA	=	10,500	NA

Recall that revenue was previously defined as an economic benefit a company obtains by providing customers with goods and services. In this case the economic benefit is a decrease in the liability account Unearned Revenue. **Revenue** can therefore be more precisely defined as *an increase in assets or a decrease in liabilities that a company obtains by providing customers with goods or services.*

CHECK *Yourself* 2.3

Sanderson & Associates received a $24,000 cash advance as a retainer to provide legal services to a client. The contract called for Sanderson to render services during a one-year period beginning October 1, 2010. Based on this information alone, determine the cash flow from operating activities Sanderson would report on the 2010 and 2011 statements of cash flows. Also determine the amount of revenue Sanderson would report on the 2010 and 2011 income statements.

Answer   Since Sanderson collected all of the cash in 2010, the 2010 statement of cash flows would report a $24,000 cash inflow from operating activities. The 2011 statement of cash flows would report zero cash flow from operating activities. Revenue is recognized in the period in which it is earned. In this case revenue is earned at the rate of $2,000 per month ($24,000 ÷ 12 months = $2,000 per month). Sanderson rendered services for three months in 2010 and nine months in 2011. Sanderson would report $6,000 (3 months × $2,000) of revenue on the 2010 income statement and $18,000 (9 months × $2,000) of revenue on the 2011 income statement.

Accounting for Accrued Salary Expense (Adjusting Entry)

EVENT 16   **Cato recognized $4,000 of accrued salary expense.**

The adjusting entry to recognize the accrued salary expense is a *claims exchange transaction.* One claims account, Retained Earnings, decreases and another claims account, Salaries Payable, increases. The expense recognition reduces net income. The statement of cash flows is not affected. The effects of this transaction on the financial statements are shown here.

Assets	=	Liab.	+	Stk. Equity						
		Sal. Pay.	+	Ret. Earn.	Rev.	−	Exp.	=	Net Inc.	Cash Flow
NA	=	4,000	+	(4,000)	NA	−	4,000	=	(4,000)	NA

Summary of Events

The previous section of this chapter described sixteen events Cato Consultants experienced the during the 2011 accounting period. These events are summarized below for your convenience.

Event 1   Cato paid $6,000 to the instructor to settle the salaries payable obligation.

Event 2   On March 1, Cato paid $12,000 cash to lease office space for one year.

Event 3   Cato received $18,000 cash in advance from Westberry Company for consulting services to be performed for one year beginning June 1.

Event 4   Cato purchased $800 of supplies on account.

Event 5   Cato provided $96,400 of consulting services on account.

Event 6   Cato collected $105,000 cash from customers as partial settlement of accounts receivable.

Answers to The *Curious* Accountant

Because the Meredith Corporation receives cash from customers before actually providing any magazines to them, the company has not earned any revenue when it receives the cash. Thus, Meredith has a liability called *unearned revenue*. If it closed its books on December 31, then $3 of Sarah's subscription would be recognized as revenue in 2010. The remaining $9 would appear on the balance sheet as a liability.

Meredith Corporation actually ends its accounting year on June 30 each year. A copy of a recent balance sheet for the company is presented in Exhibit 2.6. The liability for unearned subscription revenue was $239.8 ($127.4 + $112.4) million—which represented about 28.5 percent of Meredith's total liabilities!

Will Meredith need cash to pay these subscription liabilities? Not exactly. The liabilities will not be paid directly with cash. Instead, they will be satisfied by providing magazines to the subscribers. However, Meredith will need cash to pay for producing and distributing the magazines supplied to the customers. Even so, the amount of cash required to provide magazines will probably differ significantly from the amount of unearned revenues. In most cases, subscription fees do not cover the cost of producing and distributing magazines. By collecting significant amounts of advertising revenue, publishers can provide magazines to customers at prices well below the cost of publication. The amount of unearned revenue is not likely to coincide with the amount of cash needed to cover the cost of satisfying the company's obligation to produce and distribute magazines. Even though the association between unearned revenues and the cost of providing magazines to customers is not direct, a knowledgeable financial analyst can use the information to make estimates of future cash flows and revenue recognition.

Event 7   Cato paid $32,000 cash for salary expense.

Event 8   Cato incurred $21,000 of other operating expenses on account.

Event 9   Cato paid $18,200 in partial settlement of accounts payable.

Event 10   Cato paid $79,500 to purchase land it planned to use in the future as a building site for its home office.

Event 11   Cato paid $21,000 in cash dividends to its stockholders.

Event 12   Cato acquired $2,000 cash from issuing additional shares of common stock.

The year-end adjustments are:

Event 13   After determining through a physical count that it had $150 of unused supplies on hand as of December 31, Cato recognized supplies expense.

Event 14   Cato recognized rent expense for the office space used during the accounting period.

Event 15   Cato recognized the portion of the unearned revenue it earned during the accounting period.

Event 16   Cato recognized $4,000 of accrued salary expense.

EXHIBIT 2.6	Balance Sheet for Meredith Corporation

CONSOLIDATED BALANCE SHEETS
Meredith Corporation and Subsidiaries
As of June 30 (amounts in thousands)

Assets

Current assets

Cash and cash equivalents	$ 29,788
Accounts receivable (net of allowances of $15,205)	176,669
Inventories	41,562
Current portion of subscription and acquisition costs	27,777
Current portion of broadcast rights	13,539
Other current assets	15,160
Total current assets	304,495

Property, plant and equipment

Land	19,261
Buildings and improvements	106,112
Machinery and equipment	256,380
Leasehold improvements	8,863
Construction in progress	8,266
Total property, plant and equipment	398,882
Less accumulated depreciation	(205,926)
Net property, plant and equipment	192,956
Subscription acquisition costs	24,722
Broadcast rights	7,096
Other assets	58,589
Intangibles, net	707,068
Goodwill	196,382
Total assets	$1,491,308

Liabilities and Shareholders' Equity

Current liabilities

Current portion of long-term debt	$ 125,000
Current portion of long-term broadcast rights payable	18,676
Accounts payable	48,462
Accrued expenses	
Compensation and benefits	42,162
Distribution expenses	17,546
Other taxes and expenses	59,818
Total accrued expenses	119,526
Current portion of unearned subscription revenues	127,416
Total current liabilities	439,080
Long-term debt	125,000
Long-term broadcast rights payable	17,208
Unearned subscription revenues	112,358
Deferred income taxes	93,929
Other noncurrent liabilities	51,906
Total liabilities	839,481

Shareholders' equity

Common stock, par value $1 per share	39,700
Class B stock, par value $1 per share, convertible to common stock	9,596
Additional paid-in capital	55,346
Retained earnings	550,115
Accumulated other comprehensive loss	(1,025)
Unearned compensation	(1,905)
Total shareholders' equity	651,827
Total liabilities and shareholders' equity	$1,491,308

The General Ledger

Exhibit 2.7 shows Cato Consultants' 2011 transaction data recorded in general ledger form. The account balances at the end of 2010, shown in Exhibit 2.3, become the beginning balances for the 2011 accounting period. The 2011 transaction data are referenced to the accounting events with numbers in parentheses. The information in the ledger accounts is the basis for the financial statements in Exhibit 2.8. Before reading further, trace each event in the summary of events into Exhibit 2.7.

Organize general ledger accounts under an accounting equation.

EXHIBIT 2.7

Ledger Accounts with 2011 Transaction Data

Assets	=	Liabilities	+	Stockholders' Equity

Cash

Bal.	53,000
(1)	(6,000)
(2)	(12,000)
(3)	18,000
(6)	105,000
(7)	(32,000)
(9)	(18,200)
(10)	(79,500)
(11)	(21,000)
(12)	2,000
Bal.	9,300

Accounts Receivable

Bal.	24,000
(5)	96,400
(6)	(105,000)
Bal.	15,400

Supplies

Bal.	0
(4)	800
(13)	(650)
Bal.	150

Prepaid Rent

Bal.	0
(2)	12,000
(14)	(10,000)
Bal.	2,000

Land

Bal.	0
(10)	79,500
Bal.	79,500

Accounts Payable

Bal.	0
(4)	800
(8)	21,000
(9)	(18,200)
Bal.	3,600

Unearned Revenue

Bal.	0
(3)	18,000
(15)	(10,500)
Bal.	7,500

Salaries Payable

Bal.	6,000
(1)	(6,000)
(16)	4,000
Bal.	4,000

Common Stock

Bal.	5,000
(12)	2,000
Bal.	7,000

Retained Earnings

Bal.	66,000

Dividends

Bal.	0
(11)	(21,000)
Bal.	(21,000)

Consulting Revenue

Bal.	0
(5)	96,400
(15)	10,500
Bal.	106,900

Other Operating Expenses

Bal.	0
(8)	(21,000)
Bal.	(21,000)

Salary Expense

Bal.	0
(7)	(32,000)
(16)	(4,000)
Bal.	(36,000)

Rent Expense

Bal.	0
(14)	(10,000)
Bal.	(10,000)

Supplies Expense

Bal.	0
(13)	(650)
Bal.	(650)

Vertical Statements Model

Financial statement users obtain helpful insights by analyzing company trends over multiple accounting cycles. Exhibit 2.8 presents for Cato Consultants a multicycle **vertical statements model** of 2010 and 2011 accounting data. To conserve space, we

Explain how business events affect financial statements over multiple accounting cycles.

have combined all the expenses for each year into single amounts labeled "Operating Expenses," determined as follows.

	2010	2011
Other operating expenses	$ 0	$21,000
Salary expense	16,000	36,000
Rent expense	0	10,000
Advertising expense	2,000	0
Supplies expense	0	650
Total operating expenses	$18,000	$67,650

Similarly, we combined the cash payments for operating expenses on the statement of cash flows as follows.

	2010	2011
Supplies and other operating expenses	$ 0	$18,200*
Salary expense	10,000	38,000
Rent expense	0	12,000
Advertising expense	2,000	0
Total cash payments for operating expenses	$12,000	$68,200

*Amount paid in partial settlement of accounts payable

Recall that the level of detail reported in financial statements depends on user information needs. Most real-world companies combine many account balances together to report highly summarized totals under each financial statement caption. Before reading further, trace the remaining financial statement items from the ledger accounts in Exhibit 2.7 to where they are reported in Exhibit 2.8.

The vertical statements model in Exhibit 2.8 shows significant interrelationships among the financial statements. For each year, trace the amount of net income from the income statement to the statement of changes in stockholders' equity. Next, trace the ending balances of common stock and retained earnings reported on the statement of changes in stockholders' equity to the stockholders' equity section of the balance sheet. Also, confirm that the amount of cash reported on the balance sheet equals the ending cash balance on the statement of cash flows.

Other relationships connect the two accounting periods. For example, trace the ending retained earnings balance from the 2010 statement of stockholders' equity to the beginning retained earnings balance on the 2011 statement of stockholders' equity. Also, trace the ending cash balance on the 2010 statement of cash flows to the beginning cash balance on the 2011 statement of cash flows. Finally, confirm that the change in cash between the 2010 and 2011 balance sheets ($53,000 − $9,300 = $43,700 decrease) agrees with the net change in cash reported on the 2011 statement of cash flows.

EXHIBIT 2.8	Vertical Statements Model

CATO CONSULTANTS
Financial Statements
Income Statements
For the Years Ended December 31

	2010	2011
Consulting revenue	$84,000	$106,900
Operating expenses	(18,000)	(67,650)
Net income	$66,000	$ 39,250

continued

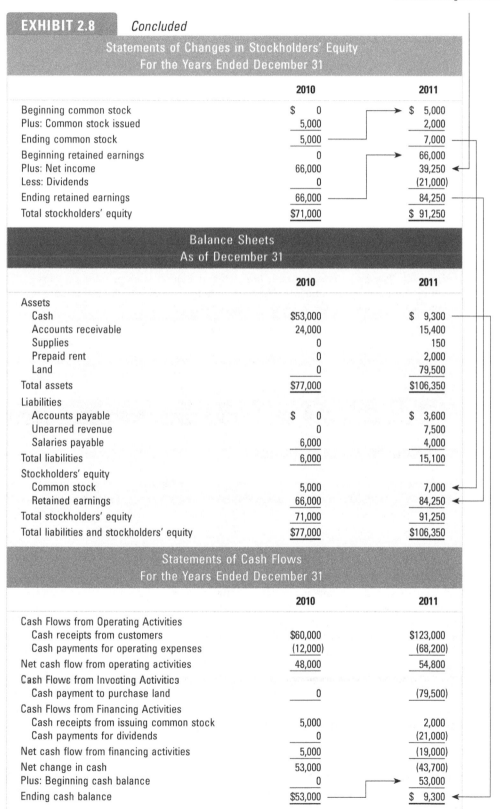

EXHIBIT 2.8	*Concluded*		

Statements of Changes in Stockholders' Equity
For the Years Ended December 31

	2010	2011
Beginning common stock	$ 0	$ 5,000
Plus: Common stock issued	5,000	2,000
Ending common stock	5,000	7,000
Beginning retained earnings	0	66,000
Plus: Net income	66,000	39,250
Less: Dividends	0	(21,000)
Ending retained earnings	66,000	84,250
Total stockholders' equity	$71,000	$ 91,250

Balance Sheets
As of December 31

	2010	2011
Assets		
Cash	$53,000	$ 9,300
Accounts receivable	24,000	15,400
Supplies	0	150
Prepaid rent	0	2,000
Land	0	79,500
Total assets	$77,000	$106,350
Liabilities		
Accounts payable	$ 0	$ 3,600
Unearned revenue	0	7,500
Salaries payable	6,000	4,000
Total liabilities	6,000	15,100
Stockholders' equity		
Common stock	5,000	7,000
Retained earnings	66,000	84,250
Total stockholders' equity	71,000	91,250
Total liabilities and stockholders' equity	$77,000	$106,350

Statements of Cash Flows
For the Years Ended December 31

	2010	2011
Cash Flows from Operating Activities		
Cash receipts from customers	$60,000	$123,000
Cash payments for operating expenses	(12,000)	(68,200)
Net cash flow from operating activities	48,000	54,800
Cash Flows from Investing Activities		
Cash payment to purchase land	0	(79,500)
Cash Flows from Financing Activities		
Cash receipts from issuing common stock	5,000	2,000
Cash payments for dividends	0	(21,000)
Net cash flow from financing activities	5,000	(19,000)
Net change in cash	53,000	(43,700)
Plus: Beginning cash balance	0	53,000
Ending cash balance	$53,000	$ 9,300

CHECK *Yourself* 2.4

Treadmore Company started the 2010 accounting period with $580 of supplies on hand. During 2010 the company paid cash to purchase $2,200 of supplies. A physical count of supplies indicated that there was $420 of supplies on hand at the end of 2010. Treadmore pays cash for supplies at the time they are purchased. Based on this information alone, determine the amount of supplies expense to be recognized on the income statement and the amount of cash flow to be shown in the operating activities section of the statement of cash flows.

Answer   The amount of supplies expense recognized on the income statement is the amount of supplies that were used during the accounting period. This amount is computed below.

Beginning balance	+	Supplies purchased	=	Supplies available	−	Ending balance	=	Supplies used
$580	+	$2,200	=	$2,780	−	$420	=	$2,360

The cash flow from operating activities is the amount of cash paid for supplies during the accounting period. In this case, Treadmore paid $2,200 cash to purchase supplies. This amount would be shown as a cash outflow.

THE FINANCIAL ANALYST

CORPORATE GOVERNANCE

LO 7

Identify the primary components of corporate governance.

Corporate governance is the set of relationships between the board of directors, management, shareholders, auditors, and other stakeholders that determines how a company is operated. Clearly, financial analysts are keenly interested in these relationships. This section discusses the key components of corporate governance.

Importance of Ethics

The accountant's role in society requires trust and credibility. Accounting information is worthless if the accountant is not trustworthy. Similarly, tax and consulting advice is useless if it comes from an incompetent person. The high ethical standards required by the profession state "a certified public accountant assumes an obligation of self-discipline above and beyond requirements of laws and regulations." The **American Institute of Certified Public Accountants** requires its members to comply with the **Code of Professional Conduct.** Section I of the Code includes six articles that are summarized in Exhibit 2.9. The importance of ethical conduct is universally recognized across a broad spectrum of accounting organizations. The Institute of Management Accountants requires its members to follow a set of Standards of Ethical Conduct. The Institute of Internal Auditors also requires its members to subscribe to the organization's Code of Ethics.

Sarbanes-Oxley Act of 2002

Credible financial reporting relies on a system of checks and balances. Corporate management is responsible for preparing financial reports while outside, independent accountants (CPAs) audit the reports. The massive surprise bankruptcies of Enron in late 2001 and WorldCom several months later suggested major audit failures on the part of the independent auditors. An audit failure means a company's auditor does

EXHIBIT 2.9

Articles of AICPA Code of Professional Conduct

Article I Responsibilities

In carrying out their responsibilities as professionals, members should exercise sensitive professional and moral judgments in all their activities.

Article II The Public Interest

Members should accept the obligation to act in a way that will serve the public interest, honor the public trust, and demonstrate commitment to professionalism.

Article III Integrity

To maintain and broaden public confidence, members should perform all professional responsibilities with the highest sense of integrity.

Article IV Objectivity and Independence

A member should maintain objectivity and be free of conflicts of interest in discharging professional responsibilities. A member in public practice should be independent in fact and appearance when providing auditing and other attestation services.

Article V Due Care

A member should observe the profession's technical and ethical standards, strive continually to improve competence and the quality of services, and discharge professional responsibility to the best of the member's ability.

Article VI Scope and Nature of Services

A member in public practice should observe the principles of the Code of Professional Conduct in determining the scope and nature of services to be provided.

not detect, or fails to report, that the company's financial reports are not in compliance with GAAP. The audit failures at Enron, WorldCom, and others prompted Congress to pass the Sarbanes-Oxley Act (SOX), which became effective on July 30, 2002.

Prior to SOX, independent auditors often provided nonaudit services, such as installing computer systems, for their audit clients. The fees they earned for these services sometimes greatly exceeded the fees charged for the audit itself. This practice had been questioned prior to the audit failures at Enron and WorldCom. Critics felt the independent audit firm was subject to pressure from the company to conduct a less rigorous audit, or risk losing lucrative nonaudit work. To strengthen the audit function SOX included the following provisions.

- Prior to the enactment of SOX, independent auditors were self-regulated by the membership of the American Institute of Certified Public Accountants and by state boards of accountancy. Beyond self-regulation, SOX establishes The Public Company Accounting Oversight Board (PCAOB) to regulate accounting professionals that audit the financial statements of public companies.

- Independent auditors must register with the PCAOB or cease all participation in public company audits and abide by the board's pronouncements.

- The PCAOB will conduct inspections of registered firms. To ensure enforcement, the board has a full range of sanctions at its disposal, including suspension or revocation of registration, censure, and significant fines.

- To reduce the likelihood of conflicts of interest, SOX prohibits all registered public accounting firms from providing audit clients, contemporaneously with the audit, certain nonaudit services, including internal audit outsourcing, financial-information-system design and implementation services, and expert services.

- SOX provides for significant corporate governance reforms regarding audit committees and their relationship to the auditor, making the audit committee responsible for the appointment, compensation, and oversight of the issuer's auditor.

Focus On INTERNATIONAL ISSUES

Ethical conduct is shaped by the cultural climate. Indeed, a business culture that focuses narrowly on shareholder interest is frequently blamed for the excesses that led to the downfall of Enron and others. The mantra was an ever-increasing stock price. Incentive packages encourage executives to take short cuts or even engage in fraudulent behavior in order to "make the numbers." The infamous quote of Gordon Gekko in the 1987 movie *Wall Street*—"Greed is Good"—epitomized a culture of self-indulgence. Gekko's quote was drawn from Sun Tzu's management treatise *The Art of War*. This treatise contained the tenets that guided corporate governance in the 1980s and 90s.

In the aftermath of the massive corporate scandals, a new view of corporate responsibility is emerging. Many leading business schools have recruited Indian educators who

Dueling Playbooks

The opposing best-practice ideas of Sun Tzu and Krishna

To Sun Tzu, author of the once-hip management treatise *The Art of War*, victory should be the "great object." Winning the battle is all about unyielding discipline. Some of Sun Tzu's key ideas:

The *Bhagavad Gita*, a Hindu text more in keeping with today's zeitgeist, contains the wisdom of Lord Krishna. Focus on your thoughts and actions, rather than the outcome. Krishna's take:

GREED IS GOOD. Troops have to see there is "advantage from defeating the enemy" in order to be motivated. Share the booty with the rank and file, and give them shares of conquered territory.	« **ON FINANCIAL INCENTIVES** »	**GREED IS BAD.** "You should never engage in action only for the desire of rewards," Krishna says. Acting on worldly desires leads to failure. Do well, and good things will come.
BE TOUGH. Sun Tzu calls for "iron discipline": If you indulge troops with too much kindness and don't maintain your authority, they'll be "useless for any practical purpose."	« **ON MANAGING UNDERLINGS** »	**BE FAIR.** Enlightened leaders are compassionate and selfless, and they "treat everyone as their equals." Followers will rally around them and follow their example.
ATTACK ONLY WHEN VICTORY IS LIKELY. Better yet, maneuver to win without a fight. If the odds are bad, retreat and wait for another opportunity. Long campaigns strain resources and make you vulnerable.	« **ON INITIATIVE** »	**ACT RATHER THAN REACT.** A leader's actions today can become the "karma" that influences his status tomorrow. Leaders accomplish "excellence by taking action," Krishna says.
BEAT THE ENEMY. War is a vital fact of life that "cannot be neglected by a responsible sovereign." Winning requires clever tactics and, in some cases, deception.	« **ON THE ULTIMATE GOAL** »	**SEEK HIGHER CONSCIOUSNESS.** Leaders should view problems within their larger contexts. Translation: Show sensitivity to multiple stakeholders including shareholders, employees, partners, and neighbors.

hold a much broader view of corporate responsibility. Their teachings are based on the Hindu text *Bhagavad Gita,* which focuses on thoughts and actions, rather than outcomes. These educators urge executives to be motivated by a broader purpose than money. They advocate a more holistic approach to business—one that takes into account the needs of shareholders, employees, customers, society, and the environment as well as the shareholders. This view has been called "Karma Capitalism."

Karma Capitalism is a gentler, more empathetic approach to business. It advances concepts such as "emotional intelligence" and "servant leadership." *BusinessWeek* observes manifestations such as "where once corporate philanthropy was an obligation, these days it's fast becoming viewed as a competitive advantage for attracting and retaining top talent." Where the rallying cry in the 1980s and 90s may have been "greed is good," today it's becoming "green is good." Certainly, this new zeitgeist is more supportive of moral conduct than a culture based largely on self-interest.

The contrasting philosophies are summarized above under the heading "Dueling Playbooks."

Other provisions of SOX clarify the legal responsibility that company management has for a company's financial reports. The company's chief executive officer (CEO) and chief financial officer (CFO) must certify in writing that they have reviewed the financial reports being issued, and that the reports present fairly the company's financial status. An executive who falsely certifies the company's financial reports is subject to a fine up to $5 million and imprisonment up to 20 years.

Common Features of Criminal and Ethical Misconduct

Unfortunately, it takes more than a code of conduct to stop fraud. People frequently engage in activities that they know are unethical or even criminal. The auditing profession has identified three elements that are typically present when fraud occurs.

1. The availability of an opportunity.
2. The existence of some form of pressure leading to an incentive.
3. The capacity to rationalize.

EXHIBIT 2.10

The Fraud Triangle

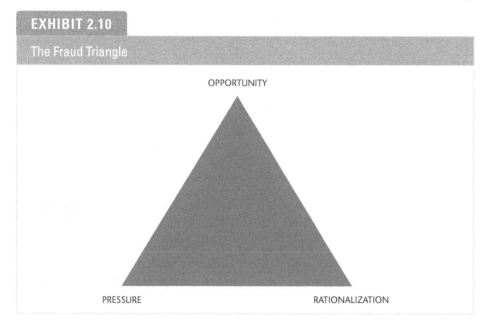

The three elements are frequently arranged in the shape of a triangle as shown in Exhibit 2.10.

Opportunity is shown at the head to the triangle because without opportunity fraud could not exist. The most effective way to reduce opportunities for ethical or criminal misconduct is to implement an effective set of internal controls. **Internal controls** are policies and procedures that a business implements to reduce opportunities for fraud and to assure that its objectives will be accomplished. Specific controls are tailored to meet the individual needs of particular businesses. For example, banks use elaborate vaults to protect cash and safety deposit boxes, but universities have little use for this type of equipment. Even so, many of the same procedures are used by a wide variety of businesses. The internal control policies and procedures that have gained widespread acceptance are discussed in a subsequent chapter.

Only a few employees turn to the dark side even when internal control is weak and opportunities abound. So, what causes one person to commit fraud and another to remain honest? The second element of the fraud triangle recognizes **pressure** as a key ingredient of misconduct. A manager who is told "either make the numbers or you are fired" is more likely to cheat than one who is told to "tell it like it is." Pressure can come from a variety of sources.

- Personal vices such as drug addiction, gambling, and promiscuity.
- Intimidation from superiors.
- Personal debt from credit cards, consumer and mortgage loans, or poor investments.
- Family expectations to provide a standard of living that is beyond one's capabilities.
- Business failure caused by poor decision making or temporary factors such as a poor economy.
- Loyalty or trying to be agreeable.

The third and final element of the fraud triangle is **rationalization.** Few individuals think of themselves as evil. They develop rationalizations to justify their misconduct. Common rationalizations include the following.

- Everybody does it.
- They are not paying me enough. I'm only taking what I deserve.

- I'm only borrowing the money. I'll pay it back.
- The company can afford it. Look what they are paying the officers.
- I'm taking what my family needs to live like everyone else.

Most people are able to resist pressure and the tendency to rationalize ethical or legal misconduct. However, some people will yield to temptation. What can accountants do to protect themselves and their companies from unscrupulous characters? The answer lies in personal integrity. The best indicator of personal integrity is past performance. Accordingly, companies must exercise due care in performing appropriate background investigations before hiring people to fill positions of trust.

Ethical misconduct is a serious offense in the accounting profession. A single mistake can destroy an accounting career. If you commit a white-collar crime, you normally lose the opportunity to hold a white-collar job. Second chances are rarely granted; it is extremely important that you learn how to recognize and avoid the common features of ethical misconduct. To help you prepare for the real-world situations you are likely to encounter, we include ethical dilemmas in the end-of-chapter materials. When working with these dilemmas, try to identify the (1) opportunity, (2) pressure, and (3) rationalization associated with the particular ethical situation described. If you are not an ethical person, accounting is not the career for you.

<< A Look Back

Classify accounting events into one of four categories:

a. asset source transactions.
b. asset use transactions.
c. asset exchange transactions.
d. claims exchange transactions.

Chapters 1 and 2 introduced four types of transactions. Although businesses engage in an infinite number of different transactions, all transactions fall into one of four types. By learning to identify transactions by type, you can understand how unfamiliar events affect financial statements. The four types of transactions are

1. *Asset source transactions:* An asset account increases, and a corresponding claims account increases.

2. *Asset use transactions:* An asset account decreases, and a corresponding claims account decreases.

3. *Asset exchange transactions:* One asset account increases, and another asset account decreases.

4. *Claims exchange transactions:* One claims account increases, and another claims account decreases.

Also, the definitions of revenue and expense have been expanded. The complete definitions of these two elements are as follows.

1. **Revenue:** Revenue is the *economic benefit* derived from operating the business. Its recognition is accompanied by an increase in assets or a decrease in liabilities resulting from providing products or services to customers.

2. **Expense:** An expense is an *economic sacrifice* incurred in the process of generating revenue. Its recognition is accompanied by a decrease in assets or an increase in liabilities resulting from consuming assets and services in an effort to produce revenue.

This chapter introduced accrual accounting. Accrual accounting distinguishes between *recognition* and *realization.* Recognition means reporting an economic item or event in the financial statements. In contrast, realization refers to collecting cash from the sale of assets or services. Recognition and realization can occur in different accounting periods. In addition, cash payments for expenses often occur in different accounting periods from when a company recognizes the expenses. Accrual accounting uses both *accruals* and *deferrals.*

- The term *accrual* applies to earnings events that are recognized before cash is exchanged. Recognizing revenue on account or accrued salaries expense are examples of accruals.

- The term *deferral* applies to earnings events that are recognized after cash has been exchanged. Supplies, prepaid items, and unearned revenue are examples of deferrals.

   Virtually all major companies operating in the United States use accrual accounting.

A Look Forward

Chapters 1 and 2 focused on businesses that generate revenue by providing services to their customers. Examples of these types of businesses include consulting, real estate sales, medical services, and legal services. The next chapter introduces accounting practices for businesses that generate revenue by selling goods. Examples of these companies include Wal-Mart, Circuit City, Office Depot, and Lowes.

 SELF-STUDY REVIEW PROBLEM

Gifford Company experienced the following accounting events during 2010.

1. Started operations on January 1 when it acquired $20,000 cash by issuing common stock.
2. Earned $18,000 of revenue on account.
3. On March 1 collected $36,000 cash as an advance for services to be performed in the future.
4. Paid cash operating expenses of $17,000.
5. Paid a $2,700 cash dividend to stockholders.
6. On December 31, 2010, adjusted the books to recognize the revenue earned by providing services related to the advance described in Event 3. The contract required Gifford to provide services for a one-year period starting March 1.
7. Collected $15,000 cash from accounts receivable.

   Gifford Company experienced the following accounting events during 2011.

1. Recognized $38,000 of cash revenue.
2. On April 1 paid $12,000 cash for an insurance policy that provides coverage for one year beginning immediately.
3. Collected $2,000 cash from accounts receivable.
4. Paid cash operating expenses of $21,000.
5. Paid a $5,000 cash dividend to stockholders.
6. On December 31, 2011, adjusted the books to recognize the remaining revenue earned by providing services related to the advance described in Event 3 of 2010.
7. On December 31, 2011, Gifford adjusted the books to recognize the amount of the insurance policy used during 2011.

Required

a. Record the events in a financial statements model like the following one. The first event is recorded as an example.

Event No.	Assets			=	Liab.	+	Stockholders' Equity							
	Cash +	Accts. Rec. −	Prep. Ins. =		Unearn. Rev. +		Com. Stk. +	Ret. Earn.		Rev. −	Exp. =	Net Inc.		Cash Flow
1	20,000 +	NA −	NA =		NA +		20,000 +	NA		NA −	NA =	NA		20,000 FA

b. What amount of revenue would Gifford report on the 2010 income statement?

c. What amount of cash flow from customers would Gifford report on the 2010 statement of cash flows?

d. What amount of unearned revenue would Gifford report on the 2010 and 2011 year-end balance sheets?

e. What are the 2011 opening balances for the revenue and expense accounts?

f. What amount of total assets would Gifford report on the December 31, 2010, balance sheet?

g. What claims on assets would Gifford report on the December 31, 2011, balance sheet?

Solution to Requirement a
The financial statements model follows.

Event No.		Assets			=	Liab.	+	Stockholders' Equity								
	Cash	+	Accts. Rec.	+	Prep. Ins.	=	Unearn. Rev.	+	Com. Stk.	+	Ret. Earn.	Rev.	−	Exp.	=	Net Inc.	Cash Flow
2010																
1	20,000	+	NA	+	NA	=	NA	+	20,000	+	NA	NA	−	NA	=	NA	20,000 FA
2	NA	+	18,000	+	NA	=	NA	+	NA	+	18,000	18,000	−	NA	=	18,000	NA
3	36,000	+	NA	+	NA	=	36,000	+	NA	+	NA	NA	−	NA	=	NA	36,000 OA
4	(17,000)	+	NA	+	NA	=	NA	+	NA	+	(17,000)	NA	−	17,000	=	(17,000)	(17,000) OA
5	(2,700)	+	NA	+	NA	=	NA	+	NA	+	(2,700)	NA	−	NA	=	NA	(2,700) FA
6*	NA	+	NA	+	NA	=	(30,000)	+	NA	+	30,000	30,000	−	NA	=	30,000	NA
7	15,000	+	(15,000)	+	NA	=	NA	+	NA	+	NA	NA	−	NA	=	NA	15,000 OA
Bal.	51,300	+	3,000	+	NA	=	6,000	+	20,000	+	28,300	48,000	−	17,000	=	31,000	51,300 NC
	Asset, liability, and equity account balances carry forward											Rev. & exp. accts. are closed					
2011																	
Bal.	51,300	+	3,000	+	NA	=	6,000	+	20,000	+	28,300	NA	−	NA	=	NA	NA
1	38,000	+	NA	+	NA	=	NA	+	NA	+	38,000	38,000	−	NA	=	38,000	38,000 OA
2	(12,000)	+	NA	+	12,000	=	NA	+	NA	+	NA	NA	−	NA	=	NA	(12,000) OA
3	2,000	+	(2,000)	+	NA	=	NA	+	NA	+	NA	NA	−	NA	=	NA	2,000 OA
4	(21,000)	+	NA	+	NA	=	NA	+	NA	+	(21,000)	NA	−	21,000	=	(21,000)	(21,000) OA
5	(5,000)	+	NA	+	NA	=	NA	+	NA	+	(5,000)	NA	−	NA	=	NA	(5,000) FA
6*	NA	+	NA	+	NA	=	(6,000)	+	NA	+	6,000	6,000	−	NA	=	6,000	NA
7†	NA	+	NA	+	(9,000)	=	NA	+	NA	+	(9,000)	NA	−	9,000	=	(9,000)	NA
Bal.	53,300	+	1,000	+	3,000	=	0	+	20,000	+	37,300	44,000	−	30,000	=	14,000	2,000 NC

*Revenue is earned at the rate of $3,000 ($36,000 ÷ 12 months) per month. Revenue recognized in 2010 is $30,000 ($3,000 × 10 months). Revenue recognized in 2011 is $6,000 ($3,000 × 2 months).

†Insurance expense is incurred at the rate of $1,000 ($12,000 ÷ 12 months) per month. Insurance expense recognized in 2011 is $9,000 ($1,000 × 9 months).

Solutions to Requirements b–g

b. Gifford would report $48,000 of revenue in 2010 ($18,000 revenue on account plus $30,000 of the $36,000 of unearned revenue).

c. The cash inflow from customers is $51,000 ($36,000 when the unearned revenue was received plus $15,000 collection of accounts receivable).

d. The December 31, 2010, balance sheet will report $6,000 of unearned revenue, which is the amount of the cash advance less the amount of revenue recognized in 2010 ($36,000 − $30,000). The December 31, 2011, unearned revenue balance is zero.

e. Since revenue and expense accounts are closed at the end of each accounting period, the beginning balances in these accounts are always zero.

f. Assets on the December 31, 2010, balance sheet are $54,300 [Gifford's cash at year end plus the balance in accounts receivable ($51,300 + $3,000)].

g. Since all unearned revenue would be recognized before the financial statements were prepared at the end of 2011, there would be no liabilities on the 2011 balance sheet. Common stock and retained earnings would be the only claims as of December 31, 2011, for a claims total of $57,300 ($20,000 + $37,300).

KEY TERMS

Accounts Receivable 44
Accrual 43
Accrual accounting 43
Accrued expenses 46
Adjusting entry 46
American Institute of Certified
    Public Accountants 64
Asset exchange transaction 44

Asset source transaction 44
Asset use transaction 45
Claims exchange
    transaction 46
Code of Professional
    Conduct 64
Conservatism 51
Cost 52

Deferral 43
Expense 49, 68
Internal controls 67
Matching concept 51
Opportunity 67
Period costs 51
Prepaid items 52
Pressure 67

Rationalization 67
Realization 42
Recognition 42
Revenue 68
Salaries Payable 46
Unearned revenue 53
Vertical statements model 61

QUESTIONS

1. What does accrual accounting attempt to accomplish?

2. Define *recognition*. How is it independent of collecting or paying cash?

3. What does the term *deferral* mean?

4. If cash is collected in advance of performing services, when is the associated revenue recognized?

5. What does the term *asset source transaction* mean?

6. What effect does the issue of common stock have on the accounting equation?

7. How does the recognition of revenue on account (accounts receivable) affect the income statement compared to its effect on the statement of cash flows?

8. Give an example of an asset source transaction. What is the effect of this transaction on the accounting equation?

9. When is revenue recognized under accrual accounting?

10. Give an example of an asset exchange transaction. What is the effect of this transaction on the accounting equation?

11. What is the effect on the claims side of the accounting equation when cash is collected in advance of performing services?

12. What does the term *unearned revenue* mean?

13. What effect does expense recognition have on the accounting equation?

14. What does the term *claims exchange transaction* mean?

15. What type of transaction is a cash payment to creditors? How does this type of transaction affect the accounting equation?

16. When are expenses recognized under accrual accounting?

17. Why may net cash flow from operating activities on the cash flow statement be different from the amount of net income reported on the income statement?

18. What is the relationship between the income statement and changes in assets and liabilities?

19. How does net income affect the stockholders' claims on the business's assets?

20. What is the difference between a cost and an expense?

21. When does a cost become an expense? Do all costs become expenses?

22. How and when is the cost of the *supplies used* recognized in an accounting period?

23. What does the term *expense* mean?

24. What does the term *revenue* mean?

25. What is the purpose of the statement of changes in stockholders' equity?

26. What is the main purpose of the balance sheet?

27. Why is the balance sheet dated *as of* a specific date when the income statement, statement of changes in stockholders' equity, and statement of cash flows are dated with the phrase *for the period ended?*

28. In what order are assets listed on the balance sheet?

29. What does the statement of cash flows explain?

30. What does the term *adjusting entry* mean? Give an example.

31. What types of accounts are closed at the end of the accounting period? Why is it necessary to close these accounts?

32. Give several examples of period costs.

33. Give an example of a cost that can be directly matched with the revenue produced by an accounting firm from preparing a tax return.

34. List and describe the four stages of the accounting cycle discussed in Chapter 2.

35. Name and comment on the three elements of the fraud triangle.

36. What is the maximum penalty and prison term that can be charged to a CEO and/or CFO under the Sarbanes-Oxley Act?

37. What are the six articles of ethical conduct set out under section I of the AICPA's Code of Professional Conduct?

EXERCISES

All applicable Exercises are available with McGraw-Hill
Connect Accounting.

Where applicable in all exercises, round computations to the nearest dollar.

LO 2, 3

Exercise 2-1   *Effect of accruals on the financial statements*

Maddox, Inc., experienced the following events in 2010, in its first year of operation.

1. Received $20,000 cash from the issue of common stock.
2. Performed services on account for $40,000.
3. Paid the utility expense of $3,500.
4. Collected $36,000 of the accounts receivable.
5. Recorded $8,000 of accrued salaries at the end of the year.
6. Paid a $2,000 cash dividend to the shareholders.

Required

a. Record the events in general ledger accounts under an accounting equation. In the last column of the table, provide appropriate account titles for the Retained Earnings amounts. The first transaction has been recorded as an example.

MADDOX INC.							
General Ledger Accounts							
Event	Assets		=	Liabilities	+	Stockholders' Equity	Acct. Titles for RE
	Cash	Accounts Receivable		Notes Payable		Common Stock	Retained Earnings	
1.	20,000					20,000		

b. Prepare the income statement, statement of changes in stockholders' equity, balance sheet, and statement of cash flows for the 2010 accounting period.

c. Why is the amount of net income different from the amount of net cash flow from operating activities?

LO 2, 3

Exercise 2-2   *Effect of collecting accounts receivable on the accounting equation and financial statements*

Venture Company earned $8,000 of service revenue on account during 2010. The company collected $5,200 cash from accounts receivable during 2010.

Required

Based on this information alone, determine the following. (*Hint:* Record the events in general ledger accounts under an accounting equation before satisfying the requirements.)

a. The balance of the accounts receivable that Venture would report on the December 31, 2010, balance sheet.

b. The amount of net income that Venture would report on the 2010 income statement.

c. The amount of net cash flow from operating activities that Venture would report on the 2010 statement of cash flows.

d. The amount of retained earnings that Venture would report on the 2010 balance sheet.

e. Why are the answers to Requirements *b* and *c* different?

LO 2, 3

Exercise 2-3   *Effect of prepaid rent on the accounting equation and financial statements*

The following events apply to 2009, the first year of operations of Howard Services.

1. Acquired $30,000 cash from the issue of common stock.
2. Paid $12,000 cash in advance for one-year rental contract for office space.
3. Provided services for $23,000 cash.
4. Adjusted the records to recognize the use of the office space. The one-year contract started on May 1, 2009. The adjustment was made as of December 31, 2009.

Required

a. Write an accounting equation and record the effects of each accounting event under the appropriate general ledger account headings.

b. Prepare an income statement and statement of cash flows for the 2009 accounting period.

c. Explain the difference between the amount of net income and amount of net cash flow from operating activities.

Exercise 2-4 *Effect of supplies on the financial statements*

LO **1, 3**

Kim's Copy Service, Inc., started the 2009 accounting period with $9,000 cash, $6,000 of common stock, and $3,000 of retained earnings. Kim's Copy Service was affected by the following accounting events during 2009.

1. Purchased $11,500 of paper and other supplies on account.

2. Earned and collected $31,000 of cash revenue.

3. Paid $9,000 cash on accounts payable.

4. Adjusted the records to reflect the use of supplies. A physical count indicated that $3,000 of supplies was still on hand on December 31, 2009.

Required

a. Show the effects of the events on the financial statements using a horizontal statements model like the following one. In the Cash Flows column, use OA to designate operating activity, IA for investing activity, FA for financing activity, and NC for net change in cash. Use NA to indicate accounts not affected by the event. The beginning balances are entered in the following example.

Event No.	Assets			=	Liab.	+	Stockholders' Equity			Rev.	−	Exp.	=	Net Inc.	Cash Flows
	Cash	+	Supplies	=	Accts. Pay	+	C. Stock	+	Ret. Earn.						
Beg. Bal.	9,000	+	0	=	0	+	6,000	+	3,000	0	−	0	=	0	0

b. Explain the difference between the amount of net income and amount of net cash flow from operating activities.

Exercise 2-5 *Effect of unearned revenue on financial statements*

LO **1**

Jordan Michael started a personal financial planning business when she accepted $80,000 cash as advance payment for managing the financial assets of a large estate. Michael agreed to manage the estate for a one-year period, beginning April 1, 2009.

Required

a. Show the effects of the advance payment and revenue recognition on the 2009 financial statements using a horizontal statements model like the following one. In the Cash Flows column, use OA to designate operating activity, IA for investing activity, FA for financing activity, and NC for net change in cash. Use NA if the account is not affected.

Event No.	Assets	=	Liab.	+	Stockholders' Equity	Rev.	−	Exp.	=	Net Inc.	Cash Flows
	Cash	=	Unearn. Rev.	+	Ret. Earn.						

b. How much revenue would Jordan recognize on the 2010 income statement?

c. What is the amount of cash flow from operating activities in 2010?

Exercise 2-6 *Unearned revenue defined as a liability*

LO **3**

Martin Gantt received $600 in advance for tutoring fees when he agreed to help Josh Smith with his introductory accounting course. Upon receiving the cash, Martin mentioned that he would have to record the transaction as a liability on his books. Smith asked, "Why a liability? You don't owe me any money, do you?"

Required

Respond to Smith's question regarding Gantt's liability.

LO 3

Exercise 2-7 *Distinguishing between an expense and a cost*

Christy Byrd tells you that the accountants where she works are real hair splitters. For example, they make a big issue over the difference between a cost and an expense. She says the two terms mean the same thing to her.

Required

a. Explain to Christy the difference between a cost and an expense from an accountant's perspective.
b. Explain whether each of the following events produces an asset or an expense.
  (1) Purchased a building for cash.
  (2) Purchased supplies on account.
  (3) Used supplies on hand to produce revenue.
  (4) Paid in advance for insurance on the building.
  (5) Recognized accrued salaries.

LO 3

Exercise 2-8 *Revenue and expense recognition*

Required

a. Describe a revenue recognition event that results in a decrease in liabilities.
b. Describe a revenue recognition event that results in an increase in assets.
c. Describe an expense recognition event that results in an increase in liabilities.
d. Describe an expense recognition event that results in a decrease in assets.

LO 3

Exercise 2-9 *Transactions that affect the elements of financial statements*

Required

Give an example of a transaction that will

a. Increase an asset and decrease another asset (asset exchange event).
b. Increase an asset and increase a liability (asset source event).
c. Decrease an asset and decrease a liability (asset use event).
d. Decrease an asset and decrease equity (asset use event).
e. Increase a liability and decrease equity (claims exchange event).
f. Increase an asset and increase equity (asset source event).
g. Decrease a liability and increase equity (claims exchange event).

LO 3

Exercise 2-10 *Identifying deferral and accrual events*

Required

Identify each of the following events as an accrual, deferral, or neither.

a. Incurred other operating expenses on account.
b. Recorded expense for salaries owed to employees at the end of the accounting period.
c. Paid a cash dividend to the stockholders.
d. Paid cash to purchase supplies to be used over the next several months.
e. Purchased land with cash.
f. Provided services on account.
g. Collected accounts receivable.
h. Paid one year's rent in advance.
i. Paid cash for utilities expense.
j. Collected $2,400 in advance for services to be performed over the next 12 months.

Exercise 2-11 *Prepaid and unearned rent*   LO 2

On August 1, 2010, Corn Products paid Warehouse Rentals $48,000 for a 12-month lease on warehouse space.

Required

a. Record the deferral and the related December 31, 2010, adjustment for Corn Products in the accounting equation.

b. Record the deferral and the related December 31, 2010, adjustment for Warehouse Rentals in the accounting equation.

Exercise 2-12 *Classifying events on the statement of cash flows*   LO 3

The following transactions pertain to the operations of Traci Company for 2011.

1. Acquired $30,000 cash from the issue of common stock.

2. Provided $40,000 of services on account.

3. Incurred $25,000 of other operating expenses on account.

4. Collected $37,000 cash from accounts receivable.

5. Paid a $2,000 cash dividend to the stockholders.

6. Paid $18,000 cash on accounts payable.

7. Performed services for $9,000 cash.

8. Paid $2,000 cash for rent expense.

9. Paid $20,000 for year's rent for office space.

10. Received $24,000 cash in advance for services to be performed over the next two years.

Required

a. Classify the cash flows from these transactions as operating activities (OA), investing activities (IA), or financing activities (FA). Use NA for transactions that do not affect the statement of cash flows.

b. Prepare a statement of cash flows. (There is no beginning cash balance.)

Exercise 2-13 *Effect of accounting events on the income statement and statement*   LO 3
                 of cash flows

Required

Explain how each of the following events and the related adjusting entry will affect the amount of *net income* and the amount of *cash flow from operating activities* reported on the year-end financial statements. Identify the direction of change (increase, decrease, or NA) and the amount of the change. Organize your answers according to the following table. The first event is recorded as an example. If an event does not have a related adjusting entry, record only the effects of the event.

	Net Income		Cash Flows from Operating Activities	
Event No.	Direction of Change	Amount of Change	Direction of Change	Amount of Change
a	NA	NA	NA	NA

a. Acquired $70,000 cash from the issue of common stock.

b. Earned $15,000 of revenue on account. Collected $12,000 cash from accounts receivable.

c. Paid $3,600 cash on October 1 to purchase a one-year insurance policy.

d. Collected $9,600 in advance for services to be performed in the future. The contract called for services to start on September 1 and to continue for one year.

e. Accrued salaries amounting to $6,000.

f. Sold land that had cost $8,000 for $8,000.

g. Provided services for $9,000 cash.

h. Purchased $1,200 of supplies on account. Paid $1,000 cash on accounts payable. The ending balance in the Supplies account, after adjustment, was $400.

i. Paid cash for other operating expenses of $2,600.

LO 1, 8   **Exercise 2-14**   *Identifying transaction type and effect on the financial statements*

Required

Identify whether each of the following transactions is an asset source (AS), asset use (AU), asset exchange (AE), or claims exchange (CE). Also show the effects of the events on the financial statements using the horizontal statements model. Indicate whether the event increases (I), decreases (D), or does not affect (NA) each element of the financial statements. In the Cash Flows column, designate the cash flows as operating activities (OA), investing activities (IA), or financing activities (FA). The first two transactions have been recorded as examples.

Event No.	Type of Event	Assets	=	Liabilities	+	Stockholders' Equity		Rev.	−	Exp.	=	Net Inc.	Cash Flows
						Common Stock	**Retained Earnings**						
a	AE	I D		NA		NA	NA	NA		NA		NA	D IA
b	AS	I		NA		I	NA	NA		NA		NA	I FA

a. Purchased land for cash.

b. Acquired cash from the issue of common stock.

c. Collected cash from accounts receivable.

d. Paid cash for operating expenses.

e. Recorded accrued salaries.

f. Paid cash for supplies.

g. Performed services on account.

h. Paid cash advance for rent on office space.

i. Performed services for cash.

j. Purchased a building with cash *and* issued a note payable.

k. Paid cash for salaries accrued at the end of a prior period.

l. Paid a cash dividend to the stockholders.

m. Adjusted books to reflect the amount of prepaid rent expired during the period.

n. Incurred operating expenses on account.

o. Paid cash on accounts payable.

p. Received cash advance for services to be provided in the future.

LO 1   **Exercise 2-15**   *Effect of accruals and deferrals on financial statements: the horizontal statements model*

G. Gabe, Attorney at Law, experienced the following transactions in 2009, the first year of operations.

1. Purchased $1,500 of office supplies on account.

2. Accepted $24,000 on February 1, 2009, as a retainer for services to be performed evenly over the next 12 months.

3. Performed legal services for cash of $66,000.

4. Paid cash for salaries expense of $22,500.

5. Paid a cash dividend to the stockholders of $5,000.

6. Paid $1,000 of the amount due on accounts payable.
7. Determined that at the end of the accounting period, $125 of office supplies remained on hand.
8. On December 31, 2010, recognized the revenue that had been earned for services performed in accordance with Transaction 2.

Required

Show the effects of the events on the financial statements using a horizontal statements model like the following one. In the Cash Flow column, use the initials OA to designate operating activity, IA for investing activity, FA for financing activity, and NC for net change in cash. Use NA to indicate accounts not affected by the event. The first event has been recorded as an example.

Event No.	Assets		=	Liabilities			+	Stk. Equity	Rev.	−	Exp.	=	Net Inc.	Cash Flow
	Cash	+ Supp.	=	Accts. Pay.	+	Unearn. Rev.	+	Ret. Earn.						
1	NA	+ 1,500	=	1,500	+	NA	+	NA	NA	−	NA	=	NA	NA

Exercise 2-16   *Effect of an error on financial statements*   LO 2, 3

On May 1, 2009, Tennessee Corporation paid $12,000 cash in advance for a one-year lease on an office building. Assume that Tennessee records the prepaid rent and that the books are closed on December 31.

Required

a. Show the payment for the one-year lease and the related adjusting entry to rent expense in the accounting equation.
b. Assume that Tennessee Corporation failed to record the adjusting entry to reflect using the office building. How would the error affect the company's 2009 income statement and balance sheet?

Exercise 2-17   *Net income versus changes in cash*   LO 2, 3

In 2010, Puckett Inc. billed its customers $60,000 for services performed. The company collected $42,000 of the amount billed. Puckett incurred $38,000 of other operating expenses on account. Puckett paid $30,000 of the accounts payable. Puckett acquired $35,000 cash from the issue of common stock. The company invested $15,000 cash in the purchase of land.

Required

Use the preceding information to answer the following questions. (*Hint:* Identify the six events described in the paragraph and record them in general ledger accounts under an accounting equation before attempting to answer the questions.)

a. What amount of revenue will Puckett report on the 2010 income statement?
b. What amount of cash flow from revenue will Puckett report on the statement of cash flows?
c. What is the net income for the period?
d. What is the net cash flow from operating activities for the period?
e. Why is the amount of net income different from the net cash flow from operating activities for the period?
f. What is the amount of net cash flow from investing activities?
g. What is the amount of net cash flow from financing activities?
h. What amounts of total assets, liabilities, and equity will Puckett report on the year-end balance sheet?

78   Chapter 2

LO 3

Exercise 2-18   *Adjusting the accounts*

Morgan Associates experienced the following accounting events during its 2010 accounting period.

1. Paid cash for an insurance policy that provides coverage during the next year.
2. Collected cash from accounts receivable.
3. Paid cash for operating expenses.
4. Paid cash to settle an account payable.
5. Paid cash to purchase land.
6. Recognized revenue on account.
7. Issued common stock.
8. Paid cash to purchase supplies.
9. Collected a cash advance for services that will be provided during the coming year.
10. Paid a cash dividend to the stockholders.

Required

a. Identify the events that would require a year-end adjusting entry.
b. Explain why adjusting entries are made at the end of the accounting period.

LO 4

Exercise 2-19   *Closing the accounts*

The following information was drawn from the accounting records of Spartan Company as of December 31, 2010, before the temporary accounts had been closed. The Cash balance was $3,000, and Notes Payable amounted to $1,300. The company had revenues of $4,500 and expenses of $2,000. The company's Land account had a $5,000 balance. Dividends amounted to $300. There was $1,000 of common stock issued.

Required

a. Identify which accounts would be classified as permanent and which accounts would be classified as temporary.
b. Assuming that Spartan's beginning balance (as of January 1, 2010) in the Retained Earnings account was $3,500, determine its balance after the nominal accounts were closed at the end of 2010.
c. What amount of net income would Spartan Company report on its 2010 income statement?
d. Explain why the amount of net income differs from the amount of the ending Retained Earnings balance.
e. What are the balances in the revenue, expense, and dividend accounts on January 1, 2011?

LO 4

Exercise 2-20   *Closing accounts and the accounting cycle*

Required

a. Identify which of the following accounts are temporary (will be closed to Retained Earnings at the end of the year) and which are permanent.
 (1) Common Stock
 (2) Notes Payable
 (3) Cash
 (4) Service Revenue
 (5) Dividends
 (6) Land
 (7) Salaries Expense
 (8) Retained Earnings
 (9) Prepaid Rent
 (10) Supplies Expense
b. List and explain the four stages of the accounting cycle. Which stage must be first? Which stage is last?

Exercise 2-21 *Closing entries*   LO **4**

Required

Which of the following accounts are closed at the end of the accounting period?

a. Dividends
b. Retained Earnings
c. Utilities Expense
d. Salaries Payable
e. Salaries Expense
f. Operating Expenses
g. Accounts Payable
h. Unearned Revenue
i. Prepaid Rent
j. Rent Expense
k. Service Revenue
l. Advertising Expense

Exercise 2-22 *Matching concept*   LO **3**

Companies make sacrifices known as *expenses* to obtain benefits called *revenues.* The accurate measurement of net income requires that expenses be matched with revenues. In some circumstances matching a particular expense directly with revenue is difficult or impossible. In these circumstances, the expense is matched with the period in which it is incurred.

Required

Distinguish the following items that could be matched directly with revenues from the items that would be classified as period expenses.

a. Sales commissions paid to employees.
b. Advertising expense.
c. Rent expense.
d. The cost of land that has been sold.

Exercise 2-23 *Identifying source, use, and exchange transactions*   LO **8**

Required

Indicate whether each of the following transactions is an asset source (AS), asset use (AU), asset exchange (AE), or claims exchange (CE) transaction.

a. Performed services for cash.
b. Performed services for clients on account.
c. Collected cash from accounts receivable.
d. Invested cash in a certificate of deposit.
e. Purchased land with cash.
f. Acquired cash from the issue of stock.
g. Paid a cash dividend to the stockholders.
h. Paid cash on accounts payable.
i. Incurred other operating expenses on account.
j. Paid cash for rent expense.

Exercise 2-24 *Identifying asset source, use, and exchange transactions*   LO **8**

Required

a. Name an asset use transaction that will affect the income statement.
b. Name an asset use transaction that will *not* affect the income statement.
c. Name an asset exchange transaction that will *not* affect the statement of cash flows.
d. Name an asset exchange transaction that will affect the statement of cash flows.
e. Name an asset source transaction that will *not* affect the income statement.

LO 3

Exercise 2-25   *Relation of elements to financial statements*

Required

Identify whether each of the following items would appear on the income statement (IS), statement of changes in stockholders' equity (SE), balance sheet (BS), or statement of cash flows (CF). Some items may appear on more than one statement; if so, identify all applicable statements. If an item would not appear on any financial statement, label it NA.

a. Accounts receivable

b. Accounts payable

c. Unearned revenue

d. Dividends

e. Beginning cash balance

f. Ending retained earnings

g. Rent expense

h. Ending cash balance

i. Prepaid rent

j. Net income

k. Utilities expense

l. Supplies

m. Cash flow from operating activities

n. Service revenue

o. Auditor's opinion

LO 7

Exercise 2-26   *Sarbanes-Oxley (SOX) Act*

In February 2006, former Senator Warren Rudman of New Hampshire completed a 17-month investigation of an $11 billion accounting scandal at Fannie Mae (a major enterprise involved in home-mortgage financing). The Rudman investigation concluded that Fannie Mae's CFO and controller used an accounting gimmick to manipulate financial statements in order to meet earning-per-share (EPS) targets. Meeting the EPS targets triggered bonus payments for the executives.

Required

Comment on the provisions of SOX that pertain to intentional misrepresentation and describe the maximum penalty that the CFO could face.

PROBLEMS

connect
|ACCOUNTING

All applicable Problems are available with McGraw-Hill
Connect Accounting.

LO 1

Problem 2-27   *Recording events in a horizontal statements model*

The following events pertain to The Mesa Company.

1. Acquired $15,000 cash from the issue of common stock.

2. Provided services for $4,000 cash.

3. Provided $13,000 of services on account.

4. Collected $9,000 cash from the account receivable created in Event 3.

5. Paid $1,100 cash to purchase supplies.

6. Had $100 of supplies on hand at the end of the accounting period.

7. Received $2,400 cash in advance for services to be performed in the future.

8. Performed one-half of the services agreed to in Event 7.

9. Paid $5,000 for salaries expense.

10. Incurred $1,500 of other operating expenses on account.

11. Paid $1,200 cash on the account payable created in Event 10.

12. Paid a $1,500 cash dividend to the stockholders.

Required

Show the effects of the events on the financial statements using a horizontal statements model like the following one. In the Cash Flows column, use the letters OA to designate operating activity, IA for investing activity, FA for financing activity, and NC for net change in cash. Use NA to indicate accounts not affected by the event. The first event is recorded as an example.

Event No.		Assets			=	Liabilities			+	Stockholders' Equity			Rev.	−	Exp.	=	Net Inc.		Cash Flows
	Cash	+	Accts. Rec.	+ Supp.	=	Accts. Pay.	+	Unearn. Rev.	+	Com. Stk.	+	Ret. Earn.							
1	15,000	+	NA	+ NA	=	NA	+	NA	+	15,000	+	NA	NA	−	NA	=	NA		15,000 FA

Problem 2-28   *Effect of deferrals on financial statements: three separate single-cycle examples*

Required

a. On February 1, 2010, Moore, Inc., was formed when it received $70,000 cash from the issue of common stock. On May 1, 2010, the company paid $42,000 cash in advance to rent office space for the coming year. The office space was used as a place to consult with clients. The consulting activity generated $80,000 of cash revenue during 2010. Based on this information alone, record the events and related adjusting entry in the general ledger accounts under the accounting equation. Determine the amount of net income and cash flows from operating activities for 2010.

b. On January 1, 2010, the accounting firm of Wayne & Associates was formed. On August 1, 2010, the company received a retainer fee (was paid in advance) of $36,000 for services to be performed monthly during the next 12 months. Assuming that this was the only transaction completed in 2010, prepare an income statement, statement of changes in stockholders' equity, balance sheet, and statement of cash flows for 2010.

c. Hal Company had $1,250 of supplies on hand on January 1, 2011. Hal purchased $6,500 of supplies on account during 2011. A physical count of supplies revealed that $1,500 of supplies was on hand as of December 31, 2011. Determine the amount of supplies expense that should be recognized in the December 31, 2011 adjusting entry. Use a financial statements model to show how the adjusting entry would affect the balance sheet, income statement, and statement of cash flows.

CHECK FIGURES
a. Net Income: $52,000
b. Net Income: $15,000

Problem 2-29   *Effect of adjusting entries on the accounting equation*

LO 2

Required

Each of the following independent events requires a year-end adjusting entry. Show how each event and its related adjusting entry affect the accounting equation. Assume a December 31 closing date. The first event is recorded as an example.

CHECK FIGURE
b. adjustment amount: $1,500

Event/ Adjustment	Total Assets			=	Liabilities	+	Stockholders' Equity		
	Cash	+	Other Assets	=	Liabilities	+	Common Stock		Retained Earnings
a	−6,000	+	+6,000	=	NA	+	NA		NA
Adj.	NA		−4,500		NA		NA		−4,500

a. Paid $6,000 cash in advance on April 1 for a one-year insurance policy.
b. Purchased $1,600 of supplies on account. At year's end, $100 of supplies remained on hand.
c. Paid $6,000 cash in advance on March 1 for a one-year lease on office space.
d. Received a $15,000 cash advance for a contract to provide services in the future. The contract required a one-year commitment starting September 1.
e. Paid $12,000 cash in advance on October 1 for a one-year lease on office space.

82   Chapter 2

LO 2, 5, 6, 8

CHECK FIGURES
a. Net Income, 2010: $42,500
b. Net Income, 2011: $53,850

Problem 2-30   *Events for two complete accounting cycles*

Ohio Mining Company was formed on January 1, 2010.

Events Affecting the 2010 Accounting Period

1. Acquired cash of $60,000 from the issue of common stock.
2. Purchased $1,600 of supplies on account.
3. Purchased land that cost $20,000 cash.
4. Paid $1,600 cash to settle accounts payable created in Event 2.
5. Recognized revenue on account of $68,000.
6. Paid $22,000 cash for other operating expenses.
7. Collected $46,000 cash from accounts receivable.

Information for 2010 Adjusting Entries

8. Recognized accrued salaries of $2,100 on December 31, 2010.
9. Had $200 of supplies on hand at the end of the accounting period.

Events Affecting the 2011 Accounting Period

1. Acquired an additional $20,000 cash from the issue of common stock.
2. Paid $2,100 cash to settle the salaries payable obligation.
3. Paid $4,800 cash in advance for a lease on office facilities.
4. Sold land that had cost $20,000 for $20,000 cash.
5. Received $6,600 cash in advance for services to be performed in the future.
6. Purchased $1,200 of supplies on account during the year.
7. Provided services on account of $56,000.
8. Collected $61,000 cash from accounts receivable.
9. Paid a cash dividend of $5,000 to the stockholders.

Information for 2011 Adjusting Entries

10. The advance payment for rental of the office facilities (see Event 3) was made on September 1 for a one-year lease term.
11. The cash advance for services to be provided in the future was collected on June 1 (see Event 5). The one-year contract started June 1.
12. Had $200 of supplies on hand at the end of the period.
13. Recognized accrued salaries of $3,200 at the end of the accounting period.

Required

a. Identify each event affecting the 2010 and 2011 accounting periods as asset source (AS), asset use (AU), asset exchange (AE), or claims exchange (CE). Record the effects of each event under the appropriate general ledger account headings of the accounting equation.
b. Prepare an income statement, statement of changes in stockholders' equity, balance sheet, and statement of cash flows for 2010 and 2011, using the vertical statements model.

LO 2, 3

CHECK FIGURES
b. $37,000
h. $(10,000)

Problem 2-31   *Effect of events on financial statements*

Oaks Company had the following balances in its accounting records as of December 31, 2010.

Assets		Claims	
Cash	$ 61,000	Accounts Payable	$ 25,000
Accounts Receivable	45,000	Common Stock	90,000
Land	27,000	Retained Earnings	18,000
Totals	$133,000		$133,000

The following accounting events apply to Oaks's 2010 fiscal year:

Jan. 1 Acquired an additional $70,000 cash from the issue of common stock.

April 1 Paid $6,600 cash in advance for a one-year lease for office space.

June   1   Paid a $3,000 cash dividend to the stockholders.

July   1   Purchased additional land that cost $25,000 cash.

Aug.   1   Made a cash payment on accounts payable of $13,000.

Sept.   1   Received $8,400 cash in advance as a retainer for services to be performed monthly during the next eight months.

Sept.   30   Sold land for $15,000 cash that had originally cost $15,000.

Oct.   1   Purchased $900 of supplies on account.

Dec.   31   Earned $80,000 of service revenue on account during the year.

        31   Received $66,000 cash collections from accounts receivable.

        31   Incurred $16,000 other operating expenses on account during the year.

        31   Recognized accrued salaries expense of $5,000.

        31   Had $250 of supplies on hand at the end of the period.

        31   The land purchased on July 1 had a market value of $28,000.

Required

Based on the preceding information, answer the following questions. All questions pertain to the 2010 financial statements. (*Hint:* Record the events in general ledger accounts under an accounting equation before answering the questions.)

a. What two additional adjusting entries need to be made at the end of the year?

b. What amount would be reported for land on the balance sheet?

c. What amount of net cash flow from operating activities would Oaks report on the statement of cash flows?

d. What amount of rent expense would Oaks report in the income statement?

e. What amount of total liabilities would Oaks report on the balance sheet?

f. What amount of supplies expense would Oaks report on the income statement?

g. What amount of unearned revenue would Oaks report on the balance sheet?

h. What amount of net cash flow from investing activities would Oaks report on the statement of cash flows?

i. What amount of total expenses would Oaks report on the income statement?

j. What total amount of service revenues would Oaks report on the income statement?

k. What amount of cash flows from financing activities would Oaks report on the statement of cash flows?

l. What amount of net income would Oaks report on the income statement?

m. What amount of retained earnings would Oaks report on the balance sheet?

Problem 2-32   *Identifying and arranging elements on financial statements*

LO 3

The following information was drawn from the records of Ruth & Associates at December 31, 2010.

Supplies	$ 3,000	Unearned revenue	$ 8,000
Consulting revenue	100,000	Notes payable	32,000
Land	63,000	Salaries payable	7,000
Dividends	10,000	Salary expense	47,000
Cash flow from fin. activities	20,000	Common stock issued	15,000
Interest revenue	4,000	Beginning common stock	25,000
Ending retained earnings	60,000	Accounts receivable	26,000
Cash	52,000	Cash flow from inv. activities	(30,000)
Interest payable	2,000	Cash flow from oper. activities	32,000
Interest expense	5,000	Prepaid rent	5,000

Required

Use the preceding information to construct an income statement, statement of changes in stockholders' equity, balance sheet, and statement of cash flows. (Show only totals for each activity on the statement of cash flows.)

84   Chapter 2

Problem 2-33 *Relationship of accounts to financial statements*

Required

Identify whether each of the following items would appear on the income statement (IS), statement of changes in stockholders' equity (SE), balance sheet (BS), or statement of cash flows (CF). Some items may appear on more than one statement; if so, identify all applicable statements. If an item would not appear on any financial statement, label it NA.

a.	Depreciation expense	t.	Cash
b.	Interest receivable	u.	Supplies
c.	Certificate of deposit	v.	Cash flow from financing activities
d.	Unearned revenue	w.	Interest revenue
e.	Service revenue	x.	Ending retained earnings
f.	Cash flow from investing activities	y.	Net income
g.	Consulting revenue	z.	Dividends
h.	Interest expense	aa.	Office equipment
i.	Ending common stock	bb.	Debt to equity ratio
j.	Total liabilities	cc.	Land
k.	Debt to assets ratio	dd.	Interest payable
l.	Cash flow from operating activities	ee.	Rent expense
m.	Operating expenses	ff.	Notes receivable
n.	Supplies expense	gg.	Accounts payable
o.	Beginning retained earnings	hh.	Total assets
p.	Beginning common stock	ii.	Salaries payable
q.	Prepaid insurance	jj.	Insurance expense
r.	Salary expense	kk.	Notes payable
s.	Accumulated depreciation	ll.	Accounts receivable

Problem 2-34 *Missing information in financial statements*

Required

Fill in the blanks (indicated by the alphabetic letters in parentheses) in the following financial statements. Assume the company started operations January 1, 2008, and all transactions involve cash.

	For the Years		
	2008	**2009**	**2010**
Income Statements			
Revenue	$ 400	$ 500	$ 800
Expense	(250)	(l)	(425)
Net income	$ (a)	$ 100	$ 375
Statement of Changes in Stockholders' Equity			
Beginning common stock	$ 0	$ (m)	$ 9,100
Plus: Common stock issued	(b)	1,100	310
Ending common stock	8,000	9,100	(s)
Beginning retained earnings	0	25	75
Plus: Net income	(c)	100	375
Less: Dividends	(d)	(50)	(150)
Ending retained earnings	25	(n)	300
Total stockholders' equity	$ (e)	$ 9,175	$ (t)

continued

Balance Sheets			
Assets			
Cash	$ (f)	$ (o)	$ (u)
Land	0	(p)	2,500
Total assets	$11,000	$11,650	$10,550
Liabilities	$ (g)	$ (q)	$ 840
Stockholders' equity			
Common stock	(h)	(r)	9,410
Retained earnings	(i)	75	300
Total stockholders' equity	8,025	9,175	9,710
Total liabilities and stockholders' equity	$11,000	$11,650	$10,550
Statements of Cash Flows			
Cash flows from operating activities			
Cash receipts from revenue	$ (j)	$ 500	$ (v)
Cash payments for expenses	(k)	(400)	(w)
Net cash flows from operating activities	150	100	375
Cash flows from investing activities			
Cash payments for land	0	(5,000)	0
Cash receipt from sale of land	0	0	2,500
Net cash flows from investing activities	0	(5,000)	2,500
Cash flows from financing activities			
Cash receipts from borrowed funds	2,975	0	0
Cash payments to reduce debt	0	(500)	(x)
Cash receipts from stock issue	8,000	1,100	(y)
Cash payments for dividends	(125)	(50)	(z)
Net cash flows from financing activities	10,850	550	(1,475)
Net change in cash	11,000	(4,350)	1,400
Beginning cash balance	0	11,000	6,650
Ending cash balance	$11,000	$ 6,650	$ 8,050

Problem 2-35   *Fraud Triangle*

LO 7

Pete Chalance is an accountant with a shady past. Suffice it to say that he owes some very unsavory characters a lot of money. Despite his past, Pete works hard at keeping up a strong professional image. He is a manager at Smith and Associates, a fast-growing CPA firm. Pete is highly regarded around the office because he is a strong producer of client revenue. Indeed, on several occasions he exceeded his authority in establishing prices with clients. This is typically a partner's job but who could criticize Pete, who is most certainly bringing in the business. Indeed, Pete is so good that he is able to pull off the following scheme. He bills clients at inflated rates and then reports the ordinary rate to his accounting firm. Say, for example, the normal charge for a job is $2,500. Pete will smooth talk the client, then charge him $3,000. He reports the normal charge of $2,500 to his firm and keeps the extra $500 for himself. He knows it isn't exactly right because his firm gets its regular charges and the client willingly pays for the services rendered. He thinks to himself, as he pockets his ill-gotten gains, who is getting hurt anyway?

Required

The text discusses three common features (conditions) that motivate ethical misconduct. Identify and explain each of the three features as they appear in the above scenario.

ANALYZE, THINK, COMMUNICATE

ATC 2-1   Business Applications Case   *Understanding real-world annual reports*

Required

Use the Topps Company annual report in Appendix B to answer the following questions.

a. Which accounts on Topps' balance sheet are accrual type accounts?

b. Which accounts on Topps' balance sheet are deferral type accounts?

c. Compare Topps' 2006 *net income* to its 2006 *cash provided by operating activities*. Which is larger?

d. First, compare Topps' 2005 net income to its 2006 net income. Next, compare Topps' 2005 cash provided by operating activities to its 2006 cash provided by operating activities. Which changed the most from 2005 to 2006, net income or cash provided by operating activities?

ATC 2-2   Group Assignment   *Missing information*

Verizon Communications, Inc., is one of the country's largest providers of communication services. The following information for 2004 through 2007 was taken from its annual reports. All amounts are in millions.

	2007	2006	2005	2004
Revenue	$93,469	$88,182	$69,518	$65,751
Operating expense	77,891	74,809	56,937	54,881

Required

a. Divide the class into groups of four or five students. Organize the groups into three sections. Assign each section of groups the financial data for one of the preceding accounting periods.

Group Tasks

(1) Determine the amount of net income for the year assigned.

(2) How does the result in item 1 above affect the retained earnings of the company?

(3) Compute the percentage growth rate in net income for each year.

(4) Speculate as to what may have caused Verizon's revenue growth from 2005 to 2006 to be so much greater than its revenue growth from 2004 to 2005 and 2006 to 2007.

(5) Have representatives from each section put the income statement for their respective year on the board.

Class Discussion

b. Have the class discuss the trend in revenue and net income.

ATC 2-3   Real-World Case   *Identifying accruals and deferrals*

The following information was drawn from the 2007 annual reports of five real-world companies.

Adidas Group, the company that makes athletic apparel, reported *trademarks* of €1,291 million. [Adidas has its headquarters in Germany and reports results in euros (€).] Trademarks is the name given to the category of assets that includes such things as the company logo.

Laboratory Corporation of America (usually called LabCorp) claims to be "the second largest independent clinical laboratory in the United States." It reported *supplies inventories of* $80.4 million.

Media General, Inc., owns, among other things, 25 daily newspapers and 23 television stations. It reported *unearned revenue* of $21,244 thousand.

Motorola, Inc., which makes cell phones and other communication equipment, reported *accounts receivables* of $5,324 million.

Palm, Inc., the company that makes the Palm Pilot personal digital assistant, reported *prepaids and others* of $10,222 thousand.

Required

a. Identify each of the accounts shown in italics above as being an accrual or deferral item, and whether it is an asset or liability.

b. Juniper Networks, Inc., designs, develops, and sells high-performance network infrastructure for Internet Protocol based networks. In 2007 it reported a liability called *accrued compensation* of $158.7 million. Write a brief explanation of what you think the company means by accrued compensation.

ATC 2-4   Business Applications Case   *Analyzing the cash flow effects of accruals and deferrals*

Make the following assumptions about Gwinn Company and Harris Company for the purpose of this problem.

1. The two companies ended 2010 with the exact same balances in all of the accounts reported on their balance sheets.

2. The two companies had the same amount of revenue and expenses during 2011, and neither company had any investing or financing cash flow activities.

Required

Shown below are changes in one balance sheet account for each company from 2010 to 2011. Based on the changes in the balances for the given account, decide which company would have ended 2011 with the highest balance in its cash account. *Consider each case independently,* and explain your answer.

a.

	Gwinn Company		Harris Company	
	2010	2011	2010	2011
Accounts receivable	$20,000	$30,000	$20,000	$25,000

b.

	Gwinn Company		Harris Company	
	2010	2011	2010	2011
Accounts payable	$10,000	$18,000	$10,000	$12,000

c.

	Gwinn Company		Harris Company	
	2010	2011	2010	2011
Prepaid rent	$12,000	$8,000	$12,000	$6,000

ATC 2-5   Business Applications Case   *Analyzing the cash flow effects of different types of expenses*

The following income statements are available for Hopi, Inc., and Zuni, Inc., for 2011.

	Hopi, Inc.	Zuni, Inc.
Revenue	$100,000	$100,000
Wages expense	70,000	55,000
Depreciation expense	10,000	25,000
Net earnings	$ 20,000	$ 20,000

Required

Assume that neither company had beginning or ending balances in its Accounts Receivable or Wages Payable accounts. Explain which company would have the lowest *net cash flows from operating activities* for 2011.

ATC 2-6   Writing Assignment   *Effects of accruals and deferrals on real-world companies' financial statements*

The following information was drawn from the 2007 annual reports of three real-world companies.

The 2006 balance sheet of Balder Electric Company reported $0.6 million of *accrued interest expense*. In 2007 it reported $27.7 million of accrued interest expense.

The 2006 balance sheet of The McGraw-Hill Companies, Inc., reported *senior long-term notes payable* of $0.3 million. In 2007 it reported $1.2 billion of these notes payables.

The 2006 balance sheet of Terra Nitrogen, L. P., reported *customer prepayments* of $35.3 million. In 2007 it reported $154.6 million of customer prepayments.

Required

For each situation presented above, write a brief explanation of how the company's 2007 financial statements would have been affected by the item in question, and whether the item is an accrual, deferral, or neither. Be sure to discuss primary and secondary effects. For example, if a company had an increase in its salaries expense, the primary effects would be the increase in expenses and decrease in net income. The secondary effects would include a decrease in retained earnings and a decrease in cash or an increase in salaries payable. Be as specific as possible.

ATC 2-7   Corporate Governance   *What is a little deceit among friends?*

Glenn's Cleaning Services Company is experiencing cash flow problems and needs a loan. Glenn has a friend who is willing to lend him the money he needs provided she can be convinced that he will be able to repay the debt. Glenn has assured his friend that his business is viable, but his friend has asked to see the company's financial statements. Glenn's accountant produced the following financial statements.

Income Statement		Balance Sheet	
Service Revenue	$ 38,000	Assets	$85,000
Operating Expenses	(70,000)	Liabilities	$35,000
Net Loss	$(32,000)	Stockholders' Equity	
		Common Stock	82,000
		Retained Earnings	(32,000)
		Total Liabilities and	
		Stockholders' Equity	$85,000

Glenn made the following adjustments to these statements before showing them to his friend. He recorded $82,000 of revenue on account from Barrymore Manufacturing Company for a contract to clean its headquarters office building that was still being negotiated for the next month. Barrymore had scheduled a meeting to sign a contract the following week, so Glenn was sure that he would get the job. Barrymore was a reputable company, and Glenn was confident that he could ultimately collect the $82,000. Also, he subtracted $30,000 of accrued salaries expense and the corresponding liability. He reasoned that since he had not paid the employees, he had not incurred any expense.

Required

a. Reconstruct the income statement and balance sheet as they would appear after Glenn's adjustments. Comment on the accuracy of the adjusted financial statements.

b. Suppose you are Glenn and the $30,000 you owe your employees is due next week. If you are unable to pay them, they will quit and the business will go bankrupt. You are sure you will be able to repay your friend when your employees perform the $82,000 of services for

Barrymore and you collect the cash. However, your friend is risk averse and is not likely to make the loan based on the financial statements your accountant prepared. Would you make the changes that Glenn made to get the loan and thereby save your company? Defend your position with a rational explanation.

c. Discuss the components of the fraud triangle as they apply to Glenn's decision to change the financial statements to reflect more favorable results.

ATC 2-8   Research Assignment   *Investigating nonfinancial information in Nike's annual report*

Although most of this course is concerned with the financial statements themselves, all sections of a company's annual report are important. A company must file various reports with the SEC, and one of these, Form 10-K, is essentially the company's annual report. The requirements below ask you to investigate sections of Nike's annual report that explain various nonfinancial aspects of its business operations.

To obtain the Form 10-K you can use either the EDGAR system following the instructions in Appendix A or the company's website.

Required

a. In what year did Nike begin operations?

b. Other than athletic shoes, what products does Nike sell?

c. Does Nike operate businesses under names other than Nike? If so, what are they?

d. How many employees does Nike have?

e. In how many countries other than the United States does Nike sell its products?

CHAPTER 3

Accounting *for* Merchandising Businesses

LEARNING OBJECTIVES

After you have mastered the material in this chapter you will be able to:

1 Identify and explain the primary features of the perpetual inventory system.

2 Show the effects of inventory transactions on financial statements.

3 Explain the meaning of terms used to describe transportation costs, cash discounts, returns or allowances, and financing costs.

4 Explain how gains and losses differ from revenues and expenses.

5 Compare and contrast single and multistep income statements.

6 Show the effect of lost, damaged, or stolen inventory on financial statements.

7 Use common size financial statements and ratio analysis to evaluate managerial performance.

8 Identify the primary features of the periodic inventory system. (Appendix)

CHAPTER OPENING

Previous chapters have discussed accounting for service businesses. These businesses obtain revenue by providing some kind of service such as medical or legal advice to their customers. Other examples of service companies include dry cleaning companies, maid service companies, and car washes. This chapter introduces accounting practices for merchandising businesses. **Merchandising businesses** generate revenue by selling goods. They buy the merchandise they sell from companies called suppliers. The goods purchased for resale are called **merchandise inventory.** Merchandising businesses include **retail companies** (companies that sell goods to the final consumer) and **wholesale companies** (companies that sell to other businesses). Sears, JCPenney, Target, and Sam's Club are real-world merchandising businesses.

The *Curious* Accountant

Diane recently purchased a gold necklace for $250 from her local Zales jewelry store. The next day she learned that Nicole bought the same necklace on-line from Blue Nile for only $200. Diane questioned how Blue Nile could sell the necklace for so much less than Zales. Nicole suggested that even though both jewelry sellers purchase their products from the same producers at about the same price, Blue Nile can charge lower prices because it does not have to operate expensive bricks-and-mortar stores, thus lowering its operating costs. Diane disagrees. She thinks the cost of operating large distribution centers and Internet server centers will offset any cost savings Blue Nile enjoys from not owning retail jewelry stores.

Exhibit 3.1 presents the income statements for Zales and Blue Nile. Based on these income statements, do you think Diane or Nicole is correct? (Answer on page 110.)

EXHIBIT 3.1	Comparative Income Statements

BLUE NILE, INC.
Consolidated Statements of Operations
(dollars in thousands)

	Fiscal Year Ended	
	Recent	Previous
Net sales	$203,169	$169,242
Cost of sales	158,025	131,590
Gross profit	45,144	37,652
Operating expenses:		
Selling, general and administrative	27,095	22,795
Restructuring charges	—	—
	27,095	22,795
Operating income	18,049	14,857
Other income (expense), net:		
Interest income	2,499	709
Interest expense	—	—
Other income	5	63
	2,504	772
Income before income taxes	20,553	15,629
Income tax expense (benefit)	7,400	5,642
Net income	$ 13,153	$ 9,987

ZALE CORPORATION AND SUBSIDIARIES
Consolidated Statements of Operations
(dollars in thousands)

	Fiscal Years Ended July 31,	
	Recent	Previous
Total revenue	$2,383,066	$2,304,440
Cost and expenses:		
Cost of sales	1,157,226	1,122,946
Selling, general and administrative expenses	982,113	942,796
Cost of insurance operations	6,084	5,963
Depreciation and amortization expense	59,840	56,381
Impairment of goodwill	—	—
Operating earnings	177,803	176,354
Interest expense, net	7,725	7,528
Cost of early retirement of debt	—	—
Earnings before income taxes	170,078	168,826
Income taxes	63,303	62,353
Net earnings (loss)	$ 106,775	$ 106,473

PRODUCT COSTS VERSUS SELLING AND ADMINISTRATIVE COSTS

LO 1

Identify and explain the primary features of the perpetual inventory system.

Companies report inventory costs on the balance sheet in the asset account Merchandise Inventory. All costs incurred to acquire merchandise and ready it for sale are included in the inventory account. Examples of inventory costs include the price of goods purchased, shipping and handling costs, transit insurance, and storage costs. Since inventory items are referred to as products, inventory costs are frequently called **product costs.**

Costs that are not included in inventory are usually called **selling and administrative costs.** Examples of selling and administrative costs include advertising, administrative salaries, sales commissions, insurance, and interest. Since selling and administrative costs are usually recognized as expenses *in the period* in which they are incurred, they are sometimes called **period costs.** In contrast, product costs are expensed when inventory is sold regardless of when it was purchased. In other words, product costs are matched directly with sales revenue, while selling and administrative costs are matched with the period in which they are incurred.

ALLOCATING INVENTORY COST BETWEEN ASSET AND EXPENSE ACCOUNTS

The cost of inventory that is available for sale during a specific accounting period is determined as follows.

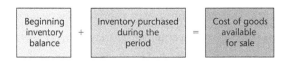

The **cost of goods available for sale** is allocated between the asset account Merchandise Inventory and an expense account called **Cost of Goods Sold.** The cost of inventory items that have not been sold (Merchandise Inventory) is reported as an asset on the balance sheet, and the cost of the items sold (Cost of Goods Sold) is expensed on the income statement. This allocation is depicted graphically as follows.

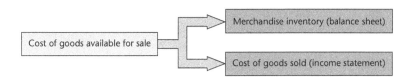

The difference between the sales revenue and the cost of goods sold is called **gross margin** or **gross profit.** The selling and administrative expenses (period costs) are subtracted from gross margin to obtain the net income.

Exhibit 3.1 displays income statements from the annual reports of Blue Nile and Zales. For each company, review the most current income statement and determine the amount of gross margin. You should find a gross profit of $45,144 for Blue Nile and a gross margin of $1,225,840 ($2,383,066 − $1,157,226) for Zales.

PERPETUAL INVENTORY SYSTEM

Most modern companies maintain their inventory records using the **perpetual inventory system,** so-called because the inventory account is adjusted perpetually (continually) throughout the accounting period. Each time merchandise is purchased, the inventory account is increased; each time it is sold, the inventory account is decreased. The following illustration demonstrates the basic features of the perpetual inventory system.

Show the effects of inventory transactions on financial statements.

June Gardener loved plants and grew them with such remarkable success that she decided to open a small retail plant store. She started June's Plant Shop (JPS) on January 1, 2010. The following discussion explains and illustrates the effects of the five events the company experienced during its first year of operation.

Effects of 2010 Events on Financial Statements

EVENT 1   JPS acquired $15,000 cash by issuing common stock.

This event is an asset source transaction. It increases both assets (cash) and stockholders' equity (common stock). The income statement is not affected. The statement of cash flows reflects an inflow from financing activities. These effects are shown here.

Assets			=	Liab.	+	Stockholders' Equity						
Cash	+ Inventory	+ Land	=	Accts. Pay.	+	Com. Stk.	+ Ret. Earn.	Rev.	− Exp.	= Net Inc.	Cash Flow
15,000	+ NA	+ NA	=	NA	+	15,000	+ NA	NA	− NA	= NA	15,000 FA

EVENT 2   JPS purchased merchandise inventory for $14,000 cash.

This event is an asset exchange transaction. One asset, cash, decreases and another asset, merchandise inventory, increases; total assets remain unchanged. Because product costs are expensed when inventory is sold, not when it is purchased, the event does not affect the income statement. The cash outflow, however, is reported in the operating activities section of the statement of cash flows. These effects are illustrated below.

Assets			=	Liab.	+	Stockholders' Equity						
Cash	+ Inventory	+ Land	=	Accts. Pay.	+	Com. Stk.	+ Ret. Earn.	Rev.	− Exp.	= Net Inc.	Cash Flow
(14,000)	+ 14,000	+ NA	=	NA	+	NA	+ NA	NA	− NA	= NA	(14,000) OA

EVENT 3A   JPS recognized sales revenue from selling inventory for $12,000 cash.

The revenue recognition is the first part of a two-part transaction. The *sales part* represents a source of assets (cash increases from earning sales revenue). Both assets (cash) and stockholders' equity (retained earnings) increase. Sales revenue on the income statement increases. The $12,000 cash inflow is reported in the operating activities section of the statement of cash flows. These effects are shown in the following financial statements model.

Assets			=	Liab.	+	Stockholders' Equity						
Cash	+ Inventory	+ Land	=	Accts. Pay.	+	Com. Stk.	+ Ret. Earn.	Rev.	− Exp.	= Net Inc.	Cash Flow
12,000	+ NA	+ NA	=	NA	+	NA	+ 12,000	12,000	− NA	= 12,000	12,000 OA

EVENT 3B   JPS recognized $8,000 of cost of goods sold.

The expense recognition is the second part of the two-part transaction. The *expense part* represents a use of assets. Both assets (merchandise inventory) and stockholders' equity (retained earnings) decrease. An expense account, Cost of Goods Sold, is reported on the income statement. This part of the transaction does not affect the statement of cash flows. A cash outflow occurred when the goods were bought, not when they were sold. These effects are shown here.

Assets			=	Liab.	+	Stockholders' Equity							
Cash	+	Inventory	+	Land	=	Accts. Pay.	+	Com. Stk.	+	Ret. Earn.	Rev.	−	Exp.	=	Net Inc.	Cash Flow
NA	+	(8,000)	+	NA	=	NA	+	NA	+	(8,000)	NA	−	8,000	=	(8,000)	NA

EVENT 4   JPS paid $1,000 cash for selling and administrative expenses.

This event is an asset use transaction. The payment decreases both assets (cash) and stockholders' equity (retained earnings). The increase in selling and administrative expenses decreases net income. The $1,000 cash payment is reported in the operating activities section of the statement of cash flows. These effects are illustrated below.

Assets			=	Liab.	+	Stockholders' Equity							
Cash	+	Inventory	+	Land	=	Accts. Pay.	+	Com. Stk.	+	Ret. Earn.	Rev.	−	Exp.	=	Net Inc.	Cash Flow
(1,000)	+	NA	+	NA	=	NA	+	NA	+	(1,000)	NA	−	1,000	=	(1,000)	(1,000) OA

EVENT 5   JPS paid $5,500 cash to purchase land for a place to locate a future store.

Buying the land increases the Land account and decreases the Cash account on the balance sheet. The income statement is not affected. The statement of cash flow shows a cash outflow to purchase land in the investing activities section of the statement of cash flows. These effects are shown below.

Assets			=	Liab.	+	Stockholders' Equity							
Cash	+	Inventory	+	Land	=	Accts. Pay.	+	Com. Stk.	+	Ret. Earn.	Rev.	−	Exp.	=	Net Inc.	Cash Flow
(5,500)	+	NA	+	5,500	=	NA	+	NA	+	NA	NA	−	NA	=	NA	(5,500) IA

Financial Statements for 2010

JPS's financial statements for 2010 are shown in Exhibit 3.2. JPS had no beginning inventory in its first year, so the cost of merchandise inventory available for sale was $14,000 (the amount of inventory purchased during the period). Recall that JPS must allocate the *Cost of Goods (Inventory) Available for Sale* between the *Cost of Goods Sold* ($8,000) and the ending balance ($6,000) in the *Merchandise Inventory* account. The cost of goods sold is reported as an expense on the income statement and the ending balance of merchandise inventory is reported as an asset on the balance sheet. The difference between the sales revenue ($12,000) and the cost of goods sold ($8,000) is labeled *gross margin* ($4,000) on the income statement.

EXHIBIT 3.2

Financial Statements

2010 Income Statement		12/31/10 Balance Sheet			2010 Statement of Cash Flows		
Sales revenue	$12,000	Assets			Operating activities		
Cost of goods sold	(8,000)	Cash	$ 6,500		Inflow from customers	$12,000	
Gross margin	4,000	Merchandise inventory	6,000		Outflow for inventory	(14,000)	
Less: Operating exp.		Land	5,500		Outflow for selling		
Selling and		Total assets		$18,000	& admin. exp.	(1,000)	
admin. exp.	(1,000)	Liabilities		$ 0	Net cash outflow for		
Net income	$ 3,000	Stockholders' equity			operating activities		$ (3,000)
		Common stock	$15,000		Investing activities		
		Retained earnings	3,000		Outflow to purchase land		(5,500)
		Total stockholders' equity		18,000	Financing activities		
		Total liab. and stk. equity		$18,000	Inflow from stock issue		15,000
					Net change in cash		6,500
					Plus: Beginning cash balance		0
					Ending cash balance		$ 6,500

CHECK *Yourself* 3.1

Phambroom Company began 2010 with $35,600 in its Inventory account. During the year, it purchased inventory costing $356,800 and sold inventory that had cost $360,000 for $520,000. Based on this information alone, determine (1) the inventory balance as of December 31, 2010, and (2) the amount of gross margin Phambroom would report on its 2010 income statement.

Answer

1. Beginning inventory + Purchases = Goods available − Ending inventory = Cost of goods sold

   $35,600 + $356,800 = $392,400 − Ending inventory = $360,000

   Ending inventory = $32,400

2. Sales revenue − Cost of goods sold = Gross margin

   $520,000 − $360,000 = $160,000

Transportation Cost, Purchase Returns and Allowances, and Cash Discounts Related to Inventory Purchases

LO 3

Explain the meaning of terms used to describe transportation costs, cash discounts, returns or allowances, and financing costs.

Purchasing inventory often involves: (1) incurring transportation costs, (2) returning inventory or receiving purchase allowances (cost reductions), and (3) taking cash discounts (also cost reductions). During its second accounting cycle, JPS encountered these kinds of events. The final account balances at the end of the 2010 fiscal year become the beginning balances for 2011: Cash, $6,500; Merchandise Inventory, $6,000; Land, 5,500; Common Stock, $15,000; and Retained Earnings, $3,000.

Effects of 2011 Events on Financial Statements

JPS experienced the following events during its 2011 accounting period. The effects of each of these events are explained and illustrated in the following discussion.

EVENT 1 JPS borrowed $4,000 cash by issuing a note payable.

JPS borrowed the money to enable it to purchase a plot of land for a future site for a store it planned to build in the near future. Borrowing the money increases the Cash account and the Note Payable account on the balance sheet. The income statement is not affected. The statement of cash flow shows a cash flow from financing activities. These effects are shown below.

Assets				=	Liabilities		+	Stockholders' Equity						
Cash +	Accts. Rec. +	Inventory +	Land =		Accts. Pay. +	Notes Pay. +		Com. Stk. +	Ret. Earn.	Rev. −	Exp. =	Net Inc.		Cash Flow
4,000 +	NA +	NA +	NA =		NA +	4,000 +		NA +	NA	NA −	NA =	NA		4,000 FA

EVENT 2 JPS purchased on account merchandise inventory with a list price of $11,000.

The inventory purchase increases both assets (merchandise inventory) and liabilities (accounts payable) on the balance sheet. The income statement is not affected until later, when inventory is sold. Since the inventory was purchased on account, there was no cash outflow. These effects are shown here.

Assets				=	Liab.		+	Stockholders' Equity						
Cash +	Accts. Rec. +	Inventory +	Land =		Accts. Pay. +	Notes Pay. +		Com. Stk. +	Ret. Earn.	Rev. −	Exp. =	Net Inc.		Cash Flow
NA +	NA +	11,000 +	NA =		11,000 +	NA +		NA +	NA	NA −	NA =	NA		NA

Accounting for Purchase Returns and Allowances

EVENT 3 JPS returned some of the inventory purchased in Event 2. The list price of the returned merchandise was $1,000.

To promote customer satisfaction, many businesses allow customers to return goods for reasons such as wrong size, wrong color, wrong design, or even simply because the purchaser changed his mind. The effect of a purchase return is the *opposite* of the original purchase. For JPS the **purchase return** decreases both assets (merchandise inventory) and liabilities (accounts payable). There is no effect on either the income statement or the statement of cash flows. These effects are shown below.

Assets				=	Liab.		+	Stockholders' Equity						
Cash +	Accts. Rec. +	Inventory +	Land =		Accts. Pay. +	Notes Pay. +		Com. Stk. +	Ret. Earn.	Rev. −	Exp. =	Net Inc.		Cash Flow
NA +	NA +	(1,000) +	NA =		(1,000) +	NA +		NA +	NA	NA −	NA =	NA		NA

Sometimes dissatisfied buyers will agree to keep goods instead of returning them if the seller offers to reduce the price. Such reductions are called allowances. **Purchase allowances** affect the financial statements the same way purchase returns do.

Purchase Discounts

EVENT 4   JPS received a cash discount on goods purchased in Event 2. The credit terms were 2/10, n/30.

To encourage buyers to pay promptly, sellers sometimes offer **cash discounts.** To illustrate, assume JPS purchased the inventory in Event 2 under terms **2/10, n/30** (two-ten, net thirty). These terms mean the seller will allow a 2 percent cash discount if the purchaser pays cash within 10 days from the date of purchase. The amount not paid within the first 10 days is due at the end of 30 days from date of purchase. Recall that JPS returned $1,000 of the inventory purchased in Event 1 leaving a $10,000 balance ($11,000 list price − $1,000 purchase return). If JPS pays for the inventory within 10 days, the amount of the discount is $200 ($10,000 × .02).

When cash discounts are applied to purchases they are called **purchases discounts.** When they are applied to sales, they are called sales discounts. Sales discounts will be discussed later in the chapter. A *purchase discount* reduces the cost of the inventory and the associated account payable on the balance sheet. A purchase discount does not directly affect the income statement or the statement of cash flow. These effects are shown here.

	Assets			=	Liab.		+	Stockholders' Equity						
Cash +	Accts. Rec. +	Inventory +	Land =		Accts. Pay. +	Notes Pay. +		Com. Stk. +	Ret. Earn.		Rev. −	Exp. =	Net Inc.	Cash Flow
NA +	NA +	(200) +	NA =		(200) +	NA +		NA +	NA		NA −	NA =	NA	NA

If JPS paid the account payable after 10 days, there would be no purchase discount. In this case the balances in the Inventory and Account Payable accounts would remain at $10,000.

EVENT 5   JPS paid the $9,800 balance due on the account payable.

The remaining balance in the accounts payable is $9,800 ($10,000 list price − $200 purchase discount). Paying cash to settle the liability reduces cash and accounts payable on the balance sheet. The income statement is not affected. The cash outflow is shown in the operating section of the statement of cash flows. These effects are shown below.

	Assets			=	Liab.		+	Stockholders' Equity						
Cash +	Accts. Rec. +	Inventory +	Land =		Accts. Pay. +	Notes Pay. +		Com. Stk. +	Ret. Earn.		Rev. −	Exp. =	Net Inc.	Cash Flow
(9,800) +	NA +	NA +	NA =		(9,800) +	NA +		NA +	NA		NA −	NA =	NA	(9,800) OA

The Cost of Financing Inventory

Suppose you buy inventory this month and sell it next month. Where do you get the money to pay for the inventory at the time you buy it? One way to finance the purchase is to buy it on account and withhold payment until the last day of the term for the account payable. For example, suppose you buy inventory under terms 2/10, net/30. Under these circumstances you could delay payment for 30 days after the day of purchase. This way you may be able to collect enough money from the inventory you sell

Reality BYTES

Many real-world companies have found it more effective to impose a penalty for late payment than to use a cash discount to encourage early payment. The invoice from Arley Water Works is an example of the penalty strategy. Notice that the amount due, if paid by the due date, is $18.14. A $1.88 late charge is imposed if the bill is paid after the due date. The $1.88 late charge is in fact interest. If Arley Water Works collects the payment after the due date, the utility will receive cash of $20.02. The collection will increase cash ($20.02), reduce accounts receivable ($18.14), and increase interest revenue ($1.88).

ARLEY WATER WORKS P.O. BOX 146 ARLEY, ALABAMA 35541 (205) 387-0156			

TYPE OF SERVICE	METER READING PRESENT	PREVIOUS	USED	CHARGES
WAT	33030	30950	2080	17.44
Sales Tax				0.70

PLEASE CLEAN OUT AROUND YOUR METER

ACCOUNT #   2054   09-26-03

METER HEAD MONTH	DAY	CLASS	TOTAL DUE UPON RECEIPT	LATE CHARGE AFTER DUE DATE	PAST DUE AMOUNT
9	17	1	18.14	1.88	20.02

to pay for the inventory you purchased. Refusing the discount allows you the time needed to generate the cash necessary to pay off the liability (account payable). Unfortunately, this is usually a very expensive way to finance the purchase of inventory.

While the amount of a cash discount may appear small, the discount period is short. Consider the terms 2/10, net/30. Since you can pay on the tenth day and still receive the discount, you obtain financing for only 20 days (30-day full credit term − 10-day discount term). In other words, you must forgo a 2 percent discount to obtain a loan with a 20-day term. What is the size of the discount in annual terms? The answer is determined by the following formula.

$$\text{Annual rate} = \text{Discount rate} \times (365 \text{ days} \div \text{term of the loan})$$

$$\text{Annual rate} = 2\% \times (365 \div 20)$$

$$\text{Annual rate} = 36.5\%$$

This means that a 2 percent discount rate for 20 days is equivalent to a 36.5 percent annual rate of interest. So, if you do not have the money to pay the account payable, but can borrow money from a bank at less than 36.5 percent annual interest, you should borrow the money and pay off the account payable within the discount period.

Accounting for Transportation Costs

EVENT 6 **The shipping terms for the inventory purchased in Event 2 were FOB shipping point. JPS paid the freight company $300 cash for delivering the merchandise.**

The terms **FOB shipping point** and **FOB destination** identify whether the buyer or the seller is responsible for transportation costs. If goods are delivered FOB shipping point, the buyer is responsible for the freight cost. If goods are delivered FOB destination, the seller is responsible. When the buyer is responsible, the freight cost is called **transportation-in.** When the seller is responsible, the cost is called **transportation-out.** The following table summarizes freight cost terms.

Responsible Party	Buyer	Seller
Freight terms	FOB shipping point	FOB destination
Account title	Merchandise inventory	Transportation-out

Event 6 indicates the inventory was delivered FOB shipping point, so JPS (the buyer) is responsible for the $300 freight cost. Since incurring transportation-in costs is necessary to obtain inventory, these costs are added to the inventory account. The freight cost increases one asset account (Merchandise Inventory) and decreases another asset account (Cash). The income statement is not affected by this transaction because transportation-in costs are not expensed when they are incurred. Instead they are expensed as part of *cost of goods sold* when the inventory is sold. However, the cash paid for transportation-in costs is reported as an outflow in the operating activities section of the statement of cash flows. The effects of *transportation-in costs* are shown here.

		Assets			=	Liab.		+	Stockholders' Equity						
Cash	+	Accts. Rec.	+ Inventory	+ Land	=	Accts. Pay.	+ Notes Pay.	+	Com. Stk.	+ Ret. Earn.	Rev.	− Exp.	= Net Inc.		Cash Flow
(300)	+	NA	+ 300	+ NA	=	NA	+ NA	+	NA	+ NA	NA	− NA	= NA		(300) OA

EVENT 7A **JPS recognized $24,750 of revenue on the cash sale of merchandise that cost $11,500.**

The sale increases assets (cash) and stockholders' equity (retained earnings). The revenue recognition increases net income. The $24,750 cash inflow from the sale is reported in the operating activities section of the statement of cash flows. These effects are shown below.

		Assets			=	Liab.		+	Stockholders' Equity						
Cash	+	Accts. Rec.	+ Inventory	+ Land	=	Accts. Pay.	+ Notes Pay.	+	Com. Stk.	+ Ret. Earn.	Rev.	− Exp.	= Net Inc.		Cash Flow
24,750	+	NA	+ NA	+ NA	=	NA	+ NA	+	NA	+ 24,750	24,750	− NA	= 24,750		24,750 OA

EVENT 7B **JPS recognized $11,500 of cost of goods sold.**

When goods are sold, the product cost—*including a proportionate share of transportation-in and adjustments for purchase returns and allowances*—is transferred from the Merchandise Inventory account to the expense account, Cost of Goods Sold. Recognizing cost of goods sold decreases both assets (merchandise inventory) and stockholders' equity (retained earnings). The expense recognition for cost of goods sold decreases net income. Cash flow is not affected. These effects are shown here.

		Assets			=	Liab.		+	Stockholders' Equity						
Cash	+	Accts. Rec.	+ Inventory	+ Land	=	Accts. Pay.	+ Notes Pay.	+	Com. Stk.	+ Ret. Earn.	Rev.	− Exp.	= Net Inc.		Cash Flow
NA	+	NA	+ (11,500)	+ NA	=	NA	+ NA	+	NA	+ (11,500)	NA	− 11,500	= (11,500)		NA

EVENT 8 **JPS paid $450 cash for freight costs on inventory delivered to customers.**

Assume the merchandise sold in Event 7A was shipped FOB destination. Also assume JPS paid the freight cost in cash. FOB destination means the seller is responsible for the freight cost, which is called transportation-out. Transportation-out is reported on the income statement as an operating expense in the section below gross margin. The cost of freight on goods shipped to customers is incurred *after* the goods are sold. It is not part of the costs to obtain goods or ready them for sale. Recognizing the expense of transportation-out reduces assets (cash) and stockholders' equity (retained earnings). Operating expenses increase and net income decreases. The cash outflow is reported in the operating activities section of the statement of cash flows. These effects are shown below.

Assets				=	Liab.		+	Stockholders' Equity						
Cash +	Accts. Rec. +	Inventory +	Land =		Accts. Pay. +	Notes Pay. +		Com. Stk. +	Ret. Earn.	Rev. −	Exp. =	Net Inc.	Cash Flow	
(450) +	NA +	NA +	NA =		NA +	NA +		NA +	(450)	NA −	450 =	(450)	(450) OA	

If the terms had been FOB shipping point, the customer would have been responsible for the transportation cost and JPS would not have recorded an expense.

EVENT 9 **JPS paid $5,000 cash for selling and administrative expenses.**

The effect on the balance sheet is to decrease both assets (cash) and stockholders' equity (retained earnings). Recognizing the selling and administrative expenses decreases net income. The $5,000 cash outflow is reported in the operating activities section of the statement of cash flows. These effects are shown below.

Assets				=	Liab.		+	Stockholders' Equity						
Cash +	Accts. Rec. +	Inventory +	Land =		Accts. Pay. +	Notes Pay. +		Com. Stk. +	Ret. Earn.	Rev. −	Exp. =	Net Inc.	Cash Flow	
(5,000) +	NA +	NA +	NA =		NA +	NA +		NA +	(5,000)	NA −	5,000 =	(5,000)	(5,000) OA	

EVENT 10 **JPS paid $360 cash for interest expense on the note described in Event 1.**

The effect on the balance sheet is to decrease both assets (cash) and stockholders' equity (retained earnings). Recognizing the interest expense decreases net income. The $360 cash outflow is reported in the operating activities section of the statement of cash flows. These effects are shown below.

Assets				=	Liab.		+	Stockholders' Equity						
Cash +	Accts. Rec. +	Inventory +	Land =		Accts. Pay. +	Notes Pay. +		Com. Stk. +	Ret. Earn.	Rev. −	Exp. =	Net Inc.	Cash Flow	
(360) +	NA +	NA +	NA =		NA +	NA +		NA +	(360)	NA −	360 =	(360)	(360) OA	

RECOGNIZING GAINS AND LOSSES

EVENT 11   JPS sold the land that had cost $5,500 for $6,200 cash.

LO 4

Explain how gains and losses differ
from revenues and expenses.

When JPS sells merchandise inventory for more than it cost, the difference between the sales revenue and the cost of the goods sold is called the *gross margin.* In contrast, when JPS sells land for more than it cost, the difference between the sales price and the cost of the land is called a **gain.** Why is one called *gross margin* and the other a *gain*? The terms are used to alert financial statement users to the fact that the nature of the underlying transactions is different.

JPS' primary business is selling inventory, not land. The term *gain* indicates profit resulting from transactions that are not likely to regularly recur. Similarly, had the land sold for less than cost the difference would have been labeled **loss** rather than expense. This term also indicates the underlying transaction is not from normal, recurring operating activities. Gains and losses are shown separately on the income statement to communicate the expectation that they are nonrecurring.

The presentation of gains and losses in the income statement is discussed in more detail in a later section of the chapter. At this point note that the sale increases cash, decreases land, and increases retained earnings on the balance sheet. The income statement shows a gain on the sale of land and net income increases. The $6,200 cash inflow is shown as an investing activity on the statement of cash flows. These effects are shown below:

Assets					=	Liab.		+	Stockholders' Equity							
Cash	+	Accts. Rec.	+	Inventory	+	Land	=	Accts. Pay.	+	Notes Pay.	+	Com. Stk.	+	Ret. Earn.	Gain	−	Exp.	=	Net Inc.	Cash Flow
6,200	+	NA	+	NA	+	(5,500)	=	NA	+	NA	+	NA	+	700	700	−	NA	=	700	6,200 IA

CHECK *Yourself* 3.2

Tsang Company purchased $32,000 of inventory on account with payment terms of 2/10, n/30 and freight terms FOB shipping point. Freight costs were $1,100. Tsang obtained a $2,000 purchase allowance because the inventory was damaged upon arrival. Tsang paid for the inventory within the discount period. Based on this information alone, determine the balance in the inventory account.

Answer

List price of inventory	$32,000
Plus: Transportation-in costs	1,100
Less: Purchase returns and allowances	(2,000)
Less: Purchase discount [($32,000 − $2,000) × .02]	(600)
Balance in inventory account	$30,500

MULTISTEP INCOME STATEMENT

LO 5

Compare and contrast single and
multistep income statements.

JPS' 2011 income statement is shown in Exhibit 3.3. Observe the form of this statement carefully. It is more informative than one which simply subtracts expenses from revenues. First, it compares sales revenue with the cost of the goods that were sold to produce that revenue. The difference between the sales revenue and the cost of goods sold is called *gross margin*. Next, the operating expenses are subtracted from the gross margin to determine the *operating income*. **Operating income** is the amount of income that is generated from the normal recurring operations of a business. Items that are not expected to recur on a regular basis are subtracted from the operating income to determine the amount of *net income.*[1]

EXHIBIT 3.3

JUNE'S PLANT SHOP	
Income Statement	
For the Period Ended December 31, 2011	
Sales revenue	$ 24,750
Cost of goods sold	(11,500)
Gross margin	13,250
Less: Operating expenses	
Selling and administrative expense	(5,000)
Transportation-out	(450)
Operating income	7,800
Nonoperating items	
Interest expense	(360)
Gain on the sale of land	700
Net income	$ 8,140

EXHIBIT 3.4

Income Statement Format Used by U.S. Companies

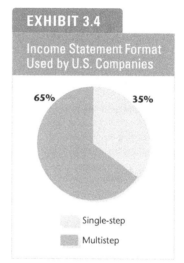

65%   35%

Single-step

Multistep

Data Source: AICPA, *Accounting Trends and Techniques.*

EXHIBIT 3.5

JUNE'S PLANT SHOP		
Balance Sheet		
As of December 31, 2011		
Assets		
Cash	$25,540	
Merchandise inventory	4,600	
Total assets		$30,140
Liabilities		
Notes payable		$ 4,000
Stockholders' equity		
Common stock	$15,000	
Retained earnings	11,140	
Total stockholders' equity		26,140
Total liabilities and stockholders' equity		$30,140

Income statements that show these additional relationships are called **multistep income statements.** Income statements that display a single comparison of all revenues minus all expenses are called **single-step income statements.** To this point in the text we have shown only single-step income statements to promote simplicity. However, the multistep form is used more frequently in practice. Exhibit 3.4 shows the percentage of companies that use the multistep versus the single-step format. Go to Exhibit 3.1 and identify the company that presents its income statement in the multistep format. You should have identified Blue Nile as the company using the multistep format. Zale's statement is shown in the single-step format.

---

[1]Revenue and expense items with special characteristics may be classified as discontinued or extraordinary items. These items are shown separately just above net income regardless of whether a company uses a single-step or multistep format. Further discussion of these items is beyond the scope of this text.

EXHIBIT 3.6

JUNE'S PLANT SHOP
Statement of Cash Flows
For the Period Ended December 31, 2011

Operating activities		
Inflow from customers	$ 24,750	
Outflow for inventory*	(10,100)	
Outflow for transportation-out	(450)	
Outflow for selling and administrative expense	(5,000)	
Outflow for interest expense	(360)	
Net cash outflow for operating activities		$ 8,840
Investing activities		
Inflow from sale of land		6,200
Financing activities		
Inflow from issue of note payable		4,000
Net change in cash		19,040
Plus beginning cash balance		6,500
Ending cash balance		$25,540

*Net cost on inventory $9,800 + transportation-in $300 = $10,100

Note that interest is reported as a *nonoperating* item on the income statement in Exhibit 3.3. In contrast, it is shown in the *operating* activities section of the statement of cash flows in Exhibit 3.6. When the FASB issued Statement of Financial Accounting Standard (SFAS) 95, it required interest to be reported in the operating activities section of the statement of cash flows. There was no corresponding requirement for the treatment of interest on the income statement. Prior to SFAS 95, interest was considered to be a nonoperating item. Most companies continued to report interest as a nonoperating item on their income statements even though they were required to change how it was reported on the statement of cash flows. As a result, there is frequent inconsistency in the way interest is reported on the two financial statements.

Also note that while the gain on the sale of land is shown on the income statement, it is not included in the operating activities section of the statement of cash flows. Since the gain is a nonoperating item, it is included in the cash inflow from the sale of land shown in the investing activities section. In this case the full cash inflow from the sale of land ($6,200) is shown in the investing activities section of the statement of cash flows in Exhibit 3.6.

LOST, DAMAGED, OR STOLEN INVENTORY

LO 6

Show the effect of lost, damaged, or stolen inventory on financial statements.

Most merchandising companies experience some level of inventory **shrinkage,** a term that reflects decreases in inventory for reasons other than sales to customers. Inventory may be stolen by shoplifters, damaged by customers or employees, or even simply lost or misplaced. Since the *perpetual* inventory system is designed to record purchases and sales of inventory as they occur, the balance in the merchandise inventory account represents the amount of inventory that *should* be on hand at any given time. By taking a physical count of the merchandise inventory at the end of the accounting period and comparing that amount with the book balance in the Merchandise Inventory account, managers can determine the amount of any inventory shrinkage. If goods have been lost, damaged, or stolen, the book balance will be higher than the actual amount of inventory on hand and an adjusting entry is required to reduce assets and equity. The Merchandise Inventory account is reduced, and an expense for the amount of the lost, damaged, or stolen inventory is recognized.

Reality BYTES

"Closed for Inventory Count" is a sign you frequently see on retail stores sometime during the month of January. Even if companies use a perpetual inventory system, the amount of inventory on hand may be unknown because of lost, damaged, or stolen goods. The only way to determine the amount of inventory on hand is to count it. Why count it in January? Christmas shoppers and many after-Christmas sales shoppers are satiated by mid-January, leaving the stores low on both merchandise and customers. Accordingly, stores have less merchandise to count and "lost sales" are minimized during January. Companies that do not depend on seasonal sales (e.g., a plumbing supplies wholesale business) may choose to count inventory at some other time during the year. Counting inventory is not a revenue-generating activity; it is a necessary evil that should be conducted when it least disrupts operations.

Adjustment for Lost, Damaged, or Stolen Inventory

To illustrate, assume that Midwest Merchandising Company maintains perpetual inventory records. Midwest determined, through a physical count, that it had $23,500 of merchandise inventory on hand at the end of the accounting period. The balance in the Inventory account was $24,000. Midwest must make an adjusting entry to write down the Inventory account so the amount reported on the financial statements agrees with the amount actually on hand at the end of the period. The write-down decreases both assets (inventory) and stockholders' equity (retained earnings). The write-down increases expenses and decreases net income. Cash flow is not affected. The effects on the statements are as follows.

Assets	=	Liab.	+	Equity	Rev.	−	Exp.	=	Net Inc.	Cash Flow
(500)	=	NA	+	(500)	NA	−	500	=	(500)	NA

Theoretically, inventory losses are operating expenses. However, because such losses are normally immaterial in amount, they are usually added to cost of goods sold for external reporting purposes.

EVENTS AFFECTING SALES

To this point we assumed JPS did not offer cash discounts to its customers. However, sales, as well as purchases of inventory, can be affected by returns, allowances, and discounts. **Sales discounts** are price reductions offered by sellers to encourage buyers to pay promptly. To illustrate, assume JPS engaged in the following selected events during January 2012.

EVENT 1A   **JPS sold on account merchandise with a list price of $8,500. Payment terms were 1/10, n/30. The merchandise had cost JPS $4,000.**

The sale increases both assets (accounts receivable) and shareholders' equity (retained earnings). Recognizing revenue increases net income. The statement of cash flows is not affected. The effects on the financial statements follow.

Assets					=	Liab.	+	Stockholders' Equity			Rev.	−	Exp.	=	Net Inc.	Cash Flow
Cash	+	Accts. Rec.	+	Inventory	=	Note Pay.	+	Com. Stk.	+	Retained Earnings						
NA	+	8,500	+	NA	=	NA	+	NA	+	8,500	8,500	−	NA	=	8,500	NA

EVENT 1B   **JPS recognized $4,000 of cost of goods sold.**

Recognizing the expense decreases assets (merchandise inventory) and stockholders' equity (retained earnings). Cost of goods sold increases and net income decreases. Cash flow is not affected. The effects on the financial statements follow.

Assets					=	Liab.	+	Stockholders' Equity			Rev.	–	Exp.	=	Net Inc.	Cash Flow
Cash	+	Accts. Rec.	+	Inventory	=	Note Pay.	+	Com. Stk.	+	Retained Earnings						
NA	+	NA	+	(4,000)	=	NA	+	NA	+	(4,000)	NA	–	4,000	=	(4,000)	NA

Accounting for Sales Returns and Allowances

EVENT 2A   **A customer from Event 1A returned inventory with a $1,000 list price. The merchandise had cost JPS $450.**

The sales return decreases both assets (accounts receivable) and stockholders' equity (retained earnings) on the balance sheet. Sales and net income decrease. Cash flow is not affected. The effects on the financial statements follow.

Assets					=	Liab.	+	Stockholders' Equity			Rev.	–	Exp.	=	Net Inc.	Cash Flow
Cash	+	Accts. Rec.	+	Inventory	=	Note Pay.	+	Com. Stk.	+	Retained Earnings						
NA	+	(1,000)	+	NA	=	NA	+	NA	+	(1,000)	(1,000)	–	NA	=	(1,000)	NA

EVENT 2B   **The cost of the goods ($450) is returned to the inventory account.**

Since JPS got the inventory back, the sales return increases both assets (merchandise inventory) and stockholders' equity (retained earnings). The expense (cost of goods sold) decreases and net income increases. Cash flow is not affected. The effects on the financial statements follow.

Assets					=	Liab.	+	Stockholders' Equity			Rev.	–	Exp.	=	Net Inc.	Cash Flow
Cash	+	Accts. Rec.	+	Inventory	=	Note Pay.	+	Com. Stk.	+	Retained Earnings						
NA	+	NA	+	450	=	NA	+	NA	+	450	NA	–	(450)	=	450	NA

Accounting for Sales Discounts

EVENT 3   **JPS collected the balance of the accounts receivable generated in Event 1A. Recall the goods were sold under terms 1/10, net/30.**

ALTERNATIVE 1   **The collection occurs before the discount period has expired (within 10 days from the date of the sale).**

JPS would give the buyer a 1 percent discount. Given the original sales amount of $8,500 and a sales return of $1,000, the amount of the discount is $75 [($8,500 − $1,000) × .01]. The sales discount reduces the amount of accounts receivable and retained earnings on the balance sheet. It also reduces the amount of revenue and the net income shown on the balance sheet. It does not affect the statement of cash flows. The effects on the financial statements follow.

Assets				=	Liab.	+	Stockholders' Equity			Rev.	−	Exp.	=	Net Inc.	Cash Flow
Cash	+	Accts. Rec.	+	Inventory	=	Note Pay.	+	Com. Stk.	+	Retained Earnings					
NA	+	(75)	+	NA	=	NA	+	NA	+	(75)	(75)	−	NA	=	(75)	NA

The balance due on the account receivable is $7,425 ($8,500 original sales − $1,000 sales return − $75 discount). The collection increases the Cash account and decreases the Accounts Receivable account. The income statement is not affected. The cash inflow is shown in the operating activities section of the statement of cash flows. The effects on the financial statements follow.

Assets				=	Liab.	+	Stockholders' Equity			Rev.	−	Exp.	=	Net Inc.	Cash Flow
Cash	+	Accts. Rec.	+	Inventory	=	Accts. Pay.	+	Com. Stk.	+	Retained Earnings					
7,425	+	(7,425)	+	NA	=	NA	+	NA	+	NA	NA	−	NA	=	NA	7,425 OA

Net Sales

The gross amount of sales minus **sales returns and allowance** and sales discounts is commonly called **net sales.** Companies are not required by GAAP to show sales returns and allowance and sales discount on their income statement. Indeed, most companies show only the amount of *net sales* on the income statement. In this case the net sales amount to $7,425 ($8,500 original sales − $1,000 sales return − $75 discount).

ALTERNATIVE 2   **The collection occurs after the discount period has expired (after 10 days from the date of the sale).**

Under these circumstances there is no sales discount. The amount collected is $7,500 ($8,500 original sale − $1,000 sales return). Net sales shown on the income statement would also be $7,500.

THE FINANCIAL ANALYST

Merchandising is a highly competitive business. In order to succeed, merchandisers develop different strategies to distinguish themselves in the marketplace. For example, some companies like Wal-Mart, Kmart, and Costco focus on price competition while others such as Neiman Marcus and Saks Fifth Avenue sell high price goods that offer high quality, style, and strong guaranties. Financial analysts have developed specific tools that are useful in scrutinizing the success or failure of a company's sales strategy. The first step in the analytical process is to develop common size statements so that comparisons can be made between companies.

LO 7

Use common size financial statements and ratio analysis to evaluate managerial performance.

Common Size Financial Statements

How good is a $1,000,000 increase in net income? The answer is not clear because there is no indication as to the size of the company. A million dollar increase may be excellent for a small company but would be virtually meaningless for a company the size of Exxon. To enable meaningful comparisons analysts prepare **common size financial statements.** Common size statements display information in percentages as well as absolute dollar amounts.

To illustrate, we expand the income statements for JPS to include percentages. The results are shown in Exhibit 3.7. The percentage data are computed by defining net sales as the base figure, or 100 percent. The other amounts on the statements are then shown as a percentage of net sales. For example, the *cost of goods sold percentage* is the dollar amount of *cost of goods sold* divided by the dollar amount of *net sales,* which produces a percentage of 66.7 percent ($8,000 ÷ $12,000) for 2010 and 46.5 percent ($11,500 ÷ $24,750) for 2011. Other income statement items are computed using the same approach.

EXHIBIT 3.7	Common Size Financial Statements

JUNE'S PLANT SHOP
Income Statement
For the Period Ended

	2010		2011	
Net sales*	$12,000	100.0%	$24,750	100.0%
Cost of goods sold	(8,000)	66.7	(11,500)	46.5
Gross margin	4,000	33.3	13,250	53.5
Less: Operating expenses				
Selling and administrative expense	(1,000)	8.3	(5,000)	20.2
Transportation-out			(450)	1.8
Operating income	3,000	25.0	7,800	31.5
Nonoperating items				
Interest expense			(360)	(1.5)
Gain on the sale of land			700	2.8
Net income	$ 3,000	25.0	$ 8,140	32.9

*Since JPS did not offer sales discounts or have sales returns and allowances during 2010 or 2011, the amount of sales revenue is equal to the amount of net sales. We use the term *net sales* here because it is more commonly used in business practice. Percentages do not add exactly because they have been rounded.

Ratio Analysis

Two of the percentages shown in Exhibit 3.7 are used frequently in business to make comparisons within a specific company or between two or more different companies. These two commonly used percentages are the **gross margin percentage** and the **net income percentage.** These percentages are calculated as follows:

$$\text{Gross margin percentage} = \frac{\text{Gross margin}}{\text{Net sales}}$$

The gross margin percentage provides insight about a company's pricing strategy. All other things being equal, a high gross margin percentage means that a company is charging high prices in relation to its cost of goods sold.

$$\text{Net income percentage} = \frac{\text{Net income}}{\text{Net sales}}$$

In practice, the *net income percentage* is frequently called the **return on sales** ratio. The return on sales ratio provides insight as to how much of each sales dollar is left as net income after all expenses are paid. All other things being equal, companies with high ratios are doing a better job of controlling expenses.

Comparisons within a Particular Company

To illustrate comparisons within a particular company, assume that JPS relocated its store in an upscale mall in early 2011. Management realized that the company would have to pay more for operating expenses but believed those expenses could be offset by charging significantly higher prices. We use the gross margin percentage and the net income percentage to assess the success of JPS's strategy. Exhibit 3.7 shows an increase in the *gross margin percentage* from 33.3 to 53.5. This confirms that JPS was able to increase prices relative to its cost of goods sold. The increase in the *return on sales* ratio (25 percent to 32.9 percent) confirms that the increase in gross margin was larger than the increase in total expenses. We therefore conclude that JPS's strategy to relocate was successful. As a side note this may also explain why JPS sold its land in late 2011. Considering the success the company experienced at the new location, there was no motive to build a store on the land.

Since net income is affected by nonoperating items, some financial analysts would prefer to use *operating income* instead of *net income* when computing the *return on sales* ratio. In this case the nonoperating items were immaterial. Indeed, to simplify the discussion in this chapter we always assume immateriality when computing this ratio. However, when nonoperating items are significant, it is more insightful to use *operating income* as the numerator of the *return on sales* ratio.

Comparisons between Companies

Does Wal-Mart sell merchandise at a higher or lower price than Target? The *gross margin percentage* is useful in answering questions such as this. Since Wal-Mart's annual report shows a gross margin percentage of 22.9 while Target's report shows a gross margin percentage of 33.6, we conclude that there is validity to Wal-Mart's claim of "always the low price." The next section of the chapter provides insight as to how the *gross margin percentage* and the *return on sales* ratio can be used to gain insight about the operations of several real world companies.

CHECK *Yourself* **3.3**

The following sales data are from the records of two retail sales companies. All amounts are in thousands.

	Company A	Company B
Sales	$21,234	$43,465
Cost of goods sold	(14,864)	(34,772)
Gross margin	$ 6,370	$ 8,693

One company is an upscale department store, and the other is a discount store. Which company is the upscale department store?

Answer The gross margin percentage for Company A is approximately 30 percent ($6,370 ÷ $21,234). The gross margin percentage for Company B is 20 percent ($8,693 ÷ $43,465). These percentages suggest that Company A is selling goods with a higher markup than Company B, which implies that Company A is the upscale department store.

Answers to The *Curious* Accountant

The income statement data show that compared to Zales, Blue Nile does save money by not operating bricks-and-mortar stores. The *gross margin percentage* gives some indication of how much a company is charging in relation to what it pays to purchase the goods it is selling (its cost of goods sold). The *return on sales ratio* reveals how much profit, as a percentage of sales, a company is making after *all* its expenses have been taken into account. For the most recent year shown, Zales' gross margin was 51.4% while Blue Nile's was 22.3%, indicating that Blue Nile really does charge less for its jewelry. However, the return on sales for Blue Nile was 6.5% while Zales was only 4.5%. This shows that while Blue Nile charges less for its products, it makes up for the lower gross margin with lower operating expenses. In fact, as a percentage of sales, Zales' operating expenses were over three times higher than those of Blue Nile. Excluding costs of goods sold, the operating expenses at Blue Nile were 13.4% of sales; Zales' were 44.0%.

Real-World Data

Exhibit 3.8 shows the gross margin percentages and return on sales ratios for 10 companies. Three of the companies are manufacturers that produce pharmaceutical products, and the remaining seven companies sell various products at the retail level.

A review of the data confirms our earlier finding that ratios for companies in the same industry are often more similar than are ratios for companies from different industries. For example, note that the manufacturers have much higher margins, both for gross profit and for net earnings, than do the retailers. Manufacturers are often able to charge higher prices than are retailers because they obtain patents which give them a legal monopoly on the products they create. When a company such as Merck develops a new drug, no one else can produce that drug until the patent expires, giving it lots of control over its price at the wholesale level. Conversely, when Walgreens sells Merck's drug at the retail level, it faces price competition from CVS, a company that is trying

EXHIBIT 3.8

Industry/Company	Gross Margin %	Return on Sales
Pharmaceutical manufacturers		
GlaxoSmithKline	78.0%	21.6%
Johnson & Johnson	72.4	20.6
Merck & Co.	76.6	21.0
Retail pharmacies		
CVS	26.8	3.3
Rite Aid	25.0	1.8
Walgreens	27.9	3.7
Department stores		
Federated	41.6	6.3
Wal-Mart	23.0	3.6
Office supplies		
Office Depot	30.8	1.9
Staples	28.5	5.2

to sell the same drug to the same consumers. One way CVS can try to get customers to shop at its store is to charge lower prices than its competitors, but this reduces its profit margins, since it must pay the same price to get Merck's drug as did Walgreens. As the data in Exhibit 3.8 show, CVS had a lower gross margin percentage than did Walgreens, indicating it is charging slightly lower prices for similar goods.

In the examples presented in Exhibit 3.8, the companies with higher gross margin percentages usually had higher return on sales ratios than their competitors, but this was not always the case. In the office supplies business, Office Depot's gross margin percentage was significantly higher than that of its rival, Staples, but its return on sales ratio was considerably lower. Federated Department Stores, the company that owns Macy's, among others, had a gross margin percentage that was 81 percent greater than Wal-Mart's ([41.6 − 23.0] ÷ 23.0) and its return on sales ratio was 75 percent higher. This is not surprising when you consider how much more luxurious, and costly, the interior of a Macy's store is compared to a Wal-Mart.

A Look Back   <<

Merchandising companies earn profits by selling inventory at prices that are higher than the cost paid for the goods. Merchandising companies include *retail companies* (companies that sell goods to the final consumer) and *wholesale companies* (companies that sell to other merchandising companies). The products sold by merchandising companies are called *inventory.* The costs to purchase inventory, to receive it, and to ready it for sale are *product costs,* which are first accumulated in an inventory account (balance sheet asset account) and then recognized as cost of goods sold (income statement expense account) in the period in which goods are sold. Purchases and sales of inventory can be recorded continually as goods are bought and sold (perpetual system) or at the end of the accounting period (periodic system, discussed in the chapter appendix).

Accounting for inventory includes the treatment of cash discounts, transportation costs, and returns and allowances. The cost of inventory is the list price less any purchase returns and allowances and purchase discounts, plus transportation-in costs. The cost of freight paid to acquire inventory (*transportation-in*) is considered a product cost. The cost of freight paid to deliver inventory to customers (*transportation-out*) is a selling expense. *Sales returns and allowances* and *sales discounts* are subtracted from sales revenue to determine the amount of *net sales* reported on the income statement. Purchase returns and allowances reduce product cost. Theoretically, the cost of lost, damaged, or stolen inventory is an operating expense. However, because these costs are usually immaterial in amount they are typically included as part of cost of goods sold on the income statement.

Some companies use a *multistep income statement* which reports product costs separately from selling and administrative costs. Cost of goods sold is subtracted from sales revenue to determine *gross margin.* Selling and administrative expenses are subtracted from gross margin to determine income from operations. Other companies report income using a *single-step format* in which the cost of goods sold is listed along with selling and administrative items in a single expense category that is subtracted in total from revenue to determine income from operations.

Managers of merchandising businesses operate in a highly competitive environment. They must manage company operations carefully to remain profitable. *Common size financial statements* (statements presented on a percentage basis) and ratio analysis are useful monitoring tools. Common size financial statements permit ready comparisons among different-size companies. Although a $1 million increase in sales may be good for a small company and bad for a large company, a 10 percent increase can apply to any size company. The two most common ratios used by merchandising companies are the *gross margin percentage* (gross margin ÷ net sales) and the *net income percentage* (net income ÷ net sales). Interpreting these ratios requires an understanding of industry characteristics. For example, a discount store such as Wal-Mart would be expected to have a much lower gross margin percentage than an upscale store such as Neiman Marcus.

Managers should be aware of the financing cost of carrying inventory. By investing funds in inventory, a firm loses the opportunity to invest them in interest-bearing assets. The cost of financing inventory is an *opportunity cost.* To minimize financing costs, a company should minimize the amount of inventory it carries, the length of time it holds the inventory, and the time it requires to collect accounts receivable after the inventory is sold.

>> A Look Forward

To this point, the text has explained the basic accounting cycle for service and merchandising businesses. Future chapters more closely address specific accounting issues. For example, in Chapter 6 you will learn how to deal with inventory items that are purchased at differing prices. Other chapters will discuss a variety of specific practices that are widely used by real-world companies.

APPENDIX

Identify the primary features of the periodic inventory system.

Periodic Inventory System

Under certain conditions, it is impractical to record inventory sales transactions as they occur. Consider the operations of a fast-food restaurant. To maintain perpetual inventory records, the restaurant would have to transfer from the Inventory account to the Cost of Goods Sold account the *cost* of each hamburger, order of fries, soft drink, or other food items as they were sold. Obviously, recording the cost of each item at the point of sale would be impractical without using highly sophisticated computer equipment (recording the selling price the customer pays is captured by cash registers; the difficulty lies in capturing inventory cost).

The **periodic inventory system** offers a practical solution for recording inventory transactions in a low-technology, high-volume environment. Inventory costs are recorded in a Purchases account at the time of purchase. Purchase returns and allowances and transportation-in are recorded in separate accounts. No entries for the cost of merchandise purchases or sales are recorded in the Inventory account during the period. The cost of goods sold is determined at the end of the period as shown in Exhibit 3.9.

The perpetual and periodic inventory systems represent alternative procedures for recording the same information. The amounts of cost of goods sold and ending inventory reported in the financial statements will be the same regardless of the method used.

The **schedule of cost of goods sold** presented in Exhibit 3.9 is used for internal reporting purposes. It is normally not shown in published financial statements. The amount of cost of goods sold is reported as a single line item on the income statement. The income statement in Exhibit 3.3 will be the same whether JPS maintains perpetual or periodic inventory records.

Advantages and Disadvantages of the Periodic System versus the Perpetual System

The chief advantage of the periodic method is recording efficiency. Recording inventory transactions occasionally (periodically) requires less effort than recording them continually (perpetually). Historically, practical limitations offered businesses like fast-food restaurants or grocery stores no alternative to using the periodic system. The sheer volume of transactions made recording individual decreases to the Inventory account balance as each item was sold impossible. Imagine the number of transactions a grocery store would have to record every business day to maintain perpetual records.

EXHIBIT 3.9

Schedule of Cost of Goods Sold for 2011

Beginning inventory	$ 6,000
Purchases	11,000
Purchase returns and allowances	(−1,000)
Purchase discounts	(200)
Transportation-in	300
Cost of goods available for sale	16,100
Ending inventory	4,600
Cost of goods sold	$11,500

Although the periodic system provides a recordkeeping advantage over the perpetual system, perpetual inventory records provide significant control advantages over periodic records. With perpetual records, the book balance in the Inventory account should agree with the amount of inventory in stock at any given time. By comparing that book balance with the results of a physical inventory count, management can determine the amount of lost, damaged, destroyed, or stolen inventory. Perpetual records also permit more timely and accurate reorder decisions and profitability assessments.

When a company uses the *periodic* inventory system, lost, damaged, or stolen merchandise is automatically included in cost of goods sold. Because such goods are not included in the year-end physical count, they are treated as sold regardless of the reason for their absence. Since the periodic system does not separate the cost of lost, damaged, or stolen merchandise from the cost of goods sold, the amount of any inventory shrinkage is unknown. This feature is a major disadvantage of the periodic system. Without knowing the amount of inventory losses, management cannot weigh the costs of various security systems against the potential benefits.

Advances in such technology as electronic bar code scanning and increased computing power have eliminated most of the practical constraints that once prevented merchandisers with high-volume, low dollar-value inventories from recording inventory transactions on a continual basis. As a result, use of the perpetual inventory system has expanded rapidly in recent years and continued growth can be expected. This text, therefore, concentrates on the perpetual inventory system.

 ## SELF-STUDY REVIEW PROBLEM

Academy Sales Company (ASC) started the 2010 accounting period with the balances given in the financial statements model shown below. During 2010 ASC experienced the following business events.

1. Purchased $16,000 of merchandise inventory on account, terms 2/10, n/30.
2. The goods that were purchased in Event 1 were delivered FOB shipping point. Freight costs of $600 were paid in cash by the responsible party.
3. Returned $500 of goods purchased in Event 1.
4a. Recorded the cash discount on the goods purchased in Event 1.
4b. Paid the balance due on the account payable within the discount period.
5a. Recognized $21,000 of cash revenue from the sale of merchandise.
5b. Recognized $15,000 of cost of goods sold.
6. The merchandise in Event 5a was sold to customers FOB destination. Freight costs of $950 were paid in cash by the responsible party.
7. Paid cash of $4,000 for selling and administrative expenses.
8. Sold the land for $5,600 cash.

Required

a. Record the above transactions in a financial statements model like the one shown below.

Event No.	Cash	+	Inventory	+	Land	=	Accts. Pay.	+	Com. Stk.	+	Ret. Earn.	Rev./ Gain	−	Exp.	=	Net Inc.	Cash Flow
Bal.	25,000	+	3,000	+	5,000	=	–0–	+	18,000	+	15,000	NA	−	NA	=	NA	NA

b. Prepare a schedule of cost of goods sold. (Appendix)
c. Prepare a multistep income statement. Include common size percentages on the income statement.

d. ASC's gross margin percentage in 2009 was 22%. Based on the common size data in the income statement, did ASC raise or lower its prices in 2010? (Appendix)

e. Assuming a 10 percent rate of growth, what is the amount of net income expected for 2011?

Answer

a.

Event No.	Cash	+	Inventory	+	Land	=	Accts. Pay.	+	Com. Stk.	+	Ret. Earn.	Rev./ Gain	−	Exp.	=	Net Inc.	Cash Flow	
Bal.	25,000	+	3,000	+	5,000	=	–0–	+	18,000	+	15,000	NA	−	NA	=	NA	NA	
1		+	16,000			=	16,000	+		+			−		=			
2	(600)	+	600			=		+		+			−		=		(600)	OA
3		+	(500)			=	(500)	+		+			−		=			
4a		+	(310)			=	(310)	+		+			−		=			
4b	(15,190)	+				=	(15,190)	+		+			−		=		(15,190)	OA
5a	21,000	+				=		+		+	21,000	21,000	−		=	21,000	21,000	OA
5b		+	(15,000)			=		+		+	(15,000)		−	15,000	=	(15,000)		
6	(950)	+				=		+		+	(950)		−	950	=	(950)	(950)	OA
7	(4,000)	+				=		+		+	(4,000)		−	4,000	=	(4,000)	(4,000)	OA
8	5,600	+			(5,000)	=		+		+	600	600	−		=	600	5,600	IA
Bal.	30,860	+	3,790		–0–	=	–0–	+	18,000	+	16,650	21,600	−	19,950	=	1,650	5,860	NC

b.

ACADEMY SALES COMPANY
Schedule of Cost of Goods Sold
For the Period Ended December 31, 2010

Beginning inventory	$ 3,000
Plus purchases	16,000
Less: Purchase returns and allowances	(500)
Less: Purchases discounts	(310)
Plus: Transportation-in	600
Goods available for sale	18,790
Less: Ending inventory	3,790
Cost of goods sold	$(15,000)

c.

ACADEMY SALES COMPANY
Income Statement*
For the Period Ended December 31, 2010

Net sales	$21,000	100.0%
Cost of goods sold	(15,000)	71.4
Gross margin	6,000	28.6
Less: Operating expenses		
Selling and administrative expense	(4,000)	19.0
Transportation-out	(950)	4.5
Operating income	1,050	5.0
Nonoperating items		
Gain on the sale of land	600	2.9
Net income	$ 1,650	7.9

*Percentages do not add exactly because they have been rounded.

d. All other things being equal, the higher the gross margin percentage, the higher the sales prices. Since the gross margin percentage increased from 22% to 28.6%, the data suggest that Academy raised its sales prices.

e. $1,155 [$1,050 + (.10 × $1,050)]. Note that the gain is not expected to recur.

KEY TERMS

Cash discount 98	Gross margin percentage 108	Perpetual inventory system 93	Selling and administrative
Common size financial	Gross profit 93	Product costs 93	costs 93
statements 108	Loss 102	Purchase discount 98	Shrinkage 104
Cost of goods available for	Merchandise inventory 90	Purchase returns and	Single-step income
sale 93	Merchandising businesses 90	allowances 97	statement 103
Cost of Goods Sold 93	Multistep income	Retail companies 90	Transportation-in
FOB (free on board)	statement 103	Return on sales 108	(freight-in) 99
destination 99	Net income percentage 108	Sales discounts 105	Transportation-out
FOB (free on board) shipping	Net sales 107	Sales returns and	(freight-out) 99
point 99	Operating income (or loss) 103	allowances 107	2/10, n/30 98
Gain 102	Period costs 93	Schedule of cost of goods	Wholesale companies 90
Gross margin 93	Periodic inventory system 112	sold 112	

QUESTIONS

1. Define *merchandise inventory*. What types of costs are included in the Merchandise Inventory account?

2. What is the difference between a product cost and a selling and administrative cost?

3. How is the cost of goods available for sale determined?

4. What portion of cost of goods available for sale is shown on the balance sheet? What portion is shown on the income statement?

5. When are period costs expensed? When are product costs expensed?

6. If PetCo had net sales of $600,000, goods available for sale of $450,000, and cost of goods sold of $375,000, what is its gross margin? What amount of inventory will be shown on its balance sheet?

7. Describe how the perpetual inventory system works. What are some advantages of using the perpetual inventory system? Is it necessary to take a physical inventory when using the perpetual inventory system?

8. What are the effects of the following types of transactions on the accounting equation? Also identify the financial statements that are affected. (Assume that the perpetual inventory system is used.)

   a. Acquisition of cash from the issue of common stock.

   b. Contribution of inventory by an owner of a company.

   c. Purchase of inventory with cash by a company.

   d. Sale of inventory for cash.

9. Northern Merchandising Company sold inventory that cost $12,000 for $20,000 cash. How does this event affect the accounting equation? What financial statements and accounts are affected? (Assume that the perpetual inventory system is used.)

10. If goods are shipped FOB shipping point, which party (buyer or seller) is responsible for the shipping costs?

11. Define *transportation-in*. Is it a product or a period cost?

12. Quality Cellular Co. paid $80 for freight on merchandise that it had purchased for resale to customers (transportation-in) and paid $135 for freight on merchandise delivered to customers (transportation-out). What account is debited for the $80 payment? What account is debited for the $135 payment?

13. Why would a seller grant an allowance to a buyer of the seller's merchandise?

14. Dyer Department Store purchased goods with the terms 2/10, n/30. What do these terms mean?

15. Eastern Discount Stores incurred a $5,000 cash cost. How does the accounting for this cost differ if the cash were paid for inventory versus commissions to sales personnel?

16. What is the purpose of giving a cash discount to charge customers?

17. Define *transportation-out*. Is it a product cost or a period cost for the seller?

18. Ball Co. purchased inventory with a list price of $4,000 with the terms 2/10, n/30. What amount will be debited to the Merchandise Inventory account?

19. Explain the difference between purchase returns and sales returns. How do purchase returns affect the financial statements of both buyer and seller? How do sales returns affect the financial statements of both buyer and seller?

20. Explain the difference between gross margin and a gain.

21. What is the difference between a multistep income statement and a single-step income statement?

22. What is the advantage of using common size income statements to present financial information for several accounting periods?

23. What information is provided by the net income percentage (return on sales ratio)?

24. What is the purpose of preparing a schedule of cost of goods sold?

25. Explain how the periodic inventory system works. What are some advantages of using the periodic inventory system? What are some disadvantages of using the periodic

inventory system? Is it necessary to take a physical inventory when using the periodic inventory system?

26. Why does the periodic inventory system impose a major disadvantage for management in accounting for lost, stolen, or damaged goods?

EXERCISES

connect
|ACCOUNTING

All applicable Exercises are available with McGraw-Hill *Connect Accounting*.

When the instructions for *any* exercise or problem call for the preparation of an income statement, use the *multistep format* unless otherwise indicated.

LO 1, 2

Exercise 3-1 *Comparing a merchandising company with a service company*

The following information is available for two different types of businesses for the 2010 accounting period. Madison Consulting is a service business that provides consulting services to small businesses. Books For Less is a merchandising business that sells books to college students.

Data for Madison Consulting

1. Borrowed $40,000 from the bank to start the business.
2. Performed services for customers and collected $30,000 cash.
3. Paid salary expense of $19,200.

Data for Books For Less

1. Borrowed $40,000 from the bank to start the business.
2. Purchased $19,000 of inventory for cash.
3. Inventory costing $16,800 was sold for $30,000 cash.
4. Paid $2,400 cash for operating expenses.

Required

a. Prepare an income statement, balance sheet, and statement of cash flows for each of the companies.
b. What is different about the income statements of the two businesses?
c. What is different about the balance sheets of the two businesses?
d. How are the statements of cash flow different for the two businesses?

LO 2

Exercise 3-2 *Effect of inventory transactions on financial statements: perpetual system*

Chris Daniels started a small merchandising business in 2010. The business experienced the following events during its first year of operation. Assume that Daniels uses the perpetual inventory system.

1. Acquired $60,000 cash from the issue of common stock.
2. Purchased inventory for $50,000 cash.
3. Sold inventory costing $36,000 for $56,000 cash.

Required

a. Record the events in a statements model like the one shown below.

Assets			=	Equity			Rev.	–	Exp.	=	Net Inc.	Cash Flow
Cash	+	Inv.	=	Com. Stk.	+	Ret. Earn.						

b. Prepare an income statement for 2010 (use the multistep format).

c. What is the amount of total assets at the end of the period?

Exercise 3-3 *Effect of inventory transactions on the income statement and*   LO 2
statement of cash flows: perpetual system

During 2011, Lang Merchandising Company purchased $20,000 of inventory on account. The company sold inventory on account that cost $15,000 for $22,500. Cash payments on accounts payable were $12,500. There was $20,000 cash collected from accounts receivable. Lang also paid $4,000 cash for operating expenses. Assume that Lang started the accounting period with $18,000 in both cash and common stock.

Required

a. Identify the events described in the preceding paragraph and record them in a horizontal statements model like the following one.

Assets			=	Liab.	+	Equity			Rev.	−	Exp.	=	Net inc.	Cash Flow
Cash	+ Accts. Rec.	+ Inv.	=	Accts. Pay.	+	Com. Stk.	+	Ret. Earn.						
18,000	+ NA	+ NA	=	NA	+	18,000	+	NA	NA	− NA	=	NA		NA

b. What is the balance of accounts receivable at the end of 2011?

c. What is the balance of accounts payable at the end of 2011?

d. What are the amounts of gross margin and net income for 2011?

e. Determine the amount of net cash flow from operating activities.

f. Explain any differences between net income and net cash flow from operating activities.

Exercise 3-4 *Recording inventory transactions in a financial statements model*   LO 2

David's Paint Supply experienced the following events during 2012, its first year of operation:

1. Acquired $30,000 cash from the issue of common stock.

2. Purchased inventory for $24,000 cash.

3. Sold inventory costing $13,000 for $22,000 cash.

4. Paid $1,600 for advertising expense.

Required

Record the events in a statements model like the one shown below.

Assets		=	Equity			Rev.	−	Exp.	=	Net Inc.	Cash Flow
Cash	+ Inv.	=	Com. Stk.	+	Ret. Earn.						

Exercise 3-5 *Understanding the freight terms FOB shipping point and*   LO 3
FOB destination

Required

For each of the following events, indicate whether the freight terms are FOB destination or FOB shipping point.

a. Sold merchandise and paid the freight costs.

b. Purchased merchandise and paid the freight costs.

c. Sold merchandise and the buyer paid the freight costs.

d. Purchased merchandise and the seller paid the freight costs.

LO 2, 3

Exercise 3-6   *Effect of purchase returns and allowances and freight costs on the journal, ledger, and financial statements: perpetual system*

The trial balance for The Photo Hut as of January 1, 2011, was as follows:

Account Titles	Debit	Credit
Cash	$6,000	
Inventory	3,000	
Common Stock		$7,500
Retained Earnings		1,500
Total	$9,000	$9,000

The following events affected the company during the 2011 accounting period:

1. Purchased merchandise on account that cost $4,100.
2. Purchased goods in Event 1. FOB shipping point with freight cost of $300 cash.
3. Returned $500 of damaged merchandise for credit on account.
4. Agreed to keep other damaged merchandise for which the company received a $250 allowance.
5. Sold merchandise that cost $2,750 for $4,750 cash.
6. Delivered merchandise to customers under terms FOB destination with freight costs amounting to $200 cash.
7. Paid $3,000 on the merchandise purchased in Event 1.

Required

a. Organize appropriate ledger accounts under an accounting equation. Record the beginning balances and the transaction data in the accounts.
b. Prepare an income statement and statement of cash flows for 2011.
c. Explain why a difference does or does not exist between net income and net cash flow from operating activities.

LO 2, 3

Exercise 3-7   *Accounting for product costs: perpetual inventory system*

Which of the following would be *debited* to the Inventory account for a merchandising business using the perpetual inventory system?

Required

a. Purchase of inventory.
b. Allowance received for damaged inventory.
c. Transportation-in.
d. Cash discount given on goods sold.
e. Transportation-out.
f. Purchase of office supplies.

LO 1, 2, 3

Exercise 3-8   *Effect of product cost and period cost: horizontal statements model*

Nigil Co. experienced the following events for the 2010 accounting period:

1. Acquired $10,000 cash from the issue of common stock.
2. Purchased $18,000 of inventory on account.
3. Received goods purchased in Event 2 FOB shipping point. Freight cost of $500 paid in cash.
4. Returned $4,000 of goods purchased in Event 2 because of poor quality.
5. Sold inventory on account that cost $14,300 for $44,000.
6. Freight cost on the goods sold in Event 5 was $100. The goods were shipped FOB destination. Cash was paid for the freight cost.
7. Collected $16,500 cash from accounts receivable.
8. Paid $12,000 cash on accounts payable.

9. Paid $2,200 for advertising expense.

10. Paid $4,400 cash for insurance expense.

Required

a. Which of these transactions result in period (selling and administrative) costs? Which result in product costs? If neither, label the transaction NA.

b. Record each event in a horizontal statements model like the following one. The first event is recorded as an example.

Assets				=	Liab.	+	Equity				Rev.	−	Exp.	=	Net Inc.	Cash Flow
Cash	+	Accts. Rec.	+	Inv.	=	Accts. Pay.	+	C. Stk.	+	Ret. Earn.						
10,000	+	NA	+	NA	=	NA	+	10,000	+	NA	NA	−	NA	=	NA	10,000 FA

Exercise 3-9   *Cash discounts and purchase returns*   LO 3

On March 6, 2010, Ed's Imports purchased merchandise from Watches Inc. with a list price of $31,000, terms 2/10, n/45. On March 10, Ed's returned merchandise to Watches Inc. for credit. The list price of the returned merchandise was $6,400. Ed's paid cash to settle the accounts payable on March 15, 2010.

Required

a. What is the amount of the check that Ed's must write to Watches Inc. on March 15?

b. Record the events in a horizontal statements model like the following one.

Assets			=	Liab.	+	Equity				Rev.	−	Exp.	=	Net Inc.	Cash Flow
Cash	+	Inv.	=	Accts. Pay.	+	C. Stk.	+	Ret. Earn.							

c. How much would Ed's pay for the merchandise purchased if the payment is not made until March 20, 2010?

d. Record the payment of the merchandise in Event *c* in a horizontal statements model like the one shown above.

e. Why would Watches Inc. sell merchandise with the terms 2/10, n/45?

Exercise 3-10   *Effect of sales returns and allowances and freight costs on the journal, ledger, and financial statements: perpetual system*   LO 2, 3

Sans Company began the 2010 accounting period with $18,000 cash, $60,000 inventory, $50,000 common stock, and $28,000 retained earnings. During the 2010 accounting period, Sans experienced the following events.

1. Sold merchandise costing $38,200 for $74,500 on account to Hughes's General Store.

2. Delivered the goods to Hughes under terms FOB destination. Freight costs were $400 cash.

3. Received returned goods from Hughes. The goods cost Sans $2,000 and were sold to Hughes for $3,800.

4. Granted Hughes a $1,000 allowance for damaged goods that Hughes agreed to keep.

5. Collected partial payment of $52,000 cash from accounts receivable.

Required

a. Record the events in a statements model like the one shown below.

Assets					=	Equity				Rev.	−	Exp.	=	Net Inc.	Cash Flow
Cash	+	Accts. Rec.	+	Inv.	=	Com. Stk.	+	Ret. Earn.							

    b. Prepare an income statement, balance sheet, and statement of cash flows.

    c. Why would Sans grant the $2,000 allowance to Hughes? Who benefits more?

LO 2, 3

Exercise 3-11   *Effect of cash discounts on financial statements: perpetual system (gross method)*

Digital Sales was started in 2011. The company experienced the following accounting events during its first year of operation.

1. Started business when it acquired $80,000 cash from the issue of common stock.
2. Purchased merchandise with a list price of $64,000 on account, terms 2/10, n/30.
3. Paid off one-half of the accounts payable balance within the discount period.
4. Sold merchandise on account that had a list price of $52,000. Credit terms were 1/20, n/30. The merchandise had cost Digital $31,000.
5. Collected cash from the account receivable within the discount period.
6. Paid $9,600 cash for operating expenses.
7. Paid the balance due on accounts payable. The payment was not made within the discount period.

Required

    a. Record the events in a horizontal statements model like the following one.

Assets			=	Liab.	+	Equity			Rev.	−	Exp.	=	Net Inc.	Cash Flow
Cash	+ Accts. Rec.	+ Inv.	=	Accts. Pay.	+	Com. Stk.	+	Ret. Earn.						

    b. What is the amount of gross margin for the period? What is the net income for the period?

    c. Why would Digital Sales sell merchandise with the terms 1/20, n/30?

    d. What do the terms 2/10, n/30 in Event 2 mean to Digital Sales?

LO 2, 3

Exercise 3-12   *Effect of inventory transactions on the financial statements: comprehensive exercise with sales and purchase returns and discounts*

Yoder Sales Company had the following balances in its accounts on January 1, 2012.

Cash	$ 60,000
Merchandise Inventory	40,000
Land	100,000
Common Stock	80,000
Retained Earnings	120,000

Yoder experienced the following events during 2012.

1. Sold merchandise inventory that cost $32,000 for $68,000.
2. Sold land that cost $40,000 for $75,000.

Required

    a. Determine the amount of gross margin recognized by Yoder.

    b. Determine the amount of the gain on the sale of land recognized by Yoder.

    c. Comment on how the gross margin versus the gain will be recognized on the income statement.

    d. Comment on how the gross margin versus the gain will be recognized on the statement of cash flows.

LO 2, 5

Exercise 3-13   *Effect of inventory losses: perpetual system*

Cox Sales experienced the following events during 2010, its first year of operation.

1. Started the business when it acquired $50,000 cash from the issue of common stock.
2. Paid $21,000 cash to purchase inventory.

3. Sold inventory costing $12,500 for $26,500 cash.

4. Physically counted inventory showing $7,900 inventory was on hand at the end of the accounting period.

Required

a. Determine the amount of the difference between book balance and the actual amount of inventory as determined by the physical count.

b. Explain how differences between the book balance and the physical count of inventory could arise. Why is being able to determine whether differences exist useful to management?

Exercise 3-14 *Determining the effect of inventory transactions on the horizontal statements model: perpetual system*   LO 2

Ramsey Company experienced the following events.

1. Purchased merchandise inventory on account.

2. Purchased merchandise inventory for cash.

3. Sold merchandise inventory on account. Label the revenue recognition 3a and the expense recognition 3b.

4. Returned merchandise purchased on account.

5. Sold merchandise inventory for cash. Label the revenue recognition 5a and the expense recognition 5b.

6. Paid cash on accounts payable within the discount period.

7. Paid cash for selling and administrative expenses.

8. Collected cash from accounts receivable not within the discount period.

9. Paid cash for transportation-out.

10. Paid cash for transportation-in.

Required

Identify each event as asset source (AS), asset use (AU), asset exchange (AE), or claims exchange (CE). Also explain how each event affects the financial statements by placing a + for increase, − for decrease, or NA for not affected under each of the components in the following statements model. Assume the company uses the perpetual inventory system. The first event is recorded as an example.

Event No.	Event Type	Assets	=	Liab.	+	Equity	Rev.	−	Exp.	=	Net Inc.	Cash Flow
1	AS	+	=	+	+	NA	NA	−	NA	=	NA	NA

Exercise 3-15 *Single-step and multistep income statements*   LO 4

The following information was taken from the accounts of Helen's Groceries, a delicatessen. The accounts are listed in alphabetical order, and each has a normal balance.

Accounts payable	$600
Accounts receivable	400
Advertising expense	200
Cash	410
Common stock	200
Cost of goods sold	600
Interest expense	70
Merchandise inventory	450
Prepaid rent	40
Retained earnings (Beginning balance)	635
Sales revenue	1,000
Salaries expense	130
Supplies expense	110
Loss on sale of land	25

Required

First, prepare an income statement using the single-step approach. Then prepare another income statement using the multistep approach.

LO 2

Exercise 3-16   *Determining the cost of financing inventory*

On January 1, 2012, Sam started a small sailboat merchandising business that he named Sam's Boats. The company experienced the following events during the first year of operation.

1. Started the business by issuing common stock for $30,000 cash.
2. Paid $22,000 cash to purchase inventory.
3. Sold a sailboat that cost $12,000 for $24,000 on account.
4. Collected $14,000 cash from accounts receivable.
5. Paid $5,800 for operating expenses.

Required

a. Organize ledger accounts under an accounting equation and record the events in the accounts.
b. Prepare an income statement, balance sheet, and statement of cash flows.
c. Since Sam sold inventory for $24,000, he will be able to recover more than half of the $30,000 he invested in the stock. Do you agree with this statement? Why or why not?

LO 3

Exercise 3-17   *Inventory financing costs*

Jerry Guardino comes to you for advice. He has just purchased a large amount of inventory with the terms 1/10, n/30. The amount of the invoice is $320,000. He is currently short of cash but has good credit. He can borrow the money needed to settle the account payable at an annual interest rate of 7%. Guardino is sure he will have the necessary cash by the due date of the invoice but not by the last day of the discount period.

Required

a. Convert the discount rate into an annual interest rate.
b. Make a recommendation regarding whether Guardino should borrow the money and pay off the account payable within the discount period.

LO 8

Exercise 3-18   *Effect of inventory transactions on the income statement and balance sheet: periodic system (Appendix)*

Daniel Jackson is the owner of ABC Cleaning. At the beginning of the year, Jackson had $2,400 in inventory. During the year, Jackson purchased inventory that cost $13,000. At the end of the year, inventory on hand amounted to $3,600.

Required

Calculate the following.

a. Cost of goods available for sale during the year.
b. Cost of goods sold for the year.
c. Inventory amount ABC Cleaning would report on its year-end balance sheet.

LO 8

Exercise 3-19   *Determining cost of goods sold: periodic system (Appendix)*

Laura's Clothing Co. uses the periodic inventory system to account for its inventory transactions. The following account titles and balances were drawn from Laura's records for the year 2009: beginning balance in inventory, $24,900; purchases, $306,400; purchase returns and allowances, $12,400; sales, $720,000; sales returns and allowances, $6,370; transportation-in, $1,820; and operating expenses, $51,400. A physical count indicated that $24,800 of merchandise was on hand at the end of the accounting period.

Required

a. Prepare a schedule of cost of goods sold.
b. Prepare a multistep income statement.

Exercise 3-20 *Performing ratio analysis using real-world data*   LO 7

The following data were taken from Microsoft Corporation's 2007 annual report. All dollar
amounts are in millions.

	Fiscal Years Ending	
	June 30, 2007	June 30, 2006
Revenue	$51,122	$44,282
Cost of Goods Sold	10,693	7,650
Net Income	14,065	12,599

Required

a. Compute Microsoft's gross margin percentage for 2007 and 2006.

b. Compute Microsoft's return on sales percentage for 2007 and 2006.

c. Based on the percentages computed in Requirements *a* and *b*, did Microsoft's performance
get better or worse from 2006 to 2007?

d. Compare Microsoft's gross margin percentages and return on sales percentages to those of
the other real-world companies discussed in this chapter and discuss whether or not it
appears to have better-than-average financial performance or not.

PROBLEMS

**All applicable Problems are available with McGraw-Hill
Connect Accounting.**

connect
|ACCOUNTING

Problem 3-21 *Basic transactions for three accounting cycles: perpetual system*   LO 2

Ferguson Company was started in 2008 when it acquired $60,000 from the issue of common
stock. The following data summarize the company's first three years' operating activities.
Assume that all transactions were cash transactions.

CHECK FIGURES
2008 Net Income: $7,100
2010 Total Assets: $76,300

	2008	2009	2010
Purchases of inventory	$24,000	$12,000	$20,500
Sales	26,000	30,000	36,000
Cost of goods sold	13,400	18,500	20,000
Selling and administrative expenses	5,500	8,200	10,100

Required

Prepare an income statement (use the multistep format) and balance sheet for each fiscal year.
(*Hint:* Record the transaction data for each accounting period in the accounting equation before
preparing the statements for that year.)

Problem 3-22 *Identifying product and period costs*

Required

Indicate whether each of the following costs is a product cost or a period (selling and administrative) cost.

a. Transportation-in.

b. Insurance on the office building.

c. Office supplies.

d. Costs incurred to improve the quality of goods available for sale.

e. Goods purchased for resale.

f. Salaries of salespersons.

g. Advertising costs.

h. Transportation-out.

i. Rent expense.

j. Salary of the company president.

LO 3

CHECK FIGURE

Event (b): Freight Cost is zero

Problem 3-23   *Identifying freight costs*

Required

For each of the following events, determine the amount of freight paid by The Book Shop. Also indicate whether the freight cost would be classified as a product or period (selling and administrative) cost.

a. Purchased merchandise with freight costs of $700. The merchandise was shipped FOB shipping point.

b. Shipped merchandise to customers, freight terms FOB shipping point. The freight costs were $100.

c. Purchased inventory with freight costs of $1,000. The goods were shipped FOB destination.

d. Sold merchandise to a customer. Freight costs were $900. The goods were shipped FOB destination.

LO 2, 3

CHECK FIGURES

a. Ending Cash: $26,592

d. Net Income: $4,750

Problem 3-24   *Effect of purchase returns and allowances and purchase discounts on the financial statements: perpetual system (gross method)*

The following events were completed by John's Hobby Shop in September 2012.

Sept. 1   Acquired $40,000 cash from the issue of common stock.

1   Purchased $28,000 of merchandise on account with terms 2/10, n/30.

5   Paid $600 cash for freight to obtain merchandise purchased on September 1.

8   Sold merchandise that cost $9,000 to customers for $17,000 on account, with terms 1/10, n/30.

8   Returned $900 of defective merchandise from the September 1 purchase to the supplier.

10   Paid cash for the balance due on the merchandise purchased on September 1.

20   Received cash from customers of September 8 sale in settlement of the account balances, but not within the discount period.

30   Paid $3,250 cash for selling expenses.

Required

a. Record each event in a statements model like the following one. The first event is recorded as an example.

Assets			=	Liab.	+	Equity			Rev.	−	Exp.	=	Net Inc.	Cash Flow
Cash	+ Accts. Rec.	+ Inv.	=	Accts. Pay.	+	Com. Stk.	+	Ret. Earn.						
30,000	+ NA	+ NA	=	NA	+	30,000	+	NA	NA	−	NA	=	NA	30,000 FA

b. Prepare an income statement for the month ending September 30.

c. Prepare a statement of cash flows for the month ending September 30.

d. Explain why there is a difference between net income and cash flow from operating activities.

Problem 3-25 *Comprehensive cycle problem: perpetual system*

LO **2, 3, 5, 6**

At the beginning of 2012, D & L Enterprises had the following balances in its accounts:

CHECK FIGURES
d. Net Income: $1,584
Total Assets: $11,984

Cash	$8,400
Inventory	2,000
Common stock	8,000
Retained earnings	2,400

During 2012, D & L Enterprises experienced the following events:

1. Purchased inventory costing $5,600 on account from Smoot Company under terms 2/10, n/30. The merchandise was delivered FOB shipping point. Freight costs of $500 were paid in cash.
2. Returned $400 of the inventory that it had purchased because the inventory was damaged in transit. The freight company agreed to pay the return freight cost.
3. Paid the amount due on its account payable to Smoot Company within the cash discount period.
4. Sold inventory that had cost $6,000 for $9,000. The sale was on account under terms 2/10, n/45.
5. Received returned merchandise from a customer. The merchandise had originally cost $520 and had been sold to the customer for $840 cash. The customer was paid $840 cash for the returned merchandise.
6. Delivered goods in Event 4 FOB destination. Freight costs of $600 were paid in cash.
7. Collected the amount due on accounts receivable within the discount period.
8. Took a physical count indicating that $1,800 of inventory was on hand at the end of the accounting period.

Required

a. Identify these events as asset source (AS), asset use (AU), asset exchange (AE), or claims exchange (CE).
b. Record each event in a statements model like the following one.

Event	Balance Sheet				Income Statement			Statement of Cash Flows
	Assets	=	Liab.	= Equity	Rev.	− Exp.	= Net Inc.	
	Cash + Accts. Rec. + Mdse. Inv.	=	Accts. Pay.	+ Ret. Earn.				

c. Prepare an income statement, a statement of changes in stockholders' equity, a balance sheet, and a statement of cash flows.

Problem 3-26 *Using common size income statements to make comparisons*

LO **6**

The following income statements were drawn from the annual reports of Pierro Sales Company.

	2010*	2011*
Net Sales	$426,500	$520,600
Cost of Goods Sold	(312,000)	(369,600)
Gross Margin	114,500	151,000
Less: Operating Expense		
Selling and Administrative Expenses	(50,200)	(64,800)
Net Income	$ 64,300	$ 86,200

*All dollar amounts are reported in thousands.

The president's message in the company's annual report stated that the company had implemented a strategy to increase market share by spending more on advertising. The president indicated that prices held steady and sales grew as expected. Write a memo indicating whether you agree with the president's statements. How has the strategy affected profitability? Support your answer by measuring growth in sales and selling expenses. Also prepare common size income statements and make appropriate references to the differences between 2010 and 2011.

LO 5, 8

CHECK FIGURES
a. Cost of Goods Available for
   Sale: $171,500
b. Net Income: $55,400

Problem 3-27   *Preparing a schedule of cost of goods sold and multistep and single-step income statements: periodic system (Appendix)*

The following account titles and balances were taken from the adjusted trial balance of Wright Sales Co. at December 31, 2012. The company uses the periodic inventory method.

Account Title	Balance
Advertising expense	$ 10,400
Income taxes	8,200
Interest expense	5,000
Merchandise inventory, January 1	18,000
Merchandise inventory, December 31	20,100
Miscellaneous expense	800
Purchases	150,000
Purchase returns and allowances	2,700
Rent expense	18,000
Salaries expense	53,000
Sales	320,000
Sales returns and allowances	8,000
Transportation-in	6,200
Transportation-out	10,800
Gain on sale of land	4,000

Required

a. Prepare a schedule to determine the amount of cost of goods sold.
b. Prepare a multistep income statement.
c. Prepare a single-step income statement.

LO 8

CHECK FIGURES
b. Ending Cash: $57,640
c. Cost of Goods Sold: $50,810

Problem 3-28   *Comprehensive cycle problem: periodic system (Appendix)*

The following trial balance pertains to Mitchell Home Products as of January 1, 2010.

Account Title	Debit	Credit
Cash	$14,000	
Accounts receivable	9,000	
Merchandise inventory	60,000	
Accounts payable		$ 5,000
Common stock		70,000
Retained earnings		8,000
Total	$83,000	$83,000

The following events occurred in 2010. Assume that Mitchell Home Products uses the periodic inventory system.

1. Purchased land for $8,000 and a building for $53,000 cash.
2. Purchased merchandise on account for $23,000, terms 2/10 n/30.
3. The merchandise purchased was shipped FOB shipping point for $230 cash.
4. Returned $2,000 of defective merchandise purchased in Event 2.
5. Sold merchandise for $27,000 cash.

6. Sold merchandise on account for $50,000, terms 1/20 n/30.

7. Paid cash within the discount period on accounts payable due on merchandise purchased in Event 2.

8. Paid $1,200 cash for selling expenses.

9. Collected $35,000 of accounts receivable within the discount period.

10. Collected $12,000 of accounts receivable but not within the discount period.

11. Performed a physical count indicating that $30,000 of inventory was on hand at the end of the accounting period.

Required

a. Record the above transactions in a horizontal statements model like the following one.

Event	Balance Sheet								Income Statement			Statement of Cash Flows
	Assets				=	Equity			Rev. − Exp. = Net Inc.			
	Cash +	Accts. Rec. +	Mdse. Inv. +	Land =		Accts. Pay. +	Com. Stock +	Ret. Earn.				

b. Prepare a schedule of cost of goods sold and an income statement.

Problem 3-29 *Performing ratio analysis using real-world data*

LO 7

Supervalu, Inc., claims to be the largest publicly held food wholesaler in the United States. In addition to being a food wholesaler, it operates "extreme value" retail grocery stores under the name Save-A-Lot. Most of these discount stores are located in inner-city areas not served by others. Whole Food Markets claims to be the world's largest retailer of natural and organic foods. Unlike Save-A-Lot stores that focuses on low-income customers, Whole Foods offers specialty products to customers with sufficient disposal income to spend on such goods. The following data were taken from these companies' 2007 annual reports. All dollar amounts are in millions.

	Supervalu, Inc. February 24, 2007	Whole Foods September 30, 2007
Sales	$37,406	$6,592
Cost of Goods Sold	29,267	4,295
Net Income	452	183

Required

a. Before performing any calculations, speculate as to which company will have the highest gross margin and return on sales percentage. Explain the rationale for your decision.

b. Calculate the gross margin percentages for Supervalu and Whole Foods Market.

c. Calculate the return on sales percentages for Supervalu and Whole Foods Market.

d. Do the calculations from Requirements *b* and *c* confirm your speculations in Requirement *a*?

ANALYZE, THINK, COMMUNICATE

ATC 3-1 Business Applications Case *Understanding real world annual reports*

Required

Use the Topps Company's annual report in Appendix B to answer the following questions.

a. What was Topps' gross margin percentage for 2006 and 2005?

b. What was Topps' return on sales percentage for 2006 and 2005?

c. Topps' Gross Profit on Sales was about $9 million lower in 2006 than in 2005 and this caused its Net Income to be lower as well. However, its gross margin percentage also decreased in 2006. Ignoring taxes, how much higher would its 2006 net income have been if the gross margin percentage in 2006 had been the same as for 2005?

ATC 3-2   Group Exercise   *Multistep income statement*

The following quarterly information is given for Raybon for the year ended 2010 (amounts shown are in millions).

	First Quarter	Second Quarter	Third Quarter	Fourth Quarter
Net Sales	$736.0	$717.4	$815.2	$620.1
Gross Margin	461.9	440.3	525.3	252.3
Net Income	37.1	24.6	38.6	31.4

Required

a. Divide the class into groups and organize the groups into four sections. Assign each section financial information for one of the quarters.

   (1) Each group should compute the cost of goods sold and operating expenses for the specific quarter assigned to its section and prepare a multistep income statement for the quarter.

   (2) Each group should compute the gross margin percentage and cost of goods sold percentage for its specific quarter.

   (3) Have a representative of each group put that quarter's sales, cost of goods sold percentage, and gross margin percentage on the board.

Class Discussion

b. Have the class discuss the change in each of these items from quarter to quarter and explain why the change might have occurred. Which was the best quarter and why?

ATC 3-3   Real-World Case   *Identifying companies based on financial statement information*

Presented here is selected information from the 2005 fiscal-year 10-K reports of four companies. The four companies, in alphabetical order, are Caterpillar, Inc., a manufacturer of heavy machinery; Oracle Corporation, a company that develops software; Starbucks, a company that sells coffee products; and Tiffany & Company, a company that operates high-end jewelry and department stores. The data for the companies, presented in the order of the amount of their sales in millions of dollars, follow.

	A	B	C	D
Sales	$2,395	$6,369	$11,799	$36,339
Cost of Goods Sold	1,052	2,605	2,651	26,558
Net Earnings	255	495	2,886	2,854
Inventory	1,060	546	0	5,224
Accounts Receivable	142	191	2,900	13,968
Total Assets	$2,777	$3,514	$20,687	$47,069

Required

Based on these financial data and your knowledge and assumptions about the nature of the businesses that the companies operate, determine which data relate to which companies. Write a memorandum explaining your decisions. Include a discussion of which ratios you used in your analysis, and show the computations of these ratios in your memorandum.

ATC 3-4   Business Applications Case   *Using ratios to make comparisons*

The following income statements were drawn from the annual reports of Design Company and Royal Company.

	Design	Royal
Net Sales	$95,700	$52,300
Cost of Goods Sold	68,900	31,400
Gross Margin	26,800	20,900
Less: Selling and Admin. Expenses	22,000	18,800
Net Income	$ 4,800	$ 2,100

Note: All figures are reported in thousands of dollars.

Required

a. One of the companies is a high-end retailer that operates in exclusive shopping malls. The other operates discount stores located in low-cost stand-alone buildings. Identify the high-end retailer and the discounter. Support your answer with appropriate ratios.

b. If Design and Royal have equity of $40,000 and $21,000, respectively, which company is the more profitable?

ATC 3-5   Business Applications Case   *Using common size statements and ratios to make comparisons*

At the end of 2009, the following information is available for Chicago and St. Louis companies:

	Chicago	St. Louis
Sales	$3,000,000	$3,000
Cost of Goods Sold	1,800,000	2,100
Selling and Administrative Expenses	960,000	780
Total Assets	3,750,000	3,750
Stockholders' Equity	1,000,000	1,200

Required

a. Prepare common size income statements for each company.

b. Compute the return on assets and return on equity for each company.

c. Which company is more profitable from the stockholders' perspective?

d. One company is a high-end retailer, and the other operates a discount store. Which is the discounter? Support your selection by referring to appropriate ratios.

ATC 3-6   Written Assignment, Critical Thinking   *Effect of sales returns on financial statements*

Bell Farm and Garden Equipment reported the following information for 2010:

Net Sales of Equipment	$2,450,567
Other Income	6,786
Cost of Goods Sold	1,425,990
Selling, General, and Administrative Expense	325,965
Net Operating Income	$ 705,398

Selected information from the balance sheet as of December 31, 2010, follows.

Cash and Marketable Securities	$113,545
Inventory	248,600
Accounts Receivable	82,462
Property, Plant, and Equipment—Net	335,890
Other Assets	5,410
Total Assets	$785,907

Assume that a major customer returned a large order to Bell on December 31, 2010. The amount of the sale had been $146,800 with a cost of sales of $94,623. The return was recorded in the books on January 1, 2011. The company president does not want to correct the books. He argues that it makes no difference as to whether the return is recorded in 2010 or 2011. Either way, the return has been duly recognized.

Required

a. Assume that you are the CFO for Bell Farm and Garden Equipment Co. Write a memo to the president explaining how omitting the entry on December 31, 2010, could cause the financial statements to be misleading to investors and creditors. Explain how omitting the return from the customer would affect net income and the balance sheet.

b. Why might the president want to record the return on January 1, 2011, instead of December 31, 2010?

c. Would the failure to record the customer return violate the AICPA Code of Professional Conduct? (See Exhibit 1.4 in Chapter 1.)

d. If the president of the company refuses to correct the financial statements, what action should you take?

ATC 3-7 Corporate Governance *Wait until I get mine*

Ada Fontanez is the chief executive officer (CEO) of a large company that owns a chain of athletic shoe stores. The company was in dire financial condition when she was hired three years ago. To motivate Fontanez, the board of directors included a bonus plan as part of her compensation package. According to her employment contract, on January 15 of each year, Fontanez is paid a cash bonus equal to 5 percent of the amount of net income reported on the preceding December 31 income statement. Fontanez was sufficiently motivated. Through her leadership, the company prospered. Her efforts were recognized throughout the industry, and she received numerous lucrative offers to leave the company. One offer was so enticing that she decided to change jobs. Her decision was made in late December 2010. However, she decided to resign effective February 1, 2011, to ensure the receipt of her January bonus. On December 31, 2010, the chief financial officer (CFO), Walter Smith, advised Fontanez that the company had a sizable quantity of damaged inventory. A warehouse fire had resulted in smoke and water damage to approximately $600,000 of inventory. The warehouse was not insured, and the accountant recommended that the loss be recognized immediately. After examining the inventory, Fontanez argued that it could be sold as *damaged goods* to customers at reduced prices. She refused to allow the write-off the accountant recommended. She stated that so long as she is president, the inventory stays on the books at cost. She told the accountant that he could take up the matter with the new president in February.

Required

a. How would an immediate write-off of the damaged inventory affect the December 31, 2010, income statement, balance sheet, and statement of cash flows?

b. How would the write-off affect Fontanez's bonus?

c. If the new president is given the same bonus plan, how will Fontanez's refusal to recognize the loss affect his or her bonus?

d. Assume Walter Smith (CFO) yields to the pressure exerted by Ada Fontanez (CEO) and certifies the financial statements without requiring the write-off. What penalties may he face under the Sarbanes-Oxley Act?

e. Assume that Walter Smith is a CPA. Explain how signing off on the financial statements without recognizing the write-off violates Article II of the AICPA Code of Professional Conduct (see Chapter 2, Exhibit 2.7).

ATC 3-8   Research Assignment   *Analyzing Alcoa's profit margins*

Using either Alcoa's most current Form 10-K or the company's annual report, answer the questions below. To obtain the Form 10-K you can use either the EDGAR system following the instructions in Appendix A, or the company's website. The company's annual report is available on its website.

Required

a. What was Alcoa's gross margin percentage for the most current year?

b. What was Alcoa's gross margin percentage for the previous year? Has it changed significantly?

c. What was Alcoa's return on sales percentage for the most current year?

d. What percentage of Alcoa's total sales for the most current year was from operations in the United States?

e. Comment on the appropriateness of comparing Alcoa's gross margin with that of Ford Motor Company. If Ford has a higher/lower margin, does that mean that Ford is a better managed company?

CHAPTER 4

Accounting *for* Inventories

LEARNING OBJECTIVES

After you have mastered the material in this chapter you will be able to:

1 Explain how different inventory cost flow methods (specific identification, FIFO, LIFO, and weighted average) affect financial statements.

2 Demonstrate the computational procedures for FIFO, LIFO, and weighted average.

3 Identify the key elements of a strong system of internal control.

4 Identify special internal controls for cash.

5 Prepare a bank reconciliation.

6 Explain the importance of inventory turnover to a company's profitability.

CHAPTER OPENING

In the previous chapter, we used the simplifying assumption that identical inventory items cost the same amount. In practice, businesses often pay different amounts for identical items. Suppose The Mountain Bike Company (TMBC) sells high-end Model 201 helmets. Even though all Model 201 helmets are identical, the price TMBC pays for each helmet frequently charges.

Assume TMBC purchases one Model 201 helmet at a cost of $100. Two weeks later, TMBC purchases a second Model 201 helmet. Because the supplier has raised prices, the second helmet costs $110. If TMBC sells one of its two helmets, should it record $100 or $110 as cost of goods sold? The following section of this chapter discusses several acceptable alternative methods for determining the amount of cost of goods sold from which companies may choose under generally accepted accounting principles.

The *Curious* Accountant

Albertson's is one of the largest food store chains in the United States, operating about 2,500 stores. As of February 2, 2006, the company had approximately $3 billion of inventory reported on its balance sheet. In the footnotes to its financial statements, Albertson's reported that it uses an inventory method that assumes its newest goods are sold first and its oldest goods are kept in inventory.

Can you think of any reason why a company selling perishable goods such as milk and vegetables uses an inventory method that assumes older goods are kept while newer goods are sold? (Answer on page 150.)

INVENTORY COST FLOW METHODS

LO 1

Explain how different inventory cost flow methods (specific identification, FIFO, LIFO, and weighted average) affect financial statements.

Recall that when goods are sold, product costs flow (are transferred) from the Inventory account to the Cost of Goods Sold account. Four acceptable methods for determining the amount of cost to transfer are (1) specific identification; (2) first-in, first-out (FIFO); (3) last-in, first-out (LIFO); and weighted average.

Specific Identification

Suppose TMBC tags inventory items so that it can identify which one is sold at the time of sale. TMBC could then charge the actual cost of the specific item sold to cost of goods sold. Recall that the first inventory item TMBC purchased cost $100 and the second item cost $110. Using **specific identification,** cost of goods sold would be $100 if the first item purchased were sold or $110 if the second item purchased were sold.

When a company's inventory consists of many low-priced, high-turnover goods, the record keeping necessary to use specific identification isn't practical. Imagine the difficulty of recording the cost of each specific food item in a grocery store. Another disadvantage of the specific identification method is the opportunity for managers to manipulate the income statement. For example, TMBC can report a lower cost of goods sold by selling the first instead of the second item. Specific identification is, however, frequently used for high-priced, low-turnover inventory items such as automobiles. For big ticket items like cars, customer demands for specific products limit management's ability to select which merchandise is sold and volume is low enough to manage the recordkeeping.

First-In, First-Out (FIFO)

The **first-in, first-out (FIFO) cost flow method** requires that the cost of the items purchased *first* be assigned to cost of goods sold. Using FIFO, TMBC's cost of goods sold is $100.

Last-In, First-Out (LIFO)

The **last-in, first-out (LIFO) cost flow method** requires that the cost of the items purchased *last* be charged to cost of goods sold. Using LIFO, TMBC's cost of goods sold is $110.

Weighted Average

To use the **weighted-average cost flow method,** first calculate the average cost per unit by dividing the *total cost* of the inventory available by the *total number* of units available. In the case of TMBC, the average cost per unit of the inventory is $105 ([$100 + $110] ÷ 2). Cost of goods sold is then calculated by multiplying the average cost per unit by the number of units sold. Using weighted average, TMBC's cost of goods sold is $105 ($105 × 1).

Physical Flow

The preceding discussion pertains to the flow of *costs* through the accounting records, *not* the actual **physical flow of goods.** Goods usually move physically on a FIFO basis, which means that the first items of merchandise acquired by a company (first-in) are the first items sold to its customers (first-out). The inventory items on hand at the end of the accounting period are typically the last items in (the most recently acquired goods). If companies did not sell their oldest inventory items first, inventories would include dated, less marketable merchandise. *Cost flow,* however, can differ from *physical flow.* For example, a company may use LIFO or weighted average for financial reporting even if its goods flow physically on a FIFO basis.

EFFECT OF COST FLOW ON FINANCIAL STATEMENTS

Effect on Income Statement

The cost flow method a company uses can significantly affect the gross margin reported in the income statement. To demonstrate, assume that TMBC sold the inventory item discussed previously for $120. The amounts of gross margin using the FIFO, LIFO, and weighted-average cost flow assumptions are shown in the following table.

	FIFO	LIFO	Weighted Average
Sales	$120	$120	$120
Cost of goods sold	(100)	(110)	(105)
Gross margin	$ 20	$ 10	$ 15

Even though the physical flow is assumed to be identical for each method, the gross margin reported under FIFO is double the amount reported under LIFO. Companies experiencing identical economic events (same units of inventory purchased and sold) can report significantly different results in their financial statements. Meaningful financial analysis requires an understanding of financial reporting practices.

Effect on Balance Sheet

Since total product costs are allocated between costs of goods sold and ending inventory, the cost flow method a company uses affects its balance sheet as well as its income statement. Since FIFO transfers the first cost to the income statement, it leaves the last cost on the balance sheet. Similarly, by transferring the last cost to the income statement, LIFO leaves the first cost in ending inventory. The weighted-average method bases both cost of goods sold and ending inventory on the average cost per unit. To illustrate, the ending inventory TMBC would report on the balance sheet using each of the three cost flow methods is shown in the following table.

	FIFO	LIFO	Weighted Average
Ending inventory	$110	$100	$105

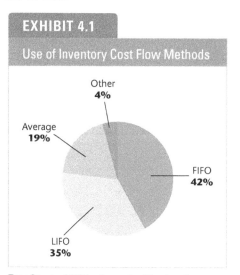

EXHIBIT 4.1

Use of Inventory Cost Flow Methods

Data Source: AICPA, *Accounting Trends and Techniques.*

The FIFO, LIFO, and weighted-average methods are all used extensively in business practice. The same company may even use one cost flow method for some of its products and different cost flow methods for other products. Exhibit 4.1 illustrates the relative use of the different cost flow methods among U.S. companies.

CHECK *Yourself* 4.1

Nash Office Supply (NOS) purchased two Model 303 copiers at different times. The first copier purchased cost $400 and the second copier purchased cost $450. NOS sold one of the copiers for $600. Determine the gross margin on the sale and the ending inventory balance assuming NOS accounts for inventory using (1) FIFO, (2) LIFO, and (3) weighted average.

Answer

	FIFO	LIFO	Weighted Average
Sales	$600	$600	$600
Cost of goods sold	(400)	(450)	(425)
Gross margin	$200	$150	$175
Ending inventory	$450	$400	$425

INVENTORY COST FLOW UNDER A PERPETUAL SYSTEM

Multiple Layers with Multiple Quantities

Demonstrate the computational procedures for FIFO, LIFO, and weighted average.

The previous example illustrates different **inventory cost flow methods** using only two cost layers ($100 and $110) with only one unit of inventory in each layer. Actual business inventories are considerably more complex. Most real-world inventories are composed of multiple cost layers with different quantities of inventory in each layer. The underlying allocation concepts, however, remain unchanged.

For example, a different inventory item The Mountain Bike Company (TMBC) carries in its stores is a bike called the Eraser. TMBC's beginning inventory and two purchases of Eraser bikes are described below.

Jan. 1	Beginning inventory	10 units @ $200	=	$ 2,000
Mar. 18	First purchase	20 units @ $220	=	4,400
Aug. 21	Second purchase	25 units @ $250	=	6,250
Total cost of the 55 bikes available for sale				$12,650

The accounting records for the period show that TMBC paid cash for all Eraser bike purchases and that it sold 43 bikes at a cash price of $350 each.

Allocating Cost of Goods Available for Sale

The following discussion shows how to determine the cost of goods sold and ending inventory amounts under FIFO, LIFO, and weighted average. We show all three methods to demonstrate how they affect the financial statements differently; TMBC would actually use only one of the methods.

Regardless of the cost flow method chosen, TMBC must allocate the cost of goods available for sale ($12,650) between cost of goods sold and ending inventory. The amounts assigned to each category will differ depending on TMBC's cost flow method. Computations for each method are shown below.

FIFO Inventory Cost Flow

Recall that TMBC sold 43 Eraser bikes during the accounting period. The FIFO method transfers to the Cost of Goods Sold account the *cost of the first 43 bikes* TMBC had available to sell. The first 43 bikes acquired by TMBC were the 10 bikes in the beginning inventory (these were purchased in the prior period) plus the 20 bikes purchased in March and 13 of the bikes purchased in August. The expense recognized for the cost of these bikes ($9,650) is computed as follows.

Jan. 1	Beginning inventory	10 units @ $200	=	$2,000
Mar. 18	First purchase	20 units @ $220	=	4,400
Aug. 21	Second purchase	13 units @ $250	=	3,250
Total cost of the 43 bikes sold				$9,650

Since TMBC had 55 bikes available for sale it would have 12 bikes (55 available − 43 sold) in ending inventory. The cost assigned to these 12 bikes (the ending balance in the Inventory account) equals the cost of goods available for sale minus the cost of goods sold as shown below.

Cost of goods available for sale	$12,650
Cost of goods sold	(9,650)
Ending inventory balance	$ 3,000

We show the allocation of the cost of goods available for sale between cost of goods sold and ending inventory graphically below.

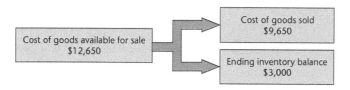

LIFO Inventory Cost Flow

Under LIFO, the cost of goods sold is the cost of the last 43 bikes acquired by TMBC, computed as follows.

Aug. 21	Second purchase	25 units @ $250	=	$ 6,250
Mar. 18	First purchase	18 units @ $220	=	3,960
	Total cost of the 43 bikes sold			$10,210

The LIFO cost of the 12 bikes in ending inventory is computed as shown below.

Cost of goods available for sale	$12,650
Cost of goods sold	(10,210)
Ending inventory balance	$ 2,440

We show the allocation of the cost of goods available for sale between cost of goods sold and ending inventory graphically below.

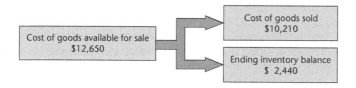

Weighted-Average Cost Flow

The weighted-average cost per unit is determined by dividing the *total cost of goods available for sale* by the *total number of units* available for sale. For TMBC, the weighted-average cost per unit is $230 ($12,650 ÷ 55). The weighted-average cost of goods sold is determined by multiplying the average cost per unit by the number of units sold ($230 × 43 = $9,890). The cost assigned to the 12 bikes in ending inventory is $2,760 (12 × $230).

We show the allocation of the cost of goods available for sale between cost of goods sold and ending inventory graphically below.

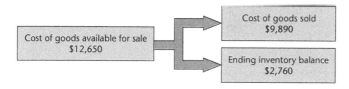

Effect of Cost Flow on Financial Statements

Exhibit 4.2 displays partial financial statements for The Mountain Bike Company (TMBC). This exhibit includes only information pertaining to the Eraser bikes inventory item described above. Other financial statement data are omitted.

EXHIBIT 4.2			
TMBC COMPANY			
Comparative Financial Statements			
Partial Income Statements			

	FIFO	LIFO	Weighted Average
Sales	$15,050	$15,050	$15,050
Cost of goods sold	(9,650)	(10,210)	(9,890)
Gross margin	5,400	4,840	5,160

Partial Balance Sheets

	FIFO	LIFO	Weighted Average
Assets			
Cash	$ xx	$ xx	$ xx
Accounts receivable	xx	xx	xx
Inventory	3,000	2,440	2,760

Partial Statements of Cash Flows

	FIFO	LIFO	Weighted Average
Operating Activities			
Cash inflow from customers	$15,050	$15,050	$15,050
Cash outflow for inventory	(10,650)	(10,650)	(10,650)

Recall that assets are reported on the balance sheet in order of liquidity (how quickly they are expected to be converted to cash). Since companies frequently sell inventory on account, inventory is less liquid than accounts receivable. As a result, companies commonly report inventory below accounts receivable on the balance sheet.

Exhibit 4.2 demonstrates that the amounts reported for gross margin on the income statement and inventory on the balance sheet differ significantly. The cash flow from operating activities on the statement of cash flows, however, is identical under all three methods. Regardless of cost flow reporting method, TMBC paid $10,650 cash ($4,400 first purchase + $6,250 second purchase) to purchase inventory and received $15,050 cash for inventory sold.

The Impact of Income Tax

Based on the financial statement information in Exhibit 4.2, which cost flow method should TMBC use? Most people initially suggest FIFO because FIFO reports the highest gross margin and the largest balance in ending inventory. However, other factors are relevant. FIFO produces the highest gross margin; it also produces the highest net income and the highest income tax expense. In contrast, LIFO results in recognizing the lowest gross margin, lowest net income, and the lowest income tax expense.

Will investors favor a company with more assets and higher net income or one with lower tax expense? Recognize that specific identification, FIFO, LIFO, and weighted average are *different methods of reporting the same information.* TMBC experienced only one set of events pertaining to Eraser bikes. Exhibit 4.2 reports those same events three different ways. However, if the FIFO reporting method causes TMBC to pay more taxes than the LIFO method, using FIFO will cause a real reduction in the value of the company. Paying more money in taxes leaves less money in the company. Knowledgeable investors would be more attracted to TMBC if it uses LIFO because the lower tax payments allow the company to keep more value in the business.

Research suggests that, as a group, investors are knowledgeable. They make investment decisions based on economic substance regardless of how information is reported in financial statements.

The Income Statement versus the Tax Return

In some instances companies may use one accounting method for financial reporting and a different method to compute income taxes (the tax return must explain any differences). With respect to LIFO, however, the Internal Revenue Service requires that companies using LIFO for income tax purposes must also use LIFO for financial reporting. A company could not, therefore, get both the lower tax benefit provided by LIFO and the financial reporting advantage offered under FIFO.

Inflation versus Deflation

Our illustration assumes an inflationary environment (rising inventory prices). In a deflationary environment, the impact of using LIFO versus FIFO is reversed. LIFO produces tax advantages in an inflationary environment, while FIFO produces tax advantages in a deflationary environment. Companies operating in the computer industry where prices are falling would obtain a tax advantage by using FIFO. In contrast, companies that sell medical supplies in an inflationary environment would obtain a tax advantage by using LIFO.

Full Disclosure and Consistency

Generally accepted accounting principles allow each company to choose the inventory cost flow method best suited to its reporting needs. Because results can vary considerably among methods, however, the GAAP principle of **full disclosure** requires that financial statements disclose the method chosen. In addition, so that a company's financial statements are comparable from year to year, the GAAP principle of **consistency** generally requires that companies use the same cost flow method each period. The limited exceptions to the consistency principle are described in more advanced accounting courses.

CHECK *Yourself* 4.2

The following information was drawn from the inventory records of Fields, Inc.

Beginning inventory	200 units @ $20
First purchase	400 units @ $22
Second purchase	600 units @ $24

Assume that Fields sold 900 units of inventory.

1. Determine the amount of cost of goods sold using FIFO.
2. Would using LIFO produce a higher or lower amount of cost of goods sold? Why?

Answer

1. Cost of goods sold using FIFO

Beginning inventory	200 units @ $20	=	$ 4,000
First purchase	400 units @ $22	=	8,800
Second purchase	300 units @ $24	=	7,200
Total cost of goods sold			$20,000

2. The inventory records reflect an inflationary environment of steadily rising prices. Since LIFO charges the latest costs (in this case the highest costs) to the income statement, using LIFO would produce a higher amount of cost of goods sold than would using FIFO.

Reality BYTES

To avoid spoilage or obsolescence, most companies use a first-in, first-out (FIFO) approach for the flow of physical goods. The older goods (first units purchased) are sold before the newer goods are sold. For example, Albertson's and other food stores stack older merchandise at the front of the shelf where customers are more likely to pick it up first. As a result, merchandise is sold before it becomes dated. However, when timing is not an issue, convenience may dictate the use of the last-in, first-out (LIFO) method. Examples of products that frequently move on a LIFO basis include rock, gravel, dirt, or other nonwasting assets. Indeed, rock, gravel, and dirt are normally stored in piles that are unprotected from weather. New inventory is simply piled on top of the old. Inventory that is sold is taken from the top of the pile because it is convenient to do so. Accordingly, the last inventory purchased is the first inventory sold. For example, Vulcan Materials Co., which claims to be the nation's largest producer of construction aggregates (stone and gravel), uses LIFO. Regardless of whether the flow of physical goods occurs on a LIFO or FIFO basis, costs can flow differently. The flow of inventory through the physical facility is a separate issue from the flow of costs through the accounting system.

KEY FEATURES OF INTERNAL CONTROL SYSTEMS

Identify the key elements of a strong system of internal control.

Suppose Wal-Mart's corporate-level executives establish a policy to ensure that inventory items have a short shelf life. More specifically, the executives decide to discount the price of any inventory item that is not sold within 30 days. How do the executives know that the store managers around the world will implement this policy? The answer: by establishing an effective set of internal controls.

Internal controls are the policies and procedures used to provide reasonable assurance that the objectives of an enterprise will be accomplished.[1]

Internal controls can be divided into two categories: (1) **accounting controls** are designed to safeguard company assets and ensure reliable accounting records; and (2) **administrative controls** are concerned with evaluating performance and assessing the degree of compliance with company policies and public laws.

Internal control systems vary from company to company. However, most systems include certain basic policies and procedures that have proven effective over time. A discussion of the more common features of a strong system of internal control follows.

Separation of Duties

The likelihood of fraud or theft is reduced if collusion is required to accomplish it. Clear **separation of duties** is frequently used as a deterrent to corruption. When duties are separated, the work of one employee can act as a check on the work of another employee. For example, a person selling seats to a movie may be tempted to steal money received from customers who enter the theater. This temptation is reduced if the person staffing the box office is required to issue tickets that a second employee collects as people enter the theater. If ticket stubs collected by the second employee are compared with the cash receipts from ticket sales, any cash shortages would become apparent. Furthermore, friends and relatives of the ticket agent could not easily enter the theater without paying. Theft or unauthorized entry would require collusion between the ticket agent and the usher who collects the tickets. Both individuals would have to be dishonest enough to steal, yet trustworthy enough to convince each other they would keep the embezzlement secret. Whenever possible, the functions of *authorization, recording,* and *custody of assets* should be performed by separate individuals.

[1] *AICPA Professional Standards,* vol. 1, sec. 320, par. 6 (June 1, 1989).

Quality of Employees

A business is only as good as the people it employs. Cheap labor is not a bargain if the employees are incompetent. Employees should be properly trained. In fact, they should be trained to perform a variety of tasks. The ability of employees to substitute for one another prevents disruptions when co-workers are absent because of illnesses, vacations, or other commitments. The capacity to rotate jobs also relieves boredom and increases respect for the contributions of other employees. Every business should strive to maximize the productivity of every employee. Ongoing training programs are essential to a strong system of internal control.

Bonded Employees

The best way to ensure employee honesty is to hire individuals with *high levels of personal integrity.* Employers should screen job applicants using interviews, background checks, and recommendations from prior employers or educators. Even so, screening programs may fail to identify character weaknesses. Further, unusual circumstances may cause honest employees to go astray. Therefore, employees in positions of trust should be bonded. A **fidelity bond** provides insurance that protects a company from losses caused by employee dishonesty.

Required Absences

Employees should be required to take regular vacations and their duties should be rotated periodically. Employees may be able to cover up fraudulent activities if they are always present at work. Consider the case of a parking meter collection agent who covered the same route for several years with no vacation. When the agent became sick, a substitute collected more money each day than the regular reader usually reported. Management checked past records and found that the ill meter reader had been understating the cash receipts and pocketing the difference. If management had required vacations or rotated the routes, the embezzlement would have been discovered much earlier.

Procedures Manual

Appropriate accounting procedures should be documented in a **procedures manual.** The manual should be routinely updated. Periodic reviews should be conducted to ensure that employees are following the procedures outlined in the manual.

Authority and Responsibility

Employees are motivated by clear lines of authority and responsibility. They work harder when they have the authority to use their own judgment and they exercise reasonable caution when they are held responsible for their actions. Businesses should prepare an **authority manual** that establishes a definitive *chain of command.* The authority manual should guide both specific and general authorizations. **Specific authorizations** apply to specific positions within the organization. For example, investment decisions are authorized at the division level while hiring decisions are authorized at the departmental level. In contrast, **general authority** applies across different levels of management. For example, employees at all levels may be required to fly coach or to make purchases from specific vendors.

Prenumbered Documents

How would you know if a check were stolen from your check book? If you keep a record of your check numbers, the missing number would tip you off immediately. Businesses also use prenumbered checks to avoid the unauthorized use of their bank accounts. In fact, prenumbered forms are used for all important documents such as purchase orders, receiving reports, invoices, and checks. To reduce errors, prenumbered forms should be as simple and easy to use as possible. Also, the documents should allow for authorized signatures. For example, credit sales slips should be signed by the customer to clearly establish who made the purchase, reducing the likelihood of unauthorized transactions.

Physical Control

Employees walk away with billions of dollars of business assets each year. To limit losses, companies should establish adequate physical control over valuable assets. For example, inventory should be kept in a storeroom and not released without proper authorization. Serial numbers on equipment should be recorded along with the name of the individual who is responsible for the equipment. Unannounced physical counts should be conducted randomly to verify the presence of company-owned equipment. Certificates of deposit and marketable securities should be kept in fireproof vaults. Access to these vaults should be limited to authorized personnel. These procedures protect the documents from fire and limit access to only those individuals who have the appropriate security clearance to handle the documents.

In addition to safeguarding assets, there should be physical control over the accounting records. The accounting journals, ledgers, and supporting documents should be kept in a fireproof safe. Only personnel responsible for recording transactions in the journals should have access to them. With limited access, there is less chance that someone will change the records to conceal fraud or embezzlement.

Performance Evaluations

Because few people can evaluate their own performance objectively, internal controls should include independent verification of employee performance. For example, someone other than the person who has control over inventory should take a physical count of inventory. Internal and external audits serve as independent verification of performance. Auditors should evaluate the effectiveness of the internal control system as well as verify the accuracy of the accounting records. In addition, the external auditors attest to the company's use of generally accepted accounting principles in the financial statements.

Limitations

A system of internal controls is designed to prevent or detect errors and fraud. However, no control system is foolproof. Internal controls can be circumvented by collusion among employees. Two or more employees working together can hide embezzlement by covering for each other. For example, if an embezzler goes on vacation, fraud will not be reported by a replacement who is in collusion with the embezzler. No system can prevent all fraud. However, a good system of internal controls minimizes illegal or unethical activities by reducing temptation and increasing the likelihood of early detection.

CHECK  4.3

What are nine features of an internal control system?

Answer

The nine features follow.

1. Separating duties so that fraud or theft requires collusion.
2. Hiring and training competent employees.
3. Bonding employees to recover losses through insurance.
4. Requiring employees to be absent from their jobs so that their replacements can discover errors or fraudulent activity that might have occurred.
5. Establishing proper procedures for processing transactions.
6. Establishing clear lines of authority and responsibility.
7. Using prenumbered documents.
8. Implementing physical controls such as locking cash in a safe.
9. Conducting performance evaluations through independent internal and external audits.

ACCOUNTING FOR CASH

For financial reporting purposes, **cash** generally includes currency and other items that are payable *on demand,* such as checks, money orders, bank drafts, and certain savings accounts. Savings accounts that impose substantial penalties for early withdrawal should be classified as *investments* rather than cash. Postdated checks or IOUs represent *receivables* and should not be included in cash. As illustrated in Exhibit 4.3, most companies combine currency and other payable on demand items in a single balance sheet account with varying titles.

Identify special internal controls for cash.

Companies must maintain a sufficient amount of cash to pay employees, suppliers, and other creditors. When a company fails to pay its legal obligations, its creditors can force the company into bankruptcy. Even so, management should avoid accumulating more cash than is needed. The failure to invest excess cash in earning assets reduces profitability. Cash inflows and outflows must be managed to prevent a shortage or surplus of cash.

Controlling Cash

Controlling cash, more than any other asset, requires strict adherence to internal control procedures. Cash has universal appeal. A relatively small suitcase filled with high-denomination currency can represent significant value. Furthermore, the rightful owner of currency is difficult to prove. In most cases, possession constitutes ownership. As a result, cash is highly susceptible to theft and must be carefully protected. Cash is most susceptible to embezzlement when it is received or disbursed. The following controls should be employed to reduce the likelihood of theft.

Cash Receipts

A record of all cash collections should be prepared immediately upon receipt. The amount of cash on hand should be counted regularly. Missing amounts of money can be detected by comparing the actual cash on hand with the book balance. Employees who receive cash should give customers a copy of a written receipt. Customers usually review their receipts to ensure they have gotten credit for the amount paid and call any errors to the receipts clerk's attention. This not only reduces errors but also provides a control on the clerk's honesty. Cash receipts should be deposited in a bank on a timely basis. Cash collected late in the day should be deposited in a night depository. Every effort should be made to minimize the amount of cash on hand. Keeping large amounts of cash on hand not only increases the risk of loss from theft but also places employees in danger of being harmed by criminals who may be tempted to rob the company.

Cash Payments

To effectively control cash, a company should make all disbursements using checks, thereby providing a record of cash payments. All checks should be prenumbered, and unused checks should be locked up. Using prenumbered checks allows companies to easily identify lost or stolen checks by comparing the numbers on unused and canceled checks with the numbers used for legitimate disbursements.

The duties of approving disbursements, signing checks, and recording transactions should be separated. If one person is authorized to approve, sign, and record checks, he or she could falsify supporting documents, write an unauthorized check, and record a cover-up transaction in the accounting records. By separating these duties, the check signer reviews the documentation provided by the approving individual before signing the check. Likewise, the recording clerk reviews the work of both the approving person and the check signer when the disbursement is recorded in the accounting records. Thus writing unauthorized checks requires trilevel collusion.

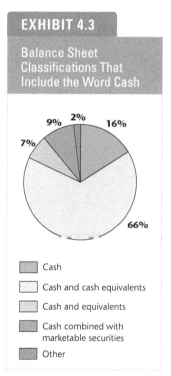

EXHIBIT 4.3

Balance Sheet Classifications That Include the Word Cash

9% 2% 16%

7%

66%

- Cash
- Cash and cash equivalents
- Cash and equivalents
- Cash combined with marketable securities
- Other

Data Source: AICPA, *Accounting Trends and Techniques,* 2006.

Supporting documents with authorized approval signatures should be required when checks are presented to the check signer. For example, a warehouse receiving order should be matched with a purchase order before a check is approved to pay a bill from a supplier. Before payments are approved, invoice amounts should be checked and payees verified as valid vendors. Matching supporting documents with proper authorization discourages employees from creating phony documents for a disbursement to a friend or fictitious business. Also, the approval process serves as a check on the accuracy of the work of all employees involved.

Supporting documents should be marked *Paid* when the check is signed. If the documents are not indelibly marked, they could be retrieved from the files and resubmitted for a duplicate, unauthorized payment. A payables clerk could collude with the payee to split extra cash paid out by submitting the same supporting documents for a second payment.

Reality BYTES

THE COST OF PROTECTING CASH

Could you afford to buy a safe like the one shown here? The vault is only one of many expensive security devices used by banks to safeguard cash. By using checking accounts, companies are able to avoid many of the costs associated with keeping cash safe. In addition to providing physical control, checking accounts enable companies to maintain a written audit trail of cash receipts and payments. Checking accounts represent the most widely used internal control device in modern society. It is difficult to imagine a business operating without the use of checking accounts.

All spoiled and voided checks should be defaced and retained. If defaced checks are not retained, an employee could steal a check and then claim that it was written incorrectly and thrown away. The clerk could then use the stolen check to make an unauthorized payment.

Checking Account Documents

The previous section explained the need for businesses to use checking accounts. A description of four main types of forms associated with a bank checking account follows.

Signature Card

A bank **signature card** shows the bank account number and the signatures of the people authorized to sign checks. The card is retained in the bank's files. If a bank employee is unfamiliar with the signature on a check, he or she can refer to the signature card to verify the signature before cashing the check.

Deposit Ticket

Each deposit of cash or checks is accompanied by a **deposit ticket,** which normally identifies the account number and the name of the account. The depositor lists the individual amounts of currency, coins, and checks, as well as the total deposited, on the deposit ticket.

Bank Check

A written check affects three parties: (1) the person or business writing the check (the *payer*); (2) the bank on which the check is drawn; and (3) the person or business to whom the check is payable (the *payee*). Companies often write **checks** using multicopy, prenumbered forms, with the name of the issuing business preprinted on the face of each check. A remittance notice is usually attached to the check forms. This portion of the form provides the issuer space to record what the check is for (e.g., what invoices are being paid), the amount being disbursed, and the date of payment. When signed by the person whose signature is on the signature card, the check authorizes the bank to transfer the face amount of the check from the payer's account to the payee.

Bank Statement

Periodically, the bank sends the depositor a **bank statement.** The bank statement is presented from the bank's point of view. Checking accounts are liabilities to a bank because the bank is obligated to pay back the money that customers have deposited in their accounts. Therefore, in the bank's accounting records a customer's checking account has a *credit* balance. As a result, **bank statement debit memos** describe transactions that reduce the customer's account balance (the bank's liability). **Bank statement credit memos** describe activities that increase the customer's account balance (the bank's liability). Since a checking account is an asset (cash) to the depositor, a *bank statement debit memo* requires a *credit entry* to the cash account on the depositor's books. Likewise, when a bank tells you that it has credited your account, you will debit your cash account in response.

Bank statements normally report (a) the balance of the account at the beginning of the period; (b) additions for customer deposits made during the period; (c) other additions described in credit memos (e.g., for interest earned); (d) subtractions for the payment of checks drawn on the account during the period; (e) other subtractions described in debit memos (e.g., for service charges); (f) a running balance of the account; and (g) the balance of the account at the end of the period. The sample bank statement in Exhibit 4.4 on the next page illustrates these items with references to the preceding letters in parentheses. Normally, the canceled checks or copies of them are enclosed with the bank statement.

Reconciling the Bank Account

Usually the ending balance reported on the bank statement differs from the balance in the depositor's cash account as of the same date. The discrepancy is normally attributable to timing differences. For example, a depositor deducts the amount of a check from its cash account when it writes the check. However, the bank does not deduct the amount of the check from the depositor's account until the payee presents it for payment, which may be days, weeks, or even months after the check is written. As a result, the balance on the depositor's books is lower than the balance on the bank's books. Companies prepare a **bank reconciliation** to explain the differences between the cash balance reported on the bank statement and the cash balance recorded in the depositor's accounting records.

Prepare a bank reconciliation.

Determining True Cash Balance

A bank reconciliation normally begins with the cash balance reported by the bank which is called the **unadjusted bank balance.** The adjustments necessary to determine the amount of cash that the depositor actually owns as of the date of the bank statement are then added to and subtracted from the unadjusted bank balance. The final total is the **true cash balance.** The true cash balance is independently reached a second time by making adjustments to the **unadjusted book balance.** The bank account is reconciled when the true cash balance determined from the perspective of the unadjusted *bank* balance agrees with the true cash balance determined from the perspective of the unadjusted *book* balance. The procedures a company uses to determine the *true cash balance* from the two different perspectives are outlined here.

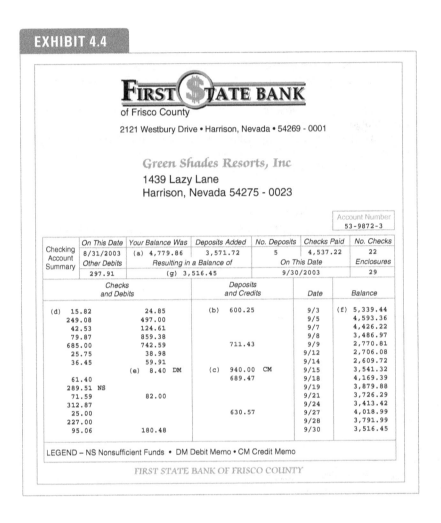

EXHIBIT 4.4

FIRST $ TATE BANK						
of Frisco County						
2121 Westbury Drive • Harrison, Nevada • 54269 - 0001						

Green Shades Resorts, Inc
1439 Lazy Lane
Harrison, Nevada 54275 - 0023

Account Number
53-9872-3

Checking Account Summary	On This Date	Your Balance Was	Deposits Added	No. Deposits	Checks Paid	No. Checks
	8/31/2003	(a) 4,779.86	3,571.72	5	4,537.22	22
	Other Debits	Resulting in a Balance of		On This Date		Enclosures
	297.91	(g) 3,516.45		9/30/2003		29

Checks and Debits			Deposits and Credits		Date	Balance
(d) 15.82	24.85		(b) 600.25		9/3	(f) 5,339.44
249.08	497.00				9/5	4,593.36
42.53	124.61				9/7	4,426.22
79.87	859.38				9/8	3,486.97
685.00	742.59		711.43		9/9	2,770.81
25.75	38.98				9/12	2,706.08
36.45	59.91				9/14	2,609.72
	(e) 8.40 DM		(c) 940.00 CM		9/15	3,541.32
61.40			689.47		9/18	4,169.39
289.51 NS					9/19	3,879.88
71.59	82.00				9/21	3,726.29
312.87					9/24	3,413.42
25.00			630.57		9/27	4,018.99
227.00					9/28	3,791.99
95.06	180.48				9/30	3,516.45

LEGEND – NS Nonsufficient Funds • DM Debit Memo • CM Credit Memo

FIRST STATE BANK OF FRISCO COUNTY

Adjustments to the Bank Balance

A typical format for determining the true cash balance beginning with the unadjusted bank balance is

Unadjusted bank balance
+ Deposits in transit
− Outstanding checks
= True cash balance

Deposits in transit.   Companies frequently leave deposits in the bank's night depository or make them on the day following the receipt of cash. Such deposits are called **deposits in transit.** Since these deposits have been recorded in the depositor's accounting records but have not yet been added to the depositor's account by the bank, they must be added to the unadjusted bank balance.

Outstanding checks.   These are disbursements that have been properly recorded as cash deductions on the depositor's books. However, the bank has not deducted the amounts from the depositor's bank account because the checks have not yet been presented by the payee to the bank for payment; that is, the checks have not cleared the bank. **Outstanding checks** must be subtracted from the unadjusted bank balance to determine the true cash balance.

Adjustments to the Book Balance

A typical format for determining the true cash balance beginning with the unadjusted book balance is as follows.

```
    Unadjusted book balance
  + Accounts receivable collections
  + Interest earned
  − Bank service charges
  − Non-sufficient-funds (NSF) checks
  = True cash balance
```

Accounts receivable collections.   To collect cash as quickly as possible, many companies have their customers send payments directly to the bank. The bank adds the collection directly to the depositor's account and notifies the depositor about the collection through a credit memo that is included on the bank statement. The depositor adds the amount of the cash collections to the unadjusted book balance in the process of determining the true cash balance.

Interest earned.   Banks pay interest on certain checking accounts. The amount of the interest is added directly to the depositor's bank account. The bank notifies the depositor about the interest through a credit memo that is included on the bank statement. The depositor adds the amount of the interest revenue to the unadjusted book balance in the process of determining the true cash balance.

Service charges.   Banks frequently charge depositors fees for services performed. They may also charge a penalty if the depositor fails to maintain a specified minimum cash balance throughout the period. Banks deduct such fees and penalties directly from the depositor's account and advise the depositor of the deduction through a debit memo that is included on the bank statement. The depositor deducts such **service charges** from the unadjusted book balance to determine the true cash balance.

Non-sufficient-funds (NSF) checks.   **NSF checks** are checks that a company obtains from its customers and deposits in its checking account. However, when the checks are submitted to the customers' banks for payment, the banks refuse payment because there is insufficient money in the customers' accounts. When such checks are returned, the amounts of the checks are deducted from the company's bank account balance. The company is advised of NSF checks through debit memos that appear on the bank statement. The depositor deducts the amounts of the NSF checks from the unadjusted book balance in the process of determining the true cash balance.

Correction of Errors

In the course of reconciling the bank statement with the cash account, the depositor may discover errors in the bank's records, the depositor's records, or both. If an error is found on the bank statement, an adjustment for it is made to the unadjusted bank balance to determine the true cash balance, and the bank should be notified immediately to correct its records. Errors made by the depositor require adjustments to the book balance to arrive at the true cash balance.

Certified Checks

A **certified check** is guaranteed for payment by a bank. Whereas a regular check is deducted from the customer's account when it is presented for payment, a certified check is deducted from the customer's account when the bank certifies that the check is good. Certified checks, therefore, *have* been deducted by the bank in determining the unadjusted bank balance, whether they have cleared the bank or remain outstanding as of the date of the bank statement. Since certified checks are deducted both from bank and depositor records immediately, they do not cause differences between the depositor and bank balances. As a result, certified checks are not included in a bank reconciliation.

Illustrating a Bank Reconciliation

The following example illustrates preparing the bank reconciliation for Green Shades Resorts, Inc. (GSRI). The bank statement for GSRI is displayed in Exhibit 4.4. Exhibit 4.5 illustrates the completed bank reconciliation. The items on the reconciliation are described below.

Adjustments to the Bank Balance

As of September 30, 2010, the bank statement showed an unadjusted balance of $3,516.45. A review of the bank statement disclosed three adjustments that had to be made to the unadjusted bank balance to determine GSRI's true cash balance.

1. Comparing the deposits on the bank statement with deposits recorded in GSRI's accounting records indicated there was $724.11 of deposits in transit.

2. An examination of the returned checks disclosed that the bank had erroneously deducted a $25 check written by Green Valley Resorts from GSRI's bank account. This amount must be added back to the unadjusted bank balance to determine the true cash balance.

3. The checks returned with the bank statement were sorted and compared to the cash records. Three checks with amounts totaling $235.25 were outstanding.

After these adjustment are made GSRI's true cash balance is determined to be $4,030.31.

EXHIBIT 4.5

GREEN SHADES RESORTS, INC.
Bank Reconciliation
September 30, 2010

Unadjusted bank balance, September 30, 2010			$3,516.45
Add: Deposits in transit			724.11
Bank error: Check drawn on Green Valley Resorts charged to GSRI			25.00
Less: Outstanding checks			

Check No.	Date	Amount
639	Sept. 18	$ 13.75
646	Sept. 20	29.00
672	Sept. 27	192.50

Total	(235.25)
True cash balance, September 30, 2010	$4,030.31
Unadjusted book balance, September 30, 2010	$3,361.22
Add: Receivable collected by bank	940.00
Error made by accountant (Check no. 633 recorded as $63.45 instead of $36.45)	27.00
Less: Bank service charges	(8.40)
NSF check	(289.51)
True cash balance, September 30, 2010	$4,030.31

Adjustments to the Book Balance

As indicated in Exhibit 4.5, GSRI's unadjusted book balance as of September 30, 2010, was $3,361.22. This balance differs from GSRI's true cash balance because of four unrecorded accounting events:

1. The bank collected a $940 account receivable for GSRI.
2. GSRI's accountant made a $27 recording error.
3. The bank charged GSRI an $8.40 service fee.
4. GSRI had deposited a $289.51 check from a customer who did not have sufficient funds to cover the check.

Two of these four adjustments increase the unadjusted cash balance. The other two decrease the unadjusted cash balance. After the adjustments have been recorded, the cash account reflects the true cash balance of $4,030.31 ($3,361.22 unadjusted cash balance + $940.00 receivable collection + $27.00 recording error − $8.40 service charge − $289.51 NSF check). Since the true balance determined from the perspective of the bank statement agrees with the true balance determined from the perspective of GSRI's books, the bank statement has been successfully reconciled with the accounting records.

Updating GSRI's Accounting Records

Each of the adjustments to the book balance must be recorded in GSRI's financial records. The effects of each adjustment on the financial statements are as follows.

ADJUSTMENT 1   *Recording the $940 receivable collection increases cash and reduces accounts receivable.*

The event is an asset exchange transaction. The effect of the collection on GSRI's financial statements is

Assets			=	Liab.	+	Equity	Rev.	−	Exp.	=	Net Inc.	Cash Flow	
Cash	+	Accts. Rec.											
940	+	(940)	=	NA	+	NA	NA	−	NA	=	NA	940	OA

ADJUSTMENT 2   *Assume the $27 recording error occurred because GSRI's accountant accidentally transposed two numbers when recording check no. 633 for utilities expense.*

The check was written to pay utilities expense of $36.45 but was recorded as a $63.45 disbursement. Since cash payments are overstated by $27.00 ($63.45 − $36.45), this amount must be added back to GSRI's cash balance and deducted from the utilities expense account, which increases net income. The effects on the financial statements are

Assets	=	Liab.	+	Equity	Rev.	−	Exp.	=	Net Inc.	Cash Flow	
Cash	=			Ret. Earn.							
27	=	NA	+	27	NA	−	(27)	=	27	27	OA

ADJUSTMENT 3   *The $8.40 service charge is an expense that reduces assets, stockholders' equity, net income, and cash.*

The effects are

Assets	=	Liab.	+	Equity	Rev.	–	Exp.	=	Net Inc.	Cash Flow
Cash	=			Ret. Earn.						
(8.40)	=	NA	+	(8.40)	NA	–	8.40	=	(8.40)	(8.40) OA

ADJUSTMENT 4   *The $289.51 NSF check reduces GSRI's cash balance.*

When it originally accepted the customer's check, GSRI increased its cash account. Since there is not enough money in the customer's bank account to pay the check, GSRI didn't actually receive cash so GSRI must reduce its cash account. GSRI will still try to collect the money from the customer. In the meantime, it will show the amount of the NSF check as an account receivable. The adjusting entry to record the NSF check is an asset exchange transaction. Cash decreases and accounts receivable increases. The effect on GSRI's financial statements is

Assets			=	Liab.	+	Equity	Rev.	–	Exp.	=	Net Inc.	Cash Flow
Cash	+	Accts. Rec.										
(289.51)	+	289.51	=	NA	+	NA	NA	–	NA	=	NA	(289.51) OA

Answers to The *Curious* Accountant

Even though Albertson's uses the last-in, first-out cost flow assumption for financial reporting purposes, it, like most other companies, actually sells its oldest inventory first. As explained in the text material, GAAP allows a company to report its costs of goods sold in an order that is different from the actual physical flow of its goods. The primary reason some companies use the LIFO assumption is to reduce income taxes. Over the years, Albertson's has saved approximately $100 million in taxes by using the LIFO versus the FIFO cost flow assumption when computing its taxable income.

THE FINANCIAL ANALYST

LO 6

Explain the importance of inventory turnover to a company's profitability.

Assume a grocery store sells two brands of kitchen cleansers, Zjax and Cosmos. Zjax costs $1 and sells for $1.25, resulting in a gross margin of $0.25 ($1.25 − $1.00). Cosmos costs $1.20 and sells for $1.60, resulting in a gross margin of $0.40 ($1.60 − $1.20). Is it more profitable to stock Cosmos than Zjax? Not if the store can sell significantly more cans of Zjax.

Suppose the lower price results in higher customer demand for Zjax. If the store can sell 7,000 units of Zjax but only 3,000 units of Cosmos, Zjax will provide a total gross profit of $1,750 (7,000 units × $0.25 per unit), while Cosmos will provide only $1,200 (3,000 units × $0.40 per unit). How fast inventory sells is as important as the spread between cost and selling price. To determine how fast inventory is selling, financial analysts calculate a ratio that measures the *average number of days it takes to sell inventory.*

Average Number of Days to Sell Inventory

The first step in calculating the average number of days it takes to sell inventory is to compute the **inventory turnover,** as follows.

$$\frac{\text{Cost of goods sold}}{\text{Inventory}}$$

The result of this computation is the number of times the balance in the Inventory account is turned over (sold) each year. To more easily interpret the inventory turnover ratio, analysts often take a further step and determine the **average number of days to sell inventory** (also called the **average days in inventory**), computed as

$$\frac{365}{\text{Inventory turnover}}$$

Is It a Marketing or an Accounting Decision?

As suggested, overall profitability depends upon two elements: gross margin and inventory turnover. The most profitable combination would be to carry high-margin inventory that turns over rapidly. To be competitive, however, companies must often concentrate on one or the other of the elements. For example, *discount merchandisers* such as Costco offer lower prices to stimulate greater sales. In contrast, fashionable stores such as Neiman Marcus charge higher prices to compensate for their slower inventory turnover. These upscale stores justify their higher prices by offering superior style, quality, convenience, service, etc. While decisions about pricing, advertising, service, and so on are often viewed as marketing decisions, effective choices require understanding the interaction between the gross margin percentage and inventory turnover.

Real-World Data

Exhibit 4.6 shows the *average number of days to sell inventory* for eight real-world companies in three different industries. The data raise several questions.

First, why do Concha y Toro and Willamette Valley Vineyards take so long to sell their inventories compared to the other companies? Both of these companies produce and sell wine. Quality wine is aged before it is sold; time spent in inventory is actually a part of the production process. In the wine world, wines produced by Willamette Valley are, on average, considered to be of higher quality than those produced by Concha y Toro. This higher quality results, in part, from the longer time Willamette Valley wines spend aging prior to sale.

EXHIBIT 4.6

Industry	Company	Average Number of Days to Sell Inventory
Fast Food	McDonald's	10
	Starbucks	77
	Yum! Brands	12
Office Supplies	Office Depot	50
	OfficeMax	50
	Staples	54
Wine	Concha y Toro	203
	Willamette Valley Vineyards	348

Why does Starbucks hold its inventory so much longer than the other two fast-food businesses? Starbucks' inventory is mostly coffee. It is more difficult for Starbucks to obtain coffee than it is for McDonald's to obtain beef or Yum! Brands to obtain flour, cheese, and fresh vegetables. Very little coffee is grown in the United States (Hawaii is the only state that produces coffee). Since purchasing coffee requires substantial delivery time, Starbucks cannot order its inventory at the last minute. This problem is further complicated by the fact that coffee harvests are seasonal. Cattle, on the other hand, can be processed into hamburgers year-round. As a result, Starbucks must hold inventory longer than McDonald's or Yum! Brands.

Finally, why do companies in the office supply business take longer to sell inventory than those in the fast-food business? Part of the answer is that food is perishable and stationery is not. But there is also the fact that office supply stores carry many more inventory items than do fast-food restaurants. It is much easier to anticipate customer demand if a company sells only 20 different items than if the company sells 20,000 different items. The problem of anticipating customer demand is solved by holding larger quantities of inventory.

Effects of Cost Flow on Ratio Analysis

Since the amounts of ending inventory and cost of goods sold are affected by the cost flow method (FIFO, LIFO, etc.) a company uses, the gross margin and inventory turnover ratios are also affected by the cost flow method used. Further, since cost of goods sold affects the amount of net income and retained earnings, many other ratios are also affected by the inventory cost flow method that a company uses. Financial analysts must consider that the ratios they use can be significantly influenced by which accounting methods a company chooses.

<< A Look Back

This chapter discussed the inventory cost flow methods of first-in, first-out (FIFO), last-in, first-out (LIFO), weighted average, and specific identification. Under *FIFO,* the cost of the items purchased first is reported on the income statement, and the cost of the items purchased last is reported on the balance sheet. Under *LIFO,* the cost of the items purchased last is reported on the income statement, and the cost of the items purchased first is reported on the balance sheet. Under the *weighted-average method,* the average cost of inventory is reported on both the income statement and the balance sheet. Finally, under specific identification the actual cost of the goods is reported on the income statement and the balance sheet.

The policies and procedures used to provide reasonable assurance that the objectives of an enterprise will be accomplished are called *internal controls,* which can be subdivided into two categories: accounting controls and administrative controls. *Accounting controls* are composed of procedures designed to safeguard the assets and ensure that the accounting records contain reliable information. *Administrative controls* are designed to evaluate performance and the degree of compliance with company policies and public laws. While the mechanics of internal control systems vary from company to company, the more prevalent features include the following.

1. *Separation of duties.* Whenever possible, the functions of authorization, recording, and custody should be exercised by different individuals.

2. *Quality of employees.* Employees should be qualified to competently perform the duties that are assigned to them. Companies must establish hiring practices to screen out unqualified candidates. Furthermore, procedures should be established to ensure that employees receive appropriate training to maintain their competence.

3. *Bonded employees.* Employees in sensitive positions should be covered by a fidelity bond that provides insurance to reimburse losses due to illegal actions committed by employees.

4. *Required absences.* Employees should be required to take extended absences from their jobs so that they are not always present to hide unscrupulous or illegal activities.

5. *Procedures manual.* To promote compliance, the procedures for processing transactions should be clearly described in a manual.

6. *Authority and responsibility.* To motivate employees and promote effective control, clear lines of authority and responsibility should be established.

7. *Prenumbered documents.* Prenumbered documents minimize the likelihood of missing or duplicate documents. Prenumbered forms should be used for all important documents such as purchase orders, receiving reports, invoices, and checks.

8. *Physical control.* Locks, fences, security personnel, and other physical devices should be employed to safeguard assets.

9. *Performance evaluations.* Because few people can evaluate their own performance objectively, independent performance evaluations should be performed. Substandard performance will likely persist unless employees are encouraged to take corrective action.

Because cash is such an important business asset and because it is tempting to steal, much of the discussion of internal controls in this chapter focused on cash controls. Special procedures should be employed to control the receipts and payments of cash. One of the most common control policies is to use *checking accounts* for all payments except petty cash disbursements.

A *bank reconciliation* should be prepared each month to explain differences between the bank statement and a company's internal accounting records. A common reconciliation format determines the true cash balance based on both bank and book records. Items that typically appear on a bank reconciliation include the following:

Unadjusted bank balance	xxx	Unadjusted book balance	xxx
Add		Add	
Deposits in transit	xxx	Interest revenue	xxx
		Collection of receivables	xxx
Subtract		Subtract	
Outstanding checks	xxx	Bank service charges	xxx
		NSF checks	xxx
True cash balance	xxx	True cash balance	xxx

Agreement of the two true cash balances provides evidence that accounting for cash transactions has been accurate.

Finally, this chapter explains how to calculate the time it takes a company to sell its inventory. The measure of how fast inventory sells is called *inventory turnover;* it is computed by dividing cost of goods sold by inventory. The result of this computation is the number of times the balance in the inventory account is turned over each year. The *average number of days to sell inventory* can be determined by dividing the number of days in a year (365) by the inventory turnover ratio.

A Look Forward »

Accounting for receivables and payables was introduced in Chapter 2 using relatively simple illustrations. For example, we assumed that customers who purchased services on account always paid their bills. In real business practice, some customers do not pay their bills. Among other topics, Chapter 5 examines how companies account for uncollectible accounts receivable.

SELF-STUDY REVIEW PROBLEM 1

Erie Jewelers sells gold earrings. Its beginning inventory of Model 407 gold earrings consisted of 100 pairs of earrings at $50 per pair. Erie purchased two batches of Model 407 earrings during the year. The first batch purchased consisted of 150 pairs at $53 per pair; the second batch consisted of 200 pairs at $56 per pair. During the year, Erie sold 375 pairs of Model 407 earrings.

Required

Determine the amount of product cost Erie would allocate to cost of goods sold and ending inventory assuming that Erie uses (a) FIFO, (b) LIFO, and (c) weighted average.

Solution to Requirements a–c

Goods Available for Sale					
Beginning inventory	100	@	$50	=	$ 5,000
First purchase	150	@	53	=	7,950
Second purchase	200	@	56	=	11,200
Goods available for sale	450				$24,150

a. FIFO

Cost of Goods Sold	Pairs		Cost per Pair		Cost of Goods Sold
From beginning inventory	100	@	$50	=	$ 5,000
From first purchase	150	@	53	=	7,950
From second purchase	125	@	56	=	7,000
Total pairs sold	375				$19,950

Ending inventory = Goods available for sale − Cost of goods sold

Ending inventory = $24,150 − $19,950 = $4,200

b. LIFO

Cost of Goods Sold	Pairs		Cost per Pair		Cost of Goods Sold
From second purchase	200	@	$56	=	$11,200
From first purchase	150	@	53	=	7,950
From beginning inventory	25	@	50	=	1,250
Total pairs sold	375				$20,400

Ending inventory = Goods available for sale − Cost of goods sold

Ending inventory = $24,150 − $20,400 = $3,750

c. Weighted average

Goods available for sale ÷ Total pairs = Cost per pair

$24,150   ÷   450   = $53.6667

Cost of goods sold   375 units @ $53.6667 = $20,125

Ending inventory   75 units @ $53.6667 = $4,025

SELF-STUDY REVIEW PROBLEM 2

The following information pertains to Terry's Pest Control Company (TPCC) for July:

1. The unadjusted bank balance at July 31 was $870.
2. The bank statement included the following items:
   (a) A $60 credit memo for interest earned by TPCC.
   (b) A $200 NSF check made payable to TPCC.
   (c) A $110 debit memo for bank service charges.
3. The unadjusted book balance at July 31 was $1,400.
4. A comparison of the bank statement with company accounting records disclosed the following:
   (a) A $400 deposit in transit at July 31.
   (b) Outstanding checks totaling $120 at the end of the month.

Required

Prepare a bank reconciliation.

Solution

TERRY'S PEST CONTROL COMPANY Bank Reconciliation July 31	
Unadjusted bank balance	$ 870
Add: Deposits in transit	400
Less: Outstanding checks	(120)
True cash balance	$1,150
Unadjusted book balance	$1,400
Add: Interest revenue	60
Less: NSF check	(200)
Less: Bank service charges	(110)
True cash balance	$1,150

KEY TERMS

Accounting controls 140
Administrative controls 140
Authority manual 141
Average number of days to sell inventory (average days in inventory) 151
Bank reconciliation 145
Bank statement 145
Bank statement credit memo 145
Bank statement debit memo 145

Cash 143
Certified check 147
Checks 145
Consistency 139
Deposit ticket 144
Deposits in transit 146
Fidelity bond 141
First-in, first-out (FIFO) cost flow method 134
Full disclosure 139
General authority 141
Internal controls 140

Inventory cost flow methods 136
Inventory turnover 151
Last-in, first-out (LIFO) cost flow method 134
Non-sufficient-funds (NSF) checks 147
Outstanding checks 146
Physical flow of goods 134
Procedures manual 141
Separation of duties 140

Service charges 147
Signature card 144
Specific authorizations 141
Specific identification 134
True cash balance 145
Unadjusted bank balance 145
Unadjusted book balance 145
Weighted-average cost flow method 134

QUESTIONS

1. Name and describe the four cost flow methods discussed in this chapter.
2. What are some advantages and disadvantages of the specific identification method of accounting for inventory?
3. What are some advantages and disadvantages of using the FIFO method of inventory valuation?
4. What are some advantages and disadvantages of using the LIFO method of inventory valuation?

5. In an inflationary period, which inventory cost flow method will produce the highest net income? Explain.

6. In an inflationary period, which inventory cost flow method will produce the largest amount of total assets on the balance sheet? Explain.

7. What is the difference between the flow of costs and the physical flow of goods?

8. Does the choice of cost flow method (FIFO, LIFO, or weighted average) affect the statement of cash flows? Explain.

9. Assume that Key Co. purchased 1,000 units of merchandise in its first year of operations for $25 per unit. The company sold 850 units for $40. What is the amount of cost of goods sold using FIFO? LIFO? Weighted average?

10. Assume that Key Co. purchased 1,500 units of merchandise in its second year of operation for $27 per unit. Its beginning inventory was determined in Question 9. Assuming that 1,500 units are sold, what is the amount of cost of goods sold using FIFO? LIFO? Weighted average?

11. Refer to Questions 9 and 10. Which method might be preferable for financial statements? For income tax reporting? Explain.

12. In an inflationary period, which cost flow method, FIFO or LIFO, produces the larger cash flow? Explain.

13. Which inventory cost flow method produces the highest net income in a deflationary period?

14. What are the policies and procedures called that are used to provide reasonable assurance that the objectives of an enterprise will be accomplished?

15. What is the difference between accounting controls and administrative controls?

16. What are several features of an effective internal control system?

17. What is meant by *separation of duties?* Give an illustration.

18. What are the attributes of a high-quality employee?

19. What is a fidelity bond? Explain its purpose.

20. Why is it important that every employee periodically take a leave of absence or vacation?

21. What are the purpose and importance of a procedures manual?

22. What is the difference between specific and general authorizations?

23. Why should documents (checks, invoices, receipts) be prenumbered?

24. What procedures are important in the physical control of assets and accounting records?

25. What is the purpose of independent verification of performance?

26. What items are considered cash?

27. Why is cash more susceptible to theft or embezzlement than other assets?

28. Giving written copies of receipts to customers can help prevent what type of illegal acts?

29. What procedures can help to protect cash receipts?

30. What procedures can help protect cash disbursements?

31. What effect does a debit memo in a bank statement have on the Cash account? What effect does a credit memo in a bank statement have on the Cash account?

32. What information is normally included in a bank statement?

33. Why might a bank statement reflect a balance that is larger than the balance recorded in the depositor's books? What could cause the bank balance to be smaller than the book balance?

34. What is the purpose of a bank reconciliation?

35. What is an outstanding check?

36. What is a deposit in transit?

37. What is a certified check?

38. How is an NSF check accounted for in the accounting records?

39. What information does inventory turnover provide?

40. What is an example of a business that would have a high inventory turnover? A low inventory turnover?

EXERCISES

connect
|ACCOUNTING

All applicable Exercises are available with McGraw-Hill
Connect Accounting.

LO 1

Exercise 4-1 *Effect of inventory cost flow assumption on financial statements*

Required

For each of the following situations, fill in the blank with *FIFO, LIFO,* or *weighted average.*

a. _____ would produce the highest amount of net income in an inflationary environment.

b. _____ would produce the highest amount of assets in an inflationary environment.

c. _____ would produce the lowest amount of net income in a deflationary environment.

d. _____ would produce the same unit cost for assets and cost of goods sold in an inflationary environment.

e. _____ would produce the lowest amount of net income in an inflationary environment.

f. _____ would produce an asset value that was the same regardless of whether the environment was inflationary or deflationary.

g. _____ would produce the lowest amount of assets in an inflationary environment.

h. _____ would produce the highest amount of assets in a deflationary environment.

Exercise 4-2   *Allocating product cost between cost of goods sold and ending inventory*

LO 1, 2

Ming Co. started the year with no inventory. During the year, it purchased two identical inventory items. The inventory was purchased at different times. The first purchase cost $2,400 and the other, $3,000. One of the items was sold during the year.

Required

Based on this information, how much product cost would be allocated to cost of goods sold and ending inventory on the year-end financial statements, assuming use of

a. FIFO?

b. LIFO?

c. Weighted average?

Exercise 4-3   *Allocating product cost between cost of goods sold and ending inventory: multiple purchases*

LO 1, 2

Rainey Company sells coffee makers used in business offices. Its beginning inventory of coffee makers was 200 units at $25 per unit. During the year, Rainey made two batch purchases of coffee makers. The first was a 300-unit purchase at $30 per unit; the second was a 250-unit purchase at $35 per unit. During the period, Rainey sold 700 coffee makers.

Required

Determine the amount of product costs that would be allocated to cost of goods sold and ending inventory, assuming that Rainey uses

a. FIFO.

b. LIFO.

c. Weighted average.

Exercise 4-4   *Effect of inventory cost flow (FIFO, LIFO, and weighted average) on gross margin*

LO 1, 2

The following information pertains to Boone Company for 2009.

Beginning inventory	70 units @ $26
Units purchased	280 units @ $30

Ending inventory consisted of 30 units. Boone sold 320 units at $40 each. All purchases and sales were made with cash.

Required

a. Compute the gross margin for Boone Company using the following cost flow assumptions: (1) FIFO, (2) LIFO, and (3) weighted average.

b. What is the dollar amount of difference in net income between using FIFO versus LIFO? (Ignore income tax considerations.)

c. Determine the cash flow from operating activities, using each of the three cost flow assumptions listed in Requirement *a.* Ignore the effect of income taxes. Explain why these cash flows have no differences.

LO 1, 2

Exercise 4-5   *Effect of inventory cost flow on ending inventory balance and gross margin*

Ross Sales had the following transactions for DVDs in 2010, its first year of operations.

Jan. 20	Purchased 75 units @ $15	=	$1,125
Apr. 21	Purchased 450 units @ $20	=	9,000
July 25	Purchased 300 units @ $23	=	6,900
Sept. 19	Purchased 100 units @ $26	=	2,600

During the year, Ross Sales sold 850 DVDs for $60 each.

Required

a. Compute the amount of ending inventory Ross would report on the balance sheet, assuming the following cost flow assumptions: (1) FIFO, (2) LIFO, and (3) weighted average.
b. Compute the difference in gross margin between the FIFO and LIFO cost flow assumptions.

LO 1, 2

Exercise 4-6   *Income tax effect of shifting from FIFO to LIFO*

The following information pertains to the inventory of the Eaton Company.

Jan. 1	Beginning Inventory	600 units @ $22
Apr. 1	Purchased	2,500 units @ $25
Oct. 1	Purchased	700 units @ $28

During the year, Eaton sold 3,300 units of inventory at $40 per unit and incurred $15,000 of operating expenses. Eaton currently uses the FIFO method but is considering a change to LIFO. All transactions are cash transactions. Assume a 30 percent income tax rate.

Required

a. Prepare income statements using FIFO and LIFO.
b. Determine the amount of income taxes Eaton would save if it changed cost flow methods.
c. Determine the cash flow from operating activities under FIFO and LIFO.
d. Explain why cash flow from operating activities is lower under FIFO when that cost flow method produced the higher gross margin.

LO 1, 2

Exercise 4-7   *Effect of FIFO versus LIFO on income tax expense*

Beth Porter, Inc., had sales of $225,000 for 2009, its first year of operation. On April 2, the company purchased 200 units of inventory at $210 per unit. On September 1, an additional 150 units were purchased for $230 per unit. The company had 50 units on hand at the end of the year. The company's income tax rate is 35 percent. All transactions are cash transactions.

Required

a. The preceding paragraph describes five accounting events: (1) a sales transaction, (2) the first purchase of inventory, (3) a second purchase of inventory, (4) the recognition of cost of goods sold expense, and (5) the payment of income tax expense. Record the amounts of each event in horizontal statements models like the following ones, assuming first a FIFO and then a LIFO cost flow.

Effect of Events on Financial Statements **Panel 1: FIFO Cost Flow**													
Event No.	**Balance Sheet**							**Income Statement**					**Statement of Cash Flows**
	Cash	+	Inventory	=	C. Stk.	+	Ret. Earn.	Rev.	−	Exp.	=	Net Inc.	
Panel 2: LIFO Cost Flow													
Event No.	**Balance Sheet**							**Income Statement**					**Statement of Cash Flows**
	Cash	+	Inventory	=	C. Stk.	+	Ret. Earn.	Rev.	−	Exp.	=	Net Inc.	

b. Compute net income using FIFO.

c. Compute net income using LIFO.

d. Explain the difference, if any, in the amount of income tax expense incurred using the two cost flow assumptions.

e. How does the use of the FIFO versus the LIFO cost flow assumptions affect the statement of cash flows?

Exercise 4-8 *Features of a strong internal control system*

LO **3**

Required

List and describe nine features of a strong internal control system discussed in this chapter.

Exercise 4-9 *Internal controls for equipment*

LO **3**

Required

List the internal control procedures that pertain to the protection of business equipment.

Exercise 4-10 *Features of internal control procedures for cash*

LO **4**

Required

List and discuss effective internal control procedures that apply to cash.

Exercise 4-11 *Internal controls to prevent theft*

LO **3**

Sarah Black worked as the parts manager for Country Automobiles, a local automobile dealership. Sarah was very dedicated and never missed a day of work. Since Country was a small operation, she was the only employee in the parts department. Her duties consisted of ordering parts for stock and as needed for repairs, receiving the parts and checking them in, distributing them as needed to the shop or to customers for purchase, and keeping track of and taking the year-end inventory of parts. Country decided to expand and needed to secure additional financing. The local bank agreed to a loan contingent on an audit of the dealership. One requirement of the audit was to oversee the inventory count of both automobiles and parts on hand. Sarah was clearly nervous, explaining that she had just inventoried all parts in the parts department and supplied the auditors with a detailed list. The inventory showed parts on hand worth $225,000. This seemed a little excessive, and the accountants decided they needed to verify at least a substantial part of the inventory. When the auditors began their counts, a pattern began to develop. Each type of part seemed to be one or two items short when the actual count was taken. This raised more concern. Although Sarah assured the auditors the parts were just misplaced, the auditors continued the count. After completing the count of parts on hand, the auditors could document only $155,000 of actual parts. Suddenly, Sarah quit her job and moved to another state.

Required

a. What do you suppose caused the discrepancy between the actual count and the count that Sarah had supplied?

b. What procedures could be put into place to prevent this type of problem?

LO 3

Exercise 4-12   *Internal control procedures*

Dick Haney is opening a new business that will sell sporting goods. It will initially be a small operation, and he is concerned about the security of his assets. He will not be able to be at the business all of the time and will have to rely on his employees and internal control procedures to ensure that transactions are properly accounted for and assets are safeguarded. He will have a store manager and two other employees who will be sales personnel and stock personnel and who will also perform any other duties necessary. Dick will be in the business on a regular basis. He has come to you for advice.

Required

Write a memo to Dick outlining the procedures that he should implement to ensure that his store assets are protected and that the financial transactions are properly recorded.

LO 5

Exercise 4-13   *Treatment of NSF check*

The bank statement of Gear Supplies included a $300 NSF check that one of Gear's customers had written to pay for services that were provided by Gear.

Required

a. Show the effects of recognizing the NSF check on the financial statements by recording the appropriate amounts in a horizontal statements model like the following one.

Assets	=	Liab.	+	Equity	Rev.	−	Exp.	=	Net Inc.	Cash Flow
Cash + Accts. Rec.										

b. Is the recognition of the NSF check on Gear's books an asset source, use, or exchange transaction?

c. Suppose the customer redeems the check by giving Gear $325 cash in exchange for the bad check. The additional $25 paid a service fee charged by Gear. Show the effects on the financial statements in the horizontal statements model in Requirement *a*.

d. Is the receipt of cash referred to in Requirement *c* an asset source, use, or exchange transaction?

LO 5

Exercise 4-14   *Adjustments to the balance per books*

Required

Identify which of the following items are added to or subtracted from the unadjusted *book balance* to arrive at the true cash balance. Distinguish the additions from the subtractions by placing a + beside the items that are added to the unadjusted book balance and a − beside those that are subtracted from it. The first item is recorded as an example.

Reconciling Items	Book Balance Adjusted?	Added or Subtracted?
Interest revenue	Yes	+
Deposits in transit		
Debit memo		
Bank service charge		
Charge for checks		
NSF check from customer		
Note receivable collected by the bank		
Outstanding checks		
Credit memo		

LO 5

Exercise 4-15   *Adjustments to the balance per bank*

Required

Identify which of the following items are added to or subtracted from the unadjusted *bank balance* to arrive at the true cash balance. Distinguish the additions from the subtractions by placing a + beside the items that are added to the unadjusted bank balance and a − beside those that are subtracted from it. The first item is recorded as an example.

Reconciling Items	Bank Balance Adjusted?	Added or Subtracted?
Deposits in transit	Yes	+
Debit memo		
Credit memo		
Certified checks		
Petty cash voucher		
NSF check from customer		
Interest revenue		
Bank service charge		
Outstanding checks		

Exercise 4-16   *Adjusting the cash account*

LO 5

As of May 31, 2010, the bank statement showed an ending balance of $18,500. The unadjusted Cash account balance was $16,950. The following information is available.

1. Deposit in transit, $2,630.
2. Credit memo in bank statement for interest earned in May, $25.
3. Outstanding check, $4,208.
4. Debit memo for bank service charge, $53.

Required

Determine the true cash balance by preparing a bank reconciliation as of May 31, 2010, using the preceding information.

Exercise 4-17   *Determining the true cash balance, starting with the unadjusted bank balance*

LO 5

The following information is available for Marble Company for the month of August.

1. The unadjusted balance per the bank statement on August 31 was $57,800.
2. Deposits in transit on August 31 were $2,900.
3. A debit memo was included with the bank statement for a service charge of $20.
4. A $5,620 check written in August had not been paid by the bank.
5. The bank statement included a $1,000 credit memo for the collection of a note. The principal of the note was $950, and the interest collected was $50.

Required

Determine the true cash balance as of August 31. (*Hint:* It is not necessary to use all of the preceding items to determine the true balance.)

Exercise 4-18   *Determining the true cash balance, starting with the unadjusted book balance*

LO 5

Smith Company had an unadjusted cash balance of $8,550 as of April 30. The company's bank statement, also dated April 30, included a $100 NSF check written by one of Smith's customers. There were $920 in outstanding checks and $250 in deposits in transit as of April 30. According to the bank statement, service charges were $75, and the bank collected a $700 note receivable for Smith. The bank statement also showed $12 of interest revenue earned by Smith.

Required

Determine the true cash balance as of April 30. (*Hint:* It is not necessary to use all of the preceding items to determine the true balance.)

LO 6

Exercise 4-19 *Performing ratio analysis using real-world data*

Safeway, Inc., operated 1,743 stores as of December 29, 2007. The following data were taken from the company's annual report. All dollar amounts are in millions.

	Fiscal Years Ending	
	December 29, 2007	December 30, 2006
Revenue	$42,286.0	$40,185.0
Cost of Goods Sold	30,133.1	28,604.0
Net Income	888.4	870.6
Merchandise Inventory	2,797.8	2,642.5

Required

a. Compute Safeway's inventory turnover ratio for 2007 and 2006.

b. Compute Safeway's average days to sell inventory for 2007 and 2006.

c. Based on your computations in Requirements *a* and *b*, did Safeway's inventory management get better or worse from 2006 to 2007?

PROBLEMS

All applicable Problems are available with McGraw-Hill *Connect Accounting.*

LO 1, 2

eXcel

CHECK FIGURES
a. Cost of Goods Sold—FIFO: $28,450
b. Net Income—LIFO: $4,935

Problem 4-20 *Effect of different inventory cost flow methods on financial statements*

The accounting records of Brooks Photography, Inc., reflected the following balances as of January 1, 2012:

Cash	$19,000
Beginning inventory	6,750 (75 units @ $90)
Common stock	7,500
Retained earnings	18,250

The following five transactions occurred in 2012.

1. First purchase (cash)   100 units @ $92
2. Second purchase (cash)   175 units @ $100
3. Sales (all cash)   300 units @ $170
4. Paid $15,000 cash for operating expenses.
5. Paid cash for income tax at the rate of 30 percent of income before taxes.

Required

a. Compute the cost of goods sold and ending inventory, assuming (1) FIFO cost flow, (2) LIFO cost flow, and (3) weighted-average cost flow.

b. Use a vertical model to prepare the 2012 income statement, balance sheet, and statement of cash flows under FIFO, LIFO, and weighted average. (*Hint:* Record the events under an accounting equation before preparing the statements.)

LO 3, 4

Problem 4-21 *Using internal control to restrict illegal or unethical behavior*

Required

For each of the following fraudulent acts, describe one or more internal control procedures that could have prevented (or helped prevent) the problems.

a. Paula Wissel, the administrative assistant in charge of payroll, created a fictional employee, wrote weekly checks to the fictional employee, and then personally cashed the checks for her own benefit.

b. Larry Kent, the receiving manager of Southern Lumber, created a fictitious supplier named F&M Building Supply. F&M regularly billed Southern Lumber for supplies purchased. Kent had printed shipping slips and billing invoices with the name of the fictitious company and opened a post office box as the mailing address. Kent simply prepared a receiving report and submitted it for payment to the accounts payable department. The accounts payable clerk then paid the invoice when it was received because Kent acknowledged receipt of the supplies.

c. Holly Baker works at a local hobby shop and usually operates the cash register. She has developed a way to give discounts to her friends. When they come by, she rings a lower price or does not charge the friend for some of the material purchased. At first, Baker thought she would get caught, but no one seemed to notice. Indeed, she has become so sure that there is no way for the owner to find out that she has started taking home some supplies for her own personal use.

Problem 4-22   *Preparing a bank reconciliation*

LO 5

Tom Landry owns a construction business, Landry Supply Co. The following cash information is available for the month of October 2012.

CHECK FIGURE
True Cash Balance, October 31, 2012: $10,950

As of October 31, the bank statement shows a balance of $13,800. The October 31 unadjusted balance in the Cash account of Landry Supply Co. is $12,700. A review of the bank statement revealed the following information.

1. A deposit of $1,600 on October 31, 2012, does not appear on the October 31 bank statement.
2. A debit memo for $250 was included in the bank statement for the purchase of a new supply of checks.
3. When checks written during the month were compared with those paid by the bank, three checks amounting to $4,450 were found to be outstanding.
4. It was discovered that a check to pay for repairs was correctly written and paid by the bank for $3,100 but was recorded on the books as $1,600.

Required

Prepare a bank reconciliation at the end of October showing the true cash balance.

Problem 4-23   *Missing information in a bank reconciliation*

LO 5

The following data apply to Owens Sports, Inc., for April 2010:

1. Balance per the bank on April 30, $12,250.
2. Deposits in transit not recorded by the bank, $2,700.
3. Bank error; check written by Owens on his personal checking account was drawn on the Owens Sports, Inc., account, $900.
4. The following checks written and recorded by Owens Sports, Inc., were not included in the bank statement:

1901	$ 250
1920	580
1921	1,650

CHECK FIGURE
True Cash Balance, April 30, 2010: $13,370

5. Credit memo for note collected by the bank, $1,100.
6. Service charge for collection of note, $10.
7. The bookkeeper recorded a check written for $560 to pay for April's office supplies as $650 in the cash disbursements journal.
8. Bank service charge in addition to the note collection fee, $40.
9. NSF checks returned by the bank, $150.

Required

Determine the amount of the unadjusted cash balance per Owens Sports, Inc.'s books.

LO **5**

Problem 4-24 *Adjustments to the cash account based on the bank reconciliation*

Required

Determine whether the following items in Powers Imports' bank reconciliation require adjusting or correcting entries on Powers Imports' books.

a. The bank collected $7,000 of Powers Imports' accounts receivable. Powers Imports had instructed its customers to send their payments directly to the bank.

b. The bank mistakenly gave Imports, Inc., credit for a $500 deposit made by Powers Imports.

c. Deposits in transit were $5,600.

d. Powers Imports' bank statement contained a $750 NSF check. Powers Imports had received the check from a customer and had included it in one of its bank deposits.

e. The bank statement indicated that Powers Imports earned $80 of interest revenue.

f. Powers Imports' accountant mistakenly recorded a $230 check that was written to purchase supplies as $370.

g. Bank service charges for the month were $50.

h. The bank reconciliation disclosed the fact that $600 had been stolen from Powers Imports' business.

i. Outstanding checks amounted to $1,700.

LO **5**

Problem 4-25 *Bank reconciliation and adjustments to the Cash account*

The following information is available for River Bed Hotel for July 2010.

Bank Statement

STATE BANK

Bolta Vista, NV 10001

River Bed Hotel
10 Main Street
Bolta Vista, NV 10001

Account number
12-4567
July 31, 2010

Beginning balance 6/30/2010	$ 9,031
Total deposits and other credits	28,900
Total checks and other debits	23,902
Ending balance 7/31/2010	14,029

Checks and Debits		Deposits and Credits		
Check No.	Amount	Date		Amount
2350	$3,761	July	1	$1,102
2351	1,643	July	10	6,498
2352	8,000	July	15	4,929
2354	2,894	July	21	6,174
2355	1,401	July	26	5,963
2357	6,187	July	30	2,084
DM	16	CM		2,150

The following is a list of checks and deposits recorded on the books of the River Bed Hotel for July 2010.

Date		Check No.	Amount of Check	Date		Amount of Deposit
July	2	2351	$1,643	July	8	$6,498
July	4	2352	8,000	July	14	4,929
July	10	2353	1,700	July	21	6,174
July	10	2354	2,894	July	26	5,963
July	15	2355	1,401	July	29	2,084
July	20	2356	950	July	30	3,550
July	22	2357	6,187			

Other Information

1. Check no. 2350 was outstanding from June.
2. Credit memo was for collection of notes receivable.
3. All checks were paid at the correct amount.
4. Debit memo was for printed checks.
5. The June 30 bank reconciliation showed a deposit in transit of $1,102.
6. The unadjusted Cash account balance at July 31 was $12,795.

Required

a. Prepare the bank reconciliation for River Bed Hotel at the end of July.
b. Explain how the adjustments described above affect the cash account.

Problem 4-26   *Bank reconciliation and internal control*

Following is a bank reconciliation for Fez's Sandwich Shop for May 31, 2010.

LO **3, 4, 5**

CHECK FIGURE
a. True Cash Balance, May 31, 2010: $23,050

	Cash Account	Bank Statement
Balance as of 5/31/10	$25,500	$23,000
Deposit in transit		4,250
Outstanding checks		(1,730)
Note collected by bank	1,050	
Bank service charge	(30)	
Automatic payment on loan	(1,000)	
Adjusted cash balance as of 5/31/10	$25,520	$25,520

Because of limited funds, Fez's employed only one accountant who was responsible for receiving cash, recording receipts and disbursements, preparing deposits, and preparing the bank reconciliation. The accountant left the company on June 8, 2010, after preparing the preceding statement. His replacement compared the checks returned with the bank statement to the cash disbursements journal and found the total of outstanding checks to be $4,200.

Required

a. Prepare a corrected bank reconciliation.
b. What is the total amount of cash missing, and how was the difference between the "true cash" per the bank and the "true cash" per the books hidden on the reconciliation prepared by the former employee?
c. What could Fez's do to avoid cash theft in the future?

Problem 4-27   *Performing ratio analysis using real-world data*

LO **6**

Ruby Tuesday's, Inc., operated 834 casual dining restaurants across the United States as of June 5, 2007. As of July 31, 2007, Zale Corporation operated 1,471 retail jewelry stores and 793 kiosks throughout the United States, Canada, and Puerto Rico. The following data were taken from these companies' 2007 annual reports. All dollar amounts are in thousands.

	Ruby Tuesday's June 5, 2007	Zale Corporation July 31, 2007
Sales	$1,395,212*	$2,437,075
Cost of Goods Sold	375,836	1,187,601
Net Income	91,668	59,252
Merchandise Inventory	11,825	1,021,164

*This excludes franchise revenue.

Required

a. Before performing any calculations, speculate as to which company will take the longest to sell its inventory. Explain the rationale for your decision.

b. Calculate the inventory turnover ratios for Ruby Tuesday's and Zale Corporation.

c. Calculate the average days to sell inventory for Ruby Tuesday's and Zale Corporation.

d. Do the calculations from Requirements *b* and *c* confirm your speculations in Requirement *a?*

ANALYZE, THINK, COMMUNICATE

ATC 4-1   Business Applications Case   *Understanding real-world annual reports*

Required

Use the Topps Company's annual report in Appendix B to answer the following questions.

a. What was Topps' inventory turnover ratio and average days to sell inventory for 2006 and 2005?

b. Is the company's management of inventory getting better or worse?

c. What cost flow method(s) did Topps use to account for inventory?

ATC 4-2   Group Assignment   *Inventory cost flow*

The accounting records of Robin Co. showed the following balances at January 1, 2008:

Cash	$30,000
Beginning inventory (100 units @ $50, 70 units @ $55)	8,850
Common stock	20,000
Retained earnings	18,850

Transactions for 2008 were as follows:

Purchased 100 units @ $54 per unit.
Purchased 250 units @ $58 per unit.
Sold 220 units @ $80 per unit.
Sold 200 units @ $90 per unit.
Paid operating expenses of $3,200.
Paid income tax expense. The income tax rate is 30%.

Required

a. Organize the class into three sections, and divide each section into groups of three to five students. Assign each section one of the cost flow methods, FIFO, LIFO, or weighted average. The company uses the perpetual inventory system.

Group Tasks

Determine the amount of ending inventory, cost of goods sold, gross margin, and net income after income tax for the cost flow method assigned to your section. Also prepare an income statement using that cost flow assumption.

Class Discussion

b. Have a representative of each section put its income statement on the board. Discuss the effect that each cost flow method has on assets (ending inventory), net income, and cash flows. Which method is preferred for tax reporting? For financial reporting? What restrictions are placed on the use of LIFO for tax reporting?

ATC 4-3   Real-World Case   *Analyzing inventory management issues at Ryland Group, Inc.*

In 2005, after years of positive growth in the housing market, sales and prices began to slow down and then decline. By 2007 many large home-construction companies were reporting net losses.

The data below, for Ryland Group, Inc.'s fiscal years ending on December 31, 2006, and 2005, pertain to analyzing the company's management of inventory. All dollar amounts are in thousands.

	2006	2005
Sales*	$4,653,920	$4,725,751
Cost of goods sold	3,640,075	3,537,603
Ending inventory**	1,735,859	1,188,148
Income before taxes	567,108	721,051

*Homebuilding sales only.

**Includes "homes under construction" plus "land under development and improved lots" only.

Required

a. Compute Ryland's gross margin percentage for 2006 and 2005.

b. Compute Ryland average days to sell inventory for 2006 and 2005.

c. Was Ryland's decline in earnings from 2005 to 2006 affected by either a lower gross margin or lower inventory turnover? Explain.

d. Do you think there may have been a connection between the change in Ryland's gross margin percentage from 2005 to 2006 and the change in its average days to sell inventory for the same period? Explain.

e. How much higher or lower would Ryland's *earnings before taxes* have been in 2006 if its gross margin percentage had been the same as it was in 2005? Show all supporting computations.

ATC 4-4   Business Applications Case   *Using the average days to sell inventory ratio to make a lending decision*

Carter's Produce has applied for a loan and has agreed to use its inventory to collateralize the loan. The company currently has an inventory balance of $289,000. The cost of goods sold for the past year was $7,518,000. The average shelf life for the fruit that Carter sells is 10 days, after which time it begins to spoil and must be sold at drastically reduced prices to dispose of it rapidly. The company maintained steady sales over the past three years and expects to continue at current levels for the foreseeable future.

Required

Based on your knowledge of inventory turnover, write a memo that describes the quality of the inventory as collateral for the loan.

ATC 4-5   Business Applications Case   *Using ratios to make comparisons*

The following accounting information pertains to Clemens Corp. and Twain Inc. at the end of 2009. The only difference between the two companies is that Clemens uses FIFO while Twain uses LIFO.

	Clemens	Twain
Cash	$ 75,000	$ 75,000
Accounts receivable	200,000	200,000
Merchandise inventory	150,000	100,000
Accounts payable	160,000	160,000
Cost of goods sold	600,000	650,000
Building	250,000	250,000
Sales	1,000,000	1,000,000

Required

a. Compute the gross margin percentage for each company, and identify the company that *appears* to be charging the higher prices in relation to its costs.

b. For each company, compute the inventory turnover ratio and the average number of days to sell inventory. Identify the company that *appears* to be incurring the higher inventory financing cost.

c. Explain why the company with the lower gross margin percentage has the higher inventory turnover ratio.

ATC 4-6   Writing Assignment   *Internal control procedures*

Alison Marsh was a trusted employee of Small City State Bank. She was involved in everything. She worked as a teller, she accounted for the cash at the other teller windows, and she recorded many of the transactions in the accounting records. She was so loyal that she never would take a day off, even when she was really too sick to work. She routinely worked late to see that all the day's work was posted into the accounting records. She would never take even a day's vacation because they might need her at the bank. Tick and Tack, CPAs, were hired to perform an audit, the first complete audit that had been done in several years. Marsh seemed somewhat upset by the upcoming audit. She said that everything had been properly accounted for and that the audit was a needless expense. When Tick and Tack examined some of the bank's internal control procedures, it discovered problems. In fact, as the audit progressed, it became apparent that a large amount of cash was missing. Numerous adjustments had been made to customer accounts with credit memorandums, and many of the transactions had been posted several days late. In addition, there were numerous cash payments for "office expenses." When the audit was complete, it was determined that more than $200,000 of funds was missing or improperly accounted for. All fingers pointed to Marsh. The bank's president, who was a close friend of Marsh, was bewildered. How could this type of thing happen at this bank?

Required

Prepare a written memo to the bank president, outlining the procedures that should be followed to prevent this type of problem in the future.

ATC 4-7   Corporate Governance   *I need just a little extra money*

Terry Bailey, an accountant, has worked for the past eight years as a payroll clerk for Fairwell Furniture, a small furniture manufacturing firm in the northeast. Terry recently experienced unfortunate circumstances. Her teenage son required minor surgery and the medical bills not covered by Terry's insurance have financially strained Terry's family.

Terry works hard and is a model employee. Although she received regular performance raises during her first few years with Fairwell, Terry's wages have not increased in three years. Terry asked her supervisor, Bill Jameson, for a raise. Bill agreed that Terry deserved a raise, but told her he could not currently approve one because of sluggish sales.

A disappointed Terry returned to her duties while the financial pressures in her life continued. Two weeks later, Larry Tyler, an assembly worker at Fairwell, quit over a dispute with management. Terry conceived an idea. Terry's duties included not only processing employee terminations but also approving time cards before paychecks were issued and then distributing the paychecks to firm personnel. Terry decided to delay processing Mr. Tyler's termination, to forge timecards for Larry Tyler for the next few weeks, and to cash the checks herself. Since she distributed paychecks, no one would find out, and Terry reasoned that she was really entitled to the extra money anyway. In fact, no one did discover her maneuver and Terry stopped the practice after three weeks.

Required

a. Does Terry's scheme affect Fairwell's balance sheet? Explain your answer.

b. Review the AICPA's Code of Professional Conduct (see Chapter 2) and comment on any of the standards that have been violated.

c. The fraud triangle (see Chapter 2) identifies three common features of unethical and criminal conduct. Name these features and explain how they pertain to this case.

ATC 4-8   Research Assignment   *Analyzing inventory at Gap Company*

Using either Gap's most current Form 10-K or the company's annual report, answer the questions below. To obtain the Form 10-K use either the EDGAR system following the instructions in Appendix A, or the company's website. The company's annual report is available on its website.

Required

a. What was the average amount of inventory per store? Use *all* stores operated by The Gap, Inc., not just those called *The Gap*. (*Hint:* The answer to this question must be computed. The number of stores in operation at the end of the most recent year can be found in the MD&A of the 10-K.)

b. How many *new* stores did Gap open during the year?

c. Using the quarterly financial information in the 10-K, complete the following chart.

Quarter	Sales during Each Quarter
1	$
2	
3	
4	

d. Referring to the chart in Requirement *c*, explain why Gap's sales vary so widely throughout its fiscal year. Do you believe that Gap's inventory level varies throughout the year in relation to sales?

CHAPTER 5

Accounting *for* Receivables

LEARNING OBJECTIVES

After you have mastered the material in this chapter you will be able to:

1 Explain how the allowance method of accounting for uncollectible accounts affects financial statements.

2 Determine uncollectible accounts expense using the percent of revenue method.

3 Determine uncollectible accounts expense using the percent of receivables method.

4 Explain how accounting for notes receivable affects financial statements.

5 Explain how accounting for credit card sales affects financial statements.

6 Identify and measure the cost of extending credit to customers.

CHAPTER OPENING

Many people buy on impulse. If they must wait, the desire to buy wanes. To take advantage of impulse buyers, most merchandising companies offer customers credit because it increases their sales. A disadvantage of this strategy occurs when some customers are unable or unwilling to pay their bills. Nevertheless, the widespread availability of credit suggests that the advantages of increased sales outweigh the disadvantages of some uncollectible accounts.

When a company allows a customer to "buy now and pay later," the company's right to collect cash in the future is called an **account receivable.** Typically, amounts due from individual accounts receivable are relatively small and the collection period is short. Most accounts receivable are collected within 30 days. When a longer credit term is needed or when a receivable is large, the seller usually requires the buyer to issue a note reflecting a credit agreement between the parties. The note specifies the maturity date, interest rate, and other credit terms. Receivables evidenced by such notes are called **notes receivable.** Accounts and notes receivable are reported as assets on the balance sheet.

The *Curious* Accountant

Suppose the U.S. government purchases $10 million of fuel from Chevron. Assume the government offers to pay for the fuel on the day it receives it from Chevron (a cash purchase) or 30 days later (a purchase on account).

Assume that Chevron is absolutely sure the government will pay its account when due. Do you think Chevron should care whether the government pays for the goods upon delivery or 30 days later? Why? (Answers on page 173.)

ALLOWANCE METHOD OF ACCOUNTING FOR UNCOLLECTIBLE ACCOUNTS

LO 1

Explain how the allowance method of accounting for uncollectible accounts affects financial statements.

Most companies do not expect to collect the full amount (face value) of their accounts receivable. Even carefully screened credit customers sometimes don't pay their bills. The **net realizable value** of accounts receivable represents the amount of receivables a company estimates it will actually collect. The net realizable value is the *face value* less an *allowance for doubtful accounts.*

The **allowance for doubtful accounts** represents a company's estimate of the amount of uncollectible receivables. To illustrate, assume a company with total accounts receivable of $50,000 estimates that $2,000 of its receivables will not be collected. The net realizable value of receivables is computed as follows.

Accounts receivable	$50,000
Less: Allowance for doubtful accounts	(2,000)
Net realizable value of receivables	$48,000

A company cannot know today, of course, the exact amount of the receivables it will not be able to collect in the future. The *allowance for doubtful accounts* and the *net realizable value* are necessarily *estimated amounts.* The net realizable value, however, more closely measures the cash that will ultimately be collected than does the face value. To avoid overstating assets, companies usually report receivables on their balance sheets at the net realizable value.

Reporting accounts receivable in the financial statements at net realizable value is commonly called the **allowance method of accounting for uncollectible accounts.** The following section illustrates using the allowance method for Allen's Tutoring Services (ATS).

Accounting Events Affecting the 2010 Period

Allen's Tutoring Services is a small company that provides tutoring services to college students. Allen's started operations on January 1, 2010. During 2010, Allen's experienced three types of accounting events. These events are discussed below.

EVENT 1   Revenue Recognition
Allen's Tutoring Services recognized $14,000 of service revenue earned on account during 2010.

This is an asset source transaction. Allen's Tutoring Services obtained assets (accounts receivable) by providing services to customers. Both assets and stockholders' equity (retained earnings) increase. The event increases revenue and net income. Cash flow is not affected. These effects follow.

Event No.	Assets	=	Liab.	+	Equity	Rev.	−	Exp.	=	Net Inc.	Cash Flow
	Accts. Rec.	=			Ret. Earn.						
1	14,000	=	NA	+	14,000	14,000	−	NA	=	14,000	NA

EVENT 2   Collection of Receivables
Allen's Tutoring Services collected $12,500 cash from accounts receivable in 2010.

This event is an asset exchange transaction. The asset cash increases; the asset accounts receivable decreases. Total assets remains unchanged. Net income is not affected

Answers to The *Curious* Accountant

Chevron would definitely prefer to make the sale to the government in cash rather than on account. Even though it may be certain to collect its accounts receivable, the sooner Chevron gets its cash, the sooner the cash can be reinvested.

The interest cost related to a small account receivable of $50 that takes 30 days to collect may seem immaterial; at 4 percent, the lost interest amounts to less than $.20. However, when one considers that Chevron had approximately $17.2 billion of accounts receivable, the cost of financing receivables for a real-world company becomes apparent. At 4 percent, the cost of waiting 30 days to collect $17.2 billion of cash is $56.5 million ($17.2 billion × .04 × [30 ÷ 365]). For one full year, the cost to Chevron would be more than $688 million ($17.2 billion × 0.04). In 2005, it took Chevron approximately 32 days to collect its accounts receivable, and the weighted-average interest rate on its debt was approximately 4.2 percent.

because the revenue was recognized in the previous transaction. The cash inflow is reported in the operating activities section of the statement of cash flows.

Event No.	Assets			=	Liab.	+	Equity	Rev.	−	Exp.	=	Net Inc.	Cash Flow
	Cash	+	Accts. Rec.										
2	12,500	+	(12,500)	=	NA	+	NA	NA	−	NA	=	NA	12,500 OA

Accounting for Uncollectible Accounts Expense

EVENT 3 **Recognizing Uncollectible Accounts Expense**

Allen's Tutoring Services recognized uncollectible accounts expense for accounts expected to be uncollectible in the future.

The year-end balance in the accounts receivable account is $1,500 ($14,000 of revenue on account − $12,500 of collections). Although Allen's Tutoring Services has the legal right to receive this $1,500 in 2011, the company is not likely to collect the entire amount because some of its customers may not pay the amounts due. Allen's will not know the actual amount of uncollectible accounts until some future time when the customers default (fail to pay). However, the company can *estimate* the amount of receivables that will be uncollectible.

Suppose Allen's Tutoring Services estimates that $75 of the receivables is uncollectible. To improve financial reporting, the company can recognize the estimated expense in 2010. In this way, uncollectible accounts expense and the related revenue will be recognized in the same accounting period (2010). Recognizing an estimated expense is more useful than recognizing no expense. The *matching* of revenues and expenses is improved and the statements are, therefore, more accurate.

The estimated amount of **uncollectible accounts expense** is recognized in a year-end adjusting entry. The adjusting entry reduces the book value of total assets, reduces stockholders' equity (retained earnings), and reduces the amount of reported net income. The statement of cash flows is not affected. The effects of recognizing uncollectible accounts expense are shown here.

Event No.	Assets			=	Liab.	+	Equity	Rev.	−	Exp.	=	Net Inc.	Cash Flow
	Accts. Rec.	−	Allow.	=			Ret. Earn.						
3	NA	−	75	=	NA	+	(75)	NA	−	75	=	(75)	NA

Instead of decreasing the receivables account directly, the asset reduction is recorded in the **contra asset account,** Allowance for Doubtful Accounts. Recall that the contra account is subtracted from the accounts receivable balance to determine the net realizable value of receivables, as follows for ATS.

Accounts receivable	$1,500
Less: Allowance for doubtful accounts	(75)
Net realizable value of receivables	$1,425

Generally accepted accounting principles require disclosure of both the net realizable value and the amount of the allowance account. Many companies disclose these amounts directly in the balance sheet in a manner similar to that shown in the text box above. Other companies disclose this information in the footnotes to the financial statements.

Financial Statements

The financial statements for Allen's Tutoring Services' 2010 accounting period are shown in Exhibit 5.1. As previously indicated, estimating uncollectible accounts improves the usefulness of the 2010 financial statements in two ways. First, the balance sheet reports the amount of cash ($1,500 − $75 = $1,425) the company actually expects to collect (net realizable value of accounts receivable). Second, the income statement provides a clearer picture of managerial performance because it better *matches* the uncollectible accounts expense with the revenue it helped produce. The statements in Exhibit 5.1 show that the cash flow from operating activities ($12,500)

EXHIBIT 5.1

Financial Statements for 2010

Income Statement		Balance Sheet			Statement of Cash Flows	
Service revenue	$14,000	Assets			Operating Activities	
Uncollectible accts. exp.	(75)	Cash		$12,500	Inflow from customers	$12,500
Net income	$13,925	Accounts receivable	$1,500		Investing Activities	0
		Less: Allowance	(75)		Financing Activities	0
		Net realizable value		1,425	Net change in cash	12,500
		Total assets		$13,925	Plus: Beginning cash balance	0
		Stockholders' equity			Ending cash balance	$12,500
		Retained earnings		$13,925		

CHECK *Yourself* 5.1

Pamlico Inc. began operations on January 1, 2011. During 2011, it earned $400,000 of revenue on account. The company collected $370,000 of accounts receivable. At the end of the year, Pamlico estimates uncollectible accounts expense will be 1 percent of sales. Based on this information alone, what is the net realizable value of accounts receivable as of December 31, 2011?

Answer   Accounts receivable at year end are $30,000 ($400,000 sales on account − $370,000 collection of receivables). The amount in the allowance for doubtful accounts would be $4,000 ($400,000 credit sales × 0.01). The net realizable value of accounts receivable is therefore $26,000 ($30,000 − $4,000).

differs from net income ($13,925). The statement of cash flows reports only cash collections, whereas the income statement reports revenues earned on account less the estimated amount of uncollectible accounts expense.

Accounting Events Affecting the 2011 Period

To further illustrate accounting for uncollectible accounts, we discuss six accounting events affecting Allen's Tutoring Services during 2011.

Accounting for Write-Off of Uncollectible Accounts Receivable

EVENT 1   Write-Off of Uncollectible Accounts Receivable
Allen's Tutoring Services wrote off $70 of uncollectible accounts receivable.

This is an asset exchange transaction. The amount of the uncollectible accounts is removed from the Accounts Receivable account and from the Allowance for Doubtful Accounts account. Since the balances in both the Accounts Receivable and the Allowance accounts decrease, the net realizable value of receivables—and therefore total assets—remains unchanged. The write-off does not affect the income statement. Since the uncollectible accounts expense was recognized in the previous year, the expense would be double counted if it were recognized again at the time an uncollectible account is written off. Finally, the statement of cash flows is not affected by the write-off. These effects are shown in the following statements model.

Event No.	Assets			=	Liab.	+	Equity	Rev.	−	Exp.	=	Net Inc.	Cash Flow
	Accts. Rec.	−	Allow.										
1	(70)	−	(70)	=	NA	+	NA	NA	−	NA	=	NA	NA

The computation of the *net realizable value*, before and after the write-off, is shown below.

	Before Write-Off	After Write-Off
Accounts receivable	$1,500	$1,430
Less: Allowance for doubtful accounts	(75)	(5)
Net realizable value	$1,425	$1,425

EVENT 2   Revenue Recognition
Allen's Tutoring Services provided $10,000 of tutoring services on account during 2011.

Assets (accounts receivable) and stockholders' equity (retained earnings) increase. Recognizing revenue increases net income. Cash flow is not affected. These effects are illustrated below.

Event No.	Assets	=	Liab.	+	Equity	Rev.	−	Exp.	=	Net Inc.	Cash Flow
	Accts. Rec.	=			Ret. Earn.						
2	10,000	=	NA	+	10,000	10,000	−	NA	=	10,000	NA

EVENT 3   Collection of Accounts Receivable
Allen's Tutoring Services collected $8,430 cash from accounts receivable.

The balance in the Cash account increases, and the balance in the Accounts Receivable account decreases. Total assets are unaffected. Net income is not affected because revenue was recognized previously. The cash inflow is reported in the operating activities section of the statement of cash flows.

Event No.	Assets			=	Liab.	+	Equity	Rev.	−	Exp.	=	Net Inc.	Cash Flow
	Cash	+	Accts. Rec.										
3	8,430	+	(8,430)	=	NA	+	NA	NA	−	NA	=	NA	8,430 OA

Accounting for Recovery of an Uncollectible Account Receivable

EVENT 4   Recovery of an Uncollectible Account: Reinstate Receivable
Allen's Tutoring Services recovered a receivable that it had previously written off.

Occasionally, a company receives payment from a customer whose account was previously written off. In such cases, the customer's account should be reinstated and the cash received should be recorded the same way as any other collection on account. The account receivable is reinstated because a complete record of the customer's payment history may be useful if the customer requests credit again at some future date. To illustrate, assume that Allen's Tutoring Services received a $10 cash payment from a customer whose account had previously been written off. The first step is to **reinstate** the account receivable by reversing the previous write-off. The balances in the Accounts Receivable and the Allowance accounts increase. Since the Allowance is a contra asset account, the increase in it offsets the increase in the Accounts Receivable account, and total assets are unchanged. Net income and cash flow are unaffected. These effects are shown here.

Event No.	Assets			=	Liab.	+	Equity	Rev.	−	Exp.	=	Net Inc.	Cash Flow
	Accts. Rec.	−	Allow.										
4	10	−	10	=	NA	+	NA	NA	−	NA	=	NA	NA

EVENT 5   Recovery of an Uncollectible Account: Collection of Receivable
Allen's Tutoring Services recorded collection of the reinstated receivable.

The collection of $10 is recorded like any other collection of a receivable account. Cash increases, and accounts receivable decreases.

Event No.	Assets			=	Liab.	+	Equity	Rev.	–	Exp.	=	Net Inc.	Cash Flow
	Cash	+	Accts. Rec.										
5	10	+	(10)	=	NA	+	NA	NA	–	NA	=	NA	10 OA

ESTIMATING UNCOLLECTIBLE ACCOUNTS EXPENSE USING THE PERCENT OF REVENUE (SALES) METHOD

Companies recognize the estimated amount of uncollectible accounts expense in a period-end adjusting entry. Since Allen's Tutoring Service began operations in 2010, it had no previous credit history upon which to base its estimate. After consulting trade publications and experienced people in the same industry, ATS made an educated guess as to the amount of expense it should recognize for its first year. In its second year of operation, however, ATS can use its first-year experience as a starting point for estimating the second year (2011) uncollectible accounts expense.

LO 2

Determine uncollectible accounts expense using the percent of revenue method.

At the end of 2010 ATS estimated uncollectible accounts expense to be $75 on service revenue of $14,000. In 2011 ATS actually wrote off $70 of which $10 was later recovered. ATS therefore experienced actual uncollectible accounts of $60 on service revenue of $14,000 for an uncollectible accounts rate of approximately .43 percent of service revenue. ATS could apply this percentage to the 2011 service revenue to estimate the 2011 uncollectible accounts expense. In practice, many companies determine the percentage estimate of uncollectible accounts on a three- or five-year moving average.

Companies adjust the historical percentage for anticipated future circumstances. For example, they reduce it if they adopt more rigorous approval standards for new credit applicants. Alternatively, they may increase the percentage if economic forecasts signal an economic downturn that would make future defaults more likely. A company will also increase the percentage if it has specific knowledge one or more of its customers is financially distressed. Multiplying the service revenue by the percentage estimate of uncollectible accounts is commonly called the **percent of revenue method** of estimating uncollectible accounts expense.

EVENT 6   Adjustment for Recognition of Uncollectible Accounts Expense
Using the percent of revenue method, Allen's Tutoring Services recognized uncollectible accounts expense for 2011.

ATS must record this adjustment as of December 31, 2011, to update its accounting records before preparing the 2011 financial statements. After reviewing its credit history, economic forecasts, and correspondence with customers, management estimates uncollectible accounts expense to be 1.35 percent of service revenue, or $135 ($10,000 service revenue × .0135). Recognizing the $135 uncollectible accounts expense decreases both assets (net realizable of receivables) and stockholders' equity (retained earnings). The expense recognition decreases net income. The statement of cash flows is not affected. The financial statements are affected as shown here.

Event No.	Assets			=	Liab.	+	Equity	Rev.	–	Exp.	=	Net Inc.	Cash Flow
	Accts. Rec.	–	Allow.	=			Ret. Earn.						
6	NA	–	135	=	NA	+	(135)	NA	–	135	=	(135)	NA

Analysis of Financial Statements

Exhibit 5.2 displays the 2011 financial statements. The amount of uncollectible accounts expense ($135) differs from the ending balance of the Allowance account ($150). The balance in the Allowance account was $15 before the 2011 adjusting entry

EXHIBIT 5.2

Financial Statements for 2011

Income Statement		Balance Sheet			Statement of Cash Flows	
Service revenue	$10,000	Assets			Operating Activities	
Uncollectible accts. exp.	(135)	Cash		$20,940	Inflow from customers	$ 8,440
Net income	$ 9,865	Accounts receivable	$3,000		Investing Activities	0
		Less: Allowance	(150)		Financing Activities	0
		Net realizable value		2,850	Net change in cash	8,440
		Total assets		$23,790	Plus: Beginning cash balance	12,500
		Stockholders' equity			Ending cash balance	$20,940
		Retained earnings		$23,790		

for uncollectible accounts expense was recorded. At the end of 2010, Allen's Tutoring Services estimated there would be $75 of uncollectible accounts as a result of 2010 credit sales. Actual write-offs, however, amounted to $70 and $10 of that amount was recovered, indicating the actual uncollectible accounts expense for 2010 was only $60. Hindsight shows the expense for 2010 was overstated by $15. However, if no estimate had been made, the amount of uncollectible accounts expense would have been understated by $60. In some accounting periods estimated uncollectible accounts expense will likely be overstated; in others it may be understated. The allowance method cannot produce perfect results, but it does improve the accuracy of the financial statements.

Since no dividends were paid, retained earnings at the end of 2011 equals the December 31, 2010, retained earnings plus 2011 net income (that is, $13,925 + $9,865 = $23,790). Again, the cash flow from operating activities ($8,440) differs from net income ($9,865) because the statement of cash flows does not include the effects of revenues earned on account or the recognition of uncollectible accounts expense.

CHECK *Yourself* 5.2

Maher Company had beginning balances in Accounts Receivable and Allowance for Doubtful Accounts of $24,200 and $2,000, respectively. During the accounting period Maher earned $230,000 of revenue on account and collected $232,500 of cash from receivables. The company also wrote off $1,950 of uncollectible accounts during the period. Maher estimates uncollectible accounts expense will be 1 percent of credit sales. Based on this information, what is the net realizable value of receivables at the end of the period?

Answer   The balance in the Accounts Receivable account is $19,750 ($24,200 + $230,000 − $232,500 − $1,950). The amount of uncollectible accounts expense for the period is $2,300 ($230,000 × 0.01). The balance in the Allowance for Doubtful Accounts is $2,350 ($2,000 − $1,950 + $2,300). The net realizable value of receivables is therefore $17,400 ($19,750 − $2,350).

ESTIMATING UNCOLLECTIBLE ACCOUNTS EXPENSE USING THE PERCENT OF RECEIVABLES METHOD

LO 3

Determine uncollectible accounts expense using the percent of receivables method.

As an alternative to the percent of revenue method, which focuses on estimating the *expense* of uncollectible accounts, companies may estimate the amount of the adjusting entry to record uncollectible accounts expense using the **percent of receivables method.** The percent of receivables method focuses on estimating the most accurate amount for the balance sheet *Allowance for Doubtful Accounts* account.

EXHIBIT 5.3

PYRAMID CORPORATION
Accounts Receivable Aging Schedule
December 31, 2011

| Customer Name | Total Balance | Current | Number of Days Past Due | | | |
			0–30	31–60	61–90	Over 90
J. Davis	$ 6,700	$ 6,700				
B. Diamond	4,800	2,100	$ 2,700			
K. Eppy	9,400	9,400				
B. Gilman	2,200				$1,000	$1,200
A. Kelly	7,300	7,300				
L. Niel	8,600	1,000	6,000	$ 1,600		
L. Platt	4,600			4,600		
J. Turner	5,500			3,000	2,000	500
H. Zachry	6,900		3,000	3,900		
Total	$56,000	$26,500	$11,700	$13,100	$3,000	$1,700

The longer an account receivable remains outstanding, the less likely it is to be collected. Companies using the percent of receivables method typically determine the age of their individual accounts receivable accounts as part of estimating the allowance for doubtful accounts. An **aging of accounts receivable** schedule classifies all receivables by their due date. Exhibit 5.3 shows an aging schedule for Pyramid Corporation as of December 31, 2011.

A company estimates the required Allowance for Doubtful Accounts balance by applying different percentages to each category in the aging schedule. The percentage for each category is based on a company's previous collection experience for each of the categories. The percentages become progressively higher as the accounts become older. Exhibit 5.4 illustrates computing the allowance balance Pyramid Corporation requires.

The computations in Exhibit 5.4 mean the *ending balance* in the Allowance for Doubtful Accounts account should be $3,760. This balance represents the amount Pyramid will subtract from total accounts receivable to determine the net realizable value of receivables. To determine the amount of the adjusting entry to recognize uncollectible accounts expense, Pyramid must take into account any existing balance in the allowance account *before* recording the adjustment. For example, if Pyramid Corporation had a $500 balance in the Allowance account before the year-end adjustment,

EXHIBIT 5.4

Balance Required in the Allowance for Doubtful Accounts at December 31, 2011

Number of Days Past Due	Receivables Amount	Percentage Likely to Be Uncollectible	Required Allowance Account Balance
Current	$26,500	.01	$ 265
0–30	11,700	.05	585
31–60	13,100	.10	1,310
61–90	3,000	.25	750
Over 90	1,700	.50	850
Total	$56,000		$3,760

the adjusting entry would need to add $3,260 ($3,760 − $500) to the account. The effects on the financial statements are shown below.

Assets			= Liab.	+	Equity	Rev.	−	Exp.	=	Net Inc.	Cash Flow
Accts. Rec.	−	Allow.	=		Ret. Earn.						
NA	−	3,260	= NA	+	(3,260)	NA	−	3,260	=	3,260	NA

Matching Revenues and Expenses versus Asset Measurement

The *percent of revenue* method, with its focus on determining the uncollectible accounts expense, is often called the income statement approach. The *percent of receivables* method, focused on determining the best estimate of the allowance balance, is frequently called the balance sheet approach. Which estimating method is better? In any given year, the results will vary slightly between approaches. In the long run, however, the percentages used in either approach are based on a company's actual history of uncollectible accounts. Accountants routinely revise their estimates as more data become available, using hindsight to determine if the percentages should be increased or decreased. Either approach provides acceptable results.

ACCOUNTING FOR NOTES RECEIVABLE (PROMISSORY NOTES)

Explain how accounting for notes receivable affects financial statements.

Companies typically do not charge their customers interest on accounts receivable that are not past due. When a company extends credit for a long time or when the amount of credit it extends is large, however, the cost of granting free credit and the potential for disputes about payment terms both increase. To address these concerns, the parties frequently enter into a credit agreement, the terms of which are legally documented in a **promissory note.**

To illustrate, assume Allen's Tutoring Services (ATS) loans some of its idle cash to an individual, Stanford Cummings, so Cummings can buy a car. ATS and Cummings agree that Cummings will repay the money borrowed plus interest at the end of one year. They also agree that ATS will hold the title to the car to secure the debt. Exhibit 5.5 illustrates a promissory note that outlines this credit agreement. For ATS, the credit arrangement represents a *note receivable.*

EXHIBIT 5.5

Promissory Note

Promissory Note

$15,000 (3)   *November 1, 2012*

Amount   **Date**

For consideration received, Stanford Cummings hereby promises to pay to the order of:

Allen's Tutoring Services (2)

Fifteen thousand and no/100   **Dollars**

payable on   October 31, 2013 (5)

plus interest thereon at the rate of _6_ **percent per year.** (4)

Collateral Description   Automobile title (6)

Signature   *Stanford Cummings* (1)

Features of this note are discussed below. Each feature is cross referenced with a number that corresponds to an item on the promissory note in Exhibit 5.5. Locate each feature in Exhibit 5.5 and read the corresponding description of the feature below.

1. Maker—The person responsible for making payment on the due date is the **maker** of the note. The maker may also be called the *borrower* or *debtor.*

2. Payee—The person to whom the note is made payable is the **payee.** The payee may also be called the *creditor* or *lender.* The payee loans money to the maker and expects the return of the principal and the interest due.

3. Principal—The amount of money loaned by the payee to the maker of the note is the **principal.**

4. Interest—The economic benefit earned by the payee for loaning the principal to the maker is **interest,** which is normally expressed as an annual percentage of the principal amount. For example, a note with a 6 percent interest rate requires interest payments equal to 6 percent of the principal amount every year the loan is outstanding.

5. Maturity Date—The date on which the maker must repay the principal and make the final interest payment to the payee is the **maturity date.**

6. Collateral—Assets belonging to the maker that are assigned as security to ensure that the principal and interest will be paid when due are called **collateral.** In this example, if Cummings fails to pay ATS the amount due, ownership of the car Cummings purchased will be transferred to ATS.

How Accounting for Notes Receivable Affects Financial Statements

We illustrate accounting for notes receivable using the credit agreement evidenced by the promissory note in Exhibit 5.5. Allen's Tutoring Services engaged in many transactions during 2012; we discuss here only transactions directly related to the note receivable.

EVENT 1   Loan of Money

The note shows that ATS loaned $15,000 to Stanford Cummings on November 1, 2012. This event is an asset exchange. The asset account Cash decreases and the asset account Notes Receivable increases. The income statement is not affected. The statement of cash flows shows a cash outflow for investing activities. The effects on the financial statements are shown below.

Date	Assets			= Liab.	+	Equity	Rev.	−	Exp.	=	Net Inc.	Cash Flow
	Cash	+ Notes Rec.	+ Int. Rec. =			Ret. Earn.						
11/01/12	(15,000)	+ 15,000	+ NA =	NA	+	NA	NA	−	NA	=	NA	(15,000) IA

EVENT 2   Accrual of Interest

For ATS, loaning money to the maker of the note, Stanford Cummings, represents investing in the note receivable. Cummings will repay the principal ($15,000) plus interest of 6 percent of the principal amount (0.06 × $15,000 = $900), or a total of $15,900, on October 31, 2013, one year from the date he borrowed the money from ATS.

Conceptually, lenders *earn* interest continually even though they do not *collect* cash payment for it every day. Each day, the amount of interest due, called **accrued interest,** is greater than the day before. Companies would find it highly impractical to attempt to record (recognize) accrued interest continually as the amount due increased.

Businesses typically solve the recordkeeping problem by only recording accrued interest when it is time to prepare financial statements or when it is due. At such times, the accounts are *adjusted* to reflect the amount of interest currently due. For example, ATS recorded the asset exchange immediately upon investing in the Note Receivable on November 1, 2012. ATS did not, however, recognize any interest earned on the note until the balance sheet date, December 31, 2012. At year-end ATS made an entry to recognize the interest it had earned during the previous two months (November 1 through December 31). This entry is an **adjusting entry** because it adjusts (updates) the account balances prior to preparing financial statements.

ATS computed the amount of accrued interest by multiplying the principal amount of the note by the annual interest rate and by the length of time for which the note has been outstanding.

$$\text{Principal} \times \text{Annual interest rate} \times \text{Time outstanding} = \text{Interest revenue}$$
$$\$15{,}000 \times 0.06 \times (2/12) = \$150$$

ATS recognized the $150 of interest revenue in 2012 although ATS will not collect the cash until 2013. This practice illustrates the **matching concept.** Interest revenue is recognized in (matched with) the period in which it is earned regardless of when the related cash is collected. The adjustment is an asset source transaction. The asset account Interest Receivable increases, and the stockholders' equity account Retained Earnings increases. The income statement reflects an increase in revenue and net income. The statement of cash flows is not affected because ATS will not collect cash until the maturity date (October 31, 2013). The effects on the financial statements are shown below.

	Assets					=	Liab.	+	Equity	Rev.	–	Exp.	=	Net Inc.	Cash Flow
Date	Cash	+	Notes Rec.	+	Int. Rec.	=			Ret. Earn.						
12/31/12	NA	+	NA	+	150	=	NA	+	150	150	–	NA	=	150	NA

EVENT 3 Collection of Principal and Interest on the Maturity Date

ATS collected $15,900 cash on the maturity date. The collection included $15,000 for the principal plus $900 for the interest. Recall that ATS previously accrued interest in the December 31, 2012, adjusting entry for the two months in 2012 that the note was outstanding. Since year-end, ATS has earned an additional 10 months of interest revenue. ATS must recognize this interest revenue before recording the cash collection. The amount of interest earned in 2013 is computed as follows.

$$\text{Principal} \times \text{Annual interest rate} \times \text{Time outstanding} = \text{Interest revenue}$$
$$\$15{,}000 \times 0.06 \times (10/12) = \$750$$

The effects on the financial statements are shown below.

	Assets					=	Liab.	+	Equity	Rev.	–	Exp.	=	Net Inc.	Cash Flow
Date	Cash	+	Notes Rec.	+	Int. Rec.	=			Ret. Earn.						
10/31/13	NA	+	NA	+	750	=	NA	+	750	750	–	NA	=	750	NA

The total amount of accrued interest is now $900 ($150 accrued in 2012 plus $750 accrued in 2013). The $15,900 cash collection is an asset exchange transaction. The asset account Cash increases and two asset accounts, Notes Receivable and Interest Receivable, decrease. The income statement is not affected. The statement of cash flows shows a $15,000 inflow from investing activities (recovery of principal) and a $900 inflow from operating activities (interest collection). The effects on the financial statements are shown below.

Date	Assets						=	Liab.	+	Equity		Rev.	–	Exp.	=	Net Inc.	Cash Flow	
	Cash	+	Notes Rec.	+	Int. Rec.	=				Ret. Earn.								
10/31/13	15,900	+	(15,000)	+	(900)	=		NA	+	NA		NA	–	NA	=	NA	15,000	IA
																	900	OA

Financial Statements

The financial statements reveal key differences between the timing of revenue recognition and the exchange of cash. These differences are highlighted below.

	2012	2013	Total
Interest revenue recognized	$150	$750	$900
Cash inflow from operating activities	0	900	900

Accrual accounting calls for recognizing revenue in the period in which it is earned regardless of when cash is collected.

Income Statement

Although generally accepted accounting principles require reporting receipts of or payments for interest on the statement of cash flows as operating activities, they do not specify how to classify interest on the income statement. In fact, companies traditionally report interest on the income statement as a nonoperating item. Interest is therefore frequently reported in two different categories within the same set of financial statements.

Balance Sheet

As with other assets, companies report interest receivable and notes receivable on the balance sheet in order of their liquidity. **Liquidity** refers to how quickly assets are expected to be converted to cash during normal operations. In the preceding example, ATS expects to convert its accounts receivable to cash before it collects the interest receivable and note receivable. Companies commonly report interest and notes receivable after accounts receivable. Exhibit 5.6 shows a partial balance sheet for Southern Company to illustrate the presentation of receivables.

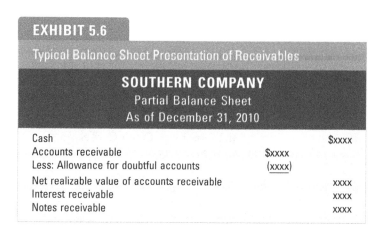

EXHIBIT 5.6

Typical Balance Sheet Presentation of Receivables

SOUTHERN COMPANY
Partial Balance Sheet
As of December 31, 2010

Cash		$xxxx
Accounts receivable	$xxxx	
Less: Allowance for doubtful accounts	(xxxx)	
Net realizable value of accounts receivable		xxxx
Interest receivable		xxxx
Notes receivable		xxxx

CHECK *Yourself* 5.3

On October 1, 2010, Mei Company accepted a promissory note for a loan it made to the Asia Pacific Company. The note had a $24,000 principal amount, a four-month term, and an annual interest rate of 4 percent. Determine the amount of interest revenue and the cash inflow from operating activities Mei will report in its 2010 and 2011 financial statements.

Answer The computation of accrued interest revenue is shown below. The interest rate is stated in annual terms even though the term of the note is only four months. Interest rates are commonly expressed as an annual percentage regardless of the term of the note. The *time outstanding* in the following formulas is therefore expressed as a fraction of a year. Mei charged annual interest of 4 percent, but the note was outstanding for only 3/12 of a year in 2010 and 1/12 of a year in 2011.

2010
Principal × Annual interest rate × Time outstanding = Interest revenue
$24,000 ×   0.04   ×   (3/12)   = $240

2011
Principal × Annual interest rate × Time outstanding = Interest revenue
$24,000 ×   0.04   ×   (1/12)   = $80

In 2010, Mei's cash inflow from interest will be zero.
In 2011, Mei will report a $320 ($240 + $80) cash inflow from operating activities for interest.

ACCOUNTING FOR CREDIT CARD SALES

Explain how accounting for credit card sales affects financial statements.

Maintaining accounts and notes receivable is expensive. In addition to uncollectible accounts expense, companies extending credit to their customers incur considerable costs for such clerical tasks as running background checks and maintaining customer records. Many businesses find it more efficient to accept third-party credit cards instead of offering credit directly to their customers. Credit card companies service the merchant's credit sales for a fee that typically ranges between 2 and 8 percent of gross sales.

The credit card company provides customers with plastic cards that permit cardholders to charge purchases at various retail outlets. When a sale takes place, the seller records the transaction on a receipt the customer signs. The receipt is forwarded to the credit card company, which immediately pays the merchant.

The credit card company deducts its service fee from the gross amount of the sale and pays the merchant the net balance (gross amount of sale less credit card fee) in cash. The credit card company collects the gross sale amount directly from the customer. The merchant avoids the risk of uncollectible accounts as well as the cost of maintaining customer credit records. To illustrate, assume that Allen's Tutoring Service experiences the following events.

EVENT 1   Recognition of Revenue and Expense on Credit Card Sales
ATS accepts a credit card payment for $1,000 of services rendered.

Assume the credit card company charges a 5 percent fee for handling the transaction ($1,000 × 0.05 = $50). ATS's income increases by the amount of revenue ($1,000) and decreases by the amount of the credit card expense ($50). Net income increases by $950. The event increases an asset, accounts receivable, due from the credit card company, and stockholders' equity (retained earnings) by $950 ($1,000 revenue − $50 credit card expense). Cash flow is not affected. These effects are shown here.

Event No.	Assets	=	Liab.	+	Equity	Rev.	−	Exp.	=	Net Inc.	Cash Flow
	Accts. Rec.	=			Ret. Earn.						
1	950	=	NA	+	950	1,000	−	50	=	950	NA

EVENT 2 Collection of Credit Card Receivable
The collection of the receivable due from the credit card company is recorded like any other receivable collection.

When ATS collects the net amount of $950 ($1,000 − $50) from the credit card company, one asset account (Cash) increases and another asset account (Accounts Receivable) decreases. Total assets are not affected. The income statement is not affected. A $950 cash inflow is reported in the operating activities section of the statement of cash flows. These effects are illustrated below.

Event No.	Assets			=	Liab.	+	Equity	Rev.	−	Exp.	=	Net Inc.	Cash Flow
	Cash	+	Accts. Rec.	=									
2	950	+	(950)	=	NA	+	NA	NA	−	NA	=	NA	950 OA

COSTS OF CREDIT SALES

As mentioned earlier, two costs of extending credit to customers are bad debts expense and record-keeping costs. These costs can be significant. Large companies spend literally millions of dollars to buy the equipment and pay the staff necessary to operate entire departments devoted to managing accounts receivable. Further, there is an implicit interest charge associated with extending credit. When a customer is permitted to delay payment, the creditor forgoes the opportunity to invest the amount the customer owes.

LO 6

Identify and measure the cost of extending credit to customers.

Exhibit 5.7 presents part of a footnote from a recent annual report of Rent-A-Center. This excerpt provides insight into the credit costs real companies incur. First, observe that Rent-A-Center was owed $23.7 million of accounts receivable. These receivables represent money that could be in the bank earning interest if all sales had been made in cash. If Rent-A-Center could have earned interest at 5 percent on that money, the opportunity cost of this lost interest is approximately $1.2 million ($23.7 million × .05) a year. Next, observe that Rent-A-Center expects to have uncollectible accounts amounting to $3.3 million (balance in the allowance account). These are indeed significant costs to a company whose net earnings were $135.8 million.

Average Number of Days to Collect Accounts Receivable

The longer it takes to collect accounts receivable, the greater the opportunity cost of lost income. Also, business experience indicates that the older an account receivable

EXHIBIT 5.7

Rent-A-Center, Inc. December 31
PARTIAL FOOTNOTE B Regarding Accounts Receivable and
Allowance for Doubtful Accounts (amounts shown in thousands)

Receivables consist of the following:

	Recent	Previous
Installment sales receivable	$18,356	$16,919
Financial service loans receivable	2,757	—
Trade receivables	2,607	1,956
Total	23,720	18,875
Less allowance for doubtful accounts	(3,317)	(2,606)
Net receivables	$20,403	$16,269

Changes in the Company's allowance for doubtful accounts are as follows:

	Recent	Previous
Beginning balance	$2,606	$1,918
Bad debt expense	1,581	1,101
Addition from acquisition	114	—
Accounts written off	(1,271)	(744)
Recoveries	287	331
Ending balance	$3,317	$2,606

becomes, the less likely it is to be collected. Finally, taking longer to collect an account typically costs more for salaries, equipment, and supplies used in the process of trying to collect it. Businesses are therefore concerned about how long it takes to collect their receivables.

Two ratios help management, or other users, measure a company's collection period. One is the **accounts receivable turnover ratio,** computed as.[1]

$$\frac{\text{Sales}}{\text{Accounts receivable}}$$

Dividing a company's sales by its accounts receivable tells how many times the accounts receivable balance is "turned over" (converted into cash) each year. The higher the turnover, the shorter the collection period. To simplify its interpretation, the accounts receivable turnover ratio is often taken one step further to determine the **average number of days to collect accounts receivable,** sometimes called the *average collection period*. This is computed as.

$$\frac{365}{\text{Accounts receivable turnover ratio}}$$

This ratio measures how many days, on average, it takes a company to collect its accounts receivable. Since longer collection periods increase costs, shorter periods are obviously more desirable. To illustrate computing the *average number of days to collect accounts receivable* for Allen's Tutoring Services, refer to the 2011 financial statements in Exhibit 5.2. On average, the company takes 104 days to collect its receivables, computed in two steps:

1. The accounts receivable turnover is 3.509 ($10,000 ÷ $2,850) times.
2. The average number of days to collect receivables is 104 (365 ÷ 3.509) days.

In the preceding computations, the net realizable value of accounts receivable was used because that is the amount typically reported in published financial statements. The results would not have been materially different had total accounts receivable been used.

Real-World Data

What is the collection period for real companies? The time required to collect receivables varies among industries and among companies within industries. Column 4 in Exhibit 5.8 displays the average number of days to collect receivables for eight companies in three different industries.

Since fast-food restaurants require customers to pay cash when they purchase hamburgers or coffee, why do these companies have accounts receivable? The accounts receivable for Yum! Brands and McDonald's arise because these companies sell goods to restaurants that are independent franchisees. So, for example, Yum's accounts receivable represents future collections from restaurant owners, not customers who purchase pepperoni pizzas at Pizza Hut restaurants.

---

[1]To be more precise, the ratio could be computed using only credit sales and average accounts receivable. Usually, however, companies do not report credit sales separately from cash sales in published financial statements. Average accounts receivable, if desired, is computed as [(beginning receivables + ending receivables) ÷ 2]. For this course, use the simpler computation shown here (sales ÷ accounts receivable).

EXHIBIT 5.8

Industry	Company	Average Days to Sell Inventory	Average Days to Collect Receivables	Length of Operating Cycle
Fast Food	McDonald's	10	14	24
	Starbucks	77	11	88
	Yum! Brands	12	9	21
Office Supplies	Office Depot	50	31	81
	OfficeMax	59	24	83
	Staples	54	13	67
Wine	Concha y Toro	203	92	295
	Willamette Valley Vineyards	348	42	390

Are the collection periods for Concha y Toro and Willamette Valley too long? The answer depends on their credit policies. If they are selling goods to customers on net 30-day terms, there may be reason for concern, but if they allow customers 90 days to pay and the cost of this policy has been built into their pricing structure, the collection periods may not be unreasonable.

Some companies allow their customers extended time to pay their bills because the customers would otherwise have difficulty coming up with the money. For example, Concha y Toro may sell to a wine retailer that does not have the cash available to pay immediately. If Concha y Toro allows the retailer sufficient time, the retailer can sell the wine to customers and obtain the cash it needs to pay Concha y Toro. Many small companies do not have cash available to pay up front. Buying on credit is the only way they can obtain the inventory they need. If a manufacturer or wholesaler wants to sell to such companies, credit sales represent the only option available.

The **operating cycle** is defined as the average time it takes a business to convert inventory to accounts receivable plus the time it takes to convert accounts receivable into cash. The average number of days to collect receivables ratio is one component of the operating cycle for a particular company. The other component is the average number of days to sell inventory ratio that will be explained in Chapter 6. The length of the operating cycles for the real-world companies discussed herein is shown in the last column of Exhibit 5.8.

What is the significance of the different operating cycle lengths in Exhibit 5.8? As previously explained, the longer the operating cycle takes, the more it costs the company. Exhibit 5.8 shows it takes OfficeMax an average of 16 days longer than Staples to complete an operating cycle. All other things being equal, approximately how much did this longer time reduce OfficeMax's earnings? Assume OfficeMax could invest excess cash at 8 percent (or alternatively, assume it pays 8 percent to finance its inventory and accounts receivable). Using the accounting information reported in OfficeMax's, financial statements, we can answer the question as follows.

$$\text{OfficeMax's investment in inventory} \times \text{Interest rate} \times \text{Time} = \text{Cost}$$

$$\$1,114,570,000 \times 8\% \times 16/365 = \$3,908,629$$

With 4.4 operating cycles per year (365 ÷ 83), the extended operating cycle costs OfficeMax $17.2 million annually. Based on the assumptions used here, OfficeMax would increase its after-tax net earnings by approximately 5 percent if it could reduce its operating cycle by 16 days. Although this illustration is a rough estimate, it demonstrates that it is important for businesses to minimize the length of their operating cycles.

Focus On INTERNATIONAL ISSUES

A ROSE BY ANY OTHER NAME . . .

If a person who studied U.S. GAAP wanted to look at the financial statements of a non-U.S. company, choosing statements of a company from another English-speaking country might seem logical. Presumably, this would eliminate language differences, and only the differences in GAAP would remain. However, this is not true.

When an accountant in the United States uses the term *turnover*, she or he is usually thinking of a financial ratio, such as the accounts receivable turnover ratio. However, in the United Kingdom, the term *turnover* refers to what U.S. accountants call *sales*. U.K. balance sheets do not usually show an account named *Inventory*; rather, they use the term *Stocks*. In the United States, accountants typically use the term *stocks* to refer to certificates representing ownership in a corporation. Finally, if an accountant or banker from the United Kingdom should ever ask you about your *gearing ratio*, he or she probably is not interested in your bicycle but in your debt to assets ratio.

CHECK *Yourself* 5.4

Randolph Corporation had sales for the year of $535,333 and an accounts receivable balance at year end of $22,000. Determine Randolph's average number of days to collect accounts receivable.

Answer The accounts receivable turnover is 24.33 ($535,333 ÷ $22,000) times per year. The average number of days to collect accounts receivable is 15 (365 ÷ 24.33).

<< A Look Back

We first introduced accounting for receivables in Chapter 2. This chapter presented additional complexities related to accounts receivable, such as the *allowance method of accounting for uncollectible accounts*. The allowance method improves matching of expenses with revenues. It also provides a more accurate measure of the value of accounts receivable on the balance sheet.

Under the allowance method, estimated uncollectible accounts expense is recorded in an adjusting entry at the end of the period in which a company has made credit sales. There are two methods commonly used to estimate the amount of uncollectible accounts expense: the percent of revenue method and the percent of receivables method. With the percent of revenue method, uncollectible accounts expense is measured as a percent of the period's sales. With the percent of receivables method, a company analyzes its accounts receivable at the end of the period, usually classifying them by age, to estimate the amount of the accounts receivable balance that is likely to be uncollectible. The balance in the Allowance for Doubtful Accounts account is then adjusted to equal the estimated amount of uncollectible accounts. Uncollectible accounts expense decreases the net realizable value of receivables (accounts receivable − allowance for doubtful accounts), stockholders' equity, and net income.

The allowance method of accounting for uncollectible accounts is conceptually superior to the *direct write-off method,* in which uncollectible accounts expense is recognized when an account is determined to be uncollectible. The direct write-off method fails to match revenues with expenses and overstates accounts receivable on the balance sheet. It is easier to use, however, and is permitted by generally accepted accounting principles if the amount of uncollectible accounts expense is immaterial.

The chapter also introduced notes receivable and accounting for *accrued interest.* When the term of a promissory note extends over more than one accounting period, companies must record adjusting entries to recognize interest in the appropriate accounting period, even if the cash exchange of interest occurs in a different accounting period.

We also discussed accounting for credit card sales, a vehicle that shifts uncollectible accounts expense to the credit card issuer. Many companies find the benefits of accepting major credit cards to be worth the credit card expense consequently incurred.

Finally, we addressed the costs of making credit sales. In addition to uncollectible accounts expense, interest is a major cost of financing receivables. The length of the collection period provides a measure of the quality of receivables. Short collection periods usually indicate lower amounts of uncollectible accounts and interest cost. Long collection periods imply higher costs. The collection period can be measured in two steps. First, divide sales by the accounts receivable balance to determine the accounts receivable turnover ratio. Then divide the number of days in the year (365) by the accounts receivable turnover ratio.

A Look Forward

Chapter 6 discusses accounting for long-term assets such as buildings and equipment. As with inventory cost flow, discussed in Chapter 4, GAAP allows companies to use different accounting methods to report on similar types of business events. Life would be easier for accounting students if all companies used the same accounting methods. However, the business world is complex. For the foreseeable future, people are likely to continue to have diverse views as to the best way to account for a variety of business transactions. To function effectively in today's business environment, it is important for you to be able to recognize differences in reporting practices.

 SELF-STUDY REVIEW PROBLEM

During 2010 Calico Company experienced the following accounting events.

1. Provided $120,000 of services on account.
2. Collected $85,000 cash from accounts receivable.
3. Wrote off $1,800 of accounts receivable that were uncollectible.
4. Loaned $3,000 to an individual, Emma Gardner, in exchange for a note receivable.
5. Paid $90,500 cash for operating expenses.
6. Estimated that uncollectible accounts expense would be 2 percent of credit sales. Recorded the year-end adjusting entry.
7. Recorded the year-end adjusting entry for accrued interest on the note receivable (see Event 4). Calico made the loan on August 1. It had a six-month term and a 6 percent rate of interest.

Calico's ledger balances on January 1, 2010, were as follows.

Event No.	Cash	+	Accts. Rec.	−	Allow.	+	Notes Rec.	+	Int. Rec.	=	Liab.	+	Com. Stk.	+	Ret. Earn.
Bal.	12,000		18,000		2,200	+	NA	+	NA	=	NA	+	20,000	+	7,800

Required

a. Record the 2010 events in ledger accounts using the horizontal format shown above.
b. Determine net income for 2010.
c. Determine net cash flow from operating activities for 2010.
d. Determine the net realizable value of accounts receivable at December 31, 2010.
e. What amount of interest revenue will Calico recognize on its note receivable in 2011?

Solution to Requirement a.

Event No.	Cash	+	Accts. Rec.	−	Allow.	+	Notes Rec.	+	Int. Rec.	=	Liab.	+	Com. Stk.	+	Ret. Earn.
Bal.	12,000	+	18,000	−	2,200	+	NA	+	NA	=	NA	+	20,000	+	7,800
1	NA	+	120,000	−	NA	+	NA	+	NA	=	NA	+	NA	+	120,000
2	85,000	+	(85,000)	−	NA	+	NA	+	NA	=	NA	+	NA	+	NA
3	NA	+	(1,800)	−	(1,800)	+	NA	+	NA	=	NA	+	NA	+	NA
4	(3,000)	+	NA	−	NA	+	3,000	+	NA	=	NA	+	NA	+	NA
5	(90,500)	+	NA	−	NA	+	NA	+	NA	=	NA	+	NA	+	(90,500)
6	NA	+	NA	−	2,400	+	NA	+	NA	=	NA	+	NA	+	(2,400)
7	NA	+	NA	−	NA	+	NA	+	75*	=	NA	+	NA	+	75
Totals	3,500	+	51,200	−	2,800	+	3,000	+	75	=	NA	+	20,000	+	34,975

*$3,000 × .06 × 5/12 = $75.

Solution to Requirements b–e.

b. Net income is $27,175 ($120,000 − $90,500 − $2,400 + $75).
c. Net cash flow from operating activities is an outflow of $5,500 ($85,000 − $90,500).
d. The net realizable value of accounts receivable is $48,400 ($51,200 − $2,800).
e. In 2011, Calico will recognize interest revenue for one month: $3,000 × .06 × 1/12 = $15.

KEY TERMS

QUESTIONS

1. What is the difference between accounts receivable and notes receivable?
2. What is the *net realizable value* of receivables?
3. What type of account is the Allowance for Doubtful Accounts?
4. What are two ways in which estimating uncollectible accounts improves the accuracy of the financial statements?
5. When using the allowance method, why is uncollectible accounts expense an estimated amount?
6. What is the most common format for reporting accounts receivable on the balance sheet? What information does this method provide beyond showing only the net amount?
7. Why is it necessary to reinstate a previously written off account receivable before the collection is recorded?
8. What are some factors considered in estimating the amount of uncollectible accounts receivable?
9. What is the effect on the accounting equation of recognizing uncollectible accounts expense?
10. What is the effect on the accounting equation of writing off an uncollectible account receivable when the allowance method is used?
11. How does the recovery of a previously written-off account affect the income statement when the allowance method is used? How does the recovery of a previously written-off account affect the statement of cash flows when the allowance method is used?
12. What is the advantage of using the allowance method of accounting for uncollectible accounts?
13. How do companies determine the percentage estimate of uncollectible accounts when using the percent of revenue method?
14. What is an advantage of using the percent of receivables method of estimating uncollectible accounts expense?
15. What is "aging of accounts receivable"?
16. What is a promissory note?

17. Define the following terms:
    a. Maker
    b. Payee
    c. Principal
    d. Interest
    e. Maturity date
    f. Collateral
18. What is the formula for computing interest revenue?
19. What is accrued interest?
20. How does the accrual of interest revenue or expense illustrate the matching concept?
21. Assets are listed on the balance sheet in the order of their liquidity. Explain this statement.
22. When is an adjusting entry for accrued interest generally recorded?
23. Assume that on July 1, 2010, Big Corp. loaned Little Corp. $12,000 for a period of one year at 6 percent interest. What amount of interest revenue will Big report for 2010? What amount of cash will Big receive upon maturity of the note?
24. In which section of the statement of cash flows will Big report the cash collected in question 23?
25. Why is it generally beneficial for a business to accept major credit cards as payment for goods and services even when the fee charged by the credit card company is substantial?
26. What types of costs do businesses avoid when they accept major credit cards as compared with handling credit sales themselves?
27. How is the accounts receivable turnover ratio computed? What information does the ratio provide?
28. How is the average number of days to collect accounts receivable computed? What information does the ratio provide?
29. Is accounting terminology standard in all countries? What term is used in the United Kingdom to refer to *sales*? What term is used to refer to *inventory*? What is a *gearing ratio*? Is it important to know about these differences?
30. What is the operating cycle of a business?

EXERCISES

All applicable Exercises are available with McGraw-Hill *Connect Accounting*.

connect
|ACCOUNTING

Exercise 5-1 *Accounting for uncollectible accounts: allowance method*

LO 1

Gold's Carpet Cleaning began operation on January 1, 2012. The company experienced the following events for its first year of operations.

1. Provided $150,000 of cleaning services on account.
2. Collected $115,000 cash from accounts receivable.
3. Paid salaries of $42,000 for the year.
4. Adjusted the accounts to reflect management's expectations that uncollectible accounts expense would be $2,300.

Required

a. Organize the transaction data in accounts under on accounting equation.

b. Prepare an income statement, balance sheet, and statement of cash flows for 2012.

LO 1

Exercise 5-2 *Analysis of financial statement effects of accounting for uncollectible accounts under the allowance method*

Businesses using the allowance method for the recognition of uncollectible accounts expense commonly experience four accounting events.

1. Recognition of revenue on account.
2. Collection of cash from accounts receivable.
3. Recognition of uncollectible accounts expense through a year-end adjusting entry.
4. Write-off of uncollectible accounts.

Required

Show the effect of each event on the elements of the financial statements, using a horizontal statements model like the one shown here. Use the following coding scheme to record your answers: increase is +, decrease is −, not affected is NA. In the cash flow column, indicate whether the item is an operating activity (OA), investing activity (IA), or financing activity (FA). The first transaction is entered as an example.

Event No.	Assets	=	Liab.	+	Equity	Rev.	−	Exp.	=	Net Inc.	Cash Flow
1	+		NA		+	+		NA		+	NA

LO 2

Exercise 5-3 *Effect of recognizing uncollectible accounts expense on financial statements: percent of revenue allowance method*

Pete's Auto Service was started on January 1, 2010. The company experienced the following events during its first year of operation.

Events affecting 2010

1. Provided $50,000 of repair services on account.
2. Collected $35,000 cash from accounts receivable.
3. Adjusted the accounting records to reflect the estimate that uncollectible accounts expense would be 1 percent of the service revenue on account.

Events affecting 2011

1. Wrote off a $350 account receivable that was determined to be uncollectible.
2. Provided $65,000 of repair services on account.
3. Collected $66,000 cash from accounts receivable.
4. Adjusted the accounting records to reflect the estimate that uncollectible accounts expense would be 1 percent of the service revenue on account.

Required

a. Organize the transaction data in accounts under an accounting equation.

b. Determine the following amounts:

(1) Net income for 2010.

(2) Net cash flow from operating activities for 2010.

(3) Balance of accounts receivable at the end of 2010.

(4) Net realizable value of accounts receivable at the end of 2010.

c. Repeat Requirement *b* for the 2011 accounting period.

Exercise 5-4   *Analyzing financial statement effects of accounting for uncollectible accounts using the percent of revenue allowance method*   LO 2

Duffy Bros. uses the allowance method to account for bad debts expense. Duffy experienced the following four events in 2008.

1. Recognition of $64,000 of service revenue on account.
2. Collection of $56,000 cash from accounts receivable.
3. Determination that $900 of its accounts were not collectible and wrote off these receivables.
4. Recognition of uncollectible accounts expense for the year. Duffy estimates that bad debts expense will be 2 percent of its sales.

Required

Show the effect of each of these events on the elements of the financial statements, using a horizontal statements model like the following one. Use + for increase, − for decrease, and NA for not affected. In the cash flow column, indicate whether the item is an operating activity (OA), investing activity (IA), or financing activity (FA).

Event No.	Assets					=	Liab.	+	Equity	Rev.	−	Exp.	=	Net Inc.	Cash Flow
	Cash	+	Accts. Rec.	−	Allow.	=			Ret. Earn.						

Exercise 5-5   *Analyzing account balances for a company using the allowance method of accounting for uncollectible accounts*   LO 1

The following account balances come from the records of Springfield Company.

	Beginning Balance	Ending Balance
Accounts receivable	$4,000	$4,500
Allowance for doubtful accounts	550	600

During the accounting period, Springfield recorded $32,000 of service revenue on account. The company also wrote off a $300 account receivable.

Required

a. Determine the amount of cash collected from receivables.
b. Determine the amount of uncollectible accounts expense recognized during the period.

Exercise 5-6   *Effect of recovering a receivable previously written off*   LO 1, 2

The accounts receivable balance for T&M Lumber at December 31, 2010, was $96,000. Also on that date, the balance in the Allowance for Doubtful Accounts was $3,600. During 2011, $2,400 of accounts receivable were written off as uncollectible. In addition, T&M Lumber unexpectedly collected $250 of receivables that had been written off in a previous accounting period. Sales on account during 2011 were $265,000, and cash collections from receivables were $275,000. Uncollectible accounts expense was estimated to be 1 percent of the sales on account for the period.

Required

a. Organize the information in accounts under an accounting equation.
b. Based on the preceding information, compute (after year-end adjustment):
    (1) Balance of Allowance for Doubtful Accounts at December 31, 2010.
    (2) Balance of Accounts Receivable at December 31, 2010.
    (3) Net realizable value of Accounts Receivable at December 31, 2010.
c. What amount of uncollectible accounts expense will T&M Lumber report for 2010?
d. Explain how the $250 recovery of receivables affected the accounting equation.

LO 2

Exercise 5-7   *Accounting for uncollectible accounts: percent of revenue allowance method*

Dixie Auto Parts sells new and used auto parts. Although a majority of its sales are cash sales, it makes a significant amount of credit sales. During 2012, its first year of operations, Dixie Auto Parts experienced the following.

Sales on account	$175,000
Cash sales	550,000
Collections of accounts receivable	168,000
Uncollectible accounts charged off during the year	1,200

Required

Assume that Dixie Auto Parts uses the allowance method of accounting for uncollectible accounts and estimates that 1 percent of its sales on account will not be collected. Answer the following questions.

a. What is the Accounts Receivable balance at December 31, 2012?
b. What is the ending balance of the Allowance for Doubtful Accounts at December 31, 2012, after all entries and adjusting entries are posted?
c. What is the amount of uncollectible accounts expense for 2012?
d. What is the net realizable value of accounts receivable at December 31, 2012?

LO 2

Exercise 5-8   *Determining account balances: allowance method of accounting for uncollectible accounts*

During the first year of operation, 2010, Holt Appliance Co. recognized $300,000 of service revenue on account. At the end of 2010, the accounts receivable balance was $58,000. For this first year in business, the owner believes uncollectible accounts expense will be about 1 percent of sales on account.

Required

a. What amount of cash did Holt collect from accounts receivable during 2010?
b. Assuming Holt uses the allowance method to account for uncollectible accounts, what amount should Holt record as uncollectible accounts expense for 2010?
c. What is the net realizable value of receivables at the end of 2010?
d. Show the effects of the above transactions *c* on the financial statements by recording the appropriate amounts in a horizontal statements model like the one shown here. In the Cash Flow column, indicate whether the item is an operating activity (OA), investing activity (IA), or financing activity (FA). Use NA for not affected.

Assets			=	Liab.	+	Equity	Rev.	−	Exp.	=	Net Inc.	Cash Flow
Cash	+	Accts. Rec.	−	Allow.								

LO 3

Exercise 5-9   *Accounting for uncollectible accounts: percent of receivables allowance method*

Posey Service Co. experienced the following transactions for 2011, its first year of operations:

1. Provided $72,000 of services on account.
2. Collected $56,000 cash from accounts receivable.
3. Paid $30,000 of salaries expense for the year.
4. Posey adjusted the accounts using the following information from an accounts receivable aging schedule.

Number of Days Past Due	Amount	Percent Likely to Be Uncollectible	Allowance Balance
Current	$12,000	.01	
0–30	2,000	.05	
31–60	500	.10	
61–90	500	.30	
Over 90 days	1,000	.50	

Required

a. Organize the information in accounts under an accounting equation.
b. Prepare the income statement for Posey Service Co. for 2011.
c. What is the net realizable value of the accounts receivable at December 31, 2011?

Exercise 5-10 *Effect of recognizing uncollectible accounts on the financial statements: percent of receivables allowance method*   LO 3

Guidry Inc. experienced the following events for the first two years of its operations.

2012:

1. Provided $80,000 of services on account.
2. Provided $35,000 of services and received cash.
3. Collected $65,000 cash from accounts receivable.
4. Paid $21,000 of salaries expense for the year.
5. Adjusted the accounting records to reflect uncollectible accounts expense for the year. Guidry estimates that 6 percent of the ending accounts receivable balance will be uncollectible.

2013:

1. Wrote off an uncollectible account of $710.
2. Provided $95,000 of services on account.
3. Provided $45,000 of services and collected cash.
4. Collected $90,000 cash from accounts receivable.
5. Paid $35,000 of salaries expense for the year.
6. Adjusted the accounts to reflect uncollectible accounts expense for the year. Guidry estimates that 6 percent of the ending accounts receivable balance will be uncollectible.

Required

a. Organize the transaction data in accounts under an accounting equation.
b. Prepare the income statement, statement of changes in stockholders' equity, balance sheet, and statement of cash flows for 2011.
c. What is the net realizable value of the accounts receivable at December 31, 2011?
d. Repeat Requirements *a, b,* and *c* for 2012.

Exercise 5-11 *Effect of credit card sales on financial statements*   LO 5

Carlos, Incorporated, provided $86,000 of services during 2010. All customers paid for the services with major credit cards. Carlos turned the credit card receipts over to the credit card company immediately. The credit card company paid Carlos cash in the amount of face value less a 2 percent service charge.

Required

a. Record the credit card sales and the subsequent collection of accounts receivable in a horizontal statements model like the one shown below. In the Cash Flow column, indicate whether the item is an operating activity (OA), investing activity (IA), or financing activity (FA). Use NA to indicate that an element is not affected by the event.

Assets		=	Liab.	+	Equity	Rev.	−	Exp.	=	Net Inc.	Cash Flow
Cash	+ Accts. Rec.										

b. Answer the following questions:

(1) What is the amount of total assets at the end of the accounting period?

(2) What is the amount of revenue reported on the income statement?

(3) What is the amount of cash flow from operating activities reported on the statement of cash flows?

(4) Why would Carlos, Incorporated, accept credit cards instead of providing credit directly to its customers? In other words, why would Carlos be willing to pay 2 percent of sales to have the credit card company handle its sales on account?

LO 5

Exercise 5-12   *Recording credit card sales*

Taylor Company accepted credit cards in payment for $7,250 of merchandise sold during March 2010. The credit card company charged Taylor a 3 percent service fee. The credit card company paid Taylor as soon as it received the invoices. Cost of goods sold amounted to $4,100.

Required

Based on this information alone, what is the amount of net income earned during the month of March?

LO 4

Exercise 5-13   *Accounting for notes receivable*

Morris Enterprises loaned $60,000 to Faello Co. on October 1, 2012, for one year at 8 percent interest.

Required

Show the effects of the following transactions in a horizontal statements model like the one shown below.

(1) The loan to Faello Co.

(2) The adjusting entry at December 31, 2012.

(3) The adjusting entry and collection of the note on September 1, 2013.

	Assets					=	Liab.	+	Equity	Rev.	−	Exp.	=	Net Inc.	Cash Flow
Date	Cash	+	Notes Rec.	+	Int. Rec.	=			Ret. Earn.						

LO 4

Exercise 5-14   *Notes receivable—accrued interest*

On March 1, 2012, Sun Co. loaned $12,000 to Silena Co. for one year at 6 percent interest.

Required

Answer the following questions.

a. What is Sun Co.'s interest income for 2012?

b. What is Sun Co.'s total amount of receivables at December 31, 2012?

c. What amounts will be reported on Sun Co.'s 2012 statement of cash flows?

d. What is Sun Co.'s interest income for 2013?

e. What is the total amount of cash that Sun Co.'s will collect in 2013 from Silena Co.?

f. What amounts will be reported on Sun Co.'s 2013 statement of cash flows?

g. What is the total amount of interest Sun Co. earned from the loan to Silena Co.?

Exercise 5-15   *Comprehensive single-cycle problem*   LO 2, 4

The following after-closing trial balance was drawn from the accounts of Oak Timber Co. as of December 31, 2011.

	Debit	Credit
Cash	$26,000	
Accounts receivable	28,000	
Allowance for doubtful accounts		$ 3,000
Inventory	25,000	
Accounts payable		19,200
Common stock		20,000
Retained earnings		36,800
Totals	$79,000	$79,000

Transactions for 2012

1. Acquired an additional $20,000 cash from the issue of common stock.
2. Purchased $80,000 of inventory on account.
3. Sold inventory that cost $65,000 for $110,000. Sales were made on account.
4. Wrote off $1,400 of uncollectible accounts.
5. On September 1, Oak loaned $12,000 to Pine Co. The note had a 8 percent interest rate and a one-year term.
6. Paid $19,600 cash for salaries expense.
7. Collected $96,000 cash from accounts receivable.
8. Paid $91,000 cash on accounts payable.
9. Paid a $5,000 cash dividend to the stockholders.
10. Estimated uncollectible accounts expense to be 1 percent of sales on account.
11. Recorded the accrued interest at December 31, 2012.

Required

a. Organize the transaction data in accounts under an accounting equation.
b. Prepare an income statement, statement of changes in stockholders' equity, balance sheet, and statement of cash flows for 2012.

Exercise 5-16   *Performing ratio analysis using real-world data*   LO 6

The following data were taken from Hershey Foods Corporation's 2007 annual report. All dollar amounts are in thousands.

	Fiscal Years Ending	
	December 31, 2007	December 31, 2006
Sales	$4,946,716	$4,944,230
Accounts Receivable	487,285	522,673

Required

a. Compute Hershey's accounts receivable ratios for 2007 and 2006.
b. Compute Hershey's average days to collect accounts receivables for 2007 and 2006.
c. Based on the ratios computed in Requirements *a* and *b*, did Hershey's performance get better or worse from 2006 to 2007?
d. In 2007 the average interest rate on Hershey's long-term debt was approximately 6.4 percent. Assume it took Hershey 30 days to collect its receivables. Using an interest rate of 6.4 percent, calculate how much it cost Hershey to finance its receivables for 30 days in 2007.

198   Chapter 5

PROBLEMS

|ACCOUNTING

LO 2

**All applicable Problems are available with McGraw-Hill
Connect Accounting.**

**Problem 5-17   *Accounting for uncollectible accounts—two cycles using the percent
of revenue allowance method***

The following transactions apply to Puretz Consulting for 2010, the first year of operation.

1. Recognized $75,000 of service revenue earned on account.
2. Collected $62,000 from accounts receivable.
3. Adjusted accounts to recognize uncollectible accounts expense. Puretz uses the allowance
   method of accounting for uncollectible accounts and estimates that uncollectible accounts
   expense will be 2 percent of sales on account.

The following transactions apply to Puretz Consulting for 2011.

1. Recognized $86,500 of service revenue on account.
2. Collected $85,000 from accounts receivable.
3. Determined that $1,120 of the accounts receivable were uncollectible and wrote them off.
4. Collected $500 of an account that had been previously written off.
5. Paid $52,600 cash for operating expenses.
6. Adjusted accounts to recognize uncollectible accounts expense for 2011. Puretz estimates
   that uncollectible accounts expense will be 1 percent of sales on account.

Required

Complete all the following requirements for 2010 and 2011. Complete all requirements for 2010
prior to beginning the requirements for 2011.

a. Identify the type of each transaction (asset source, asset use, asset exchange, or claims
   exchange).
b. Show the effect of each transaction on the elements of the financial statements, using a
   horizontal statements model like the one shown here. Use + for increase, − for decrease,
   and NA for not affected. Also, in the Cash Flow column, indicate whether the item is an
   operating activity (OA), investing activity (IA), or financing activity (FA). The first transaction is entered as an example. (*Hint:* Closing entries do not affect the statements model.)

Event No.	Assets	=	Liab.	+	Equity	Rev.	−	Exp.	=	Net Inc.	Cash Flow
1	+		NA		+	+		NA		+	NA

c. Organize the transaction data in accounts under an accounting equation.
d. Prepare the income statement, statement of changes in stockholders' equity, balance sheet,
   and statement of cash flows.

LO 2

**Problem 5-18   *Determining account balances: percent of revenue allowance
method of accounting for uncollectible accounts***

The following information pertains to Royal Carpet Company's sales on account and accounts
receivable.

Accounts receivable balance, January 1, 2010	$ 64,500
Allowance for doubtful accounts, January 1, 2010	2,800
Sales on account, 2010	756,000
Cost of goods sold, 2010	505,000
Collections of accounts receivable, 2010	782,000

After several collection attempts, Royal Carpet Company wrote off $2,600 of accounts that could not be collected. Royal estimates that bad debts expense will be 0.5 percent of sales on account.

Required

a. Compute the following amounts.

    (1) Using the allowance method, the amount of uncollectible accounts expense for 2010.

    (2) Net realizable value of receivables at the end of 2010.

b. Explain why the uncollectible accounts expense amount is different from the amount that was written off as uncollectible.

Problem 5-19 *Accounting for uncollectible accounts: percent of receivables allowance method*

LO **3**

Huggins Inc. experienced the following transactions for 2010, its first year of operations.

CHECK FIGURES
b. Net Income: $46,910
Total Assets: $120,910

1. Issued common stock for $60,000 cash.

2. Purchased $210,000 of merchandise on account.

3. Sold merchandise that cost $130,000 for $245,000 on account.

4. Collected $215,000 cash from accounts receivable.

5. Paid $196,000 on accounts payable.

6. Paid $38,000 of salaries expense for the year.

7. Paid other operating expenses of $28,000.

8. Huggins adjusted the accounts using the following information from an accounts receivable aging schedule.

Number of Days Past Due	Amount	Percent Likely to Be Uncollectible	Allowance Balance
Current	$19,000	.01	
0–30	3,000	.05	
31–60	4,500	.10	
61–90	1,500	.20	
Over 90 days	2,000	.50	

Required

a. Organize the transaction data in accounts under an accounting equation.

b. Prepare the income statement, statement of changes in stockholders' equity, balance sheet, and statement of cash flows for Huggins Inc. for 2010.

c. What is the net realizable value of the accounts receivable at December 31, 2010?

Problem 5-20 *Determination of account balances—percent of receivables allowance method of accounting for uncollectible accounts*

LO **2**

During the first year of operation, 2012, Steve's Garage recognized $256,000 of service revenue on account. At the end of 2012, the accounts receivable balance was $62,300. Even though this is his first year in business, the owner believes he will collect all but about 5 percent of the ending balance.

CHECK FIGURE
c. Net Realizable Value $59,185

Required

a. What amount of cash was collected by Steve's during 2012?

b. Assuming the use of an allowance system to account for uncollectible accounts, what amount should Steve record as uncollectible accounts expense in 2012?

c. What is the net realizable value of receivables at the end of 2012?

d. Show the effect of the above transactions *c* on the financial statements by recording the appropriate amounts in a horizontal statements model like the one shown here. When you record amounts in the Cash Flow column, indicate whether the item is an operating activity

(OA), investing activity (IA), or financing activity (FA). The letters NA indicate that an element is not affected by the event.

Assets			=	Liab.	+	Equity	Rev.	−	Exp.	=	Net Inc.	Cash Flow
Cash	+	Accts. Rec.	−	Allow.								

LO **3, 5**

e**X**cel

CHECK FIGURES
b. Net Income: $43,400
   Total Assets: $93,400

Problem 5-21 *Accounting for credit card sales and uncollectible accounts: percent of receivables allowance method*

Morris Supply Company had the following transactions in 2010.

1. Acquired $50,000 cash from the issue of common stock.
2. Purchased $210,000 of merchandise for cash in 2010.
3. Sold merchandise that cost $140,000 for $265,000 during the year under the following terms.

$ 60,000	Cash sales
175,000	Credit card sales (The credit card company charges a 3 percent service fee.)
30,000	Sales on account

4. Collected all the amount receivable from the credit card company.
5. Collected $23,000 of accounts receivable.
6. Paid selling and administrative expenses of $76,000.
7. Determined that 5 percent of the ending accounts receivable balance would be uncollectible.

Required

a. Record the above events in a horizontal statements model like the following one. When you record amounts in the Cash Flow column, indicate whether the item is an operating activity (OA), an investing activity (IA), or a financing activity (FA). The letters NA indicate that an element is not affected by the event.

	Balance Sheet								Income Statement				Statemt. of
Event	Assets					=	Equity		Rev.	−	Exp.	= Net Inc.	Cash Flows
	Cash	+	Accts. Rec.	−	Allow.	+	Mdse. Inv.	=	Com. Stk.	+	Ret. Earn.		

b. Prepare an income statement, statement of changes in stockholders' equity, balance sheet, and statement of cash flows for 2010.

LO **2, 4**

Problem 5-22 *Accounting for notes receivable and uncollectible accounts using the percent of sales allowance method*

The following transactions apply to Baker Co. for 2010, its first year of operations.

1. Issued $60,000 of common stock for cash.
2. Provided $128,000 of services on account.
3. Collected $113,200 cash from accounts receivable.
4. Loaned $12,000 to BBC on September 1, 2010. The note had a one-year term to maturity and an 8 percent interest rate.
5. Paid $28,000 of salaries expense for the year.
6. Paid a $2,000 dividend to the stockholders.

7. Recorded the accrued interest on December 31, 2010 (see item 4).

8. Uncollectible accounts expense is estimated to be 1 percent of sales on account.

Required

a. Show the effects of the above transactions in a horizontal statements model like the one shown below.

	Assets					Equity		Rev. − Exp. = Net Inc.	Cash Flows
Event	Cash +	Accts. Rec. − Allow. for Doubtful Accts.	+ Notes Rec.	+ Int. Rec. =		Com. Stk. +	Ret. Earn.		

b. Prepare the income statement, balance sheet, and statement of cash flows for 2010.

Problem 5-23   *Effect of transactions on the elements of financial statements*   LO 1, 4, 5

Required

Identify each of the following independent transactions as asset source (AS), asset use (AU), asset exchange (AE), or claims exchange (CE). Also explain how each event affects assets, liabilities, stockholders' equity, net income, and cash flow by placing a + for increase, − for decrease, or NA for not affected under each of the categories. The first event is recorded as an example.

Event	Type of Event	Assets	Liabilities	Common Stock	Retained Earnings	Net Income	Cash Flow
a	AE	+/−	NA	NA	NA	NA	−

a. Paid cash for land.

b. Sold merchandise at a price above cost. Accepted payment by credit card. The credit card company charges a service fee. The receipts have not yet been forwarded to the credit card company.

c. Submitted receipts to the credit card company (see *b* above) and collected cash.

d. Recovered an uncollectible account that was previously written off (assume direct write-off method was used).

e. Provided services for cash.

f. Paid cash for other operating expenses.

g. Paid cash for salaries expense.

h. Loaned Carl Maddox cash. The loan had a 5 percent interest rate and a one-year term to maturity.

i. Paid cash to creditors on accounts payable.

j. Provided services on account.

k. Sold land for cash at its cost.

l. Paid cash to satisfy salaries payable.

m. Accrued three months' interest on the note receivable (see *h* above).

n. Collected cash from customers paying their accounts.

o. Wrote off an uncollectible account (use allowance method).

Problem 5-24   *Multistep income statement and balance sheet*   LO 1, 4

Required

Use the following information to prepare a multistep income statement and a classified balance sheet for Reza Equipment Co. for 2010. (*Hint:* Some of the items will *not* appear on either statement, and ending retained earnings must be calculated.)

Salaries expense	$ 96,000	Interest receivable (short term)	$ 500
Common stock	40,000	Beginning retained earnings	18,100
Notes receivable (short term)	12,000	Operating expenses	70,000
Allowance for doubtful accounts	4,000	Cash flow from investing activities	80,000
Accumulated depreciation	30,000	Prepaid rent	9,600
Notes payable (long term)	103,600	Land	36,000
Salvage value of building	4,000	Cash	17,800
Interest payable (short term)	1,800	Inventory	122,800
Uncollectible accounts expense	10,800	Accounts payable	46,000
Supplies	1,600	Interest expense	24,000
Equipment	60,000	Salaries payable	9,200
Interest revenue	4,200	Unearned revenue	52,600
Sales revenue	396,000	Cost of goods sold	143,000
Dividends	8,000	Accounts receivable	90,000
Rent expense	3,400		

LO 2, 4

Problem 5-25   *Missing information*

The following information comes from the accounts of Jersey Company.

Account Title	Beginning Balance	Ending Balance
Accounts receivable	$30,000	$34,000
Allowance for doubtful accounts	1,800	1,700
Notes receivable	40,000	40,000
Interest receivable	1,200	3,600

Required

a. There were $170,000 in sales on account during the accounting period. Write-offs of uncollectible accounts were $1,400. What was the amount of cash collected from accounts receivable? What amount of uncollectible accounts expense was reported on the income statement? What was the net realizable value of receivables at the end of the accounting period?

b. The note has a 6 percent interest rate and 24 months to maturity. What amount of interest revenue was recognized during the period? How much cash was collected for interest?

LO 2, 4, 5

Problem 5-26   *Comprehensive accounting cycle problem (uses percent of revenue allowance method)*

The following trial balance was prepared for Gifts, Etc., Inc., on December 31, 2010, after the closing entries were posted.

	Debit	Credit
Cash	$110,000	
Accounts receivable	136,000	
Allowance for doubtful accounts		$ 10,000
Inventory	690,000	
Accounts payable		98,000
Common stock		720,000
Retained earnings		108,000
Totals	$936,000	$936,000

Gifts, Etc. had the following transactions in 2011.

1. Purchased merchandise on account for $360,000.
2. Sold merchandise that cost $250,000 for $465,000 on account.
3. Sold for $240,000 cash merchandise that had cost $144,000.

4. Sold merchandise for $180,000 to credit card customers. The merchandise had cost $108,000. The credit card company charges a 3 percent fee.

5. Collected $526,000 cash from accounts receivable.

6. Paid $430,000 cash on accounts payable.

7. Paid $134,000 cash for selling and administrative expenses.

8. Collected cash for the full amount due from the credit card company.

9. Issued a $48,000 face value, interest-bearing note with an 8 percent interest rate and a one-year term to maturity.

10. Wrote off $7,200 of accounts as uncollectible.

11. Made the following adjusting entries:

    (a) Recorded uncollectible accounts expense estimated at 1 percent of sales on account.

    (b) Recorded seven months of accrued interest on the note at December 31, 2011.

Required

a. Organize the transaction data in accounts under an accounting equation.

b. Prepare an income statement, a statement of changes in stockholders' equity, a balance sheet, and a statement of cash flows for 2011.

Problem 5-27 *Performing ratio analysis using real-world data*

LO 6

AutoZone, Inc., claims to be "the nation's leading specialty retailer and a leading distributor of automotive replacement parts and accessories." It sells replacement auto parts directly to the consumer. BorgWarner, Inc., has over 17,000 employees and produces automobile parts, such as transmissions and cooling systems, for the world's vehicle manufacturers. The following data were taken from these companies' 2007 annual reports. All dollar amounts are in thousands.

	AutoZone August 25, 2007	BorgWarner December 31, 2007
Sales	$6,169,804	$5,328,600
Accounts receivable	59,876	802,400

Required

a. Before performing any calculations, speculate as to which company will take the longest to collect its accounts receivable. Explain the rationale for your decision.

b. Calculate the accounts receivable turnover ratios for AutoZone and BorgWarner.

c. Calculate the average days to collect accounts receivables for AutoZone and BorgWarner.

d. Do the calculations from Requirements *b* and *c* confirm your speculations in Requirement *a*?

ANALYZE, THINK, COMMUNICATE

ATC 5-1 Business Applications Case *Understanding real-world annual reports*

Required

Use the Topps Company's annual report in Appendix B to answer the following questions.

a. How long did it take Topps to collect accounts receivable during the year ended February 25, 2006?

b. Approximately what percentage of accounts receivable, as of February 25, 2006, does the company think will not be collected (see Note 4)? Caution, "Reserve for returns," also shown in Note 4, is not related to uncollectible accounts receivable.

c. What do you think the balance in the Reserve for Returns account represents?

ATC 5-2 Group Assignment *Missing information*

The following selected financial information is available for three companies.

	Bell	Card	Zore
Total sales	$125,000	$210,000	?
Cash sales	?	26,000	$120,000
Sales on account	40,000	?	75,000
Accounts receivable, January 1, 2012	6,200	42,000	?
Accounts receivable, December 31, 2012	5,600	48,000	7,500
Allowance for doubtful accounts, January 1, 2012	?	?	405
Allowance for doubtful accounts, December 31, 2012	224	1,680	?
Uncollectible accounts expense, 2012	242	1,200	395
Uncollectible accounts written off	204	1,360	365
Collections of accounts receivable, 2012	?	?	75,235

Required

a. Divide the class into three sections and divide each section into groups of three to five students. Assign one of the companies to each of the sections.

Group Tasks

(1) Determine the missing amounts for your company.

(2) Determine the percentage of accounts receivable estimated to be uncollectible at the end of 2011 and 2012 for your company.

(3) Determine the percentage of total sales that are sales on account for your company.

(4) Determine the accounts receivable turnover for your company.

Class Discussion

b. Have a representative of each section put the missing information on the board and explain how it was determined.

c. Which company has the highest percentage of sales that are on account?

d. Which company is doing the best job of collecting its accounts receivable? What procedures and policies can a company use to better collect its accounts receivable?

ATC 5-3 Real-World Case *Time needed to collect accounts receivable*

Presented here are the average days to collect accounts receivable for four companies in different industries. The data are for 2007.

Company	Average Days to Collect Accounts Receivables
Boeing (aircraft manufacturer)	32 days
Ford (automobile manufacturer—automotive operations only)	11
Haverty's (furniture retailer)	31
Whirlpool (household appliance manufacturer)	49

Required

Write a brief memorandum that provides answers to the following questions.

a. Why would a company that manufactures large expensive items such as cars (Ford) collect its accounts receivables faster than a company that makes appliances (Whirlpool)?

b. Why would a company that manufactures airplanes (Boeing) collect its accounts receivables as quickly as a company that sells furniture (Haverty's)?

ATC 5-4   Business Applications Case   *Using average number of days to collect accounts receivable to make comparisons*

The following information was drawn from the accounting records of Hedges and Latour.

Account Title	Hedges	Latour
Accounts receivable (year end)	$ 80,000	$ 50,000
Sales on account	920,000	450,000

Required

a. Determine the average number of days to collect accounts receivable for each company.
b. Which company is likely to incur more costs associated with extending credit?
c. Identify and discuss some of the costs associated with extending credit.
d. Explain why a company would be willing to accept the costs of extending credit to its customers.

ATC 5-5   Business Applications Case   *Using ratios to make comparisons*

The following accounting information exists for Anjou and Bartlett companies at the end of 2010.

	Anjou	Bartlett
Cash	$ 25,000	$ 70,000
Accounts receivable	105,000	260,000
Allowance for doubtful accounts	5,000	10,000
Merchandise inventory	75,000	150,000
Accounts payable	80,000	200,000
Cost of goods sold	475,000	630,000
Sales	650,000	1,000,000

Required

a. For each company, compute the gross margin percentage and the average number of days to collect accounts receivable (use the net realizable value of receivables to compute the average days to collect accounts receivable).
b. In relation to cost, which company is charging more for its merchandise?
c. Which company is likely to incur higher financial costs associated with the granting of credit to customers? Explain.
d. Which company appears to have more restrictive credit standards when authorizing credit to its customers? (*Hint:* There is no specific answer to this question. Use your judgment and general knowledge of ratios to answer.)

ATC 5-6   Writing Assignment   *Cost of charge sales*

Paul Smith is opening a plumbing supply store in University City. He plans to sell plumbing parts and materials to both wholesale and retail customers. Since contractors (wholesale customers) prefer to charge parts and materials and pay at the end of the month, Paul expects he will have to offer charge accounts. He plans to offer charge sales to the wholesale customers only and to require retail customers to pay with either cash or credit cards. Paul wondered what expenses his business would incur relative to the charge sales and the credit cards.

Required

a. What issues will Paul need to consider if he allows wholesale customers to buy plumbing supplies on account?
b. Write a memo to Paul Smith outlining the potential cost of accepting charge customers. Discuss the difference between the allowance method for uncollectible accounts and the direct write-off method. Also discuss the cost of accepting credit cards.

ATC 5-7   Corporate Governance   *How bad can it be?*

Alonzo Saunders owns a small training services company that is experiencing growing pains. The company has grown rapidly by offering liberal credit terms to its customers. Although his competitors require payment for services within 30 days, Saunders permits his customers to delay payment for up to 90 days. Saunders' customers thereby have time to fully evaluate the training that employees receive before they must pay for that training. Saunders guarantees satisfaction. If a customer is unhappy, the customer does not have to pay. Saunders works with reputable companies, provides top-quality training, and rarely encounters dissatisfied customers.

The long collection period, however, has created a cash flow problem. Saunders has a $100,000 accounts receivable balance, but needs cash to pay current bills. He has recently negotiated a loan agreement with National Bank of Brighton County that should solve his cash flow problems. The loan agreement requires that Saunders pledge the accounts receivable as collateral for the loan. The bank agreed to loan Saunders 70 percent of the receivables balance, thereby giving him access to $70,000 cash. Saunders is satisfied with this arrangement because he estimates he needs approximately $60,000.

On the day Saunders was to execute the loan agreement, he heard a rumor that his biggest customer was experiencing financial problems and might declare bankruptcy. The customer owed Saunders $45,000. Saunders promptly called the customer's chief accountant and learned "off the record" that the rumor was true. The accountant told Saunders that the company's net worth was negative and most of its assets were pledged as collateral for bank loans. In his opinion, Saunders was unlikely to collect the balance due. Saunders' immediate concern was the impact the circumstances would have on his loan agreement with the bank.

Saunders uses the direct write-off method to recognize uncollectible accounts expense. Removing the $45,000 receivable from the collateral pool would leave only $55,000 of receivables, reducing the available credit to $38,500 ($55,000 × 0.70). Even worse, recognizing the uncollectible accounts expense would so adversely affect his income statement that the bank might further reduce the available credit by reducing the percentage of receivables allowed under the loan agreement. Saunders will have to attest to the quality of the receivables at the date of the loan but reasons that since the information he obtained about the possible bankruptcy was "off the record" he is under no obligation to recognize the uncollectible accounts expense until the receivable is officially uncollectible.

Required

a. How are income and assets affected by the decision not to act on the bankruptcy information?

b. Review the AICPA's Articles of Professional Conduct (see Chapter 2) and comment on any of the standards that would be violated by the actions Saunders is contemplating.

c. How do the elements of the fraud triangle (see Chapter 2) apply to this case?

ATC 5-8   Research Assignment   *Comparing Toro Company's time to collect accounts receivable*

Using the most current annual reports or the Forms 10-K for Toro Company, complete the requirements below. To obtain the Forms 10-K use either the EDGAR system following the instructions in Appendix A or the companies' websites. The annual reports can be found on the companies' websites.

Required

a. What was Toro's average days to collect accounts receivable? Show your computations.

b. What percentage of accounts receivable did Toro estimate would not be collected?

c. Did Toro provide any information about warranties that it provides to customers? If so, what information was provided? (*Hint:* Look at the accrued warranty footnote.)

d. Does it appear that Toro's warranty costs have been decreasing or increasing?

CHAPTER *6*

Accounting *for* Long-Term Operational Assets

LEARNING OBJECTIVES

After you have mastered the material in this chapter you will be able to:

1 Identify different types of long-term operational assets.

2 Determine the cost of long-term operational assets.

3 Explain how different depreciation methods affect financial statements.

4 Determine how gains and losses on disposals of long-term operational assets affect financial statements.

5 Show how revising estimates affects financial statements.

6 Explain how continuing expenditures for operational assets affect financial statements.

7 Explain how expense recognition for natural resources (depletion) affects financial statements.

8 Explain how expense recognition for intangible assets (amortization) affects financial statements.

9 Understand how expense recognition choices and industry characteristics affect financial performance measures.

CHAPTER OPENING

Companies use assets to produce revenue. Some assets, like inventory or office supplies, are called **current assets** because they are used relatively quickly (within a single accounting period). Other assets, like equipment or buildings, are used for extended periods of time (two or more accounting periods). These assets are called **long-term operational assets.**[1] Accounting for long-term assets raises several questions. For example, what is the cost of the asset? Is it the list price only or should the cost of transportation, transit insurance,

[1] Classifying assets as current versus long term is explained in more detail in Chapter 7.

Financial

setup, and so on be added to the list price? Should the cost of a long-term asset be recognized as expense in the period the asset is purchased or should the cost be expensed over the useful life of the asset? What happens in the accounting records when a long-term asset is retired from use? This chapter answers these questions. It explains accounting for long-term operational assets from the date of purchase through the date of disposal.

The *Curious* Accountant

In the normal course of operations, most companies acquire long-term assets each year. The way in which a company hopes to make money with these assets varies according to the type of business and the asset acquired. During a recent accounting period, Weyerhaeuser Company made cash acquisitions of property and equipment of $861 million and cash acquisitions of timber and timberlands of $96 million.

Can you think of how Weyerhaeuser's use of trees to produce revenue differs from its use of trucks? Do you think the procedures used to account for timber should be similar to or different from those used to account for trucks, and if so, how? (Answers on page 213.)

TANGIBLE VERSUS INTANGIBLE ASSETS

LO 1

Identify different types of long-term operational assets.

Long-term assets may be tangible or intangible. **Tangible assets** have a physical presence; they can be seen and touched. Tangible assets include equipment, machinery, natural resources, and land. In contrast, intangible assets have no physical form. Although they may be represented by physical documents, **intangible assets** are, in fact, rights or privileges. They cannot be seen or touched. For example, a patent represents an exclusive legal *privilege* to produce and sell a particular product. It protects inventors by making it illegal for others to profit by copying their inventions. Although a patent may be represented by legal documents, the privilege is the actual asset. Since the privilege cannot be seen or touched, the patent is an intangible asset.

Tangible Long-Term Assets

Tangible long-term assets are classified as (1) property, plant, and equipment; (2) natural resources, or (3) land.

Property, Plant, and Equipment

Property, plant, and equipment is sometimes called *plant assets* or *fixed assets.* Examples of property, plant, and equipment include furniture, cash registers, machinery, delivery trucks, computers, mechanical robots, and buildings. The level of detail used to account for these assets varies. One company may include all office equipment in one account, whereas another company might divide office equipment into computers, desks, chairs, and so on. The term used to recognize expense for property, plant, and equipment is **depreciation.**

Natural Resources

Mineral deposits, oil and gas reserves, timber stands, coal mines, and stone quarries are examples of **natural resources.** Conceptually, natural resources are inventories. When sold, the cost of these assets is frequently expensed as *cost of goods sold.* Although inventories are usually classified as short-term assets, natural resources are normally classified as long term because the resource deposits generally have long lives. For example, it may take decades to extract all of the diamonds from a diamond mine. The term used to recognize expense for natural resources is **depletion.**

Land

Land is classified separately from other property because land is not subject to depreciation or depletion. Land has an infinite life. It is not worn out or consumed as it is used. When buildings or natural resources are purchased simultaneously with land, the amount paid must be divided between the land and the other assets because of the nondepreciable nature of the land.

Intangible Assets

Intangible assets fall into two categories, those with *identifiable useful lives* and those with *indefinite useful lives.*

Intangible Assets with Identifiable Useful Lives

Intangible assets with identifiable useful lives include patents and copyrights. These assets may become obsolete (a patent may become worthless if new technology provides a superior product) or may reach the end of their legal lives. The term used when recognizing expense for intangible assets with identifiable useful lives is called **amortization.**

Intangible Assets with Indefinite Useful Lives

The benefits of some intangible assets may extend so far into the future that their useful lives cannot be estimated. For how many years will the Coca-Cola trademark attract customers? When will the value of a McDonald's franchise end? There are no answers to these questions. Intangible assets such as renewable franchises, trademarks, and goodwill have indefinite useful lives. The costs of such assets are not expensed unless the value of the assets becomes impaired.

DETERMINING THE COST OF LONG-TERM ASSETS

The **historical cost concept** requires that an asset be recorded at the amount paid for it. This amount includes the purchase price plus any costs necessary to get the asset in the location and condition for its intended use. Common cost components are:

Determine the cost of long-term operational assets.

- **Buildings:** (1) purchase price, (2) sales taxes, (3) title search and transfer document costs, (4) realtor's and attorney's fees, and (5) remodeling costs.
- **Land:** (1) purchase price, (2) sales taxes, (3) title search and transfer document costs, (4) realtor's and attorney's fees, (5) costs for removal of old buildings, and (6) grading costs.
- **Equipment:** (1) purchase price (less discounts), (2) sales taxes, (3) delivery costs, (4) installation costs, and (5) costs to adapt for intended use.

The cost of an asset does not include payments for fines, damages, and so on that could have been avoided.

CHECK *Yourself* 6.1

Sheridan Construction Company purchased a new bulldozer that had a $260,000 list price. The seller agreed to allow a 4 percent cash discount in exchange for immediate payment. The bulldozer was delivered FOB shipping point at a cost of $1,200. Sheridan hired a new employee to operate the dozer for an annual salary of $36,000. The employee was trained to operate the dozer for a one-time training fee of $800. The cost of the company's theft insurance policy increased by $300 per year as a result of adding the dozer to the policy. The dozer had a five-year useful life and an expected salvage value of $26,000. Determine the asset's cost.

Answer

List price	$260,000
Less: Cash discount ($260,000 × 0.04)	(10,400)
Shipping cost	1,200
Training cost	800
Total asset cost (amount capitalized)	$251,600

Basket Purchase Allocation

Acquiring a group of assets in a single transaction is known as a **basket purchase.** The total price of a basket purchase must be allocated among the assets acquired. Accountants commonly allocate the purchase price using the **relative fair market value method.** To illustrate, assume that Beatty Company purchased land and a building for $240,000 cash. A real estate appraiser determined the fair market value of each asset to be

Building	$270,000
Land	90,000
Total	$360,000

212   Chapter 6

The appraisal indicates that the land is worth 25 percent ($90,000 ÷ $360,000) of the total value and the building is worth 75 percent ($270,000 ÷ $360,000). Using these percentages, the actual purchase price is allocated as follows.

Building	0.75 × $240,000 =	$180,000
Land	0.25 × $240,000 =	60,000
Total		$240,000

METHODS OF RECOGNIZING DEPRECIATION EXPENSE

LO 3

Explain how different depreciation methods affect financial statements.

EXHIBIT 6.1

Life Cycle of an Operational Asset

EXHIBIT 6.2

Depreciation Methods Used by U.S. Companies

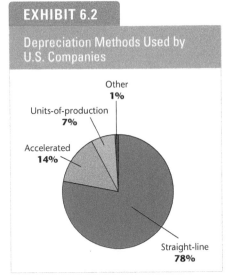

Data Source: AICPA Accounting Trends and Techniques.

The life cycle of an operational asset involves (1) acquiring the funds to buy the asset, (2) purchasing the asset, (3) using the asset, and (4) retiring (disposing of) the asset. These stages are illustrated in Exhibit 6.1. The stages involving (1) acquiring funds and (2) purchasing assets have been discussed previously. This section of the chapter describes how accountants recognize the *use* of assets (Stage 3). As they are used, assets suffer from wear and tear called *depreciation*. Ultimately, assets depreciate to the point that they are no longer useful in the process of earning revenue. This process usually takes several years. The amount of an asset's cost that is allocated to expense during an accounting period is called **depreciation expense.**

An asset that is fully depreciated by one company may still be useful to another company. For example, a rental car that is no longer useful to Hertz may still be useful to a local delivery company. As a result, companies are frequently able to sell their fully depreciated assets to other companies or individuals. The expected market value of a fully depreciated asset is called its **salvage value.** The total amount of depreciation a company recognizes for an asset, its **depreciable cost,** is the difference between its original cost and its salvage value.

For example, assume a company purchases an asset for $5,000. The company expects to use the asset for 5 years (the **estimated useful life**) and then to sell it for $1,000 (salvage value). The depreciable cost of the asset is $4,000 ($5,000 − $1,000). The portion of the depreciable cost ($4,000) that represents its annual usage is recognized as depreciation expense.

Accountants must exercise judgment to estimate the amount of depreciation expense to recognize each period. For example, suppose you own a personal computer. You know how much the computer cost, and you know you will eventually need to replace it. How would you determine the amount the computer depreciates each year you use it? Businesses may use any of several acceptable methods to estimate the amount of depreciation expense to recognize each year.

The method used to recognize depreciation expense should match the asset's usage pattern. More expense should be recognized in periods when the asset is used more and less in periods when the asset is used less. Since assets are used to produce revenue, matching expense recognition with asset usage also matches expense recognition with revenue recognition. Three alternative methods for recognizing depreciation expense are (1) straight-line, (2) double-declining-balance, and (3) units-of-production.

The *straight-line* method produces the same amount of depreciation expense each accounting period. *Double-declining-balance,* an accelerated method, produces more depreciation expense in the early years of an asset's life, with a declining amount of expense in later years. *Units-of-production* produces varying amounts of depreciation expense in different accounting periods (more in some accounting periods and less in others). Exhibit 6.2 contrasts the different depreciation methods that U.S. companies use.

Answers to The *Curious* Accountant

Equipment is a long-term asset used for the purpose of producing revenue. A portion of the equipment's cost is recognized as depreciation expense each accounting period. The expense recognition for the cost of equipment is therefore spread over the useful life of the asset. Timber, however, is not used until the trees are grown. Conceptually, the costs of the trees should be treated as inventories and expensed as cost of goods sold at the time the products made from trees are sold. Even so, some timber companies recognize a periodic charge called *depletion* in a manner similar to that used for depreciation.

Accounting for unusual long-term assets such as timber requires an understanding of specialized "industry practice" accounting rules that are beyond the scope of this course. Many industries have unique accounting problems, and business managers in such industries must understand specialized accounting rules that relate to their companies.

Dryden Enterprises Illustration

To illustrate the different depreciation methods, consider a van purchased by Dryden Enterprises. Dryden plans to use the van as rental property. The van had a list price of $23,500. Dryden obtained a 10 percent cash discount from the dealer. The van was delivered FOB shipping point, and Dryden paid an additional $250 for transportation costs. Dryden also paid $2,600 for a custom accessory package to increase the van's appeal as a rental vehicle. The cost of the van is computed as follows.

List price	$23,500	
Less: Cash discount	(2,350)	$23,500 × 0.10
Plus: Transportation costs	250	
Plus: Cost of customization	2,600	
Total	$24,000	

The van has an estimated *salvage value* of $4,000 and an *estimated useful life* of four years. The following section examines three different patterns of expense recognition for this van.

Straight-Line Depreciation

The first scenario assumes the van is used evenly over its four-year life. The revenue from renting the van is assumed to be $8,000 per year. The matching concept calls for the expense recognition pattern to match the revenue stream. Since the same amount of revenue is recognized in each accounting period, Dryden should use **straight-line depreciation** because it produces equal amounts of depreciation expense each year.

Life Cycle Phase 1

The first phase of the asset life cycle is to acquire funds to purchase the asset. Assume Dryden acquired $25,000 cash on January 1, 2008, by issuing common stock. The effects on the financial statements follow.

Assets				=	Equity			Rev.	−	Exp.	=	Net Inc.	Cash Flow
Cash	+ Van	−	Acc. Dep.	=	Com. Stk.	+	Ret. Earn.						
25,000	+ NA	−	NA	=	25,000	+	NA	NA	−	NA	=	NA	25,000 FA

Life Cycle Phase 2

The second phase of the life cycle is to purchase the van. Assume Dryden bought the van on January 1, 2008, using funds from the stock issue. The cost of the van, previously computed, was $24,000 cash. The effects on the financial statements are:

Assets				=	Equity			Rev.	−	Exp.	=	Net Inc.	Cash Flow
Cash	+ Van	−	Acc. Dep.	=	Com. Stk.	+	Ret. Earn.						
(24,000)	+ 24,000	−	NA	=	NA	+	NA	NA	−	NA	=	NA	(24,000) IA

Life Cycle Phase 3

Dryden used the van by renting it to customers. The rent revenue each year is $8,000 cash. The effects on the financial statements are shown next.

Assets				=	Equity			Rev.	−	Exp.	=	Net Inc.	Cash Flow
Cash	+ Van	−	Acc. Dep.	=	Com. Stk.	+	Ret. Earn.						
8,000	+ NA	−	NA	=	NA	+	8,000	8,000	−	NA	=	8,000	8,000 OA

Although illustrated only once, these effects occur four times—once for each year Dryden earns revenue by renting the van.

At the end of each year, Dryden adjusts its accounts to recognize depreciation expense. The amount of depreciation recognized using the straight-line method is calculated as follows.

$$(\text{Asset cost} - \text{Salvage value}) \div \text{Useful life} = \text{Depreciation expense}$$
$$(\$24,000 - \$4,000) \div 4 \text{ years} = \$5,000 \text{ per year}$$

Recognizing depreciation expense is an asset use transaction that reduces assets and equity. The asset reduction is reported using a **contra asset account** called **Accumulated Depreciation.** Recognizing depreciation expense *does not affect cash flow.* The entire cash outflow for this asset occurred in January 2008 when Dryden purchased the van. Depreciation reflects *using* tangible assets, not spending cash to purchase them. The effects on the financial statements are as follows.

Assets				=	Equity			Rev.	−	Exp.	=	Net Inc.	Cash Flow
Cash	+ Van	−	Acc. Dep.	=	Com. Stk.	+	Ret. Earn.						
NA	+ NA	−	5,000	=	NA	+	(5,000)	NA	−	5,000	=	(5,000)	NA

The Depreciation *Expense* account, like other expense accounts, is closed to the Retained Earnings account at the end of each year. The *Accumulated* Depreciation account, in contrast, increases each year, *accumulating* the total amount of depreciation recognized on the asset to date.

Life Cycle Phase 4

The final stage in the life cycle of a tangible asset is its disposal and removal from the company's records. Dryden retired the van from service on January 1, 2012, selling it for $4,500 cash. The van's **book value** (cost − accumulated depreciation) when it was sold was $4,000 ($24,000 cost − $20,000 accumulated depreciation), so Dryden recognized a $500 gain ($4,500 − $4,000) on the sale.

Determine how gains and losses on disposals of long-term operational assets affect financial statements.

Gains are *like* revenues in that they increase assets or decrease liabilities. Gains are *unlike* revenues in that gains result from peripheral (incidental) transactions rather than routine operating activities. Dryden is not in the business of selling vans. Dryden's normal business activity is renting vans. Since selling vans is incidental to Dryden's normal operations, gains are reported separately, after operating income, on the income statement.

If Dryden had sold the asset for less than book value, the company would have recognized a loss on the asset disposal. Losses are similar to expenses in that they decrease assets or increase liabilities. However, like gains, losses result from peripheral transactions. Losses are also reported as nonoperating items on the income statement.

The effects of the asset disposal on the financial statements are shown next.

Assets				=	Equity			Rev. or Gain	−	Exp. or Loss	=	Net Inc.	Cash Flow
Cash	+	Van	− Acc. Dep.	=	Com. Stk.	+	Ret. Earn.						
4,500	+	(24,000)	− (20,000)	=	NA	+	500	500	−	NA	=	500	4,500 IA

Although the gain reported on the 2012 income statement is $500, the cash inflow from selling the van is $4,500. Gains and losses are not reported on the statement of cash flows. Instead they are included in the total amount of cash collected from the sale of the asset. In this case, the entire $4,500 is shown in the cash flow from investing activities section of the 2012 statement of cash flows.

Financial Statements

Exhibit 6.3 displays a vertical statements model that shows the financial results for the Dryden illustration from 2008 through 2012. Study the exhibit until you understand how all the figures were derived. The amount of depreciation expense ($5,000) reported on the income statement is constant each year from 2008 through 2011. The amount of accumulated depreciation reported on the balance sheet grows from $5,000 to $10,000, to $15,000, and finally to $20,000. The Accumulated Depreciation account is a *contra asset account* that is subtracted from the Van account in determining total assets.

Study the timing differences between cash flow and net income. Dryden spent $24,000 cash to acquire the van. Over the van's life cycle, Dryden collected $36,500 [($8,000 revenue × 4 years = $32,000) plus ($4,500 from the asset disposal) = $36,500]. The $12,500 difference between the cash collected and the cash paid ($36,500 − $24,000) equals the total net income earned during the van's life cycle.

Although the amounts are the same, the timing of the cash flows and the income recognition are different. For example, in 2008 there was a $24,000 cash outflow to purchase the van and an $8,000 cash inflow from customers. In contrast, the income statement reports net income of $3,000. In 2012, Dryden reported a $500 gain on the asset disposal, but the amount of operating income and the cash flow from operating

EXHIBIT 6.3	Financial Statements under Straight-Line Depreciation

DRYDEN ENTERPRISES
Financial Statements

	2008	2009	2010	2011	2012
Income Statements					
Rent revenue	$ 8,000	$ 8,000	$ 8,000	$ 8,000	$ 0
Depreciation expense	(5,000)	(5,000)	(5,000)	(5,000)	0
Operating income	3,000	3,000	3,000	3,000	0
Gain on sale of van	0	0	0	0	500
Net income	$ 3,000	$ 3,000	$ 3,000	$ 3,000	$ 500
Balance Sheets					
Assets					
Cash	$ 9,000	$17,000	$25,000	$33,000	$37,500
Van	24,000	24,000	24,000	24,000	0
Accumulated depreciation	(5,000)	(10,000)	(15,000)	(20,000)	0
Total assets	$28,000	$31,000	$34,000	$37,000	$37,500
Stockholders' equity					
Common stock	$25,000	$25,000	$25,000	$25,000	$25,000
Retained earnings	3,000	6,000	9,000	12,000	12,500
Total stockholders' equity	$28,000	$31,000	$34,000	$37,000	$37,500
Statements of Cash Flows					
Operating Activities					
Inflow from customers	$ 8,000	$ 8,000	$ 8,000	$ 8,000	$ 0
Investing Activities					
Outflow to purchase van	(24,000)				
Inflow from sale of van					4,500
Financing Activities					
Inflow from stock issue	25,000				
Net Change in Cash	9,000	8,000	8,000	8,000	4,500
Beginning cash balance	0	9,000	17,000	25,000	33,000
Ending cash balance	$ 9,000	$17,000	$25,000	$33,000	$37,500

activities is zero for that year. The gain is only indirectly related to cash flows. The $4,500 of cash received on disposal is reported as a cash inflow from investing activities. Since gains and losses result from peripheral transactions, they do not affect operating income or cash flow from operating activities.

Double-Declining-Balance Depreciation

Explain how different depreciation methods affect financial statements.

For the second scenario, assume demand for the van is strong when it is new, but fewer people rent the van as it ages. As a result, the van produces smaller amounts of revenue as time goes by. To match expenses with revenues, it is reasonable to recognize more depreciation expense in the van's early years and less as it ages.

Double-declining-balance depreciation produces a large amount of depreciation in the first year of an asset's life and progressively smaller levels of expense in each succeeding year. Since the double-declining-balance method recognizes depreciation expense more rapidly than the straight-line method does, it is called an **accelerated**

depreciation method. Depreciation expense recognized using double-declining-balance is computed in three steps.

1. *Determine the straight-line rate.* Divide one by the asset's useful life. Since the estimated useful life of Dryden's van is four years, the straight-line rate is 25 percent ($1 \div 4$) per year.

2. *Determine the double-declining-balance rate.* Multiply the straight-line rate by 2 (*double* the rate). The double-declining-balance rate for the van is 50 percent (25 percent $\times$ 2).

3. *Determine the depreciation expense.* Multiply the double-declining-balance rate by the book value of the asset *at the beginning of the period* (recall that book value is historical cost minus *accumulated depreciation*). The following table shows the amount of depreciation expense Dryden will recognize over the van's useful life (2008–2011).

Year	Book Value at Beginning of Period	×	Double the Straight-Line Rate	=	Annual Depreciation Expense	
2008	($24,000 − $ 0)	×	0.50	=	$12,000	
2009	(24,000 − 12,000)	×	0.50	=	6,000	
2010	(24,000 − 18,000)	×	0.50	=	~~3,000~~	2,000
2011	(24,000 − 20,000)	×	0.50	=	~~2,000~~	0

Regardless of the depreciation method used, *an asset cannot be depreciated below its salvage value.* This restriction affects depreciation computations for the third and fourth years. Because the van had a cost of $24,000 and a salvage value of $4,000, the total amount of depreciable cost (historical cost − salvage value) is $20,000 ($24,000 − $4,000). Since $18,000 ($12,000 + $6,000) of the depreciable cost is recognized in the first two years, only $2,000 ($20,000 − $18,000) remains to be recognized after the second year. Depreciation expense recognized in the third year is therefore $2,000 even though double-declining-balance computations suggest that $3,000 should be recognized. Similarly, zero depreciation expense is recognized in the fourth year even though the computations indicate a $2,000 charge.

CHECK *Yourself* 6.2

Olds Company purchased an asset that cost $36,000 on January 1, 2010. The asset had an expected useful life of five years and an estimated salvage value of $5,000. Assuming Olds uses the double-declining-balance method, determine the amount of depreciation expense and the amount of accumulated depreciation Olds would report on the 2012 financial statements.

Answer

Year	Book Value at Beginning of Period ×	Double the Straight-Line Rate* =	Annual Depreciation Expense
2010	($36,000 − $ 0) ×	0.40 =	$14,400
2011	(36,000 − 14,400) ×	0.40 =	8,640
2012	(36,000 − 23,040) ×	0.40 =	5,184
Total accumulated depreciation at December 31, 2012			$28,224

*Double-declining-balance rate = 2 × Straight-line rate = 2 × (1 ÷ 5 years) = 0.40

EXHIBIT 6.4	Financial Statements under Double-Declining-Balance Depreciation				
DRYDEN ENTERPRISES					
Financial Statements					
	2008	2009	2010	2011	2012
Income Statements					
Rent revenue	$15,000	$ 9,000	$ 5,000	$ 3,000	$ 0
Depreciation expense	(12,000)	(6,000)	(2,000)	0	0
Operating income	3,000	3,000	3,000	3,000	0
Gain on sale of van	0	0	0	0	500
Net income	$ 3,000	$ 3,000	$ 3,000	$ 3,000	$ 500
Balance Sheets					
Assets					
Cash	$16,000	$25,000	$30,000	$33,000	$37,500
Van	24,000	24,000	24,000	24,000	0
Accumulated depreciation	(12,000)	(18,000)	(20,000)	(20,000)	0
Total assets	$28,000	$31,000	$34,000	$37,000	$37,500
Stockholders' equity					
Common stock	$25,000	$25,000	$25,000	$25,000	$25,000
Retained earnings	3,000	6,000	9,000	12,000	12,500
Total stockholders' equity	$28,000	$31,000	$34,000	$37,000	$37,500
Statements of Cash Flows					
Operating Activities					
Inflow from customers	$15,000	$ 9,000	$ 5,000	$ 3,000	$ 0
Investing Activities					
Outflow to purchase van	(24,000)				
Inflow from sale of van					4,500
Financing Activities					
Inflow from stock issue	25,000				
Net Change in Cash	16,000	9,000	5,000	3,000	4,500
Beginning cash balance	0	16,000	25,000	30,000	33,000
Ending cash balance	$16,000	$25,000	$30,000	$33,000	$37,500

Effects on the Financial Statements

Exhibit 6.4 displays financial statements for the life of the asset assuming Dryden uses double-declining-balance depreciation. The illustration assumes a cash revenue stream of $15,000, $9,000, $5,000, and $3,000 for the years 2008, 2009, 2010, and 2011, respectively. Trace the depreciation expense from the table above to the income statements. Reported depreciation expense is greater in the earlier years and smaller in the later years of the asset's life.

The double-declining-balance method smooths the amount of net income reported over the asset's useful life. In the early years, when heavy asset use produces higher revenue, depreciation expense is also higher. Similarly, in the later years, lower levels of revenue are matched with lower levels of depreciation expense. Net income is constant at $3,000 per year.

The depreciation method a company uses *does not* affect how it acquires the financing, invests the funds, and retires the asset. For Dryden's van, the accounting effects of these life cycle phases are the same as under the straight-line approach. Similarly, the *recording procedures* are not affected by the depreciation method. Different depreciation methods affect only the amounts of depreciation expense recorded each year, not which accounts are used.

Units-of-Production Depreciation

Suppose rental demand for Dryden's van depends on general economic conditions. In a robust economy, travel increases, and demand for renting vans is high. In a stagnant economy, demand for van rentals declines. In such circumstances, revenues fluctuate from year to year. To accomplish the matching objective, depreciation should also fluctuate from year to year. A method of depreciation known as **units-of-production depreciation** accomplishes this goal by basing depreciation expense on actual asset usage.

Explain how different depreciation methods affect financial statements.

Computing depreciation expense using units-of-production begins with identifying a measure of the asset's productive capacity. For example, the number of miles Dryden expects its van to be driven may be a reasonable measure of its productive capacity. If the depreciable asset were a saw, an appropriate measure of productive capacity could be the number of board feet the saw was expected to cut during its useful life. In other words, the basis for measuring production depends on the nature of the depreciable asset.

To illustrate computing depreciation using the units-of-production depreciation method, assume that Dryden measures productive capacity based on the total number of miles the van will be driven over its useful life. Assume Dryden estimates this productive capacity to be 100,000 miles. The first step in determining depreciation expense is to compute the cost per unit of production. For Dryden's van, this amount is total depreciable cost (historical cost − salvage value) divided by total units of expected productive capacity (100,000 miles). The depreciation cost per mile is therefore $0.20 ([$24,000 cost − $4,000 salvage] ÷ 100,000 miles). Annual depreciation expense is computed by multiplying the cost per mile by the number of miles driven. Odometer readings indicate the van was driven 40,000 miles, 20,000 miles, 30,000 miles, and 15,000 miles in 2008, 2009, 2010, and 2011, respectively. Dryden developed the following schedule of depreciation charges.

Year	Cost per Mile (a)	Miles Driven (b)	Depreciation Expense (a × b)
2008	$.20	40,000	$8,000
2009	.20	20,000	4,000
2010	.20	30,000	6,000
2011	.20	15,000	~~3,000~~ 2,000

As pointed out in the discussion of the double-declining-balance method, an asset cannot be depreciated below its salvage value. Since $18,000 of the $20,000 ($24,000 cost − $4,000 salvage) depreciable cost is recognized in the first three years of using the van, only $2,000 ($20,000 − $18,000) remains to be charged to depreciation in the fourth year, even though the depreciation computations suggest the charge should be $3,000. As the preceding table indicates, the general formula for computing units-of-production depreciation is

$$\frac{\text{Cost} - \text{Salvage value}}{\text{Total estimated units of production}} \times \frac{\text{Units of production}}{\text{in current}} = \frac{\text{Annual}}{\text{depreciation}}$$
$$\text{year} \qquad \text{expense}$$

| EXHIBIT 6.5 | Financial Statements under Units-of-Production Depreciation |

DRYDEN ENTERPRISES
Financial Statements

	2008	2009	2010	2011	2012
Income Statements					
Rent revenue	$11,000	$ 7,000	$ 9,000	$ 5,000	$ 0
Depreciation expense	(8,000)	(4,000)	(6,000)	(2,000)	0
Operating income	3,000	3,000	3,000	3,000	0
Gain on sale of van	0	0	0	0	500
Net income	$ 3,000	$ 3,000	$ 3,000	$ 3,000	$ 500
Balance Sheets					
Assets					
Cash	$12,000	$19,000	$28,000	$33,000	$37,500
Van	24,000	24,000	24,000	24,000	0
Accumulated depreciation	(8,000)	(12,000)	(18,000)	(20,000)	0
Total assets	$28,000	$31,000	$34,000	$37,000	$37,500
Stockholders' equity					
Common stock	$25,000	$25,000	$25,000	$25,000	$25,000
Retained earnings	3,000	6,000	9,000	12,000	12,500
Total stockholders' equity	$28,000	$31,000	$34,000	$37,000	$37,500
Statements of Cash Flows					
Operating Activities					
Inflow from customers	$11,000	$ 7,000	$ 9,000	$ 5,000	$ 0
Investing Activities					
Outflow to purchase van	(24,000)				
Inflow from sale of van					4,500
Financing Activities					
Inflow from stock issue	25,000				
Net Change in Cash	12,000	7,000	9,000	5,000	4,500
Beginning cash balance	0	12,000	19,000	28,000	33,000
Ending cash balance	$12,000	$19,000	$28,000	$33,000	$37,500

Exhibit 6.5 displays financial statements that assume Dryden uses units-of-production depreciation. The exhibit assumes a cash revenue stream of $11,000, $7,000, $9,000, and $5,000 for 2008, 2009, 2010, and 2011, respectively. Trace the depreciation expense from the schedule above to the income statements. Depreciation expense is greater in years the van is driven more and smaller in years the van is driven less, providing a reasonable matching of depreciation expense with revenue produced. Net income is again constant at $3,000 per year.

Comparing the Depreciation Methods

LO 3

Explain how different depreciation methods affect financial statements.

The total amount of depreciation expense Dryden recognized using each of the three methods was $20,000 ($24,000 cost − $4,000 salvage value). The different methods affect the *timing,* but not the *total amount,* of expense recognized. The different methods simply assign the $20,000 to different accounting periods. Exhibit 6.6 presents graphically the differences among the three depreciation methods discussed above. A company should use the method that most closely matches expenses with revenues.

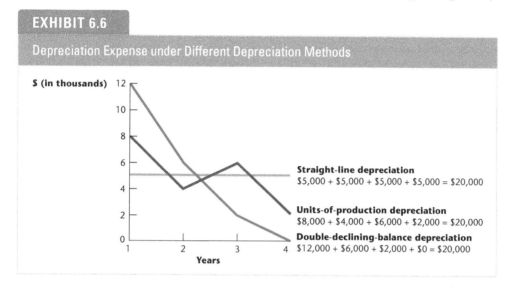

EXHIBIT 6.6

Depreciation Expense under Different Depreciation Methods

Straight-line depreciation
$5,000 + $5,000 + $5,000 + $5,000 = $20,000

Units-of-production depreciation
$8,000 + $4,000 + $6,000 + $2,000 = $20,000

Double-declining-balance depreciation
$12,000 + $6,000 + $2,000 + $0 = $20,000

REVISION OF ESTIMATES

In order to report useful financial information on a timely basis, accountants must make many estimates of future results, such as the salvage value and useful life of depreciable assets and uncollectible accounts expense. Estimates are frequently revised when new information surfaces. Because revisions of estimates are common, generally accepted accounting principles call for incorporating the revised information into present and future calculations. Prior reports are not corrected.

Show how revising estimates affects financial statements.

To illustrate, assume that McGraw Company purchased a machine on January 1, 2010, for $50,000. McGraw estimated the machine would have a useful life of 8 years and a salvage value of $3,000. Using the straight-line method, McGraw determined the annual depreciation charge as follows:

$$(\$50,000 - \$3,000) \div 8 \text{ years} = \$5,875 \text{ per year}$$

At the beginning of the fifth year, accumulated depreciation on the machine is $23,500 ($5,875 × 4). The machine's book value is $26,500 ($50,000 − $23,500). At this point, what happens if McGraw changes its estimates of useful life or the salvage value? Consider the following revision examples independently of each other.

Revision of Life

Assume McGraw revises the expected life to 14, rather than 8, years. The machine's *remaining* life would then be 10 more years instead of 4 more years. Assume salvage value remains $3,000. Depreciation for each remaining year is:

$$(\$26,500 \text{ book value} - \$3,000 \text{ salvage}) \div 10\text{-year remaining life} = \$2,350$$

Revision of Salvage

Alternatively, assume the original expected life remained 8 years, but McGraw revised its estimate of salvage value to $6,000. Depreciation for each of the remaining four years would be

$$(\$26,500 \text{ book value} - \$6,000 \text{ salvage}) \div 4\text{-year remaining life} = \$5,125$$

The revised amounts are determined for the full year, regardless of when McGraw revised its estimates. For example, if McGraw decides to change the estimated useful life on October 1, 2015, the change would be effective as of January 1, 2015. The year-end adjusting entry for depreciation would include a full year's depreciation calculated on the basis of the revised estimated useful life.

CONTINUING EXPENDITURES FOR PLANT ASSETS

Explain how continuing expenditures for operational assets affect financial statements.

Most plant assets require additional expenditures for maintenance or improvement during their useful lives. Accountants must determine if these expenditures should be expensed or capitalized (recorded as assets).

Costs That Are Expensed

The costs of routine maintenance and minor repairs that are incurred to *keep* an asset in good working order are expensed in the period in which they are incurred. Because they reduce net income when incurred, accountants often call repair and maintenance costs **revenue expenditures** (companies subtract them from revenue).

With respect to the previous example, assume McGraw spent $500 for routine lubrication and to replace minor parts. The effects on the financial statements follow.

Assets	=	Equity			Rev.	−	Exp.	=	Net Inc.	Cash Flow
Cash	=	Com. Stk.	+	Ret. Earn.						
(500)	=	NA	+	(500)	NA	−	500	=	(500)	(500) OA

Costs That Are Capitalized

Substantial amounts spent to improve the quality or extend the life of an asset are described as **capital expenditures.** Capital expenditures are accounted for in one of two ways, depending on whether the cost incurred *improves the quality* or *extends the life* of the asset.

Improving Quality

Expenditures such as adding air conditioning to an existing building or installing a trailer hitch on a vehicle improve the quality of service these assets provide. If a capital expenditure improves an asset's quality, the amount is added to the historical cost of the asset. The additional cost is expensed through higher depreciation charges over the asset's remaining useful life.

To demonstrate, return to the McGraw Company example. Recall that the machine originally cost $50,000, had an estimated salvage of $3,000, and had a predicted life of 8 years. Recall further that accumulated depreciation at the beginning of the fifth year is $23,500 ($5,875 × 4) so the book value is $26,500 ($50,000 − $23,500). Assume McGraw makes a major expenditure of $4,000 in the machine's fifth year to improve its productive capacity. The effects on the financial statements follow.

	Assets			=	Equity			Rev.	−	Exp.	=	Net Inc.	Cash Flow
Cash	+	Mach.	−	Acc. Dep.	=	Com. Stk.	+	Ret. Earn.					
(4,000)	+	4,000	−	NA	=	NA	+	NA	NA	−	NA	=	NA	(4,000) IA

After recording the expenditure, the machine account balance is $54,000 and the asset's book value is $30,500 ($54,000 − $23,500). The depreciation charges for each of the remaining four years are

($30,500 book value − $3,000 salvage) ÷ 4-year remaining life = $6,875

Extending Life

Expenditures such as replacing the roof of an existing building or putting a new engine in an older vehicle extend the useful life of these assets. If a capital expenditure extends the life of an asset rather than improving the asset's quality of service, account-ants view the expenditure as canceling some of the depreciation previously charged to expense. The event is still an asset exchange; cash decreases, and the book value of the machine increases. However, the increase in the book value of the machine results from reducing the balance in the contra asset account, Accumulated Depreciation.

To illustrate, assume that instead of increasing productive capacity, McGraw's $4,000 expenditure had extended the useful life of the machine by two years. The effects of the expenditure on the financial statements follow.

Assets				=	Equity			Rev.	−	Exp.	=	Net Inc.	Cash Flow	
Cash	+	Mach.	−	Acc. Dep.	=	Com. Stk.	+	Ret. Earn.						
(4,000)	+	NA	−	(4,000)	=	NA	+	NA	NA	−	NA	=	NA	(4,000)	IA

After the expenditure is recognized, the book value is the same as if the $4,000 had been added to the Machine account ($50,000 cost − $19,500 adjusted balance in Accumulated Depreciation = $30,500). Depreciation expense for each of the remaining six years follows.

($30,500 book value − $3,000 salvage) ÷ 6-year remaining life = $4,583

CHECK *Yourself* 6.3

On January 1, 2010, Dager Inc. purchased an asset that cost $18,000. It had a five-year useful life and a $3,000 salvage value. Dager uses straight-line depreciation. On January 1, 2012, it incurred a $1,200 cost related to the asset. With respect to this asset, determine the amount of expense and accumulated depreciation Dager would report in the 2012 financial statements under each of the following assumptions.

1. The $1,200 cost was incurred to repair damage resulting from an accident.

2. The $1,200 cost improved the operating capacity of the asset. The total useful life and salvage value remained unchanged.

3. The $1,200 cost extended the useful life of the asset by one year. The salvage value remained unchanged.

Answer

1. Dager would report the $1,200 repair cost as an expense. Dager would also report depreciation expense of $3,000 ([$18,000 − $3,000] ÷ 5). Total expenses related to this asset in 2012 would be $4,200 ($1,200 repair expense + $3,000 depreciation expense). Accumulated depreciation at the end of 2012 would be $9,000 ($3,000 depreciation expense × 3 years).

2. The $1,200 cost would be capitalized in the asset account, increasing both the book value of the asset and the annual depreciation expense.

	After Effects of Capital Improvement
Amount in asset account ($18,000 + $1,200)	$19,200
Less: Salvage value	(3,000)
Accumulated depreciation on January 1, 2012	(6,000)
Remaining depreciable cost before recording 2012 depreciation	$10,200
Depreciation for 2012 ($10,200 ÷ 3 years)	$ 3,400
Accumulated depreciation at December 31, 2012 ($6,000 + $3,400)	$ 9,400

(continued)

3. The $1,200 cost would be subtracted from the Accumulated Depreciation account, increasing the book value of the asset. The remaining useful life would increase to four years, which would decrease the depreciation expense.

	After Effects of Capital Improvement
Amount in asset account	$18,000
Less: Salvage value	(3,000)
Accumulated depreciation on January 1, 2012 ($6,000 − $1,200)	(4,800)
Remaining depreciable cost before recording 2012 depreciation	$10,200
Depreciation for 2012 ($10,200 ÷ 4 years)	$ 2,550
Accumulated depreciation at December 31, 2012 ($4,800 + $2,550)	$ 7,350

NATURAL RESOURCES

Explain how expense recognition for natural resources (depletion) affects financial statements.

The cost of natural resources includes not only the purchase price but also related items such as the cost of exploration, geographic surveys, and estimates. The process of expensing natural resources is commonly called depletion.[2] The most common method used to calculate depletion is units-of-production.

To illustrate, assume Apex Coal Mining paid $4,000,000 cash to purchase a mine with an estimated 16,000,000 tons of coal. The unit depletion charge is

$$\$4,000,000 \div 16,000,000 \text{ tons} = \$0.25 \text{ per ton}$$

If Apex mines 360,000 tons of coal in the first year, the depletion charge is:

$$360,000 \text{ tons} \times \$0.25 \text{ per ton} = \$90,000$$

The depletion of a natural resource has the same effect on the accounting equation as other expense recognition events. Assets (in this case, a *coal mine*) and stockholders' equity decrease. The depletion expense reduces net income. The effects on the financial statements follow.

Assets			=	Equity			Rev.	−	Exp.	=	Net Inc.	Cash Flow	
Cash	+	Coal Mine	=	Com. Stk.	+	Ret. Earn.							
(4,000,000)	+	4,000,000	=	NA	+	NA	NA	−	NA	=	NA	(4,000,000)	IA
NA	+	(90,000)	=	NA	+	(90,000)	NA	−	90,000	=	(90,000)	NA	

INTANGIBLE ASSETS

Explain how expense recognition for intangible assets (amortization) affects financial statements.

Intangible assets provide rights, privileges, and special opportunities to businesses. Common intangible assets include trademarks, patents, copyrights, franchises, and goodwill. Some of the unique characteristics of these intangible assets are described in the following sections.

Trademarks

A **trademark** is a name or symbol that identifies a company or a product. Familiar trademarks include the Polo emblem, the name *Coca-Cola*, and the Nike slogan, "Just

---

[2]In practice, the depletion charge is considered a product cost and allocated between inventory and cost of goods sold. This text uses the simplifying assumption that all resources are sold in the same accounting period in which they are extracted. The full depletion charge is therefore expensed in the period in which the resources are extracted.

do it." Trademarks are registered with the federal government and have an indefinite legal lifetime.

The costs incurred to design, purchase, or defend a trademark are capitalized in an asset account called Trademarks. Companies want their trademarks to become familiar but also face the risk of a trademark being used as the generic name for a product. To protect a trademark, companies in this predicament spend large sums on legal fees and extensive advertising programs to educate consumers. Well-known trademarks that have been subject to this problem include Coke, Xerox, Kleenex, and Vaseline.

Patents

A **patent** grants its owner an exclusive legal right to produce and sell a product that has one or more unique features. Patents issued by the U.S. Patent Office have a legal life of 20 years. Companies may obtain patents through purchase, lease, or internal development. The costs capitalized in the Patent account are usually limited to the purchase price and legal fees to obtain and defend the patent. The research and development costs that are incurred to develop patentable products are usually expensed in the period in which they are incurred.

$\mathscr{Focus}$ $\mathscr{On}$ INTERNATIONAL ISSUES

U.S. GAAP: A COMPETITIVE DISADVANTAGE?

As discussed earlier in this textbook, the diversity of accounting rules is decreasing among industrialized nations. This is due in large part to the fact that so many countries require their publicly listed companies to follow the accounting rules of the International Accounting Standards Board (IASB) and the efforts between the FASB and the IASB to bring their rules into closer agreement. However, there continue to be areas where significant differences exist between the accounting rules for companies in the United States and companies in other countries. Furthermore, in the opinion of the managers of some companies involved in global competition, these differences put U.S. companies at a competitive disadvantage. Accounting for research and development costs (R&D) is a good example of this situation.

Suppose that Microbiotech, Inc., is a pharmaceutical company that spent $10 million in 2011 on R&D of a new drug. If Microbiotech is a U.S. company, it is required to expense the $10 million immediately under U.S. GAAP. However, if Microbiotech is a Japanese company, using Japanese GAAP, it is allowed to capitalize the costs in an asset account and then expense it gradually, through amortization, over the useful life of the asset. As a result, in the year the R&D costs are incurred a U.S. company reports more expense, and less earnings, than its Japanese counterpart.

Some businesspeople believe that U.S. GAAP can put U.S. companies at a competitive disadvantage in the search for capital. Certainly the rules pertaining to R&D demonstrate how Microbiotech, as a U.S. company, may be required to report lower earnings in 2011 than if it had been a Japanese company, even though each company is in the same economic position. South Korea, whose companies present significant competition to U.S. companies, also permits R&D costs to be capitalized.

Keep in mind that well-informed business professionals know how different accounting rules affect a company's financial statements. If they believe that U.S. GAAP cause a company's earnings to be understated, they can take this into consideration when making business decisions.

Copyrights

A **copyright** protects writings, musical compositions, works of art, and other intellectual property for the exclusive benefit of the creator or persons assigned the right by the creator. The cost of a copyright includes the purchase price and any legal costs associated with obtaining and defending the copyright. Copyrights granted by the federal government extend for the life of the creator plus 70 years. A radio commercial could legally use a Bach composition as background music; it could not, however, use the theme song from the movie, *The Matrix,* without obtaining permission from the copyright owner. The cost of a copyright is often expensed early because future royalties may be uncertain.

Franchises

Franchises grant exclusive rights to sell products or perform services in certain geographic areas. Franchises may be granted by governments or private businesses. Franchises granted by governments include federal broadcasting licenses. Private business franchises include fast-food restaurant chains and brand labels such as Healthy Choice. The legal and useful lives of a franchise are frequently difficult to determine. Judgment is often crucial to establishing the estimated useful life for franchises.

Reality BYTES

On July 24, 2006, a group of three private equity investors offered to pay approximately $21 billion to acquire HCA, one of the nations largest hospital concerns. At the time, HCA's balance sheet showed net assets (assets minus liabilities) of approximately $4.9 billion. Why would the investors offer to pay the owners of HCA four times the value of the assets shown on the company's balance sheet?

They were willing to pay four times the book value of the assets for at least two reasons. First, the value of the assets on HCA's balance sheet represented the historical cost of the assets. The current market value of many of these assets was probably higher than their historical cost. Second, the investors probably believed that HCA had *goodwill,* which enables a company to generate above-average earnings from using its assets. In other words, they were agreeing to pay for a hidden asset not shown on HCA's balance sheet.

Goodwill

Goodwill is the value attributable to favorable factors such as reputation, location, and superior products. Consider the most popular restaurant in your town. If the owner sold the restaurant, do you think the purchase price would be simply the total value of the chairs, tables, kitchen equipment, and building? Certainly not, because much of the restaurant's value lies in its popularity; in other words, its ability to generate a high return is based on the goodwill (reputation) of the business.

Calculating goodwill can be complex; here we present a simple example to illustrate how it is determined. Suppose the accounting records of a restaurant named Bendigo's show

Assets   = Liabilities + Stockholders' Equity
$200,000 = $50,000   + $150,000

Assume a buyer agrees to purchase the restaurant by paying the owner $300,000 cash and assuming the existing liabilities. In other words, the restaurant is purchased at a price of $350,000 ($300,000 cash + $50,000 assumed liabilities). Now assume that the assets of the business (tables, chairs, kitchen equipment, etc.) have a fair market value of only $280,000. Why would the buyer pay $350,000 to purchase assets with a market value of $280,000? Obviously, the buyer is purchasing more than just the assets. The buyer is purchasing the business's goodwill. The amount of the goodwill is the difference between the purchase price and the fair market value of the assets. In this case, the goodwill is $70,000 ($350,000 − $280,000). The effects of the purchase on the financial statements of the buyer follow.

Assets					=	Liab.	+	Equity	Rev.	−	Exp.	=	Net Inc.	Cash Flow	
Cash	+	Rest. Assets	+	Goodwill											
(300,000)	+	280,000	+	70,000	=	50,000	+	NA	NA	−	NA	=	NA	(300,000)	IA

The fair market value of the restaurant assets represents the historical cost to the new owner. It becomes the basis for future depreciation charges.

EXPENSE RECOGNITION FOR INTANGIBLE ASSETS

As mentioned earlier, intangible assets fall into two categories, those with *identifiable useful lives* and those with *indefinite useful lives*. Expense recognition for intangible assets depends on which classification applies.

Expensing Intangible Assets with Identifiable Useful Lives

The costs of intangible assets with identifiable useful lives are normally expensed on a straight-line basis using a process called *amortization*. An intangible asset should be amortized over the shorter of two possible time periods: (1) its legal life or (2) its useful life.

To illustrate, assume that Flowers Industries purchased a newly granted patent for $44,000 cash. Although the patent has a legal life of 20 years, Flowers estimates that it will be useful for only 11 years. The annual amortization charge is therefore $4,000 ($44,000 ÷ 11 years). The effects on the financial statements follow.

Assets			=	Equity			Rev.	−	Exp.	=	Net Inc.	Cash Flow	
Cash	+	Patent	=	Com. Stk.	+	Ret. Earn.							
(44,000)	+	44,000	=	NA	+	NA	NA	−	NA	=	NA	(44,000)	IA
NA	+	(4,000)	=	NA	+	(4,000)	NA	−	4,000	=	(4,000)	NA	

Impairment Losses for Intangible Assets with Indefinite Useful Lives

Intangible assets with indefinite useful lives must be tested for impairment annually. The impairment test consists of comparing the fair value of the intangible asset to its carrying value (book value). If the fair value is less than the book value, an impairment loss must be recognized.

To illustrate, return to the example of the Bendigo's restaurant purchase. Recall that the buyer of Bendigo's paid $70,000 for goodwill. Assume the restaurant experiences a significant decline in revenue because many of its former regular customers are dissatisfied with the food prepared by the new chef. Suppose the decline in revenue is so substantial that the new owner believes the Bendigo's name is permanently impaired. The owner decides to hire a different chef and change the name of the restaurant. In this case, the business has suffered a permanent decline in value of goodwill. The company must recognize an impairment loss.

The restaurant's name has lost its value, but the owner believes the location continues to provide the opportunity to produce above-average earnings. Some, but not all, of the goodwill has been lost. Assume the fair value of the remaining goodwill is determined to be $40,000. The impairment loss to recognize is $30,000 ($70,000 − $40,000). The loss reduces the intangible asset (goodwill), stockholder's equity (retained earnings), and net income. The statement of cash flows would not be affected. The effects on the financial statements follow.

Assets	=	Liab.	+	Equity	Rev.	−	Exp./Loss	=	Net Inc.	Cash Flow
Goodwill	=			Ret. Earn.						
(30,000)	=	NA	+	(30,000)	NA	−	30,000	=	(30,000)	NA

BALANCE SHEET PRESENTATION

This chapter has explained accounting for the acquisition, expense recognition, and disposal of a wide range of long-term assets. Exhibit 6.7 illustrates typical balance sheet presentation of many of the assets discussed.

EXHIBIT 6.7
Balance Sheet Presentation of Operational Assets
Partial Balance Sheet

Long-Term Assets			
Plant and equipment			
Buildings	$4,000,000		
Less: Accumulated depreciation	(2,500,000)	$1,500,000	
Equipment	1,750,000		
Less: Accumulated depreciation	(1,200,000)	550,000	
Total plant and equipment			$2,050,000
Land			850,000
Natural resources			
Mineral deposits (Less: Depletion)		2,100,000	
Oil reserves (Less: Depletion)		890,000	
Total natural resources			2,990,000
Intangibles			
Patents (Less: Amortization)		38,000	
Goodwill		175,000	
Total intangible assets			213,000
Total long-term assets			$6,103,000

THE FINANCIAL ANALYST

LO 9

Understand how expense recognition choices and industry characteristics affect financial performance measures.

Managers may have differing opinions about which allocation method (straight-line, accelerated, or units-of-production) best matches expenses with revenues. As a result, one company may use straight-line depreciation while another company in similar circumstances uses double-declining-balance. Since the allocation method a company uses affects the amount of expense it recognizes, analysts reviewing financial statements must consider the accounting procedures companies use in preparing the statements.

EFFECT OF JUDGMENT AND ESTIMATION

Assume that two companies, Alpha and Zeta, experience identical economic events in 2009 and 2010. Both generate revenue of $50,000 and incur cost of goods sold of $30,000 during each year. In 2009, each company pays $20,000 for an asset with an expected useful life of five years and no salvage value. How will the companies' financial statements differ if one uses straight-line depreciation and the other uses the double-declining-balance method? To answer this question, first compute the depreciation expense for both companies for 2009 and 2010.

If Alpha Company uses the straight-line method, depreciation for 2009 and 2010 is

$$(\text{Cost} - \text{Salvage}) \div \text{Useful life} = \text{Depreciation expense per year}$$

$$(\$20{,}000 - \$0) \div 5 \text{ years} = \$4{,}000$$

In contrast, if Zeta Company uses the double-declining-balance method, Zeta recognizes the following amounts of depreciation expense for 2009 and 2010.

	(Cost − Accumulated Depreciation)	×	2 × (Straight-Line Rate)	=	Depreciation Expense
2009	($20,000 − $ 0)	×	[2 × (1 ÷ 5)]	=	$8,000
2010	($20,000 − $8,000)	×	[2 × (1 ÷ 5)]	=	$4,800

Based on these computations, the income statements for the two companies are:

Income Statements				
	2009		**2010**	
	Alpha Co.	Zeta Co.	Alpha Co.	Zeta Co.
Sales	$50,000	$50,000	$50,000	$50,000
Cost of goods sold	(30,000)	(30,000)	(30,000)	(30,000)
Gross margin	20,000	20,000	20,000	20,000
Depreciation expense	(4,000)	(8,000)	(4,000)	(4,800)
Net income	$16,000	$12,000	$16,000	$15,200

The relevant sections of the balance sheets are

Plant Assets				
	2009		**2010**	
	Alpha Co.	Zeta Co.	Alpha Co.	Zeta Co.
Assets	$20,000	$20,000	$20,000	$20,000
Accumulated depreciation	(4,000)	(8,000)	(8,000)	(12,800)
Book value	$16,000	$12,000	$12,000	$ 7,200

The depreciation method is not the only aspect of expense recognition that can vary between companies. Companies may also make different assumptions about the useful lives and salvage values of long-term operational assets. Thus, even if the same depreciation method is used, depreciation expense may still differ.

Since the depreciation method and the underlying assumptions regarding useful life and salvage value affect the determination of depreciation expense, they also affect the amounts of net income, retained earnings, and total assets. Financial statement analysis is affected if it is based on ratios that include these items. Previously defined ratios that are affected include the (1) debt to assets ratio, (2) return on assets ratio, (3) return on equity ratio, and (4) return on sales ratio.

To promote meaningful analysis, public companies are required to disclose all significant accounting policies used to prepare their financial statements. This disclosure is usually provided in the footnotes that accompany the financial statements.

EFFECT OF INDUSTRY CHARACTERISTICS

As indicated in previous chapters, industry characteristics affect financial performance measures. For example, companies in manufacturing industries invest heavily in machinery while insurance companies rely more on human capital. Manufacturing companies therefore have relatively higher depreciation charges than insurance companies. To illustrate how the type of industry affects financial reporting, examine Exhibit 6.8. This exhibit compares the ratio of sales to property, plant, and equipment for two companies in each of three different industries.

The table indicates that for every $1.00 invested in property, plant, and equipment, Kelly Services produced $31.91 of sales. In contrast, Cox Communications and United Airlines produced only $0.73 and $1.31, respectively, for each $1.00 they invested in operational assets. Does this mean the management of Kelly is doing a better job than the management of Cox Communications or United Airlines? Not necessarily. It means that these companies operate in different economic environments. In other words, it takes significantly more equipment to operate a cable company or an airline than it takes to operate an employment agency.

Effective financial analysis requires careful consideration of industry characteristics, accounting policies, and the reasonableness of assumptions such as useful life and salvage value.

EXHIBIT 6.8

Industry Data Reflecting the Use of Long-Term Tangible Assets

Industry	Company	Sales ÷ Property, Plant, and Equipment
Cable Companies	Charter Communications	0.90
	Cox Communications	0.73
Airlines	American	1.35
	United	1.31
Employment Agencies	Kelly Services	31.91
	Robert Half	30.20

<< A Look Back

This chapter explains that the primary objective of recognizing depreciation is to match the cost of a long-term tangible asset with the revenues the asset is expected to generate. The matching concept also applies to natural resources (depletion) and intangible assets (amortization). The chapter explains how alternative methods can be used to account for the same event (e.g., straight-line versus double-declining-balance depreciation).

Companies experiencing exactly the same business events could produce different financial statements. The alternative accounting methods for depreciating, depleting, or amortizing assets include the (1) straight-line, (2) double-declining-balance, and (3) units-of-production methods.

The *straight-line method* produces equal amounts of expense in each accounting period. The amount of the expense recognized is determined using the formula [(cost − salvage) ÷ number of years of useful life]. The *double-declining-balance method* produces proportionately larger amounts of expense in the early years of an asset's useful life and increasingly smaller amounts of expense in the later years of the asset's useful life. The formula for calculating double-declining-balance depreciation is [book value at beginning of period × (2 × the straight-line rate)]. The *units-of-production method* produces expense in direct proportion to the number of units produced during an accounting period. The formula for the amount of expense recognized each period is [(cost − salvage) ÷ total estimated units of production = allocation rate × units of production in current accounting period].

This chapter showed how to account for *changes in estimates* such as the useful life or the salvage value of a depreciable asset. Changes in estimates do not affect the amount of depreciation recognized previously. Instead, the remaining book value of the asset is expensed over its remaining useful life.

After an asset has been placed into service, companies typically incur further costs for maintenance, quality improvement, and extensions of useful life. *Maintenance costs are expensed in the period in which they are incurred. Costs that improve the quality* of an asset are added to the cost of the asset, increasing the book value and the amount of future depreciation charges. *Costs that extend the useful life* of an asset are subtracted from the asset's Accumulated Depreciation account, increasing the book value and the amount of future depreciation charges.

A Look Forward

In Chapter 7 we move from the assets section of the balance sheet to issues in accounting for liabilities.

 ## SELF-STUDY REVIEW PROBLEM

The following information pertains to a machine purchased by Bakersfield Company on January 1, 2010.

Purchase price	$ 63,000
Delivery cost	$ 2,000
Installation charge	$ 3,000
Estimated useful life	8 years
Estimated units the machine will produce	130,000
Estimated salvage value	$ 3,000

The machine produced 14,400 units during 2010 and 17,000 units during 2011.

Required

Determine the depreciation expense Bakersfield would report for 2010 and 2011 using each of the following methods.

a. Straight-line.

b. Double-declining-balance.

c. Units-of-production.

Solution to Requirements a–c.

a. Straight-line

Purchase price	$63,000
Delivery cost	2,000
Installation charge	3,000
Total cost of machine	68,000
Less: Salvage value	(3,000)
	$65,000 ÷ 8 = $8,125 Depreciation per year
2010	$ 8,125
2011	$ 8,125

b. Double-declining-balance

Year	Cost	−	Accumulated Depreciation at Beginning of Year	×	2 × S-L Rate	=	Annual Depreciation
2010	$68,000	−	$ 0	×	(2 × 0.125)	=	$17,000
2011	68,000	−	17,000	×	(2 × 0.125)	=	12,750

c. Units-of-production

(1) (Cost − Salvage value) ÷ Estimated units of production = Depreciation cost per unit produced

$$\frac{\$68,000 - \$3,000}{130,000} = \$0.50 \text{ per unit}$$

(2) Cost per unit × Annual units produced = Annual depreciation expense

$$2005 \quad \$0.50 \times 14,400 = \$7,200$$

$$2006 \quad 0.50 \times 17,000 = 8,500$$

KEY TERMS

Accelerated depreciation method 216	Current assets 208	Goodwill 226	Relative fair market value method 211
Accumulated Depreciation 214	Depletion 210	Historical cost concept 211	Revenue expenditures 222
Amortization 210	Depreciable cost 212	Intangible assets 210	Salvage value 212
Basket purchase 211	Depreciation 210	Long-term operational assets 208	Straight-line depreciation 213
Book value 215	Depreciation expense 212		Tangible assets 210
Capital expenditures 222	Double-declining-balance depreciation 216	Natural resources 210	Trademark 224
Contra asset account 214	Estimated useful life 212	Patent 225	Units-of-production depreciation 219
Copyright 225	Franchise 226	Property, plant, and equipment 210	

QUESTIONS

1. What is the difference between the functions of long-term operational assets and investments?

2. What is the difference between tangible and intangible assets? Give an example of each.

3. What is the difference between goodwill and specifically identifiable intangible assets?

4. Define *depreciation*. What kind of asset depreciates?

5. Why are natural resources called *wasting assets?*

6. Is land a depreciable asset? Why or why not?

7. Define *amortization*. What kind of assets are *amortized?*

8. Explain the historical cost concept as it applies to long-term operational assets. Why is the book value of an asset likely to be different from the current market value of the asset?

9. What different kinds of expenditures might be included in the recorded cost of a building?

10. What is a basket purchase of assets? When a basket purchase is made, how is cost assigned to individual assets?

11. What are the stages in the life cycle of a long-term operational asset?

12. Explain straight-line, units-of-production, and double-declining-balance depreciation. When is it appropriate to use each of these depreciation methods?

13. What effect does the recognition of depreciation expense have on total assets? On total equity?

14. Does the recognition of depreciation expense affect cash flows? Why or why not?

15. MalMax purchased a depreciable asset. What would be the difference in total assets at the end of the first year if MalMax chooses straight-line depreciation versus double-declining-balance depreciation?

16. John Smith mistakenly expensed the cost of a long-term tangible fixed asset. Specifically, he charged the cost of a truck to a delivery expense account. How will this error affect the income statement and the balance sheet in the year in which the mistake is made?

17. What is *salvage value?*

18. What type of account (classification) is Accumulated Depreciation?

19. How is the book value of an asset determined?

20. Why is depreciation that has been recognized over the life of an asset shown in a contra account? Why not just reduce the asset account?

21. Assume that a piece of equipment cost $5,000 and had accumulated depreciation recorded of $3,000. What is the book value of the equipment? Is the book value equal to the fair market value of the equipment? Explain.

22. Why would a company choose to depreciate one piece of equipment using the double-declining-balance method and another piece of equipment using straight-line depreciation?

23. Why may it be necessary to revise the estimated life of a plant asset? When the estimated life is revised, does it affect the amount of depreciation per year? Why or why not?

24. How are capital expenditures made to improve the quality of a capital asset accounted for? Would the answer change if the expenditure extended the life of the asset but did not improve quality? Explain.

25. When a long-term operational asset is sold at a gain, how is the balance sheet affected? Is the statement of cash flows affected? If so, how?

26. Define *depletion.* What is the most commonly used method of computing depletion?

27. List several common intangible assets. How is the life determined that is to be used to compute amortization?

28. List some differences between U.S. GAAP and GAAP of other countries.

29. How do differences in expense recognition and industry characteristics affect financial performance measures?

EXERCISES

All applicable Exercises are available with McGraw-Hill Connect Accounting.

connect
|ACCOUNTING

Unless specifically included, ignore income tax considerations in all exercises and problems.

Exercise 6-1   *Long-term operational assets used in a business*   LO 1

Required

Give some examples of long-term operational assets that each of the following companies is likely to own: (*a*) Chico's, (*b*) John Deere, (*c*) Amtrak, and (*d*) Malco Theatre.

Exercise 6-2   *Identifying long-term operational assets*   LO 1

Required

Which of the following items should be classified as long-term operational assets?

a. Prepaid insurance	**g.** Delivery van
b. Coal mine	**h.** Land held for investment
c. Office equipment	**i.** 10-year treasury note
d. Notes receivable (short-term)	**j.** Cash
e. Supplies	**k.** Filing cabinet
f. Copyright	**l.** Inventory

LO 1

Exercise 6-3   *Classifying tangible and intangible assets*

Required

Identify each of the following long-term operational assets as either tangible (T) or intangible (I).

a. Pizza oven

b. Land

c. Franchise

d. Filing cabinet

e. Copyright

f. Silver mine

g. Office building

h. Drill press

i. Patent

j. Oil well

k. Desk

l. Goodwill

LO 2

Exercise 6-4   *Determining the cost of an asset*

Pine Logging Co. purchased an electronic saw to cut various types and sizes of logs. The saw had a list price of $160,000. The seller agreed to allow a 5 percent discount because Pine paid cash. Delivery terms were FOB shipping point. Freight cost amounted to $4,200. Pine had to hire an individual to operate the saw. Pine had to build a special platform to mount the saw. The cost of the platform was $2,500. The saw operator was paid an annual salary of $65,000. The cost of the company's theft insurance policy increased by $2,000 per year as a result of the acquisition of the saw. The saw had a four-year useful life and an expected salvage value of $10,000.

Required

Determine the amount to be capitalized in an asset account for the purchase of the saw.

LO 2

Exercise 6-5   *Allocating costs on the basis of relative market values*

Illinois Company purchased a building and the land on which the building is situated for a total cost of $1,200,000 cash. The land was appraised at $600,000 and the building at $1,000,000.

Required

a. What is the accounting term for this type of acquisition?

b. Determine the amount of the purchase cost to allocate to the land and the amount to allocate to the building.

c. Would Illinois Company recognize a gain on the purchase? Why or why not?

d. Record the purchase in a statements model like the following one.

Assets	= Liab. + Equity	Rev. − Exp. = Net Inc.	Cash Flow
Cash + Land + Building			

LO 2

Exercise 6-6   *Allocating costs for a basket purchase*

Keenum Company purchased a restaurant building, land, and equipment for $900,000. Keenum paid $100,000 in cash and issued a 20-year, 8 percent note to First Bank for the balance. The appraised value of the assets was as follows.

Land	$ 240,000
Building	600,000
Equipment	360,000
Total	$1,200,000

Required

a. Compute the amount to be recorded on the books for each of the assets.
b. Record the purchase in a horizontal statements model like the following one.

Assets				=	Liab.	+	Equity	Rev.	−	Exp.	=	Net Inc.	Cash Flow
Cash	+ Land	+ Building	+ Equip.		N. Payable								

Exercise 6-7 *Effect of depreciation on the accounting equation and financial statements*

LO 3

The following events apply to R&L Logging Company for the 2010 fiscal year.

1. The company started when it acquired $80,000 cash from the issue of common stock.
2. Purchased a new skidder that cost $75,000 cash.
3. Earned $98,000 in cash revenue.
4. Paid $52,000 cash for salaries expense.
5. Paid $12,000 cash for operating expenses.
6. Adjusted the records to reflect the use of the skidder. The skidder, purchased on January 1, 2010, has an expected useful life of five years and an estimated salvage value of $5,000. Use straight-line depreciation. The adjusting entry was made as of December 31, 2010.

Required

a. Record the above transactions in a horizontal statements model like the following one.

Event	Balance Sheet							Income Statement					Statemt. of Cash Flows
	Assets			=	Equity			Rev.	−	Exp.	=	Net Inc.	
	Cash	+ Equip.	− A. Depr.	=	Com. Stock	+	Ret. Earn.						

b. What amount of depreciation expense would R&L Logging Co. report on the 2011 income statement?
c. What amount of accumulated depreciation would R&L Logging Co. report on the December 31, 2011, balance sheet?
d. Would the cash flow from operating activities be affected by depreciation in 2011?

Exercise 6-8 *Effect of double-declining-balance depreciation on financial statements*

LO 3

Miller Company started operations by acquiring $200,000 cash from the issue of common stock. The company purchased equipment that cost $200,000 cash on January 1, 2010. The equipment had an expected useful life of five years and an estimated salvage value of $20,000. Miller Company earned $92,000 and $76,000 of cash revenue during 2010 and 2011, respectively. Miller Company uses double-declining-balance depreciation.

Required

a. Record the above transactions in a horizontal statements model like the following one.

Event	Balance Sheet							Income Statement					Statemt. of Cash Flows
	Assets			=	Equity			Rev.	−	Exp.	=	Net Inc.	
	Cash	+ Equip.	− A. Depr.	=	Com. Stock	+	Ret. Earn.						

b. Prepare income statements, balance sheets, and statements of cash flows for 2010 and 2011. Use a vertical statements format.

LO 3, 4

Exercise 6-9   *Events related to the acquisition, use, and disposal of a tangible plant asset: straight-line depreciation*

Cook Wrecker Co. purchased a truck on January 1, 2010, for $37,000. In addition, Cook paid sales tax and title fees of $2,000 for the truck. The truck is expected to have a four-year life and a salvage value of $7,000.

Required

a. Using the straight-line method, compute the depreciation expense for 2010 and 2011.

b. Assume the truck was sold on January 1, 2013, for $15,000. Determine the amount of gain or loss that would be recognized on the asset disposal.

LO 3

Exercise 6-10   *Computing and recording straight-line versus double-declining-balance depreciation*

At the beginning of 2009, Expert Manufacturing purchased a new computerized drill press for $65,000. It is expected to have a five-year life and a $5,000 salvage value.

Required

a. Compute the depreciation for each of the five years, assuming that the company uses

  (1) Straight-line depreciation.

  (2) Double-declining-balance depreciation.

b. Record the purchase of the drill press and the depreciation expense for the first year under the straight-line and double-declining-balance methods in a financial statements model like the following one.

Assets					=	Equity	Rev.	−	Exp.	=	Net Inc.	Cash Flow
Cash	+	Drill Press	−	Acc. Dep.	=	Ret. Earn						

LO 4

Exercise 6-11   *Effect of the disposal of plant assets on the financial statements*

A plant asset with a cost of $50,000 and accumulated depreciation of $42,000 is sold for $6,000.

Required

a. What is the book value of the asset at the time of sale?

b. What is the amount of gain or loss on the disposal?

c. How would the sale affect net income (increase, decrease, no effect) and by how much?

d. How would the sale affect the amount of total assets shown on the balance sheet (increase, decrease, no effect) and by how much?

e. How would the event affect the statement of cash flows (inflow, outflow, no effect) and in what section?

LO 4

Exercise 6-12   *Effect of gains and losses on the accounting equation and financial statements*

On January 1, 2010, Reese Enterprises purchased a parcel of land for $22,000 cash. At the time of purchase, the company planned to use the land for future expansion. In 2011, Reese Enterprises changed its plans and sold the land.

Required

a. Assume that the land was sold for $25,000 in 2010.
  (1) Show the effect of the sale on the accounting equation.
  (2) What amount would Reese report on the income statement related to the sale of the land?
  (3) What amount would Reese report on the statement of cash flows related to the sale of the land?

b. Assume that the land was sold for $21,500 in 2011.
  (1) Show the effect of the sale on the accounting equation.
  (2) What amount would Reese report on the income statement related to the sale of the land?
  (3) What amount would Reese report on the statement of cash flows related to the sale of the land?

Exercise 6-13   *Double-declining-balance and units-of-production depreciation: gain or loss on disposal*   LO **3, 4**

Copy Service Co. purchased a new color copier at the beginning of 2010 for $42,000. The copier is expected to have a five-year useful life and a $6,000 salvage value. The expected copy production was estimated at 2,000,000 copies. Actual copy production for the five years was as follows.

2010	550,000
2011	480,000
2012	380,000
2013	390,000
2014	240,000
Total	2,040,000

The copier was sold at the end of 2014 for $5,200.

Required

a. Compute the depreciation expense for each of the five years, using double-declining-balance depreciation.
b. Compute the depreciation expense for each of the five years, using units-of-production depreciation. (Round cost per unit to three decimal places.)
c. Calculate the amount of gain or loss from the sale of the asset under each of the depreciation methods.

Exercise 6-14   *Revision of estimated useful life*   LO **5**

On January 1, 2010, Miller Machining Co. purchased a compressor and related installation equipment for $56,000. The equipment had a three-year estimated life with a $5,000 salvage value. Straight-line depreciation was used. At the beginning of 2012, Miller revised the expected life of the asset to four years rather than three years. The salvage value was revised to $4,000.

Required

Compute the depreciation expense for each of the four years.

Exercise 6-15   *Distinguishing between revenue expenditures and capital expenditures*   LO **6**

Uber's Shredding Service has just completed a minor repair on a shredding machine. The repair cost was $1,200, and the book value prior to the repair was $5,000. In addition, the company spent $9,000 to replace the roof on a building. The new roof extended the life of the building by five years. Prior to the roof replacement, the general ledger reflected the Building account at $90,000 and related Accumulated Depreciation account at $36,000.

Required

After the work was completed, what book value should Uber's report on the balance sheet for the shredding machine and the building?

LO **6**   **Exercise 6-16**   *Effect of revenue expenditures versus capital expenditures on financial statements*

Commercial Construction Company purchased a forklift for $115,000 cash. It had an estimated useful life of four years and a $5,000 salvage value. At the beginning of the third year of use, the company spent an additional $10,000 that was related to the forklift. The company's financial condition just prior to this expenditure is shown in the following statements model.

Assets					Equity			Rev.	−	Exp.	=	Net Inc.	Cash Flow
Cash	+	Forklift	−	Acc. Dep.	=	Com. Stk.	+	Ret. Earn.					
12,000	+	115,000	−	55,000	=	24,000	+	48,000	NA	−	NA	=	NA	NA

Required

Record the $10,000 expenditure in the statements model under each of the following *independent* assumptions.

a. The expenditure was for routine maintenance.

b. The expenditure extended the forklift's life.

c. The expenditure improved the forklift's operating capacity.

LO **6**   **Exercise 6-17**   *Effect of revenue expenditures versus capital expenditures on financial statements*

On January 1, 2010, Grayson Construction Company overhauled four cranes resulting in a slight increase in the life of the cranes. Such overhauls occur regularly at two-year intervals and have been treated as maintenance expense in the past. Management is considering whether to capitalize this year's $26,000 cash cost in the Cranes asset account or to expense it as a maintenance expense. Assume that the cranes have a remaining useful life of two years and no expected salvage value. Assume straight-line depreciation.

Required

a. Determine the amount of additional depreciation expense Grayson would recognize in 2010 and 2011 if the cost were capitalized in the Cranes account.

b. Determine the amount of expense Grayson would recognize in 2010 and 2011 if the cost were recognized as maintenance expense.

c. Determine the effect of the overhaul on cash flow from operating activities for 2010 and 2011 if the cost were capitalized and expensed through depreciation charges.

d. Determine the effect of the overhaul on cash flow from operating activities for 2010 and 2011 if the cost were recognized as maintenance expense.

LO **7**   **Exercise 6-18**   *Computing and recording depletion expense*

Southwest Sand and Gravel paid $800,000 to acquire 1,000,000 cubic yards of sand reserves. The following statements model reflects Southwest's financial condition just prior to purchasing the sand reserves. The company extracted 420,000 cubic yards of sand in year 1 and 360,000 cubic yards in year 2.

Assets			=	Equity			Rev.	–	Exp.	=	Net Inc.	Cash Flow
Cash	+	Sand Res.	=	Com. Stk.	+	Ret. Earn.						
900,000	+	NA	=	900,000	+	NA	NA	–	NA	=	NA	NA

Required

a. Compute the depletion charge per unit.

b. Record the acquisition of the sand reserves and the depletion expense for years 1 and 2 in a financial statements model like the preceding one.

Exercise 6-19 *Computing and recording the amortization of intangibles*   LO 8

Nevada's Manufacturing paid cash to purchase the assets of an existing company. Among the assets purchased were the following items.

Patent with 5 remaining years of legal life	$32,000
Goodwill	36,000

Nevada's financial condition just prior to the purchase of these assets is shown in the following statements model:

Assets					=	Liab.	+	Equity	Rev.	–	Exp.	=	Net Inc.	Cash Flow
Cash	+	Patent	+	Goodwill										
94,000	+	NA	+	NA	=	NA	+	94,000	NA	–	NA	=	NA	NA

Required

a. Compute the annual amortization expense for these items if applicable.

b. Record the purchase of the intangible assets and the related amortization expense for year 1 in a horizontal statements model like the preceding one.

Exercise 6-20 *Computing and recording goodwill*   LO 8

Ben Sands purchased the business Regional Supply Co. for $285,000 cash and assumed all liabilities at the date of purchase. Regional's books showed assets of $280,000, liabilities of $40,000, and equity of $240,000. An appraiser assessed the fair market value of the tangible assets at $270,000 at the date of purchase. Sands's financial condition just prior to the purchase is shown in the following statements model.

Assets					=	Liab.	+	Equity	Rev.	–	Exp.	=	Net Inc.	Cash Flow
Cash	+	Assets	+	Goodwill										
325,000	+	NA	+	NA	=	NA	+	325,000	NA	–	NA	=	NA	NA

Required

a. Compute the amount of goodwill purchased.

b. Record the purchase in a financial statements model like the preceding one.

LO 9

Exercise 6-21 *Performing ratio analysis using real-world data*

American Greetings Corporation manufactures and sells greeting cards and related items such as gift wrapping paper. CSX Corporation is one of the largest railway networks in the nation. The following data were taken from one of the companies' December 28, 2007, annual report and from the other's February 28, 2007, annual report. Revealing which data relate to which company was intentionally omitted. For one company, the dollar amounts are in thousands, while for the other they are in millions.

	Company 1	Company 2
Sales	$10,030	$1,744,603
Depreciation costs	883	46,975
Net earnings	1,336	42,378
Current assets	2,491	799,281
Property, plant, and equipment	21,780	285,072
Total assets	$25,534	$1,778,214

Required

a. Calculate depreciation costs as a percentage of sales for each company.

b. Calculate property, plant, and equipment as a percentage of total assets for each company.

c. Based on the information now available to you, decide which data relate to which company. Explain the rationale for your decision.

d. Which company appears to be using its assets most efficiently? Explain your answer.

PROBLEMS

connect
|ACCOUNTING

All applicable Problems are available with McGraw-Hill *Connect Accounting*.

LO 2

Problem 6-22 *Accounting for acquisition of assets including a basket purchase*

Moon Co., Inc., made several purchases of long-term assets in 2010. The details of each purchase are presented here.

New Office Equipment

1. List price: $60,000; terms: 2/10 n/30; paid within discount period.
2. Transportation-in: $1,600.
3. Installation: $2,200.
4. Cost to repair damage during unloading: $1,000.
5. Routine maintenance cost after six months: $300.

Basket Purchase of Copier, Computer, and Scanner for $15,000 with Fair Market Values

1. Copier, $10,000.
2. Computer, $6,000.
3. Scanner, $4,000.

Land for New Warehouse with an Old Building Torn Down

1. Purchase price, $200,000.
2. Demolition of building, $10,000.
3. Lumber sold from old building, $7,000.
4. Grading in preparation for new building, $14,000.
5. Construction of new building, $500,000.

Required

In each of these cases, determine the amount of cost to be capitalized in the asset accounts.

Problem 6-23 *Accounting for depreciation over multiple accounting cycles:*
straight-line depreciation

LO **3, 4**

NEC Company began operations when it acquired $60,000 cash from the issue of common
stock on January 1, 2008. The cash acquired was immediately used to purchase equipment for
$60,000 that had a $5,000 salvage value and an expected useful life of four years. The equipment was used to produce the following revenue stream (assume all revenue transactions are
for cash). At the beginning of the fifth year, the equipment was sold for $4,500 cash. NEC
uses straight-line depreciation.

CHECK FIGURES
Net Income, 2008: $1,250
Total Assets, 2012: $65,900

	2008	2009	2010	2011	2012
Revenue	$15,000	$16,000	$16,400	$14,000	$0

Required

Prepare income statements, statements of changes in stockholders' equity, balance sheets, and
statements of cash flows for each of the five years.

Problem 6-24 *Purchase and use of tangible asset: three accounting cycles,*
double-declining-balance depreciation

LO **2, 3, 5, 6**

The following transactions pertain to ALFA Solutions, Inc. Assume the transactions for the
purchase of the computer and any capital improvements occur on January 1 each year.

CHECK FIGURES
b. Net Income, 2010: $25,400
Total Assets, 2012: $127,860

2010

1. Acquired $50,000 cash from the issue of common stock.
2. Purchased a computer system for $30,000. It has an estimated useful life of five years and
a $5,000 salvage value.
3. Paid $2,000 sales tax on the computer system.
4. Collected $40,000 in data entry fees from clients.
5. Paid $1,800 in fees to service the computers.
6. Recorded double-declining-balance depreciation on the computer system for 2010.

2011

1. Paid 1,000 for repairs to the computer system.
2. Bought a case of toner cartridges for the printers that are part of the computer system,
$1,500.
3. Collected $38,000 in data entry fees from clients.
4. Paid $1,100 in fees to service the computers.
5. Recorded double-declining-balance depreciation for 2011.

2012

1. Paid $4,800 to upgrade the computer system, which extended the total life of the system
to six years.
2. Paid $1,100 in fees to service the computers.
3. Collected $35,000 in data entry fees from clients.
4. Recorded double-declining-balance depreciation for 2012.

Required

a. Record the above transactions in a horizontal statements model like the following one.

	Balance Sheet						Income Statement					Statemt. of
Event	**Assets**			=	**Equity**		**Rev.**	−	**Exp.**	=	**Net Inc.**	**Cash Flows**
	Cash	+ Equip.	− A. Depr.	=	Com. Stock	+ Ret. Earn.						

b. Use a vertical model to present financial statements for 2010, 2011, and 2012.

LO 3

CHECK FIGURES

b. Depreciation Expense, 2011:
$4,600

c. Depreciation Expense, 2012:
$4,625

Problem 6-25   *Calculating depreciation expense using three different methods*

Swanson Service Company purchased a copier on January 1, 2011, for $18,000 and paid an additional $500 for delivery charges. The copier was estimated to have a life of four years or 800,000 copies. Salvage was estimated at $2,500. The copier produced 230,000 copies in 2011 and 250,000 copies in 2012.

Required

Compute the amount of depreciation expense for the copier for calendar years 2011 and 2012, using these methods.

a. Straight-line.

b. Units-of-production.

c. Double-declining-balance.

LO 3, 4

CHECK FIGURES

a. Depreciation Expense, Year 2:
$8,000

b. Depreciation Expense, Year 2:
$10,800

Problem 6-26   *Effect of straight-line versus double-declining-balance depreciation on the recognition of expense and gains or losses*

One Hour Laundry Services purchased a new steam press machine on January 1, for $45,000. It is expected to have a five-year useful life and a $5,000 salvage value. One Hour expects to use the equipment more extensively in the early years.

Required

a. Calculate the depreciation expense for each of the five years, assuming the use of straight-line depreciation.

b. Calculate the depreciation expense for each of the five years, assuming the use of double-declining-balance depreciation.

c. Would the choice of one depreciation method over another produce a different amount of annual cash flow for any year? Why or why not?

d. Assume that One Hour Laundry Services sold the steam press machine at the end of the third year for $26,000. Compute the amount of gain or loss using each depreciation method.

LO 3, 4

Problem 6-27   *Computing and recording units-of-production depreciation*

Brees Corporation purchased a delivery van for $35,500 in 2010. The firm's financial condition immediately prior to the purchase is shown in the following horizontal statements model.

Assets				=	Equity			Rev.	−	Exp.	=	Net Inc.	Cash Flow
Cash	+	Van	−	Acc. Dep.	=	Com. Stk.	+	Ret. Earn.					
50,000	+	NA	−	NA	=	50,000	+	NA	NA	−	NA	=	NA	NA

CHECK FIGURES

a. Depreciation Expense, 2010:
$10,000

c. Loss on Sale: $(1,500)

The van was expected to have a useful life of 150,000 miles and a salvage value of $5,500. Actual mileage was as follows.

2010	50,000
2011	70,000
2012	58,000

Required

a. Compute the depreciation for each of the three years, assuming the use of units-of-production depreciation.

b. Assume that Brees earns $21,000 of cash revenue during 2010. Record the purchase of the van and the recognition of the revenue and the depreciation expense for the first year in a financial statements model like the preceding one.

c. Assume that Brees sold the van at the end of the third year for $4,000. Calculate the amount of gain or lose from the sale.

Problem 6-28 *Determining the effect of depreciation expense on financial statements*

LO 3

Three different companies each purchased a machine on January 1, 2008, for $42,000. Each machine was expected to last five years or 200,000 hours. Salvage value was estimated to be $2,000. All three machines were operated for 50,000 hours in 2008, 55,000 hours in 2009, 40,000 hours in 2010, 44,000 hours in 2011, and 31,000 hours in 2012. Each of the three companies earned $30,000 of cash revenue during each of the five years. Company A uses straight-line depreciation, company B uses double-declining-balance depreciation, and company C uses units-of-production depreciation.

CHECK FIGURES
a. Company A, Net Income: $22,000
c. Company A, Highest Book Value: $18,000

Required

Answer each of the following questions. Ignore the effects of income taxes.

a. Which company will report the highest amount of net income for 2008?
b. Which company will report the lowest amount of net income for 2010?
c. Which company will report the highest book value on the December 31, 2010, balance sheet?
d. Which company will report the highest amount of retained earnings on the December 31, 2011, balance sheet?
e. Which company will report the lowest amount of cash flow from operating activities on the 2010 statement of cash flows?

Problem 6-29 *Accounting for depletion*

LO 7

Favre Exploration Corporation engages in the exploration and development of many types of natural resources. The company has engaged in the following activities:

CHECK FIGURES
a. Coal Mine Depletion, 2010: $279,000
b. Total Natural Resources: $3,056,000

Jan. 1, 2010   Purchased a coal mine estimated to contain 200,000 tons of coal for $900,000.
Feb. 1, 2010   Purchased a silver mine estimated to contain 30,000 tons of silver for $750,000.
July 1, 2010   Purchased for $2,500,000 a tract of timber estimated to yield 3,000,000 board feet of lumber and to have a residual land value of $250,000.
Aug. 1, 2010   Purchased for $720,000 oil reserves estimated to contain 380,000 barrels of oil, of which 20,000 would be unprofitable to pump.

Required

a. Determine the amount of depletion expense to recognize on the 2010 income statement for each of the four reserves, assuming 62,000 tons of coal, 1,200,000 board feet of lumber, 9,000 tons of silver, and 80,000 barrels of oil are extracted.
b. Prepare the portion of the December 31, 2010, balance sheet that reports natural resources.

Problem 6-30 *Recognizing continuing expenditures for plant assets*

LO 3, 4, 5, 6

Sam's Outdoor, Inc., recorded the following transactions over the life of a piece of equipment purchased in 2010.

CHECK FIGURES
b. 2012 Depreciation Expense: $8,000
d. Loss on Sale: $4,000

Jan. 1, 2010   Purchased the equipment for $39,000 cash. The equipment is estimated to have a five-year life and $4,000 salvage value and was to be depreciated using the straight-line method.
Dec. 31, 2010   Recorded depreciation expense for 2010.
May 5, 2011   Undertook routine repairs costing $800.
Dec. 31, 2011   Recorded depreciation expense for 2011.
Jan. 1, 2012   Made an adjustment costing $3,000 to the equipment. It improved the quality of the output but did not affect the life estimate.
Dec. 31, 2012   Recorded depreciation expense for 2012.
Mar. 1, 2013   Incurred $520 cost to oil and clean the equipment.
Dec. 31, 2013   Recorded depreciation expense for 2013.
Jan. 1, 2014   Had the equipment completely overhauled at a cost of $9,000. The overhaul was estimated to extend the total life to seven years and revised the salvage value to $3,000.
Dec. 31, 2014   Recorded depreciation expense for 2014.
July 1, 2015   Sold the equipment for $8,000 cash.

Required

a. Use a horizontal statements model like the following one to show the effects of these transactions on the elements of the financial statements. Use + for increase, − for decrease, and NA for not affected. The first event is recorded as an example.

Date	Assets	=	Liabilities	+	Equity	Net Inc.	Cash Flow
Jan. 1, 2010	+ −		NA		NA	NA	− IA

b. Determine the amount of depreciation expense Sam's will report on the income statements for the years 2010 through 2014.

c. Determine the book value (cost − accumulated depreciation) Sam's will report on the balance sheets at the end of the years 2010 through 2014.

d. Determine the amount of the gain or loss Sam's will report on the disposal of the equipment on July 1, 2015.

LO 5, 6, 7

CHECK FIGURE
Depreciation Expense: $8,500

Problem 6-31 *Accounting for continuing expenditures*

Shaw Manufacturing paid $62,000 to purchase a computerized assembly machine on January 1, 2008. The machine had an estimated life of eight years and a $2,000 salvage value. Shaw's financial condition as of January 1, 2011, is shown in the following financial statements model. Shaw uses the straight-line method for depreciation.

Assets				=	Equity			Rev.	−	Exp.	=	Net Inc.	Cash Flow
Cash	+	Mach.	−	Acc. Dep.	=	Com. Stk.	+	Ret. Earn.					
15,000	+	62,000	−	22,500	=	8,000	+	46,500	NA	−	NA	=	NA	NA

Shaw Manufacturing made the following expenditures on the computerized assembly machine in 2011.

Jan. 2   Added an overdrive mechanism for $6,000 that would improve the overall quality of the performance of the machine but would not extend its life. The salvage value was revised to $3,000.

Aug. 1   Performed routine maintenance, $1,150.

Oct. 2   Replaced some computer chips (considered routine), $950.

Dec. 31 Recognized 2011 depreciation expense.

Required

Record the 2011 transactions in a statements model like the preceding one.

LO 8

CHECK FIGURE
Goodwill Purchased: $210,000

Problem 6-32 *Accounting for intangible assets*

Le Gormet Company purchased a fast-food restaurant for $1,700,000. The fair market values of the assets purchased were as follows. No liabilities were assumed.

Equipment	$420,000
Land	300,000
Building	650,000
Franchise (5-year life)	120,000

Required

Calculate the amount of goodwill purchased.

Problem 6-33 *Accounting for goodwill*

LO 8

Green Leaf purchased the assets of Flower Co. for $1,200,000 in 2010. The estimated fair market value of the assets at the purchase date was $1,000,000. Goodwill of $200,000 was recorded at purchase. In 2012, because of negative publicity, one-half of the goodwill purchased from Flower Co. was judged to be permanently impaired.

CHECK FIGURE
Impairment Loss: $100,000

Required

Explain how the recognition of the impairment of the goodwill will affect the 2012 balance sheet, income statement, and statement of cash flows.

Problem 6-34 *Performing ratio analysis using real-world data*

LO 9

Cooper Tire Rubber Company claims to be the fourth largest tire manufacturer in North America. Goodyear Tire & Rubber Company is the largest tire manufacturer in North America. The following information was taken from these companies' December 31, 2007, annual reports. All dollar amounts are in thousands.

	Cooper Tire	Goodyear Tire
Sales	$2,932,575	$19,644,000
Depreciation costs	131,007	610,000
Buildings, machinery, and equipment		
(net of accumulated depreciation)	949,458	4,383,000
Total assets	2,296,868	17,028,000
Depreciation method	"Straight-line or accelerated"	Straight-line
Estimated life of assets:		
Buildings	10 to 40 years	8 to 45 years
Machinery and equipment	4 to 14 years	3 to 30 years

Required

a. Calculate depreciation costs as a percentage of sales for each company.
b. Calculate buildings, machinery, and equipment as a percentage of total assets for each company.
c. Which company appears to be using its assets most efficiently? Explain your answer.
d. Identify some of the problems a financial analyst encounters when trying to compare the use of long-term assets of Cooper versus Goodyear.

ANALYZE, THINK, COMMUNICATE

ATC 6-1 Business Applications Case *Understanding real-world annual reports*

Required

Use the Topps Company's annual report in Appendix B to answer the following questions.

The Topps Company, Inc.

a. What method of depreciation does Topps use?
b. What types of intangible assets does Topps have?
c. What are the estimated lives that Topps uses for the various types of long-term assets?
d. As of February 25, 2006, what is the original cost of Topps': Land; Buildings and improvements; and Machinery, equipment and software (see the footnotes)?
e. What was Topps' depreciation expense and amortization expense for 2006 (see the footnotes)?

ATC 6-2   Group Assignment   *Different depreciation methods*

Sweet's Bakery makes cakes, pies, and other pastries that it sells to local grocery stores. The company experienced the following transactions during 2010.

1. Started business by acquiring $60,000 cash from the issue of common stock.
2. Purchased bakery equipment for $46,000.
3. Had sales in 2010 amounting to $42,000.
4. Paid $8,200 of cash for supplies which were all used during the year to make baked goods.
5. Incurred other operating expenses of $12,000 for 2010.

Required

a. Organize the class into two sections and divide each section into groups of three to five students. Assign each section a depreciation method: straight-line or double-declining-balance.

Group Task

Prepare an income statement and balance sheet using the preceding information and the depreciation method assigned to your group.

Class Discussion

b. Have a representative of each section put its income statement on the board. Are there differences in net income? In the amount of income tax paid? How will these differences in the amount of depreciation expense change over the life of the equipment?

ATC 6-3   Real-World Case   *Different numbers for different industries*

The following ratios are for four companies in different industries. Some of these ratios have been discussed in the textbook; others have not, but their names explain how the ratio was computed. The four sets of ratios, presented randomly, are

Ratio	Company 1	Company 2	Company 3	Company 4
Current assets ÷ total assets	12%	18%	20%	72%
Operating cycle	42 days	35 days	19 days	409 days
Return on assets	12%	19%	5%	5%
Gross margin	35%	55%	46%	24%
Sales ÷ property, plant and equipment	1.89 times	38.97 times	1.97 times	6.08 times
Sales ÷ number of full-time employees	$540,883	$29,942	$55,687	$413,252

The four companies to which these ratios relate, listed in alphabetical order, are

1. Anheuser Bush Companies, Inc., is a company that produces beer and related products. Its fiscal year-end was December 31, 2007.
2. Wendy's International, Inc., operates 1,414 of the 6,645 Wendy's restaurants in the United States and 19 other countries. Its fiscal year-end was December 30, 2007.
3. Deere & Company is a company that manufactures heavy construction equipment. Its fiscal year-end was December 31, 2007.
4. Weight Watchers International, Inc., is a company that provides weight loss services and products. Its fiscal year-end was December 31, 2007.

Required

Determine which company should be matched with each set of ratios. Write a memorandum explaining the rationale for your decisions.

ATC 6-4   Business Applications Case   *Effect of depreciation on the return on assets ratio*

Campus Video Games (CVG) was started on January 1, 2010, when it acquired $62,500 cash from the issue of common stock. The company immediately purchased video games that cost $62,500 cash. The games had an estimated salvage value of $7,500 and an expected useful life of five years. CVG used the games during 2010 to produce $25,000 of cash revenue. Assume that these were the only events affecting CVG during 2010.

Required

(*Hint:* Prepare an income statement and a balance sheet prior to completing the following requirements.)

a. Compute the return on assets ratio as of December 31, 2010, assuming CVG uses the straight-line depreciation method.

b. Recompute the ratio assuming CVG uses the double-declining-balance method.

c. Which depreciation method makes it *appear* that CVG is utilizing its assets more effectively?

ATC 6-5   Business Applications Case   *Effect of depreciation on financial statement analysis: straight-line versus double-declining-balance*

Rucky Company and Stone Company experienced the exact same set of economic events during 2010. Both companies purchased machines on January 1, 2010. Except for the effects of this purchase, the accounting records of both companies had the following accounts and balances.

As of January 1, 2010	
Total Assets	$400,000
Total Liabilities	160,000
Total Stockholders' Equity	240,000
During 2010	
Total Sales Revenue	200,000
Total Expenses (not including depreciation)	120,000
Liabilities were not affected by transactions in 2010.	

The machines purchased by the companies each cost $80,000 cash. The machines had expected useful lives of five years and estimated salvage values of $8,000. Rucky uses straight-line depreciation. Stone uses double-declining-balance depreciation.

Required

a. For both companies, calculate the balances in the preceding accounts on December 31, 2010, after the effects of the purchase and depreciation of the machines have been applied. [*Hint:* The purchases of the machines are asset exchange transactions that do not affect total assets. However, the effect of depreciating the machines changes the amounts in total assets, expense, and equity (retained earnings).]

b. Based on the revised account balances determined in Requirement *a*, calculate the following ratios for both companies.

(1) Debt to assets ratio.

(2) Return on assets ratio.

(3) Return on equity ratio.

c. Disregarding the effects of income taxes, which company produced the higher increase in real economic wealth during 2010?

ATC 6-6   Writing Assignment   *Impact of historical cost on asset presentation on the balance sheet*

Assume that you are examining the balance sheets of two companies and note the following information.

	Company A	Company B
Equipment	$1,130,000	$900,000
Accumulated Depreciation	(730,000)	(500,000)
Book Value	$ 400,000	$400,000

Maxie Smith, a student who has had no accounting courses, remarks that Company A and Company B have the same amount of equipment.

Required

In a short paragraph, explain to Maxie that the two companies do not have equal amounts of equipment. You may want to include in your discussion comments regarding the possible age of each company's equipment, the impact of the historical cost concept on balance sheet information, and the impact of different depreciation methods on book value.

ATC 6-7   Corporate Governance   *What's an expense?*

Several years ago, Wilson Blowhard founded a communications company. The company became successful and grew by expanding its customer base and acquiring some of its competitors. In fact, most of its growth resulted from acquiring other companies. Mr. Blowhard is adamant about continuing the company's growth and increasing its net worth. To achieve these goals, the business's net income must continue to increase at a rapid pace.

If the company's net worth continues to rise, Mr. Blowhard plans to sell the company and retire. He is, therefore, focused on improving the company's profit any way he can.

In the communications business, companies often use the lines of other communications companies. This line usage is a significant operating expense for Mr. Blowhard's company. Generally accepted accounting principles require operating costs like line use to be expensed as they are incurred each year. Each dollar of line cost reduces net income by a dollar.

After reviewing the company's operations, Mr. Blowhard concluded that the company did not currently need all of the line use it was paying for. It was really paying the owner of the lines now so that the line use would be available in the future for all of Mr. Blowhard's expected new customers. Mr. Blowhard instructed his accountant to capitalize all of the line cost charges and depreciate them over 10 years. The accountant reluctantly followed Mr. Blowhard's instructions and the company's net income for the current year showed a significant increase over the prior year's net income. Mr. Blowhard had found a way to report continued growth in the company's net income and increase the value of the company.

Required

a. How does Mr. Blowhard's scheme affect the amount of income that the company would otherwise report in its financial statements and how does the scheme affect the company's balance sheet? Explain your answer.

b. Review the AICPA's Articles of Professional Conduct (see Chapter 2) and comment on any of the standards that were violated.

c. Review the fraud triangle discussed in Chapter 2 and comment on which of the features are evident in this case.

ATC 6-8   Research Assignment   *Comparing Microsoft's and Intel's operational assets*

This chapter discussed how companies in different industries often use different proportions of current versus long-term assets to accomplish their business objective. The technology revolution resulting from the silicon microchip has often been led by two well-known companies: Microsoft and Intel. Although often thought of together, these companies are really very different. Using either the most current Forms 10-K or annual reports for Microsoft Corporation and Intel Corporation, complete the requirements below. To obtain the Forms 10-K, use either the

EDGAR system following the instructions in Appendix A or the company's website. Microsoft's annual report is available on its website; Intel's annual report is its Form 10-K.

Required

a. Fill in the missing data in the following table. The percentages must be computed; they are not included in the companies 10-Ks. (*Note:* The percentages for current assets and property, plant, and equipment will not sum to 100.)

	Current Assets	Property, Plant, and Equipment	Total Assets
Microsoft	74,918		
Dollar Amount	$ 5W	$ 8162	$ 108-704
% of Total Assets	69 %	7.5 %	100%
Intel			
Dollar Amount	$ 71,119,000,000	$ 23,627,000,000	$ 71,119
% of Total Assets	1. %	33 %	100%

b. Briefly explain why these two companies have different percentages of their assets in current assets versus property, plant, and equipment.

$$
\begin{array}{r}
\overset{6\;\;10}{71,119,000,000} \\
-\; 23,627,000,000 \\
\hline
47,492,000,000
\end{array}
$$

25,872

Mic

74,918

CHAPTER 7

Accounting *for* Liabilities

LEARNING OBJECTIVES

After you have mastered the material in this chapter you will be able to:

1 Show how notes payable and related interest expense affect financial statements.

2 Show how sales tax liabilities affect financial statements.

3 Define contingent liabilities and explain how they are reported in financial statements.

4 Explain how warranty obligations affect financial statements.

5 Show how installment notes affect financial statements.

6 Show how a line of credit affects financial statements.

7 Explain how to account for bonds and their related interest costs.

8 Distinguish between current and noncurrent assets and liabilities.

9 Prepare a classified balance sheet.

10 Use the current and debt to assets ratios to assess the level of liquidity.

CHAPTER OPENING

Chapter 5 explained the need to estimate the net realizable value of receivables (the amount of receivables a company expects to actually collect). Do companies also estimate the net realizable value of payables (the amount they expect to actually pay)? The answer is no. Unless there is evidence to the contrary, companies are assumed to be going concerns that will continue to operate. Under this **going concern assumption,** companies expect to pay their obligations in full. Accounts and notes payable are therefore reported at face value. In addition to reporting liabilities for which the amounts due are known, companies report liabilities for which the amounts due are uncertain. Liabilities that are uncertain as to amount are contingent liabilities.

Chapter 2 discussed several types of liabilities with known amounts due, including accounts payable, salaries payable, and unearned revenue. This chapter introduces other liabilities with known amounts due: notes payable, sales taxes payable, lines of credit, and bond liabilities. We also discuss a contingent liability called warranties payable. We begin with a discussion of **current liabilities,** those that are payable within one year or the operating cycle, whichever is longer.

The *Curious* Accountant

CBS Corporation recently reported a net loss of $7.1 billion. The previous year it had reported an even greater loss, $17.5 billion. The company had $721 million of interest expense in recent period and $694 million in the previous year.

With such huge losses on its income statements, do you think CBS was able to make the interest payments on its debt? If so, how? (Answers on page 259.)

ACCOUNTING FOR CURRENT LIABILITIES

Accounting for Notes Payable

Our discussion of promissory notes in Chapter 5 focused on the payee, the company
with a note receivable on its books. In this chapter we focus on the maker of the note,
the company with a note payable on its books. Since the maker of the note issues
(gives) the note to the payee, the maker is sometimes called the **issuer.**

To illustrate, assume that on September 1, 2010, Herrera Supply Company (HSC)
borrowed $90,000 from the National Bank. As evidence of the debt, Herrera issued
a **note payable** that had a one-year term and an annual interest rate of 9 percent.

Issuing the note is an asset source transaction. The asset account Cash increases
and the liability account Notes Payable increases. The income statement is not affected.
The statement of cash flows shows a $90,000 cash inflow from financing activities.
The effects on the financial statements are as follows.

	Assets	=	Liabilities			+	Stockholders' Equity			Rev.	–	Exp.	=	Net Inc.	Cash Flow
Date	Cash	=	Notes Pay.	+	Int. Pay.	+	Com. Stk.	+	Ret. Earn.						
09/01/10	90,000	=	90,000	+	NA	+	NA	+	NA	NA	–	NA	=	NA	90,000 FA

On December 31, 2010, HSC would recognize four months (September 1 through
December 31) of accrued interest expense. The accrued interest is $2,700 [$90,000 ×
0.09 × (4 ÷ 12)]. Recognizing the accrued interest expense increases the liability
account Interest Payable and decreases retained earnings. It is a claims exchange event.
The income statement would report interest expense although HSC had not paid any
cash for interest in 2010. The effects on the financial statements are as follows.

	Assets	=	Liabilities			+	Stockholders' Equity			Rev.	–	Exp.	=	Net Inc.	Cash Flow
Date	Cash	=	Notes Pay.	+	Int. Pay.	+	Com. Stk.	+	Ret. Earn.						
12/31/10	NA	=	NA	+	2,700	+	NA	+	(2,700)	NA	–	2,700	=	(2,700)	NA

HSC would record three events on August 31, 2011 (the maturity date). The first event
recognizes $5,400 of interest expense that accrued in 2011 from January 1 through
August 31 [$90,000 × 0.09 × (8 ÷ 12)]. The effects on the financial statements are
as follows.

	Assets	=	Liabilities			+	Stockholders' Equity			Rev.	–	Exp.	=	Net Inc.	Cash Flow
Date	Cash	=	Notes Pay.	+	Int. Pay.	+	Com. Stk.	+	Ret. Earn.						
08/31/11	NA	=	NA	+	5,400	+	NA	+	(5,400)	NA	–	5,400	=	(5,400)	NA

The second event recognizes HSC's cash payment for interest on August 31, 2011.
This event is an asset use transaction that reduces both the Cash and Interest Payable
accounts for the total amount of interest due, $8,100 [$90,000 × 0.09 × (12 ÷ 12)].
The interest payment includes the four months' interest accrued in 2010 and the eight
months accrued in 2011 ($2,700 + $5,400 = $8,100). There is no effect on the income
statement because HSC recognized the interest expense in two previous journal entries.

The statement of cash flows would report an $8,100 cash outflow from operating activities. The effects on the financial statements follow.

	Assets	=	Liabilities			+	Stockholders' Equity			Rev.	−	Exp.	=	Net Inc.	Cash Flow
Date	Cash	=	Notes Pay.	+	Int. Pay.	+	Com. Stk.	+	Ret. Earn.						
08/31/11	(8,100)	=	NA	+	(8,100)	+	NA	+	NA	NA	−	NA	=	NA	(8,100) OA

The third event on August 31, 2011, reflects repaying the principal. This event is an asset use transaction. The Cash account and the Notes Payable account each decrease by $90,000. There is no effect on the income statement. The statement of cash flows would show a $90,000 cash outflow from financing activities. Recall that paying interest is classified as an operating activity even though repaying the principal is a financing activity. The effects on the financial statements are as follows.

	Assets	=	Liabilities			+	Stockholders' Equity			Rev.	−	Exp.	=	Net Inc.	Cash Flow
Date	Cash	=	Notes Pay.	+	Int. Pay.	+	Com. Stk.	+	Ret. Earn.						
08/31/11	(90,000)	=	(90,000)	+	NA	+	NA	+	NA	NA	−	NA	=	NA	(90,000) FA

CHECK *Yourself* 7.1

On October 1, 2010, Mellon Company issued an interest-bearing note payable to Better Banks Inc. The note had a $24,000 principal amount, a four-month term, and an annual interest rate of 4 percent. Determine the amount of interest expense and the cash outflow from operating activities Mellon will report in its 2010 and 2011 financial statements.

Answer The computation of accrued interest expense is shown below. Unless otherwise specified, the interest rate is stated in annual terms even though the term of the note is only four months. Interest rates are commonly expressed as an annual percentage regardless of the term of the note. The *time outstanding* in the following formulas is therefore expressed as a fraction of a year. Mellon paid interest at an annual rate of 4 percent, but the note was outstanding for only 3/12 of a year in 2010 and 1/12 of a year in 2011.

2010
Principal × Annual interest rate × Time outstanding = Interest expense
$24,000 × 0.04 × (3/12) = $240

2011
Principal × Annual interest rate × Time outstanding = Interest expense
$24,000 × 0.04 × (1/12) = $80

Mellon will report a $320 ($240 + $80) cash outflow from operating activities for interest in 2011.

Accounting for Sales Tax

Most states require retail companies to collect a sales tax on items sold to their customers. The retailer collects the tax from its customers and remits the tax to the state at regular intervals. The retailer has a current liability for the amount of sales tax collected but not yet paid to the state.

LO 2

Show how sales tax liabilities affect financial statements.

To illustrate, assume Herrera Supply Company (HSC) sells merchandise to a customer for $2,000 cash in a state where the sales tax rate is 6 percent. The effects on the financial statements are shown below.[1]

Assets =	Liab.	+		Equity		Rev.	− Exp.	= Net Inc.	Cash Flow
Cash	= Sales Tax Pay.	+	Com. Stk.	+	Ret. Earn.				
2,120 =	120	+	NA	+	2,000	2,000	− NA	= 2,000	2,120 OA

Remitting the tax (paying cash to the tax authority) is an asset use transaction. Both the Cash account and the Sales Tax Payable account decrease. The effects on the financial statements are as follows.

Assets =	Liab.	+		Equity		Rev.	− Exp.	= Net Inc.	Cash Flow
Cash	= Sales Tax Pay.	+	Com. Stk.	+	Ret. Earn.				
(120) =	(120)	+	NA	+	NA	NA	− NA	= NA	(120) OA

Contingent Liabilities

LO 3

Define contingent liabilities and explain how they are reported in financial statements.

A **contingent liability** is a potential obligation arising from a past event. The amount or existence of the obligation depends on some future event. A pending lawsuit, for example, is a contingent liability. Depending on the outcome, a defendant company could be required to pay a large monetary settlement or could be relieved of any obligation. Generally accepted accounting principles require that companies classify contingent liabilities into three different categories depending on the likelihood of their becoming actual liabilities. The categories and the accounting for each are described below.

1. If the likelihood of a future obligation arising is *probable* (likely) and its amount can be *reasonably estimated,* a liability is recognized in the financial statements. Contingent liabilities in this category include warranties, vacation pay, and sick leave.

2. If the likelihood of a future obligation arising is *reasonably possible* but not likely or if it is probable but *cannot be reasonably estimated,* no liability is reported on the balance sheet. The potential liability is, however, disclosed in the footnotes to the financial statements. Contingent liabilities in this category include legal challenges, environmental damages, and government investigations.

3. If the likelihood of a future obligation arising is *remote,* no liability need be recognized in the financial statements or disclosed in the footnotes to the statements.[2]

Determining whether a contingent liability is probable, reasonably possible, or remote requires professional judgment. Even seasoned accountants seek the advice of attorneys, engineers, insurance agents, and government regulators before classifying significant contingent liabilities. Professional judgment is also required to distinguish between contingent liabilities and **general uncertainties.** All businesses face uncertainties such as competition and damage from floods or storms. Such uncertainties are not contingent liabilities, however, because they do not arise from past events.

---

[1]The entry to record cost of goods sold for this sale is intentionally omitted.

[2]Companies may, if desired, voluntarily disclose contingent liabilities classified as remote.

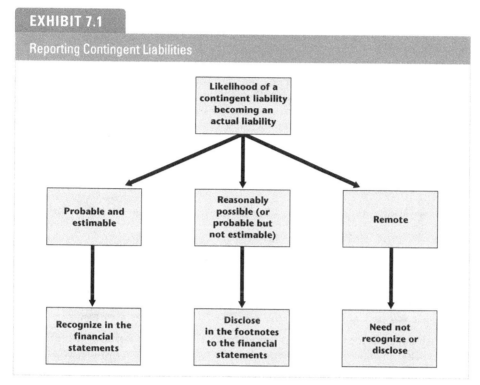

EXHIBIT 7.1

Reporting Contingent Liabilities

Exhibit 7.1 summarizes the three categories of contingent liabilities and the accounting for each category.

Warranty Obligations

To attract customers, many companies guarantee their products or services. Such guarantees are called **warranties.** Warranties take many forms. Usually, they extend for a specified period of time. Within this period, the seller promises to replace or repair defective products without charge. Although the amount and timing of warranty obligations are uncertain, warranties usually represent liabilities that must be reported in the financial statements.

Explain how warranty obligations affect financial statements.

To illustrate accounting for warranty obligations, assume Herrera Supply Company (HSC) had cash of $2,000, inventory of $6,000, common stock of $5,000, and retained earnings of $3,000 on January 1, 2009. The 2009 accounting period is affected by three accounting events: (1) sale of merchandise under warranty; (2) recognition of warranty obligations to customers who purchased the merchandise; and (3) settlement of a customer's warranty claim.

EVENT 1   Sale of Merchandise
HSC sold for $7,000 cash merchandise that had cost $4,000.

In the following statements model, revenue from the sale is referenced as 1a and the cost of the sale as 1b. The effects of the sales transaction on the financial statements are shown below.

Event No.	Assets			=	Liab.	+	Equity	Rev.	−	Exp.	=	Net Inc.	Cash Flow
	Cash	+	Inventory	=		+	Ret. Earn.						
1a	7,000	+	NA	=	NA	+	7,000	7,000	−	NA	=	7,000	7,000 OA
1b	NA	+	(4,000)	=	NA	+	(4,000)	NA	−	4,000	=	(4,000)	NA

EVENT 2   Recognition of Warranty Expense
HSC guaranteed the merchandise sold in Event 1 to be free from defects for one year following the date of sale.

Although the exact amount of future warranty claims is unknown, HSC must inform financial statement users of the company's obligation. HSC must estimate the amount of the warranty liability and report the estimate in the 2009 financial statements. Assume the warranty obligation is estimated to be $100. Recognizing this obligation increases liabilities (warranties payable) and reduces stockholders' equity (retained earnings). Recognizing the warranty expense reduces net income. The statement of cash flows is not affected when the obligation and the corresponding expense are recognized. The effects on the financial statements follow.

Event No.	Assets	=	Liab.	+	Equity	Rev.	−	Exp.	=	Net Inc.	Cash Flow
			Warr. Pay.	+	Ret. Earn.						
2	NA	=	100	+	(100)	NA	−	100	=	(100)	NA

EVENT 3   Settlement of Warranty Obligation
HSC paid $40 cash to repair defective merchandise returned by a customer.

The cash payment for the repair is not an expense. Warranty expense was recognized in the period in which the sale was made (when the Warranties Payable account was credited). The payment reduces an asset (cash) and a liability (warranties payable). The income statement is not affected by the repairs payment. However, there is a $40 cash outflow reported in the operating activities section of the statement of cash flows. The effects on the financial statements follow.

Event No.	Assets	=	Liab.	+	Equity	Rev.	−	Exp.	=	Net Inc.	Cash Flow
	Cash	=	Warr. Pay.	+	Ret. Earn.						
3	(40)	=	(40)	+	NA	NA	−	NA	=	NA	(40) OA

Financial Statements

The financial statements for HSC's 2009 accounting period are shown in Exhibit 7.2.

EXHIBIT 7.2

Financial Statements for 2009

Income Statement		Balance Sheet		Statement of Cash Flows	
Sales revenue	$7,000	Assets		**Operating Activities**	
Cost of goods sold	(4,000)	Cash	$ 8,960	Inflow from customers	$7,000
Gross margin	3,000	Inventory	2,000	Outflow for warranty	(40)
Warranty expense	(100)	Total assets	$10,960	Net inflow from	
Net income	$2,900	Liabilities		operating activities	6,960
		Warranties payable	$ 60	**Investing Activities**	0
		Stockholders' equity		**Financing Activities**	0
		Common stock	5,000	Net change in cash	6,960
		Retained earnings	5,900	Plus: Beginning cash balance	2,000
		Total liab. and stockholders' equity	$10,960	Ending cash balance	$8,960

CHECK *Yourself* 7.2

Flotation Systems, Inc. (FSI) began operations in 2010. Its sales were $360,000 in 2010 and $410,000 in 2011. FSI estimates the cost of its one-year product warranty will be 2 percent of sales. Actual cash payments for warranty claims amounted to $5,400 during 2010 and $8,500 during 2011. Determine the amount of warranty expense that FSI would report on its 2010 and 2011 year-end income statements. Also, determine the amount of warranties payable FSI would report on its 2010 and 2011 year-end balance sheet.

Answer FSI would report Warranty Expense on the December 31, 2010, income statement of $7,200 ($360,000 × .02). Warranty Expense on the December 31, 2011, income statement is $8,200 ($410,000 × .02).

FSI would report Warranties Payable on the December 31, 2010, balance sheet of $1,800 ($7,200 − $5,400). Warranties Payable on the December 31, 2011, balance sheet is $1,500 ($1,800 + $8,200 − $8,500).

Reality BYTES

Most electrical appliances come with a manufacturer's warranty that obligates the manufacturer to pay for defects that occur during some designated period of time after the point of sale. Why would Circuit City issue warranties that obligate it to pay for defects that occur after the manufacturer's warranty has expired? Warranties are in fact insurance policies that generate profits. Circuit City recently reported that the gross dollar sales from extended warranty programs were 3.8 percent of its total sales. Even more important, Circuit City notes that gross profit margins on products sold with extended warranties are higher than the gross profit margins on products sold without extended warranties. Warranties produce revenues for manufacturers as well as retailers. The only difference is that the revenues generated from manufacturer's warranties are embedded in the sales price. Products with longer, more comprehensive warranties usually sell at higher prices than products with shorter, less extensive warranties.

ACCOUNTING FOR LONG-TERM DEBT

Most businesses finance their investing activities with long-term debt. Recall that current liabilities mature within one year or a company's operating cycle, whichever is longer. Other liabilities are **long-term liabilities.** Long-term debt agreements vary with respect to requirements for paying interest charges and repaying principal (the amount borrowed). Interest payments may be due monthly, annually, at some other interval, or at the maturity date. Interest charges may be based on a **fixed interest rate** that remains constant during the term of the loan or may be based on a **variable interest rate** that fluctuates up or down during the loan period.

Principal repayment is generally required either in one lump sum at the maturity date or in installments that are spread over the life of the loan. For example, each monthly payment on your car loan probably includes both paying interest and repaying some of the principal. Repaying a portion of the principal with regular payments that also include interest is often called loan **amortization.**[3] This section explains accounting for interest and principal with respect to the major forms of long-term debt financing.

Installment Notes Payable

Show how installment notes affect financial statements.

Loans that require payments of principal and interest at regular intervals (amortizing loans) are typically represented by **installment notes.** The terms of installment notes usually range from two to five years. To illustrate accounting for installment notes, assume Blair Company was started on January 1, 2010, when it borrowed $100,000 cash from the National Bank. In exchange for the money, Blair issued the bank a five-year installment note with a 9 percent fixed interest rate. The effects on the financial statements are as follows.

	Assets	=	Liab.	+		Equity			Rev.	−	Exp.	=	Net Inc.	Cash Flow
Date	Cash	=	Note Pay.	+	Com. Stk.	+	Ret. Earn.							
2010 Jan. 1	100,000	=	100,000	+	NA	+	NA		NA	−	NA	=	NA	100,000 FA

The loan agreement required Blair to pay five equal installments of $25,709[4] on December 31 of each year from 2010 through 2014. Exhibit 7.3 shows the allocation of each payment between principal and interest. When Blair pays the final installment, both

EXHIBIT 7.3

Amortization Schedule for Installment Note Payable

Accounting Period Column A	Principal Balance on Jan. 1 Column B	Cash Payment on Dec. 31 Column C	Interest Expense Column D	Principal Repayment Column E	Principal Balance on Dec. 31 Column F
2010	$100,000	$25,709	$9,000	$16,709	$83,291
2011	83,291	25,709	7,496	18,213	65,078
2012	65,078	25,709	5,857	19,852	45,226
2013	45,226	25,709	4,070	21,639	23,587
2014	23,587	25,710*	2,123	23,587	0

*All computations are rounded to the nearest dollar. To fully liquidate the liability, the final payment is one dollar more than the others because of rounding differences.

[3]In Chapter 6 the term *amortization* described the expense recognized when the *cost of an intangible asset* is systematically allocated to expense over the useful life of the asset. This chapter shows that the term amortization refers more broadly to a variety of allocation processes. Here it means the systematic process of allocating the *principal repayment* over the life of a loan.

[4]The amount of the annual payment is determined using the present value concepts presented in a later chapter. Usually the lender (bank or other financial institution) calculates the amount of the payment for the customer. In this chapter we provide the amount of the annual payment.

Answers to The *Curious* Accountant

CBS Corporation was able to make its interest payments for two reasons. (1) Remember that interest is paid with cash, not accrual earnings. Many of the expenses on the company's income statement did not require the use of cash. Indeed, the company's statement of cash flows shows that net cash flows from operating activities, *after making interest payments,* was a positive $3.5 billion in the recent report and $3.6 billion in the previous report. (2) The net loss the company incurred was *after* interest expense had been deducted. The capacity of operations to support interest payments is measured by the amount of earnings before interest deductions. For example, look at the 2008 income statement for Blair in Exhibit 7.4. This statement shows only $3,000 of net income, but $12,000 of cash revenue was available for the payment of interest. Similarly, CBS's net losses are not an indication of the company's ability to pay interest in the short run.

the principal and interest will be paid in full. The amounts shown in Exhibit 7.3 are computed as follows.

1. The Interest Expense (Column D) is computed by multiplying the Principal Balance on Jan. 1 (Column B) by the interest rate. For example, interest expense for 2010 is $100,000 \times .09 = $9,000; for 2011 it is $83,291 \times .09 = $7,496; and so on.

2. The Principal Repayment (Column E) is computed by subtracting the Interest Expense (Column D) from the Cash Payment on Dec. 31 (Column C). For example, the Principal Repayment for 2010 is $25,709 − $9,000 = $16,709; for 2011 it is $25,709 − $7,496 = $18,213; and so on.

3. The Principal Balance on Dec. 31 (Column F) is computed by subtracting the Principal Repayment (Column E) from the Principal Balance on Jan. 1 (Column B). For example, the Principal Balance on Dec. 31 for 2010 is $100,000 − $16,709 = $83,291; on December 31, 2011, the principal balance is $83,291 − $18,213 = $65,078; and so on. The Principal Balance on Dec. 31 (ending balance) for 2010 ($83,291) is also the Principal Balance on Jan. 1 (beginning balance) for 2011; the principal balance on December 31, 2011, is the principal balance on January 1, 2012; and so on.

Although the amounts for interest expense and principal repayment differ each year, the effects of the annual payment on the financial statements are the same. On the balance sheet, assets (cash) decrease by the total amount of the payment; liabilities (note payable) decrease by the amount of the principal repayment; and stockholders' equity (retained earnings) decreases by the amount of interest expense. Net income decreases from recognizing interest expense. On the statement of cash flows, the portion of the cash payment applied to interest is reported in the operating activities section and the portion applied to principal is reported in the financing activities section. The effects on the financial statements are as follows.

Date	Assets	=	Liab.	+		Equity		Rev.	−	Exp.	=	Net Inc.	Cash Flow	
	Cash	=	Note Pay.	+	Com. Stk.	+	Ret. Earn.							
2010 Dec. 31	(25,709)	=	(16,709)	+	NA	+	(9,000)	NA	−	9,000	=	(9,000)	(9,000) (16,709)	OA FA

EXHIBIT 7.4					
BLAIR COMPANY Financial Statements					
	2010	2011	2012	2013	2014
Income Statements					
Rent revenue	$12,000	$12,000	$12,000	$12,000	$12,000
Interest expense	(9,000)	(7,496)	(5,857)	(4,070)	(2,123)
Net income	$ 3,000	$ 4,504	$ 6,143	$ 7,930	$ 9,877
Balance Sheets					
Assets					
Cash	$86,291	$72,582	$58,873	$45,164	$31,454
Liabilities					
Note payable	$83,291	$65,078	$45,226	$23,587	$ 0
Stockholders' equity					
Retained earnings	3,000	7,504	13,647	21,577	31,454
Total liabilities and stk. equity	$86,291	$72,582	$58,873	$45,164	$31,454
Statements of Cash Flows					
Operating Activities					
Inflow from customers	$ 12,000	$12,000	$12,000	$12,000	$12,000
Outflow for interest	(9,000)	(7,496)	(5,857)	(4,070)	(2,123)
Investing Activities	0	0	0	0	0
Financing Activities					
Inflow from note issue	100,000	0	0	0	0
Outflow to repay note	(16,709)	(18,213)	(19,852)	(21,639)	(23,587)
Net change in cash	86,291	(13,709)	(13,709)	(13,709)	(13,710)
Plus: Beginning cash balance	0	86,291	72,582	58,873	45,164
Ending cash balance	$ 86,291	$72,582	$58,873	$45,164	$31,454

Exhibit 7.4 displays income statements, balance sheets, and statements of cash flows for Blair Company for the accounting periods 2010 through 2014. The illustration assumes that Blair earned $12,000 of rent revenue each year. Since some of the principal

CHECK *Yourself* **7.3**

On January 1, 2009, Krueger Company issued a $50,000 installment note to State Bank. The note had a 10-year term and an 8 percent interest rate. Krueger agreed to repay the principal and interest in 10 annual payments of $7,451.47 at the end of each year. Determine the amount of principal and interest Krueger paid during the first and second year that the note was outstanding.

Answer

Accounting Period	Principal Balance January 1 A	Cash Payment December 31 B	Applied to Interest $C = A \times 0.08$	Applied to Principal $B - C$
2009	$50,000.00	$7,451.47	$4,000.00	$3,451.47
2010	46,548.53	7,451.47	3,723.88	3,727.59

is repaid each year, the note payable amount reported on the balance sheet and the amount of the interest expense on the income statement both decline each year.

Line of Credit

A **line of credit** enables a company to borrow or repay funds as needed. For example, a business may borrow $50,000 one month and make a partial repayment of $10,000 the next month. Credit agreements usually specify a limit on the amount that can be borrowed. Exhibit 7.5 shows that credit agreements are widely used.

Show how a line of credit affects financial statements.

Interest rates on lines of credit normally vary with fluctuations in some designated interest rate benchmark such as the rate paid on U.S. Treasury bills. For example, a company may pay 4 percent interest one month and 4.5 percent the next month, even if the principal balance remains constant.

Lines of credit typically have one-year terms. Although they are classified on the balance sheet as short-term liabilities, lines of credit are frequently extended indefinitely by simply renewing the credit agreement.

To illustrate accounting for a line of credit, assume Lagoon Company owns a wholesale jet-ski distributorship. In the spring, Lagoon borrows money using a line of credit to finance building up its inventory. Lagoon repays the loan over the summer months using cash generated from jet-ski sales. Borrowing or repaying events occur on the first of the month. Interest payments occur at the end of each month. Exhibit 7.6 presents all 2011 line of credit events.

Each borrowing event (March 1, April 1, and May 1) is an asset source transaction. Both cash and the line of credit liability increase. Each repayment (June 1, July 1, and August 1) is an asset use transaction. Both cash and the line of credit liability decrease. Each month's interest expense recognition and payment is an asset use transaction. Assets (cash) and stockholders' equity (retained earnings) decrease, as does net income. The effects of the events on the financial statements are shown in Exhibit 7.7.

EXHIBIT 7.5

Percentage of U.S. Companies Disclosing Credit Agreements

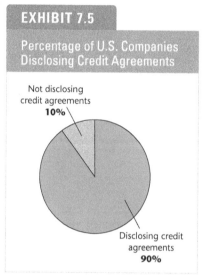

Data source: AICPA, *Accounting Trends and Techniques,* 2006.

EXHIBIT 7.6

Summary of 2011 Line of Credit Events

Date	Amount Borrowed (Repaid)	Loan Balance at End of Month	Effective Interest Rate per Month (%)	Interest Expense (rounded to nearest $1)
Mar. 1	$20,000	$ 20,000	0.09 ÷ 12	$150
Apr. 1	30,000	50,000	0.09 ÷ 12	375
May 1	50,000	100,000	0.105 ÷ 12	875
June 1	(10,000)	90,000	0.10 ÷ 12	750
July 1	(40,000)	50,000	0.09 ÷ 12	375
Aug. 1	(50,000)	0	0.09 ÷ 12	0

Bond Liabilities

Many companies borrow money directly from the public by selling **bond certificates,** otherwise called *issuing* bonds. Bond certificates describe a company's obligation to pay interest and to repay the principal. The seller, or **issuer,** of a bond is the borrower; the buyer of a bond, or **bondholder,** is the lender.

From the issuer's point of view, a bond represents an obligation to pay a sum of money to the bondholder on the bond's maturity date. The amount due at maturity

Explain how to account for bonds and their related interest costs.

EXHIBIT 7.7

Date	Assets	=	Liabilities	+	Equity	Rev.	–	Exp.	=	Net Inc.	Cash Flow	
Mar. 1	20,000	=	20,000	+	NA	NA	–	NA	=	NA	20,000	FA
31	(150)	=	NA	+	(150)	NA	–	150	=	(150)	(150)	OA
Apr. 1	30,000	=	30,000	+	NA	NA	–	NA	=	NA	30,000	FA
30	(375)	=	NA	+	(375)	NA	–	375	=	(375)	(375)	OA
May 1	50,000	=	50,000	+	NA	NA	–	NA	=	NA	50,000	FA
31	(875)	=	NA	+	(875)	NA	–	875	=	(875)	(875)	OA
June 1	(10,000)	=	(10,000)	+	NA	NA	–	NA	=	NA	(10,000)	FA
30	(750)	=	NA	+	(750)	NA	–	750	=	(750)	(750)	OA
July 1	(40,000)	=	(40,000)	+	NA	NA	–	NA	=	NA	(40,000)	FA
31	(375)	=	NA	+	(375)	NA	–	375	=	(375)	(375)	OA
Aug. 1	(50,000)	=	(50,000)	+	NA	NA	–	NA	=	NA	(50,000)	FA
31	NA	=	NA	+	NA	NA	–	NA	=	NA	NA	

is the **face value** of the bond. Most bonds also require the issuer to make cash interest payments based on a **stated interest rate** at regular intervals over the life of the bond. Exhibit 7.8 shows a typical bond certificate.

EXHIBIT 7.8

Bond Certificate

Advantages of Issuing Bonds

Bond financing offers companies the following advantages.

1. Bonds usually have longer terms than notes issued to banks. While typical bank loan terms range from 2 to 5 years, bonds normally have 20-year terms to maturity. Longer terms to maturity allow companies to implement long-term strategic plans without having to worry about frequent refinancing arrangements.

2. Bond interest rates may be lower than bank interest rates. Banks earn profits by borrowing money from the public (depositors) at low interest rates, then loaning that money to companies at higher rates. By issuing bonds directly to the public, companies can pay lower interest costs by eliminating the middle man (banks).

Fixed-Rate, Fixed-Term, Annual Interest Bonds

Assume Marsha Mason needs cash in order to seize a business opportunity. Mason knows of a company seeking a plot of land on which to store its inventory of crushed stone. Mason also knows of a suitable tract of land she could purchase for $100,000. The company has agreed to lease the land it needs from Mason for $12,000 per year. Mason lacks the funds to buy the land.

Some of Mason's friends recently complained about the low interest rates banks were paying on certificates of deposit. Mason suggested that her friends invest in bonds instead of CDs. She offered to sell them bonds with a 9 percent stated interest

 **BYTES**

On November 8, 2001, Enron Corporation announced that it would have to reduce its stockholders' equity by approximately $1.2 billion. On December 2, 2001, the company filed for Chapter 11 bankruptcy protection.

When covering this story, most of the media's attention focused on the overstatement of earnings that resulted from Enron's improper use of a form of partnerships called "special purpose entities." However, these entities were also used to improperly keep as much as $1 billion of debt off of Enron's balance sheet. Why did this matter to Enron? Enron was a very rapidly growing company and it used lots of debt to finance this growth. From 1999 to 2000 its assets grew from $33.4 billion to $65.5 billion, but its debt grew from $23.8 billion to $54.0 billion. This caused its debt to assets ratio to rise from 71.3 percent to 82.4 percent. The higher debt burden put Enron at risk of having to pay higher interest rates, an unattractive option for a company with this much debt.

rate. The terms specified in the bond agreement Mason drafted included making interest payments in cash on December 31 of each year, a five-year term to maturity, and pledging the land as collateral for the bonds.[5] Her friends were favorably impressed, and Mason issued the bonds to them in exchange for cash on January 1, 2011.

Mason used the bond proceeds to purchase the land and immediately contracted to lease it for five years. On December 31, 2015, the maturity date of the bonds, Mason sold the land for its $100,000 book value and used the proceeds from the sale to repay the bond liability.

Mason's business venture involved six distinct accounting events.

1. Received $100,000 cash from issuing five-year bonds at face value.
2. Invested proceeds from the bond issue to purchase land for $100,000 cash.
3. Earned $12,000 cash revenue annually from leasing the land.
4. Paid $9,000 annual interest on December 31 of each year.
5. Sold the land for $100,000 cash.
6. Repaid the bond principal to bondholders.

Effect of Events on Financial Statements

EVENT 1   Issue Bonds for Cash
Issuing bonds is an asset source transaction.

Assets (cash) and liabilities (bonds payable) increase. Net income is not affected. The $100,000 cash inflow is reported in the financing activities section of the statement of cash flows. These effects are shown here.

Assets	=	Liab.	+	Equity	Rev.	−	Exp.	=	Net Inc.	Cash Flow
Cash	=	Bonds Pay.								
100,000	=	100,000	+	NA	NA	−	NA	=	NA	100,000 FA

[5]In practice, bonds are usually issued for much larger sums of money, often hundreds of millions of dollars. Also, terms to maturity are normally long, with 20 years being common. Using such large amounts for such long terms is unnecessarily cumbersome for instructional purposes. The effects of bond issues can be illustrated efficiently by using smaller amounts of debt with shorter maturities, as assumed in the case of Marsha Mason.

EVENT 2   Investment in Land
Paying $100,000 cash to purchase land is an asset exchange transaction.

The asset cash decreases and the asset land increases. The income statement is not affected. The cash outflow is reported in the investing activities section of the statement of cash flows. These effects are illustrated below.

Assets			=	Liab.	+	Equity	Rev.	−	Exp.	=	Net Inc.	Cash Flow	
Cash	+	Land											
(100,000)	+	100,000	=	NA	+	NA	NA	−	NA	=	NA	(100,000)	IA

EVENT 3   Revenue Recognition
Recognizing $12,000 cash revenue from renting the property is an asset source transaction.

This event is repeated each year from 2011 through 2015. The event increases assets and stockholders' equity. Recognizing revenue increases net income. The cash inflow is reported in the operating activities section of the statement of cash flows. These effects follow.

Assets	=	Liab.	+	Equity	Rev.	−	Exp.	=	Net Inc.	Cash Flow	
Cash	=			Ret. Earn.							
12,000	=	NA	+	12,000	12,000	−	NA	=	12,000	12,000	OA

EVENT 4   Expense Recognition
Mason's $9,000 ($100,000 × 0.09) cash payment represents interest expense.

This event is also repeated each year from 2011 through 2015. The interest payment is an asset use transaction. Cash and stockholders' equity (retained earnings) decrease. The expense recognition decreases net income. The cash outflow is reported in the operating activities section of the statement of cash flows. These effects follow.

Assets	=	Liab.	+	Equity	Rev.	−	Exp.	=	Net Inc.	Cash Flow	
Cash	=			Ret. Earn.							
(9,000)	=	NA	+	(9,000)	NA	−	9,000	=	(9,000)	(9,000)	OA

EVENT 5   Sale of Investment in Land
Selling the land for cash equal to its $100,000 book value is an asset exchange transaction.

Cash increases and land decreases. Since there was no gain or loss on the sale, the income statement is not affected. The cash inflow is reported in the investing activities section of the statement of cash flows. These effects follow.

Assets			=	Liab.	+	Equity	Rev.	−	Exp.	=	Net Inc.	Cash Flow	
Cash	+	Land											
100,000	+	(100,000)	=	NA	+	NA	NA	−	NA	=	NA	100,000	IA

EVENT 6   Payoff of Bond Liability
Repaying the face value of the bond liability is an asset use transaction.

Cash and bonds payable decrease. The income statement is not affected. The cash outflow is reported in the financing activities section of the statement of cash flows.

Assets	=	Liab.	+	Equity	Rev.	−	Exp.	=	Net Inc.	Cash Flow
Cash	=	Bonds Pay.								
(100,000)	=	(100,000)	+	NA	NA	−	NA	=	NA	(100,000) FA

Financial Statements

Exhibit 7.9 displays Mason Company's financial statements. For simplicity, the income statement does not distinguish between operating and nonoperating items. Rent revenue and interest expense are constant across all accounting periods, so Mason recognizes

EXHIBIT 7.9

Mason Company Financial Statements

	Bonds Issued at Face Value				
	2011	2012	2013	2014	2015
Income Statements					
Rent revenue	$ 12,000	$ 12,000	$ 12,000	$ 12,000	$ 12,000
Interest expense	(9,000)	(9,000)	(9,000)	(9,000)	(9,000)
Net income	$ 3,000	$ 3,000	$ 3,000	$ 3,000	$ 3,000
Balance Sheets					
Assets					
Cash	$ 3,000	$ 6,000	$ 9,000	$ 12,000	$ 15,000
Land	100,000	100,000	100,000	100,000	0
Total assets	$103,000	$106,000	$109,000	$112,000	$ 15,000
Liabilities					
Bonds payable	$100,000	$100,000	$100,000	$100,000	$ 0
Stockholders' equity					
Retained earnings	3,000	6,000	9,000	12,000	15,000
Total liabilities and stockholders' equity	$103,000	$106,000	$109,000	$112,000	$ 15,000
Statements of Cash Flows					
Operating Activities					
Inflow from customers	$ 12,000	$ 12,000	$ 12,000	$ 12,000	$ 12,000
Outflow for interest	(9,000)	(9,000)	(9,000)	(9,000)	(9,000)
Investing Activities					
Outflow to purchase land	(100,000)				
Inflow from sale of land					100,000
Financing Activities					
Inflow from bond issue	100,000				
Outflow to repay bond liab.					(100,000)
Net change in cash	3,000	3,000	3,000	3,000	3,000
Plus: Beginning cash balance	0	3,000	6,000	9,000	12,000
Ending cash balance	$ 3,000	$ 6,000	$ 9,000	$ 12,000	$ 15,000

$3,000 of net income in each accounting period. On the balance sheet, cash increases by $3,000 each year because cash revenue exceeds cash paid for interest. Land remains constant each year at its $100,000 historical cost until it is sold in 2015. Similarly, the bonds payable liability is reported at $100,000 from the date the bonds were issued in 2011 until they are paid off on December 31, 2015.

Compare Blair Company's income statements in Exhibit 7.4 with Mason Company's income statements in Exhibit 7.9. Both Blair and Mason borrowed $100,000 cash at a 9 percent stated interest rate for five-year terms. Blair, however, repaid its liability under the terms of an installment note while Mason did not repay any principal until the end of the five-year bond term. Because Blair repaid part of the principal balance on the installment loan each year, Blair's interest expense declined each year. The interest expense on Mason's bond liability, however, remained constant because the full principal amount was outstanding for the entire five-year bond term.

SECURITY FOR LOAN AGREEMENTS

In general, large loans with long terms to maturity pose more risk to lenders (creditors) than small loans with short terms. To reduce the risk that they won't get paid, lenders frequently require borrowers (debtors) to pledge designated assets as **collateral** for loans. For example, when a bank makes a car loan, it usually retains legal title to the car until the loan is fully repaid. If the borrower fails to make the monthly payments, the bank repossesses the car, sells it to someone else, and uses the proceeds to pay the original owner's debt. Similarly, assets like accounts receivable, inventory, equipment, buildings, and land may be pledged as collateral for business loans.

In addition to requiring collateral, creditors often obtain additional protection by including **restrictive covenants** in loan agreements. Such covenants may restrict additional borrowing, limit dividend payments, or restrict salary increases. If the loan restrictions are violated, the borrower is in default and the loan balance is due immediately.

Finally, creditors often ask key personnel to provide copies of their personal tax returns and financial statements. The financial condition of key executives is important because they may be asked to pledge personal property as collateral for business loans, particularly for small businesses.

THE FINANCIAL **ANALYST**

Current versus Noncurrent

Distinguish between current and noncurrent assets and liabilities.

Because meeting obligations on time is critical to business survival, financial analysts and creditors are interested in whether companies will have enough money available to pay bills when they are due. Most businesses provide information about their bill-paying ability by classifying their assets and liabilities according to liquidity. The more quickly an asset is converted to cash or consumed, the more *liquid* it is. Assets are usually divided into two major classifications: *current* and *noncurrent*. Current items are also referred to as *short term* and noncurrent items as *long term*.

A **current (short-term) asset** is expected to be converted to cash or consumed within one year or an operating cycle, whichever is longer. An **operating cycle** is defined as the average time it takes a business to convert cash to inventory, inventory to accounts receivable, and accounts receivable back to cash. The financial tools used to measure the length of an operating cycle for particular businesses are discussed in Chapter 5. For most businesses, the operating cycle is less than one year. As a result, the one-year rule normally prevails with respect to classifying assets as current. The current assets section of a balance sheet typically includes the following items.

> Current Assets
> Cash
> Marketable securities
> Accounts receivable
> Short-term notes receivable
> Interest receivable
> Inventory
> Supplies
> Prepaid items

Given the definition of current assets, it seems reasonable to assume that **current (short-term) liabilities** would be those due within one year or an operating cycle, whichever is longer. This assumption is usually correct. However, an exception is made for long-term renewable debt. For example, consider a liability that was issued with a 20-year term to maturity. After 19 years, the liability becomes due within one year and is, therefore, a current liability. Even so, the liability will be classified as long term if the company plans to issue new long-term debt and to use the proceeds from that debt to repay the maturing liability. This situation is described as *refinancing short-term debt on a long-term basis.* In general, if a business does not plan to use any of its current assets to repay a debt, that debt is listed as long term even if it is due within one year. The current liabilities section of a balance sheet typically includes the following items.

> Current Liabilities
> Accounts payable
> Short-term notes payable
> Wages payable
> Taxes payable
> Interest payable

Prepare a classified balance sheet.

Balance sheets that distinguish between current and noncurrent items are called **classified balance sheets.** To enhance the usefulness of accounting information, most real-world balance sheets are classified. Exhibit 7.10 displays an example of a classified balance sheet.

Liquidity versus Solvency

Liquidity describes the ability to generate sufficient short-term cash flows to pay obligations as they come due. **Solvency** is the ability to repay liabilities in the long run. Liquidity and solvency are both important to the survival of a business. Financial analysts rely on several ratios to help them evaluate a company's liquidity and solvency. The primary ratio used to evaluate liquidity is the current ratio.

The **current ratio** is defined as

Use the current and debt to assets ratio to assess the level of liquidity.

$$\frac{\text{Current assets}}{\text{Current liabilities}}$$

Since current assets normally exceed current liabilities, this ratio is usually greater than 100 percent. For example, if a company has $250 in current assets and $100 in current liabilities, current assets are 250 percent of current liabilities. The current ratio is traditionally expressed as a decimal rather than as a percentage, however; most analysts would describe this example as a current ratio of 2.5 to 1 ($250 ÷ $100 = $2.50 in current assets for every $1 in current liabilities). This book uses the traditional format when referring to the current ratio.

EXHIBIT 7.10

LIMBAUGH COMPANY
Classified Balance Sheet
As of December 31, 2010

Assets

Current Assets

Cash	$ 20,000	
Accounts receivable	35,000	
Inventory	230,000	
Prepaid rent	3,600	
Total current assets		$288,600

Property, Plant, and Equipment

Office equipment	$ 80,000		
Less: Accumulated depreciation	(25,000)	55,000	
Building	340,000		
Less: Accumulated depreciation	(40,000)	300,000	
Land		120,000	
Total property, plant, and equipment			475,000
Total assets			$763,600

Liabilities and Stockholders' Equity

Current Liabilities

Accounts payable	$ 32,000	
Notes payable	120,000	
Salaries payable	32,000	
Unearned revenue	9,800	
Total current liabilities		$193,800

Long-Term Liabilities

Note payable		100,000
Total liabilities		293,800

Stockholders' Equity

Common stock	200,000	
Retained earnings	269,800	469,800
Total liabilities and stockholders' equity		$763,600

The current ratio is among the most widely used ratios in analyzing financial statements. Current ratios can be too high as well as too low. A low ratio suggests that the company may have difficulty paying its short-term obligations. A high ratio suggests that a company is not maximizing its earnings potential because investments in liquid assets usually do not earn as much money as investments in other assets. Companies must try to maintain an effective balance between liquid assets (so they can pay bills on time) and nonliquid assets (so they can earn a good return).

The **debt to assets ratio** is a common measure of solvency. This ratio reveals the percentage of a company's assets that is financed with borrowed money. The higher the ratio, the greater the financial risk. The debt to assets ratio is defined as

$$\frac{\text{Total debt}}{\text{Total assets}}$$

While a high debt to assets ratio suggests high risk, it may also signal an opportunity for a high return. Suppose a company earns a 12% return on investment and borrows money at 9%. The 3% spread (12% − 9%) goes into the pockets of the owners. In this case, owners benefit from high levels of debt rather than low levels. So, what is the ideal debt to assets ratio? The best ratio is the one that provides a proper balance between risk and return. Ratios that are excessively high or low suggest poor management.

Focus On INTERNATIONAL ISSUES

WHY ARE THESE BALANCE SHEETS BACKWARD?

Many of the differences in accounting rules used around the world would be difficult to detect by merely comparing financial statements of companies in different countries. For example, if a balance sheet for a U.S. company and one for a U.K. company both report an asset called *land*, it might not be clear whether the reported amounts were computed by using the same measurement rules or different measurement rules. Did both companies use historical cost as a basis for measurement? Perhaps not, but this would be difficult to determine by comparing their balance sheets.

However, one difference between financial reporting in the United Kingdom and the United States that is obvious is the arrangement of assets on the balance sheet. In this chapter, we explain that U.S. GAAP requires current assets to be shown first and noncurrent assets second; the same is true of liabilities. In the United Kingdom, noncurrent assets appear first, followed by current assets; however, liabilities are shown in the same order as in the United States. In other countries (e.g., France), both assets and liabilities are shown with noncurrent items first. The accounting rules of some countries require that equity be shown before liabilities; this is the opposite of U.S. GAAP. Therefore, to someone who learned accounting in the United States, the balance sheets of companies from some countries may appear backward or upside down.

No matter in what order the assets, liabilities, and equity accounts are arranged on a company's balance sheet, one accounting concept is true throughout the free world:

$$\text{Assets} = \text{Liabilities} + \text{Equity}$$

For a real-world example of the items discussed here, look up the financial statements of ITV, the largest commercial television network in the United Kingdom. Go to www.itvplc.com. Click on "Reports and Presentations." Next click on "Company Reports," then click on "Reports and Accounts 2007" or whatever is the most current fiscal year.

Real-World Data

Exhibit 7.11 presents the current ratios and debt to assets ratios for six companies in three different industries.

Which of these companies has the highest level of financial risk? Perhaps Dominion Resources because it has the highest debt to assets ratio. The electric utilities have higher debt to assets ratios and lower current ratios than those of the companies in the building supplies business. Does this mean that electric utilities are riskier investments? Not necessarily; since the companies are in different industries, the ratios may not be comparable. Utility companies have a more stable revenue base than building companies. If the economy turns downward, people are likely to continue to use electricity. However, they are less likely to buy a new home or to add on to their existing home. Because utility companies have a stable source of revenue, creditors are likely to feel comfortable with higher levels of debt for them than they would for building

EXHIBIT 7.11

Industry	Company	Current Ratio	Debt to Assets Ratio
Electric utilities	American Electric Power	0.72	0.75
	Dominion Resources	0.70	0.80
Grocery stores	Kroger	0.96	0.79
	Whole Foods Market	1.61	0.28
Building supplies	Home Depot	1.19	0.40
	Lowe's	1.34	0.42

companies. As previously stated, the industry must be considered when interpreting ratios, but of the companies shown in Exhibit 7.11, Whole Foods Market appears to have the lowest financial risk.

Finally, note that the debt to assets ratios, with the exception of the grocery stores, tend to be grouped by industry. Current ratios do vary somewhat among different industries, but they probably do not vary as much as the debt to assets ratios. Why? Because all companies, regardless of how they finance their total assets, must keep sufficient current assets on hand to repay current liabilities.

≪ A Look Back

Chapter 7 discussed accounting for current liabilities and long-term debt. Current liabilities are obligations due within one year or the company's operating cycle, whichever is longer. The chapter expanded the discussion of promissory notes begun in Chapter 5. Chapter 5 introduced accounting for the note payee, the lender; Chapter 7 discussed accounting for the note maker (issuer), the borrower. Notes payable and related interest payable are reported as liabilities on the balance sheet. Chapter 7 also discussed accounting for the contingent liability and warranty obligations.

Long-term notes payable mature in two to five years and usually require payments that include a return of principal plus interest. *Lines of credit* enable companies to borrow limited amounts on an as-needed basis. Although lines of credit normally have one-year terms, companies frequently renew them, extending the effective maturity date to the intermediate range of five or more years. Interest on a line of credit is normally paid monthly. Long-term debt financing for more than 10 years usually requires issuing *bonds*.

Finally, Chapter 7 discussed assessing companies' liquidity. The current ratio is current assets divided by current liabilities. The higher the current ratio, the more liquid the business.

≫ A Look Forward

A company seeking long-term financing might choose to use debt, such as the types of bonds or term loans that were discussed in this chapter. Owners' equity is another source of long-term financing. Several equity alternatives are available, depending on the type of business organization the owners choose to establish. For example, a company could be organized as a sole proprietorship, partnership, or corporation. Chapter 8 presents accounting issues related to equity transactions for each of these types of business structures.

SELF-STUDY REVIEW PROBLEM

Perfect Picture Inc. (PPI) experienced the following transactions during 2010. The transactions are summarized (transaction data pertain to the full year) and limited to those that affect the company's current liabilities.

1. PPI had cash sales of $820,000. The state requires that PPI charge customers an 8 percent sales tax (ignore cost of goods sold).
2. PPI paid the state sales tax authority $63,000.
3. On March 1, PPI issued a note payable to the County Bank. PPI received $50,000 cash (principal balance). The note had a one-year term and a 6 percent annual interest rate.
4. On December 31, PPI recognized accrued interest on the note issued in Event 3.
5. On December 31, PPI recognized warranty expense at the rate of 3 percent of sales.
6. PPI paid $22,000 cash to settle warranty claims.
7. On January 1, 2009, PPI issued a $100,000 installment note. The note had a 10-year term and an 8 percent interest rate. PPI agreed to repay the principal and interest in 10 annual interest payments of $14,902.94 at the end of each year.

Required

Prepare the liabilities section of the December 31, 2010, balance sheet.

Solution

PERFECT PICTURE INC.
Partial Balance Sheet
December 31, 2010

Current Liabilities	
Sales tax payable	$ 2,600
Notes payable	50,000
Interest payable	2,500
Warranties payable	2,600
Installment note payable	85,642
Total liabilities	$143,342

Explanations for amounts shown in the balance sheet:

1. Sales Tax Payable: $820,000 × 0.08 = $65,600 Amount Due − $63,000 Amount Paid = $2,600 Liability as of December 31, 2010.
2. Note Payable: $50,000 Borrowed with no repayment.
3. Interest Payable: $50,000 × 0.06 × 10/12 = $2,500.
4. Warranty Payable: $820,000 × 0.03 = $24,600 Estimated Warranty Liability − $22,000 Cash Paid to Settle Warranty Claims = $2,600 Remaining Liability.
5. Installment Note Payable:

Accounting Period	Principal Bal. January 1 A	Cash Payment December 31 B	Applied to Interest C = A × 0.08	Applied to Principal B − C
2009	$100,000.00	$14,902.94	$8,000.00	$6,902.94
2010	93,097.06	14,902.94	7,447.76	7,455.18
2011*	85,641.88			

*The amount due on December 31, 2010, is the same as the amount due on January 1, 2011. The amount shown on the balance sheet has been rounded to the nearest dollar.

KEY TERMS

Amortization 258	Current (short-term)	Going concern assumption 250	Operating cycle 266
Bond certificates 261	liabilities 251, 267	Installment notes 258	Restrictive covenants 266
Bondholder 261	Current ratio 267	Issuer 252, 261	Solvency 267
Classified balance sheets 267	Debt to assets ratio 268	Line of credit 261	Stated interest rate 262
Collateral 266	Face value 262	Liquidity 267	Variable interest rate 257
Contingent liability 254	Fixed interest rate 257	Long-term liabilities 257	Warranties 255
Current (short-term) asset 266	General uncertainties 254	Note payable 252	

QUESTIONS

1. What type of transaction is a cash payment to creditors? How does this type of transaction affect the accounting equation?

2. What is a current liability? Distinguish between a current liability and a long-term debt.

3. What type of entry is the entry to record accrued interest expense? How does it affect the accounting equation?

4. Who is the maker of a note payable?

5. What is the going concern assumption? Does it affect the way liabilities are reported in the financial statements?

6. Why is it necessary to make an adjustment at the end of the accounting period for unpaid interest on a note payable?

7. Assume that on October 1, 2010, Big Company borrowed $10,000 from the local bank at 6 percent interest. The note is due on October 1, 2011. How much interest does Big pay in 2010? How much interest does Big pay in 2011? What amount of cash does Big pay back in 2011?

8. When a business collects sales tax from customers, is it revenue? Why or why not?

9. What is a contingent liability?

10. List the three categories of contingent liabilities.

11. Are contingent liabilities recorded on a company's books? Explain.

12. What is the difference in accounting procedures for a liability that is probable and estimable and one that is reasonably possible but not estimable?

13. What type of liabilities are not recorded on a company's books?

14. What does the term *warranty* mean?

15. What effect does recognizing future warranty obligations have on the balance sheet? On the income statement?

16. When is warranty cost reported on the statement of cash flows?

17. What is the difference between classification of a note as short term or long term?

18. At the beginning of year 1, B Co. has a note payable of $72,000 that calls for an annual payment of $16,246, which includes both principal and interest. If the interest rate is 8 percent, what is the amount of interest expense in year 1 and in year 2? What is the balance of the note at the end of year 2?

19. What is the purpose of a line of credit for a business? Why would a company choose to obtain a line of credit instead of issuing bonds?

20. What are the primary sources of debt financing for most large companies?

21. What are some advantages of issuing bonds versus borrowing from a bank?

22. What are some disadvantages of issuing bonds?

23. Why can a company usually issue bonds at a lower interest rate than the company would pay if the funds were borrowed from a bank?

24. If Roc Co. issued $100,000 of 5 percent, 10-year bonds at the face amount, what is the effect of the issuance of the bonds on the financial statements? What amount of interest expense will Roc Co. recognize each year?

25. What is a classified balance sheet?

26. What is the difference between the liquidity and the solvency of a business?

27. The higher the company's current ratio, the better the company's financial condition. Do you agree with this statement? Explain.

EXERCISES

connect
|ACCOUNTING

All applicable Exercises are available with McGraw-Hill Connect Accounting.

LO 1

Exercise 7-1   *Recognizing accrued interest expense*

Flash Corporation borrowed $120,000 from the bank on November 1, 2010. The note had an 8 percent annual rate of interest and matured on April 30, 2011. Interest and principal were paid in cash on the maturity date.

Required

a. What amount of interest expense was paid in cash in 2010?
b. What amount of interest expense was reported on the 2010 income statement?
c. What amount of total liabilities was reported on the December 31, 2010, balance sheet?
d. What total amount of cash was paid to the bank on April 30, 2011, for principal and interest?
e. What amount of interest expense was reported on the 2011 income statement?

Exercise 7-2   *Effects of recognizing accrued interest on financial statements*

LO 1

Joe Hughes started Hughes Company on January 1, 2012. The company experienced the following events during its first year of operation.

1. Earned $2,500 of cash revenue for performing services.
2. Borrowed $3,000 cash from the bank.
3. Adjusted the accounting records to recognize accrued interest expense on the bank note. The note, issued on August 1, 2012, had a one-year term and a 6 percent annual interest rate.

Required

a. What is the amount of interest expense in 2012?
b. What amount of cash was paid for interest in 2012?
c. Use a horizontal statements model to show how each event affects the balance sheet, income statement, and statement of cash flows. Indicate whether the event increases (I), decreases (D), or does not affect (NA) each element of the financial statements. In the Cash Flows column, designate the cash flows as operating activities (OA), investing activities (IA), or financing activities (FA). The first transaction has been recorded as an example.

Event No.	Balance Sheet										Income Statement					Statement of Cash Flows
	Cash	=	Notes Pay.	+	Int. Pay.	+	Com. Stk.	+	Ret. Earn.		Rev.	−	Exp.	=	Net Inc.	
1	I	=	NA	+	NA	+	NA	+	I		I	−	NA	=	I	I OA

Exercise 7-3   *Recording sales tax expense*

LO 2

The Campus Book Store sells books and other supplies to students in a state where the sales tax rate is 7 percent. The Campus Book Store engaged in the following transactions for 2010. Sales tax of 7 percent is collected on all sales.

1. Book sales, not including sales tax, for 2010 amounted to $315,000 cash.
2. Cash sales of miscellaneous items in 2010 were $175,000, not including tax.
3. Cost of goods sold amounted to $255,000 for the year.
4. Paid $145,000 in operating expenses for the year.
5. Paid the sales tax collected to the state agency.

Required

a. What is the total amount of sales tax the Campus Book Store collected and paid for the year?
b. What is the Campus Book Store's net income for the year?

Exercise 7-4   *Recognizing sales tax payable*

LO 2

The following selected transactions apply to Quick Mart for November and December 2010. November was the first month of operations. Sales tax is collected at the time of sale but is not paid to the state sales tax agency until the following month.

1. Cash sales for November 2010 were $72,000 plus sales tax of 8 percent.
2. Quick Mart paid the November sales tax to the state agency on December 10, 2010.
3. Cash sales for December 2010 were $96,000 plus sales tax of 8 percent.

Required

a. Show the effect of the above transactions on a statements model like the one shown below.

Assets	=	Liabilities	+		Equity		Income Statement			
Cash	=	Sales Tax Pay.	+	Com. Stk.	+	Ret. Earn.	Rev. − Exp. = Net Inc.			Cash Flow

b. What was the total amount of sales tax paid in 2010?
c. What was the total amount of sales tax collected in 2010?
d. What is the amount of the sales tax liability as of December 31, 2010?
e. On what financial statement will the sales tax liability appear?

LO 3

Exercise 7-5 *Contingent liabilities*

The following three independent sets of facts relate to contingent liabilities.

1. In November of the current year an automobile manufacturing company recalled all mini-vans manufactured during the past two years. A flaw in the seat belt fastener was discovered and the recall provides for replacement of the defective fasteners. The estimated cost of this recall is $1 million.
2. The EPA has notified a company of violations of environmental laws relating to hazard-ous waste. These actions seek cleanup costs, penalties, and damages to property. The company is reasonably certain that the cleanup cost will be approximately $5 million. In addition, potential reimbursements for property damage could be as much as $2 million or as little as $100,000. There is no way to more accurately estimate the property damage at this time.
3. Big Company does not carry property damage insurance because of the cost. The com-pany suffered substantial losses each year of the past three years. However, it has had no losses for the current year. Management thinks this is too good to be true and is sure there will be significant losses in the coming year. However, the exact amount cannot be determined.

Required

a. Discuss the various categories of contingent liabilities.
b. For each item above determine the correct accounting treatment.

LO 4

Exercise 7-6 *Effect of warranties on income and cash flow*

To support herself while attending school, Kim Lee sold stereo systems to other students. During her first year of operation, she sold systems that had cost her $95,000 cash for $140,000 cash. She provided her customers with a one-year warranty against defects in parts and labor. Based on industry standards, she estimated that warranty claims would amount to 6 percent of sales. During the year she paid $200 cash to replace a defective tuner.

Required

a. Prepare an income statement and statement of cash flows for Lee's first year of operation.
b. Explain the difference between net income and the amount of cash flow from operating activities.

LO 4

Exercise 7-7 *Effect of warranty obligations and payments on financial statements*

The Cycle Company provides a 120-day parts-and-labor warranty on all merchandise it sells. Cycle estimates the warranty expense for the current period to be $1,400. During the period a customer returned a product that cost $596 to repair.

Required

a. Show the effects of these transactions on the financial statements using a horizontal state-ments model like the example shown here. Use a + to indicate increase, a − for decrease, and NA for not affected. In the Cash Flow column, indicate whether the item is an oper-ating activity (OA), investing activity (IA), or financing activity (FA).

Assets	=	Liab.	+	Equity	Rev.	−	Exp.	=	Net Inc.	Cash Flow

b. Discuss the advantage of estimating the amount of warranty expense.

Exercise 7-8   *Current liabilities*

LO 2, 4, 8

The following transactions apply to Comfort Mattress Sales for 2010.

1. The business was started when the company received $30,000 from the issue of common stock.
2. Purchased mattress inventory of $200,000 on account.
3. Sold mattresses for $300,000 cash (not including sales tax). Sales tax of 8 percent is col-lected when the merchandise is sold. The merchandise had a cost of $150,000.
4. Provided a six-month warranty on the mattresses sold. Based on industry estimates, the warranty claims would amount to 2 percent of mattress sales.
5. Paid the sales tax to the state agency on $250,000 of the sales.
6. On September 1, 2010, borrowed $30,000 from the local bank. The note had a 6 percent interest rate and matured on March 1, 2011.
7. Paid $4,600 for warranty repairs during the year.
8. Paid operating expenses of $96,000 for the year.
9. Paid $175,000 of accounts payable.
10. Record accrued interest on the note issued in transaction no. 6.

Required

a. Record the above transactions in a horizontal statements model like the following one.

	Balance Sheet								Income Statement	
Event	**Assets**	**=**	**Liabilities**					**+** **Equity**	**Rev. − Exp. = Net Inc.**	**Statemt. of Cash Flows**
	Cash + Mdse. Inv.		Acct. Pay. + Sales Tax Pay. + War. Pay. + Int. Pay. + Notes Pay.					+ Com. Stock + Ret. Earn.		

b. Prepare the income statement, balance sheet, and statement of cash flows for 2010.
c. What is the total amount of current liabilities at December 31, 2010?

Exercise 7-9   *How credit terms affect financial statements*

LO 5

Cordell Co. is planning to finance an expansion of its operations by borrowing $100,000. City Bank has agreed to loan Cordell the funds. Cordell has two repayment options: (1) to issue a note with the principal due in 10 years and with interest payable annually or (2) to issue a note to repay $10,000 of the principal each year along with the annual interest based on the unpaid principal balance. Assume the interest rate is 8 percent for each option.

Required

a. What amount of interest will Cordell pay in year 1
   (1) Under option 1?
   (2) Under option 2?

b. What amount of interest will Cordell pay in year 2

   (1) Under option 1?

   (2) Under option 2?

c. Explain the advantage of each option.

LO 5

Exercise 7-10   *Accounting for an installment note payable with annual payments that include interest and principal*

On January 1, 2010, Grant Co. borrowed $80,000 cash from First Bank by issuing a four-year, 6 percent note. The principal and interest are to be paid by making annual payments in the amount of $23,087. Payments are to be made December 31 of each year, beginning December 31, 2010.

Required

Prepare an amortization schedule for the interest and principal payments for the four-year period.

LO 5

Exercise 7-11   *Long-term installment note payable*

Jerry Posey started a business by issuing a $50,000 face value note to State National Bank on January 1, 2010. The note had a 5 percent annual rate of interest and a 10-year term. Payments of $6,475 are to be made each December 31 for 10 years.

Required

a. What portion of the December 31, 2010, payment is applied to

   (1) Interest expense?

   (2) Principal?

b. What is the principal balance on January 1, 2011?

c. What portion of the December 31, 2011, payment is applied to

   (1) Interest expense?

   (2) Principal?

LO 5

Exercise 7-12   *Amortization of a long-term loan*

A partial amortization schedule for a five-year note payable that Puro Co. issued on January 1, 2010, is shown here:

Accounting Period	Principal Balance January 1	Cash Payment	Applied to Interest	Applied to Principal
2010	$100,000	$25,046	$8,000	$17,046
2011	82,954	25,046	6,636	18,410

Required

a. What rate of interest is Puro Co. paying on the note?

b. Using a financial statements model like the one shown below, record the appropriate amounts for the following two events.

   (1) January 1, 2010, issue of the note payable.

   (2) December 31, 2010, payment on the note payable.

Event No.	Assets	=	Liab.	+	Equity	Rev.	−	Exp.	=	Net Inc.	Cash Flow
1											

c. If the company earned $75,000 cash revenue and paid $35,000 in cash expenses in addition to the interest in 2010, what is the amount of each of the following?

   (1) Net income for 2010.

   (2) Cash flow from operating activities for 2010.

   (3) Cash flow from financing activities for 2010.

d. What is the amount of interest expense on this loan for 2012?

Exercise 7-13   *Accounting for a line of credit*   LO 6

Song Co. uses an approved line of credit not to exceed $250,000 with the local bank to provide short-term financing for its business operations. Song either borrows or repays funds on the first day of a month. Interest is payable monthly at the bank's prime interest rate plus 1 percent. The following table shows the amounts borrowed and repaid for 2010 along with the bank's prime interest rate.

Month	Amount Borrowed or (Repaid)	Prime Rate for the Month, %
January	70,000	4
February	$40,000	4
March	(20,000)	4.5
April	(10,000)	5
May	(20,000)	4
June	(10,000)	4.5
July–October	0	4.5
November	40,000	5.5
December	(20,000)	5.25

Required

a. Show the effects of these transactions on the financial statements using a horizontal statements model like the one shown here. Use a + to indicate increase, a − for decrease, and NA for not affected. In the Cash Flow column, indicate whether the item is an operating activity (OA), investing activity (IA), or financing activity (FA).

Assets	=	Liabilities	+	Equity	Rev.	−	Exp.	=	Net Inc.	Cash Flow

b. What is the total amount of interest expense paid for 2010?

Exercise 7-14   *Two complete accounting cycles: bonds issued at face value with annual interest*   LO 7

Pulse Company issued $200,000 of 10-year, 6 percent bonds on January 1, 2010. The bonds were issued at face value. Interest is payable in cash on December 31 of each year. Pulse immediately invested the proceeds from the bond issue in land. The land was leased for an annual $32,000 of cash revenue, which was collected on December 31 of each year, beginning December 31, 2010.

Required

a. Organize the transaction data in accounts under the accounting equation.

b. Prepare the income statement, balance sheet, and statement of cash flows for 2010 and 2011.

Exercise 7-15   *Preparing a classified balance sheet*   LO 9

Required

Use the following information to prepare a classified balance sheet for Little Co. at the end of 2010.

Accounts receivable	$42,500
Accounts payable	12,500
Cash	16,230
Common stock	40,000
Long-term notes payable	27,000
Merchandise inventory	31,000
Office equipment (net)	27,000
Retained earnings	40,430
Prepaid insurance	3,200

LO **10**

Exercise 7-16   *Performing ratio analysis using real-world data*

Tupperware Company claims to be "a global direct seller of premium, innovative products across multiple brands and categories through an independent sales force of approximately 2.1 million." Its goods are sold in almost 100 countries through its eight brands. The following data were taken from the company's 2007 annual report. Dollar amounts are in millions.

	Fiscal Years Ending	
	December 29, 2007	**December 30, 2006**
Current assets	$ 699.5	$ 586.6
Current liabilities	450.3	359.3
Total assets	1,868.7	1,712.1
Total liabilities	1,346.0	1,311.6

Required

a. Compute Tupperware's current ratios for 2007 and 2006.

b. Compute Tupperware's debt to assets ratios for 2007 and 2006.

c. Based on the ratios computed in Requirements *a* and *b*, did Tupperware's liquidity get better or worse from 2006 to 2007?

d. Based on the ratios computed in Requirements *a* and *b*, did Tupperware's solvency get better or worse from 2006 to 2007?

PROBLEMS

All applicable Problems are available with McGraw-Hill *Connect Accounting.*

LO **1, 2, 3, 4**

CHECK FIGURE
Net Income 2010: $87,750

Problem 7-17   *Account for short-term debt and sales tax—two accounting cycles*

The following transactions apply to Allied Enterprises for 2010, its first year of operations.

1. Received $50,000 cash from the issue of a short-term note with a 6 percent interest rate and a one-year maturity. The note was made on April 1, 2010.

2. Received $180,000 cash plus applicable sales tax from performing services. The services are subject to a sales tax rate of 6 percent.

3. Paid $90,000 cash for other operating expenses during the year.

4. Paid the sales tax due on $140,000 of the service revenue for the year. Sales tax on the balance of the revenue is not due until 2010.

5. Recognized the accrued interest at December 31, 2010.

The following transactions apply to Allied Enterprises for 2011.

1. Paid the balance of the sales tax due for 2010.

2. Received $215,000 cash plus applicable sales tax from performing services. The services are subject to a sales tax rate of 6 percent.

3. Repaid the principal of the note and applicable interest on April 1, 2011.

4. Paid $125,000 of other operating expenses during the year.

5. Paid the sales tax due on $180,000 of the services revenue. The sales tax on the balance of the revenue is not due until 2012.

Required

a. Organize the transaction data in accounts under an accounting equation.

b. Prepare an income statement, statement of changes in stockholders' equity, balance sheet, and statement of cash flow for 2010 and 2011.

Problem 7-18 *Effect of accrued interest on financial statements*

LO 1

CHECK FIGURES
b. $18,500
i. $34,060

Magic Enterprises borrowed $18,000 from the local bank on July 1, 2010, when the company was started. The note had an 8 percent annual interest rate and a one-year term to maturity. Magic Enterprises recognized $42,500 of revenue on account in 2010 and $45,000 of revenue on account in 2011. Cash collections from accounts receivable were $36,000 in 2010 and $35,000 in 2011. Magic Enterprises paid $24,000 of salaries expense in 2010 and $28,000 of salaries expense in 2011. Repaid loan and interest at maturity date.

Required

a. Organize the information in accounts under an accounting equation.
b. What amount of net cash flow from operating activities would Magic report on the 2010 cash flow statement?
c. What amount of interest expense would Magic report on the 2010 income statement?
d. What amount of total liabilities would Magic report on the December 31, 2010, balance sheet?
e. What amount of retained earnings would Magic report on the December 31, 2010, balance sheet?
f. What amount of cash flow from financing activities would Magic report on the 2010 statement of cash flows?
g. What amount of interest expense would Magic report on the 2011 income statement?
h. What amount of cash flows from operating activities would Magic report on the 2011 cash flow statement?
i. What amount of total assets would Magic report on the December 31, 2011, balance sheet?

Problem 7-19 *Current liabilities*

LO 1, 2, 4

CHECK FIGURE
Total Current Liabilities: $53,300

The following selected transactions were taken from the books of Chandra Company for 2010.

1. On February 1, 2010, borrowed $60,000 cash from the local bank. The note had a 6 percent interest rate and was due on June 1, 2010.
2. Cash sales for the year amounted to $310,000 plus sales tax at the rate of 7 percent.
3. Chandra provides a 90-day warranty on the merchandise sold. The warranty expense is estimated to be 1 percent of sales.
4. Paid the sales tax to the state sales tax agency on $280,000 of the sales.
5. Paid the note due on June 1 and the related interest.
6. On November 1, 2010, borrowed $50,000 cash from the local bank. The note had a 6 percent interest rate and a one-year term to maturity.
7. Paid $2,400 in warranty repairs.
8. A customer has filed a lawsuit against Chandra for $500,000 for breach of contract. The company attorney does not believe the suit has merit.

Required

a. Answer the following questions:
   (1) What amount of cash did Chandra pay for interest during the year?
   (2) What amount of interest expense is reported on Chandra's income statement for the year?
   (3) What is the amount of warranty expense for the year?
b. Prepare the current liabilities section of the balance sheet at December 31, 2010.
c. Show the effect of these transactions on the financial statements using a horizontal statements model like the one shown here. Use a + to indicate increase, a − for decrease, and NA for not affected. In the Cash Flow column, indicate whether the item is an operating activity (OA), investing activity (IA), or financing activity (FA). The first transaction is recorded as an example.

Assets	=	Liabilities	+	Equity	Rev.	−	Exp.	=	Net Inc.	Cash Flow
+		+		NA	NA		NA		NA	+ FA

LO 3

Problem 7-20   *Contingent liabilities*

Required

How should each of the following situations be reported in the financial statements?

a. It has been determined that one of the company's products has caused a safety hazard. It is considered probable that liabilities have been incurred and a reasonable estimate of the amount can be made.

b. A company warehouse is located in a section of the city that has routinely flooded in the past. Consequently the company can no longer find a source of insurance for the warehouse. No flood has yet occurred this year.

c. Because of newly passed legislation, a company will have to upgrade its facilities over the next two years. Significant expenditures will occur, but at this time the amount has not been determined.

LO 9

e**X**cel

CHECK FIGURES
Total Current Assets: $250,300
Total Current Liabilities: $110,900

Problem 7-21   *Multistep income statement and classified balance sheet*

Required

Use the following information to prepare a multistep income statement and a classified balance sheet for Beamer Equipment Co. for 2010. (*Hint:* Some of the items will *not* appear on either statement, and ending retained earnings must be calculated.)

Salaries expense	$ 96,000	Beginning retained earnings	$ 10,400
Common stock	40,000	Warranties payable (short term)	1,300
Notes receivable (short term)	12,000	Gain on sale of equipment	6,400
Allowance for doubtful accounts	4,000	Operating expenses	70,000
Accumulated depreciation	30,000	Cash flow from investing activities	80,000
Notes payable (long term)	103,600	Prepaid rent	9,600
Salvage value of building	4,000	Land	36,000
Interest payable (short term)	1,800	Cash	17,800
Uncollectible accounts expense	10,800	Inventory	122,800
Supplies	1,600	Accounts payable	46,000
Equipment	60,000	Interest expense	24,000
Interest revenue	4,200	Salaries payable	9,200
Sales revenue	396,000	Unearned revenue	52,600
Dividends	8,000	Cost of goods sold	143,000
Warranty expense	3,400	Accounts receivable	90,000
Interest receivable (short term)	500		

LO 5

CHECK FIGURES
a. 2008 Ending Principal
   Balance: $55,116
c. 2010 Net Income: $38,006

Problem 7-22   *Effect of a term loan on financial statements*

On January 1, 2008, Holmes Co. borrowed cash from First City Bank by issuing an $80,000 face value, three-year term note that had a 7 percent annual interest rate. The note is to be repaid by making annual payments of $30,484 that include both interest and principal on December 31. Holmes invested the proceeds from the loan in land that generated lease revenues of $40,000 cash per year.

Required

a. Prepare an amortization schedule for the three-year period.

b. Organize the information in accounts under an accounting equation.

c. Prepare an income statement, balance sheet, and statement of cash flows for each of the three years.

d. Does cash outflow from operating activities remain constant or change each year? Explain.

LO 5

Problem 7-23   *Accounting for an installment note payable*

The following transactions apply to Gupta Co. for 2010, its first year of operations.

1. Received $50,000 cash in exchange for issuance of common stock.

2. Secured a $100,000, 10-year installment loan from First Bank. The interest rate was 6 percent and annual payments are $14,901.33.

3. Purchased land for $40,000.
4. Provided services for $96,000 cash.
5. Paid other operating expenses of $42,000.
6. Paid the annual payment on the loan.

Required

a. Organize the transaction data in accounts under an accounting equation.
b. Prepare an income statement and balance sheet for 2010.
c. What is the interest expense for 2011? 2012?

Problem 7-24   *Accounting for a line of credit*

LO 6

CHECK FIGURE
a. Interest Expense for
January: $250

Sayles Co. uses a line of credit to help finance its inventory purchases. Sayles sells ski equipment and uses the line of credit to build inventory for its peak sales months, which tend to be clustered in the winter months. Account balances at the beginning of 2010 were as follows.

Cash	$80,000
Inventory	65,000
Common stock	70,000
Retained earnings	75,000

Sayles experienced the following transactions for January, February, and March, 2010.

1. January 1, 2010, obtained approval for a line of credit of up to $300,000. Funds are to be obtained or repaid on the first day of each month. The interest rate is the bank prime rate plus 1 percent.
2. January 1, 2010, borrowed $50,000 on the line of credit. The bank's prime interest rate is 5 percent for January.
3. January 15, purchased inventory on account, $82,000.
4. January 31, paid other operating expenses of $12,000.
5. In January, sold inventory for $90,000 on account. The inventory had cost $62,000.
6. January 31, paid the interest due on the line of credit.
7. February 1, borrowed $80,000 on the line of credit. The bank's prime rate is 6 percent for February.
8. February 1, paid the accounts payable from transaction 3.
9. February 10, collected $81,000 of the sales on account.
10. February 20, purchased inventory on account, $96,000.
11. February sales on account were $130,000. The inventory had cost $91,000.
12. February 28, paid the interest due on the line of credit.
13. March 1, repaid $25,000 on the line of credit. The bank's prime rate is 5 percent for March.
14. March 5, paid $70,000 of the accounts payable.
15. March 10, collected $120,000 from accounts receivable.
16. March 20, purchased inventory on account, $78,000.
17. March sales on account were $165,000. The inventory had cost $87,000.
18. March 31, paid the interest due on the line of credit.

Required

a. What is the amount of interest expense for January? February? March?
b. What amount of cash was paid for interest in January? February? March?

Problem 7-25   *Effect of a line of credit on financial statements*

LO 6

Hulse Company has a line of credit with Bay Bank. Hulse can borrow up to $250,000 at any time over the course of the 2010 calendar year. The following table shows the prime rate expressed as an annual percentage along with the amounts borrowed and repaid during 2010. Hulse agreed to pay interest at an annual rate equal to 1 percent above the bank's prime rate. Funds are borrowed or repaid on the first day of each month. Interest is payable in cash on the last day of the month. The interest rate is applied to the outstanding monthly balance. For example, Hulse pays 6 percent (5 percent + 1 percent) annual interest on $70,000 for the month of January.

Month	Amount Borrowed or (Repaid)	Prime Rate for the Month, %
January	$70,000	5
February	40,000	5
March	(20,000)	6
April through October	No change	No change
November	(30,000)	6
December	(20,000)	5

Hulse earned $22,000 of cash revenue during 2010.

Required

a. Organize the information in accounts under an accounting equation.
b. Prepare an income statement, balance sheet, and statement of cash flows for 2010.
c. Write a memo discussing the advantages to a business of arranging a line of credit.

LO 1, 6, 7

Problem 7-26   *Effect of debt transactions on financial statements*

Required

Show the effect of each of the following independent accounting events on the financial statements using a horizontal statements model like the following one. Use + for increase, − for decrease, and NA for not affected. The first event is recorded as an example.

Event No.	Assets	=	Liab.	+	Equity	Rev.	−	Exp.	=	Net Inc.	Cash Flow
a	+		+		NA	NA		NA		NA	+ FA

a. Issued a bond at face value.
b. Made an interest payment on a bond that had been issued at face value.
c. Borrowed funds using a line of credit.
d. Made an interest payment for funds that had been borrowed against a line of credit.
e. Made a cash payment on a note payable for both interest and principal.

LO 10

Problem 7-27   *Performing ratio analysis using real-world data*

Texas Instruments, Inc., claims to be "the world leader in digital signal processing and analog technologies, the semiconductor engines of the Internet age." Eastman Kodak Company manufactures Kodak film, cameras and related products. The following data were taken from the companies' December 31, 2007, annual reports. Dollar amounts are in millions.

	Eastman Kodak	Texas Instruments
Current assets	$ 6,053	$ 6,918
Current liabilities	4,446	2,025
Total assets	13,659	12,667
Total liabilities	10,630	2,692

Required

a. Compute the current ratio for each company.
b. Compute the debt to assets ratio for each company.
c. Based on the ratios computed in Requirements *a* and *b*, which company had the better liquidity in 2007?
d. Based on the ratios computed in Requirements *a* and *b*, which company had the better solvency in 2007?

ANALYZE, THINK, COMMUNICATE

ATC 7-1   Business Applications Case   *Understanding real-world annual reports*

Required

Use the Topps Company's annual report in Appendix B to answer the following questions.

The Topps Company, Inc.

a. What was Topps' current ratio as of February 25, 2007?
b. Which of Topps' current assets had the largest balance as of February 25, 2007?
c. What percentage of Topps' total assets consisted of current assets?
d. Instead of "Cash," Topps' balance sheet shows an account named "Cash and cash equivalents." What do cash equivalents include? (See the footnotes.)
e. Does Topps have any restrictions placed on it by its creditors? (*Hint:* See Note 11.)

ATC 7-2   Group Assignment   *Using current ratios to make comparisons*

The following accounting information pertains to Adams and Hood companies at the end of 2010.

Account Title	Adams	Hood
Cash	$ 12,000	$ 15,000
Wages payable	10,000	12,000
Merchandise inventory	20,000	55,000
Building	90,000	80,000
Accounts receivable	22,000	25,000
Long-term notes payable	80,000	100,000
Land	35,000	40,000
Accounts payable	25,000	35,000
Sales revenue	220,000	250,000
Expenses	190,000	230,000

Required

a. Organize the class into two sections and divide each section into groups of three to five students. Assign each of the sections one of the companies.

Group Tasks

(1) Identify the current assets and current liabilities, and compute the current ratio for the particular company assigned to the group.
(2) Assuming that all assets and liabilities are listed here, compute the debt to assets ratio for the particular company assigned to the group.

Class Discussion

b. Have a representative from each section report the current ratio and debt to assets ratio for their respective companies.
c. Solicit comments regarding which company has the greater financial risk in both the short and long term.

ATC 7-3   Real-World Case   *Unusual types of liabilities*

In the liabilities section of its 2007 balance sheet, Wachovia Corporation reported "noninterest-bearing deposits" of over $60 billion. Wachovia is a very large banking company. In the liabilities section of its 2007 balance sheet, Newmont Mining Corporation reported "reclamation and remediation liabilities" of more than $623 million. Newmont Mining is involved in gold mining and refining activities. In the accrued liabilities reported on its 2007 balance sheet, Conoco Phillips included $1.1 billion for "accrued dismantlement, removal, and environmental costs."

Required

a. For each of the preceding liabilities, write a brief explanation of what you believe the nature of the liability to be and how the company will pay it off. To develop your answers, think about the nature of the industry in which each of the companies operates.

b. Of the three liabilities described, which do you think poses the most risk for the company? In other words, for which liability are actual costs most likely to exceed the liability reported on the balance sheet? Uncertainty creates risk.

ATC 7-4   Business Applications Case   *Using the current ratio*

The following information was drawn from the balance sheets of the Alberta and Ottawa Companies.

	Alberta Company	Ottawa Company
Current assets	$45,000	$72,000
Current liabilities	28,000	54,000

Required

a. Compute the current ratio for each company.

b. Which company has the greater likelihood of being able to pay its bills?

c. Assuming that both companies have the same amount of total assets, which company would produce the higher return on assets ratio?

ATC 7-5   Business Applications Case   *Debt versus equity financing*

Mack Company plans to invest $50,000 in land that will produce annual rent revenue equal to 15 percent of the investment starting on January 1, 2007. The revenue will be collected in cash at the end of each year, starting December 31, 2007. Mack can obtain the cash necessary to purchase the land from two sources. Funds can be obtained by issuing $50,000 of 10 percent, five-year bonds at their face amount. Interest due on the bonds is payable on December 31 of each year with the first payment due on December 31, 2007. Alternatively, the $50,000 needed to invest in land can be obtained from equity financing. In this case, the stockholders (holders of the equity) will be paid a $5,000 annual distribution. Mack Company is in a 30 percent income tax bracket.

Required

a. Prepare an income statement and statement of cash flows for 2007 under the two alternative financing proposals.

b. Write a short memorandum explaining why one financing alternative provides more net income but less cash flow than the other.

ATC 7-6   Writing Assignment   *Definition of elements of financial statements*

Putting "yum" on people's faces around the world is the mission of YUM Brands, Inc. Yum was spun off from PepsiCo in 1997. A spin-off occurs when a company separates its operations into two or more distinct companies. The company was originally composed of KFC, Pizza Hut, and Taco Bell and was operated as a part of PepsiCo prior to the spin-off. In 2002 YUM acquired A & W All American Foods and Long John Silver's units. YUM's long-term debt in 2007 was $2.9 billion. YUM's net income before interest and taxes in 2007 was $1.36 million.

Required

a. If YUM's debt remains constant at $2.9 billion for 2008, how much interest will YUM incur in 2008, assuming the average interest rate is 6 percent?

b. Does the debt seem excessive compared with the amount of 2007 net income before interest and taxes? Explain.

c. Assuming YUM pays tax at the rate of 25 percent, what amount of tax will YUM pay in 2007?

d. Assume you are the president of the company. Write a memo to the shareholders explaining how YUM is able to meet its obligations and increase stockholders' equity.

ATC 7-7   Corporate Governance   *Sometimes debt is not debt*

David Sheridan was a well-respected CPA in his mid-fifties. After spending 10 years at a national accounting firm, he was hired by Global, Inc., a multinational corporation headquartered in the United States. He patiently worked his way up to the top of Global's accounting department and in the early 1990s, took over as chief financial officer for the company. As the Internet began to explode, management at Global, Inc., decided to radically change the nature of its business to one of e-commerce. Two years after the transition, Internet commerce began to slow down, and Global was in dire need of cash in order to continue operations. Management turned to the accounting department.

Global, Inc., needed to borrow a substantial amount of money but couldn't afford to increase the amount of liabilities on the balance sheet for fear of the stock price dropping and banks becoming nervous and demanding repayment of existing loans. David discovered a way that would allow the company to raise the needed cash to continue operations without having to report the long-term notes payable on the balance sheet. Under an obscure rule, companies can set up separate legal organizations that do not have to be reported on the parent company's financial statements, if a third party contributes just 3 percent of the start-up capital. David called a friend, Brian Johnson, and asked him to participate in a business venture with Global. Brian agreed, and created a special purpose entity with Global named BrianCo. For his participation, Brian was awarded a substantial amount of valuable Global stock. Brian then went to a bank and used the stock as collateral to borrow a large sum of money for BrianCo. Then, Global sold some of its poor or underperforming assets to BrianCo for the cash that Brian borrowed. In the end, Global got rid of bad assets, received the proceeds of the long-term note payable, and did not have to show the liability on the balance sheet. Only the top executives and the accountants that worked closely with David knew of the scheme, and they planned to use this method only until the e-commerce portion of Global became profitable again.

Required

a. How did David's scheme affect the overall appearance of Global's financial statements? Why was this important to investors and creditors?

b. Review the AICPA's Articles of Professional Conduct (see Chapter 1) and comment on any of the standards that have been violated.

c. Name the features of the fraud triangle and explain how they materialize in this case.

ATC 7-8   Research Assignment   *Analyzing long-term debt at Union Pacific Railroad*

Many companies have a form of debt called *capital leases*. A capital lease is created when a company agrees to rent an asset, such as equipment or a building, for such a long time that GAAP treats the lease as if the asset were purchased using borrowed funds. A capital lease creates a liability for the company that acquired the leased asset because it has promised to make payments to another company for several years in the future. If a company has any capital leases, it must disclose them in the footnotes to the financial statements, and will sometimes disclose them in a separate account in the liabilities section of the balance sheet.

Using the most current Forms 10-K for Union Pacific Corporation, complete the requirements below. To obtain the 10-Ks use either the EDGAR system following the instructions in Appendix A, or the company's website.

Required

a. What was Union Pacific's debt to assets ratio? (You will need to compute total liabilities by subtracting "Common shareholders' equity" from total assets.)

b. How much interest expense did Union Pacific incur?

c. What amount of liabilities did Union Pacific have as a result of capital leases? Footnote 5 presents information about Union Pacific's leases.

d. What percentage of Union Pacific's long-term liabilities was the result of capital leases?

e. Many companies try to structure (design) leasing agreements so their leases will *not* be classified as capital leases. Explain why a company such as Union Pacific might want to avoid reporting capital leases.

CHAPTER 8

Proprietorships, Partnerships, *and* Corporations

LEARNING OBJECTIVES

After you have mastered the material in this chapter you will be able to:

1 Identify the primary characteristics of sole proprietorships, partnerships, and corporations.

2 Analyze financial statements to identify the different types of business organizations.

3 Explain the characteristics of major types of stock issued by corporations.

4 Explain how to account for different types of stock issued by corporations.

5 Show how treasury stock transactions affect a company's financial statements.

6 Explain the effects of declaring and paying cash dividends on a company's financial statements.

7 Explain the effects of stock dividends and stock splits on a company's financial statements.

8 Show how the appropriation of retained earnings affects financial statements.

9 Explain some uses of accounting information in making stock investment decisions.

CHAPTER OPENING

You want to start a business. How should you structure it? Should it be a sole proprietorship, partnership, or corporation? Each form of business structure presents advantages and disadvantages. For example, a sole proprietorship allows maximum independence and control while partnerships and corporations allow individuals to pool resources and talents with other people. This chapter discusses these and other features of the three primary forms of business structure.

The *Curious* Accountant

Imagine that a rich uncle wanted to reward you for doing so well in your first accounting course, so he gave you $10,000 to invest in the stock of one company. You narrowed your choice to two companies. After reviewing their recent annual reports, you developed the following information.

Mystery Company A: This company's stock has been trading publicly since October 1999, but it only began selling its services in 2001. Although it is an early leader in a business that both you and your grandparents could enjoy, it has not made a profit in a single year of its existence. In fact, each year it has lost more money than the year before. By the end of 2005, it had accumulated losses of $2.2 billion. This stock is currently selling for about $11.40 per share, the same price at which it was offered to the public when it first began trading. At this price, you can buy around 880 shares. A friend told you that at its current price it is a sure winner, especially, since it has recently sold for as much as $38 a share. Your friend, who uses the company's services, says "the sky is the limit for this company; just give it time."

Mystery Company B: This company has been in existence since 1892 and has made a profit most years. From 1998 through 2006, its net earnings totaled $786 million. This company produces products that both you and your grandparents could enjoy. Its stock is selling for about $10.80 per share, so you can buy around 930 shares of it. Your friend says "you would have to be bananas to invest in this company."

The descriptions apply to real-world companies, the names of which will be revealed later. Based on the information provided, which company's stock would you buy? (Answer on page 290.)

FORMS OF BUSINESS ORGANIZATIONS

Identify the primary characteristics of sole proprietorships, partnerships, and corporations.

Sole proprietorships are owned by a single individual who is responsible for making business and profit distribution decisions. If you want to be the absolute master of your destiny, you should organize your business as a proprietorship. Establishing a sole proprietorship is usually as simple as obtaining a business license from local government authorities. Usually no legal ownership agreement is required.

Partnerships allow persons to share their talents, capital, and the risks and rewards of business ownership. Since two or more individuals share ownership, partnerships require clear agreements about how authority, risks, and profits will be shared. Prudent partners minimize misunderstandings by hiring attorneys to prepare a **partnership agreement** which defines the responsibilities of each partner and describes how income or losses will be divided. Since the measurement of income affects the distribution of profits, partnerships frequently hire accountants to ensure that records are maintained in accordance with generally accepted accounting principles (GAAP). Partnerships (and sole proprietorships) also may need professional advice to deal with tax issues.

A **corporation** is a separate legal entity created by the authority of a state government. The paperwork to start a corporation is complex. For most laypersons, engaging professional attorneys and accountants to assist with the paperwork is well worth the fees charged.

Each state has separate laws governing establishing corporations. Many states follow the standard provisions of the Model Business Corporation Act. All states require the initial application to provide **articles of incorporation** which normally include the following information: (1) the corporation's name and proposed date of incorporation; (2) the purpose of the corporation; (3) the location of the business and its expected life (which can be *perpetuity,* meaning *endless*); (4) provisions for capital stock; and (5) the names and addresses of the members of the first board of directors, the individuals with the ultimate authority for operating the business. If the articles are in order, the state establishes the legal existence of the corporation by issuing a charter of incorporation. The charter and the articles are public documents.

ADVANTAGES AND DISADVANTAGES OF DIFFERENT FORMS OF BUSINESS ORGANIZATION

Each form of business organization presents a different combination of advantages and disadvantages. Persons wanting to start a business or invest in one should consider the characteristics of each type of business structure.

Regulation

Few laws specifically affect the operations of proprietorships and partnerships. Corporations, however, are usually heavily regulated. The extent of government regulation depends on the size and distribution of a company's ownership interests. Ownership interests in corporations are normally evidenced by **stock certificates.**

Ownership of corporations can be transferred from one individual to another through exchanging stock certificates. As long as the exchanges (buying and selling of shares of stock, often called *trading*) are limited to transactions between individuals, a company is defined as a **closely held corporation.** However, once a corporation reaches a certain size, it may list its stock on a stock exchange such as the New York Stock Exchange or the American Stock Exchange. Trading on a stock exchange is limited to the stockbrokers who are members of the exchange. These brokers represent buyers and sellers who are willing to pay the brokers commissions for exchanging stock certificates on their behalf. Although closely held corporations are relatively free from government regulation, companies whose stock is publicly traded on the exchanges by brokers are subject to extensive regulation.

Reality BYTES

Edward Nusbaum, CEO of Grant Thornton, a Chicago accounting firm, believes that "Sarbanes-Oxley is most likely creating the desired effect of making businesses realize that very strong responsibilities come with being a public company." However, a recent study conducted by Grant Thornton indicates that the cost of regulatory compliance is so significant that many smaller companies are taking their firms' stock off the exchanges. The study found that the number of public companies making the switch to private ownership is up 30 percent since the Sarbanes-Oxley Act went into effect July 30, 2002. A different study by Thomson Financial found similar results. The Thomson
study found 60 public companies went private in the first nine months of 2003, up from 49 during the same period in 2002 and nearly double the 32 firms that went private in 2001. Clearly, the expense of regulatory compliance is a distinct disadvantage of the corporate form of business. In contrast, ease of formation and limited regulation are clear advantages of proprietorships and, to a lesser extent, partnerships.

The extensive regulation of trading on stock exchanges began in the 1930s. The stock market crash of 1929 and the subsequent Great Depression led Congress to pass the **Securities Act of 1933** and the **Securities Exchange Act of 1934** to regulate issuing stock and to govern the exchanges. The 1934 act also created the Securities and Exchange Commission (SEC) to enforce the securities laws. Congress gave the SEC legal authority to establish accounting principles for corporations that are registered on the exchanges. However, the SEC has generally deferred its rule-making authority to private sector accounting bodies such as the Financial Accounting Standards Board (FASB), effectively allowing the accounting profession to regulate itself.

A number of high-profile business failures around the turn of the last century raised questions about the effectiveness of self-regulation and the usefulness of audits to protect the public. The **Sarbanes-Oxley Act of 2002** was adopted to address these concerns. The act creates a five-member Public Company Accounting Oversight Board (PCAOB) with the authority to set and enforce auditing, attestation, quality control, and ethics standards for auditors of public companies. The PCAOB is empowered to impose disciplinary and remedial sanctions for violations of its rules, securities laws, and professional auditing and accounting standards. Public corporations operate in a complex regulatory environment that requires the services of attorneys and professional accountants.

Double Taxation

Corporations pay income taxes on their earnings and then owners pay income taxes on distributions (dividends) received from corporations. As a result, distributed corporate profits are taxed twice—first when income is reported on the corporation's income tax return and a second time when distributions are reported on individual owners' tax returns. This phenomenon is commonly called **double taxation** and is a significant disadvantage of the corporate form of business organization.

To illustrate, assume Glide Corporation earns pretax income of $100,000. Glide is in a 30 percent tax bracket. The corporation itself will pay income tax of $30,000 ($100,000 × 0.30). If the corporation distributes the after-tax income of $70,000 ($100,000 − $30,000) to individual stockholders in 15 percent tax brackets,[1] the

[1]As a result of the Jobs and Growth Tax Relief Reconciliation Act (JGTRRA) of 2003, dividends received in tax years after 2002 are taxed at a maximum rate of 15 percent for most taxpayers. Lower income individuals pay a 5 percent tax on dividends received on December 31, 2007, or earlier. This rate falls to zero in 2008. The provisions of JGTRRA are set to expire on December 31, 2008.

Answers to The *Curious* Accountant

Mystery Company A is XM Satellite Holdings, Inc. (as of November 3, 2006). It is a company that provides XM satellite radio services on a monthly subscription basis. The origins of the company can be traced back to 1992, but it took several years to get its satellite system up and running. On October 5, 1999, XM's stock was sold to the public in an *initial public offering* (IPO) at $12 per share. Its stock, which is traded on NASDAQ, rose as high as $44.75 in 1999, but in 2002 it traded below $5.00 at times. Obviously, the people trading XM's stock were not paying much attention to its past profits. Instead, they were focusing on what the company might become.

Mystery Company B is Del Monte Foods Company, Inc. (as of November 3, 2006). Of course, only the future will tell which company will be the better investment.

$70,000 dividend will be reported on the individual tax returns, requiring tax payments of $10,500 ($70,000 × .15). Total income tax of $40,500 ($30,000 + $10,500) is due on $100,000 of earned income. In contrast, consider a proprietorship that is owned by an individual in a 30 percent tax bracket. If the proprietorship earns and distributes $100,000 profit, the total tax would be only $30,000 ($100,000 × .30).

Double taxation can be a burden for small companies. To reduce that burden, tax laws permit small closely held corporations to elect "S Corporation" status. S Corporations are taxed as proprietorships or partnerships. Also, many states have recently enacted laws permitting the formation of **limited liability companies (LLCs)** which offer many of the benefits of corporate ownership yet are in general taxed as partnerships. Since proprietorships and partnerships are not separate legal entities, company earnings are taxable to the owners rather than the company itself.

Limited Liability

Given the disadvantages of increased regulation and double taxation, why would anyone choose the corporate form of business structure over a partnership or proprietorship? A major reason is that the corporate form limits an investor's potential liability as an owner of a business venture. Because a corporation is legally separate from its owners, creditors cannot claim owners' personal assets as payment for the company's debts. Also, plaintiffs must sue the corporation, not its owners. The most that owners of a corporation can lose is the amount they have invested in the company (the value of the company's stock).

Unlike corporate stockholders, the owners of proprietorships and partnerships are *personally liable* for actions they take in the name of their companies. In fact, partners are responsible not only for their own actions but also for those taken by any other partner on behalf of the partnership. The benefit of **limited liability** is one of the most significant reasons the corporate form of business organization is so popular.

Continuity

Unlike partnerships or proprietorships, which terminate with the departure of their owners, a corporation's life continues when a shareholder dies or sells his or her stock. Because of **continuity** of existence, many corporations formed in the 1800s still thrive today.

Transferability of Ownership

The **transferability** of corporate ownership is easy. An investor simply buys or sells stock to acquire or give up an ownership interest in a corporation. Hundreds of millions of shares of stock are bought and sold on the major stock exchanges each day.

Transferring the ownership of proprietorships is much more difficult. To sell an ownership interest in a proprietorship, the proprietor must find someone willing to purchase the entire business. Since most proprietors also run their businesses, transferring ownership also requires transferring management responsibilities. Consider the difference in selling $1 million of Exxon stock versus selling a locally owned gas station. The stock could be sold on the New York Stock Exchange within minutes. In contrast, it could take years to find a buyer who is financially capable of and interested in owning and operating a gas station.

Transferring ownership in partnerships can also be difficult. As with proprietorships, ownership transfers may require a new partner to make a significant investment and accept management responsibilities in the business. Further, a new partner must accept and be accepted by the other partners. Personality conflicts and differences in management style can cause problems in transferring ownership interests in partnerships.

Management Structure

Partnerships and proprietorships are usually managed by their owners. Corporations, in contrast, have three tiers of management authority. The *owners* (**stockholders**) represent the highest level of organizational authority. The stockholders *elect* a **board of directors** to oversee company operations. The directors then *hire* professional executives to manage the company on a daily basis. Since large corporations can offer high salaries and challenging career opportunities, they can often attract superior managerial talent.

While the management structure used by corporations is generally effective, it sometimes complicates dismissing incompetent managers. The chief executive officer (CEO) is usually a member of the board of directors and is frequently influential in choosing other board members. The CEO is also in a position to reward loyal board members. As a result, board members may be reluctant to fire the CEO or other top executives even if the individuals are performing poorly. Corporations operating under such conditions are said to be experiencing **entrenched management.**

Ability to Raise Capital

Because corporations can have millions of owners (shareholders), they have the opportunity to raise huge amounts of capital. Few individuals have the financial means to build and operate a telecommunications network such as AT&T or a marketing distribution system such as Wal-Mart. However, by pooling the resources of millions of owners through public stock and bond offerings, corporations generate the billions of dollars of capital needed for such massive investments. In contrast, the capital resources of proprietorships and partnerships are limited to a relatively small number of private owners. Although proprietorships and partnerships can also obtain resources by borrowing, the amount creditors are willing to lend them is usually limited by the size of the owners' net worth.

APPEARANCE OF CAPITAL STRUCTURE IN FINANCIAL STATEMENTS

The ownership interest (equity) in a business is composed of two elements: (1) owner/investor contributions and (2) retained earnings. The way these two elements are reported in the financial statements differs for each type of business structure (proprietorship, partnership, or corporation).

LO 2

Analyze financial statements to identify the different types of business organizations.

Presentation of Equity in Proprietorships

Owner contributions and retained earnings are combined in a single Capital account on the balance sheets of proprietorships. To illustrate, assume that Worthington Sole Proprietorship was started on January 1, 2010, when it acquired a $5,000 capital contribution from its owner, Phil Worthington. During the first year of operation, the company generated $4,000 of cash revenues, incurred $2,500 of cash expenses, and distributed $1,000 cash to the owner. Exhibit 8.1 displays 2010 financial statements for Worthington's company. Note on the *capital statement* that distributions are called **withdrawals.** Verify that the $5,500 balance in the Capital account on the balance sheet includes the $5,000 owner contribution and the retained earnings of $500 ($1,500 net income − $1,000 withdrawal).

EXHIBIT 8.1

WORTHINGTON SOLE PROPRIETORSHIP
Financial Statements
As of December 31, 2010

Income Statement		Capital Statement		Balance Sheet	
Revenue	$4,000	Beginning capital balance	$ 0	Assets	
Expenses	2,500	Plus: Investment by owner	5,000	Cash	$5,500
Net income	$1,500	Plus: Net income	1,500	Equity	
		Less: Withdrawal by owner	(1,000)	Worthington, capital	$5,500
		Ending capital balance	$5,500		

CHECK *Yourself* 8.1

Weiss Company was started on January 1, 2011, when it acquired $50,000 cash from its owner(s). During 2011 the company earned $72,000 of net income. Explain how the equity section of Weiss's December 31, 2011, balance sheet would differ if the company were a proprietorship versus a corporation.

Answer *Proprietorship* records combine capital acquisitions from the owner and earnings from operating the business in a single capital account. In contrast, *corporation* records separate capital acquisitions from the owners and earnings from operating the business. If Weiss were a proprietorship, the equity section of the year-end balance sheet would report a single capital component of $122,000. If Weiss were a corporation, the equity section would report two separate equity components, most likely common stock of $50,000 and retained earnings of $72,000.

Presentation of Equity in Partnerships

The financial statement format for reporting partnership equity is similar to that used for proprietorships. Contributed capital and retained earnings are combined. However, a separate capital account is maintained for each partner in the business to reflect each partner's ownership interest.

To illustrate, assume that Sara Slater and Jill Johnson formed a partnership on January 1, 2010. The partnership acquired $2,000 of capital from Slater and $4,000 from Johnson. The partnership agreement called for each partner to receive an annual distribution equal to 10 percent of her capital contribution. Any further earnings were to be retained in the business and divided equally between the partners. During 2010, the company earned $5,000 of cash revenue and incurred $3,000 of cash expenses, for net income of $2,000 ($5,000 − $3,000). As specified by the partnership agreement, Slater received a $200 ($2,000 × 0.10) cash withdrawal and Johnson received $400 ($4,000 × 0.10). The remaining $1,400 ($2,000 − $200 − $400) of income was retained in the business and divided equally, adding $700 to each partner's capital account.

Exhibit 8.2 displays financial statements for the Slater and Johnson partnership. Again, note that distributions are called *withdrawals*. Also find on the balance sheet a *separate capital account* for each partner. Each capital account includes the amount of the partner's contributed capital plus her proportionate share of the retained earnings.

EXHIBIT 8.2

SLATER AND JOHNSON PARTNERSHIP
Financial Statements
As of December 31, 2010

Income Statement		Capital Statement		Balance Sheet	
Revenue	$5,000	Beginning capital balance	$ 0	Assets	
Expenses	3,000	Plus: Investment by owners	6,000	Cash	$7,400
Net income	$2,000	Plus: Net income	2,000	Equity	
		Less: Withdrawal by owners	(600)	Slater, capital	$2,700
		Ending capital balance	$7,400	Johnson, capital	4,700
				Total capital	$7,400

Presentation of Equity in Corporations

Corporations have more complex capital structures than proprietorships and partnerships. Explanations of some of the more common features of corporate capital structures and transactions follow.

CHARACTERISTICS OF CAPITAL STOCK

Stock issued by corporations may have a variety of different characteristics. For example, a company may issue different classes of stock that grant owners different rights and privileges. Also, the number of shares a corporation can legally issue may differ from the number it actually has issued. Further, a corporation can even buy back its own stock. Finally, a corporation may assign different values to the stock it issues. Accounting for corporate equity transactions is discussed in the next section of the text.

LO 3

Explain the characteristics of major types of stock issued by corporations.

Par Value

Many states require assigning a **par value** to stock. Historically, par value represented the maximum liability of the investors. Par value multiplied by the number of shares of stock issued represents the minimum amount of assets that must be retained in the company as protection for creditors. This amount is known as **legal capital.** To ensure that the amount of legal capital is maintained in a corporation, many states require that purchasers pay at least the par value for a share of stock initially purchased from a corporation. To minimize the amount of assets that owners must maintain in the business, many corporations issue stock with very low par values, often $1 or less. Therefore, *legal capital* as defined by par value has come to have very little relevance to investors or creditors. As a result, many states allow corporations to issue no-par stock.

Stated Value

No-par stock may have a stated value. Like par value, **stated value** is an arbitrary amount assigned by the board of directors to the stock. It also has little relevance to investors and creditors. Stock with a par value and stock with a stated value are accounted for exactly the same way. When stock has no par or stated value, accounting for it is slightly different. These accounting differences are illustrated later in this chapter.

Other Valuation Terminology

The price an investor must pay to purchase a share of stock is the **market value.** The sales price of a share of stock may be more or less than the par value. Another term analysts frequently associate with stock is *book value.* **Book value per share** is calculated by dividing total stockholders' equity (assets − liabilities) by the number of shares of stock owned by investors. Book value per share differs from market value per share because equity is measured in historical dollars and market value reflects investors' estimates of a company's current value.

Stock: Authorized, Issued, and Outstanding

As part of the regulatory function, states approve the maximum number of shares of stock corporations are legally permitted to issue. This maximum number is called **authorized stock.** Authorized stock that has been sold to the public is called **issued stock.** When a corporation buys back some of its issued stock from the public, the repurchased stock is called **treasury stock.** Treasury stock is still considered to be issued stock, but it is no longer outstanding. **Outstanding stock** (total issued stock minus treasury stock) is stock owned by investors outside the corporation. For example, assume a company that is authorized to issue 150 shares of stock issues 100 shares to investors, and then buys back 20 shares of treasury stock. There are 150 shares authorized, 100 shares issued, and 80 shares outstanding.

Classes of Stock

The corporate charter defines the number of shares of stock authorized, the par value or stated value (if any), and the classes of stock that a corporation can issue. Most stock issued is either *common* or *preferred.*

Common Stock

All corporations issue **common stock.** Common stockholders bear the highest risk of losing their investment if a company is forced to liquidate. On the other hand, they reap the greatest rewards when a corporation prospers. Common stockholders generally enjoy several rights, including: (1) the right to buy and sell stock, (2) the right to share in the distribution of profits, (3) the right to share in the distribution of corporate assets in the case of liquidation, (4) the right to vote on significant matters that affect the corporate charter, and (5) the right to participate in the election of directors.

Focus On INTERNATIONAL ISSUES

The accounting rules in a country are affected by who provides financing to businesses in that country. Equity (versus debt) financing is a major source of financing for most businesses in the United States. The stock (equity ownership) of most large U.S. companies is said to be *widely held.* This means that many different institutional investors (e.g., pension funds) and individuals own stock. At the other extreme is a country in which the government owns most industries. In between might be a country in which large banks provide a major portion of business financing, such as Japan or Germany.

It is well beyond the scope of this course to explain specifically how a country's accounting principles are affected by who provides the financing for the country's major industries. Nevertheless, a businessperson should be aware that the source of a company's financing affects its financial reporting. Do not assume that business practices or accounting rules in other countries are like those in the United States.

Preferred Stock

Many corporations issue **preferred stock** in addition to common stock. Holders of preferred stock receive certain privileges relative to holders of common stock. In exchange for special privileges in some areas, preferred stockholders give up rights in other areas. Preferred stockholders usually have no voting rights and the amount of their dividends is usually limited. Preferences granted to preferred stockholders include the following.

1. *Preference as to assets.* Preferred stock often has a liquidation value. In case of bankruptcy, preferred stockholders must be paid the liquidation value before any assets are distributed to common stockholders. However, preferred stockholder claims still fall behind creditor claims.

2. *Preference as to dividends.* Preferred shareholders are frequently guaranteed the right to receive dividends before common stockholders. The amount of the preferred dividend is normally stated on the stock certificate. It may be stated as a dollar value (say, $5) per share or as a percentage of the par value. Most preferred stock has **cumulative dividends,** meaning that if a corporation is unable to pay the preferred dividend in any year, the dividend is not lost but begins to accumulate. Cumulative dividends that have not been paid are called **dividends in arrears.** When a company pays dividends, any preferred stock arrearages must be paid before any other dividends are paid. Noncumulative preferred stock is not often issued because preferred stock is much less attractive if missed dividends do not accumulate.

To illustrate the effects of preferred dividends, consider Dillion, Incorporated, which has the following shares of stock outstanding.

> Preferred stock, 4%, $10 par, 10,000 shares
> Common stock, $10 par, 20,000 shares

Assume the preferred stock dividend has not been paid for two years. If Dillion pays $22,000 in dividends, how much will each class of stock receive? It depends on whether the preferred stock is cumulative.

Allocation of Distribution for Cumulative Preferred Stock		
	To Preferred	To Common
Dividends in arrears	$ 8,000	$ 0
Current year's dividends	4,000	10,000
Total distribution	$12,000	$10,000
Allocation of Distribution for Noncumulative Preferred Stock		
	To Preferred	To Common
Dividends in arrears	$ 0	$ 0
Current year's dividends	4,000	18,000
Total distribution	$ 4,000	$18,000

EXHIBIT 8.3

Presence of Preferred Stock in the Capital Structure of U.S. Companies

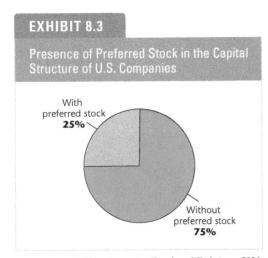

With preferred stock
25%

Without preferred stock
75%

Data source: AICPA, *Accounting Trends and Techniques,* 2006.

The total annual dividend on the preferred stock is $4,000 (0.04 × $10 par × 10,000 shares). If the preferred stock is cumulative, the $8,000 in arrears must be paid first. Then $4,000 for the current year's dividend is paid next. The remaining $10,000 goes to common stockholders. If the preferred stock is noncumulative, the $8,000 of dividends from past periods is ignored. This year's $4,000 preferred dividend is paid first, with the remaining $18,000 going to common.

Other features of preferred stock may include the right to participate in distributions beyond the established amount of the preferred dividend, the right to convert preferred stock to common stock or to bonds, and the potential for having the preferred stock called (repurchased) by the corporation. Detailed discussion of these topics is left to more advanced courses. Exhibit 8.3 indicates that roughly 25 percent of U.S. companies have preferred shares outstanding.

ACCOUNTING FOR STOCK TRANSACTIONS ON THE DAY OF ISSUE

Explain how to account for different types of stock issued by corporations.

Issuing stock with a par or stated value is accounted for differently from issuing no-par stock. For stock with either a par or stated value, the total amount acquired from the owners is divided between two separate equity accounts. The amount of the par or stated value is recorded in the stock account. Any amount received above the par or stated value is recorded in an account called **Paid-in Capital in Excess of Par** (or **Stated**) **Value.**

Issuing Par Value Stock

To illustrate the issue of common stock with a par value, assume that Nelson Incorporated is authorized to issue 250 shares of common stock. During 2010, Nelson issued 100 shares of $10 par common stock for $22 per share. The event increases assets and stockholders' equity by $2,200 ($22 × 100 shares). The increase in stockholders' equity is divided into two parts, $1,000 of par value ($10 per share × 100 shares) and $1,200 ($2,200 − $1,000) received in excess of par value. The income statement is not affected. The $2,200 cash inflow is reported in the financing activities section of the statement of cash flows. The effects on the financial statements follow.

Assets	=	Liab.	+		Equity			Rev.	−	Exp.	=	Net Inc.	Cash Flow
Cash	=			Com. Stk.	+	PIC in Excess							
2,200	=	NA	+	1,000	+	1,200		NA	−	NA	=	NA	2,200 FA

The *legal capital* of the corporation is $1,000, the total par value of the issued common stock. The number of shares issued can be easily verified by dividing the total amount in the common stock account by the par value ($1,000 ÷ $10 = 100 shares).

Stock Classification

Assume Nelson Incorporated obtains authorization to issue 400 shares of Class B, $20 par value common stock. The company issues 150 shares of this stock at $25 per share. The event increases assets and stockholders' equity by $3,750 ($25 × 150 shares). The increase in stockholders' equity is divided into two parts, $3,000 of par value ($20 per share × 150 shares) and $750 ($3,750 − $3,000) received in excess of par value. The income statement is not affected. The $3,750 cash inflow is reported in the financing activities section of the statement of cash flows. The effects on the financial statements follow.

Assets	=	Liab.	+		Equity			Rev.	−	Exp.	=	Net Inc.	Cash Flow
Cash	=			Com. Stk.	+	PIC in Excess							
3,750	=	NA	+	3,000	+	750		NA	−	NA	=	NA	3,750 FA

As the preceding event suggests, companies can issue numerous classes of common stock. The specific rights and privileges for each class are described in the individual stock certificates.

Stock Issued at Stated Value

Assume Nelson is authorized to issue 300 shares of a third class of stock, 7 percent cumulative preferred stock with a stated value of $10 per share. Nelson issued 100 shares of the preferred stock at a price of $22 per share. The effects on the financial statements are identical to those described for the issue of the $10 par value common stock.

Assets	=	Liab.	+		Equity			Rev.	−	Exp.	=	Net Inc.	Cash Flow
Cash	=			Pfd. Stk.	+	PIC in Excess							
2,200	=	NA	+	1,000	+	1,200		NA	−	NA	=	NA	2,200 FA

Stock Issued with No Par Value

Assume that Nelson Incorporated is authorized to issue 150 shares of a fourth class of stock. This stock is no-par common stock. Nelson issues 100 shares of this no-par stock at $22 per share. The entire amount received ($22 × 100 = $2,200) is recorded in the stock account. The effects on the financial statements follow.

Assets	=	Liab.	+		Equity			Rev.	−	Exp.	=	Net Inc.	Cash Flow
Cash	=			Com. Stk.	+	PIC in Excess							
2,200	=	NA	+	2,200	+	NA		NA	−	NA	=	NA	2,200 FA

Financial Statement Presentation

Exhibit 8.4 displays Nelson Incorporated's balance sheet after the four stock issuances described above. The exhibit assumes that Nelson earned and retained $5,000 of cash income during 2010. The stock accounts are presented first, followed by the paid-in capital in excess of par (or stated) value accounts. A wide variety of reporting formats is used in practice. For example, another popular format is to group accounts by stock class, with the paid-in capital in excess accounts listed with their associated stock accounts. Alternatively, many companies combine the different classes of stock into a single amount and provide the detailed information in footnotes to the financial statements.

EXHIBIT 8.4

NELSON INCORPORATED
Balance Sheet
As of December 31, 2010

Assets	
Cash	$15,350
Stockholders' equity	
Preferred stock, $10 stated value, 7% cumulative,	
300 shares authorized, 100 issued and outstanding	$ 1,000
Common stock, $10 par value, 250 shares authorized,	
100 issued and outstanding	1,000
Common stock, class B, $20 par value, 400 shares	
authorized, 150 issued and outstanding	3,000
Common stock, no par, 150 shares authorized,	
100 issued and outstanding	2,200
Paid-in capital in excess of stated value—preferred	1,200
Paid-in capital in excess of par value—common	1,200
Paid-in capital in excess of par value—class B common	750
Total paid-in capital	10,350
Retained earnings	5,000
Total stockholders' equity	$15,350

STOCKHOLDERS' EQUITY TRANSACTIONS AFTER THE DAY OF ISSUE

Treasury Stock

Show how treasury stock transactions affect a company's financial statements.

When a company buys its own stock, the stock purchased is called *treasury stock*. Why would a company buy its own stock? Common reasons include (1) to have stock available to give employees pursuant to stock option plans, (2) to accumulate stock in preparation for a merger or business combination, (3) to reduce the number of shares outstanding in order to increase earnings per share, (4) to keep the price of the stock high when it appears to be falling, and (5) to avoid a hostile takeover (removing shares from the open market reduces the opportunity for outsiders to obtain enough voting shares to gain control of the company).

Conceptually, purchasing treasury stock is the reverse of issuing stock. When a business issues stock, the assets and equity of the business increase. When a business buys treasury stock, the assets and equity of the business decrease. To illustrate, return to the Nelson Incorporated example. Assume that in 2011 Nelson paid $20 per share to buy back 50 shares of the $10 par value common stock that it originally issued at $22 per share. The purchase of treasury stock is an asset use transaction. Assets and stockholders' equity decrease by the cost of the purchase ($20 × 50 shares = $1,000). The income statement is not affected. The cash outflow is reported in the financing activities section of the statement of cash flows. The effects on the financial statements follow.

Assets	=	Liab.	+	Equity			Rev.	−	Exp.	=	Net Inc.	Cash Flow
Cash	=			Other Equity Accts.	−	Treasury Stk.						
(1,000)	=	NA	+	NA	−	1,000	NA	−	NA	=	NA	(1,000) FA

The Treasury Stock account is a contra equity account. It is deducted from the other equity accounts in determining total stockholders' equity. In this example, the Treasury Stock account is debited for the full amount paid ($1,000). The original issue price and the par value of the stock have no effect on the entry. Recording the full amount paid in the treasury stock account is called the **cost method of accounting for treasury stock** transactions. Although other methods could be used, the cost method is the most common.

Assume Nelson reissues 30 shares of treasury stock at a price of $25 per share. As with any other stock issue, the sale of treasury stock is an asset source transaction. In this case, assets and stockholders' equity increase by $750 ($25 × 30 shares). The income statement is not affected. The cash inflow is reported in the financing activities section of the statement of cash flows. The effects on the financial statements follow.

Assets	=	Liab.	+	Equity					Rev.	−	Exp.	=	Net Inc.	Cash Flow
Cash	=			Other Equity Accounts	−	Treasury Stock	+	PIC from Treasury Stk.						
750	=	NA	+	NA	−	(600)	+	150	NA	−	NA	=	NA	750 FA

The decrease in the Treasury Stock account increases stockholders' equity. The $150 difference between the cost of the treasury stock ($20 per share × 30 shares = $600) and the sales price ($750) is *not* reported as a gain. The sale of treasury stock is a capital acquisition, not a revenue transaction. The $150 is additional paid-in capital. *Corporations do not recognize gains or losses on the sale of treasury stock.*

After selling 30 shares of treasury stock, 20 shares remain in Nelson's possession. These shares cost $20 each, so the balance in the Treasury Stock account is now $400 ($20 × 20 shares). Treasury stock is reported on the balance sheet directly below retained earnings. Although this placement suggests that treasury stock reduces retained earnings, the reduction actually applies to the entire stockholders' equity section. Exhibit 8.5 on page 302 shows the presentation of treasury stock in the balance sheet.

CHECK *Yourself* 8.2

On January 1, 2010, Janell Company's Common Stock account balance was $20,000. On April 1, 2010, Janell paid $12,000 cash to purchase some of its own stock. Janell resold this stock on October 1, 2010, for $14,500. What is the effect on the company's cash and stockholders' equity from both the April 1 purchase and the October 1 resale of the stock?

Answer   The April 1 purchase would reduce both cash and stockholders' equity by $12,000. The treasury stock transaction represents a return of invested capital to those owners who sold stock back to the company.

The sale of the treasury stock on October 1 would increase both cash and stockholders' equity by $14,500. The difference between the sales price of the treasury stock and its cost ($14,500 − $12,000) represents additional paid-in capital from treasury stock transactions. The stockholders' equity section of the balance sheet would include Common Stock, $20,000, and Additional Paid-in Capital from Treasury Stock Transactions, $2,500.

Explain the effects of declaring and paying cash dividends on a company's financial statements.

Cash Dividend

Cash dividends are affected by three significant dates: *the declaration date, the date of record,* and *the payment date.* Assume that on October 15, 2011, the board of Nelson Incorporated declared a 7% cash dividend on the 100 outstanding shares of its $10 stated value preferred stock. The dividend will be paid to stockholders of record as of November 15, 2011. The cash payment will be made on December 15, 2011.

Declaration Date

Although corporations are not required to declare dividends, they are legally obligated to pay dividends once they have been declared. They must recognize a liability on the **declaration date** (in this case, October 15, 2011). The increase in liabilities is accompanied by a decrease in retained earnings. The income statement and statement of cash flows are not affected. The effects on the financial statements of *declaring* the $70 (0.07 × $10 × 100 shares) dividend follow.

Assets	=	Liab.	+			Equity			Rev.	−	Exp.	=	Net Inc.	Cash Flow
Cash	=	Div. Pay.	+	Com. Stk.	+	Ret. Earn.								
NA	=	70	+	NA	+	(70)			NA	−	NA	=	NA	NA

Date of Record

Cash dividends are paid to investors who owned the preferred stock on the **date of record** (in this case November 15, 2011). Any stock sold after the date of record but before the payment date (in this case December 15, 2011) is traded **ex-dividend,** meaning the buyer will not receive the upcoming dividend. The date of record is merely a cutoff date. It does not affect the financial statements.

Payment Date

Nelson actually paid the cash dividend on the **payment date.** This event has the same effect as paying any other liability. Assets (cash) and liabilities (dividends payable) both decrease. The income statement is not affected. The cash outflow is reported in the financing activities section of the statement of cash flows. The effects of the cash payment on the financial statements follow.

Assets	=	Liab.	+			Equity			Rev.	−	Exp.	=	Net Inc.	Cash Flow
Cash	=	Div. Pay.	+	Com. Stk.	+	Ret. Earn.								
(70)	=	(70)	+	NA	+	NA			NA	−	NA	=	NA	(70) FA

Stock Dividend

Explain the effects of stock dividends and stock splits on a company's financial statements.

Dividends are not always paid in cash. Companies sometimes choose to issue **stock dividends,** wherein they distribute additional shares of stock to the stockholders. To illustrate, assume that Nelson Incorporated decided to issue a 10 percent stock dividend on its class B, $20 par value common stock. Since dividends apply to outstanding shares only, Nelson will issue 15 (150 outstanding shares × 0.10) additional shares of class B stock.

Assume the new shares are distributed when the market value of the stock is $30 per share. As a result of the stock dividend, Nelson will transfer $450 ($30 × 15 new shares) from retained earnings to paid-in capital.[2] The stock dividend is an equity exchange

---

[2]The accounting here applies to small stock dividends. Accounting for large stock dividends is explained in a more advanced course.

transaction. The income statement and statement of cash flows are not affected. The effects of the stock dividend on the financial statements follow.

Assets	=	Liab.	+	Equity							Rev.	−	Exp.	=	Net Inc.	Cash Flow
				Com. Stk.	+	PIC in Excess	+	Ret. Earn.								
NA	=	NA	+	300	+	150	+	(450)			NA	−	NA	=	NA	NA

Stock dividends have no effect on assets. They merely increase the number of shares of stock outstanding. Since a greater number of shares represents the same ownership interest in the same amount of assets, the market value per share of a company's stock normally declines when a stock dividend is distributed. A lower market price makes the stock more affordable and may increase demand for the stock, which benefits both the company and its stockholders.

Stock Split

A corporation may also reduce the market price of its stock through a **stock split.** A stock split replaces existing shares with a greater number of new shares. Any par or stated value of the stock is proportionately reduced to reflect the new number of shares outstanding. For example, assume Nelson Incorporated declared a 2-for-1 stock split on the 165 outstanding shares (150 originally issued + 15 shares distributed in a stock dividend) of its $20 par value, class B common stock. Nelson notes in the accounting records that the 165 old $20 par shares are replaced with 330 new $10 par shares. Investors who owned the 165 shares of old common stock would now own 330 shares of the new common stock.

Stock splits have no effect on the dollar amounts of assets, liabilities, and stockholders' equity. They only affect the number of shares of stock outstanding. In Nelson's case, the ownership interest that was previously represented by 165 shares of stock is now represented by 330 shares. Since twice as many shares now represent the same ownership interest, the market value per share should be one-half as much as it was prior to the split. However, as with a stock dividend, the lower market price will probably stimulate demand for the stock. As a result, doubling the number of shares will likely reduce the market price to slightly more than one-half of the pre-split value. For example, if the stock were selling for $30 per share before the 2-for-1 split, it might sell for $15.50 after the split.

Appropriation of Retained Earnings

The board of directors may restrict the amount of retained earnings available to distribute as dividends. The restriction may be required by credit agreements, or it may be discretionary. A retained earnings restriction, often called an *appropriation,* is an equity exchange event. It transfers a portion of existing retained earnings to **Appropriated Retained Earnings.** Total retained earnings remains unchanged. To illustrate, assume that Nelson appropriates $1,000 of retained earnings for future expansion. The income statement and the statement of cash flows are not affected. The effects on the financial statements of appropriating $1,000 of retained earnings follow.

Show how the appropriation of retained earnings affects financial statements.

Assets	=	Liab.	+	Equity						Rev.	−	Exp.	=	Net Inc.	Cash Flow
				Com. Stk.	+	Ret. Earn.	+	App. Ret. Earn.							
NA	=	NA	+	NA	+	(1,000)	+	1,000		NA	−	NA	=	NA	NA

FINANCIAL STATEMENT PRESENTATION

The 2010 and 2011 events for Nelson Incorporated are summarized below. Events 1 through 8 are cash transactions. The results of the 2010 transactions (nos. 1–5) are reflected in Exhibit 8.4. The results of the 2011 transactions (nos. 6–9) are shown in Exhibit 8.5.

1. Issued 100 shares of $10 par value common stock at a market price of $22 per share.
2. Issued 150 shares of class B, $20 par value common stock at a market price of $25 per share.
3. Issued 100 shares of $10 stated value, 7 percent cumulative preferred stock at a market price of $22 per share.
4. Issued 100 shares of no-par common stock at a market price of $22 per share.
5. Earned and retained $5,000 cash from operations.
6. Purchased 50 shares of $10 par value common stock as treasury stock at a market price of $20 per share.
7. Sold 30 shares of treasury stock at a market price of $25 per share.
8. Declared and paid a $70 cash dividend on the preferred stock.
9. Issued a 10 percent stock dividend on the 150 shares of outstanding class B, $20 par value common stock (15 additional shares). The additional shares were issued when the market price of the stock was $30 per share. There are 165 (150 + 15) class B common shares outstanding after the stock dividend.
10. Issued a 2-for-1 stock split on the 165 shares of class B, $20 par value common stock. After this transaction, there are 330 shares outstanding of the class B common stock with a $10 par value.
11. Appropriated $1,000 of retained earnings.

EXHIBIT 8.5

NELSON INCORPORATED
Balance Sheet
As of December 31, 2011

Assets		
Cash		$21,030
Stockholders' equity		
Preferred stock, $10 stated value, 7% cumulative,		
300 shares authorized, 100 issued and outstanding	$1,000	
Common stock, $10 par value, 250 shares authorized,		
100 issued, and 80 outstanding	1,000	
Common stock, class B, $10 par, 800 shares authorized,		
330 issued and outstanding	3,300	
Common stock, no par, 150 shares authorized,		
100 issued and outstanding	2,200	
Paid-in capital in excess of stated value—preferred	1,200	
Paid-in capital in excess of par value—common	1,200	
Paid-in capital in excess of par value—class B common	900	
Paid-in capital in excess of cost of treasury stock	150	
Total paid-in capital		$10,950
Retained earnings		
Appropriated	1,000	
Unappropriated	9,480	
Total retained earnings		10,480
Less: Treasury stock, 20 shares @ $20 per share		(400)
Total stockholders' equity		$21,030

The illustration assumes that Nelson earned net income of $6,000 in 2011. The ending retained earnings balance is determined as follows: Beginning Balance $5,000 − $70 Cash Dividend − $450 Stock Dividend + $6,000 Net Income = $10,480.

THE FINANCIAL ANALYST

Stockholders may benefit in two ways when a company generates earnings. The company may distribute the earnings directly to the stockholders in the form of dividends. Alternatively, the company may retain some or all of the earnings to finance growth and increase its potential for future earnings. If the company retains earnings, the market value of its stock should increase to reflect its greater earnings prospects. How can analysts use financial reporting to help assess the potential for dividend payments or growth in market value?

Explain some uses of accounting information in making stock investment decisions.

Receiving Dividends

Is a company likely to pay dividends in the future? The financial statements can help answer this question. They show if dividends were paid in the past. Companies with a history of paying dividends usually continue to pay dividends. Also, to pay dividends in the future, a company must have sufficient cash and retained earnings. These amounts are reported on the balance sheet and the statement of cash flows.

Increasing the Price of Stock

Is the market value (price) of a company's stock likely to increase? Increases in a company's stock price occur when investors believe the company's earnings will grow. Financial statements provide information that is useful in predicting the prospects for earnings growth. Here also, a company's earnings history is an indicator of its growth potential. However, because published financial statements report historical information, investors must recognize their limitations. Investors want to know about the future. Stock prices are therefore influenced more by forecasts than by history.

For example:

■ On July 11, 2006, Alcoa, Inc., announced that its profits for the second quarter of the 2006 fiscal year were 62 percent higher than profits in the same quarter of 2005. Its sales were up 19 percent during the second quarter. In reaction to this news, the price of Alcoa's stock *fell* by 4.5 percent. Why did the stock market respond in this way? Because many analysts who follow the company were expecting revenues to grow more than 19 percent.

■ On July 26, 2006, General Motors Corporation announced a second quarter *loss* of $3.2 billion. This loss was over three times greater than its loss had been for the second quarter of the 2005 fiscal year. The stock market's reaction to the news was to *increase* the price of GM's stock by over 4 percent to its highest price in ten months. The market reacted this way because in that same announcement the company reported strong revenue growth, which made investors more optimistic about the future, and the investors had expected an even greater second quarter loss.

In each case, investors reacted to the potential for earnings growth rather than the historical earnings reports. Because investors find forecasted statements more relevant to decision making than historical financial statements, most companies provide forecasts in addition to historical financial statements.

The value of a company's stock is also influenced by nonfinancial information that financial statements cannot provide. For example, suppose ExxonMobil announced in the middle of its fiscal year that it had just discovered substantial oil reserves on property to which it held drilling rights. Consider the following questions:

- What would happen to the price of ExxonMobil's stock on the day of the announcement?
- What would happen to ExxonMobil's financial statements on that day?

The price of ExxonMobil's stock would almost certainly increase as soon as the discovery was made public. However, nothing would happen to its financial statements on that day. There would probably be very little effect on its financial statements for that year. Only after the company began to develop the oil field and sell the oil would its financial statements reflect the discovery. Changes in financial statements tend to lag behind the announcements companies make regarding their earnings potential.

Stock prices are also affected by general economic conditions and consumer confidence as well as the performance measures reported in financial statements. For example, the stock prices of virtually all companies declined sharply immediately after the September 11, 2001, terrorist attacks on the World Trade Center and the Pentagon. Historically based financial statements are of little benefit in predicting general economic conditions or changes in consumer confidence.

Price-earnings Ratio

The most commonly reported measure of a company's value is the price-earnings ratio, frequently called the P/E ratio. The P/E ratio is a company's market price per share of stock divided by the company's annual earnings per share (EPS). In general, high P/E ratios indicate that investors are optimistic about a company's earnings growth potential.

Exercising Control through Stock Ownership

The more influence an investor has over the operations of a company, the more the investor can benefit from owning stock in the company. For example, consider a power company that needs coal to produce electricity. The power company may purchase some common stock in a coal mining company to ensure a stable supply of coal. What percentage of the mining company's stock must the power company acquire to exercise significant influence over the mining company? The answer depends on how many investors own stock in the mining company and how the number of shares is distributed among the stockholders.

The greater its number of stockholders, the more *widely held* a company is. If stock ownership is concentrated in the hands of a few persons, a company is *closely held*. Widely held companies can generally be controlled with smaller percentages of ownership than closely held companies. Consider a company in which no existing investor owns more than 1 percent of the voting stock. A new investor who acquires a 5 percent interest would immediately become, by far, the largest shareholder and would likely be able to significantly influence board decisions. In contrast, consider a closely held company in which one current shareholder owns 51 percent of the company's stock. Even if another investor acquired the remaining 49 percent of the company, that investor could not control the company.

Financial statements contain some, but not all, of the information needed to help an investor determine ownership levels necessary to permit control. For example, the financial statements disclose the total number of shares of stock outstanding, but they normally contain little information about the number of shareholders and even less information about any relationships between shareholders. Relationships between shareholders are critically important because related shareholders, whether bound by family or business interests, might exercise control by voting as a block. For publicly traded companies, information about the number of shareholders and the identity of some large shareholders is disclosed in reports filed with the Securities and Exchange Commission.

A Look Back

Starting a business requires obtaining financing; it takes money to make money. Although some money may be borrowed, lenders are unlikely to make loans to businesses that lack some degree of owner financing. Equity financing is therefore critical to virtually all profit-oriented businesses. This chapter has examined some of the issues related to accounting for equity transactions.

The idea that a business must obtain financing from its owners was one of the first events presented in this textbook. This chapter discussed the advantages and disadvantages of organizing a business as a sole proprietorship versus a partnership versus a corporation. These advantages and disadvantages include the following.

1. *Double taxation*—Income of corporations is subject to double taxation, but that of proprietorships and partnerships is not.

2. *Regulation*—Corporations are subject to more regulation than are proprietorships and partnerships.

3. *Limited liability*—An investor's personal assets are not at risk as a result of owning corporate securities. The investor's liability is limited to the amount of the investment. In general proprietorships and partnerships do not offer limited liability. However, laws in some states permit the formation of limited liability companies which operate like proprietorships and partnerships yet place some limits on the personal liability of their owners.

4. *Continuity*—Proprietorships and partnerships dissolve when one of the owners leaves the business. Corporations are separate legal entities that continue to exist regardless of changes in ownership.

5. *Transferability*—Ownership interests in corporations are easier to transfer than those of proprietorships or partnerships.

6. *Management structure*—Corporations are more likely to have independent professional managers than are proprietorships or partnerships.

7. *Ability to raise capital*—Because they can be owned by millions of investors, corporations have the opportunity to raise more capital than proprietorships or partnerships.

Corporations issue different classes of common stock and preferred stock as evidence of ownership interests. In general, *common stock* provides the widest range of privileges including the right to vote and participate in earnings. *Preferred stockholders* usually give up the right to vote in exchange for preferences such as the right to receive dividends or assets upon liquidation before common stockholders. Stock may have a *par value* or *stated value,* which relates to legal requirements governing the amount of capital that must be maintained in the corporation. Corporations may also issue *no-par stock,* avoiding some of the legal requirements that pertain to par or stated value stock.

Stock that a company issues and then repurchases is called *treasury stock.* Purchasing treasury stock reduces total assets and stockholders' equity. Reselling treasury stock represents a capital acquisition. The difference between the reissue price and the cost of the treasury stock is recorded directly in the equity accounts. Treasury stock transactions do not result in gains or losses on the income statement.

Companies may issue *stock splits* or *stock dividends.* These transactions increase the number of shares of stock without changing the net assets of a company. The per share market value usually drops when a company issues stock splits or dividends.

A Look Forward

The Financial Analyst sections of the previous chapters have discussed several procedures and ratios used to analyze financial statements. Financial statement analysis is so important that Chapter 9 is devoted solely to a more detailed discussion of this subject. The expanded coverage in Chapter 9 includes new ratios and additional detail about many of the ratios previously introduced. The chapter also covers vertical analysis (analyzing relationships within a specific statement) and horizontal analysis (analyzing relationships across accounting periods). Finally, the chapter discusses limitations associated with financial statement analysis.

SELF-STUDY REVIEW PROBLEM

Edwards Inc. experienced the following events:

1. Issued common stock for cash.
2. Declared a cash dividend.
3. Issued noncumulative preferred stock for cash.
4. Appropriated retained earnings.
5. Distributed a stock dividend.
6. Paid cash to purchase treasury stock.
7. Distributed a 2-for-1 stock split.
8. Issued cumulative preferred stock for cash.
9. Paid a cash dividend that had previously been declared.
10. Sold treasury stock for cash at a higher amount than the cost of the treasury stock.

Required

Show the effect of each event on the elements of the financial statements using a horizontal statements model like the one shown here. Use + for increase, − for decrease, and NA for not affected. In the Cash Flow column, indicate whether the item is an operating activity (OA), investing activity (IA), or a financing activity (FA). The first transaction is entered as an example.

Event	Assets	=	Liab.	+	Equity	Rev.	−	Exp.	=	Net Inc.	Cash Flow
1	+		NA		+	NA		NA		NA	+ FA

Solution to Self-Study Review Problem

Event	Assets	=	Liab.	+	Equity	Rev.	−	Exp.	=	Net Inc.	Cash Flow
1	+		NA		+	NA		NA		NA	+ FA
2	NA		+		−	NA		NA		NA	NA
3	+		NA		+	NA		NA		NA	+ FA
4	NA		NA		− +	NA		NA		NA	NA
5	NA		NA		− +	NA		NA		NA	NA
6	−		NA		−	NA		NA		NA	− FA
7	NA		NA		NA	NA		NA		NA	NA
8	+		NA		+	NA		NA		NA	+ FA
9	−		−		NA	NA		NA		NA	− FA
10	+		NA		+	NA		NA		NA	+ FA

KEY TERMS

Appropriated Retained
  Earnings 301
Articles of incorporation 288
Authorized stock 294
Board of directors 291
Book value per share 294
Closely held corporation 288
Common stock 294
Continuity 290
Corporation 288
Cost method of accounting
  for treasury stock 299

Cumulative dividends 295
Date of record 300
Declaration date 300
Dividends in arrears 295
Double taxation 289
Entrenched management 291
Ex-dividend 300
Issued stock 294
Legal capital 293
Limited liability 290
Limited liability companies
  (LLCs) 290

Market value 294
Outstanding stock 294
Paid-in Capital in Excess of
  Par Value 296
Par value 293
Partnerships 288
Partnership
  agreement 288
Payment date 300
Preferred stock 295
Sarbanes-Oxley Act of
  2002 289

Securities Act of 1933 and
  Securities Exchange Act
  of 1934 289
Sole proprietorships 288
Stated value 294
Stock certificates 288
Stock dividends 300
Stockholders 291
Stock split 301
Transferability 291
Treasury stock 294
Withdrawals 292

QUESTIONS

1. What are the three major forms of business organizations? Describe each.

2. How are sole proprietorships formed?

3. Discuss the purpose of a partnership agreement. Is such an agreement necessary for partnership formation?

4. What is meant by the phrase *separate legal entity?* To which type of business organization does it apply?

5. What is the purpose of the articles of incorporation? What information do they provide?

6. What is the function of the stock certificate?

7. What prompted Congress to pass the Securities Act of 1933 and the Securities Exchange Act of 1934? What is the purpose of these laws?

8. What are the advantages and disadvantages of the corporate form of business organization?

9. What is a limited liability company? Discuss its advantages and disadvantages.

10. How does the term *double taxation* apply to corporations? Give an example of double taxation.

11. What is the difference between contributed capital and retained earnings for a corporation?

12. What are the similarities and differences in the equity structure of a sole proprietorship, a partnership, and a corporation?

13. Why is it easier for a corporation to raise large amounts of capital than it is for a partnership?

14. What is the meaning of each of the following terms with respect to the corporate form of organization?
  (a) Legal capital
  (b) Par value of stock
  (c) Stated value of stock
  (d) Market value of stock
  (e) Book value of stock
  (f) Authorized shares of stock
  (g) Issued stock
  (h) Outstanding stock

  (i) Treasury stock
  (j) Common stock
  (k) Preferred stock
  (l) Dividends

15. What is the difference between cumulative preferred stock and noncumulative preferred stock?

16. What is no-par stock? How is it recorded in the accounting records?

17. Assume that Best Co. has issued and outstanding 1,000 shares of $100 par value, 10 percent, cumulative preferred stock. What is the dividend per share? If the preferred dividend is two years in arrears, what total amount of dividends must be paid before the common shareholders can receive any dividends?

18. If Best Co. issued 10,000 shares of $20 par value common stock for $30 per share, what amount is credited to the Common Stock account? What amount of cash is received?

19. What is the difference between par value stock and stated value stock?

20. Why might a company repurchase its own stock?

21. What effect does the purchase of treasury stock have on the equity of a company?

22. Assume that Day Company repurchased 1,000 of its own shares for $30 per share and sold the shares two weeks later for $35 per share. What is the amount of gain on the sale? How is it reported on the balance sheet? What type of account is treasury stock?

23. What is the importance of the declaration date, record date, and payment date in conjunction with corporate dividends?

24. What is the difference between a stock dividend and a stock split?

25. Why would a company choose to distribute a stock dividend instead of a cash dividend?

26. What is the primary reason that a company would declare a stock split?

27. If Best Co. had 10,000 shares of $20 par value common stock outstanding and declared a 5-for-1 stock split, how

many shares would then be outstanding and what would be their par value after the split?

28. When a company appropriates retained earnings, does the company set aside cash for a specific use? Explain.

29. What is the largest source of financing for most U.S. businesses?

30. What is meant by *equity financing?* What is meant by *debt financing?*

31. What is a widely held corporation? What is a closely held corporation?

32. What are some reasons that a corporation might not pay dividends?

EXERCISES

connect
|ACCOUNTING

All applicable Exercises are available with McGraw-Hill Connect Accounting.

LO 1, 2

Exercise 8-1   *Effect of accounting events on the financial statements of a sole proprietorship*

A sole proprietorship was started on January 1, 2010, when it received $80,000 cash from Derek Hughes, the owner. During 2010, the company earned $50,000 in cash revenues and paid $22,400 in cash expenses. Hughes withdrew $5,000 cash from the business during 2010.

Required

Prepare an income statement, capital statement (statement of changes in equity), balance sheet, and statement of cash flows for Hughes's 2010 fiscal year.

LO 1, 2

Exercise 8-2   *Effect of accounting events on the financial statements of a partnership*

Wes Poole and Ross King started the PK partnership on January 1, 2010. The business acquired $60,000 cash from Poole and $90,000 from King. During 2010, the partnership earned $56,000 in cash revenues and paid $32,000 for cash expenses. Poole withdrew $2,000 cash from the business, and King withdrew $3,000 cash. The net income was allocated to the capital accounts of the two partners in proportion to the amounts of their original investments in the business.

Required

Prepare an income statement, capital statement, balance sheet, and statement of cash flows for the PK partnership for the 2010 fiscal year.

LO 1, 2

Exercise 8-3   *Effect of accounting events on the financial statements of a corporation*

Premo Corporation was started with the issue of 8,000 shares of $10 par common stock for cash on January 1, 2010. The stock was issued at a market price of $18 per share. During 2010, the company earned $58,000 in cash revenues and paid $39,000 for cash expenses. Also, a $4,000 cash dividend was paid to the stockholders.

Required

Prepare an income statement, statement of changes in stockholders' equity, balance sheet, and statement of cash flows for Premo Corporation's 2010 fiscal year.

LO 4

Exercise 8-4   *Effect of issuing common stock on the balance sheet*

Newly formed Health First Corporation has 100,000 shares of $5 par common stock authorized. On March 1, 2010, Health First issued 20,000 shares of the stock for $12 per share. On May 2 the company issued an additional 30,000 shares for $15 per share. Health First was not affected by other events during 2010.

Required

a. Record the transactions in a horizontal statements model like the following one. In the Cash Flow column, indicate whether the item is an operating activity (OA), investing activity

(IA), or financing activity (FA). Use NA to indicate that an element was not affected by the event.

Assets	=	Liab.	+	Equity			Rev.	−	Exp.	=	Net Inc.	Cash Flow
Cash	=		+	Com. Stk.	+	Paid-in Excess						

b. Determine the amount Health First would report for common stock on the December 31, 2010, balance sheet.

c. Determine the amount Health First would report for paid-in capital in excess of par.

d. What is the total amount of capital contributed by the owners?

e. What amount of total assets would Health First report on the December 31, 2010, balance sheet?

Exercise 8-5   *Recording and reporting common and preferred stock transactions*

LO 4

Farmer, Inc., was organized on June 5, 2010. It was authorized to issue 400,000 shares of $10 par common stock and 50,000 shares of 5 percent cumulative class A preferred stock. The class A stock had a stated value of $30 per share. The following stock transactions pertain to Farmer, Inc.

1. Issued 20,000 shares of common stock for $14 per share.

2. Issued 10,000 shares of the class A preferred stock for $32 per share.

3. Issued 30,000 shares of common stock for $18 per share.

Required

Prepare the stockholders' equity section of the balance sheet immediately after these transactions have been recognized.

Exercise 8-6   *Effect of no-par common and par preferred stock on the horizontal statements model*

LO 4

Collins Corporation issued 10,000 shares of no-par common stock for $20 per share. Collins also issued 2,000 shares of $50 par, 5 percent noncumulative preferred stock at $55 per share.

Required

Record these events in a horizontal statements model like the following one. In the cash flow column, indicate whether the item is an operating activity (OA), investing activity (IA), or financing activity (FA). Use NA to indicate that an element was not affected by the event.

Assets	=			Equity			Rev.	−	Exp.	=	Net Inc.	Cash Flow
Cash	=	Pfd. Stk.	+	Com. Stk.	+	PIC in Excess						

Exercise 8-7   *Issuing stock for assets other than cash*

LO 4

Gaines Corporation was formed when it issued shares of common stock to two of its shareholders. Gaines issued 5,000 shares of $10 par common stock to S. Gaines in exchange for $75,000 cash (the issue price was $15 per share). Gaines also issued 2,000 shares of stock to J. Caldwell in exchange for a one-year-old delivery van on the same day. Caldwell had originally paid $42,000 for the van.

a. What was the market value of the delivery van on the date of the stock issue?

b. Show the effect of the two stock issues on Gaine's books in a horizontal statements model like the following one. In the Cash Flow column, indicate whether the item is an operating activity (OA), investing activity (IA), or financing activity (FA). Use NA to indicate that an element was not affected by the event.

Assets	=	Equity			Rev.	−	Exp.	=	Net Inc.	Cash Flow
Cash	+ Van	= Com. Stk.	+	PIC in Excess						

LO 5

Exercise 8-8 *Treasury stock transactions*

Woodard Corporation repurchased 3,000 shares of its own stock for $40 per share. The stock has a par of $10 per share. A month later Woodard resold 1,500 shares of the treasury stock for $45 per share.

Required

What is the balance of the treasury stock account after these transactions are recognized?

LO 5

Exercise 8-9 *Recording and reporting treasury stock transactions*

The following information pertains to Kwon Corp. at January 1, 2010.

Common stock, $10 par, 50,000 shares authorized,	
2,000 shares issued and outstanding	$20,000
Paid-in capital in excess of par, common stock	15,000
Retained earnings	65,000

Kwon Corp. completed the following transactions during 2010:

1. Issued 2,000 shares of $10 par common stock for $25 per share.
2. Repurchased 200 shares of its own common stock for $22 per share.
3. Resold 50 shares of treasury stock for $26 per share.

Required

a. How many shares of common stock were outstanding at the end of the period?
b. How many shares of common stock had been issued at the end of the period?
c. Organize the transactions data in accounts under the accounting equation.
d. Prepare the stockholders' equity section of the balance sheet reflecting these transactions. Include the number of shares authorized, issued, and outstanding in the description of the common stock.

LO 6

Exercise 8-10 *Effect of cash dividends on financial statements*

On October 1, 2011, Evans Corporation declared a $50,000 cash dividend to be paid on December 30 to shareholders of record on November 20.

Required

Record the events occurring on October 1, November 20, and December 30 in a horizontal statements model like the following one. In the Cash Flow column, indicate whether the item is an operating activity (OA), investing activity (IA), or financing activity (FA).

Date	Assets = Liab. + Com. Stock + Ret. Earn.	Rev. − Exp. = Net Inc.	Cash Flow

LO 6

Exercise 8-11 *Accounting for cumulative preferred dividends*

When Collum Corporation was organized in January 2011, it immediately issued 10,000 shares of $60 par, 5 percent, cumulative preferred stock and 20,000 shares of $10 par common stock. The company's earnings history is as follows: 2011, net loss of $15,000; 2012, net income of $120,000; 2013, net income of $95,000. The corporation did not pay a dividend in 2011.

Required

a. How much is the dividend arrearage as of January 1, 2012?
b. Assume that the board of directors declares an $80,000 cash dividend at the end of 2012 (remember that the 2011 and 2012 preferred dividends are due). How will the dividend be divided between the preferred and common stockholders?

Exercise 8-12   *Cash dividends for preferred and common shareholders*   LO 6

J&J Corporation had the following stock issued and outstanding at January 1, 2010.

1. 50,000 shares of $5 par common stock.
2. 5,000 shares of $100 par, 5 percent, noncumulative preferred stock.

On May 10, J&J Corporation declared the annual cash dividend on its 5,000 shares of preferred stock and a $1 per share dividend for the common shareholders. The dividends will be paid on June 15 to the shareholders of record on May 30.

Required

Determine the total amount of dividends to be paid to the preferred shareholders and common shareholders.

Exercise 8-13   *Cash dividends: common and preferred stock*   LO 6

Hu Corp. had the following stock issued and outstanding at January 1, 2010.

1. 50,000 shares of no-par common stock.
2. 10,000 shares of $100 par, 3 percent, cumulative preferred stock. (Dividends are in arrears for one year, 2009.)

On February 1, 2010, Hu declared a $100,000 cash dividend to be paid March 31 to shareholders of record on March 10.

Required

What amount of dividends will be paid to the preferred shareholders versus the common shareholders?

Exercise 8-14   *Accounting for stock dividends*   LO 7

Magee Corporation issued a 4 percent stock dividend on 30,000 shares of its $10 par common stock. At the time of the dividend, the market value of the stock was $30 per share.

Required

a. Compute the amount of the stock dividend.
b. Show the effects of the stock dividend on the financial statements using a horizontal statements model like the following one.

Assets	=	Liab.	+	Com. Stk.	+	PIC in Excess	+	Ret. Earn.	Rev.	−	Exp.	=	Net Inc.	Cash Flow

Exercise 8-15   *Determining the effects of stock splits on the accounting records*   LO 7

The market value of Lan Corporation's common stock had become excessively high. The stock was currently selling for $160 per share. To reduce the market price of the common stock, Lan declared a 2-for-1 stock split for the 400,000 outstanding shares of its $10 par common stock.

Required

a. How will Lan Corporation's books be affected by the stock split?
b. Determine the number of common shares outstanding and the par value after the split.
c. Explain how the market value of the stock will be affected by the stock split.

LO 9

Exercise 8-16   *Corporate announcements*

Mighty Drugs (one of the three largest drug makers) just reported that its 2010 third quarter profits are essentially the same as the 2009 third quarter profits. In addition to this announcement, the same day, Mighty Drugs also announced that the Food and Drug Administration had just approved a new drug used to treat high blood pressure that Mighty Drugs developed. This new drug has been shown to be extremely effective and has few or no side effects. It will also be less expensive than the other drugs currently on the market.

Required

Using the above information, answer the following questions.

a. What do you think will happen to the stock price of Mighty Drugs on the day these two announcements are made? Explain your answer.
b. How will the balance sheet be affected on that day by the above announcements?
c. How will the income statement be affected on that day by the above announcements?
d. How will the statement of cash flows be affected on that day by the above announcements?

LO 9

Exercise 8-17   *Performing ratio analysis using real-world data*

Merck & Company is one of the world's largest pharmaceutical companies. The following data were taken from the company's 2007 annual report.

	Fiscal Years Ending	
	December 31, 2007	**December 31, 2006**
Net earnings (in millions)	$3,275.4	$4,433.8
Earnings per share	$1.51	$2.04

The following data were taken from public stock-price quotes.

Stock price per share on March 3, 2008: $44.06
(Two months after the end of Merck's 2007 fiscal year.)

Stock price per share on March 1, 2007: $43.99
(Two months after the end of Merck's 2007 fiscal year.)

Required

a. Compute Merck's price-earnings ratio for March 3, 2008, and March 1, 2007.
b. Did the financial markets appear to be more optimistic about Merck's future performance on March 1, 2007, or March 3, 2008?
c. Based on the information provided, estimate approximately how many shares of stock Merck had outstanding as of December 31, 2007.

PROBLEMS

connect
|ACCOUNTING

All applicable Problems are available with McGraw-Hill
Connect Accounting.

LO 1, 2

Problem 8-18   *Effect of business structure on financial statements*

Upton Company was started on January 1, 2011, when the owners invested $160,000 cash in the business. During 2011, the company earned cash revenues of $120,000 and incurred cash expenses of $82,000. The company also paid cash distributions of $15,000.

Required

Prepare a 2011 income statement, capital statement (statement of changes in equity), balance sheet, and statement of cash flows using each of the following assumptions. (Consider each assumption separately.)

CHECK FIGURES
a. Net Income: $38,000
b. Dan Upton Capital: $106,200

a. Upton is a sole proprietorship owned by J. Upton.

b. Upton is a partnership with two partners, Dan and Nancy Upton. Dan invested $100,000 and Nancy invested $60,000 of the $160,000 cash that was used to start the business. Nancy was expected to assume the vast majority of the responsibility for operating the business. The partnership agreement called for Nancy to receive 60 percent of the profits and Dan the remaining 40 percent. With regard to the $15,000 distribution, Nancy withdrew $6,000 from the business and Dan withdrew $9,000.

c. Upton is a corporation. The owners were issued 10,000 shares of $10 par common stock when they invested the $160,000 cash in the business.

Problem 8-19 *Recording and reporting stock transactions and cash dividends across two accounting cycles*

LO 4-6

Flesher Corporation was authorized to issue 100,000 shares of $5 par common stock and 50,000 shares of $50 par, 5 percent, cumulative preferred stock. Flesher Corporation completed the following transactions during its first two years of operation.

CHECK FIGURES
b. Preferred Stock, 2010: $100,000
c. Common Shares Outstanding, 2011: 34,500

2010

Jan.   2   Issued 15,000 shares of $5 par common stock for $8 per share.
      15   Issued 2,000 shares of $50 par preferred stock for $55 per share.
Feb. 14   Issued 20,000 shares of $5 par common stock for $9 per share.
Dec. 31   During the year, earned $310,000 of cash service revenue and paid $240,000 of cash operating expenses.
      31   Declared the cash dividend on outstanding shares of preferred stock for 2010. The dividend will be paid on January 31 to stockholders of record on January 15, 2011.

2011

Jan. 31   Paid the cash dividend declared on December 31, 2010.
Mar. 1   Issued 3,000 shares of $50 par preferred stock for $60 per share.
June 1   Purchased 500 shares of common stock as treasury stock at $9 per share.
Dec. 31   During the year, earned $250,000 of cash service revenue and paid $175,000 of cash operating expenses.
      31   Declared the dividend on the preferred stock and a $0.50 per share dividend on the common stock.

Required

a. Organize the transaction data in accounts under an accounting equation.
b. Prepare the stockholders' equity section of the balance sheet at December 31, 2010.
c. Prepare the balance sheet at December 31, 2011.

Problem 8-20 *Recording and reporting treasury stock transactions*

LO 5, 6, 8

Millsaps Corp. completed the following transactions in 2010, the first year of operation.

CHECK FIGURE
b. Total Paid-In Capital: $366,900

1. Issued 30,000 shares of $10 par common stock at par.
2. Issued 2,000 shares of $30 stated value preferred stock at $33 per share.
3. Purchased 1,000 shares of common stock as treasury stock for $12 per share.
4. Declared a 5 percent dividend on preferred stock.
5. Sold 300 shares of treasury stock for $15 per share.
6. Paid the cash dividend on preferred stock that was declared in Event 4.

7. Earned cash service revenue of $75,000 and incurred cash operating expenses of $42,000.
8. Appropriated $6,000 of retained earnings.

Required

a. Organize the transaction in accounts under an accounting equation.
b. Prepare the stockholders' equity section of the balance sheet as of December 31, 2010.

LO 5

Problem 8-21 *Recording and reporting treasury stock transactions*

Carter Corporation reports the following information in its January 1, 2010, balance sheet:

Stockholders' equity	
Common stock, $10 par value,	
50,000 shares authorized, 30,000 shares issued and outstanding	$300,000
Paid-in capital in excess of par value	150,000
Retained earnings	100,000
Total stockholders' equity	$550,000

During 2010, Carter was affected by the following accounting events.

1. Purchased 1,000 shares of treasury stock at $20 per share.
2. Reissued 600 shares of treasury stock at $22 per share.
3. Earned $64,000 of cash service revenues.
4. Paid $38,000 of cash operating expenses.

Required

Prepare the stockholders' equity section of the year-end balance sheet.

LO 4, 6, 7

Problem 8-22 *Recording and reporting stock dividends*

Davis Corp. completed the following transactions in 2010, the first year of operation.

1. Issued 30,000 shares of $20 par common stock for $30 per share.
2. Issued 5,000 shares of $50 par, 4 percent, preferred stock at $51 per share.
3. Paid the annual cash dividend to preferred shareholders.
4. Issued a 5 percent stock dividend on the common stock. The market value at the dividend declaration date was $40 per share.
5. Later that year, issued a 2-for-1 split on the 31,500 shares of outstanding common stock.
6. Earned $195,000 of cash service revenues and paid $120,000 of cash operating expenses.

Required

a. Record each of these events in a horizontal statements model like the following one. In the Cash Flow column, indicate whether the item is an operating activity (OA), investing activity (IA), or financing activity (FA). Use NA to indicate that an element is not affected by the event.

Assets = Liab. +	Equity					Rev. − Exp. = Net Inc.	Cash Flow
	Pfd. Stk. +	Com. Stk. +	PIC in Excess PS +	PIC in Excess CS +	Ret. Earn.		

b. Prepare the stockholders' equity section of the balance sheet at the end of 2010.

Problem 8-23   *Analyzing the stockholders' equity section of the balance sheet*   LO 4, 7

The stockholders' equity section of the balance sheet for Atkins Company at December 31, 2011, is as follows.

Stockholders' Equity		
Paid-in capital		
Preferred stock, ? par value, 6% cumulative,		
50,000 shares authorized,		
40,000 shares issued and outstanding	$400,000	
Common stock, $10 stated value,		
150,000 shares authorized,		
60,000 shares issued and ? outstanding	600,000	
Paid-in capital in excess of par–preferred	30,000	
Paid-in capital in excess of par–common	200,000	
Total paid-in capital		$1,230,000
Retained earnings		250,000
Treasury stock, 2,000 shares		(50,000)
Total stockholders' equity		$1,430,000

Note: The market value per share of the common stock is $25, and the market value per share of the preferred stock is $12.

Required

a. What is the par value per share of the preferred stock?

b. What is the dividend per share on the preferred stock?

c. What is the number of common stock shares outstanding?

d. What was the average issue price per share (price for which the stock was issued) of the common stock?

e. Explain the difference between the average issue price and the market price of the common stock.

f. If Atkins declared a 2-for-1 stock split on the common stock, how many shares would be outstanding after the split? What amount would be transferred from the retained earnings account because of the stock split? Theoretically, what would be the market price of the common stock immediately after the stock split?

Problem 8-24   *Different forms of business organization*   LO 1

Brian Walter was working to establish a business enterprise with four of his wealthy friends. Each of the five individuals would receive a 20 percent ownership interest in the company. A primary goal of establishing the enterprise was to minimize the amount of income taxes paid. Assume that the five investors are taxed at the rate of 15% on dividend income received from corporations and that the corporate tax rate is 30 percent. Also assume that the new company is expected to earn $400,000 of cash income before taxes during its first year of operation. All earnings are expected to be immediately distributed to the owners.

Required

Calculate the amount of after-tax cash flow available to each investor if the business is established as a partnership versus a corporation. Write a memo explaining the advantages and disadvantages of these two forms of business organization. Explain why a limited liability company may be a better choice than either a partnership or a corporation.

Problem 8-25   *Effects of equity transactions on financial statements*   LO 4–8

The following events were experienced by Baskin, Inc.

1. Issued common stock for cash.

2. Paid cash to purchase treasury stock.

3. Declared a cash dividend.

4. Issued cumulative preferred stock.

5. Issued noncumulative preferred stock.

6. Appropriated retained earnings.

7. Sold treasury stock for an amount of cash that was more than the cost of the treasury stock.

8. Distributed a stock dividend.

9. Declared a 2-for-1 stock split on the common stock.

10. Paid a cash dividend that was previously declared.

Required

Show the effect of each event on the elements of the financial statements using a horizontal statements model like the following one. Use + for increase, − for decrease, and NA for not affected. In the Cash Flow column, indicate whether the item is an operating activity (OA), investing activity (IA), or financing activity (FA). The first transaction is entered as an example.

Event No.	Assets	=	Liab.	+	Equity	Rev.	−	Exp.	=	Net Inc.	Cash Flow
1	+		NA		+	NA		NA		NA	+ FA

LO 9

Problem 8-26   *Performing ratio analysis using real-world data*

Google, Inc., operates the world's largest Internet search engine. International Business Machines Corporation (IBM) is one of the world's largest computer hardware and software companies. The following data were taken from the companies' December 31, 2007, annual reports.

	Google, Inc.	IBM
Net earnings (in thousands)	$4,203.7	$10,418.0
Earnings per share	$5.31	$7.32

The following data were taken from public stock-price quotes.

Stock price per share on March 3, 2007: (Two months after the end of their 2007 fiscal years.)	$457.02	$114.23

Required

a. Compute the price-earnings ratios for each company as of March 3, 2008.

b. Which company's future performance did the financial markets appear to be more optimistic about as of March 3, 2008?

c. Provide some reasons why the market may view one company's future more optimistically than the other's.

ANALYZE, THINK, COMMUNICATE

ATC 8-1   Business Applications Case   *Understanding real-world annual reports*

Required

Use the Topps Company's annual report in Appendix B to answer the following questions.

a. Does Topps' common stock have a par value, and if so how much is it?

b. How many shares of Topps' common stock were *outstanding* as of February 25, 2006? Do not forget to consider treasury stock.

c. The dollar-value balance in Topps' Treasury Stock account is larger than the balance in its Common Stock and Additional Paid-In-Capital accounts. How can this be?

d. How many members of Topps' Board of Directors are also officers (employees) of the company as of February 25, 2006?

e. What was the highest and lowest price per share that Topps' common stock sold for during the fiscal year ending on February 25, 2006?

ATC 8-2   Group Assignment   *Missing information*

Listed here are the stockholders' equity sections of three public companies for years ending in 2007 and 2006.

	2007	2006
Wendy's (dollar amounts are presented in thousands)		
Stockholders' Equity		
Common stock, ?? Stated Value per share, authorized: 200,000,000; 130,241,000 in 2007 and 129,548,000 in 2006 shares issued, respectively	$ 13,024	$ 12,955
Capital in Excess of Stated Value	1,110,363	1,089,825
Retained Earnings	1,287,963	1,241,489
Acc. Other Comp. Income (Exp.)	9,959	(13,446)
Treasury Stock, at cost: (42,844,000 shares in 2007; 33,847,000 shares in 2006)	(1,617,178)	1,319,146
Coca-Cola (amounts are presented in millions)		
Stockholders' Equity		
Common Stock, ?? Par Value per share, authorized: 5,600; issued: 3,519 shares in 2007 and 3,511 shares in 2006	$ 880	$ 878
Capital Surplus	7,378	5,983
Reinvested Earnings	36,235	33,468
Acc. Other Comp. Inc. (loss)	626	(1,291)
Treasury Stock, at cost: (1,201 shares in 2007; 1,193 shares in 2006)	(23,375)	(22,118)
Harley-Davidson (dollar amounts are presented in thousands)		
Stockholders' Equity		
Common stock, ?? Par Value per share, authorized: 800,000,000, issued: 335,211,201 in 2007 and 334,328,193 shares in 2006	3,352	3,343
Additional Paid-in Capital	812,224	766,382
Retained Earnings	6,117,567	5,460,629
Acc. Other Comp. Inc. (loss)	(137,258)	(206,662)
Treasury Stock, at cost: 96,725,399 for 2007 and 76,275,837 for 2006	(4,420,394)	(3,266,955)

Required

a. Divide the class in three sections and divide each section into groups of three to five students. Assign each section one of the companies.

Group Tasks

Based on the company assigned to your group, answer the following questions.

b. What is the per share par or stated value of the common stock in 2006?

c. What was the average issue price of the common stock for each year?

d. How many shares of stock are outstanding at the end of each year?

e. What is the average cost per share of the treasury stock for 2006?

f. Do the data suggest that your company was profitable in 2006?

g. Can you determine the amount of net income from the information given? What is missing?

h. What is the total stockholders' equity of your company for each year?

Class Discussion

i. Have each group select a representative to present the information about its company. Compare the share issue price and the par or stated value of the companies.

j. Compare the average issue price to the current market price for each of the companies. Speculate about what might cause the difference.

ATC 8-3   Real-World Case   *Which stock is most valuable?*

Listed here are data for five companies. These data are from companies' annual reports for the fiscal year indicated in the parentheses. The market price per share is the closing price of the companies' stock as of November 3, 2006. Except for market price per share, all amounts are in thousands. The shares outstanding number is the weighted-average number of shares the company used to compute its basic earnings per share.

Company (Fiscal Year)	Net Earnings	Shares Outstanding	Stockholders' Equity	Market-Price per Share
Brink's (12/31/2005)	$ 142,400	58,700	$ 837,500	$52.50
Carmax (2/28/2006)	148,055	104,954	959,738	43.33
ExxonMobil (12/31/2005)	36,130,000	6,133,000	111,186,000	72.15
Garmin (12/31/2005)	311,219	216,134	1,157,264	46.57
Schering-Plough (12/31/2005)	269,000	1,480,000	7,387,000	22.28

Required

a. Compute the earnings per share (EPS) for each company.

b. Compute the P/E ratio for each company.

c. Using the P/E ratios, rank the companies' stock in the order that the stock market appears to value the companies, from most valuable to least valuable. Identify reasons the ranking based on P/E ratios may not represent the market's optimism about one or two companies.

d. Compute the book value per share for each company.

e. Compare each company's book value per share to its market price per share. Based on the data, rank the companies from most valuable to least valuable. (The higher the ratio of market value to book value, the greater the value the stock market appears to be assigning to a company's stock.)

ATC 8-4   Business Applications Case   *Finding stock market information*

Use one of the many financial information sites on the Internet, such as CNBC, CNNMoney, Google Finance, or Yahoo Finance, to complete the requirements below. Some of the sites require you to enter a company's stock trading symbol in order to retrieve information. These sites will provide a function to find a company's stock symbol based on its name.

Required

For each company listed here, provide the requested information based on the most recent data available.

Company Name	Closing Price of Stock	P/E Ratio	Dividend per Share	Dividend Yield
Berkshire Hathaway A				
ExxonMobil				
Johnson & Johnson				
Kroger				
Walgreen				

ATC 8-5   Business Applications Case   *Using the P/E ratio*

During 2010, Jason Corporation and Fitzgerald Corporation reported net incomes of $7,000 and $9,600, respectively. Each company had 2,000 shares of common stock issued and outstanding. The market price per share of Jason's stock was $50, while Fitzgerald's stock sold for $85 per share.

Required

a. Determine the P/E ratio for each company.

b. Based on the P/E ratios computed in Requirement *a*, which company do investors believe has more potential for growth in income?

ATC 8-6   Writing Assignment   *Comparison of organizational forms*

Jim Baku and Scott Hanson are thinking about opening a new restaurant. Baku has extensive marketing experience but does not know that much about food preparation. However, Hanson is an excellent chef. Both will work in the business, but Baku will provide most of the funds necessary to start the business. At this time, they cannot decide whether to operate the business as a partnership or a corporation.

Required

Prepare a written memo to Baku and Hanson describing the advantages and disadvantages of each organizational form. Also, from the limited information provided, recommend the organizational form you think they should use.

ATC 8-7   Ethical Dilemma   *Bad news versus very bad news*

Louise Stinson, the chief financial officer of Bostonian Corporation, was on her way to the president's office. She was carrying the latest round of bad news. There would be no executive bonuses this year. Corporate profits were down. Indeed, if the latest projections held true, the company would report a small loss on the year-end income statement. Executive bonuses were tied to corporate profits. The executive compensation plan provided for 10 percent of net earnings to be set aside for bonuses. No profits meant no bonuses. While things looked bleak, Stinson had a plan that might help soften the blow.

After informing the company president of the earnings forecast, Stinson made the following suggestion: Since the company was going to report a loss anyway, why not report a big loss? She reasoned that the directors and stockholders would not be much more angry if the company reported a large loss than if it reported a small one. There were several questionable assets that could be written down in the current year. This would increase the current year's loss but would reduce expenses in subsequent accounting periods. For example, the company was carrying damaged inventory that was estimated to have a value of $2,500,000. If this estimate were revised to $500,000, the company would have to recognize a $2,000,000 loss in the current year. However, next year when the goods were sold, the expense for cost of goods sold would be $2,000,000 less and profits would be higher by that amount. Although the directors would be angry this year, they would certainly be happy next year. The strategy would also have the benefit of adding $200,000 to next year's executive bonus pool ($2,000,000 × 0.10). Furthermore, it could not hurt this year's bonus pool because there would be no pool this year since the company is going to report a loss.

Some of the other items that Stinson is considering include (1) converting from straight-line to accelerated depreciation, (2) increasing the percentage of receivables estimated to be uncollectible in the current year and lowering the percentage in the following year, and (3) raising the percentage of estimated warranty claims in the current period and lowering it in the following period. Finally, Stinson notes that two of the company's department stores have been experiencing losses. The company could sell these stores this year and thereby improve earnings next year. Stinson admits that the sale would result in significant losses this year, but she smiles as she thinks of next year's bonus check.

Required

a. Explain how each of the three numbered strategies for increasing the amount of the current year's loss would affect the stockholders' equity section of the balance sheet in the current year. How would the other elements of the balance sheet be affected?

b. If Stinson's strategy were effectively implemented, how would it affect the stockholders' equity in subsequent accounting periods?

c. Comment on the ethical implications of running the company for the sake of management (maximization of bonuses) versus the maximization of return to stockholders.

d. Formulate a bonus plan that will motivate managers to maximize the value of the firm instead of motivating them to manipulate the reporting process.

e. How would Stinson's strategy of overstating the amount of the reported loss in the current year affect the company's current P/E ratio?

ATC 8-8   Research Assignment   *Analyzing PepsiCo's equity structure*

Using either PepsiCo's most current Form 10-K or the company's annual report, answer the questions below. To obtain the Form 10-K use either the EDGAR system following the instructions in Appendix A or the company's website. The company's annual report is available on its website.

Required

a. What is the *book value* of PepsiCo's stockholders' equity that is shown on the company's balance sheet?

b. What is the par value of PepsiCo's common stock?

c. Does PepsiCo have any treasury stock? If so, how many shares of treasury stock does the company hold?

d. Why does the stock of a company such as a PepsiCo have a market value that is higher than its book value?

Financial Statement Analysis

LEARNING OBJECTIVES

After you have mastered the material in this chapter you will be able to:

1 Describe factors associated with communicating useful information.

2 Differentiate between horizontal and vertical analysis.

3 Explain ratio analysis.

4 Calculate ratios for assessing a company's liquidity.

5 Calculate ratios for assessing a company's solvency.

6 Calculate ratios for assessing company management's effectiveness.

7 Calculate ratios for assessing a company's position in the stock market.

8 Explain the limitations of financial statement analysis.

CHAPTER OPENING

Expressing financial statement information in the form of ratios enhances its usefulness. Ratios permit comparisons over time and among companies, highlighting similarities, differences, and trends. Proficiency with common financial statement analysis techniques benefits both internal and external users. Before beginning detailed explanations of numerous ratios and percentages, however, we consider factors relevant to communicating useful information.

The *Curious* Accountant

On May 14, 2007, DaimlerChrysler (DC) and Cerberus announced that Cerberus, a private-equity firm, was buying 80 percent of the Chrysler Group from Daimler-Chrysler. The sale closed on August 3, 2007. Some analysts claimed the "sale" actually involved Daimler-Chrysler paying Cerberus to take Chrysler off its hands. After the sale DaimlerChrysler planned to rename itself Daimler AG and focus its efforts on its production of commercial trucks and its Mercedes brand of cars.

Three other groups in addition to Cerberus also made offers to buy Chrysler, but in the end Cerberus was the winner. The question some might ask is why would anyone have wanted to buy Chrysler? It had lost money in several years prior to the sale, including a $1.6 billion loss in 2006. Additionally, like Ford and GM, it is at a costing disadvantage to its main competitors from Japan. Some analysts estimate that when all benefits are included, American car manufacturers pay an average of $30 per hour more to their workers than do Toyota and Honda. Also, as part of the deal Cerberus agreed to assume $18 billion of liabilities related to Chrysler's pension and health-care commitments.

Why would Cerberus be so anxious to buy Chrysler? What types of analysis would the company use to make this decision? (Answers on page 327.)

FACTORS IN COMMUNICATING USEFUL INFORMATION

Describe factors associated with communicating useful information.

The primary objective of accounting is to provide information useful for decision making. To provide information that supports this objective, accountants must consider the intended users, the types of decisions users make with financial statement information, and available means of analyzing the information.

The Users

Users of financial statement information include managers, creditors, stockholders, potential investors, and regulatory agencies. These individuals and organizations use financial statements for different purposes and bring varying levels of sophistication to understanding business activities. For example, investors range from private individuals who know little about financial statements to large investment brokers and institutional investors capable of using complex statistical analysis techniques. At what level of user knowledge should financial statements be aimed? Condensing and reporting complex business transactions at a level easily understood by nonprofessional investors is increasingly difficult. Current reporting standards target users that have a reasonably informed knowledge of business, though that level of sophistication is difficult to define.

The Types of Decisions

Just as the knowledge level of potential users varies, the information needs of users varies, depending on the decision at hand. A supplier considering whether or not to sell goods on account to a particular company wants to evaluate the likelihood of getting paid; a potential investor in that company wants to predict the likelihood of increases in the market value of the company's common stock. Financial statements, however, are designed for general purposes; they are not aimed at any specific user group. Some disclosed information, therefore, may be irrelevant to some users but vital to others. Users must employ different forms of analysis to identify information most relevant to a particular decision.

Financial statements can provide only highly summarized economic information. The costs to a company of providing excessively detailed information would be prohibitive. In addition, too much detail leads to **information overload,** the problem of having so much data that important information becomes obscured by trivial information. Users faced with reams of data may become so frustrated attempting to use it that they lose the value of *key* information that is provided.

Information Analysis

Because of the diversity of users, their different levels of knowledge, the varying information needs for particular decisions, and the general nature of financial statements, a variety of analysis techniques has been developed. In the following sections, we explain several common methods of analysis. The choice of method depends on which technique appears to provide the most relevant information in a given situation.

METHODS OF ANALYSIS

Differentiate between horizontal and vertical analysis.

Financial statement analysis should focus primarily on isolating information useful for making a particular decision. The information required can take many forms but usually involves comparisons, such as comparing changes in the same item for the same company over a number of years, comparing key relationships within the same year, or comparing the operations of several different companies in the same industry. This chapter discusses three categories of analysis methods: horizontal, vertical, and ratio. Exhibits 9.1 and 9.2 present comparative financial statements for Milavec Company. We refer to these statements in the examples of analysis techniques.

EXHIBIT 9.1

MILAVEC COMPANY
Income Statements and Statements of
Retained Earnings
For the Years Ending December 31

	2010	2009
Sales	$900,000	$800,000
Cost of goods sold		
Beginning inventory	43,000	40,000
Purchases	637,000	483,000
Goods available for sale	680,000	523,000
Ending inventory	70,000	43,000
Cost of goods sold	610,000	480,000
Gross margin	290,000	320,000
Operating expenses	248,000	280,000
Income before taxes	42,000	40,000
Income taxes	17,000	18,000
Net income	25,000	22,000
Plus: Retained earnings,		
beginning balance	137,000	130,000
Less: Dividends	0	15,000
Retained earnings,		
ending balance	$162,000	$137,000

EXHIBIT 9.2

MILAVEC COMPANY
Balance Sheets
As of December 31

	2010	2009
Assets		
Cash	$ 20,000	$ 17,000
Marketable securities	20,000	22,000
Notes receivable	4,000	3,000
Accounts receivable	50,000	56,000
Merchandise inventory	70,000	43,000
Prepaid items	4,000	4,000
Property, plant, and		
equipment (net)	340,000	310,000
Total assets	$508,000	$455,000
Liabilities and Stockholders' Equity		
Accounts payable	$ 40,000	$ 38,000
Salaries payable	2,000	3,000
Taxes payable	4,000	2,000
Bonds payable, 8%	100,000	100,000
Preferred stock, 6%,		
$100 par, cumulative	50,000	50,000
Common stock, $10 par	150,000	125,000
Retained earnings	162,000	137,000
Total liabilities and		
stockholders' equity	$508,000	$455,000

Horizontal Analysis

Horizontal analysis, also called **trend analysis,** refers to studying the behavior of individual financial statement items over several accounting periods. These periods may be several quarters within the same fiscal year or they may be several different years. The analysis of a given item may focus on trends in the absolute dollar amount of the item or trends in percentages. For example, a user may observe that revenue increased from one period to the next by $42 million (an absolute dollar amount) or that it increased by a percentage such as 15 percent.

Absolute Amounts

The **absolute amounts** of particular financial statement items have many uses. Various national economic statistics, such as gross domestic product and the amount spent to replace productive capacity, are derived by combining absolute amounts reported by businesses. Financial statement users with expertise in particular industries might evaluate amounts reported for research and development costs to judge whether a company is spending excessively or conservatively. Users are particularly concerned with how amounts change over time. For example, a user might compare a pharmaceutical company's revenue before and after the patent expired on one of its drugs.

Comparing only absolute amounts has drawbacks, however, because *materiality* levels differ from company to company or even from year to year for a given company. The **materiality** of information refers to its relative importance. An item is considered material if knowledge of it would influence the decision of a reasonably informed user. Generally accepted accounting principles permit companies to account for *immaterial* items in the most convenient way, regardless of technical accounting rules. For example, companies may expense, rather than capitalize and depreciate, relatively inexpensive long-term assets like pencil sharpeners or waste baskets even if the assets have useful lives of many years. The concept of materiality, which has both quantitative and qualitative aspects, underlies all accounting principles.

It is difficult to judge the materiality of an absolute financial statement amount without considering the size of the company reporting it. For reporting purposes, Exxon Corporation's financial statements are rounded to the nearest million dollars. For Exxon, a $400,000 increase in sales is not material. For a small company, however, $400,000 could represent total sales, a highly material amount. Meaningful comparisons between the two companies' operating performance are impossible using only absolute amounts. Users can surmount these difficulties with percentage analysis.

Percentage Analysis

Percentage analysis involves computing the percentage relationship between two amounts. In horizontal percentage analysis, a financial statement item is expressed as a percentage of the previous balance for the same item. Percentage analysis sidesteps the materiality problems of comparing different size companies by measuring changes in percentages rather than absolute amounts. Each change is converted to a percentage of the base year. Exhibit 9.3 presents a condensed version of Milavec's income statement with horizontal percentages for each item.

The percentage changes disclose that, even though Milavec's net income increased slightly more than sales, products may be underpriced. Cost of goods sold increased much more than sales, resulting in a lower gross margin. Users would also want to investigate why operating expenses decreased substantially despite the increase in sales.

EXHIBIT 9.3

MILAVEC COMPANY
Comparative Income Statements
For the Years Ending December 31

	2010	2009	Percentage Difference
Sales	$900,000	$800,000	+12.5%*
Cost of goods sold	610,000	480,000	+27.1
Gross margin	290,000	320,000	−9.4
Operating expenses	248,000	280,000	−11.4
Income before taxes	42,000	40,000	+5.0
Income taxes	17,000	18,000	−5.6
Net income	$ 25,000	$ 22,000	+13.6

*($900,000 − $800,000) ÷ $800,000; all changes expressed as percentages of previous totals.

Whether basing their analyses on absolute amounts, percentages, or ratios, users must avoid drawing overly simplistic conclusions about the reasons for the results. Numerical relationships flag conditions requiring further study. A change that appears favorable on the surface may not necessarily be a good sign. Users must evaluate the underlying reasons for the change.

CHECK *Yourself* 9.1

The following information was drawn from the annual reports of two retail companies (amounts are shown in millions). One company is an upscale department store; the other is a discount store. Based on this limited information, identify which company is the upscale department store.

	Jenkins Co.	Horn's Inc.
Sales	$325	$680
Cost of goods sold	130	408
Gross margin	$195	$272

Answer   Jenkins' gross margin represents 60 percent ($195 ÷ $325) of sales. Horn's gross margin represents 40 percent ($272 ÷ $680) of sales. Since an upscale department store would have higher margins than a discount store, the data suggest that Jenkins is the upscale department store.

Answers to The *Curious* Accountant

Obviously, Cerberus agreed to purchase Chrysler believing it could make a profit on its investment. In its public comments it did not explain exactly how it planned to make the company profitable when DaimlerChrysler could not. Being a private-equity company it is not obligated to make public disclosures about how well its businesses are doing or what its plans are, unlike companies whose stock is publicly traded. Many analysts believe that getting the workers to grant concessions on wages and/or benefits is essential if Cerberus is to have success with Chrysler.

Cerberus does have other opportunities to cut costs. Before buying Chrysler Cerberus had purchased the General Motors Acceptance Corporation (GMAC), which finances automobiles and home mortgages. Chrysler Financial is the arm of Chrysler that also finances auto purchases, so there is the potential to merge some of its operations with GMAC, though Cerberus did not disclose any plans of doing this. Cerberus also owns some automotive parts supply companies, so the opportunity for vertical integration exists.

Cerberus' optimism about its purchase of Chrysler does not guarantee that the investment will be successful. Remember that Daimler was optimistic when it purchased Chrysler through a merger in 1998 for $36 billion. Less than 10 years later it was sold to Cerberus for what has to be considered a substantial loss. However the deal turns out, we can be sure that Cerberus' team of analysts, lawyers, accountants, and investment bankers put thousands of hours into analyzing every aspect of the deal. But then, so did Daimler's in 1998.

The point here is that financial analysis techniques can help managers make decisions, but these tools cannot guarantee success. Before tools such as ratios and trend analysis can be used, the decision maker must understand the business being evaluated and he or she must make assumptions about future events. Only the future will tell us whether Cerberus made a wise investment in Chrysler, but we can be sure that a lot of ratio analysis and capital budgeting computations were made before the deal was done.

Sources: DaimlerChrysler's filings with the SEC; "Chrysler Deal Heralds New Direction for Detroit," *The Wall Street Journal,* May 15, 2007, pp. A-1 and A-14; and "After Pact to Shed Chrysler, Daimler Turns Focus to Other Challenges," *The Wall Street Journal,* May 15, 2007, p. A-14.

When comparing more than two periods, analysts use either of two basic approaches: (1) choosing one base year from which to calculate all increases or decreases or (2) calculating each period's percentage change from the preceding figure. For example, assume Milavec's sales for 2007 and 2008 were $600,000 and $750,000, respectively.

	2010	2009	2008	2007
Sales	$900,000	$800,000	$750,000	$600,000
Increase over 2007 sales	50.0%	33.3%	25.0%	–
Increase over preceding year	12.5%	6.7%	25.0%	–

Analysis discloses that Milavec's 2010 sales represented a 50 percent increase over 2007 sales, and a large increase (25 percent) occurred in 2008. From 2008 to 2009, sales increased only 6.7 percent but in the following year increased much more (12.5 percent).

Vertical Analysis

Vertical analysis uses percentages to compare individual components of financial statements to a key statement figure. Horizontal analysis compares items over many time periods; vertical analysis compares many items within the same time period.

Vertical Analysis of the Income Statement

Vertical analysis of an income statement (also called a *common size* income statement) involves converting each income statement component to a percentage of sales. Although vertical analysis suggests examining only one period, it is useful to compare common size income statements for several years. Exhibit 9.4 presents Milavec's income statements, along with vertical percentages, for 2010 and 2009. This analysis discloses that cost of goods sold increased significantly as a percentage of sales. Operating expenses and income taxes, however, decreased in relation to sales. Each of these observations indicates a need for more analysis regarding possible trends for future profits.

EXHIBIT 9.4

MILAVEC COMPANY
Vertical Analysis of Comparative Income Statements

| | 2010 | | 2009 | |
	Amount	Percentage* of Sales	Amount	Percentage* of Sales
Sales	$900,000	100.0%	$800,000	100.0%
Cost of goods sold	610,000	67.8	480,000	60.0
Gross margin	290,000	32.2	320,000	40.0
Operating expenses	248,000	27.6	280,000	35.0
Income before taxes	42,000	4.7	40,000	5.0
Income taxes	17,000	1.9	18,000	2.3
Net income	$ 25,000	2.8%	$ 22,000	2.8%

*Percentages may not add exactly due to rounding.

Vertical Analysis of the Balance Sheet

Vertical analysis of the balance sheet involves converting each balance sheet component to a percentage of total assets. The vertical analysis of Milavec's balance sheets in Exhibit 9.5 discloses few large percentage changes from the preceding year. Even small individual percentage changes, however, may represent substantial dollar increases. For example, inventory constituted 9.5% of total assets in 2009 and 13.5% in 2010. While this appears to be a small increase, it actually represents a 62.8% increase in the inventory account balance ([$70,000 − $43,000] ÷ $43,000) from 2009 to 2010. Careful analysis requires considering changes in both percentages *and* absolute amounts.

Ratio Analysis

Ratio analysis involves studying various relationships between different items reported in a set of financial statements. For example, net earnings (net income) reported on the income statement may be compared to total assets reported on the balance sheet. Analysts calculate many different ratios for a wide variety of purposes. The remainder of this chapter is devoted to discussing some of the more commonly used ratios.

LO 3

Explain ratio analysis.

EXHIBIT 9.5

MILAVEC COMPANY
Vertical Analysis of Comparative Balance Sheets

	2010	Percentage* of Total	2009	Percentage* of Total
Assets				
Cash	$ 20,000	3.9%	$ 17,000	3.7%
Marketable securities	20,000	3.9	22,000	4.8
Notes receivable	4,000	0.8	3,000	0.7
Accounts receivable	50,000	9.8	56,000	12.3
Merchandise inventory	70,000	13.8	43,000	9.5
Prepaid items	4,000	0.8	4,000	0.9
Total current assets	168,000	33.1	145,000	31.9
Property, plant, and equipment	340,000	66.9	310,000	68.1
Total assets	$508,000	100.0%	$455,000	100.0%
Liabilities and Stockholders' Equity				
Accounts payable	$ 40,000	7.9%	$ 38,000	8.4%
Salaries payable	2,000	0.4	3,000	0.7
Taxes payable	4,000	0.8	2,000	0.4
Total current liabilities	46,000	9.1	43,000	9.5
Bonds payable, 8%	100,000	19.7	100,000	22.0
Total liabilities	146,000	28.7	143,000	31.4
Preferred stock 6%, $100 par	50,000	9.8	50,000	11.0
Common stock, $10 par	150,000	29.5	125,000	27.5
Retained earnings	162,000	31.9	137,000	30.1
Total stockholders' equity	362,000	71.3	312,000	68.6
Total liabilities and stockholders' equity	$508,000	100.0%	$455,000	100.0%

*Percentages may not add exactly due to rounding.

Objectives of Ratio Analysis

As suggested earlier, various users approach financial statement analysis with many different objectives. Creditors are interested in whether a company will be able to pay its debts on time. Both creditors and stockholders are concerned with how the company is financed, whether through debt, equity, or earnings. Stockholders and potential investors analyze past earnings performance and dividend policy for clues to the future value of their investments. In addition to using internally generated data to analyze operations, company managers find much information prepared for external purposes useful for examining past operations and planning future policies. Although many of these objectives are interrelated, it is convenient to group ratios into categories such as measures of debt-paying ability and measures of profitability.

MEASURES OF DEBT-PAYING ABILITY

Liquidity Ratios

Liquidity ratios indicate a company's ability to pay short-term debts. They focus on current assets and current liabilities. The examples in the following section use the financial statement information reported by Milavec Company.

Working Capital

Working capital is current assets minus current liabilities. Current assets include assets most likely to be converted into cash or consumed in the current operating period.

LO 4

Calculate ratios for assessing a company's liquidity.

Current liabilities represent debts that must be satisfied in the current period. Working capital therefore measures the excess funds the company will have available for operations, excluding any new funds it generates during the year. Think of working capital as the cushion against short-term debt-paying problems. Working capital at the end of 2010 and 2009 for Milavec Company was as follows.

	2010	2009
Current assets	$168,000	$145,000
− Current liabilities	46,000	43,000
Working capital	$122,000	$102,000

Milavec's working capital increased from 2009 to 2010, but the numbers themselves say little. Whether $122,000 is sufficient or not depends on such factors as the industry in which Milavec operates, its size, and the maturity dates of its current obligations. We can see, however, that the increase in working capital is primarily due to the increase in inventories.

Current Ratio

Working capital is an absolute amount. Its usefulness is limited by the materiality difficulties discussed earlier. It is hard to draw meaningful conclusions from comparing Milavec's working capital of $122,000 with another company that also has working capital of $122,000. By expressing the relationship between current assets and current liabilities as a ratio, however, we have a more useful measure of the company's debt-paying ability relative to other companies. The **current ratio,** also called the **working capital ratio,** is calculated as follows.

$$\text{Current ratio} = \frac{\text{Current assets}}{\text{Current liabilities}}$$

To illustrate using the current ratio for comparisons, consider Milavec's current position relative to Laroque's, a larger firm with current assets of $500,000 and current liabilities of $378,000.

	Milavec	Laroque
Current assets (a)	$168,000	$500,000
− Current liabilities (b)	46,000	378,000
Working capital	$122,000	$122,000
Current ratio (a ÷ b)	3.65:1	1.32:1

The current ratio is expressed as the number of dollars of current assets for each dollar of current liabilities. In the above example, both companies have the same amount of working capital. Milavec, however, appears to have a much stronger working capital position. Any conclusions from this analysis must take into account the circumstances of the particular companies; there is no single ideal current ratio that suits all companies. In recent years the average current ratio of the 30 companies that constitute the Dow Jones Industrial Average was around 1.21:1; the individual company ratios, however, ranged from .05:1 to 3.0:1. A current ratio can be too high. Money invested in factories and developing new products is usually more profitable than money held as large cash balances or invested in inventory.

Quick Ratio

The **quick ratio,** also known as the **acid-test ratio,** is a conservative variation of the current ratio. The quick ratio measures a company's *immediate* debt-paying ability.

Only cash, receivables, and current marketable securities *(quick assets)* are included in the numerator. Less liquid current assets, such as inventories and prepaid items, are omitted. Inventories may take several months to sell; prepaid items reduce otherwise necessary expenditures but do not lead eventually to cash receipts. The quick ratio is computed as follows.

$$\text{Quick ratio} = \frac{\text{Quick assets}}{\text{Current liabilities}}$$

Milavec Company's current ratios and quick ratios for 2010 and 2009 follow.

	2010	2009
Current ratio	$168,000 ÷ $46,000	$145,000 ÷ $43,000
	3.65:1	3.37:1
Quick ratio	$94,000 ÷ $46,000	$98,000 ÷ $43,000
	2.04:1	2.28:1

The decrease in the quick ratio from 2009 to 2010 reflects both a decrease in quick assets and an increase in current liabilities. The result indicates that the company is less liquid (has less ability to pay its short-term debt) in 2010 than it was in 2009.

Accounts Receivable Ratios

Offering customers credit plays an enormous role in generating revenue, but it also increases expenses and delays cash receipts. To minimize uncollectible accounts expense and collect cash for use in current operations, companies want to collect receivables as quickly as possible without losing customers. Two relationships are often examined to assess a company's collection record: *accounts receivable turnover* and *average number of days to collect receivables (average collection period)*.

Accounts receivable turnover is calculated as follows.

$$\text{Accounts receivable turnover} = \frac{\text{Net credit sales}}{\text{Average accounts receivable}}$$

Net credit sales refers to total sales on account less sales discounts, allowances, and returns. When most sales are credit sales or when a breakdown of total sales between cash sales and credit sales is not available, the analyst must use total sales in the numerator. The denominator is based on *net accounts receivable* (receivables after subtracting the allowance for doubtful accounts). Since the numerator represents a whole period, it is preferable to use average receivables in the denominator if possible. When comparative statements are available, the average can be based on the beginning and ending balances. Milavec Company's accounts receivable turnover is computed as follows.

	2010	2009
Net sales (assume all on account) (a)	$900,000	$800,000
Beginning receivables (b)	$ 56,000	$ 55,000*
Ending receivables (c)	50,000	56,000
Average receivables (d) = (a + c) ÷ 2	$ 53,000	$ 55,500
Accounts receivable turnover (a ÷ d)	16.98	14.41

*The beginning receivables balance was drawn from the 2008 financial statements, which are not included in the illustration.

The 2010 accounts receivable turnover of 16.98 indicates Milavec collected its average receivables almost 17 times that year. The higher the turnover, the faster the collections. A company can have cash flow problems and lose substantial purchasing power if resources are tied up in receivables for long periods.

Average number of days to collect receivables is calculated as follows.

$$\text{Average number of days to collect receivables} = \frac{365 \text{ days}}{\text{Accounts receivable turnover}}$$

This ratio offers another way to look at turnover by showing the number of days, on average, it takes to collect a receivable. If receivables were collected 16.98 times in 2010, the average collection period was 21 days, 365 ÷ 16.98 (the number of days in the year divided by accounts receivable turnover). For 2009, it took an average of 25 days (365 ÷ 14.41) to collect a receivable.

Although the collection period improved, no other conclusions can be reached without considering the industry, Milavec's past performance, and the general economic environment. In recent years the average time to collect accounts receivable for the 25 nonfinancial companies that make up the Dow Jones Industrial Average was around 49 days. (Financial firms are excluded because, by the nature of their business, they have very long collection periods.)

Inventory Ratios

A fine line exists between having too much and too little inventory in stock. Too little inventory can result in lost sales and costly production delays. Too much inventory can use needed space, increase financing and insurance costs, and become obsolete. To help analyze how efficiently a company manages inventory, we use two ratios similar to those used in analyzing accounts receivable.

Inventory turnover indicates the number of times, on average, that inventory is totally replaced during the year. The relationship is computed as follows.

$$\text{Inventory turnover} = \frac{\text{Cost of goods sold}}{\text{Average inventory}}$$

The average inventory is usually based on the beginning and ending balances that are shown in the financial statements. Inventory turnover for Milavec was as follows.

	2010	2009
Cost of goods sold (a)	$610,000	$480,000
Beginning inventory (b)	$ 43,000	$ 40,000*
Ending inventory (c)	70,000	43,000
Average inventory (d) = (b + c) ÷ 2	$ 56,500	$ 41,500
Inventory turnover (a ÷ d)	10.80	11.57

*The beginning inventory balance was drawn from the company's 2008 financial statements, which are not included in the illustration.

Generally, a higher turnover indicates that merchandise is being handled more efficiently. Trying to compare firms in different industries, however, can be misleading. Inventory turnover for grocery stores and many retail outlets is high. Because of the nature of the goods being sold, inventory turnover is much lower for appliance and jewelry stores. We look at this issue in more detail when we discuss return on investment.

Average number of days to sell inventory is determined by dividing the number of days in the year by the inventory turnover as follows.

$$\text{Average number of days to sell inventory} = \frac{365 \text{ days}}{\text{Inventory turnover}}$$

The result approximates the number of days the firm could sell inventory without purchasing more. For Milavec, this figure was 34 days in 2010 (365 ÷ 10.80) and 32 days in 2009 (365 ÷ 11.57). In recent years it took around 72 days, on average, for the companies in the Dow Jones Industrial Average that have inventory to sell their inventory.

The time it took individual companies to sell their inventory varied by industry, ranging from 10 days to 292 days.

Solvency Ratios

Solvency ratios are used to analyze a company's long-term debt-paying ability and its financing structure. Creditors are concerned with a company's ability to satisfy outstanding obligations. The larger a company's liability percentage, the greater the risk that the company could fall behind or default on debt payments. Stockholders, too, are concerned about a company's solvency. If a company is unable to pay its debts, the owners could lose their investment. Each user group desires that company financing choices minimize its investment risk, whether their investment is in debt or stockholders' equity.

Calculate ratios for assessing a company's solvency.

Debt Ratios

The following ratios represent two different ways to express the same relationship. Both are frequently used.

Debt to assets ratio.   This ratio measures the percentage of a company's assets that are financed by debt.

Debt to equity ratio.   As used in this ratio, *equity* means stockholders' equity. The debt to equity ratio compares creditor financing to owner financing. It is expressed as the dollar amount of liabilities for each dollar of stockholders' equity.

These ratios are calculated as follows.

$$\text{Debt to assets} = \frac{\text{Total liabilities}}{\text{Total assets}}$$

$$\text{Debt to equity} = \frac{\text{Total liabilities}}{\text{Total stockholders' equity}}$$

Applying these formulas to Milavec Company's results produces the following.

	2010	2009
Total liabilities (a)	$146,000	$143,000
Total stockholders' equity (b)	362,000	312,000
Total assets (liabilities + stockholders' equity) (c)	$508,000	$455,000
Debt to assets (a ÷ c)	29%	31%
Debt to equity ratio (a ÷ b)	0.40:1	0.46:1

Each year less than one-third of the company's assets were financed with debt. The amount of liabilities per dollar of stockholders' equity declined by 0.06. It is difficult to judge whether the reduced percentage of liabilities is favorable. In general, a lower level of liabilities provides greater security because the likelihood of bankruptcy is reduced. Perhaps, however, the company is financially strong enough to incur more liabilities and benefit from financial leverage. The 25 nonfinancial companies that make up the Dow Jones Industrial Average report around 33 percent of their assets, on average, are financed through borrowing.

Number of Times Interest Is Earned

The **times interest earned** ratio measures the burden a company's interest payments represent. Users often consider times interest is earned along with the debt ratios when evaluating financial risk. The numerator of this ratio uses *earnings before interest and taxes (EBIT),* rather than net earnings, because the amount of earnings *before* interest and income taxes is available for paying interest.

$$\text{Times interest earned} = \frac{\text{Earnings before interest expense and taxes}}{\text{Interest expense}}$$

Dividing EBIT by interest expense indicates how many times the company could have made its interest payments. Obviously, interest is paid only once, but the more times it *could* be paid, the bigger the company's safety net. Although interest is paid from cash, not accrual earnings, it is standard practice to base this ratio on accrual-based EBIT, not a cash-based amount. For Milavec, this calculation is as follows.

	2010	2009
Income before taxes	$42,000	$40,000
Interest expense (b)	8,000	8,000*
Earnings before interest and taxes (a)	$50,000	$48,000
Times interest earned (a ÷ b)	6.25 times	6 times

*Interest on bonds: $100,000 × .08 = $8,000.

Any expense or dividend payment can be analyzed this way. Another frequently used calculation is the number of times the preferred dividend is earned. In that case, the numerator is net income (after taxes) and the denominator is the amount of the annual preferred dividend.

CHECK *Yourself* 9.2

Selected data for Riverside Corporation and Academy Company follow (amounts are shown in millions).

	Riverside Corporation	Academy Company
Total liabilities (a)	$650	$450
Stockholders' equity (b)	300	400
Total liabilities + stockholders' equity (c)	$950	$850
Interest expense (d)	$ 65	$ 45
Income before taxes (e)	140	130
Earnings before interest and taxes (f)	$205	$175

Based on this information alone, which company would likely obtain the less favorable interest rate on additional debt financing?

Answer Interest rates vary with risk levels. Companies with less solvency (long-term debt-paying ability) generally must pay higher interest rates to obtain financing. Two solvency measures for the two companies follow. Recall:

Total assets = Liabilities + Stockholders' equity

	Riverside Corporation	Academy Company
Debt to assets ratio (a ÷ c)	68.4%	52.9%
Times interest earned (f ÷ d)	3.15 times	3.89 times

Since Riverside has a higher percentage of debt and a lower times interest earned ratio, the data suggest that Riverside is less solvent than Academy. Riverside would therefore likely have to pay a higher interest rate to obtain additional financing.

Plant Assets to Long-Term Liabilities

Companies often pledge plant assets as collateral for long-term liabilities. Financial statement users may analyze a firm's ability to obtain long-term financing on the strength of its asset base. Effective financial management principles dictate that asset purchases should be financed over a time span about equal to the expected lives of the assets. Short-term assets should be financed with short-term liabilities; the current ratio, introduced earlier, indicates how well a company manages current debt. Long-lived assets should be financed with long-term liabilities, and the **plant assets to long-term liabilities** ratio suggests how well long-term debt is managed. It is calculated as follows.

$$\text{Plant assets to long-term liabilities} = \frac{\text{Net plant assets}}{\text{Long-term liabilities}}$$

For Milavec Company, these ratios follow.

	2010	2009
Net plant assets (a)	$340,000	$310,000
Bonds payable (b)	100,000	100,000
Plant assets to long-term liabilities (a ÷ b)	3.4:1	3.1:1

MEASURES OF PROFITABILITY

Profitability refers to a company's ability to generate earnings. Both management and external users desire information about a company's success in generating profits and how these profits are used to reward investors. Some of the many ratios available to measure different aspects of profitability are discussed in the following two sections.

Measures of Managerial Effectiveness

The most common ratios used to evaluate managerial effectiveness measure what percentage of sales results in earnings and how productive assets are in generating those sales. As mentioned earlier, the *absolute amount* of sales or earnings means little without also considering company size.

Calculate ratios for assessing company management's effectiveness.

Net Margin (or Return on Sales)

Gross margin and *gross profit* are alternate terms for the amount remaining after subtracting the expense cost of goods sold from sales. **Net margin,** sometimes called *operating margin, profit margin,* or the *return on sales ratio,* describes the percent remaining of each sales dollar after subtracting other expenses as well as cost of goods sold. Net margin can be calculated in several ways; some of the more common methods only subtract normal operating expenses or all expenses other than income tax expense. For simplicity, our calculation uses net income (we subtract all expenses). Net income divided by net sales expresses net income (earnings) as a percentage of sales, as follows.

$$\text{Net margin} = \frac{\text{Net income}}{\text{Net sales}}$$

For Milavec Company, the net margins for 2010 and 2009 were as follows.

	2010	2009
Net income (a)	$ 25,000	$ 22,000
Net sales (b)	900,000	800,000
Net margin (a ÷ b)	2.78%	2.75%

Milåvec has maintained approximately the same net margin. Obviously, the larger the percentage, the better; a meaningful interpretation, however, requires analyzing the company's history and comparing the net margin to other companies in the same industry. The average net margin for the 30 companies that make up the Dow Jones Industrial Average has been around 12 percent in recent years; some companies, such as Pfizer with 40 percent, have been much higher than the average. Of course, if a company has a net loss, its net margin for that year will be negative.

Asset Turnover Ratio

The **asset turnover ratio** (sometimes called *turnover of assets ratio*) measures how many sales dollars were generated for each dollar of assets invested. As with many ratios used in financial statement analysis, users may define the numerator and denominator of this ratio in different ways. For example, they may use total assets or only include operating assets. Since the numerator represents a whole period, it is preferable to use average assets in the denominator if possible, especially if the amount of assets changed significantly during the year. We use average total assets in our illustration.

$$\text{Asset turnover} = \frac{\text{Net sales}}{\text{Average total assets}}$$

For Milavec, the asset turnover ratios were as follows.

	2010	2009
Net sales (a)	$900,000	$800,000
Beginning assets (b)	$455,000	$420,000*
Ending assets (c)	508,000	455,000
Average assets (d) = (b + c) ÷ 2	$481,500	$437,500
Asset turnover (a ÷ d)	1.87	1.83

*The beginning asset balance was drawn from the 2008 financial statements, which are not included in the illustration.

As with most ratios, the implications of a given asset turnover ratio are affected by other considerations. Asset turnover will be high in an industry that requires only minimal investment to operate, such as real estate sales companies. On the other hand, industries that require large investments in plant and machinery, like the auto industry, are likely to have lower asset turnover ratios. The asset turnover ratios of the companies that make up the Dow Jones Industrial Average have averaged around 0.90 in recent years. This means that annual sales have averaged 90 percent of their assets.

Return on Investment

Return on investment (ROI), also called *return on assets* or *earning power,* is the ratio of wealth generated (net income) to the amount invested (average total assets) to generate the wealth. ROI can be calculated as follows.[1]

$$\text{ROI} = \frac{\text{Net income}}{\text{Average total assets}}$$

[1] Detailed coverage of the return on investment ratio is provided in Chapter 15. As discussed in that chapter, companies frequently manipulate the formula to improve managerial motivation and performance. For example, instead of using net income, companies frequently use operating income because net income may be affected by items that are not controllable by management such as loss on a plant closing, storm damage, and so on.

For Milavec, ROI was as follows.

2010

$25,000 ÷ $481,500* = 5.19%

2009

$22,000 ÷ $437,500* = 5.03%

*The computation of average assets is shown above.

In general, higher ROIs suggest better performance. The ROI of the large companies that make up the Dow Jones Industrial Average averaged around 9 percent. These data suggest that Milavec is performing below average, and therefore signals a need for further evaluation that would lead to improved performance.

Return on Equity

Return on equity (ROE) is often used to measure the profitability of the stockholders' investment. ROE is usually higher than ROI because of financial leverage. Financial leverage refers to using debt financing to increase the assets available to a business beyond the amount of assets financed by owners. As long as a company's ROI exceeds its cost of borrowing (interest expense), the owners will earn a higher return on their investment in the company by using borrowed money. For example, if a company borrows money at 8 percent and invests it at 10 percent, the owners will enjoy a return that is higher than 10 percent. ROE is computed as follows.

$$ ROE = \frac{Net\ income}{Average\ total\ stockholders'\ equity} $$

If the amount of stockholders' equity changes significantly during the year, it is desirable to use average equity rather than year-end equity in the denominator. The ROE figures for Milavec Company were as follows.

	2010	2009
Net income (a)	$ 25,000	$ 22,000
Preferred stock, 6%, $100 par, cumulative	50,000	50,000
Common stock, $10 par	150,000	125,000
Retained earnings	162,000	137,000
Total stockholders' equity (b)	$362,000	$312,000
ROE (a ÷ b)	6.9%	7.1%

The slight decrease in ROE is due primarily to the increase in common stock. The effect of the increase in total stockholders' equity offsets the effect of the increase in earnings. This information does not disclose whether Milavec had the use of the additional stockholder investment for all or part of the year. If the data are available, calculating a weighted average amount of stockholders' equity provides more meaningful results.

We mentioned earlier the companies that make up the Dow Jones Industrial Average had an average ROI of 9 percent. The average ROE for the companies in the Dow was 25 percent, indicating effective use of financial leverage.

Stock Market Ratios

LO 7

Calculate ratios for assessing a company's position in the stock market.

Existing and potential investors in a company's stock use many common ratios to analyze and compare the earnings and dividends of different size companies in different industries. Purchasers of stock can profit in two ways: through receiving dividends and through increases in stock value. Investors consider both dividends and overall earnings performance as indicators of the value of the stock they own.

Earnings per Share

Perhaps the most frequently quoted measure of earnings performance is **earnings per share (EPS).** EPS calculations are among the most complex in accounting, and more advanced textbooks devote entire chapters to the subject. At this level, we use the following basic formula.

$$\text{Earnings per share} = \frac{\text{Net earnings available for common stock}}{\text{Average number of outstanding common shares}}$$

EPS pertains to shares of *common stock.* Limiting the numerator to earnings available for common stock eliminates the annual preferred dividend ($0.06 \times \$50,000 = \$3,000$) from the calculation. Exhibit 9.1 shows that Milavec did not pay the preferred dividends in 2010. Since the preferred stock is cumulative, however, the preferred dividend is in arrears and not available to the common stockholders. The number of common shares outstanding is determined by dividing the book value of the common stock by its par value per share ($\$150,000 \div \$10 = 15,000$ for 2010 and $\$125,000 \div \$10 = 12,500$ for 2009). Using these data, Milavec's 2010 EPS is calculated as follows.

$$\frac{\$25,000 \text{ (net income)} - \$3,000 \text{ (preferred dividend)}}{(15,000 + 12,500)/2 \text{ (average outstanding common shares)}} = \$1.60 \text{ per share}$$

Investors attribute a great deal of importance to EPS figures. The amounts used in calculating EPS, however, have limitations. Many accounting choices, assumptions, and estimates underlie net income computations, including alternative depreciation methods, different inventory cost flow assumptions, and estimates of future uncollectible accounts or warranty expenses, to name only a few. The denominator is also inexact because various factors (discussed in advanced accounting courses) affect the number of shares to include. Numerous opportunities therefore exist to manipulate EPS figures. Prudent investors consider these variables in deciding how much weight to attach to earnings per share.

Book Value

Book value per share is another frequently quoted measure of a share of stock. It is calculated as follows.

$$\text{Book value per share} = \frac{\text{Stockholders' equity} - \text{Preferred rights}}{\text{Outstanding common shares}}$$

Instead of describing the numerator as stockholders' equity, we could have used assets minus liabilities, the algebraic computation of a company's "net worth." Net worth is a misnomer. A company's accounting records reflect book values, not worth. Because assets are recorded at historical costs and different methods are used to transfer asset costs to expense, the book value of assets after deducting liabilities means little if anything. Nevertheless, investors use the term *book value per share* frequently.

Preferred rights represents the amount of money required to satisfy the claims of preferred stockholders. If the preferred stock has a call premium, the call premium amount is subtracted. In our example, we assume the preferred stock can be retired at par. Book value per share for 2010 was therefore as follows.

$$\frac{\$362,000 - \$50,000}{15,000 \text{ shares}} = \$20.80 \text{ per share}$$

Price-Earnings Ratio

The **price-earnings ratio,** or *P/E ratio,* compares the earnings per share of a company to the market price for a share of the company's stock. Assume Avalanche Company and Brushfire Company each report earnings per share of $3.60. For the same year, Cyclone Company reports EPS of $4.10. Based on these data alone, Cyclone stock may seem to be the best investment. Suppose, however, that the price for one share of stock in each company is $43.20, $36.00, and $51.25, respectively. Which stock would you buy? Cyclone's stock price is the highest, but so is its EPS. The P/E ratio provides a common base of comparison.

$$\text{Price-earnings ratio} = \frac{\text{Market price per share}}{\text{Earnings per share}}$$

The P/E ratios for the three companies are

Avalanche	Brushfire	Cyclone
12.0	10.0	12.5

Brushfire might initially seem to be the best buy for your money. Yet there must be some reason that Cyclone's stock is selling at 12½ times earnings. In general, a higher P/E ratio indicates the market is more optimistic about a company's growth potential than it is about a company with a lower P/E ratio. The market price of a company's stock reflects judgments about both the company's current results and expectations about future results. Investors cannot make informed use of these ratios for investment decisions without examining the reasons behind the ratios. Recently the average P/E ratio for the companies in the Dow Jones Industrial Average was around 18.

Dividend Yield

There are two ways to profit from a stock investment. One, investors can sell the stock for more than they paid to purchase it (if the stock price rises). Two, the company that issued the stock can pay cash dividends to the shareholders. Most investors view rising stock prices as the primary reward for investing in stock. The importance of receiving dividends, however, should not be overlooked. Evaluating dividend payments is more complex than simply comparing the dividends per share paid by one company to the dividends per share paid by another company. Receiving a $1 dividend on a share purchased for $10 is a much better return than receiving a $1.50 dividend on stock bought for $100. Computing the **dividend yield** simplifies comparing dividend payments. Dividend yield measures dividends received as a percentage of a stock's market price.

$$\text{Dividend yield} = \frac{\text{Dividends per share}}{\text{Market price per share}}$$

To illustrate, consider Dragonfly Inc. and Elk Company. The information for calculating dividend yield follows.

	Dragonfly	Elk
Dividends per share (a)	$ 1.80	$ 3.00
Market price per share (b)	40.00	75.00
Dividend yield (a ÷ b)	4.5%	4.0%

Even though the dividend per share paid by Elk Company is higher, the yield is lower (4.5 percent versus 4.0 percent) because Elk's stock price is so high. The dividend yields for the companies included in the Dow Jones Industrial Average were averaging around 2.3 percent.

Other Ratios

Investors can also use a wide array of other ratios to analyze profitability. Most **profitability ratios** use the same reasoning. For example, you can calculate the *yield* of a variety of financial investments. Yield represents the percentage the amount received is of the amount invested. The dividend yield explained above could be calculated for either common or preferred stock. Investors could measure the earnings yield by calculating earnings per share as a percentage of market price. Yield on a bond can be calculated the same way: interest received divided by the price of the bond.

The specific ratios presented in this chapter are summarized in Exhibit 9.6.

EXHIBIT 9.6

Summary of Key Relationships

Liquidity Ratios	1. Working capital	Current assets − Current liabilities
	2. Current ratio	Current assets ÷ Current liabilities
	3. Quick (acid-test) ratio	(Current assets − Inventory − Prepaid Items) ÷ Current liabilities
	4. Accounts receivable turnover	Net credit sales ÷ Average receivables
	5. Average number of days to collect receivables	365 ÷ Accounts receivable turnover
	6. Inventory turnover	Cost of goods sold ÷ Average inventory
	7. Average number of days to sell inventory	365 ÷ Inventory turnover
Solvency Ratios	8. Debt to assets ratio	Total liabilities ÷ Total assets
	9. Debt to equity ratio	Total liabilities ÷ Total stockholders' equity
	10. Times interest earned	Earnings before interest expense and taxes ÷ Interest expense
	11. Plant assets to long-term liabilities	Net plant assets ÷ Long-term liabilities
Profitability Ratios	12. Net margin	Net income ÷ Net sales
	13. Asset turnover	Net sales ÷ Average total assets
	14. Return on investment (also: return on assets)	Net income ÷ Average total assets
	15. Return on equity	Net income ÷ Average total stockholders' equity
Stock Market Ratios	16. Earnings per share	Net earnings available for common stock ÷ Average outstanding common shares
	17. Book value per share	(Stockholders' equity − Preferred rights) ÷ Outstanding common shares
	18. Price-earnings ratio	Market price per share ÷ Earnings per share
	19. Dividend yield	Dividends per share ÷ Market price per share

PRESENTATION OF ANALYTICAL RELATIONSHIPS

To communicate with users, companies present analytical information in endless different ways in annual reports. Although providing diagrams and illustrations in annual reports is not usually required, companies often include various forms of graphs and charts along with the underlying numbers to help users interpret financial statement data more easily. Common types presented include bar charts, pie charts, and line graphs. Exhibits 9.7, 9.8, and 9.9 show examples of these forms.

EXHIBIT 9.7

Earnings and Dividends on Common Stock

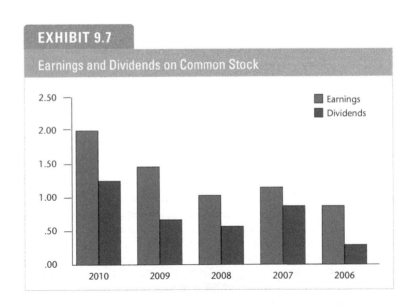

EXHIBIT 9.8
Percentage of Sales Dollar

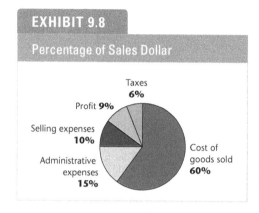

Taxes **6%**
Profit **9%**
Selling expenses **10%**
Administrative expenses **15%**
Cost of goods sold **60%**

EXHIBIT 9.9
Profits by Major Industry Segment

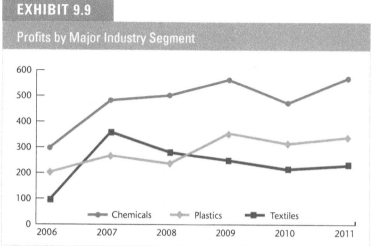

Chemicals — Plastics — Textiles

LIMITATIONS OF FINANCIAL STATEMENT ANALYSIS

Analyzing financial statements is analogous to choosing a new car. Each car is different, and prospective buyers must evaluate and weigh a myriad of features: gas mileage, engine size, manufacturer's reputation, color, accessories, and price, to name a few. Just as it is difficult to compare a Toyota minivan to a Ferrari sports car, so it is difficult to compare a small textile firm to a giant oil company. To make a meaningful assessment, the potential car buyer must focus on key data that can be comparably expressed for each car, such as gas mileage. The superior gas mileage of the minivan may pale in comparison to the thrill of driving the sports car, but the price of buying and operating the sports car may be the characteristic that determines the ultimate choice.

External users can rely on financial statement analysis only as a general guide to the potential of a business. They should resist placing too much weight on any

LO 8

Explain the limitations of financial statement analysis.

Reality BYTES

The most important source of financial information comes from companies' reports, but decision makers should also consult other sources. Interested persons can access quarterly and annual reports through the SEC's EDGAR database and often from company websites. Many companies will provide printed versions of these reports upon request. Companies also post information on their websites that is not included in their annual reports. For example, some automobile companies provide detailed production data on their websites.

Users can frequently obtain information useful in analyzing a particular company from independent sources as well as from the company itself. For example, the websites of popular news services such as CNN (*money.cnn.com*) and CNBC (*moneycentral.msn.com*) provide archived news stories and independent financial information about many companies. The websites of brokerage houses like *www.schwab.com* offer free financial information about companies. Finally, libraries often subscribe to independent services that evaluate companies as potential investments. One example worth reviewing is *Value Line Investment Survey*.

particular figure or trend. Many factors must be considered simultaneously before making any judgments. Furthermore, the analysis techniques discussed in this chapter are all based on historical information. Future events and unanticipated changes in conditions will also influence a company's operating results.

Different Industries

Different industries may be affected by unique social policies, special accounting procedures, or other individual industry attributes. Ratios of companies in different industries are not comparable without considering industry characteristics. A high debt to assets ratio is more acceptable in some industries than others. Even within an industry, a particular business may require more or less working capital than the industry average. If so, the working capital and quick ratios would mean little compared to those of other firms, but may still be useful for trend analysis.

Because of industry-specific factors, most professional analysts specialize in one, or only a few, industries. Financial institutions such as brokerage houses, banks, and insurance companies typically employ financial analysts who specialize in areas such as mineral or oil extraction, chemicals, banking, retail, insurance, bond markets, or automobile manufacturing.

Changing Economic Environment

When comparing firms, analysts must be alert to changes in general economic trends from year to year. Significant changes in fuel costs and interest rates in recent years make old rule-of-thumb guidelines for evaluating these factors obsolete. In addition, the presence or absence of inflation affects business prospects.

Accounting Principles

Financial statement analysis is only as reliable as the data on which it is based. Although most companies follow generally accepted accounting principles, a wide variety of acceptable accounting methods is available from which to choose, including different inventory and depreciation methods, different schedules for recognizing revenue, and different ways to account for oil and gas exploration costs. Analyzing statements of companies that seem identical may produce noncomparable ratios if the companies used different accounting methods. Analysts may seek to improve comparability by trying to recast different companies' financial statements as if the same accounting methods had been applied.

Accrual accounting requires the use of many estimates; uncollectible accounts expense, warranty expense, asset lives, and salvage value are just a few. The reliability of the resulting financial reports depends on the expertise and integrity of the persons who make the estimates.

The quality and usefulness of accounting information are influenced by underlying accounting concepts. Two particular concepts, *conservatism* and *historical cost,* have a tremendous impact on financial reporting. Conservatism dictates recognizing estimated losses as soon as they occur, but gain recognition is almost always deferred until the gains are actually realized. Conservatism produces a negative bias in financial statements. There are persuasive arguments for the conservatism principle, but users should be alert to distortions it may cause in accounting information.

The pervasive use of the historical cost concept is probably the greatest single cause of distorted financial statement analysis results. The historical cost of an asset does not represent its current value. The asset purchased in 1980 for $10,000 is not comparable in value to the asset purchased in 2010 for $10,000 because of changes in the value of the dollar. Using historical cost produces financial statements that report dollars with differing purchasing power in the same statement. Combining these differing dollar values is akin to adding miles to kilometers. To get the most from analyzing financial statements, users should be cognizant of these limitations.

CHECK *Yourself* 9.3

The return on equity for Gup Company is 23.4 percent and for Hunn Company is 17 percent. Does this mean Gup Company is better managed than Hunn Company?

Answer No single ratio can adequately measure management performance. Even analyzing a wide range of ratios provides only limited insight. Any useful interpretation requires the analyst to recognize the limitations of ratio analysis. For example, ratio norms typically differ between industries and may be affected by changing economic factors. In addition, companies' use of different accounting practices and procedures produces different ratio results even when underlying circumstances are comparable.

A Look Back

Financial statement analysis involves many factors, among them user characteristics, information needs for particular types of decisions, and how financial information is analyzed. Analytical techniques include *horizontal, vertical,* and *ratio analysis.* Users commonly calculate ratios to measure a company's liquidity, solvency, and profitability. The specific ratios presented in this chapter are summarized in Exhibit 9.6. Although ratios are easy to calculate and provide useful insights into business operations, when interpreting analytical results, users should consider limitations resulting from differing industry characteristics, differing economic conditions, and the fundamental accounting principles used to produce reported financial information.

A Look Forward

This chapter concludes the *financial* accounting portion of the text. Beginning with Chapter 10, we introduce various tools from a branch of the field called *managerial* accounting. Managerial accounting focuses on meeting the accounting information needs of decision makers inside, rather than outside, a company. In addition to financial statement data, inside users require detailed, forward looking information that includes nonfinancial as well as financial components. We begin with a chapter that discusses the value management accounting adds to the decision making process.

 SELF-STUDY REVIEW PROBLEM

Financial statements for Stallings Company follow.

INCOME STATEMENTS For the Years Ended December 31		
	2011	**2010**
Revenues		
Net sales	$315,000	$259,000
Expenses		
Cost of goods sold	(189,000)	(154,000)
General, selling, and administrative expenses	(54,000)	(46,000)
Interest expense	(4,000)	(4,500)
Income before taxes	68,000	54,500
Income tax expense (40%)	(27,200)	(21,800)
Net income	$ 40,800	$ 32,700

Balance Sheets as of December 31		
	2011	**2010**
Assets		
Current assets		
Cash	$ 6,500	$ 11,500
Accounts receivable	51,000	49,000
Inventories	155,000	147,500
Total current assets	212,500	208,000
Plant and equipment (net)	187,500	177,000
Total assets	$400,000	$385,000
Liabilities and Stockholders' Equity		
Liabilities		
Current liabilities		
Accounts payable	$ 60,000	$ 81,500
Other	25,000	22,500
Total current liabilities	85,000	104,000
Bonds payable	100,000	100,000
Total liabilities	185,000	204,000
Stockholders' equity		
Common stock (50,000 shares, $3 par)	150,000	150,000
Paid-in capital in excess of par value	20,000	20,000
Retained earnings	45,000	11,000
Total stockholders' equity	215,000	181,000
Total liabilities and stockholders' equity	$400,000	$385,000

Required

a. Use horizontal analysis to determine which expense item increased by the highest percentage from 2010 to 2011.

b. Use vertical analysis to determine whether the inventory balance is a higher percentage of total assets at the end of 2010 or 2011.

c. Calculate the following ratios for 2010 and 2011. When data limitations prohibit computing averages, use year-end balances in your calculations.

   (1) Net margin
   (2) Return on investment
   (3) Return on equity
   (4) Earnings per share
   (5) Price-earnings ratio (market price per share at the end of 2011 and 2010 was $12.04 and $8.86, respectively)
   (6) Book value per share of common stock
   (7) Times interest earned
   (8) Working capital
   (9) Current ratio
   (10) Acid-test ratio
   (11) Accounts receivable turnover
   (12) Inventory turnover
   (13) Debt to equity

Solution to Requirement *a*

Income tax expense increased by the greatest percentage. Computations follow.

Cost of goods sold ($189,000 − $154,000) ÷ $154,000 = 22.73%

General, selling, and administrative ($54,000 − $46,000) ÷ $46,000 = 17.39%

Interest expense decreased.

Income tax expense ($27,200 − $21,800) ÷ $21,800 = 24.77%

Solution to Requirement *b*

2010: $147,500 ÷ $385,000 = 38.31%

2011: $155,000 ÷ $400,000 = 38.75%

Inventory is slightly larger relative to total assets at the end of 2011.

Solution to Requirement *c*

		2011	2010
1.	$\dfrac{\text{Net income}}{\text{Net sales}}$	$\dfrac{\$40,800}{\$315,000} = 12.95\%$	$\dfrac{\$32,700}{\$259,000} = 12.63\%$
2.	$\dfrac{\text{Net income}}{\text{Average total assets}}$	$\dfrac{\$40,800}{\$392,500} = 10.39\%$	$\dfrac{\$32,700}{\$385,000} = 8.49\%$
3.	$\dfrac{\text{Net income}}{\text{Average total stockholders' equity}}$	$\dfrac{\$40,800}{\$198,000} = 20.61\%$	$\dfrac{\$32,700}{\$181,000} = 18.07\%$
4.	$\dfrac{\text{Net income}}{\text{Average common shares outstanding}}$	$\dfrac{\$40,800}{50,000 \text{ shares}} = \$0.816$	$\dfrac{\$32,700}{50,000 \text{ shares}} = \$0.654$
5.	$\dfrac{\text{Market price per share}}{\text{Earnings per share}}$	$\dfrac{\$12.04}{\$0.816} = 14.75 \text{ times}$	$\dfrac{\$8.86}{\$0.654} = 13.55 \text{ times}$
6.	$\dfrac{\text{Stockholders' equity} - \text{Preferred rights}}{\text{Outstanding common shares}}$	$\dfrac{\$215,000}{50,000 \text{ shares}} = \$4.30$	$\dfrac{\$181,000}{50,000 \text{ shares}} = \$3.62$
7.	$\dfrac{\text{Net income} + \text{Taxes} + \text{Interest expense}}{\text{Interest expense}}$	$\dfrac{\$40,800 + \$27,200 + \$4,000}{\$4,000} = 18 \text{ times}$	$\dfrac{\$32,700 + \$21,800 + \$4,500}{\$4,500} = 13.1 \text{ times}$
8.	Current assets − Current liabilities	$\$212,500 - \$85,000 = \$127,500$	$\$208,000 - \$104,000 = \$104,000$
9.	$\dfrac{\text{Current assets}}{\text{Current liabilities}}$	$\dfrac{\$212,500}{\$85,000} = 2.5:1$	$\dfrac{\$208,000}{\$104,000} = 2:1$
10.	$\dfrac{\text{Quick assets}}{\text{Current liabilities}}$	$\dfrac{\$57,500}{\$85,000} = 0.68:1$	$\dfrac{\$60,500}{\$104,000} = 0.58:1$
11.	$\dfrac{\text{Net credit sales}}{\text{Average accounts receivable}}$	$\dfrac{\$315,000}{\$50,000} = 6.3 \text{ times}$	$\dfrac{\$259,000}{\$49,000} = 5.29 \text{ times}$
12.	$\dfrac{\text{Cost of goods sold}}{\text{Average inventory}}$	$\dfrac{\$189,000}{\$151,250} = 1.25 \text{ times}$	$\dfrac{\$154,000}{\$147,500} = 1.04 \text{ times}$
13.	$\dfrac{\text{Total liabilities}}{\text{Total stockholders' equity}}$	$\dfrac{\$185,000}{\$215,000} = 86.05\%$	$\dfrac{\$204,000}{\$181,000} = 112.71\%$

KEY TERMS

Absolute amounts 325
Accounts receivable
  turnover 331
Acid-test ratio 330
Asset turnover ratio 336
Average number of days to
  collect receivables 332
Average number of days to
  sell inventory 332

Book value per share 338
Current ratio 330
Debt to assets ratio 333
Debt to equity ratio 333
Dividend yield 339
Earnings per share 338
Horizontal analysis 325
Information overload 324
Inventory turnover 332

Liquidity ratios 329
Materiality 325
Net margin 335
Percentage analysis 326
Plant assets to long-term
  liabilities 335
Price-earnings ratio 338
Profitability ratios 339
Quick ratio 330

Ratio analysis 328
Return on equity 337
Return on investment 336
Solvency ratios 333
Times interest earned 333
Trend analysis 325
Vertical analysis 328
Working capital 329
Working capital ratio 330

QUESTIONS

1. Why are ratios and trends used in financial analysis?

2. What do the terms *liquidity* and *solvency* mean?

3. What is apparent from a horizontal presentation of financial statement information? A vertical presentation?

4. What is the significance of inventory turnover, and how is it calculated?

5. What is the difference between the current ratio and the quick ratio? What does each measure?

6. Why are absolute amounts of limited use when comparing companies?

7. What is the difference between return on investment and return on equity?

8. Which ratios are used to measure long-term debt-paying ability? How is each calculated?

9. What are some limitations of the earnings per share figure?

10. What is the formula for calculating return on investment (ROI)?

11. What is information overload?

12. What is the price-earnings ratio? Explain the difference between it and the dividend yield.

13. What environmental factors must be considered in analyzing companies?

14. How do accounting principles affect financial statement analysis?

EXERCISES

All applicable Exercises are available with McGraw-Hill
Connect Accounting.

LO 4

Exercise 9-1 *Inventory turnover*

Selected financial information for Atwell Company for 2009 follows.

Sales	$1,500,000
Cost of goods sold	1,200,000
Merchandise inventory	
Beginning of year	180,000
End of year	220,000

Required

Assuming that the merchandise inventory buildup was relatively constant, how many times did the merchandise inventory turn over during 2009?

LO 5

Exercise 9-2 *Times interest earned*

The following data come from the financial records of Linton Corporation for 2008.

Sales	$135,000
Interest expense	3,800
Income tax expense	22,500
Net income	30,700

Required

How many times was interest earned in 2008?

LO 4

Exercise 9-3 *Current ratio*

Piper Corporation wrote off a $900 uncollectible account receivable against the $9,600 balance in its allowance account.

Required

Explain the effect of the write-off on Piper's current ratio.

LO 4

Exercise 9-4 *Working capital and current ratio*

On June 30, 2008, Thorpe Company's total current assets were $250,000 and its total current liabilities were $125,000. On July 1, 2008, Thorpe issued a short-term note to a bank for $25,000 cash.

Required

a. Compute Thorpe's working capital before and after issuing the note.

b. Compute Thorpe's current ratio before and after issuing the note.

LO 4

Exercise 9-5 *Working capital and current ratio*

On June 30, 2008, Thorpe Company's total current assets were $250,000 and its total current liabilities were $125,000. On July 1, 2008, Thorpe issued a long-term note to a bank for $25,000 cash.

Required

a. Compute Thorpe's working capital before and after issuing the note.
b. Compute Thorpe's current ratio before and after issuing the note.

Exercise 9-6   *Horizontal analysis*

LO **2**

Hammond Corporation reported the following operating results for two consecutive years.

	2008	2007	Percentage Change
Sales	$1,250,000	$1,000,000	
Cost of goods sold	750,000	600,000	
Gross margin	500,000	400,000	
Operating expenses	300,000	200,000	
Income before taxes	200,000	200,000	
Income taxes	61,000	53,000	
Net income	$ 139,000	$ 147,000	

Required

a. Compute the percentage changes in Hammond Corporation's income statement components between the two years.
b. Comment on apparent trends disclosed by the percentage changes computed in Requirement *a*.

Exercise 9-7   *Vertical analysis*

LO **2**

Garcia Company reported the following operating results for two consecutive years.

2008	Amount	Percent of Sales
Sales	$600,000	
Cost of goods sold	400,000	
Gross margin	200,000	
Operating expenses	130,000	
Income before taxes	70,000	
Income taxes	30,000	
Net income	$ 40,000	

2009	Amount	Percent of Sales
Sales	$580,000	
Cost of goods sold	377,000	
Gross margin	203,000	
Operating expenses	150,000	
Income before taxes	53,000	
Income taxes	23,000	
Net income	$ 30,000	

Required

Express each income statement component for each of the two years as a percent of sales.

Exercise 9-8   *Ratio analysis*

LO **4, 5**

Balance sheet data for Ramsey Corporation follow.

Current assets	$ 150,000
Long-term assets (net)	850,000
Total assets	$1,000,000
Current liabilities	$ 84,000
Long-term liabilities	492,000
Total liabilities	576,000
Total stockholders' equity	424,000
Total liabilities and stockholders' equity	$1,000,000

Required

Compute the following:

Working capital	_____
Current ratio	_____
Debt to assets ratio	_____
Debt to equity ratio	_____

LO 7

Exercise 9-9 *Ratio analysis*

For 2008, Orchard Corporation reported after-tax net income of $5,800,000. During the year, the number of shares of stock outstanding remained constant at 10,000 of $100 par, 9 percent preferred stock and 400,000 shares of common stock. The company's total stockholders' equity was $23,000,000 at December 31, 2008. Orchard Corporation's common stock was selling at $52 per share at the end of its fiscal year. All dividends for the year had been paid, including $4.80 per share to common stockholders.

Required

Compute the following:

a. Earnings per share
b. Book value per share of common stock
c. Price-earnings ratio
d. Dividend yield

LO 4, 5, 6, 7

Exercise 9-10 *Ratio analysis*

Required

Match each of the following ratios with the formula used to compute it.

_____ 1. Working capital
_____ 2. Current ratio
_____ 3. Quick ratio
_____ 4. Accounts receivable turnover
_____ 5. Average number of days to collect receivables
_____ 6. Inventory turnover
_____ 7. Average number of days to sell inventory
_____ 8. Debt to assets ratio
_____ 9. Debt to equity ratio
_____ 10. Return on investment
_____ 11. Return on equity
_____ 12. Earnings per share

a. Net income ÷ Average total stockholders' equity
b. Cost of goods sold ÷ Average inventory
c. Current assets − Current liabilities
d. 365 ÷ Inventory turnover
e. Net income ÷ Average total assets
f. (Net income − Preferred dividends) ÷ Average outstanding common shares
g. (Current assets − Inventory − Prepaid items) ÷ Current liabilities
h. Total liabilities ÷ Total assets
i. 365 days ÷ Accounts receivable turnover
j. Total liabilities ÷ Total stockholders' equity
k. Net credit sales ÷ Average accounts receivables
l. Current assets ÷ Current liabilities

Exercise 9-11   *Horizontal and vertical analysis*   LO 2

Income statements for Sennett Company for 2008 and 2009 follow.

	2009	2008
Sales	$121,000	$92,000
Cost of goods sold	75,000	51,000
Selling expenses	20,000	11,000
Administrative expenses	12,000	14,000
Interest expense	3,000	5,000
Total expenses	110,000	81,000
Income before taxes	11,000	11,000
Income taxes expense	3,000	2,000
Net income	$ 8,000	$ 9,000

Required

a. Perform a horizontal analysis, showing the percentage change in each income statement component between 2008 and 2009.

b. Perform a vertical analysis, showing each income statement component as a percent of sales for each year.

Exercise 9-12   *Ratio analysis*   LO 4, 5, 6, 7

Compute the specified ratios using Bryce Company's balance sheet at December 31, 2008.

Assets	
Cash	$ 18,000
Marketable securities	8,000
Accounts receivable	13,000
Inventory	11,000
Property and equipment	170,000
Accumulated depreciation	(12,500)
Total assets	$207,500
Equities	
Accounts payable	$ 8,500
Current notes payable	3,500
Mortgage payable	7,500
Bonds payable	21,500
Common stock, $50 par	110,000
Paid-in capital in excess of par value	4,000
Retained earnings	52,500
Total liabilities and stockholders' equity	$207,500

The average number of common stock shares outstanding during 2008 was 880 shares. Net income for the year was $15,000.

Required

Compute each of the following:

a. Current ratio

b. Earnings per share

c. Quick (acid-test) ratio

d. Return on investment

e. Return on equity

f. Debt to equity ratio

LO **4, 5, 6, 7**

Exercise 9-13   *Comprehensive analysis*

Required

Indicate the effect of each of the following transactions on (1) the current ratio, (2) working capital, (3) stockholders' equity, (4) book value per share of common stock, (5) retained earnings. Assume that the current ratio is greater than 1.0.

a. Collected account receivable.
b. Wrote off account receivable.
c. Purchased treasury stock.
d. Purchased inventory on account.
e. Declared cash dividend.
f. Sold merchandise on account at a profit.
g. Issued stock dividend.
h. Paid account payable.
i. Sold building at a loss.

LO **4, 6**

Exercise 9-14   *Accounts receivable turnover, inventory turnover, and net margin*

Selected data from Anthony Company follow.

Balance Sheet Data As of December 31		
	2008	**2007**
Accounts receivable	$490,000	$380,000
Allowance for doubtful accounts	(40,000)	(30,000)
Net accounts receivable	$450,000	$350,000
Inventories, lower of cost or market	$600,000	$480,000

Income Statement Data For the Year Ended December 31		
	2008	**2007**
Net credit sales	$2,000,000	$1,760,000
Net cash sales	400,000	320,000
Net sales	2,400,000	2,080,000
Cost of goods sold	1,600,000	1,440,000
Selling, general, and administrative expenses	240,000	216,000
Other expenses	40,000	24,000
Total operating expenses	$1,880,000	$1,680,000

Required

Compute the following:

a. The accounts receivable turnover for 2008.
b. The inventory turnover for 2008.
c. The net margin for 2008.

LO **4, 5**

Exercise 9-15   *Comprehensive analysis*

The December 31, 2007, balance sheet for Grogan Inc. is presented here. These are the only accounts on Grogan's balance sheet. Amounts indicated by question marks (?) can be calculated using the additional information following the balance sheet.

Assets	
Cash	$ 25,000
Accounts receivable (net)	?
Inventory	?
Property, plant, and equipment (net)	294,000
	$432,000

Liabilities and Stockholders' Equity	
Accounts payable (trade)	$?
Income taxes payable (current)	25,000
Long-term debt	?
Common stock	300,000
Retained earnings	?
	$?

Additional Information

Current ratio (at year end)	1.5 to 1.0
Total liabilities ÷ Total stockholders' equity	0.8
Gross margin percent	30%
Inventory turnover (Cost of goods sold ÷ Ending inventory)	10.5 times
Gross margin for 2007	$315,000

Required

Determine the following.

a. The balance in trade accounts payable as of December 31, 2007.

b. The balance in retained earnings as of December 31, 2007.

c. The balance in the inventory account as of December 31, 2007.

PROBLEMS

All applicable Problems are available with McGraw-Hill
Connect Accounting.

Problem 9-16   *Vertical analysis*

The following percentages apply to Walton Company for 2007 and 2008.

	2008	2007
Sales	100.0%	100.0%
Cost of goods sold	61.0	64.0
Gross margin	39.0	36.0
Selling and administrative expenses	26.5	20.5
Interest expense	2.5	2.0
Total expenses	29.0	22.5
Income before taxes	10.0	13.5
Income tax expense	5.5	7.0
Net income	4.5%	6.5%

Required

Assuming that sales were $480,000 in 2007 and $640,000 in 2008, prepare income statements
for the two years.

352   Chapter 9

Problem 9-17 *Ratio analysis*

Hood Company's income statement information follows.

	2009	2008
Net sales	$210,000	$130,000
Income before interest and taxes	55,000	42,500
Net income after taxes	27,500	31,500
Interest expense	4,500	4,000
Stockholders' equity, December 31 (2007: $100,000)	158,500	117,500
Common stock, par $50, December 31	130,000	115,000

The average number of shares outstanding was 2,600 for 2009 and 2,300 for 2008.

Required

Compute the following ratios for Hood for 2009 and 2008.

a. Times interest earned.
b. Earnings per share based on the average number of shares outstanding.
c. Price-earnings ratio (market prices: 2009, $116 per share; 2008, $96 per share).
d. Return on average equity.
e. Net margin.

Problem 9-18 *Effect of transactions on current ratio and working capital*

Gilchrist Manufacturing has a current ratio of 3:1 on December 31, 2008. Indicate whether each of the following transactions would increase (+), decrease (−), or have no affect (NA) Gilchrist's current ratio and its working capital.

Required

a. Paid cash for a trademark.
b. Wrote off an uncollectible account receivable.
c. Sold equipment for cash.
d. Sold merchandise at a profit (cash).
e. Declared a cash dividend.
f. Purchased inventory on account.
g. Scrapped a fully depreciated machine (no gain or loss).
h. Issued a stock dividend.
i. Purchased a machine with a long-term note.
j. Paid a previously declared cash dividend.
k. Collected accounts receivable.
l. Invested in current marketable securities.

Problem 9-19 *Ratio analysis*

Selected data for Koch Company for 2007 and additional information on industry averages follow.

Earnings (net income)		$ 289,000
Preferred stock (19,800 shares at $50 par, 4%)		$ 990,000
Common stock (45,000 shares at $1 par, market value $56)		45,000
Paid-in capital in excess of par value—Common		720,000
Retained earnings		843,750
		2,598,750
Less: Treasury stock		
Preferred (1,800 shares)	$81,000	
Common (1,800 shares)	36,000	117,000
Total stockholders' equity		$2,481,750

Note: Dividends in arrears on preferred stock: $36,000. The preferred stock can be called for $51 per share.

Industry averages
Earnings per share $ 5.20
Price-earnings ratio   9.50
Return on equity   11.20%

Required

a. Calculate and compare Koch Company's ratios with the industry averages.

b. Discuss factors you would consider in deciding whether to invest in the company.

Problem 9-20   *Supply missing balance sheet numbers*   LO 2

The bookkeeper for Andy's Country Music Bar went insane and left this incomplete balance sheet. Andy's working capital is $95,000 and its debt to assets ratio is 40 percent.

CHECK FIGURES
d. $342,500
f. $99,500

Assets	
Current assets	
Cash	$ 21,000
Accounts receivable	42,000
Inventory	(A)
Prepaid items	9,000
Total current assets	(B)
Long-term assets	
Building	(C)
Less: Accumulated depreciation	(39,000)
Total long-term assets	210,000
Total assets	$ (D)
Liabilities and Stockholders' Equity	
Liabilities	
Current liabilities	
Accounts payable	$ (E)
Notes payable	12,000
Income tax payable	10,500
Total current liabilities	37,500
Long-term liabilities	
Mortgage payable	(F)
Total liabilities	(G)
Stockholders' equity	
Common stock	105,000
Retained earnings	(H)
Total stockholders' equity	(I)
Total liabilities and stockholders' equity	$ (J)

Required

Complete the balance sheet by supplying the missing amounts.

Problem 9-21   *Ratio analysis*   LO 4, 5, 6, 7

The following financial statements apply to Keating Company.

CHECK FIGURES
d. 2009: $0.72
k. 2008: 5.47 times

	2009	2008
Revenues		
Net sales	$210,000	$175,000
Other revenues	4,000	5,000
Total revenues	214,000	180,000

continued

	2009	2008
Expenses		
Cost of goods sold	126,000	103,000
Selling expenses	21,000	19,000
General and administrative expenses	11,000	10,000
Interest expense	3,000	3,000
Income tax expense	21,000	18,000
Total expenses	182,000	153,000
Earnings from continuing operations		
before extraordinary items	32,000	27,000
Extraordinary gain (net of $3,000 tax)	4,000	0
Net earnings	$ 36,000	$ 27,000
Assets		
Current assets		
Cash	$ 4,000	$ 8,000
Marketable securities	1,000	1,000
Accounts receivable	35,000	32,000
Inventories	100,000	96,000
Prepaid items	3,000	2,000
Total current assets	143,000	139,000
Plant and equipment (net)	105,000	105,000
Intangibles	20,000	0
Total assets	$268,000	$244,000
Liabilities and Stockholders' Equity		
Liabilities		
Current liabilities		
Accounts payable	$ 40,000	$ 54,000
Other	17,000	15,000
Total current liabilities	57,000	69,000
Bonds payable	66,000	67,000
Total liabilities	123,000	136,000
Stockholders' equity		
Common stock ($2 par)	100,000	100,000
Paid-in capital in excess of par value	15,000	15,000
Retained earnings	30,000	(7,000)
Total stockholders' equity	145,000	108,000
Total liabilities and stockholders' equity	$268,000	$244,000

Required

Calculate the following ratios for 2008 and 2009. When data limitations prohibit computing averages, use year-end balances in your calculations.

a. Net margin
b. Return on investment
c. Return on equity
d. Earnings per share
e. Price-earnings ratio (market prices at the end of 2008 and 2009 were $5.94 and $4.77, respectively)
f. Book value per share of common stock
g. Times interest earned

h. Working capital

i. Current ratio

j. Quick (acid-test) ratio

k. Accounts receivable turnover

l. Inventory turnover

m. Debt to equity ratio

n. Debt to assets ratio

Problem 9-22   *Horizontal analysis*

LO 2

Financial statements for Thorn Company follow.

THORN COMPANY
Balance Sheets
As of December 31

	2008	2007
Assets		
Current assets		
Cash	$ 16,000	$ 12,000
Marketable securities	20,000	6,000
Accounts receivable (net)	54,000	46,000
Inventories	135,000	143,000
Prepaid items	25,000	10,000
Total current assets	250,000	217,000
Investments	27,000	20,000
Plant (net)	270,000	255,000
Land	29,000	24,000
Total assets	$576,000	$516,000
Liabilities and Stockholders' Equity		
Liabilities		
Current liabilities		
Notes payable	$ 17,000	$ 6,000
Accounts payable	113,800	100,000
Salaries payable	21,000	15,000
Total current liabilities	151,800	121,000
Noncurrent liabilities		
Bonds payable	100,000	100,000
Other	32,000	27,000
Total noncurrent liabilities	132,000	127,000
Total liabilities	283,800	248,000
Stockholders' equity		
Preferred stock, par value $10, 4% cumulative, non-participating; 7,000 shares authorized and issued; no dividends in arrears	70,000	70,000
Common stock, $5 par value; 50,000 shares authorized; 10,000 shares issued	50,000	50,000
Paid-in capital in excess of par value—Preferred	10,000	10,000
Paid-in capital in excess of par value—Common	30,000	30,000
Retained earnings	132,200	108,000
Total stockholders' equity	292,200	268,000
Total liabilities and stockholders' equity	$576,000	$516,000

THORN COMPANY
Statements of Income and Retained Earnings
For the Years Ended December 31

	2008	2007
Revenues		
Sales (net)	$230,000	$210,000
Other revenues	8,000	5,000
Total revenues	238,000	215,000
Expenses		
Cost of goods sold	120,000	103,000
Selling, general, and administrative expenses	55,000	50,000
Interest expense	8,000	7,200
Income tax expense	23,000	22,000
Total expenses	206,000	182,200
Net earnings (net income)	32,000	32,800
Retained earnings, January 1	108,000	83,000
Less: Preferred stock dividends	2,800	2,800
Common stock dividends	5,000	5,000
Retained earnings, December 31	$132,200	$108,000

Required

Prepare a horizontal analysis of both the balance sheet and income statement.

LO 2, 3, 4, 5, 6, 7   **Problem 9-23   *Ratio analysis***

eXcel

CHECK FIGURES
k. 2008: 2.05:1
p. 2007: $3.00

Required

Use the financial statements for Thorn Company from Problem 9-22 to calculate the following ratios for 2008 and 2007.

a. Working capital
b. Current ratio
c. Quick ratio
d. Accounts receivable turnover (beginning receivables at January 1, 2007, were $47,000)
e. Average number of days to collect accounts receivable
f. Inventory turnover (beginning inventory at January 1, 2007, was $140,000)
g. Average number of days to sell inventory
h. Debt to assets ratio
i. Debt to equity ratio
j. Times interest earned
k. Plant assets to long-term debt
l. Net margin
m. Asset turnover
n. Return on investment
o. Return on equity
p. Earnings per share
q. Book value per share of common stock
r. Price-earnings ratio (market price per share: 2007, $11.75; 2008, $12.50)
s. Dividend yield on common stock

LO 2   **Problem 9-24   *Vertical analysis***

eXcel

CHECK FIGURE
2008 Retained Earnings: 23%

Required

Use the financial statements for Thorn Company from Problem 9-22 to perform a vertical analysis of both the balance sheets and income statements for 2008 and 2007.

ANALYZE, THINK, COMMUNICATE

ATC 9-1   **Business Applications Case**   *Analyzing Best Buy Company and Circuit City Stores*

The following information relates to Best Buy Company and Circuit City Stores, Inc., for their 2007 and 2006 fiscal years.

BEST BUY COMPANY Selected Financial Information (Amounts in millions, except per share amounts)		
	March 3, 2007	February 25, 2006
Total current assets	$9,081	$7,985
Merchandise inventories	4,028	3,338
Property and equipment, net of depreciation	2,938	2,712
Total assets	13,570	11,864
Total current liabilities	6,301	6,056
Total long-term liabilities	590	178
Total liabilities	7,369	6,607
Total shareholders equity	6,201	5,257
Revenue	35,934	30,848
Cost of goods sold	27,165	23,122
Gross profit	8,769	7,726
Operating income	1,999	1,644
Earnings from continuing operations before income tax expense	2,130	1,721
Income tax expense	752	581
Net earnings	1,377	1,140
Basic earnings per share	$2.86	$2.33

CIRCUIT CITY STORES Selected Financial Information (Amounts in millions except per share data)		
	February 28, 2007	February 28, 2006
Total current assets	$2,884	$2,833
Merchandise inventory	1,637	1,698
Property and equipment, net of depreciation	921	839
Total assets	4,007	4,069
Total current liabilities	1,714	1,622
Total long-term liabilities	502	492
Total liabilities	2,216	2,114
Total stockholders' equity	1,791	1,955
Revenues	12,430	11,598
Cost of sales, buying and warehousing	9,501	8,767
Gross profit	2,928	2,831
Earnings from continuing operations before income taxes	20	239
Provision for income taxes	31	88
Earnings from continuing operations	−10	151
Net earnings	−8	140
Basic earnings per share— Continuing operations:	($0.05)	$0.79

Required

a. Compute the following ratios for the companies' 2007 fiscal years:

   (1) Current ratio.

   (2) Average number of days to sell inventory. (Use average inventory.)

   (3) Debt to assets ratio.

   (4) Return on investment. (Use average assets and use "earnings from continuing operations" rather than "net earnings.")

   (5) Gross margin percentage.

   (6) Asset turnover. (Use average assets.)

   (7) Return on sales. (Use "earnings from continuing operations" rather than "net earnings.")

   (8) Plant assets to long-term debt ratio.

b. Which company appears to be more profitable? Explain your answer and identify which of the ratio(s) from Requirement *a* you used to reach your conclusion.

c. Which company appears to have the higher level of financial risk? Explain your answer and identify which of the ratio(s) from Requirement *a* you used to reach your conclusion.

d. Which company appears to be charging higher prices for its goods? Explain your answer and identify which of the ratio(s) from Requirement *a* you used to reach your conclusion.

e. Which company appears to be the more efficient at using its assets? Explain your answer and identify which of the ratio(s) from Requirement *a* you used to reach your conclusion.

ATC 9-2   Group Assignment   *Ratio analysis and logic*

Presented here are selected data from the 10-K reports of four companies for the 2007 fiscal year. The four companies in alphabetical order are:

1. AT&T, a large telecommunications company.

2. Deere & Co., a manufacturer of heavy machinery.

3. Dollar General Corporation, a company that owns and operates discount stores.

4. Starbucks Corporation, the world's largest specialty coffee-shop chain.

The data, presented below in the order of the amount of sales, are as follows. Dollar amounts are in millions.

	A	B	C	D
Sales	$118,928	$24,082.2	$9,411.5	$9,169.8
Cost of goods sold	46,055	16,252.8	3,999.1	6,801.6
Net earnings	11,951	1,821.7	672.6	137.9
Merchandise inventory	N/A	2,337.3	691.7	1,432.3
Accounts receivable	16,185	3,084.6	287.9	NA
Total assets	275,644	38,575.7	5,343.9	3,040.5

Required

a. Divide the class into groups of four or five students per group and then organize the groups into four sections. Assign Task 1 to the first section of groups, Task 2 to the second section, Task 3 to the third section, and Task 4 to the fourth section.

Group Tasks

   (1) Assume that you represent AT&T. Identify the set of financial data (Column A, B, C, or D) that relates to your company.

   (2) Assume that you represent Deere & Co. Identify the set of financial data (Column A, B, C, or D) that relates to your company.

   (3) Assume that you represent Dollar General Corporation. Identify the set of financial data (Column A, B, C, or D) that relates to your company.

(4) Assume that you represent Starbucks Corporation. Identify the set of financial data (Column A, B, C, or D) that relates to your company.

Hint: Use a gross margin ratio (gross margin ÷ sales), a net margin ratio (net income ÷ sales), and return on assets (net income ÷ total assets) to facilitate identifying the financial data related to your particular company.

b. Select a representative from each section. Have the representatives explain the rationale for the group's selection. The explanation should include a set of ratios that support the group's conclusion.

ATC 9-3   Research Assignment   *Analyzing Whirlpool's Acquisition of Maytag*

To complete the requirements below you will need to obtain Whirlpool's income statements for 2005 and 2006, and its balance sheets for 2004, 2005, and 2006. The easiest way to obtain these income statements is to retrieve the company's 2006 and 2005 Form 10-Ks. To obtain the Form 10-Ks you can use either the EDGAR system following the instructions in Appendix A, or they can be found under the "Investors" link on the company's corporate website, www.whirlpoolcorp.com. On March 31, 2006, Whirlpool Corporation acquired Maytag, another manufacturer of home appliances. The company's 2006 financial statements include the activities of Maytag; its 2005 and 2004 statements do not.

Required

a. Compute the following ratios for 2006 and 2005. Show your calculations.

Gross margin percentage	Net margin
Return on investment	Return on equity
Current ratio	Debt to assets ratio

b. Based on the ratios computed in Requirement *a*, comment on the apparent effects of Whirlpool's acquisition of Maytag. Assume any significant change in these ratios was the result of the acquisition.

c. Based on this limited analysis, does it appear that the short-term effects of the acquisition were good or bad for Whirlpool?

ATC 9-4   Writing Assignment   *Interpreting ratios*

The following table provides the net earnings, total assets, and total liabilities for four companies from two different industries. The data are for the fiscal years ending in 2006. All numbers are millions of dollars.

	Net Earnings	Total Assets	Total Liabilities
Banking Industry			
Sun Trust Bank	$2,110	$182,162	$164,348
Wells Fargo & Co.	8,482	481,996	436,120
Home Construction Industry			
Pulte Homes	687	13,177	6,600
Ryland Group	360	3,417	1,724

Required

a. Briefly explain which company appears to be using its assets most efficiently. Be sure to include the computations of ratios you used to reach your conclusions.

b. Briefly explain which company appears to be earning the best return for its owners. Be sure to include the computations of ratios you used to reach your conclusions.

c. Briefly explain which company appears to have the greatest financial risk. Be sure to include the computations of ratios you used to reach your conclusions.

ATC 9-5   Ethical Dilemma   *Making the ratios look good*

J. Talbot is the accounting manager for Kolla Waste Disposal Corporation. Kolla is having its worst financial year since its inception. The company is expected to report a net loss. In the midst of such bad news, Ms. Talbot surprised the company president, Mr. Winston, by suggesting that the company write off approximately 25 percent of its garbage trucks. Mr. Winston responded by noting that the trucks could still be operated for another two or three years. Ms. Talbot replied, "We may use them for two or three more years, but you couldn't sell them on the street if you had to. Who wants to buy a bunch of old garbage trucks and besides, it will make next year's financials so sweet. No one will care about the additional write-off this year. We are already showing a loss. Who will care if we lose a little bit more?"

Required

a. How will the write-off affect the following year's return on assets ratio?

b. How will the write-off affect the asset and income growth percentages?

c. Would writing off the garbage trucks for the reasons stated present any ethical concerns for Kolla? Explain.

Comprehensive financial statements analysis projects are available at www.mhhe.com/edmonds/survey2e.

CHAPTER *12*

Statement of Cash Flows

LEARNING OBJECTIVES

After you have mastered the material in this chapter, you will be able to:

1 Prepare the operating activities section of a statement of cash flows using the indirect method.

2 Prepare the operating activities section of a statement of cash flows using the direct method.

3 Prepare the investing activities section of a statement of cash flows.

4 Prepare the financing activities section of a statement of cash flows.

LP12

CHAPTER OPENING

To make informed investment and credit decisions, financial statement users need information to help them assess the amounts, timing, and uncertainty of a company's prospective cash flows. This chapter explains more about the items reported on the statement of cash flows and describes a more practical way to prepare the statement than analyzing every entry in the cash account. As previously shown, the statement of cash flows reports how a company obtained and spent cash during an accounting period. Sources of cash are *cash inflows*, and uses are *cash outflows*. Cash receipts (inflows) and payments (outflows) are reported as either operating activities, investing activities, or financing activities.

The *Curious* Accountant

Sirius XM Radio, Inc., was created by a merger between Sirius Radio and XM Radio, in July 2008. Sirius Radio was formed in 1990, and XM Radio began in 1992, although these companies did not generate any significant amounts of revenue in the early years of their existence. Even though their revenues grew steadily over the years, neither XM, Sirius, nor the combined company, Sirius XM Radio, has ever earned a profit. Its cumulative net losses totaled $9.7 billion by the end of 2008, with $5.5 billion of that coming in 2008 alone.

How could Sirius XM lose so much money and still be able to pay its bills? (Answer on page 625.)

AN OVERVIEW OF THE STATEMENT OF CASH FLOWS

The statement of cash flows provides information about cash coming into and going out of a business during an accounting period. Cash flows are classified into one of three categories: operating activities, investing activities, or financing activities. A separate section also displays any significant noncash investing and financing activities. Descriptions of these categories and how they are presented in the statement of cash flows follow.

Operating Activities

Routine cash inflows and outflows resulting from running (operating) a business are reported in the **operating activities** section of the statement of cash flows. Cash flows reported as operating activities include:

1. Cash receipts from revenues including interest and dividend revenue.
2. Cash payments for expenses including interest expense. Recall that dividend payments are not expenses. Dividend payments are reported in the financing activities section.

EXHIBIT 12.1

Operating Activities—Direct Method

Cash Flows from Operating Activities	
Cash receipts from customers	$400
Cash payments for expenses	(350)
Net cash flow from operating activities	$ 50

Under generally accepted accounting principles, the operating activities section of the statement of cash flows can be presented using either the *direct* or the *indirect* method. The **direct method** explicitly (*directly*) identifies the major *sources* and *uses* of cash. To illustrate, assume that during 2011 New South Company earns revenue on account of $500 and collects $400 cash from customers. Further assume the company incurs $390 of expenses on account and pays $350 cash to settle accounts payable. Exhibit 12.1 shows the operating activities section of the statement of cash flows using the *direct method.*

In contrast, the **indirect method** starts with net income as reported on the income statement followed by the adjustments necessary to convert the accrual-based net income figure to a cash-basis equivalent. To illustrate, begin with New South Company's income statement based on the above assumptions.

Revenues	$500
Expenses	(390)
Net income	$110

Converting the net income of $110 to the net cash flow from operating activities of $50 requires the following adjustments.

1. New South earned $500 of revenue but collected only $400 in cash. The remaining $100 will be collected in the next accounting period. This $100 *increase in accounts receivable* must be *subtracted* from net income to determine cash flow because it increased net income but did not increase cash.

2. New South incurred $390 of expense but paid only $350 in cash. The remaining $40 will be paid in the next accounting period. This $40 *increase in accounts payable* must be *added* back to net income to determine cash flow because it decreased net income but did not use cash.

EXHIBIT 12.2

Operating Activities—Indirect Method

Cash Flows from Operating Activities	
Net income	$110
Subtract: Increase in accounts receivable	(100)
Add: Increase in accounts payable	40
Net cash flow from operating activities	$ 50

Exhibit 12.2 shows the operating activities section of the statement of cash flows using the indirect method.

Compare the direct method presented in Exhibit 12.1 with the indirect method presented in Exhibit 12.2. Both methods report $50 of net cash flow from operating activities. They represent two different approaches to computing the same amount.

Because people typically find the direct method easier to understand, the Financial Accounting Standards Board (FASB) recommends it. Most companies, however, use the indirect method. Why? Back when the FASB adopted a requirement for companies to include a statement of cash flows in their annual reports, most companies used accounting systems that were compatible with the indirect method. It was therefore easier to prepare the new statement under the indirect method using existing systems than to create new record-keeping systems compatible with the direct method.

The FASB continues to advocate the direct method and a growing number of companies use it. Since the majority of companies continue to use the indirect method, however, financial statement users should understand both methods.

CHECK *Yourself* 12.1

Hammer, Inc., had a beginning balance of $22,400 in its Accounts Receivable account. During the accounting period, Hammer earned $234,700 of net income. The ending balance in the Accounts Receivable account was $18,200. Based on this information alone, determine the amount of cash flow from operating activities.

Answer

Account Title	Ending	Beginning	Change
Accounts receivable	$18,200	$22,400	$(4,200)

Applicable Rule	Cash Flow from Operating Activities	Amount
Rule 1	Net Income	$234,700
	Add: Decrease in accounts receivable	4,200
	Cash flow from operating activities	$238,900

Investing Activities

For a business, long-term assets are investments. Cash flows related to acquiring or disposing of long-term assets are therefore reported in the **investing activities** section of the statement of cash flows. Cash flows reported as investing activities include:

1. Cash receipts (inflows) from selling property, plant, equipment, or marketable securities as well as collections from long-term credit instruments such as notes or mortgages receivable.
2. Cash payments (outflows) for purchasing property, plant, equipment, or marketable securities as well as long-term loans to borrowers.

Financing Activities

Cash flows related to borrowing (short- or long-term) and stockholders' equity are reported in the **financing activities** section of the statement of cash flows. Cash flows reported as financing activities include:

1. Cash receipts (inflows) from borrowing money and issuing stock.
2. Cash payments (outflows) to repay debt, purchase treasury stock, and pay dividends.

The classification of cash flows is based on the type of activity, not the type of account. For example, buying another company's common stock is an investing activity, but issuing a company's own common stock is a financing activity. Receiving dividends from a common stock investment is an operating activity, and paying dividends to a company's own stockholders is a financing activity. Similarly, loaning money is an investing activity, although borrowing it is a financing activity. Focus on the type of activity rather than the type of account when classifying cash flows as operating, investing, or financing activities.

Noncash Investing and Financing Activities

Companies sometimes undertake significant **noncash investing and financing activities** such as acquiring a long-term asset in exchange for common stock. Since these types of transactions do not involve exchanging cash they are not reported in the main body of the statement of cash flows. However, because the FASB requires that all material investing and financing activities be disclosed, whether or not they involve exchanging cash, companies must include with the statement of cash flows a separate schedule of any noncash investing and financing activities.

Reporting Format for the Statement of Cash Flows

Cash flow categories are reported in the following order: (1) operating activities; (2) investing activities; and (3) financing activities. In each category, the difference between the inflows and outflows is presented as a net cash inflow or outflow for the category. These net amounts are combined to determine the net change (increase or decrease) in the company's cash for the period. The net change in cash is combined with the beginning cash balance to determine the ending cash balance. The ending cash balance on the statement of cash flows is the same as the cash balance reported on the balance sheet. The schedule of noncash investing and financing activities is typically presented at the bottom of the statement of cash flows. Exhibit 12.3 outlines this format.

EXHIBIT 12.3	Format for Statement of Cash Flows

WESTERN COMPANY
Statement of Cash Flows
For the Year Ended December 31, 2011

Cash flows from operating activities	
Net increase (decrease) from operating activities	XXX
Cash flows from investing activities	
Net increase (decrease) from investing activities	XXX
Cash flows from financing activities	
Net increase (decrease) from financing activities	XXX
Net increase (decrease) in cash	XXX
Plus: Beginning cash balance	XXX
Ending cash balance	XXX
Schedule of Noncash Investing and Financing Activities	
List of significant noncash transactions	XXX

As indicated in Exhibit 12.4, most companies present the statement of cash flows as the last of the four primary financial statements. However, a sizable number of companies present it after the income statement and balance sheet but before the statement of changes in stockholders' equity. Some companies place the statement of cash flows first, before the other three statements.

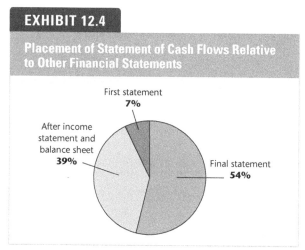

EXHIBIT 12.4

Placement of Statement of Cash Flows Relative to Other Financial Statements

First statement
7%

After income statement and balance sheet
39%

Final statement
54%

Data Source: AICPA, *Accounting Trends and Techniques.*

PREPARING A STATEMENT OF CASH FLOWS

Most of the data needed to construct a statement of cash flows can be obtained from two successive balance sheets and the intervening income statement. Certain information from the long-term asset records is also usually required. To illustrate, refer to the financial statements for New South Company presented in Exhibit 12.5. Notice that cash decreased from $400 at the end of 2011 to $300 at the end of 2012. The statement of cash flows explains what caused this $100 decrease.

EXHIBIT 12.5 Financial Statements for New South Company

NEW SOUTH COMPANY
Balance Sheets
As of December 31

	2012	2011
Current assets:		
Cash	$ 300	$ 400
Accounts receivable	1,000	1,200
Interest receivable	400	300
Inventory	8,900	8,200
Prepaid insurance	1,100	1,400
Total current assets	11,700	$11,500
Long-term assets		
Investment securities	5,100	3,500
Store fixtures	5,400	4,800
Accumulated depreciation	(900)	(1,200)
Land	8,200	6,000
Total long-term assets	17,800	13,100
Total assets	$29,500	$24,600
Current liabilities:		
Accounts payable—inventory purchases	$ 800	$ 1,100
Salaries payable	1,000	900
Other operating expenses payable	1,500	1,300
Interest payable	300	500
Unearned rent revenue	600	1,600
Total current liabilities	4,200	5,400

continued

EXHIBIT 12.5	*concluded*

NEW SOUTH COMPANY
Balance Sheets
As of December 31

	2012	2011
Long-term liabilities		
Mortgage payable	2,200	0
Bonds payable	1,000	4,000
Total long-term liabilities	3,200	4,000
Stockholders' equity		
Common stock	10,000	8,000
Retained earnings	12,700	7,200
Treasury stock	(600)	0
Total stockholders' equity	22,100	15,200
Total liabilities and stockholders' equity	$29,500	$24,600

NEW SOUTH COMPANY
Income Statement
For the Year Ended December 31, 2012

Sales revenue		$20,600
Cost of goods sold		(10,500)
Gross margin		10,100
Operating expenses		
Depreciation expense	$(1,000)	
Salaries expense	(2,700)	
Insurance expense	(1,300)	
Other operating expenses	(1,400)	
Total operating expenses		(6,400)
Income from sales business		3,700
Other income—rent revenue		2,400
Operating income		6,100
Nonoperating revenue and expense		
Interest revenue	700	
Interest expense	(400)	
Gain on sale of store fixtures	600	
Total nonoperating items		900
Net income		$ 7,000

Note 1: No investment securities were sold during 2012.

Note 2: During 2012, New South sold store fixtures that had originally cost $1,700. At the time of sale, accumulated depreciation on the fixtures was $1,300.

Note 3: Land was acquired during 2012 by issuing a mortgage note payable. No land sales occurred during 2012.

PREPARING THE OPERATING ACTIVITIES SECTION OF A STATEMENT OF CASH FLOWS USING THE INDIRECT METHOD

LO 1

Prepare the operating activities section of a statement of cash flows using the indirect method.

Recall that the indirect approach begins with the amount of net income. Many aspects of accrual accounting, such as recognizing revenues and expenses on account, can cause differences between the amount of net income reported on a company's income statement and the amount of net cash flow it reports from operating activities. Most of the differences between revenue and expense recognition and cash flows are related to changes in the balances of the noncash current assets and current liabilities.

Answers to The *Curious* Accountant

First, it should be remembered that GAAP requires earnings and losses to be computed on an accrual basis. A company can have negative earnings and still have positive cash flows from operating activities. This was not the case at Sirius XM Radio (Sirius). From 2005 through 2008 the company's cash flows from operating activities totaled a negative $1 billion. Although this is much less than the $7.8 billion of cumulative net losses the company incurred during the same period, negative cash flows do not pay the bills.

In its early years of operations, Sirius, like many new companies, was able to stay in business because of the cash it raised through financing activities. In the most recent years, however, it has raised cash primarily through its investing activities, most notably, through the cash it received in 2008 as a part of the merger. Obviously, a company cannot operate indefinitely without generating cash from operating activities. Individuals and institutions who are willing to buy a company's stock or loan it cash in its early years will disappear if they do not believe the company will eventually begin earning profits and positive cash flows from operations. Exhibit 12.6 presents Sirius's statements of cash flows from 2005 through 2008.

EXHIBIT 12.6

SIRIUS XM RADIO INC. AND SUBSIDIARIES
Consolidated Statements of Cash Flows
(dollar amounts in thousands)

	For the Years Ended December 31			
	2008	2007	2006	2005
Cash Flows from Operating Activities:				
Net loss	$(5,313,288)	$(565,252)	$(1,104,867)	$(862,997)
Adjustments to reconcile net loss to net cash used in operating activities:				
Depreciation and amortization	203,752	106,780	105,749	98,555
Impairment of goodwill	4,766,190	—	—	—
Noncash interest expense, net of amortization of premium	(6,311)	4,269	3,107	3,169
Provision for doubtful accounts	21,589	9,002	9,370	4,311
Noncash income (expense) from affiliate	—	—	—	3,192
Noncash loss from redemption of debt	98,203	—	—	712
Amortization of deferred income related to equity method investment	(1,156)	—	—	—
Loss on disposal of assets	4,879	(428)	1,661	1,028
Equity granted to third parties and employees	—	—	—	163,078
Impairment loss	—	—	10,917	—
Loss on investments, net	28,999	—	4,445	—
Shared-based payment expense	87,405	78,900	437,918	—
Deferred income taxes	2,476	2,435	2,065	2,311
Other noncash purchase price adjustments	(68,330)	—	—	—
Other	1,643	—	—	—

continued

EXHIBIT 12.6	concluded

SIRIUS XM RADIO INC. AND SUBSIDIARIES
Consolidated Statements of Cash Flows
(dollar amounts in thousands)

	For the Years Ended December 31			
	2008	2007	2006	2005
Changes in operating assets and liabilities, net of assets and liabilities acquired:				
Marketable securities	—	—	—	16
Accounts receivable	(32,121)	(28,881)	(1,871)	(28,440)
Inventory	8,291	4,965	(20,246)	(6,329)
Receivables from distributors	14,401	(13,179)	(20,312)	—
Related party assets	(22,249)	(1,241)	(1,189)	—
Prepaid expenses and other current assets	(19,953)	11,118	(42,132)	(29,129)
Other long-term assets	(5,490)	13,691	(18,377)	6,476
Accounts payable and accrued expenses	(65,481)	66,169	26,366	145,052
Accrued interest	23,081	(8,920)	1,239	17,813
Deferred revenue	55,778	169,905	181,003	210,947
Related party liabilities	34,646	—	—	—
Other long-term liabilities	30,249	1,901	3,452	(3,505)
Net cash used in operating activities	(152,797)	(148,766)	(421,702)	(273,740)
Cash Flows from Investing Activities:				
Additions to property and equipment	(130,551)	(65,264)	(92,674)	(49,888)
Sales of property and equipment	105	641	127	72
Purchases of restricted and other investments	(3,000)	(310)	(12,339)	(21,291)
Release of restricted investments	—	—	—	10,997
Acquisition of acquired entity cash	819,521	—	—	—
Merger related costs	(23,519)	(29,444)	—	—
Purchase of available-for-sale securities	—	—	(123,500)	(148,900)
Sale of restricted and other investments	65,869	40,191	255,715	31,850
Maturities of available-for-sale securities	—	—	—	5,085
Net cash provided by (used in) investing activities	728,425	(54,186)	27,329	(172,075)
Cash Flows from Financing Activities:				
Proceeds from exercise of warrants and stock options and from share borrow arrangement	471	4,097	25,787	18,543
Long-term borrowings, net of related costs	531,743	244,879	—	493,005
Redemption of debt	—	—	—	(57,609)
Payment of premiums on redemption of debt	(18,693)	—	—	—
Payments to minority interest holder	(1,479)	—	—	—
Repayment of long-term borrowings	(1,146,044)	(625)	—	—
Other	—	—	—	(8)
Net cash (used in) provided by financing activities	(634,002)	(248,351)	25,787	453,931
Net (decrease) increase in cash and cash equivalents	(58,374)	45,399	(368,586)	8,116
Cash and cash equivalents at beginning of period	438,820	393,421	762,007	753,891
Cash and cash equivalents at end of period	$ 380,446	$438,820	$393,421	$762,007

Indirect Method—Reconciliation Approach

The following section of this chapter examines the relationships between items reported on the income statement and the related assets and liabilities. Begin by reconciling the *noncash* current asset and current liability amounts shown on the balance sheets in Exhibit 12.5. *Do not include Cash in this analysis.* The amount of the change in the cash balance is the result of not only operating activities but also investing and financing activities.

Reconciliation of Accounts Receivable

Use the information in Exhibit 12.5 to prepare the following reconciliation of Accounts Receivable. The beginning and ending balances appear on the balance sheets. The *increase due to revenue recognized on account* is the sales revenue reported on the income statement.

Table 1 Reconciliation of Accounts Receivable	
Beginning balance	$ 1,200
Increase due to revenue recognized on account	20,600
Decrease due to cash collections from customers	? = (20,800)
Ending balance	$ 1,000

$200 Decrease

To balance Accounts Receivable, the *decrease due to cash collections from customers* must be $20,800.[1]

The reconciliation shows that the $200 decrease in the accounts receivable balance occurred because *cash collections from customers* were $200 more than the amount of *revenue recognized on account* ($20,800 versus $20,600). Since the amount of cash collected is more than the amount of revenue recognized, we add $200 to the amount of net income to determine net cash flow from operating activities (Reference No. 1 in Exhibit 12.7).

Reconciliation of Interest Receivable

The beginning and ending balances appear on the balance sheets in Exhibit 12.5. The *increase due to interest revenue recognized on account* is the interest revenue reported on the income statement.

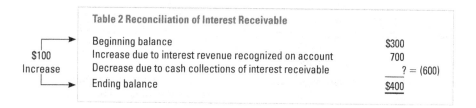

Table 2 Reconciliation of Interest Receivable	
Beginning balance	$300
Increase due to interest revenue recognized on account	700
Decrease due to cash collections of interest receivable	? = (600)
Ending balance	$400

$100 Increase

To balance Interest Receivable, the *decrease due to cash collections of interest receivable* must be $600.

The reconciliation shows that the $100 increase in the interest receivable balance occurred because *cash collections of interest* were $100 less than the *interest revenue recognized on account* ($600 versus $700). Since the amount of cash collected is less than the amount of revenue recognized, we subtract the $100 from the amount of net income to determine net cash flow from operating activities (Reference No. 2 in Exhibit 12.7).

Reconciliation of Inventory and Accounts Payable

To simplify computing the amount of cash paid for inventory purchases, assume that all inventory purchases are made on account. The computation requires two steps. First, Inventory must be analyzed to determine the amount of inventory purchased. Second, Accounts Payable must be analyzed to determine the amount of cash paid to purchase inventory.

Use the financial statement information in Exhibit 12.5 to prepare the following Inventory reconciliation. The beginning and ending balances appear on the balance sheets. The *decrease due to recognizing cost of goods sold* is the cost of goods sold reported on the income statement.

---

[1]This text uses the simplifying assumption that all sales occur on account.

Table 3 Reconciliation of Inventory

Beginning balance	$ 8,200
Increase due to inventory purchases	? = 11,200
Decrease due to recognizing cost of goods sold	(10,500)
Ending balance	$ 8,900

$700 Increase

To balance Inventory, the *increase due to inventory purchases* must be $11,200.

Assuming the inventory was purchased on account, the $11,200 of inventory purchases determined above equals the *increase due to inventory purchases* used in the reconciliation of Accounts Payable below. The beginning and ending balances appear on the balance sheets in Exhibit 12.5.

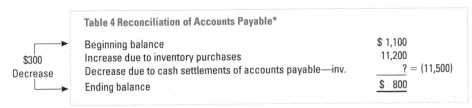

Table 4 Reconciliation of Accounts Payable*

Beginning balance	$ 1,100
Increase due to inventory purchases	11,200
Decrease due to cash settlements of accounts payable—inv.	? = (11,500)
Ending balance	$ 800

$300 Decrease

*Assume that Accounts Payable is used for purchases of inventory only.

To balance Accounts Payable, the *decrease due to cash settlements of accounts payable—inventory* (cash paid to purchase inventory) must be $11,500.

Since the amount of *cash paid to purchase inventory* is $1,000 more than the amount of *cost of goods sold* recognized on the income statement ($11,500 versus $10,500), we subtract the $1,000 difference from the amount of net income to determine net cash flow from operating activities. In Exhibit 12.7 the $1,000 subtraction is divided between a $700 increase in inventory (Reference No. 3 in Exhibit 12.7) and a $300 decrease in accounts payable (Reference No. 4 in Exhibit 12.7).

Reconciliation of Prepaid Insurance

Use the financial statement information in Exhibit 12.5 to reconcile Prepaid Insurance. The beginning and ending balances appear on the balance sheets. The *decrease due to recognizing insurance expense* is the insurance expense reported on the income statement.

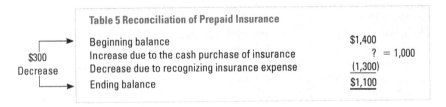

Table 5 Reconciliation of Prepaid Insurance

Beginning balance	$1,400
Increase due to the cash purchase of insurance	? = 1,000
Decrease due to recognizing insurance expense	(1,300)
Ending balance	$1,100

$300 Decrease

To balance Prepaid Insurance, the amount of the *increase due to the cash purchase of insurance* must be $1,000.

The reconciliation shows that the $300 decrease in the prepaid insurance balance occurred because *cash paid to purchase insurance* was $300 less than the amount of *insurance expense recognized* ($1,000 versus $1,300). Since the amount of cash paid is less than the amount of expense recognized, we add $300 to the amount of net income to determine the net cash flow from operating activities (Reference No. 5 in Exhibit 12.7).

Reconciliation of Salaries Payable

Use the financial statement information in Exhibit 12.5 to reconcile Salaries Payable. The beginning and ending balance appear on the balance sheets. The *increase due to recognizing salary expense on account* is the salaries expense reported on the income statement.

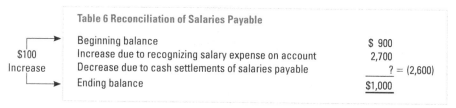

Table 6 Reconciliation of Salaries Payable

Beginning balance	$ 900
Increase due to recognizing salary expense on account	2,700
Decrease due to cash settlements of salaries payable	? = (2,600)
Ending balance	$1,000

$100 Increase

To balance Salaries Payable, the amount of the *decrease due to cash settlements of salaries payable* (cash paid for salaries expense) must be $2,600. The reconciliation shows that the $100 increase in the salaries payable balance occurred because the *cash paid for salary expense* is $100 less than the amount of *salary expense recognized on account* ($2,600 versus $2,700). Since the amount of cash paid is less than the amount of expense recognized, we add $100 to the amount of net income to determine the cash flow from operating activities (Reference No. 6 in Exhibit 12.7).

Reconciliation of Other Operating Expenses Payable

Use the financial statement information in Exhibit 12.5 to reconcile Other Operating Expenses Payable. The beginning and ending balances appear on the balance sheets. The *increase due to recognizing other operating expenses on account* is the other operating expenses amount reported on the income statement.

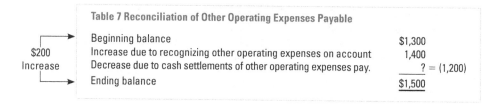

Table 7 Reconciliation of Other Operating Expenses Payable

Beginning balance	$1,300
Increase due to recognizing other operating expenses on account	1,400
Decrease due to cash settlements of other operating expenses pay.	? = (1,200)
Ending balance	$1,500

$200 Increase

To balance Other Operating Expenses Payable, the amount of the *decrease due to cash settlements of other operating expenses payable* must be $1,200.

The reconciliation shows that the $200 increase in the other operating expenses payable balance occurred because the *cash paid for other operating expenses* was $200 less than the amount of *other operating expenses recognized on account* ($1,200 versus $1,400). Since the amount of cash paid is less than the amount of expense recognized, we add $200 to the amount of net income to determine the net cash flow from operating activities (Reference No. 7 in Exhibit 12.7).

Reconciliation of Interest Payable

Use the financial statement information in Exhibit 12.5 to reconcile Interest Payable. The beginning and ending balances appear on the balance sheets. The *increase due to recognizing interest expense on account* is the interest expense reported on the income statement.

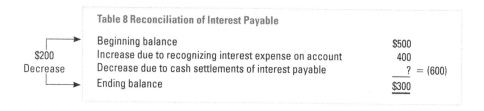

Table 8 Reconciliation of Interest Payable

Beginning balance	$500
Increase due to recognizing interest expense on account	400
Decrease due to cash settlements of interest payable	? = (600)
Ending balance	$300

$200 Decrease

To balance Interest Payable, the amount of the *decrease due to cash settlements of interest payable* (cash paid for interest expense) must be $600.

The reconciliation shows that the $200 decrease in the interest payable balance occurred because the amount of *cash paid for interest expense* is $200 more than the amount of *interest expense recognized on account* ($600 versus $400). Since the amount of cash paid is more than the amount of interest expense recognized, we subtract $200 from the amount of net income to determine the net cash flow from operating activities (Reference No. 8 in Exhibit 12.7).

Reconciliation of Unearned Rent Revenue

Use the financial statement information in Exhibit 12.5 to reconcile Unearned Rent Revenue. The beginning and ending balances appear on the balance sheets. The *decrease due to recognizing other income—rent revenue* is the other income—rent revenue reported on the income statement.

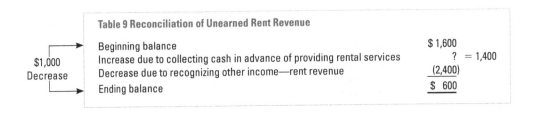

Table 9 Reconciliation of Unearned Rent Revenue

Beginning balance	$ 1,600
Increase due to collecting cash in advance of providing rental services	? = 1,400
Decrease due to recognizing other income—rent revenue	(2,400)
Ending balance	$ 600

$1,000 Decrease

To balance Unearned Rent Revenue, the amount of the *increase due to collecting cash in advance of providing rental services* must be $1,400.

The reconciliation shows that the $1,000 decrease in the unearned rent revenue balance occurred because the amount of *cash collected in advance of providing rental services* is $1,000 less than the amount of *rent revenue recognized* ($1,400 versus $2,400). Since the amount of cash collected is less than the amount of revenue recognized, we subtract $1,000 from the amount of net income to determine the net cash flow from operating activities (Reference No. 9 in Exhibit 12.7).

Noncash Expenses

The calculation of accrual-based net income frequently includes noncash expenses such as depreciation expense. Since noncash expenses are deducted in determining net income, they must be added back to the amount of net income when computing net cash flow from operating activities (Reference No. 10 in Exhibit 12.7).

Gains and Losses

When a company retires a long-term asset, the company may receive cash from the sale of the asset being retired. If the asset is sold for more than book value (cost − accumulated depreciation), the gain increases net income; if the asset is sold for less than book value, the loss decreases net income. In either case, the cash inflow is the total amount of cash collected from selling the asset, not the amount of the gain or loss, and this cash inflow is reported in the investing activities section of the statement of cash flows. Since gains increase net income and losses decrease net income, but neither represents the amount of cash received from an asset sale, gains must be subtracted from and losses added back to net income to determine net cash flow from operating activities (Reference No. 11 in Exhibit 12.7).

Indirect Method—Rule-Based Approach

The reconciliation process described in the previous section of this chapter leads to a set of rules that can be used to convert accrual-based revenues and expenses to their cash flow equivalents. These rules are summarized in Exhibit 12.8.

Although the rule-based approach offers less insight, it is easy to apply. To illustrate, return to the financial statement data in Exhibit 12.5. The *noncash* current assets

EXHIBIT 12.7

Cash Flows from Operating Activities—Indirect Method

Reference No.	Cash Flows from Operating Activities	
	Net income	$7,000
	Adjustments to reconcile net income to net cash flow from operating activities:	
1	Decrease in accounts receivable	200
2	Increase in interest receivable	(100)
3	Increase in inventory	(700)
4	Decrease in accounts payable for inventory purchases	(300)
5	Decrease in prepaid insurance	300
6	Increase in salaries payable	100
7	Increase in other operating expenses payable	200
8	Decrease in interest payable	(200)
9	Decrease in unearned rent revenue	(1,000)
10	Depreciation expense	1,000
11	Gain on sale of store fixtures	(600)
	Net cash flow from operating activities	$5,900

EXHIBIT 12.8

Cash Flows from Operating Activities—Indirect Method

	Net income	XXX
Rule 1	Add decreases and subtract increases in noncash current assets.	XXX
Rule 2	Add increases and subtract decreases in noncash current liabilities.	XXX
Rule 3	Add noncash expenses (e.g., depreciation).	XXX
Rule 4	Add losses and subtract gains.	XXX
	Net cash flow from operating activities	XXX

and current liabilities reported on the balance sheets are summarized in Exhibit 12.9 for your convenience. The amount of the change in each balance is shown in the *Change* column.

Refer to the income statement to identify the amounts of net income, noncash expenses, gains, and losses. The income statement for New South Company in Exhibit 12.5 includes three relevant figures: net income of $7,000; depreciation expense of $1,000;

EXHIBIT 12.9

Noncash Current Assets and Current Liabilities

Account Title	2012	2011	Change
Accounts receivable	$1,000	$1,200	$ (200)
Interest receivable	400	300	100
Inventory	8,900	8,200	700
Prepaid insurance	1,100	1,400	(300)
Accounts payable—inventory purchases	800	1,100	(300)
Salaries payable	1,000	900	100
Other operating expenses payable	1,500	1,300	200
Interest payable	300	500	(200)
Unearned rent revenue	600	1,600	(1,000)

EXHIBIT 12.10	Cash Flows from Operating Activities—Indirect Method, Operating Activities

NEW SOUTH COMPANY
Statement of Cash Flows
For the Year Ended December 31, 2012

Applicable Rule	Cash Flows from Operating Activities	
	Net income	$7,000
	Adjustments to reconcile net income to net cash flow from operating activities:	
Rule 1	Decrease in accounts receivable	200
Rule 1	Increase in interest receivable	(100)
Rule 1	Increase in inventory	(700)
Rule 2	Decrease in accounts payable for inventory purchases	(300)
Rule 1	Decrease in prepaid insurance	300
Rule 2	Increase in salaries payable	100
Rule 2	Increase in other operating expenses payable	200
Rule 2	Decrease in interest payable	(200)
Rule 2	Decrease in unearned rent revenue	(1,000)
Rule 3	Depreciation expense	1,000
Rule 4	Gain on sale of store fixtures	(600)
	Net cash flow from operating activities	$5,900

and a $600 gain on sale of store fixtures. Applying the rules in Exhibit 12.8 produces the operating activities section of the statement of cash flows shown in Exhibit 12.10. The applicable rule for each item is referenced in the first column of the exhibit.

The operating activities section of the statements of cash flows shown in Exhibits 12.10 and 12.7 are identical. The rule-based approach is an alternative way to prepare this section when using the indirect method.

CHECK *Yourself* 12.2

Q Magazine, Inc., reported $369,000 of net income for the month. At the beginning of the month, its Unearned Revenue account had a balance of $78,000. At the end of the month, the account had a balance of $67,000. Based on this information alone, determine the amount of net cash flow from operating activities.

Answer

Account Title	Ending	Beginning	Change
Unearned revenue	$67,000	$78,000	$(11,000)

Applicable Rule	Cash Flows from Operating Activities	Amount
	Net income	$369,000
Rule 2	Deduct: Decrease in unearned revenue	(11,000)
	Net cash flow from operating activities	$358,000

CHECK *Yourself* 12.3

The following account balances were drawn from the accounting records of Loeb, Inc.

Account Title	Ending Balance	Beginning Balance
Prepaid rent	$3,000	$4,200
Interest payable	2,650	2,900

Loeb reported $7,400 of net income during the accounting period. Based on this information alone, determine the amount of net cash flow from operating activities.

Answer   Based on Rule 1, the $1,200 decrease ($3,000 − $4,200) in Prepaid Rent (current asset) must be added to net income to determine the amount of net cash flow from operating activities. Rule 2 requires that the $250 decrease ($2,650 − $2,900) in interest Payable (current liability) must be deducted from net income. Accordingly, the cash flow from operating activities is $8,350 ($7,400 + $1,200 − $250). Note that paying interest is defined as an operating activity and should not be confused with dividend payments, which are classified as financing activities.

CHECK *Yourself* 12.4

Arley Company's income statement reported net income (all amounts are in millions) of $326 for the year. The income statement included depreciation expense of $45 and a net loss on the sale of long-term assets of $22. Based on this information alone, determine the net cash flow from operating activities.

Answer   Based on Rule 3 and Rule 4, both the depreciation expense and the loss would have to be added to net income to determine net cash flow from operating activities. Net cash flow from operating activities would be $393 million ($326 + $45 + $22).

PREPARING THE OPERATING ACTIVITIES SECTION OF A STATEMENT OF CASH FLOWS USING THE DIRECT METHOD

The reconciliation tables developed earlier to determine net cash flow from operating activities under the *indirect method* also disclose the information needed to present the amount of net cash flow from operating activities under the *direct method*. Remember that the amount of net cash flow from operating activities is the same whether it is presented using the indirect or the direct method.

The direct method shows the specific sources and uses of cash that are associated with operating activities. It does not show adjustments to net income. To illustrate, examine Exhibit 12.11. The information in the reference column identifies the reconciliation table from which the cash flow amounts were drawn. The page number indicates where the reconciliation table is located in this chapter.

Table 3 is not included above because it does not directly involve a cash flow. Also, noncash expenses, gains, and losses are not used in the determination of net cash flow from operating activities when using the direct method.

LO 2

Prepare the operating activities section of a statement of cash flows using the direct method.

EXHIBIT 12.11

Cash Flows from Operating Activities—Direct Method

Reference	Cash Flows from Operating Activities	
Table 1, page 627	Inflow from customers	$ 20,800
Table 2, page 627	Inflow from interest revenue	600
Table 4, page 628	Outflow for inventory purchases	(11,500)
Table 5, page 628	Outflow to purchase insurance	(1,000)
Table 6, page 629	Outflow to pay salary expense	(2,600)
Table 7, page 629	Outflow for other operating expenses	(1,200)
Table 8, page 629	Outflow to pay interest expense	(600)
Table 9, page 630	Inflow from rent revenue	1,400
	Net cash flow from operating activities	$ 5,900

PREPARING THE INVESTING ACTIVITIES SECTION OF A STATEMENT OF CASH FLOWS

LO 3

Prepare the investing activities section of a statement of cash flows.

The direct and indirect methods discussed above pertain only to the presentation of operating activities. The *investing activities* section of the statement of cash flows is the same regardless of whether the direct or indirect method is used for operating activities. The information necessary to identify cash inflows and outflows from investing activities is obtained by reconciling changes in a company's long-term assets. In general:

■ Increases in long-term asset balances suggest cash outflows to purchase assets.

■ Decreases in long-term asset balances suggest cash inflows from selling assets.

It is usually necessary to analyze data from the long-term asset records to determine details about long-term asset purchases and sales. In the New South Company example, these details are presented as notes at the bottom of the balance sheets.

To illustrate, return to the financial statements in Exhibit 12.5. New South Company reports the following three long-term assets on its balance sheets. *It is not necessary to reconcile accumulated depreciation since it does not affect cash flow.*

Long-term Asset	2012	2011
Investment securities	$5,100	$3,500
Store fixtures	5,400	4,800
Land	8,200	6,000

For each long-term asset, reconcile the beginning and ending balances by identifying purchases and sales affecting it. Review the notes for additional relevant information. Begin with investment securities.

Reconciliation of Investment Securities

Reconciliation of Investment Securities

Beginning balance in investment securities	$3,500
Increase due to purchase of investment securities	? = 1,600
Decrease due to sale of investment securities	0
Ending balance in investment securities	$5,100

Because Note 1 below the balance sheets indicates no investment securities were sold during 2012, the *decrease due to sale of investment securities* is zero. To balance Investment Securities, the *increase due to purchase of investment securities* must be $1,600. In the absence of contrary information, assume New South used cash to purchase the investment securities. This cash outflow is reported in the investing activities section of the statement of cash flows in Exhibit 12.12.

Reconciliation of Store Fixtures

Reconciliation of Store Fixtures	
Beginning balance in store fixtures	$4,800
Increase due to purchase of store fixtures	? = 2,300
Decrease due to sale of store fixtures	(1,700)
Ending balance in store fixtures	$5,400

Note 2 below the balance sheets indicates that the *decrease due to sale of store fixtures* is $1,700. What is the cash flow from this sale? The book value of these fixtures was $400 ($1,700 cost − $1,300 accumulated depreciation). Since the income statement reports a $600 gain on the sale of store fixtures, the cash collected from the sale was more than the book value of the store fixtures. Compute the amount of cash collected from the sale of store fixtures as follows:

$$\text{Cash inflow} = \text{book value} + \text{gain} = \$400 + \$600 = \$1,000$$

The $1,000 cash inflow from the sale of store fixtures is reported in the investing activities section of the statement of cash flows in Exhibit 12.12.

To balance Store Fixtures, the *increase due to purchase of store fixtures* must be $2,300. In the absence of contrary information, assume New South used cash to purchase store fixtures. The cash outflow is reported in the investing activities section of the statement of cash flows in Exhibit 12.12.

Reconciliation of Land

Reconciliation of Land	
Beginning balance in land	$6,000
Increase due to purchase of land	? = 2,200
Decrease due to sale of land	0
Ending balance in land	$8,200

Because Note 3 below the balance sheets indicates no land was sold during 2012, the *decrease due to sale of land* is zero. To balance Land, the *increase due to purchase of land* must be $2,200. Since the land was acquired by issuing a mortgage note payable, New South did not use cash for the purchase. This type of transaction is reported in the *noncash investing and financing activities* section of the statement of cash flows, discussed in more detail later in the chapter. The cash inflows and outflows from investing activities are summarized in Exhibit 12.12.

EXHIBIT 12.12

Cash Flows from Investing Activities

Cash Flows from Investing Activities

Cash outflow to purchase investment securities	$(1,600)
Cash inflow from the sale of store fixtures	1,000
Cash outflow to purchase store fixtures	(2,300)
Net cash outflow from investing activities	$(2,900)

CHECK *Yourself* 12.5

On January 1, 2011, Wyatt Company had an Equipment balance of $124,000. During 2011, Wyatt purchased equipment that cost $50,000. The balance in Equipment on December 31, 2011, was $90,000. The 2011 income statement included a $7,000 loss from the sale of equipment. On the date of sale, accumulated depreciation on the equipment sold was $49,000.

Required

a. Determine the cost of the equipment sold during 2011.

b. Determine the amount of cash flow from the sale of equipment that should be reported in the investing activities section of the 2011 statement of cash flows.

Solution

a.

Reconciliation of Equipment

Beginning balance	$124,000
Increase due to the purchase of equipment	50,000
Decrease due to sale of equipment	? = (84,000)
Ending balance	$ 90,000

To balance Equipment, *decrease due to sale of equipment* must be $84,000.

b. The book value of the equipment sold was $35,000 ($84,000 − $49,000 accumulated depreciation). Since Wyatt recognized a loss on the equipment sale, the amount of cash collected from the sale was less than the book value of the equipment. The cash collected from the sale of the equipment was $28,000 ($35,000 book value − $7,000 loss on sale).

PREPARING THE FINANCING ACTIVITIES SECTION OF A STATEMENT OF CASH FLOWS

LO 4

Prepare the financing activities section of a statement of cash flows.

Because the differences between the direct and the indirect methods of presenting the statement of cash flows pertain only to operating activities, the *financing activities* section is the same under either approach. The information necessary to identify cash inflows and outflows from financing activities is obtained by reconciling changes in short-term notes payable, long-term liabilities, and stockholders' equity. In general:

■ Increases in short-term notes payable or long-term debt balances suggest cash inflows occurred from issuing debt instruments (notes or bonds).

■ Decreases in short-term notes payable or long-term debt balances suggest cash outflows occurred for payment of debt (notes or bonds).

■ Increases in contributed capital (common stock, preferred stock, or paid-in capital) suggest cash inflows occurred from issuing equity instruments.

■ Increases or decreases in treasury stock suggest cash outflows or inflows occurred to purchase or sell a company's own stock.

■ Decreases in retained earnings from cash dividends suggest cash outflows occurred to pay dividends.

To illustrate, return to the financial statements of the New South Company in Exhibit 12.5. The following long-term liability and stockholders' equity balances are reported on the New South balance sheets.

Account Title	2012	2011
Mortgage payable	$ 2,200	$ 0
Bonds payable	1,000	4,000
Common stock	10,000	8,000
Retained earnings	12,700	7,200
Treasury stock	600	0

For each account, reconcile the beginning and ending balances by identifying the increases and decreases affecting it. Review the notes for additional relevant information. Begin with the mortgage payable liability.

Reconciliation of Mortgage Payable

Reconciliation of Mortgage Payable	
Beginning balance in mortgage payable	$ 0
Increase due to issuing mortgage payable	2,200
Decrease due to payment of mortgage payable	0
Ending balance in mortgage payable	$2,200

As previously discussed, Note 3 indicates a mortgage payable was issued to acquire land. The *increase due to issuing mortgage payable* is $2,200. Since New South received land, not cash, by issuing the mortgage, the transaction is reported in the noncash investing and financing activities section of the statement of cash flows.

Reconciliation of Bonds Payable

Bonds Payable	
Beginning balance in bonds payable	$4,000
Increase due to issuing bonds payable	0
Decrease due to payment of bonds payable	? = (3,000)
Ending balance in bonds payable	$1,000

Since there is no indication that New South issued bonds during 2012, assume the *increase due to issuing bonds payable* is zero. To balance Bonds Payable, the *decrease due to payment of bonds payable* must be $3,000. The cash outflow is reported in the financing activities section in Exhibit 12.13.

Reconciliation of Common Stock

Reconciliation of Common Stock	
Beginning balance in common stock	$ 8,000
Increase due to issuing common stock	? = 2,000
Ending balance in common stock	$10,000

To balance Common Stock, the *increase due to issuing common stock* has to be $2,000. The cash inflow is reported in the financing activities section in Exhibit 12.13.

Reconciliation of Retained Earnings

Reconciliation of Retained Earnings	
Beginning balance in retained earnings	$ 7,200
Increase due to net income	7,000
Decrease due to payment of dividends	? = (1,500)
Ending balance in retained earnings	$12,700

The *increase due to net income* comes from the income statement. To balance Retained Earnings, the decrease due to payment of dividends must be $1,500. In the absence of information to the contrary, assume the decrease is due to the cash payment of dividends. The cash outflow for payment of dividends is reported in the financing activities section of the statement of cash flows in Exhibit 12.13.

Reconciliation of Treasury Stock

Reconciliation of Treasury Stock	
Beginning balance in treasury stock	$ 0
Increase due to purchasing treasury stock	? = 600
Decrease due to reissuing treasury stock	0
Ending balance in treasury stock	$600

Since there is no indication that New South reissued treasury stock during 2012, the *decrease due to reissuing treasury stock* is zero. To balance Treasury Stock, the increase due to purchasing treasury stock must be $600. The cash outflow is reported in the financing activities section in Exhibit 12.13.

EXHIBIT 12.13

Cash Flows from Financing Activities

Cash Flows from Financing Activities	
Cash outflow to reduce bonds payable	$(3,000)
Cash inflow from issuing common stock	2,000
Cash outflow to pay dividends	(1,500)
Cash outflow to purchase treasury stock	(600)
Net cash outflow from financing activities	$(3,100)

Exhibits 12.14 and 12.15 illustrate the complete statement of cash flows for New South Company under the two alternative methods. Exhibit 12.14 presents operating activities using the indirect method. Exhibit 12.15 presents operating activities using the direct method. The investing and financing activities do not differ between methods. Under either method the combined effects of operating, investing, and financing activities result in a net decrease in cash of $100 for 2012. This $100 decrease is necessarily consistent with the difference between the December 31, 2012, and the December 31, 2011, cash balances shown in the balance sheets in Exhibit 12.5.

EXHIBIT 12.14	Statement of Cash Flows—Indirect Method

NEW SOUTH COMPANY
Statement of Cash Flows
For the Year Ended December 31, 2012

Cash Flows from Operating Activities

Net income	$7,000	
Adjustments to reconcile net income to net cash flow from operating activities:		
Decrease in accounts receivable	200	
Increase in interest receivable	(100)	
Increase in inventory	(700)	
Decrease in accounts payable for inventory purchases	(300)	
Decrease in prepaid insurance	300	
Increase in salaries payable	100	
Increase in other operating expenses payable	200	
Decrease in interest payable	(200)	
Decrease in unearned rent revenue	(1,000)	
Depreciation expense	1,000	
Gain on sale of store fixtures	(600)	
Net cash flow from operating activities		$5,900
Cash Flows from Investing Activities		
Cash outflow to purchase investment securities	(1,600)	
Cash inflow from the sale of store fixtures	1,000	
Cash outflow to purchase store fixtures	(2,300)	
Net cash outflow from investing activities		(2,900)
Cash Flows from Financing Activities		
Cash outflow to reduce bonds payable	(3,000)	
Cash inflow from issuing common stock	2,000	
Cash outflow to pay dividends	(1,500)	
Cash outflow to purchase treasury stock	(600)	
Net cash outflow from financing activities		(3,100)
Net decrease in cash		(100)
Plus: Beginning cash balance		400
Ending cash balance		$300
Schedule of Noncash Investing and Financing Activities		
Issue mortgage for land		$2,200

EXHIBIT 12.15	Statement of Cash Flows—Direct Method

NEW SOUTH COMPANY
Statement of Cash Flows
For the Year Ended December 31, 2012

Cash Flows from Operating Activities

Inflow from customers	$20,800	
Inflow from interest revenue	600	
Outflow for inventory purchases	(11,500)	
Outflow to purchase insurance	(1,000)	
Outflow to pay salary expense	(2,600)	
Outflow for other operating expenses	(1,200)	
Outflow to pay interest expense	(600)	
Inflow from rent revenue	1,400	
Net cash flow from operating activities		$5,900

continued

EXHIBIT 12.15	*concluded*

NEW SOUTH COMPANY
Statement of Cash Flows
For the Year Ended December 31, 2012

Cash Flows from Investing Activities		
Cash outflow to purchase investment securities	(1,600)	
Cash inflow from the sale of store fixtures	1,000	
Cash outflow to purchase store fixtures	(2,300)	
Net cash outflow from investing activities		(2,900)
Cash Flows from Financing Activities		
Cash outflow to reduce bonds payable	(3,000)	
Cash inflow from issuing common stock	2,000	
Cash outflow to pay dividends	(1,500)	
Cash outflow to purchase treasury stock	(600)	
Net cash outflow from financing activities		(3,100)
Net decrease in cash		(100)
Plus: Beginning cash balance		400
Ending cash balance		$ 300
Schedule of Noncash Investing and Financing Activities		
Issue mortgage for land		$2,200

CHECK *Yourself* 12.6

On January 1, 2011, Sterling Company had a balance of $250,000 in Bonds Payable. During 2011, Sterling issued bonds with a $75,000 face value. The bonds were issued at face value. The balance in Bonds Payable on December 31, 2011, was $150,000.

Required

a. Determine the cash outflow for repayment of bond liabilities assuming the bonds were retired at face value.

b. Prepare the financing activities section of the 2011 statement of cash flows.

Solution

a.

Reconciliation of Bonds Payable	
Beginning balance	$250,000
Increase due to issuing bonds payable	75,000
Decrease due to payment of bonds payable	? = (175,000)
Ending balance	$150,000

In order to balance Bonds Payable, the decrease due to payment of bonds payable must be $175,000. In the absence of information to the contrary, assume cash was used to pay the bond liabilities.

b.

Cash Flows from Financing Activities	
Inflow from issuing bond liabilities	$ 75,000
Outflow for reduction of bond liabilities	(175,000)
Net cash outflow from financing activities	$(100,000)

PREPARING THE SCHEDULE OF NONCASH INVESTING AND FINANCING ACTIVITIES

As mentioned earlier, companies may engage in significant noncash investing and financing activities. For example, New South Company acquired land by issuing a $2,200 mortgage note. Since these types of transactions do not involve exchanging cash, they are not reported in the main body of the statement of cash flows. However, the Financial Accounting Standards Board (FASB) requires disclosure of all material investing and financing activities whether or not they involve exchanging cash. Companies must therefore include with the statement of cash flows a separate schedule that reports noncash investing and financing activities. See the *Schedule of Noncash Investing and Financing Activities* at the bottom of Exhibits 12.14 and 12.15 for an example.

Reality BYTES

How did Dillard's, Inc., the department store chain, acquire $22 million of property, plant, and equipment in its 2006 fiscal year *without* spending any cash? Oddly enough, the answer can be found on its statement of cash flows.

The supplemental "noncash transactions" information included at the bottom of Dillard's statement of cash flows revealed that it acquired the assets by exchanging debt directly for assets. Capital lease transactions, a form of borrowing, were responsible for $19.5 million of these purchases. The remaining $2.5 million was purchased through "accrued capital transactions."

Had Dillard's borrowed $22 million from a bank and then used this cash to purchase $22 million of assets, it would have reported two separate cash events in the body of its statement of cash flows. A cash inflow would have been reported in the financing activities for the borrowing transaction, and a cash outflow would have been reported in the investing activities section for the purchase transaction. Acquiring large amounts of assets is considered important, even if there is no immediate exchange of cash, so generally accepted accounting principles require such events to be reported as a part of the statement of cash flows.

THE *Financial* ANALYST

Why are financial analysts interested in the statement of cash flows? Understanding the cash flows of a business is essential because cash is used to pay the bills. A company, especially one experiencing rapid growth, can be short of cash in spite of earning substantial net income. To illustrate, assume you start a computer sales business. You borrow $2,000 and spend the money to purchase two computers for $1,000 each. You sell one of the computers on account for $1,500. If your loan required a payment at this time, you could not make it. Even though you have net income of $500 ($1,500 sales − $1,000 cost of goods sold), you have no cash until you collect the $1,500 account receivable. A business cannot survive without managing cash flow carefully. It is little wonder that financial analysts are keenly interested in cash flow.

Real-World Data

The statement of cash flows frequently provides a picture of business activity that would otherwise be lost in the complexities of accrual accounting. For example, IBM Corporation's combined operating losses (before taxes) for 1991, 1992, and 1993 were more than $17.9 *billion*. During this same period, IBM reported "restructuring charges"

of more than $24 billion. Restructuring costs relate to reorganizing a company. They may include the costs of closing facilities and losses on asset disposals. Without the restructuring charges, IBM would have reported operating *profits* of about $6 billion (before taxes). Do restructuring charges signal positive or negative changes? Different financial analysts have different opinions about this issue. However, one aspect of IBM's performance during these years is easily understood. The company produced over $21 billion in positive cash flow from operating activities. It had no trouble paying its bills.

Investors consider cash flow information so important that they are willing to pay for it, even when the FASB discourages its use. The FASB *prohibits* companies from disclosing *cash flow per share* in audited financial statements. However, one prominent stock analysis service, *Value Line Investment Survey,* sells this information to a significant customer base. Clearly, Value Line's customers value information about cash flows.

Exhibit 12.16 compares income from operations to cash flows from operating activities for six real-world companies for 2003 through 2005 and 2007 and 2008. These first three years were a time of economic expansion in the United States, but the economy had slowed and eventually entered into a recession in 2007 and 2008.

Several things are apparent from Exhibit 12.16. The cash flow from operating activities exceeds income from operations for all but four of the 30 comparisons, and three of these four are for one company, Pulte Homes. Cash flows often exceed income because depreciation, a noncash expense, is usually significant. Excluding Pulte Homes, which will be discussed separately, the most dramatic example of the differences between cash flow and income is Alaska Air Group, the company that owns Alaska Airlines. For the five years shown in Exhibit 12.16, its net income totals $71.8 million, but its cash flows from operations were $1.6 billion. The difference between cash flow from operating activities and operating income helps explain how some companies can have significant losses over a few years and continue to stay in business and pay their bills.

EXHIBIT 12.16

Operating Income versus Cash Flow from Operations (Amounts in $000)

	2008	2007	2005	2004	2003
Alaska Air Group					
Operating income	$ (135,900)	$ 125,000	$ 84,500	$ (15,300)	$ 13,500
Cash flow—operations	164,300	482,000	271,900	334,000	355,200
Boeing					
Operating income	2,654,000	4,058,000	2,562,000	1,820,000	718,000
Cash flow—operations	(401,000)	9,584,000	7,000,000	3,458,000	3,881,000
Johnson & Johnson					
Operating income	12,949,000	10,576,000	10,411,000	8,509,000	7,197,000
Cash flow—operations	14,972,000	15,249,000	11,877,000	11,131,000	10,595,000
McAfee					
Operating income	172,209	166,980	138,828	225,065	70,242
Cash flow—operations	308,322	393,415	419,457	358,913	156,304
McDonalds					
Operating income	4,313,200	2,335,000	2,602,200	2,278,500	1,508,200
Cash flow—operations	5,917,200	4,876,300	4,336,800	3,903,600	3,268,800
Pulte Homes, Inc.					
Operating income	(1,473,113)	(2,274,417)	1,436,888	998,008	617,322
Cash flow—operations	1,220,392	1,218,255	18,704	(698,280)	(301,848)

The exhibit also shows that cash flow from operating activities can be more stable than operating income. Results for Alaska Air Group also demonstrate this clearly. For the five years presented, Alaska Air earned a profit in three years, but had a loss in two years. However, its operating cash flows were not only positive for all five years, but they were never lower than $164.3 million.

What could explain why Pulte Homes had *less* cash flow from operating activities than operating income in 2003, 2004, and 2005, but not in 2007 and 2008? In the early years, when the housing market was strong, Pulte was experiencing the kind of growth described earlier for your computer business. Its cash outflows were supporting growth in inventory. Pulte is one of the nation's largest new-home construction companies. Its growth rates, based on sales of new homes, were 25%, 31%, and 28% for 2003, 2004, and 2005, but sales declined by 35% and 33% in 2007 and 2008. Notice that in the years of declining sales, its cash flows from operating activities *exceeded* its net income.

Finally, why did Boeing have negative cash flow from operations in 2008 even though its revenue and operating income were also declining? It was because of a growth in inventory, but not due to revenue growth. This situation was significant enough that Boeing explained it in the footnotes of its 2008 annual report, as follows.

In 2008 inventory grew at a faster rate than customer advances. The 2008 increase in inventories was driven by continued spending on production materials, airplane engines, and supplier advances during the IAM strike, lower commercial airplane deliveries and the continued ramp-up of the 787 program. We expect to generate positive operating cash flows in 2009.

The Pulte Homes situation highlights a potential weakness in the format of the statement of cash flows. Some accountants consider it misleading to classify all increases in long-term assets as *investing activities* and all changes in inventory as affecting cash flow from operating activities. They argue that the increase in inventory at Pulte that results from building more houses should be classified as an investing activity, just as the cost of a new building is. Although inventory is classified as a current asset and buildings are classified as long-term assets, in reality there is a certain level of inventory a company must permanently maintain to stay in business. The GAAP format of the statement of cash flows penalizes cash flow from operating activities for increases in inventory that are really a permanent investment in assets.

Conversely, the same critics might argue that some purchases of long-term assets are not actually *investments* but merely replacements of old, existing property, plant, and equipment. In other words, the *investing activities* section of the statement of cash flows makes no distinction between expenditures that expand the business and those that simply replace old equipment (sometimes called *capital maintenance* expenditures).

Users of the statement of cash flows must exercise the same care interpreting it as when they use the balance sheet or the income statement. Numbers alone are insufficient. Users must evaluate numbers based on knowledge of the particular business and industry they are analyzing.

Accounting information alone cannot guide a businessperson to a sound decision. Making good business decisions requires an understanding of the business in question, the environmental and economic factors affecting the operation of that business, and the accounting concepts on which the financial statements of that business are based.

A Look Back

This chapter examined in detail only one financial statement, the statement of cash flows. The chapter provided a more comprehensive discussion of how accrual accounting relates to cash-based accounting. Effective use of financial statements requires understanding not only accrual and cash-based accounting systems but also how they relate to each other. That relationship is why a statement of cash flows can begin with a reconciliation of net income, an accrual measurement, to net cash flow from operating activities, a cash measurement. Finally, this chapter explained how the conventions for classifying cash flows as operating, investing, or financing activities require analysis and understanding to make informed decisions with the financial information.

644   Chapter 12

A Look Forward

The next chapter presents a detailed explanation of the statement of cash flows. In that chapter, you will learn how to classify cash receipts and payments as financing activities, investing activities, or operating activities. The chapter explains how to use the T-account method to prepare a statement of cash flows and the difference between the direct method of presenting cash flows from operating activities and the indirect method of presenting cash flows from operating activities. The depth and timing of statement of cash flows coverage varies among colleges. Your instructor may or may not cover this chapter.

SELF-STUDY REVIEW PROBLEM

DP 12

A step-by-step audio-narrated series of slides is provided on the text website at www.mhhe.com/edmonds7e.

The following financial statements pertain to Schlemmer Company.

Balance Sheets As of December 31		
	2012	2011
Cash	$48,400	$ 2,800
Accounts receivable	2,200	1,200
Inventory	5,600	6,000
Equipment	18,000	22,000
Accumulated depreciation—equip.	(13,650)	(17,400)
Land	17,200	10,400
Total assets	$77,750	$25,000
Accounts payable (inventory)	$ 5,200	$ 4,200
Long-term debt	5,600	6,400
Common stock	19,400	10,000
Retained earnings	47,550	4,400
Total liabilities and equity	$77,750	$25,000

Income Statement For the Year Ended December 31, 2012	
Sales revenue	$67,300
Cost of goods sold	(24,100)
Gross margin	43,200
Depreciation expense	(1,250)
Operating income	41,950
Gain on sale of equipment	2,900
Loss on disposal of land	(100)
Net income	$44,750

Additional Data

1. During 2012 equipment that had originally cost $11,000 was sold. Accumulated depreciation on this equipment was $5,000 at the time of sale.

2. Common stock was issued in exchange for land valued at $9,400 at the time of the exchange.

Required

Using the indirect method, prepare in good form a statement of cash flows for the year ended December 31, 2012.

Solution

SCHLEMMER COMPANY		
Statement of Cash Flows		
For the Year Ended December 31, 2012		
Cash Flows from Operating Activities		
Net income	$44,750	
Add:		
Decrease in inventory (1)	400	
Increase in accounts payable (2)	1,000	
Depreciation expense (3)	1,250	
Loss on disposal of land (4)	100	
Subtract:		
Increase in accounts receivable (1)	(1,000)	
Gain on sale of equipment (4)	(2,900)	
Net cash inflow from operating activities		$43,600
Cash Flows from Investing Activities		
Cash inflow from the sale of equipment (5)	8,900	
Cash outflow for the purchase of equipment (5)	(7,000)	
Cash inflow from sale of land (6)	2,500	
Net cash outflow from investing activities		4,400
Cash Flows from Financing Activities		
Cash outflow to repay long-term debt (7)	(800)	
Cash outflow to pay dividends (8)	(1,600)	
Net cash outflow from financing activities		(2,400)
Net Increase in Cash		45,600
Plus: Beginning cash balance		2,800
Ending cash balance		$48,400
Schedule of Noncash Investing and Financing Activities		
Issue of common stock for land (9)		$ 9,400

(1) Add decreases and subtract increases in current asset account balances to net income.

(2) Add increases and subtract decreases in current liability account balances to net income.

(3) Add noncash expenses (depreciation) to net income.

(4) Add losses on the sale of noncurrent assets to net income and subtract gains on the sale of long-term assets from net income.

(5) Information regarding the Equipment account is summarized in the following table.

Equipment Account Information	
Beginning balance in equipment	$22,000
Purchases of equipment (cash outflows)	?
Sales of equipment (cash inflows)	(11,000)
Ending balance in equipment	$18,000

To balance the account, equipments costing $7,000 must have been purchased. In the absence of information to the contrary, we assume cash was used to make the purchase.

Note 1 to the financial statement shows that equipment sold had a book value of $6,000 ($11,000 cost − $5,000 accumulated depreciation). The amount of the cash inflow from this sale is computed as follows:

$$\text{Cash inflow} = \text{book value} + \text{gain} = \$6,000 + \$2,900 = \$8,900$$

(6) The information regarding the Land account is as follows:

Land Account Information	
Beginning balance in land	$10,400
Purchases of land (issue of common stock)	9,400
Sales of land (cash inflows)	?
Ending balance in land	$17,200

Note 2 indicates that land valued at $9,400 was acquired by issuing common stock. Since there was no cash flow associated with this purchase, the event is shown in the *noncash investing and financing activities* section of the statement of cash flows.

To balance the account, the cost (book value) of land sold had to be $2,600. Since the income statement shows a $100 loss on the sale of land, the cash collected from the sale is computed as follows:

$$\text{Cash inflow} = \text{book value} - \text{less} = \$2,600 - \$100 = \$2,500$$

(7) The information regarding the Long-term Debt account is as follows:

Long-term Debt Information	
Beginning balance in long-term debt	$6,400
Issue of long-term debt instruments (cash inflow)	0
Payment of long-term debt (cash outflow)	?
Ending balance in long-term debt	$5,600

There is no information in the financial statements that suggest that long-term debt was issued. Therefore, to balance the account, $800 of long-term debt had to be paid off, thereby resulting in a cash outflow.

(8) The information regarding the Retained Earnings account is as follows:

Retained Earnings Information	
Beginning balance in retained earnings	$ 4,400
Net income	44,750
Dividends (cash outflow)	?
Ending balance in retained earnings	$47,550

To balance the account, $1,600 of dividends had to be paid, thereby resulting in a cash outflow.

(9) Note 2 states that common stock was issue to acquire land valued at $9,400. This is a noncash investing and financing activity.

KEY TERMS

QUESTIONS

1. What is the purpose of the statement of cash flows?

2. What are the three categories of cash flows reported on the cash flow statement?

Discuss each and give an example of an inflow and an outflow for each category.

3. What are noncash investing and financing activities? Provide an example. How are such transactions shown on the statement of cash flows?

4. Albring Company had a beginning balance in accounts receivable of $12,000 and an ending balance of $14,000. Net income amounted to $110,000. Based on this information alone, determine the amount of net cash flow from operating activities.

5. Forsyth Company had a beginning balance in utilities payable of $3,300 and an ending balance of $5,200. Net income amounted to $87,000. Based on this information alone, determine the amount of net cash flow from operating activities.

6. Clover Company had a beginning balance in unearned revenue of $4,300 and an ending balance of $3,200. Net income amounted to $54,000. Based on this information alone, determine the amount of net cash flow from operating activities.

7. Which of the following activities are financing activities?

   (a) Payment of accounts payable.

   (b) Payment of interest on bonds payable.

   (c) Sale of common stock.

   (d) Sale of preferred stock at a premium.

   (e) Payment of a cash dividend.

8. Does depreciation expense affect net cash flow? Explain.

9. If Best Company sold land that cost $4,200 at a $500 gain, how much cash did it collect from the sale of land?

10. If Best Company sold office equipment that originally cost $7,500 and had $7,200 of accumulated depreciation at a $100 loss, what was the selling price for the office equipment?

11. In which section of the statement of cash flows would the following transactions be reported?

(a) The amount of the change in the balance of accounts receivable.

(b) Cash purchase of investment securities.

(c) Cash purchase of equipment.

(d) Cash sale of merchandise.

(e) Cash sale of common stock.

(f) The amount of net income.

(g) Cash proceeds from loan.

(h) Cash payment on bonds payable.

(i) Cash receipt from sale of old equipment.

(j) The amount of the change in the balance of accounts payable.

12. What is the difference between preparing the statement of cash flows using the direct method and using the indirect method?

13. Which method (direct or indirect) of presenting the statement of cash flows is more intuitively logical? Why?

14. What is the major advantage of using the indirect method to present the statement of cash flows?

15. What is the advantage of using the direct method to present the statement of cash flows?

16. How would Best Company report the following transactions on the statement of cash flows?

   (a) Purchased new equipment for $46,000 cash.

   (b) Sold old equipment for $8,700 cash. The equipment had a book value of $4,900.

17. Can a company report negative net cash flows from operating activities for the year on the statement of cash flows but still have positive net income on the income statement? Explain.

MULTIPLE-CHOICE QUESTIONS

Multiple-choice questions are provided on the text website at www.mhhe.com/edmonds7e.

Quiz 12

EXERCISES—SERIES A

All applicable Exercises in Series A are available with McGraw-Hill's *Connect Accounting*.

connect

|ACCOUNTING

Exercise 12-1A *Use the indirect method to determine cash flows from operating activities*

LO 1

An accountant for Golden Enterprise Companies (GEC) computed the following information by making comparisons between GEC's 2011 and 2012 balance sheets. Further information was determined by examining the company's 2011 income statement.

1. The amount of an increase in the balance of the Accounts Receivable account.
2. The amount of a loss arising from the sale of land.
3. The amount of an increase in the balance of the other Operating Expenses Payable account.
4. The amount of a decrease in the balance of the Bonds Payable account.
5. The amount of depreciation expense shown on the income statement.
6. The amount of cash dividends paid to the stockholders.
7. The amount of a decrease in the balance of an Unearned Revenue account.
8. The amount of an increase in the balance of an Inventory account.
9. The amount of an increase in the balance of a Land account.
10. The amount of a decrease in the balance of a Prepaid Rent account.
11. The amount of an increase in the balance of a Treasury Stock account.

Required

For each item described above indicate whether the amount should be added to or subtracted from the amount of net income when determining the amount of net cash flow from operating activities. If an item does not affect net cash flow from operating activities, identify it as being not affected.

LO 1

Exercise 12-2A   *Use the indirect method to determine cash flows from operating activities*

Mendez Incorporated presents its statement of cash flows using the indirect method. The following accounts and corresponding balances were drawn from the company's 2012 and 2011 year-end balance sheets.

Account Title	2012	2011
Accounts receivable	$15,200	$16,500
Accounts payable	8,800	9,200

The 2012 income statement showed net income of $27,200.

Required

a. Prepare the operating activities section of the statement of cash flows.
b. Explain why the change in the balance in accounts receivable was added to or subtracted from the amount of net income when you completed Requirement *a*.
c. Explain why the change in the balance in accounts payable was added to or subtracted from the amount of net income when you completed Requirement *a*.

LO 1

Exercise 12-3A   *Use the indirect method to determine cash flows from operating activities*

Chang Company presents its statement of cash flows using the indirect method. The following accounts and corresponding balances were drawn from Chang's 2012 and 2011 year-end balance sheets.

Account Title	2012	2011
Accounts receivable	$28,000	$32,000
Prepaid rent	1,800	1,500
Interest receivable	700	500
Accounts payable	8,500	9,800
Salaries payable	3,600	3,200
Unearned revenue	4,000	6,000

The income statement contained a $1,200 gain on the sale of equipment, a $900 loss on the sale of land, and $2,500 of depreciation expense. Net income for the period was $52,000.

Required

Prepare the operating activities section of the statement of cash flows.

Exercise 12-4A *Use the direct method to determine cash flows from operating activities*

LO 2

The following accounts and corresponding balances were drawn from Widjaja Company's 2012 and 2011 year-end balance sheets.

Account Title	2012	2011
Unearned revenue	$6,500	$5,000
Prepaid rent	1,800	2,400

During the year, $68,000 of unearned revenue was recognized as having been earned. Rent expense for 2012 was $15,000.

Required

Based on this information alone, prepare the operating activities section of the statement of cash flows assuming the direct approach is used.

Exercise 12-5A *Use the direct method to determine cash flows from operating activities*

LO 2

The following accounts and corresponding balances were drawn from Berry Company's 2012 and 2011 year-end balance sheets.

Account Title	2012	2011
Accounts receivable	$46,000	$42,000
Interest receivable	5,000	6,000
Other operating expenses payable	27,000	22,000
Salaries payable	12,000	15,000

The 2012 income statement is shown below:

Income Statement	
Sales	$680,000
Salary expense	(172,000)
Other operating expenses	(270,000)
Operating income	238,000
Nonoperating items: Interest revenue	24,000
Net income	$262,000

Required

a. Use the direct method to compute the amount of cash inflows from operating activities.
b. Use the direct method to compute the amount of cash outflows from operating activities.

Exercise 12-6A *Direct versus indirect method of determining cash flows from operating activities*

LO 1, 2

Master Mechanics, Inc. (MMI), recognized $1,200 of sales revenue on account and collected $1,100 of cash from accounts receivable. Further, MMI recognized $700 of operating expenses on account and paid $500 cash as partial settlement of accounts payable.

Required

Based on this information alone:

a. Prepare the operating activities section of the statement of cash flows under the direct method.
b. Prepare the operating activities section of the statement of cash flows under the indirect method.

LO 1, 2

Exercise 12-7A *The direct versus the indirect method of determining cash flows from operating activities*

The following accounts and corresponding balances were drawn from Larry Company's 2012 and 2011 year-end balance sheets.

Account Title	2012	2011
Accounts receivable	$78,000	$75,000
Prepaid rent	800	900
Utilities payable	1,500	1,200
Other operating expenses payable	34,000	33,000

The 2012 income statement is shown below:

Income Statement	
Sales	$272,000
Rent expense	(24,000)
Utilities expense	(36,400)
Other operating expenses	(168,000)
Net Income	$ 43,600

Required

a. Prepare the operating activities section of the statement of cash flows using the direct method.

b. Prepare the operating activities section of the statement of cash flows using the indirect method.

LO 3

Exercise 12-8A *Determining cash flow from investing activities*

On January 1, 2011, Webber Company had a balance of $278,000 in its Land account. During 2011, Webber sold land that had cost $94,000 for $120,000 cash. The balance in the Land account on December 31, 2011, was $300,000.

Required

a. Determine the cash outflow for the purchase of land during 2011.

b. Prepare the investing activities section of the 2011 statement of cash flows.

LO 3

Exercise 12-9A *Determining cash flows from investing activities*

On January 1, 2011, Duncan Company had a balance of $59,600 in its Delivery Equipment account. During 2011, Duncan purchased delivery equipment that cost $18,500. The balance in the Delivery Equipment account on December 31, 2011, was $60,000. The 2011 income statement reported a gain from the sale of equipment for $3,000. On the date of sale, accumulated depreciation on the equipment sold amounted to $10,000.

Required

a. Determine the cost of the equipment that was sold during 2011.

b. Determine the amount of cash flow from the sale of delivery equipment that should be shown in the investing activities section of the 2011 statement of cash flows.

LO 3

Exercise 12-10A *Determining cash flows from investing activities*

The following accounts and corresponding balances were drawn from Winston Company's 2012 and 2011 year-end balance sheets.

Account Title	2012	2011
Investment securities	$102,000	$112,000
Machinery	520,000	425,000
Land	140,000	90,000

Other information drawn from the accounting records:

1. Winston incurred a $2,000 loss on the sale of investment securities during 2012.
2. Old machinery with a book value of $5,000 (cost of $25,000 minus accumulated depreciation of $20,000) was sold. The income statement showed a gain on the sale of machinery of $4,000.
3. Winston did not sell land during the year.

Required

a. Compute the amount of cash flow associated with the sale of investment securities.
b. Compute the amount of cash flow associated with the purchase of machinery.
c. Compute the amount of cash flow associated with the sale of machinery.
d. Compute the amount of cash flow associated with the purchase of land.
e. Prepare the investing activities section of the statement of cash flows.

Exercise 12-11A   *Determining cash flows from financing activities*   LO 4

On January 1, 2011, BGA Company had a balance of $500,000 in its Bonds Payable account. During 2011, BGA issued bonds with a $150,000 face value. There was no premium or discount associated with the bond issue. The balance in the Bonds Payable account on December 31, 2011, was $300,000.

Required

a. Determine the cash outflow for the repayment of bond liabilities assuming that the bonds were retired at face value.
b. Prepare the financing activities section of the 2011 statement of cash flows.

Exercise 12-12A   *Determining cash flows from financing activities*   LO 4

On January 1, 2011, Parker Company had a balance of $120,000 in its Common Stock account. During 2011, Parker paid $18,000 to purchase treasury stock. Treasury stock is accounted for using the cost method. The balance in the Common Stock account on December 31, 2011, was $130,000. Assume that the common stock is no par stock.

Required

a. Determine the cash inflow from the issue of common stock.
b. Prepare the financing activities section of the 2011 statement of cash flows.

Exercise 12-13A   *Determining cash flows from financing activities*   LO 4

The following accounts and corresponding balances were drawn from Berry Company's 2012 and 2011 year-end balance sheets.

Account Title	2012	2011
Bonds payable	$210,000	$300,000
Common stock	370,000	275,000

Other information drawn from the accounting records:

1. Dividends paid during the period amounted to $30,000.
2. There were no bond liabilities issued during the period.

Required

a. Compute the amount of cash flow associated with the repayment of bond liabilities.
b. Compute the amount of cash flow associated with the issue of common stock.
c. Prepare the financing activities section of the statement of cash flows.

PROBLEMS—SERIES A

LO 1, 2

CHECK FIGURE
Net cash flow from operating
activities: $28,700

All applicable Problems in Series A are available with McGraw-Hill's
Connect Accounting.

Problem 12-14A   *The direct versus the indirect method to determine cash flow from*
operating activities

Top Brands, Inc. (TBI), presents its statement of cash flows using the indirect method. The
following accounts and corresponding balances were drawn from TBI's 2012 and 2011 year-end
balance sheets.

Account Title	2012	2011
Accounts receivable	$24,000	$26,000
Merchandise inventory	56,000	52,000
Prepaid insurance	19,000	24,000
Accounts payable	23,000	20,000
Salaries payable	4,600	4,200
Unearned service revenue	1,000	2,700

The 2012 income statement is shown below:

Income Statement	
Sales	$ 603,000
Cost of goods sold	(383,000)
Gross margin	220,000
Service revenue	4,000
Insurance expense	(40,000)
Salaries expense	(160,000)
Depreciation expense	(6,000)
Operating income	18,000
Gain on sale of equipment	3,000
Net income	$ 21,000

Required

a. Prepare the operating activities section of the statement of cash flows using the direct
method.

b. Prepare the operating activities section of the statement of cash flows using the indirect
method.

LO 3

CHECK FIGURES
b. $5,000
c. $35,000

Problem 12-15A   *Determining cash flows from investing activities*

The following information was drawn from the year-end balance sheets of Desoto Company:

Account Title	2012	2011
Investment securities	$ 33,500	$ 30,000
Equipment	235,000	220,000
Buildings	845,000	962,000
Land	80,000	69,000

Additional information regarding transactions occurring during 2012:

1. Investment securities that had cost $5,600 were sold. The 2012 income statement contained a
loss on the sale of investment securities of $600.

2. Equipment with a cost of $50,000 was purchased.

3. The income statement showed a gain on the sale of equipment of $6,000. On the date of sale, accumulated depreciation on the equipment sold amounted to $8,000.
4. A building that had originally cost $158,000 was demolished.
5. Land that had cost $25,000 was sold for $22,000.

Required

a. Determine the amount of cash flow for the purchase of investment securities during 2012.
b. Determine the amount of cash flow from the sale of investment securities during 2012.
c. Determine the cost of the equipment that was sold during 2012.
d. Determine the amount of cash flow from the sale of equipment during 2012.
e. Determine the amount of cash flow for the purchase of buildings during 2012.
f. Determine the amount of cash flow for the purchase of land during 2012.
g. Prepare the investing activities section of the 2012 statement of cash flows.

Problem 12-16A *Determining cash flows from financing activities*

LO 4

The following information was drawn from the year-end balance sheets of Pet Doors, Inc.:

Account Title	2012	2011
Bonds payable	$800,000	$900,000
Common stock	197,000	140,000
Treasury stock	25,000	10,000
Retained earnings	80,000	69,000

Additional information regarding transactions occurring during 2012:

1. Pet Doors, Inc., issued $50,000 of bonds during 2012. The bonds were issued at face value. All bonds retired were retired at face value.
2. Common stock did not have a par value.
3. Pet Doors, Inc., uses the cost method to account for treasury stock.
4. The amount of net income shown on the 2012 income statement was $27,000.

Required

a. Determine the amount of cash flow for the retirement of bonds that should appear on the 2012 statement of cash flows.
b. Determine the amount of cash flow from the issue of common stock that should appear on the 2012 statement of cash flows.
c. Determine the amount of cash flow for the purchase of treasury stock that should appear on the 2012 statement of cash flows.
d. Determine the amount of cash flow for the payment of dividends that should appear on the 2012 statement of cash flows.
e. Prepare the financing activities section of the 2012 statement of cash flows.

Problem 12-17A *Preparing a statement of cash flows*

LO 1, 3, 4

The following information can be obtained by examining a company's balance sheet and income statement information.

a. Decreases in noncash current asset account balances.
b. Cash outflows to repay long-term debt.
c. Increases in noncash current asset account balances.
d. Cash outflows made to purchase long-term assets.
e. Decreases in current liability account balances.
f. Noncash expenses (depreciation).
g. Cash outflows to purchase treasury stock.
h. Gains recognized on the sale of long-term assets.

 i. Cash outflows to pay dividends.

 j. Cash inflows from the issue of common stock.

 k. Cash inflows from the sale of long-term assets.

 l. Increases in current liability account balances.

 m. Cash inflows from the issue of long-term debt.

 n. Losses incurred from the sale of long-term assets.

Required

Construct a table like the one shown below. For each item, indicate whether it would be used in the computation of net cash flows from operating, investing, or financing activities. Also, indicate whether the item would be added or subtracted when determining the net cash flow from operating, investing, or financing activities. Assume the indirect method is used to prepare the operating activities section of the statement of cash flows. The first item has been completed as an example.

Item	Type of Activity	Add or Subtract
a.	Operating	Add
b.		
c.		
d.		
e.		
f.		
g.		
h.		
i.		
j.		
k.		
l.		
m.		
n.		

LO 1, 3, 4

Problem 12-18A   *Using financial statements to prepare a statements of cash flows— Indirect method*

The comparative balance sheets and income statements for Pacific Company follow.

Balance Sheets As of December 31		
	2012	2011
Assets		
Cash	$24,200	$ 2,800
Accounts receivable	2,000	1,200
Inventory	6,400	6,000
Equipment	19,000	42,000
Accumulated depreciation—equipment	(9,000)	(17,400)
Land	18,400	10,400
Total assets	$61,000	$45,000
Liabilities and equity		
Accounts payable (inventory)	$ 2,600	$ 4,200
Long-term debt	2,800	6,400
Common stock	22,000	10,000
Retained earnings	33,600	24,400
Total liabilities and equity	$61,000	$45,000

Income Statement For the Year Ended December 31, 2012	
Sales revenue	$35,700
Cost of goods sold	(14,150)
Gross margin	21,550
Depreciation expense	(3,600)
Operating income	17,950
Gain on sale of equipment	500
Loss on disposal of land	(50)
Net income	$18,400

Additional Data

1. During 2012, the company sold equipment for $18,500; it had originally cost $30,000. Accumulated depreciation on this equipment was $12,000 at the time of the sale. Also, the company purchased equipment for $7,000 cash.
2. The company sold land that had cost $4,000. This land was sold for $3,950, resulting in the recognition of a $50 loss. Also, common stock was issued in exchange for title to land that was valued at $12,000 at the time of exchange.
3. Paid dividends of $9,200.

Required

Prepare a statement of cash flows using the indirect method.

Problem 12-19A   *Using financial statements to prepare a statement of cash flows—*
                        Indirect method

The comparative balance sheets and an income statement for Redwood Corporation follow.

LO 1, 3, 4

Balance Sheets As of December 31		
	2012	2011
Assets		
Cash	$ 68,800	$ 40,600
Accounts receivable	30,000	22,000
Merchandise inventory	160,000	176,000
Prepaid rent	2,400	4,800
Equipment	256,000	288,000
Accumulated depreciation	(146,800)	(236,000)
Land	192,000	80,000
Total assets	$562,400	$375,400
Liabilities		
Accounts payable (inventory)	$ 67,000	$ 76,000
Salaries payable	28,000	24,000
Stockholders' equity		
Common stock, $25 par value	250,000	200,000
Retained earnings	217,400	75,400
Total liabilities and stockholders' equity	$562,400	$375,400

	Income Statement For the Year Ended December 31, 2012
Sales	$1,500,000
Cost of goods sold	(797,200)
Gross profit	702,800
Operating expenses	
Depreciation expense	(22,800)
Rent expense	(24,000)
Salaries expense	(256,000)
Other operating expenses	(258,000)
Net income	$ 142,000

Other Information

1. Purchased land for $112,000.
2. Purchased new equipment for $100,000.
3. Sold old equipment that cost $132,000 with accumulated depreciation of $112,000 for $20,000 cash.
4. Issued common stock for $50,000.

Required

Prepare the statement of cash flows for 2012 using the indirect method.

LO 2, 3, 4

CHECK FIGURE
Net Cash Flow from Operating
Activities: $(110,775)

Problem 12-20A *Using transaction data to prepare a statement of cash flows— Direct method*

Store Company engaged in the following transactions during the 2011 accounting period. The beginning cash balance was $28,600 and ending cash balance was $6,025.

1. Sales on account were $250,000. The beginning receivables balance was $87,000 and the ending balance was $83,000.
2. Salaries expense for the period was $56,000. The beginning salaries payable balance was $3,500 and the ending balance was $2,000.
3. Other operating expenses for the period were $125,000. The beginning other operating expenses payable balance was $4,500 and the ending balance was $8,500.
4. Recorded $19,500 of depreciation expense. The beginning and ending balances in the Accumulated Depreciation account were $14,000 and $33,500, respectively.
5. The Equipment account had beginning and ending balances of $210,000 and $240,000 respectively. There were no sales of equipment during the period.
6. The beginning and ending balances in the Notes Payable account were $50,000 and $150,000, respectively. There were no payoffs of notes during the period.
7. There was $6,000 of interest expense reported on the income statement. The beginning and ending balances in the Interest Payable account were $1,500 and $1,000, respectively.
8. The beginning and ending Merchandise Inventory account balances were $90,000 and $108,000, respectively. The company sold merchandise with a cost of $156,000 (cost of goods sold for the period was $156,000). The beginning and ending balances of Accounts Payable were $9,500 and $11,500, respectively.
9. The beginning and ending balances of Notes Receivable were $5,000 and $10,000, respectively. Notes receivable result from long-term loans made to employees. There were no collections from employees during the period.
10. The beginning and ending balances of the Common Stock account were $100,000 and $120,000, respectively. The increase was caused by the issue of common stock for cash.
11. Land had beginning and ending balances of $50,000 and $41,000, respectively. Land that cost $9,000 was sold for $12,200, resulting in a gain of $3,200.

12. The tax expense for the period was $7,700. The Taxes Payable account had a $950 beginning balance and an $875 ending balance.

13. The Investments account had beginning and ending balances of $25,000 and $29,000, respectively. The company purchased investments for $18,000 cash during the period, and investments that cost $14,000 were sold for $9,000, resulting in a $5,000 loss.

Required

a. Determine the amount of cash flow for each item and indicate whether the item should appear in the operating, investing, or financing activities section of a statement of cash flows. If an item does not affect the cash flow statement, make a statement indicating that the cash statement will not be affected. Assume Store Company uses the direct method for showing net cash flow from operating activities.

b. Prepare a statement of cash flows based on the information you developed in Requirement *a*.

Problem 12-21A *Using financial statements to prepare a statement of cash flows—Direct method*

LO 2, 3, 4

The following financial statements were drawn from the records of Raceway Sports:

CHECK FIGURES
Net Cash Flow from Operating Activities: $86,800
Net Increase in Cash: $95,400

Balance Sheets As of December 31		
	2012	2011
Assets		
Cash	$123,600	$ 28,200
Accounts receivable	57,000	66,000
Inventory	126,000	114,000
Notes receivable (long-term)	0	30,000
Equipment	147,000	255,000
Accumulated depreciation-equipment	(74,740)	(141,000)
Land	82,500	52,500
Total assets	$461,360	$404,700
Liabilities and equity		
Accounts payable (inventory)	$ 42,000	$ 48,600
Salaries payable	30,000	24,000
Utilities payable	600	1,200
Interest payable	0	1,800
Notes payable (long-term)	0	60,000
Common stock	300,000	240,000
Retained earnings	88,760	29,100
Total liabilities and equity	$461,360	$404,700

Income Statement For the Year Ended December 31, 2012	
Sales revenue	$580,000
Cost of goods sold	(288,000)
Gross margin	292,000
Operating expenses	
Salary expense	(184,000)
Depreciation expense	(17,740)
Utilities expense	(12,200)
Operating income	78,060
Nonoperating items	
Interest expense	(3,000)
Loss on the sale of equipment	(1,800)
Net income	$ 73,260

Additional Information

1. Sold equipment costing $108,000 with accumulated depreciation of $84,000 for $22,200 cash.
2. Paid a $13,600 cash dividend to owners.

Required

Analyze the data and prepare a statement of cash flows using the direct method.

EXERCISES—SERIES B

LO 1

Exercise 12-1B   *Use the indirect method to determine cash flows from operating activities*

An accountant for Farve Enterprise Companies (FEC) computed the following information by making comparisons between FEC's 2012 and 2011 balance sheets. Further information was determined by examining the company's 2012 income statement.

1. The amount of cash dividends paid to the stockholders.
2. The amount of an increase in the balance of an Unearned Revenue account.
3. The amount of a decrease in the balance of an Inventory account.
4. The amount of a decrease in the balance of a Land account.
5. The amount of an increase in the balance of a Prepaid Rent account.
6. The amount of an increase in the balance of a Treasury Stock account.
7. The amount of a decrease in the balance of the Accounts Receivable account.
8. The amount of a gain arising from the sale of land.
9. The amount of an increase in the balance of the Salaries Payable account.
10. The amount of an increase in the balance of the Bonds Payable account.
11. The amount of depreciation expense shown on the income statement.

Required

For each item described above, indicate whether the amount should be added to or subtracted from the amount of net income when determining the amount of net cash flow from operating activities using the indirect method. If an item does not affect net cash flow from operating activities, identify it as being not affected.

LO 1

Exercise 12-2B   *Use the indirect method to determine cash flows from operating activities*

Haughton Incorporated presents its statement of cash flows using the indirect method. The following accounts and corresponding balances were drawn from the company's 2012 and 2011 year-end balance sheets:

Account Title	2012	2011
Accounts receivable	$26,200	$21,400
Accounts payable	9,700	9,300

The 2012 income statement showed net income of $36,300.

Required

a. Prepare the operating activities section of the statement of cash flows.
b. Explain why the change in the balance in accounts receivable was added to or subtracted from the amount of net income when you completed Requirement *a*.
c. Explain why the change in the balance in accounts payable was added to or subtracted from the amount of net income when you completed Requirement *a*.

Exercise 12-3B *Use the indirect method to determine cash flows from operating activities*   LO 1

Hong Company presents its statement of cash flows using the indirect method. The following accounts and corresponding balances were drawn from Hong's 2012 and 2011 year-end balance sheets:

Account Title	2012	2011
Accounts receivable	$46,000	$38,000
Prepaid rent	2,400	2,800
Interest receivable	900	1,000
Accounts payable	10,500	9,000
Salaries payable	4,200	4,800
Unearned revenue	5,000	4,500

The income statement contained a $500 loss on the sale of equipment, a $700 gain on the sale of land, and $3,200 of depreciation expense. Net income for the period was $47,000.

Required

Prepare the operating activities section of the statement of cash flows.

Exercise 12-4B *Use the direct method to determine cash flows from operating activities*   LO 2

The following accounts and corresponding balances were drawn from Pizzazz Company's 2012 and 2011 year-end balance sheets:

Account Title	2012	2011
Unearned revenue	$5,000	$6,500
Prepaid rent	2,400	1,800

During the year, $72,000 of unearned revenue was recognized as having been earned. Rent expense for 2012 was $20,000.

Required

Based on this information alone, prepare the operating activities section of the statement of cash flows assuming the direct approach is used.

Exercise 12-5B *Use the direct method to determine cash flows from operating activities*   LO 2

The following accounts and corresponding balances were drawn from Hughes Company's 2012 and 2011 year-end balance sheets:

Account Title	2012	2011
Accounts receivable	$56,000	$41,000
Interest receivable	6,000	5,000
Other operating expenses payable	22,000	28,000
Salaries payable	15,000	13,000

The 2012 income statement is shown below:

Income Statement	
Sales	$725,000
Salary expense	(180,000)
Other operating expenses	(310,000)
Operating income	235,000
Nonoperating items: Interest revenue	18,000
Net income	$253,000

Required

a. Use the direct method to compute the amount of cash inflows from operating activities.

b. Use the direct method to compute the amount of cash outflows from operating activities.

LO 1, 2

Exercise 12-6B   *Direct versus indirect method of determining cash flows from operating activities*

Security Services, Inc. (SSI), recognized $2,400 of sales revenue on account and collected $1,900 of cash from accounts receivable. Further, SSI recognized $900 of operating expenses on account and paid $400 cash as partial settlement of accounts payable.

Required

Based on this information alone:

a. Prepare the operating activities section of the statement of cash flows under the direct method.

b. Prepare the operating activities section of the statement of cash flows under the indirect method.

LO 1, 2

Exercise 12-7B   *The direct versus the indirect method of determining cash flows from operating activities*

The following accounts and corresponding balances were drawn from Littlejohn Company's 2012 and 2011 year-end balance sheets:

Account Title	2012	2011
Accounts receivable	$89,000	$92,000
Prepaid rent	1,100	1,500
Utilities payable	2,100	2,600
Other operating expenses payable	42,000	49,000

The 2012 income statement is shown below:

Income Statement	
Sales	$312,000
Rent expense	(36,000)
Utilities expense	(41,900)
Other operating expenses	(189,000)
Net income	$ 45,100

Required

a. Prepare the operating activities section of the statement of cash flows using the direct method.

b. Prepare the operating activities section of the statement of cash flows using the indirect method.

LO 3

Exercise 12-8B   *Determining cash flow from investing activities*

On January 1, 2011, Oswalt Company had a balance of $156,000 in its Land account. During 2011, Oswalt sold land that had cost $66,000 for $98,000 cash. The balance in the Land account on December 31, 2011, was $220,000.

Required

a. Determine the cash outflow for the purchase of land during 2011.

b. Prepare the investing activities section of the 2011 statement of cash flows.

Exercise 12-9B   *Determining cash flow from investing activities*   LO 3

On January 1, 2011, Artex Company had a balance of $65,600 in its Office Equipment account. During 2011, Artex purchased office equipment that cost $21,600. The balance in the Office Equipment account on December 31, 2011, was $65,000. The 2011 income statement contained a gain from the sale of equipment for $5,000. On the date of sale, accumulated depreciation on the equipment sold amounted to $8,300.

Required

a. Determine the cost of the equipment that was sold during 2011.
b. Determine the amount of cash flow from the sale of office equipment that should be shown in the investing activities section of the 2011 statement of cash flows.

Exercise 12-10B   *Determining cash flows from investing activities*   LO 3

The following accounts and corresponding balances were drawn from Callon Company's 2012 and 2011 year-end balance sheets:

Account Title	2012	2011
Investment securities	$ 98,000	$106,000
Machinery	565,000	520,000
Land	90,000	140,000

Other information drawn from the accounting records:

1. Callon incurred a $4,000 loss on the sale of investment securities during 2012.
2. Old machinery with a book value of $7,000 (cost of $32,000 minus accumulated depreciation of $25,000) was sold. The income statement showed a gain on the sale of machinery of $5,500.
3. Callon incurred a loss of $2,500 on the sale of land in 2012.

Required

a. Compute the amount of cash flow associated with the sale of investment securities.
b. Compute the amount of cash flow associated with the purchase of machinery.
c. Compute the amount of cash flow associated with the sale of machinery.
d. Compute the amount of cash flow associated with the sale of land.
e. Prepare the investing activities section of the statement of cash flows.

Exercise 12-11B   *Determining cash flows from financing activities*   LO 4

On January 1, 2011, MMC Company had a balance of $700,000 in its Bonds Payable account. During 2011, MMC issued bonds with a $200,000 face value. There was no premium or discount associated with the bond issue. The balance in the Bonds Payable account on December 31, 2011, was $400,000.

Required

a. Determine the cash outflow for the repayment of bond liabilities assuming that the bonds were retired at face value.
b. Prepare the financing activities section of the 2011 statement of cash flows.

Exercise 12-12B   *Determining cash flows from financing activities*   LO 4

On January 1, 2011, Graves Company had a balance of $200,000 in its Common Stock account. During 2011, Graves paid $15,000 to purchase treasury stock. Treasury stock is accounted for using the cost method. The balance in the Common Stock account on December 31, 2011, was $240,000. Assume that the common stock is no par stock.

Required

a. Determine the cash inflow from the issue of common stock.
b. Prepare the financing activities section of the 2011 statement of cash flows.

LO 4

Exercise 12-13B   *Determining cash flows from financing activities*

The following accounts and corresponding balances were drawn from Poole Company's 2012 and 2011 year-end balance sheets:

Account Title	2012	2011
Bonds payable	$300,000	$210,000
Common stock	550,000	450,000

Other information drawn from the accounting records:

1. Dividends paid during the period amounted to $40,000.
2. There were no bond liabilities repaid during the period.

Required

a. Compute the amount of cash flow associated with the issue of bond liabilities.
b. Compute the amount of cash flow associated with the issue of common stock.
c. Prepare the financing activities section of the statement of cash flows.

PROBLEMS—SERIES B

LO 1, 2

Problem 12-14B   *The direct versus the indirect method to determine cash flows from operating activities*

The following accounts and corresponding balances were drawn from Bryan Sports, Inc.'s 2012 and 2011 year-end balance sheets:

Account Title	2012	2011
Accounts receivable	$36,000	$45,000
Merchandise inventory	65,000	62,000
Prepaid insurance	24,000	20,000
Accounts payable	20,000	25,000
Salaries payable	4,500	3,900
Unearned service revenue	9,500	8,600

The 2012 income statement is shown below:

Income Statement	
Sales	$651,500
Cost of goods sold	(402,000)
Gross margin	249,500
Service revenue	15,000
Insurance expense	(38,000)
Salaries expense	(175,000)
Depreciation expense	(8,000)
Operating income	43,500
Gain on sale of equipment	2,500
Net income	$ 46,000

Required

a. Prepare the operating activities section of the statement of cash flows using the direct method.
b. Prepare the operating activities section of the statement of cash flows using the indirect method.

Problem 12-15B   *Determining cash flows from investing activities*   LO 3

The following information was drawn from the year-end balance sheets of Madison Company:

Account Title	2012	2011
Investment securities	$ 46,500	$ 50,000
Equipment	275,000	260,000
Buildings	950,000	920,000
Land	110,000	90,000

Additional information regarding transactions occurring during 2012:

1. Investment securities that had cost $7,800 were sold. The 2012 income statement contained a loss on the sale of investment securities of $1,200.
2. Equipment with a cost of $75,000 was purchased.
3. The income statement showed a gain on the sale of equipment of $10,000. On the date of sale, accumulated depreciation on the equipment sold amounted to $52,000.
4. A building that had originally cost $70,000 was demolished.
5. Land that had cost $15,000 was sold for $20,000.

Required

a. Determine the amount of cash flow for the purchase of investment securities during 2012.
b. Determine the amount of cash flow from the sale of investment securities during 2012.
c. Determine the cost of the equipment that was sold during 2012.
d. Determine the amount of cash flow from the sale of equipment during 2012.
e. Determine the amount of cash flow for the purchase of buildings during 2012.
f. Determine the amount of cash flow for the purchase of land during 2012.
g. Prepare the investing activities section of the 2012 statement of cash flows.

Problem 12-16B   *Determining cash flows from financing activities*   LO 4

The following information was drawn from the year-end balance sheets of Sports Supply, Inc.:

Account Title	2012	2011
Bonds payable	$700,000	$800,000
Common stock	180,000	140,000
Treasury stock	40,000	25,000
Retained earnings	96,000	80,000

Additional information regarding transactions occurring during 2012:

1. Sports Supply, Inc., issued $70,000 of bonds during 2012. The bonds were issued at face value. All bonds retired were retired at face value.
2. Common stock did not have a par value.
3. Sports Supply, Inc., uses the cost method to account for treasury stock. Sports Supply, Inc., did not resell any treasury stock in 2012.
4. The amount of net income shown on the 2012 income statement was $36,000.

Required

a. Determine the amount of cash flow for the retirement of bonds that should appear on the 2012 statement of cash flows.
b. Determine the amount of cash flow from the issue of common stock that should appear on the 2012 statement of cash flows.

    c. Determine the amount of cash flow for the purchase of treasury stock that should appear on the 2012 statement of cash flows.

    d. Determine the amount of cash flow for the payment of dividends that should appear on the 2012 statement of cash flows.

    e. Prepare the financing activities section of the 2012 statement of cash flows.

LO 1, 3, 4

Problem 12-17B *Preparing a statement of cash flows*

The following information can be obtained by examining a company's balance sheet and income statement information.

    a. Gains recognized on the sale of noncurrent assets.

    b. Cash outflows to pay dividends.

    c. Cash inflows from the issue of common stock.

    d. Cash inflows from the sale of noncurrent assets.

    e. Increases in current liability account balances.

    f. Cash inflows from the issue of noncurrent debt.

    g. Losses incurred from the sale of noncurrent assets.

    h. Decreases in noncash current asset account balances.

    i. Cash outflows to repay noncurrent debt.

    j. Increases in noncash current asset account balances.

    k. Cash outflows made to purchase noncurrent assets.

    l. Decreases in current liability account balances.

    m. Noncash expenses (e.g., depreciation).

    n. Cash outflows to purchase treasury stock.

Required

Construct a table like the one shown below. For each item, indicate whether it would be used in the computation of net cash flows from operating, investing, or financing activities. Also, indicate whether the item would be added or subtracted when determining the net cash flow from operating, investing, or financing activities. Assume the indirect method is used to prepare the operating activities section of the statement of cash flows. The first item has been completed as an example.

Item	Type of Activity	Add or Subtract
a.	Operating	Subtract
b.		
c.		
d.		
e.		
f.		
g.		
h.		
i.		
j.		
k.		
l.		
m.		
n.		

Problem 12-18B   *Using financial statements to prepare a statement of cash flows—*   LO 1, 3, 4
Indirect method

The following financial statements were drawn from the records of Healthy Products Co.

Balance Sheets As of December 31		
	2012	2011
Assets		
Cash	$16,120	$ 1,940
Accounts receivable	2,400	2,000
Inventory	2,000	2,600
Equipment	13,700	17,100
Accumulated depreciation—equipment	(11,300)	(12,950)
Land	13,000	8,000
Total assets	$35,920	$18,690
Liabilities and stockholders' equity		
Accounts payable (inventory)	$ 3,600	$ 2,400
Long-term debt	3,200	4,000
Common stock	17,000	10,000
Retained earnings	12,120	2,290
Total liabilities and stockholders' equity	$35,920	$18,690

Income Statement For the Year Ended December 31, 2012	
Sales revenue	$17,480
Cost of goods sold	(6,200)
Gross margin	11,280
Depreciation expense	(1,750)
Operating income	9,530
Gain on sale of equipment	1,800
Loss on disposal of land	(600)
Net income	$10,730

Additional Data

1. During 2012, the company sold equipment for $6,800; it had originally cost $8,400. Accumulated depreciation on this equipment was $3,400 at the time of the sale. Also, the company purchased equipment for $5,000 cash.

2. The company sold land that had cost $2,000. This land was sold for $1,400, resulting in the recognition of a $600 loss. Also, common stock was issued in exchange for title to land that was valued at $7,000 at the time of exchange.

3. Paid dividends of $900.

Required

Prepare a statement of cash flows using the indirect method.

Problem 12-19B   *Using financial statements to prepare a statement of cash flows—*   LO 1, 3, 4
Indirect method

The comparative balance sheets and an income statement for Lind Beauty Products, Inc., shown on the next page.

Balance Sheets As of December 31		
	2012	**2011**
Assets		
Cash	$ 6,300	$ 48,400
Accounts receivable	10,200	7,260
Merchandise inventory	45,200	56,000
Prepaid rent	700	2,140
Equipment	140,000	144,000
Accumulated depreciation	(73,400)	(118,000)
Land	116,000	50,000
Total assets	$245,000	$189,800
Liabilities and equity		
Accounts payable (inventory)	$ 37,200	$ 40,000
Salaries payable	12,200	10,600
Stockholders' equity		
Common stock, $50 par value	150,000	120,000
Retained earnings	45,600	19,200
Total liabilities and equity	$245,000	$189,800

Income Statement For the Year Ended December 31, 2012	
Sales	$480,000
Cost of goods sold	(264,000)
Gross profit	216,000
Operating expenses	
Depreciation expense	(11,400)
Rent expense	(7,000)
Salaries expense	(95,200)
Other operating expenses	(76,000)
Net income	$ 26,400

Other Information

1. Purchased land for $66,000.
2. Purchased new equipment for $62,000.
3. Sold old equipment that cost $66,000 with accumulated depreciation of $56,000 for $10,000 cash.
4. Issued common stock for $30,000.

Required

Prepare the statement of cash flows for 2012 using the indirect method.

LO 2, 3, 4   **Problem 12-20B**   *Using transaction data to prepare a statement of cash flows— Direct method*

Greenstein Company engaged in the following transactions during 2012. The beginning cash balance was $86,000 and ending cash balance was $123,100.

1. Sales on account were $548,000. The beginning receivables balance was $128,000 and the ending balance was $90,000.
2. Salaries expense was $232,000. The beginning salaries payable balance was $16,000 and the ending balance was $8,000.
3. Other operating expenses were $236,000. The beginning other Operating Expenses Payable balance was $16,000 and the ending balance was $10,000.
4. Recorded $30,000 of depreciation expense. The beginning and ending balances in the Accumulated Depreciation account were $12,000 and $42,000, respectively.

5. The Equipment account had beginning and ending balances of $44,000 and $56,000, respectively. There were no sales of equipment during the period.

6. The beginning and ending balances in the Notes Payable account were $44,000 and $36,000, respectively. There were no notes payable issued during the period.

7. There was $4,600 of interest expense reported on the income statement. The beginning and ending balances in the Interest Payable account were $8,400 and $7,500, respectively.

8. The beginning and ending Merchandise Inventory account balances were $22,000 and $29,400, respectively. The company sold merchandise with a cost of $83,600. The beginning and ending balances of Accounts Payable were $8,000 and $6,400, respectively.

9. The beginning and ending balances of Notes Receivable were $100,000 and $60,000, respectively. Notes receivable result from long-term loans made to creditors. There were no loans made to creditors during the period.

10. The beginning and ending balances of the Common Stock account were $120,000 and $160,000, respectively. The increase was caused by the issue of common stock for cash.

11. Land had beginning and ending balances of $24,000 and $14,000, respectively. Land that cost $10,000 was sold for $6,000, resulting in a loss of $4,000.

12. The tax expense for the period was $6,600. The Tax Payable account had a $2,400 beginning balance and a $2,200 ending balance.

13. The Investments account had beginning and ending balances of $20,000 and $60,000, respectively. The company purchased investments for $50,000 cash during the period, and investments that cost $10,000 were sold for $22,000, resulting in a $12,000 gain.

Required

a. Determine the amount of cash flow for each item and indicate whether the item should appear in the operating, investing, or financing activities section of a statement of cash flows. If an item does not affect the cash flow statement, make a statement indicating that the cash flow statement will not be affected. Assume Greenstein Company uses the direct method for showing net cash flow from operating activities.

b. Prepare a statement of cash flows based on the information you developed in Requirement *a*.

Problem 12-21B *Using financial statements to prepare a statement of cash flows—Direct method*   LO 2, 3, 4

The following financial statements were drawn from the records of Norton Materials, Inc.

Balance Sheets As of December 31		
	2012	2011
Assets		
Cash	$ 94,300	$ 14,100
Accounts receivable	36,000	40,000
Inventory	72,000	64,000
Notes receivable (long-term)	0	16,000
Equipment	98,000	170,000
Accumulated depreciation—equipment	(47,800)	(94,000)
Land	46,000	30,000
Total assets	$298,500	$240,100
Liabilities and equity		
Accounts payable	$ 24,000	$ 26,400
Salaries payable	15,000	10,000
Utilities payable	800	1,400
Interest payable	0	1,000
Notes payable (long-term)	0	24,000
Common stock	150,000	110,000
Retained earnings	108,700	67,300
Total liabilities and equity	$298,500	$240,100

Income Statement For the Year Ended December 31, 2012	
Sales revenue	$300,000
Cost of goods sold	(144,000)
Gross margin	156,000
Operating expenses	
Salary expense	(88,000)
Depreciation expense	(9,800)
Utilities expense	(6,400)
Operating income	51,800
Nonoperating items	
Interest expense	(2,400)
Loss on sale of equipment	(800)
Net income	$ 48,600

Additional Information

1. Sold equipment costing $72,000 with accumulated depreciation of $56,000 for $15,200 cash.
2. Paid a $7,200 cash dividend to owners.

Required

Analyze the data and prepare a statement of cash flows using the direct method.

ANALYZE, THINK, COMMUNICATE

ATC 12-1   Business Applications Case   *Understanding real-world annual reports*

Required

Use the Target Corporation's annual report in Appendix B to answer the following questions.

a. For the 2008 fiscal year, which was larger, Target's *net income* or its *cash flow from operating activities*? By what amount did they differ?

b. What two items are most responsible for the difference between Target's *net income* and its *cash flow from operating activities* in 2008?

c. In 2008 Target generated approximately $4.4 billion of cash from operating activities, and its cash balance decreased by about $1.6 billion. How did the company use this $6 billion of cash?

ATC 12-2   Real-World Case   *Following the cash*

Vonage Holding Corporation provides telecommunication services using voice over internet technology. It began operations in 2002 and has never made a profit. By the end of 2008 it had cumulative losses of $1 billion. Vonage's statements of cash flows for 2006, 2007, and 2008 follow.

VONAGE HOLDINGS CORP. Statements of Cash Flows (amounts in thousands)			
	For the Years Ended		
	2008	**2007**	**2006**
Cash Flows from Operating Activities			
Net income (loss)	$ (64,576)	$(267,428)	$(338,573)
Depreciation and amortization and impairment charges	45,796	33,574	22,709
Amortization of intangibles	2,816	2,144	968
			continued

	For the Years Ended		
	2008	2007	2006
Loss on early extinguishment of notes	30,570	—	—
Beneficial conversion on interest in kind on convertible notes	108	42	32
Amortization of discount on debt	882	—	—
Accrued interest	3,014	846	4,002
Allowance for doubtful accounts	207	1,852	266
Allowance for obsolete inventory	1,519	2,799	1,441
Amortization of deferred financing costs	—	4,689	1,999
Amortization of debt-related costs	3,237	—	—
Loss (gain) on disposal of fixed assets	12	283	320
Share-based expense	12,238	7,542	26,980
Other adjustments	—	—	(49)
Accounts receivable	2,028	(5,296)	(10,196)
Inventory	7,472	2,196	(10,133)
Prepaid expenses and other current assets	(282)	(6,185)	(6,218)
Deferred customer acquisition costs	13,322	(10,796)	(21,053)
Due from related parties	2	74	32
Other assets	(7,498)	(81)	(294)
Accounts payable	(22,029)	(2,966)	42,407
Accrued expenses	(12,738)	(77,770)	62,281
Deferred revenue	(10,124)	20,509	34,181
Other liability	(5,321)	23,046	—
Net cash flows from operating activities	655	(270,926)	(188,898)
Cash Flows from Investing Activities			
Capital expenditures	(11,386)	(20,386)	(48,601)
Purchase of intangible assets	(560)	(5,500)	(5,268)
Purchase of marketable securities	(21,375)	(236,875)	(639,707)
Maturities and sales of marketable securities	101,317	446,949	484,116
Acquisition and development of software assets	(26,530)	(21,346)	(4060)
Decrease (increase) in restricted cash	(980)	(31,385)	(543)
Net cash flows from investing activities	40,486	131,457	(210,798)
Cash Flows from Financing Activities			
Principal payments on capital lease obligations	(1,036)	(1,020)	(826)
Principal payments on debt	(326)	—	—
Proceeds from issuance of debt	223,200	—	2,047
Discount on notes payable	(7,167)	—	—
Early extinguishment of notes	(253,460)	—	—
Debt-related costs	(26,799)	—	(283)
Proceeds from subscription receivable, net	9	279	169
Proceeds from common stock issuance, net	—	—	493,040
Purchase of treasury stock	—	—	(11,723)
Proceeds (payments) for directed-share program, net	62	169	(5,426)
Proceeds from exercise of stock options	47	817	431
Net cash flows from financing activities	(65,470)	245	477,429
Effect of exchange rate changes on cash	(1,079)	513	(29)
Net change in cash and cash equivalents	(25,408)	(138,711)	77,704
Cash and cash equivalents, beginning of period	71,542	210,253	132,549
Cash and cash equivalents, end of period	$ 46,134	$ 71,542	$ 210,253

Required

a. This chapter explained that many companies that report net losses on their earnings statements report positive cash flows from operating activities. How does Vonage's net income for each year compare to its cash flows from operating activities?

b. Based only on the information in the statements of cash flows, does Vonage appear to be improving its position in the telecommunications business? Explain.

c. In 2008 Vonage paid off over $250 million in debt. Where did it get the funds to repay this debt?

d. All things considered, based on the information in its statements of cash flows, did Vonage's cash position appear to be improving or deteriorating?

ATC 12-3   Group Assignment   *Preparing a statement of cash flows*

The following financial statements and information are available for Blythe Industries Inc.

Balance Sheets As of December 31		
	2011	2012
Assets		
Cash	$120,600	$ 160,200
Accounts receivable	85,000	103,200
Inventory	171,800	186,400
Marketable securities (available for sale)	220,000	284,000
Equipment	490,000	650,000
Accumulated depreciation	(240,000)	(310,000)
Land	120,000	80,000
Total assets	$967,400	$1,153,800
Liabilities and equity		
Liabilities		
Accounts payable (inventory)	$ 66,200	$ 36,400
Notes payable—Long-term	250,000	230,000
Bonds payable	100,000	200,000
Total liabilities	416,200	466,400
Stockholders' equity		
Common stock, no par	200,000	240,000
Preferred stock, $50 par	100,000	110,000
Paid-in capital in excess of par—Preferred stock	26,800	34,400
Total paid-In capital	326,800	384,400
Retained earnings	264,400	333,000
Less: Treasury stock	(40,000)	(30,000)
Total stockholders' equity	551,200	687,400
Total liabilities and stockholders' equity	$967,400	$1,153,800

Income Statement For the Year Ended December 31, 2012		
Sales revenue		$1,050,000
Cost of goods sold		(766,500)
Gross profit		283,500
Operating expenses		
Supplies expense	$20,400	
Salaries expense	92,000	
Depreciation expense	90,000	
Total operating expenses		(202,400)
Operating income		81,100
Nonoperating items		
Interest expense		(16,000)
Gain from the sale of marketable securities		30,000
Gain from the sale of land and equipment		12,000
Net income		$ 107,100

Additional Information

1. Sold land that cost $40,000 for $44,000.
2. Sold equipment that cost $30,000 and had accumulated depreciation of $20,000 for $18,000.
3. Purchased new equipment for $190,000.
4. Sold marketable securities, classified as available-for-sale, that cost $40,000 for $70,000.
5. Purchased new marketable securities, classified as available-for-sale, for $104,000.
6. Paid $20,000 on the principal of the long-term note.
7. Paid off a $100,000 bond issue and issued new bonds for $200,000.
8. Sold 100 shares of treasury stock at its cost.
9. Issued some new common stock.
10. Issued some new $50 par preferred stock.
11. Paid dividends. (*Note:* The only transactions to affect retained earnings were net income and dividends.)

Required

Organize the class into three sections, and divide each section into groups of three to five students. Assign each section of groups an activity section of the statement of cash flows (operating activities, investing activities, or financing activities).

Group Task

Prepare your assigned portion of the statement of cash flows. Have a representative of your section put your activity section of the statement of cash flows on the board. As each section adds its information on the board, the full statement of cash flows will be presented.

Class Discussion

Have the class finish the statement of cash flows by computing the net change in cash. Also have the class answer the following questions:

a. What is the cost per share of the treasury stock?
b. What was the issue price per share of the preferred stock?
c. What was the book value of the equipment sold?

ATC 12-4 Business Applications Case *Identifying different presentation formats*

In *Statement of Financial Accounting Standards No. 95,* the Financial Accounting Standards Board (FASB) recommended but did not require that companies use the direct method. In Appendix B, Paragraphs 106–121, of the standard, the FASB discussed its reasons for this recommendation.

Required

Obtain a copy of *Standard No. 95* and read Appendix B Paragraphs 106–121. Write a brief response summarizing the issues that the FASB considered and its specific reaction to those issues. Your response should draw heavily on paragraphs 119–121.

ATC 12-5 Writing Assignment *Explaining discrepancies between cash flow and operating income*

The following selected information was drawn from the records of Fleming Company:

Assets	2011	2012
Accounts receivable	$ 400,000	$ 840,200
Merchandise inventory	720,000	1,480,000
Equipment	1,484,000	1,861,200
Accumulated depreciation	(312,000)	(402,400)

Fleming is experiencing cash flow problems. Despite the fact that it reported significant increases in operating income, operating activities produced a net cash outflow. Recent financial forecasts predict that Fleming will have insufficient cash to pay its current liabilities within three months.

Required

Write an explanation of Fleming's cash shortage. Include a recommendation to remedy the problem.

ATC 12-6   Ethical Dilemma   *Would I lie to you, baby?*

Andy and Jean Crocket are involved in divorce proceedings. When discussing a property settlement, Andy told Jean that he should take over their investment in an apartment complex because she would be unable to absorb the loss that the apartments are generating. Jean was somewhat distrustful and asked Andy to support his contention. He produced the following income statement, which was supported by a CPA's unqualified opinion that the statement was prepared in accordance with generally accepted accounting principles.

CROCKET APARTMENTS		
Income Statement		
For the Year Ended December 31, 2011		
Rent revenue		$580,000
Less: Expenses		
Depreciation expense	$280,000	
Interest expense	184,000	
Operating expense	88,000	
Management fees	56,000	
Total expenses		(608,000)
Net loss		$(28,000)

All revenue is earned on account. Interest and operating expenses are incurred on account. Management fees are paid in cash. The following accounts and balances were drawn from the 2010 and 2011 year-end balance sheets.

Account Title	2010	2011
Rent receivable	$40,000	$44,000
Interest payable	12,000	18,000
Accounts payable (oper. exp.)	6,000	4,000

Jean is reluctant to give up the apartments but feels that she must do so because her present salary is only $40,000 per year. She says that if she takes the apartments, the $28,000 loss would absorb a significant portion of her salary, leaving her only $12,000 with which to support herself. She tells you that while the figures seem to support her husband's arguments, she believes that she is failing to see something. She knows that she and her husband collected a $20,000 distribution from the business on December 1, 2011. Also, $150,000 cash was paid in 2011 to reduce the principal balance on a mortgage that was taken out to finance the purchase of the apartments two years ago. Finally, $24,000 cash was paid during 2011 to purchase a computer system used in the business. She wonders, "If the apartments are losing money, where is my husband getting all the cash to make these payments?"

Required

a. Prepare a statement of cash flows for the 2011 accounting period.

b. Compare the cash flow statement prepared in Requirement *a* with the income statement and provide Jean Crocket with recommendations.

c. Comment on the value of an unqualified audit opinion when using financial statements for decision-making purposes.

ATC 12-7   Research Assignment   *Analyzing cash flow information*

In 2008 Time Warner, Inc., reported a net loss of $13.4 billion. This loss occurred predominantly because Time Warner took a charge for "asset impairments" of $24,309 million, ($24.3 billion). (These amounts do not include tax benefits.) Without these special charges, Time Warner's net income would have been a positive $10.9 billion. Using the company's 2008 Form 10-K, complete the requirements below. Be sure to use the Form 10-K for *Time Warner, Inc.,* not *Time Warner Cable, Inc.* The Form 10-K can be found on the company's website. It can also be obtained using the EDGAR system following the instructions in Appendix A.

Required

a. How much cash flow from operating activities did Time Warner generate?

b. Based on the statement of cash flows, how much cash did the company pay out as a result of the asset impairments?

c. How much cash did Time Warner spend on investing activities (net)?

d. How much cash did the company use the repay debt? Where did it get the cash to make these payments?

CHAPTER *3*

The Double-Entry Accounting System

LEARNING OBJECTIVES

After you have mastered the material in this chapter, you will be able to:

1 Describe business events using debit/credit terminology.

2 Record transactions in T-accounts and show their effect on financial statements.

3 Record transactions using the general journal format and show their effect on financial statements.

4 Prepare a trial balance and explain how it is used to prepare financial statements.

5 Use a return on assets ratio, debt to assets ratio, and a return on equity ratio to analyze financial statements.

LP3

CHAPTER OPENING

To prepare financial statements, a company must have a system for accurately capturing the vast numbers of business transactions in which it engages each year. The most widely used such system, double-entry accounting, is so effective it has been in use for hundreds of years! This chapter explains the rules for recording transactions using double-entry accounting.

Double-entry accounting rules are analogous to other rules people adopt to achieve various goals, such as rules governing traffic signals. A red signal means "stop," but it could just as easily mean "go." What matters is that all drivers agree on what red means. Similarly, double-entry accounting rules could have developed differently. In fact, the rules sometimes seem backwards at first. You likely use accounting terms like "debit" or "credit" from a consumer's point of view. To learn the accounting rules, however, you must view them from a business perspective. With practice, they will become second nature and you will know them as well as you know traffic signals.

The *Curious* Accountant

Most companies prepare financial statements at least once each year. The year about which financial statements report is called a **fiscal year**. Illustrations in this textbook usually assume the fiscal year coincides with the calendar year; that is, it ends on December 31. In practice, the fiscal years of many companies do not end on December 31. For example, Levi Strauss, a company that produces clothing, ends its fiscal year on the last Sunday in November. Gap, Inc., a company that sells clothing, ends its fiscal year on the last Saturday in January or the first Saturday in February.

Why would these companies choose these dates to end their fiscal years? (Answers on pages 139 and 140.)

Describe business events using
debit/credit terminology.

DEBIT/CREDIT TERMINOLOGY

An account form known as a **T-account** is a good starting point for learning double-entry recording procedures. A T-account looks like the letter "T" drawn on a piece of paper. The account title is written across the top of the horizontal bar of the T. The left side of the vertical bar is the **debit** side, and the right side is the **credit** side. An account has been *debited* when an amount is written on the left side and *credited* when an amount is written on the right side. Accountants often abbreviate the term *debit* as "dr." and *credit* as "cr." For any given account, the difference between the total debit and credit amounts is the **account balance.**

The rules for using debits and credits to record transactions in T-accounts are as follows:

			Claims			
Assets		**=**	**Liabilities**	**+**	**Equity**	
Debit	Credit		Debit	Credit	Debit	Credit
+	−		−	+	−	+

Notice that a debit can represent an increase or a decrease. Likewise, a credit can represent an increase or a decrease. Whether a debit or credit is an increase or a decrease depends on the type of account (asset, liability, or stockholders' equity) in question. The rules of debits and credits are summarized as follows:

1. Debits increase asset accounts; credits decrease asset accounts.
2. Debits decrease liability and stockholders' equity accounts; credits increase liability and stockholders' equity accounts.

RECORDING TRANSACTIONS IN T-ACCOUNTS

Record transactions in T-accounts
and show their effect on financial
statements.

To illustrate the rules for debits and credits we record the 2011 accounting events for a small business, Collins Brokerage Services, Inc. Collins begins the accounting period with the following balances in its permanent accounts: cash, $5,000; common stock, $4,000; and retained earnings, $1,000. The beginning balances for the temporary accounts (revenues, expenses, and dividends) are zero because these accounts were closed at the end of the previous period. The events are organized into four categories including: asset source, asset exchange, asset use, and claims exchange.

Asset Source Transactions

A business may obtain assets from three primary sources: (1) from stockholders, (2) from creditors, or (3) through operating activities (earning revenue). An asset source transaction increases an asset account and a corresponding liability or stockholders' equity account. The increase in the asset account is recorded with a debit entry. The increase in a liability or stockholders' equity account is recorded with a credit entry. The following section demonstrates recording procedures for common asset source transactions.

EVENT 1   **Acquired $25,000 cash from the issue of common stock.**

This accounting event increases both assets and stockholders' equity. The increase in assets (Cash) is recorded with a debit, and the increase in stockholders' equity (Common Stock) with a credit, shown in T-account form as follows:

Assets		=	Liabilities	+	Equity	
Cash					Common Stock	
Debit	Credit				Debit	Credit
+						+
(1) 25,000						25,000 (1)

Notice the entry included both debiting an account and crediting an account. This system is called **double-entry accounting.** Recording any transaction requires at least one debit and at least one credit. The total of the debit amounts must equal the total of the credit amounts. These requirements provide accountants with a built-in error detection tool. For your convenience, the event number is shown parenthetically beside the transactions amounts.

This entry has the following effects on the financial statements:

Assets	=	Liab.	+	Equity	Rev.	−	Exp.	=	Net Inc.	Cash Flow
Cash	=			Com. Stk.						
25,000	=	NA	+	25,000	NA	−	NA	=	NA	25,000 FA

EVENT 2   Purchased $850 of supplies on account.

Purchasing supplies on account increases both assets and liabilities. The increase in assets (Supplies) is recorded with a debit, and the increase in liabilities (Accounts Payable) is recorded with a credit, as shown in the following T-accounts:

Assets		=	Liabilities		+	Equity
Supplies			Accounts Payable			
Debit	Credit		Debit	Credit		
+				+		
(2) 850				850 (2)		

This entry has the following effects on the financial statements:

Assets	=	Liab.	+	Equity	Rev.	−	Exp.	=	Net Inc.	Cash Flow
Supplies	−	Accts. Pay.								
850	=	850	+	NA	NA	−	NA	=	NA	NA

EVENT 3   Collected $1,800 cash as an advance to provide future services over a one year period starting March 1.

Accepting the $1,800 in advance creates an obligation for Collins. The obligation is to provide future services to a customer. Collins will recognize a liability called *unearned revenue.* Recording the event increases both assets and liabilities. The increase in assets

(Cash) is recorded with a debit, and the increase in liabilities (Unearned Revenue) is recorded with a credit, as shown in the following T-accounts:

Assets		=	Liabilities		+	Equity	
Cash			**Unearned Revenue**				
Debit	Credit		Debit	Credit			
+				+			
(3) 1,800				1,800 (3)			

This entry has the following effects on the financial statements:

Assets	=	Liab.	+	Equity	Rev.	−	Exp.	=	Net Inc.	Cash Flow	
		Unearned									
Cash	=	Revenue									
1,800	=	1,800	+	NA	NA	−	NA	=	NA	1,800	OA

EVENT 4   **Provided $15,760 of services on account.**

Recognizing revenue earned on account increases both assets and stockholders' equity. The increase in assets (Accounts Receivable) is recorded with a debit, and the increase in stockholders' equity (Service Revenue) is recorded with a credit, as shown in the following T-accounts:

Assets		=	Liabilities	+	Equity	
Accounts Receivable					**Service Revenue**	
Debit	Credit				Debit	Credit
+						+
(4) 15,760						15,760 (4)

This entry has the following effects on the financial statements:

Assets	=	Liab.	+	Equity	Rev.	−	Exp.	=	Net Inc.	Cash Flow
Accts. Rec.	=			Ret. Earn.						
15,760	=	NA	+	15,760	15,760	−	NA	=	15,760	NA

Summary of the Previous Asset Source Transactions

Events 1 through 4 are asset source transactions. In each case, an asset account and a corresponding claims account increased. The increase in the asset account was recorded with a debit and the increase in the liability or stockholders' equity account was recorded with a credit. Any transaction that provides assets to a business is recorded similarly.

CHECK *Yourself* 3.1

What are the three sources of assets? Which accounts are debited and credited when a business acquires an asset?

Answer   The three sources of assets are creditors, investors, and earnings. When a company acquires an asset, the asset account is debited and the source account is credited. For example, if a company earns revenue on account, the receivables account is debited and the revenue account is credited.

Asset Exchange Transactions

Asset exchange transactions involve trading one asset for another asset. One asset account increases; the other decreases. The total amount of assets remains unchanged. Asset exchange transactions are recorded by debiting the asset account that is increasing and crediting the asset account that is decreasing. In T-account form, asset exchange transactions have the following effects on the accounting equation:

Assets				=	Claims
Asset 1		**Asset 2**			
Debit	Credit	Debit	Credit		
+			−		

EVENT 5   **Purchased land for \$26,000 cash.**

The increase in assets (Land) is recorded with a debit, and the decrease in assets (Cash) is recorded with a credit, as shown in the following T-accounts:

Assets				=	Claims
Cash		**Land**			
Debit	Credit	Debit	Credit		
	−	+			
	26,000 (5)	(5) 26,000			

This entry has the following effects on the financial statements:

Assets			=	Liab.	+	Equity	Rev.	−	Exp.	=	Net Inc.	Cash Flow
Cash	+	Land										
(26,000)	+	26,000	=	NA	+	NA	NA	−	NA	=	NA	(26,000) IA

EVENT 6   Paid $1,200 cash for a one-year insurance policy with coverage starting August 1.

The increase in assets (Prepaid Insurance) is recorded with a debit, and the decrease in assets (Cash) is recorded with a credit, as shown in the following T-accounts:

Assets				=	Claims
Cash		**Prepaid Insurance**			
Debit	Credit	Debit	Credit		
	—	+			
	1,200 (6)	(6) 1,200			

This entry has the following effects on the financial statements:

Assets		=	Liab.	+	Equity	Rev.	−	Exp.	=	Net Inc.	Cash Flow
Cash	+ Prepaid Insurance										
(1,200) +	(1,200)	=	NA	+	NA	NA	−	NA	=	NA	(1,200) OA

EVENT 7   Collected $13,400 cash from accounts receivable.

The increase in assets (Cash) is recorded with a debit, and the decrease in assets (Accounts Receivable) is recorded with a credit, as shown in the following T-accounts:

Assets				=	Claims
Cash		**Accounts Receivable**			
Debit	Credit	Debit	Credit		
+			—		
(7) 13,400			13,400 (7)		

This entry has the following effects on the financial statements:

Assets		=	Liab.	+	Equity	Rev.	−	Exp.	=	Net Inc.	Cash Flow
Cash	+ Accts. Rec.										
13,400 +	(13,400)	=	NA	+	NA	NA	−	NA	=	NA	13,400 OA

Summary of the Previous Asset Exchange Transactions

Events 6 and 7 are both asset exchange transactions. In each case, one asset account increased and another decreased. The asset account that increased was debited, and the asset account that decreased was credited. These asset exchange transactions did not affect the total amounts of either assets or claims.

Asset Use Transactions

There are three primary asset use transactions: (1) expenses may use assets, (2) settling liabilities may use assets, or (3) paying dividends may use assets. An asset use transaction decreases an asset account and also decreases a claims account. The decrease in the asset account is recorded with a credit and the decrease in the claims account is recorded with a debit.

EVENT 8   Paid $9,500 cash for salaries expense.

The decrease in assets (Cash) is recorded with a credit, and the decrease in stockholders' equity (Salaries Expense) is recorded with a debit, as shown in the following T-accounts:

Assets		=	Liabilities	+	Equity	
Cash					**Salaries Expense**	
Debit	Credit				Debit	Credit
	—				+ Expense	
	9,500 (8)				− Equity	
					(8) 9,500	

The debit to Salaries Expense represents an *increase* in the salaries expense account which is actually a *decrease* in stockholders' equity (Retained Earnings). Debit entries increase expense accounts. Expenses, however, decrease stockholders' equity (Retained Earnings). Debiting an expense account, therefore, reduces stockholders' equity.

This entry has the following effects on the financial statements:

Assets	=	Liab.	+	Equity	Rev.	−	Exp.	=	Net Inc.	Cash Flow
Cash	=			Ret. Earn.						
(9,500)	=	NA	+	(9,500)	NA	−	9,500	=	(9,500)	(9,500) OA

EVENT 9   Paid an $800 cash dividend.

The decrease in assets (Cash) is recorded with a credit, and the decrease in stockholders' equity (Dividends) is recorded with a debit, as shown in the following T-accounts:

Assets		=	Liabilities	+	Equity	
Cash					**Dividends**	
Debit	Credit				Debit	Credit
	—				+ Div	
	800 (9)				− Equity	
					(9) 800	

The debit to Dividends represents both an *increase* in the dividends account and a decrease in stockholders' equity (Retained Earnings). Since dividends decrease stockholders' equity, an increase in the dividends account reduces stockholders' equity. Recall that dividends are wealth transfers, not expenses.

This entry has the following effects on the financial statements:

Assets	=	Liab.	+	Equity	Rev.	−	Exp.	=	Net Inc.	Cash Flow
Cash	=			Ret. Earn.						
(800)	=	NA	+	(800)	NA	−	NA	=	NA	(800) FA

EVENT 10   Paid $850 cash to settle accounts payable.

The decrease in assets (Cash) is recorded with a credit, and the decrease in liabilities (Accounts Payable) is recorded with a debit, as shown in the following T-accounts:

Assets		=	Liabilities		+	Equity
Cash			**Accounts Payable**			
Debit	Credit		Debit	Credit		
	—		—			
	850 (10)		(10) 850			

This entry has the following effects on the financial statements:

Assets	=	Liab.	+	Equity	Rev.	−	Exp.	=	Net Inc.	Cash Flow
Cash	=	Accts. Pay.								
(850)	=	(850)	+	NA	NA	−	NA	=	NA	(850) OA

Summary of Asset Use Transactions

Events 8 through 10 each reduced an asset account and also either a liability or stockholders' equity account. Even though debit entries to expense and dividends accounts represent increases in those accounts, the balances in expense and dividends accounts reduce stockholders' equity. Any asset use transaction is recorded with a debit to a liability or a stockholders' equity account and a credit to an asset account.

Claims Exchange Transactions

Certain transactions involve exchanging one claims account for another claims account. The total amount of claims remains unchanged. Such transactions are recorded by debiting the claims account which is decreasing and crediting the claims account which is increasing.

EVENT 11   Recognized $1,900 other operating expenses on account.

The event increases liabilities and decreases stockholders' equity. The increase in liabilities (Accounts Payable) is recorded with a credit, and the decrease in stockholders' equity (Advertising Expense) is recorded with a debit, as shown in the following T-accounts:

Assets		=	Liabilities		+	Equity	
			Accounts Payable			**Other Operating Expense**	
			Debit	Credit		Debit	Credit
				+		+ Expense	
				1,900 (11)		− Equity	
						(11) 1,900	

This entry has the following effects on the financial statements:

Assets	=	Liab.	+	Equity	Rev.	−	Exp.	=	Net Inc.	Cash Flow
		Accts. Pay.	+	Ret. Earn.						
NA	=	1,900	+	(1,900)	NA	−	1,900	=	(1,900)	NA

Summary of Claims Exchange Transactions

Event 11 reflects an exchange on the claims side of the accounting equation. In each case, one claims account was debited, and another claims account was credited. Claims exchange transactions do not affect the total amounts of either assets or claims.

Adjusting the Accounts

Assume Collins' fiscal year ends on December 31, 2011. Collins has several unrecorded accruals and deferrals that be recognized before the financial statements can be prepared. The appropriate adjustments are discussed below.

ADJUSTMENT 1   As of December 31, 2011 Collins had earned $750 of accrued interest revenue.

Recognizing the revenue increases both assets and stockholders' equity. The increase in assets (Accrued Interest Receivable) is recorded with a debit, and the increase in stockholders' equity (Accrued Interest Revenue) is recorded with a credit, as shown in the following T-accounts:

Assets	=	Liabilities	+	Equity
Accrued Interest Receivable				**Accrued Interest Revenue**

Debit	Credit			Debit	Credit
+					+
(Adj. 1) 750					750 (Adj. 1)

This entry has the following effects on the financial statements:

Assets	=	Liab.	+	Equity		Rev.	–	Exp.	=	Net Inc.		Cash Flow
Int. Rec.	=			Ret. Earn.								
750	=	NA	+	750		750	–	NA	=	750		750 OA

ADJUSTMENT 2   As of December 31, 2011 Collins had earned $1,500 of the $1,800 of the revenue it deferred in Event 3.

Recall that Collins collected $1,800 in advance for a one-year contract starting March 1. By December 31, 2011, Collins would have provided professional services for 10 months, earning $1,500 ($1,800 ÷ 12 = $150 × 10 = $1,500) of the revenue during 2011. This amount must be transferred from the liability account (Unearned Revenue) to an equity account (Service Revenue). Recognizing the revenue decreases liabilities and increases stockholders' equity. The decrease in liabilities (Unearned Revenue) is recorded with a debit, and the increase in stockholders' equity (Service Revenue) is recorded with a credit, as shown in the following T-accounts:

Assets	=	Liabilities	+	Equity
		Unearned Revenue		**Service Revenue**

		Debit	Credit		Debit	Credit
		–				+
		(Adj. 2) 1,500				1,500 (Adj. 2)

This adjustment has the following effects on the financial statements:

Assets	=	Liab.	+	Equity	Rev.	−	Exp.	=	Net Inc.	Cash Flow
		Unearned Revenue	+	Ret. Earn.						
NA	=	(1,500)	+	1,500	1,500	−	NA	=	1,500	NA

ADJUSTMENT 3   As of December 31, 2011 Collins had $800 of accrued salary expenses that will be paid in 2012.

Assume that Collins owes $800 more to employees for work done in 2011 since September 4. Collins will pay these salaries in 2012. The required adjusting entry increases liabilities and decreases stockholders' equity. The increase in liabilities (Salaries Payable) is recorded with a credit, and the decrease in stockholders' equity (Salaries Expense) is recorded with a debit, as shown in the following T-accounts:

Assets	=	Liabilities	+	Equity
		Salaries Payable		**Salaries Expense**
		Debit | Credit		Debit | Credit
		+		+ Expense
		800 (Adj. 3)		− Equity
				(Adj. 3) 800

This adjustment has the following effects on the financial statements:

Assets	=	Liab.	+	Equity	Rev.	−	Exp.	=	Net Inc.	Cash Flow
		Sal. Pay.	+	Ret. Earn.						
NA	=	800	+	(800)	NA	−	800	=	(800)	NA

ADJUSTMENT 4   As of December 31, 2011 Collins had used $500 of the $1,200 of insurance coverage that was prepaid in Event 6.

Recall that Collins paid $1,200 in advance for insurance coverage for one year. The monthly insurance cost is therefore $100 ($1,200 ÷ 12 months). By December 31, Collins had *used* the insurance coverage for five months in 2011. Insurance expense for those five months is therefore $500 ($100 × 5). Recognizing the insurance expense decreases both assets and stockholders' equity. The decrease in assets (Prepaid Insurance) is recorded with a credit, and the decrease in stockholders' equity (Insurance Expense) is recorded with a debit, as shown in the following T-accounts:

Assets	=	Liabilities	+	Equity
Prepaid Insurance				**Insurance Expense**
Debit | Credit				Debit | Credit
−				+ Expense
500 (Adj. 4)				− Equity
				(Adj. 4) 500

This adjustment has the following effects on the financial statements:

Assets	=	Liab.	+	Equity	Rev.	–	Exp.	=	Net Inc.	Cash Flow
Prep. Ins.	=			Ret. Earn.						
(500)	=	NA	+	(500)	NA	–	500	=	(500)	NA

ADJUSTMENT 5   As of December 31, 2011 a physical count of the supplies on hand revealed that $125 of unused supplies were available for future use.

Collins used $725 ($850 − $125) of supplies during the period. Recognizing the supplies expense decreases both assets and stockholders' equity. The decrease in assets (Supplies) is recorded with a credit and the decrease in stockholders' equity (Supplies Expense) is recorded with a debit, as shown in the following T-accounts:

Assets	=	Liabilities	+	Equity

Supplies				Supplies Expense	
Debit	Credit			Debit	Credit
	–			+ Expense	
	725 (Adj. 5)			− Equity	
				(Adj. 5) 725	

This adjustment has the following effects on the financial statements:

Assets	=	Liab.	+	Equity	Rev.	–	Exp.	=	Net Inc.	Cash Flow
Supplies	=			Ret. Earn.						
(725)	=	NA	+	(725)	NA	–	725	=	(725)	NA

CHECK *Yourself* 3.2

Can an asset exchange transaction be an adjusting entry?

Answer   No. Adjusting entries always involve revenue or expense accounts. Since an asset exchange transaction involves only asset accounts, it cannot be an adjusting entry.

Overview of Debit/Credit Relationships

Panel A of Exhibit 3.1 summarizes the rules for debits and credits. Panel B illustrates these rules in T-account form.

The balance in each account, which is the difference between all the debit entries and all the credit entries, is written on the plus (increase) side of that account. Asset, expense, and dividend accounts normally have *debit balances;* liability, stockholders' equity, and revenue accounts normally have *credit balances.*

THE GENERAL JOURNAL

LO 3

Businesses find it impractical to record every individual transaction directly into general ledger accounts. Imagine the number of cash transactions a grocery store has each day. To simplify recordkeeping, businesses rely on **source documents** such as cash register

Record transactions using the general journal format and show their effect on financial statements.

EXHIBIT 3.1

Debit/Credit Relationships

Panel A

Account	Debits	Credits
Assets	Increase	Decrease
Liabilities	Decrease	Increase
Equity	Decrease	Increase
Common Stock	Decrease	Increase
Revenue	Decrease	Increase
Expenses	Increase	Decrease
Dividends	Increase	Decrease

Panel B

Assets		=	Liabilities		+	Equity	
Debit	Credit		Debit	Credit		Debit	Credit
+	−		−	+		−	+

Common Stock	
Debit	Credit
−	+

Dividends	
Debit	Credit
− Equity	+ Equity
+ Div.	− Div.

Revenue	
Debit	Credit
−	+

Expense	
Debit	Credit
− Equity	+ Equity
+ Exp.	− Exp.

tapes as the basis for entering transaction data into the accounting system. Other source documents include invoices, time cards, check registers, and deposit tickets.

Accountants further simplify recordkeeping by initially recording data from source documents into **journals.** Journals provide a chronological record of business transactions. *Transactions are recorded in journals before they are entered into ledger accounts.* Journals are therefore **books of original entry.** Companies may use different **special journals** to record specific types of recurring transactions. For example, a company may use one special journal to record sales on account, another to record purchases on account, a third to record cash receipts, and a fourth to record cash payments. Transactions that do not fall into any of these categories are recorded in the **general journal.** Although special journals are useful, companies can keep records without them by recording all transactions in the general journal. For simplicity, this text illustrates a general journal only.

At a minimum, the general journal shows the dates, the account titles, and the amounts of each transaction. The date is recorded in the first column, followed by the title of the account to be debited. The title of the account to be credited is indented and written on the line directly below the account to be debited. The dollar amount of the transaction is recorded in the Debit and Credit columns. Dollar signs are not used when recording journal entries. For example, providing services for $1,000 cash on August 1 would be recorded in general journal format as follows:

Date	Account Title	Debit	Credit
Aug. 1	Cash	1,000	
	Service Revenue		1,000

Exhibit 3.2 shows a summary of Collins's 2011 transactions and demonstrates how the transactions are recorded in general journal format. For easy reference the journal column normally used for the transaction date contains the event numbers and the references for the adjusting entries. After transactions are initially recorded in a journal, the dollar amounts of each debit and credit are copied into the ledger accounts through a process called **posting.**

Most companies today use computer technology to record transactions and prepare financial statements. Computers can record and post data pertaining to vast numbers of transactions with incredible speed and unparalleled accuracy. Both manual and computerized accounting systems, however, use the same underlying design. Analyzing a manual accounting system is a useful way to gain insight into how computer-based systems work.

The collection of all the accounts used by a particular business is called the **general ledger.** The general ledger for Collins is displayed in Exhibit 3.3. In a manual system, the ledger could be a book with pages for each account where entries are recorded by hand. In more sophisticated systems, the general ledger is maintained in electronic form. Data is entered into electronic ledgers using computer keyboards or scanners. Companies typically assign each ledger account a name and a number. A list of all ledger accounts and their account numbers is called the **chart of accounts.**

Reality BYTES

Do all accounting systems require using debits and credits? The answer is a definite no. Many small businesses use a single-entry system. A checkbook constitutes a sufficient accounting system for many business owners. Deposits represent revenues, and payments constitute expenses. Many excellent automated accounting systems do not require data entry through a debit/credit recording scheme. **QuickBooks** is a good example of this type of system. Data are entered into the QuickBooks software program through a user-friendly computer interface that does not require knowledge of debit/credit terminology. Even so, the QuickBooks program produces traditional financial reports such as an income statement, balance sheet, and statement of cash flows. How is this possible? Before you become too ingrained in the debit/credit system, recall that throughout the first two chapters of this text, we illustrated accounting records without using debits and credits. Financial reports can be produced in many ways without using a double-entry system. Having recognized this point, we also note that the vast majority of medium- to large-size companies use the double-entry system. Indeed, debit/credit terminology is a part of common culture. Most people have an understanding of what is happening when a business tells them that their account is being debited or credited. It is important for you to embrace the double-entry system as well as other financial reporting systems.

EXHIBIT 3.2

Transaction Summary

Event 1 Acquired $25,000 cash from the issue of common stock.
Event 2 Purchased $850 of supplies on account.
Event 3 Collected $1,800 cash as an advance to provide future services over a one year period starting March 1.
Event 4 Provided $15,760 of services on account.
Event 5 Purchased land for $26,000 cash.
Event 6 Paid $1,200 cash for a one-year insurance policy with coverage starting August 1.
Event 7 Collected $13,400 cash from accounts receivable.
Event 8 Paid $9,500 cash for salaries expense.
Event 9 Paid an $800 cash dividend.
Event 10 Paid $850 cash to settle accounts payable.
Event 11 Recognized $1,900 other operating expenses on account.

Adjustments

Adj. 1   Recognized $750 of accrued interest revenue.
Adj. 2   Recognized $1,500 of deferred service revenue.
Adj. 3   Recognized $800 of accrued salaries expense.
Adj. 4   Recognized $500 of deferred insurance expense.
Adj. 5   Recognized $725 of deferred supplies expense.

General Journal Entries

Event No.	Account Titles	Debit	Credit
1	Cash	25,000	
	Common Stock		25,000
2	Supplies	850	
	Accounts Payable		850
3	Cash	1,800	
	Unearned Service Revenue		1,800
4	Accounts Receivable	15,760	
	Service Revenue		15,760
5	Land	26,000	
	Cash		26,000
6	Prepaid Insurance	1,200	
	Cash		1,200
7	Cash	13,400	
	Accounts Receivable		13,400
8	Salaries Expense	9,500	
	Cash		9,500
9	Dividends	800	
	Cash		800
10	Accounts Payable	850	
	Cash		850
11	Other Operating Expenses	1,900	
	Accounts Payable		1,900
Adj. 1	Accrued Interest Receivable	750	
	Accrued Interest Revenue		750
Adj. 2	Unearned Service Revenue	1,500	
	Service Revenue		750
Adj. 3	Salaries Expense	800	
	Salaries Payable		800
Adj. 4	Insurance Expense	500	
	Prepaid Insurance		500
Adj. 5	Supplies Expense	725	
	Supplies		725

EXHIBIT 3.3

General Ledger

Assets = **Liabilities** + **Stockholders' Equity**

Cash

Bal.	5,000	26,000	(5)
(1)	25,000	1,200	(6)
(3)	1,800	9,500	(8)
(7)	13,400	800	(9)
		850	(10)
Bal.	6,850		

Accounts Receivable

(4)	15,760	13,400	(7)
Bal.	2,360		

Accrued Interest Receivable

Adj. 1	750	

Prepaid Insurance

(6)	1,200	500	(Adj. 4)
Bal.	700		

Supplies

(2)	850	725	(Adj. 5)
Bal.	125		

Land

(5)	26,000	

Accounts Payable

(10)	850	850	(2)
		1,900	(11)
		1,900	Bal.

Salaries Payable

		800	(Adj. 3)

Unearned Service Revenue

(Adj. 2)	1,500	1,800	(3)
		300	Bal.

Common Stock

		4,000	Bal.
		25,000	(1)
		29,000	Bal.

Retained Earnings

		1,000	Bal.

Dividends

(9)	800	

Service Revenue

		15,760	(4)
		1,500	(Adj. 2)
		17,260	Bal.

Accrued Interest Revenue

		750	(Adj. 1)

Salaries Expense

(8)	9,500	
(Adj. 3)	800	
Bal.	10,300	

Other Operating Expenses

(11)	1,900	

Insurance Expense

(Adj. 4)	500	

Supplies Expense

(Adj. 5)	725	

TRIAL BALANCE AND FINANCIAL STATEMENTS

To test whether debits equal credits in the general ledger, accountants regularly prepare an internal accounting schedule called a **trial balance.** A trial balance lists every ledger account and its balance. Debit balances are listed in one column and credit balances are listed in an adjacent column. The columns are totaled and the totals are compared. Exhibit 3.4 displays the trial balance for Collins Brokerage Services, Inc. after the adjusting entries have been posted to the ledger.

Prepare a trial balance and explain how it is used to prepare financial statements.

If the debit total does not equal the credit total, the accountant knows to search for an error. Even if the totals are equal, however, there may be errors in the accounting records. For example, equal trial balance totals would not disclose errors like the following: failure to record transactions; misclassifications, such as debiting the wrong account; or incorrectly recording the amount of a transaction, such as recording a $200 transaction as $2,000. Equal debits and credits in a trial balance provide evidence rather than proof of accuracy.

Supplemented with details from the Cash and Common Stock ledger accounts, the adjusted trial balance (Exhibit 3.4) provides the information to prepare the financial statements for Collins Brokerage Services, Inc. The income statement, statement of changes in stockholders' equity, balance sheet, and statement of cash flows are shown in Exhibits 3.5, 3.6, 3.7, and 3.8.

138   Chapter 3

EXHIBIT 3.4

COLLINS BROKERAGE SERVICES, INC.
Adjusted Trial Balance
December 31, 2011

Account Title	Debit	Credit
Cash	$ 6,850	
Accounts receivable	2,360	
Accrued interest receivable	750	
Prepaid insurance	700	
Supplies	125	
Land	26,000	
Accounts payable		$ 1,900
Salaries payable		800
Unearned service revenue		300
Common stock		29,000
Retained earnings		1,000
Dividends	800	
Service revenue		17,260
Accrued interest revenue		750
Salaries expense	10,300	
Insurance expense	500	
Supplies expense	725	
Other operating expense	1,900	
Totals	$51,010	$51,010

EXHIBIT 3.5

COLLINS BROKERAGE SERVICES, INC.
Income Statement
For the Year Ended December 31, 2011

Revenues		
Service revenue	$17,260	
Interest revenue	750	
Total revenue		$18,010
Expenses		
Salaries expense	(10,300)	
Other operating expenses	(1,900)	
Insurance expense	(500)	
Supplies expense	(725)	
Total expenses		(13,425)
Net income		$ 4,585

EXHIBIT 3.6

COLLINS BROKERAGE SERVICES, INC.
Statement of Changes in Stockholders' Equity
For the Year Ended December 31, 2011

Beginning common stock	$ 4,000	
Plus: Common stock issued	25,000	
Ending common stock		$29,000
Beginning retained earnings	1,000	
Plus: Net income	4,585	
Less: Dividends	(800)	
Ending retained earnings		4,785
Total Stockholders' equity		$33,785

EXHIBIT 3.7

COLLINS BROKERAGE SERVICES, INC.
Balance Sheet
As of December 31, 2011

Assets		
Cash	$ 6,850	
Accounts receivable	2,360	
Accrued interest receivable	750	
Prepaid insurance	700	
Supplies	125	
Land	26,000	
Total assets		$36,785
Liabilities:		
Accounts payable	$ 1,900	
Unearned service revenue	300	
Salaries payable	800	
Total liabilities		$ 3,000
Stockholders equity		
Common stock	29,000	
Retained earnings	4,785	
Total stockholders' equity		33,785
Total liabilities and stockholders' equity		$36,785

EXHIBIT 3.8

COLLINS BROKERAGE SERVICES, INC.
Statement of Cash Flows
For the Year Ended December 31, 2011

Cash flows from operating activities		
Cash receipts from customers	$15,200*	
Cash payments for salaries expense	(9,500)	
Cash payments for insurance expense	(1,200)	
Cash payments for supplies	(850)	
Net cash flow from operating activities		$ 3,650
Cash flows from investing activities		
Cash payment to purchase land		(26,000)
Cash flows from financing activities		
Cash receipts from issue of common stock	25,000	
Cash payment for dividends	(800)	
Net cash flow from financing activities		24,200
Net decrease in cash		1,850
Plus: Beginning cash balance		5,000
Ending cash balance		$ 6,850

*$13,400 accounts receivable collections + $1,800 unearned service revenue collection.

Answers to The *Curious* Accountant

Part 1

The process of closing the books and going through a year-end audit is time consuming for a business. Also, it is time spent that does not produce revenue. Thus, companies whose business is highly seasonal often choose "slow" periods to end their fiscal year. Gap, Inc. does heavy business during the Christmas season, so it might find December 31 an inconvenient time to close its books. Toward the end of January, business activity is slow, and inventory levels are at their low points. This is a good time to count the inventory and to assess the financial condition of the company. For these reasons, Gap, Inc. has chosen to close its books to end its fiscal year around the end of January.

Now that you know why a business like Gap, Inc. might choose to end its fiscal year at the end of January, can you think of a reason why Levi Strauss closes its books at the end of November? (See page 140.)

Closing Entries

Exhibit 3.9 shows **closing entries** for Collins Brokerage Services, Inc. These entries move all 2011 data from the temporary accounts (revenues, expenses, and dividends) into the Retained Earnings account. For example, the first closing entry in Exhibit 3.9 moves the balance in the Service Revenue account to the Retained Earnings account. As shown in the adjusted trial balance (Exhibit 3.4), the Service Revenue account has a $17,260 credit balance before it is closed. Debiting the account for $17,260 brings its after-closing balance to zero. The corresponding $17,260 credit to Retained Earnings increases the balance in that account.

The third closing entry moves the balance in the Salaries Expense account to the Retained Earnings account. Before closing, the Salaries Expense account has a $10,300 debit balance; crediting the account for $10,300 leaves it with an after-closing balance of zero. The corresponding $10,300 debit to the Retained Earnings account reduces the balance in that account. The remaining entries close the other revenue, expense and the dividends accounts to the Retained Earnings account.

EXHIBIT 3.9

Closing Entries

Date	Account Titles	Debit	Credit
Dec. 31	Service Revenue	17,260	
	Retained Earnings		17,260
31	Accrued Interest Revenue	750	
	Retained Earnings		750
31	Retained Earnings	10,300	
	Salaries Expense		10,300
31	Retained Earnings	1,900	
	Other Operating Expenses		1,900
31	Retained Earnings	500	
	Insurance Expense		500
31	Retained Earnings	725	
	Supplies Expense		725
31	Retained Earnings	800	
	Dividends		800

Answers to The *Curious* Accountant

Part 2

Levi Strauss does not sell its clothes directly to consumers; rather, it sells most of its clothes through retailers.

Levi Strauss must deliver its jeans to retailers before Thanksgiving if the stores are going to have goods available to sell during the Christmas season. So, Levi's "Christmas season" is probably over by early November, making the end of November a good time to end its fiscal year. Some clothing manufacturers, such as Tommy Hilfiger and Polo Ralph Lauren, close their books around the end of March. By then, goods for both the Christmas and spring seasons have been shipped to retailers.

Closing entries can be recorded more efficiently than in Exhibit 3.9. For example, the two revenue accounts could be closed with one compound journal entry, like the one below.

Date	Account Title	Debit	Credit
Dec. 31	Service Revenue	17,260	
	Accrued Interest Revenue	750	
	Retained Earnings		18,010

Furthermore, revenue, expense, and dividend accounts could all be closed in a single compound journal entry. The form of the closing entries is not important. What matters is that all revenue, expense, and dividend amounts be moved to the Retained Earnings account. After the closing entries are posted to the ledger accounts, all revenue, expense, and dividends accounts have zero balances. The temporary accounts are then ready to capture revenue, expense, and dividend data for the next fiscal year.

If all companies closed their books on December 31 each year, accountants, printers, lawyers, government agencies, and others would be overburdened by the effort to produce the accounting reports of all companies at the same time. In an effort to balance the workload, many companies close their books at the end of the natural business year. A natural business year ends when operating activities are at their lowest point. For many companies the lowest point in the operating cycle occurs on a date other than December 31. A recent survey found that almost one-half of the companies sampled closed their books in months other than December (see Exhibit 3.10).

Post-Closing Trial Balance

How often should companies prepare a trial balance? Some companies prepare a trial balance daily; others may prepare one monthly, quarterly, or annually, depending on the needs of management. The heading of a trial balance describes the status of the account balances

EXHIBIT 3.10

Distribution of Fiscal Closing Dates

Data Source: AICPA Accounting Trends and Techniques.

in it. For example, the trial balance in Exhibit 3.11 is described as a *Post-Closing Trial Balance* because it reflects the account balances immediately after the closing entries were posted. In contrast, the trial balance in Exhibit 3.4 is described as an *Adjusted Trial Balance* because it shows the account balances immediately after the adjusting entries were posted. A trial balance prepared at the end of each day may be described as a *Daily Trial Balance*.

CHECK *Yourself* 3.3

Describe an error that would not cause a trial balance to be out of balance.

Answer Many potential errors would not cause a trial balance to be out of balance, such as debiting or crediting the wrong account. For example, if revenue earned on account were recorded with a debit to Cash instead of Accounts Receivable, total assets would be correct and the totals in the trial balance would equal each other even though the balances in the Cash and Accounts Receivable accounts would be incorrect. Recording the same incorrect amount in both the debit and credit part of an entry also would not cause a trial balance to be out of balance. For example, if $20 of revenue earned on account were recorded as a $200 debit to Accounts Receivable and a $200 credit to Consulting Revenue, the totals in the trial balance would equal each other although Accounts Receivable and Consulting Revenue amounts would be incorrect.

THE *Financial* ANALYST

Suppose a company earned net income of $1,000,000. Is the company's performance good or poor? If the company is Comcast, the performance is poor. If it is a small shoe store, the performance is outstanding. So, how do financial analysts compare the performance of differing size companies? Financial ratios are helpful in this regard.

LO 5

Use a return on assets ratio, debt to assets ratio, and a return on equity ratio to analyze financial statements.

Assessing the Effective Use of Assets

Evaluating performance requires considering the size of the investment base used to produce the income. In other words, you expect someone who has a $10 million investment base to earn more than someone who has a $10 thousand base. The relationship between the level of income and the size of the investment can be expressed as the **return on assets ratio,** as follows:

$$\frac{\text{Net income}^{[1]}}{\text{Total assets}}$$

This ratio permits meaningful comparisons between different-size companies. Compare Blue Nile, Inc., a large online retailer of fine jewelry, with Comcast. In 2008, Blue Nile's net income was $11.6 million and Comcast's was $2.5 billion, more than 215 times the earnings of Blue Nile. However, the return on asset ratios for the two companies reveal that Blue Nile produced higher earnings

EXHIBIT 3.11		
COLLINS BROKERAGE SERVICES, INC.		
Post-Closing Trial Balance		
December 31, 2011		
Account Title	**Debit**	**Credit**
Cash	$ 6,050	
Accounts receivable	2,360	
Accrued interest receivable	750	
Prepaid insurance	700	
Supplies	125	
Land	26,000	
Accounts payable		$ 1,900
Salaries payable		800
Unearned service revenue		300
Common stock		29,000
Retained earnings		4,785
Totals	$36,785	$36,785

[1]The use of net income in this ratio ignores the effects of debt financing and income taxation. The effect of these variables on the return on assets ratio is explained in a later chapter.

relative to the assets invested. Comcast's ratio was 2.2 percent while Blue Nile's was 13 percent. Even though Blue Nile earned fewer dollars of net income, the company did a better job than Comcast of managing its assets.

The preceding example demonstrates the usefulness of the relationship between income and assets. Two more ratios that enhance financial statement analysis are discussed in the following paragraphs.

Assessing Debt Risk

Borrowing money can be a risky business. To illustrate, assume two companies have the following financial structures:

	Assets	=	Liabilities	+	Stockholders' Equity
Eastern Company	100	=	20	+	80
Western Company	100	=	80	+	20

Which company has the greater financial risk? If each company incurred a $30 loss, the financial structures would change as follows:

	Assets	=	Liabilities	+	Stockholders' Equity
Eastern Company	70	=	20	+	50
Western Company	70	=	80	+	(10)

Clearly, Western Company is at greater risk. Eastern Company could survive a $30 loss that reduced assets and stockholders' equity. It would still have a $50 balance in stockholders' equity and more than enough assets ($70) to satisfy the creditors' $20 claim. In contrast, a $30 loss would throw Western Company into bankruptcy. The company would have a $10 deficit (negative) balance in stockholders' equity and the remaining assets ($70) would be less than the creditors' $80 claim on assets.

The level of debt risk can be measured in part by using a **debt to assets ratio,** as follows:

$$\frac{\text{Total debt}}{\text{Total assets}}$$

For example, Eastern Company's debt to assets ratio is 20 percent ($20 ÷ $100) while Western Company's is 80 percent ($80 ÷ $100). Why would the owners of Western Company be willing to accept greater debt risk? Assume that both companies produce $12 of revenue and each must pay 10 percent interest on money owed to creditors. Income statements for the two companies appear as follows:[2]

	Eastern Company	Western Company
Revenue	$12	$12
Interest Expense	2	8
Net Income	$10	$ 4

At first glance, the owners of Eastern Company appear better off because Eastern produced higher net income. In fact, however, the owners of *Western* Company are better off. The owners of Eastern Company get $10 of income for investing $80 of their own money into the business, a return on their invested funds of 12.5 percent ($10 ÷ $80).

---

[2]This illustration ignores the effect of income taxes on debt financing. This subject is discussed in a later chapter.

Focus On INTERNATIONAL ISSUES

HOW DO IFRS DIFFER FROM U.S. GAAP?

Chapter 1 discussed the progression toward a single global GAAP in the form of International Financial Reporting Standards (IFRS). That discussion noted that the United States does not currently allow domestic companies to use IFRS; they must follow GAAP. Let's briefly consider just how U.S. GAAP differs from IFRS.

The differences can be summarized in a few broad categories. First, some differences are relatively minor. Consider the case of bank overdrafts. Under IFRS some bank overdrafts are included as a cash inflow and reported on the statement of cash flows. U.S. GAAP does not permit this. Conversely, some differences relate to very significant issues. Both IFRS and GAAP use historical cost as their primary method for reporting information on financial statements, but both allow exceptions in some circumstances. However, IFRS permit more exceptions to historical cost than do GAAP. Some of these differences will be discussed in later chapters.

Some of the differences affect how financial statements are presented in annual reports. IFRS require companies to report all financial statements for the current year and the prior year—two years of comparative data. Rules of the Securities and Exchange Commission require U.S. companies to report two years of balance sheets, the current and prior year, and three years of all other statements. See the financial statements of Target Corporation in Appendix B as an example. Of course, companies can show additional years if they wish.

As you would expect in the first course of accounting, some of the differences between IFRS and GAAP are simply too complex to be covered. Examples of such items relate to business combinations (when one company buys another) and to foreign currency translations (when a company has subsidiaries that operate outside the United States).

Do not be overwhelmed by the differences between IFRS and GAAP. There are many more rules that are alike than that are different. A person who has a reasonable understanding of U.S. GAAP should be able to read financial statements prepared under IFRS without too much difficulty. If you wish more detailed, up-to-date information about IFRS versus GAAP, the large international accounting firms have websites that can help. Two examples are: www.iasplus.com, which is presented by the firm of Deloitte Touche Tohmatsu, and www.kpmgifrg.com, which is presented by the firm of KPMG.

In contrast, the owners of Western Company obtain $4 of net income for their $20 investment, a return on invested funds of 20 percent ($4 ÷ $20).

The relationship between net income and stockholders' equity used above is the **return on equity ratio,** computed as:

$$\frac{\text{Net income}}{\text{Stockholders' equity}}$$

Using borrowed money to increase the return on stockholders' investment is called **financial leverage.** Financial leverage explains why companies are willing to accept the risk of debt. Companies borrow money to make money. If a company can borrow money at 10 percent and invest it at 12 percent, the owners will be better off by 2 percent of the amount borrowed. A business that does not borrow may be missing an opportunity to increase its return on equity.

EXHIBIT 3.12

Three Ratios (in Percentages) for Six Real-World Companies

Industry	Company	Debt to Assets	Return on Assets	Return on Equity
Insurance	Aetna	77	3.9	16.9
	Aflac	92	1.6	18.9
	MetLife	95	0.6	13.0
Oil	Chevron	46	14.8	27.6
	Exxon Mobil	50	19.8	40.0
	Marathon Oil	50	8.3	16.5

Real-World Data

Exhibit 3.12 shows the debt to assets, return on assets, and return on equity ratios for six real-world companies in two different industries. The data are drawn from the companies' 2008 financial reports. Notice Aflac's return on assets ratio was 1.6 percent and MetLife's was 0.6 percent. Neither ratio seems good; banks often pay more than 1.6 percent interest on deposits in savings accounts. The *return on equity* ratios, however, show a different picture; Aflac's was 18.9 percent and MetLife's was 13.0 percent—much better than banks pay depositors.

Exhibit 3.12 shows that while Chevron's return on assets ratio was 25 times higher than Metlife's (14.8 percent versus 0.6 percent), its return on equity ratio was only double that of MetLife (27.6 percent versus 13.0 percent). How can this happen? Compare the debt to assets ratios. MetLife financed 95 percent of its assets with debt compared to Chevron's 46 percent. Financial leverage is a contributing factor. While financial leverage can boost the return on equity, it is not the only factor that affects this ratio.

Since financial leverage offers the opportunity to increase return on equity, why doesn't every company leverage itself to the maximum? There is a down side. When the economy turns down, companies may not be able to produce investment returns that exceed interest rates. A company that has borrowed money at a fixed rate of 8 percent that can only earn 6 percent on its investments will suffer from financial leverage. In other words, financial leverage is a double-edged sword. It can have a negative as well as a positive impact on a company's return on equity ratio.

Finally, compare the ratios in Exhibit 3.12 for companies in the oil industry to the same ratios for companies in the insurance industry. There are significant differences *between* industries, but there are considerable similarities *within* each industry. The debt to assets ratio is much higher for the insurance industry than for the oil industry. However, within each industry, the ratios are clustered fairly close together. Distinct differences between industries and similarities within industries are common business features. When you compare accounting information for different companies, you must consider the industries in which those companies operate.

SCOPE OF COVERAGE

Throughout this text, we introduce ratios directly related to chapter topics. Only a few of the many ratios available to users of financial statements are introduced. Introductory finance courses typically include a more extensive study of ratios and other topics related to financial statement analysis. Many business programs offer an entire course on financial statement analysis. These courses help students learn to judge whether the ratio results signal good or poor performance. Developing such judgment requires understanding how accounting policies and procedures can affect financial ratios. The ratios introduced in this text will enhance your understanding of accounting as a basis for studying more advanced topics in subsequent courses.

A Look Back

This chapter introduced the *double-entry accounting system*. This system was first documented in the 1400s, and is used by most companies today. Key components of the double-entry system are summarized below.

1. Business events can be classified concisely using debit/credit terminology. *Debits* are used to record increases in asset accounts and decreases in liability and stockholders' equity accounts. *Credits* are used to record decreases in asset accounts and increases in liability and stockholders' equity accounts.

2. *T-accounts* are frequently used to analyze and communicate account activity. The account title is placed at the top of the horizontal bar of the T, and increases and decreases are placed on either side of the vertical bar. In a T-account, debits are recorded on the left side and credits are recorded on the right side.

3. Accountants initially record transaction data in journals. The *general journal* is used not only for data entry but also as a shorthand communication tool. Each journal entry includes at least one debit and one credit. An entry is recorded using at least two lines, with the debit recorded on the top line and the credit on the bottom line. The credit is indented to distinguish it from the debit. The general journal format is illustrated here:

Debit	xxx	
Credit		xxx

4. Information is posted (copied) from the journals to *ledger* accounts. The ledger accounts provide the information used to prepare the financial statements.

5. *Trial balances* are used to check the mathematical accuracy of the recording process. Ledger accounts with their associated debit and credit balances are listed in the trial balance. The debit and credit amounts are totaled and compared. An equal amount of debits and credits provides evidence that transactions have been recorded correctly, although errors may still exist. If the debits and credits are *not* equal, it is proof that errors exist.

The double-entry system is just a way to organize accounting data. No matter how we organize the data, the objective is to summarize and report it in a way that is useful for making decisions.

A Look Forward

Chapters 1 through 3 focused on businesses that generate revenue by providing services to their customers. Examples of these types of businesses include consulting, real estate sales, medical services, and legal services. The next chapter introduces accounting practices for businesses that generate revenue by selling goods. Examples of these companies include Wal-Mart, Circuit City, Office Depot, and Lowe's.

SELF-STUDY REVIEW PROBLEM

DP 3

A step-by-step audio-narrated series of slides is provided on the text website at www.mhhe.com/edmonds7e.

The following events apply to the first year of operations for Mestro Financial Services Company:

1. Acquired $28,000 cash by issuing common stock on January 1, 2011.
2. Purchased $1,100 of supplies on account.
3. Paid $12,000 cash in advance for a one-year lease on office space.
4. Earned $23,000 of consulting revenue on account.
5. Incurred $16,000 of general operating expenses on account.
6. Collected $20,000 cash from receivables.
7. Paid $13,000 cash on accounts payable.
8. Paid a $1,000 cash dividend to stockholders.

Information for Adjusting Entries

9. There was $200 of supplies on hand at the end of the accounting period.
10. The one-year lease on the office space was effective beginning on October 1, 2011.
11. There was $1,200 of accrued salaries at the end of 2011.

Required

a. Record the preceding events in general journal format.
b. Post the transaction data from the general journal into general ledger T-accounts.
c. Prepare an adjusted trial balance.
d. Prepare an income statement, statement of changes in stockholders' equity, balance sheet, and statement of cash flows.
e. Prepare the appropriate closing entries in general journal format.

Solution to Requirement a

Event No.	Account Title	Debit	Credit
1	Cash	28,000	
	Common Stock		28,000
2	Supplies	1,100	
	Accounts Payable		1,100
3	Prepaid Rent	12,000	
	Cash		12,000
4	Accounts Receivable	23,000	
	Consulting Revenue		23,000
5	General Operating Expenses	16,000	
	Accounts Payable		16,000
6	Cash	20,000	
	Accounts Receivable		20,000
7	Accounts Payable	13,000	
	Cash		13,000
8	Dividends	1,000	
	Cash		1,000
9	Supplies Expense	900	
	Supplies		900
10	Rent Expense	3,000	
	Prepaid Rent		3,000
11	Salaries Expense	1,200	
	Salaries Payable		1,200

Solution to Requirement b

MESTRO FINANCIAL SERVICES COMPANY
T-Accounts, 2011

Assets = Liabilities + Equity

Cash

1.	28,000	3.	12,000
6.	20,000	7.	13,000
		8.	1,000
Bal.	22,000		

Accounts Receivable

| 4. | 23,000 | 6. | 20,000 |
| Bal. | 3,000 | | |

Supplies

| 2. | 1,100 | 9. | 900 |
| Bal. | 200 | | |

Prepaid Rent

| 3. | 12,000 | 10. | 3,000 |
| Bal. | 9,000 | | |

Accounts Payable

7.	13,000	2.	1,100
		5.	16,000
		Bal.	4,100

Salaries Payable

| | | 11. | 1,200 |
| | | Bal. | 1,200 |

Common Stock

| | | 1. | 28,000 |
| | | Bal. | 28,000 |

Dividends

| 8. | 1,000 | |

Consulting Revenue

| | | 4. | 23,000 |

General Operating Expenses

| 5. | 16,000 | |

Salaries Expense

| 11. | 1,200 | |

Supplies Expense

| 9. | 900 | |

Rent Expense

| 10. | 3,000 | |

Solution to Requirement c

MESTRO FINANCIAL SERVICES COMPANY
Trial Balance
December 31, 2011

Account Titles	Debit	Credit
Cash	$22,000	
Accounts receivable	3,000	
Supplies	200	
Prepaid rent	9,000	
Accounts payable		$ 4,100
Salaries payable		1,200
Common stock		28,000
Dividends	1,000	
Consulting revenue		23,000
General operating expenses	16,000	
Salaries expense	1,200	
Supplies expense	900	
Rent expense	3,000	
Totals	$56,300	$56,300

Solution to Requirement d

MESTRO FINANCIAL SERVICES COMPANY
Financial Statements
For 2011

Income Statement
For the Year Ended December 31, 2011

Consulting revenue		$23,000
Expenses		
General operating expenses	$16,000	
Salaries expense	1,200	
Supplies expense	900	
Rent expense	3,000	
Total expenses		(21,100)
Net income		$ 1,900

Statement of Changes in Stockholders' Equity
For the Year Ended December 31, 2011

Beginning common stock	$ 0	
Plus: Common stock issued	28,000	
Ending common stock		$28,000
Beginning retained earnings	0	
Plus: Net income	1,900	
Less: Dividends	(1,000)	
Ending retained earnings		900
Total stockholders' equity		$28,900

Balance Sheet
As of December 31, 2011

Assets		
Cash	$22,000	
Accounts receivable	3,000	
Supplies	200	
Prepaid rent	9,000	
Total assets		$34,200
Liabilities		
Accounts payable	$ 4,100	
Salaries payable	1,200	
Total liabilities		$ 5,300
Stockholders' equity		
Common stock	28,000	
Retained earnings	900	
Total stockholders' equity		28,900
Total liabilities and stockholders' equity		$34,200

continued

Statement of Cash Flows For the Year Ended December 31, 2011		
Cash Flows from Operating Activities		
Inflow from customers	$20,000	
Outflow for expenses	(25,000)	
Net cash flow for operating activities		$ (5,000)
Cash flows from investing activities		0
Cash flows from financing activities		
Inflow from issue of common stock	28,000	
Outflow for dividends	(1,000)	
Net cash flow from financing activities		27,000
Net change in cash		22,000
Plus: Beginning cash balance		0
Ending cash balance		$22,000

Solution to Requirement e

Date	Account Title	Debit	Credit
Dec. 31	Consulting Revenue	23,000	
	Retained Earnings		23,000
Dec. 31	Retained Earnings	21,100	
	General Operating Expenses		16,000
	Salaries Expense		1,200
	Supplies Expense		900
	Rent Expense		3,000
Dec. 31	Retained Earnings	1,000	
	Dividends		1,000

KEY TERMS

account balance 124
books of original entry 134
chart of accounts 135
closing entries 139
credit 124

debit 124
debt to assets ratio 142
double-entry accounting 125
financial leverage 143
fiscal year 123

general journal 134
general ledger 135
journals 134
posting 135
return on assets ratio 141

return on equity ratio 143
source documents 133
special journals 134
T-account 124
trial balance 137

QUESTIONS

1. What are the two fundamental equality requirements of the double-entry accounting system?

2. Define *debit* and *credit*. How are assets, liabilities, common stock, retained earnings, revenues, expenses, and dividends affected (increased or decreased) by debits and by credits?

3. How is the balance of an account determined?

4. What are the three primary sources of business assets?

5. What are the three primary ways a business may use assets?

6. Give an example of an asset exchange transaction.

7. How does a debit to an expense account ultimately affect retained earnings? Stockholders' equity?

8. What accounts normally have debit balances? What accounts normally have credit balances?

9. What is the primary source of information for preparing the financial statements?

10. What is the purpose of a journal?

11. What is the difference between the *general journal* and special journals?

12. What is a ledger? What is its function in the accounting system?

13. What is the purpose of closing entries?

14. Do all companies close their books on December 31? Why or why not?

15. At a minimum, what information is recorded in the general journal?

16. What is the purpose of a trial balance?

17. When should a trial balance be prepared?

18. What does the term *posting* mean?

19. What information does the return on assets ratio provide about a company?

20. What information does the debt to assets ratio provide about a company?

21. What is financial leverage?

22. Explain how financial leverage impacts the return on equity ratio.

MULTIPLE-CHOICE QUESTIONS

Quiz 3

Multiple-choice questions are provided on the text website at www.mhhe.com/edmonds7e.

EXERCISES—SERIES A

All applicable Exercises in Series A are available with McGraw-Hill's *Connect Accounting*.

LO 1

Exercise 3-1A   *Matching debit and credit terminology with accounting elements*

Required

Complete the following table by indicating whether a debit or credit is used to increase or decrease the balance of accounts belonging to each category of financial statement elements. The appropriate debit/credit terminology has been identified for the first category (assets) as an example.

Category of Elements	Used to Increase This Element	Used to Decrease This Element
Assets	Debit	Credit
Liabilities		
Common Stock		
Retained Earnings		
Revenue		
Expense		
Dividends		

LO 1

Exercise 3-2A   *Debit/credit terminology*

Two introductory accounting students were arguing about how to record a transaction involving an exchange of cash for land. Trisha stated that the transaction should have a debit to Land and a credit to Cash; Tony argued that the reverse (debit to Cash and credit to Land) represented the appropriate treatment.

Required

Which student was correct? Defend your position.

Exercise 3-3A *Matching debit and credit terminology with account titles*

Required

Indicate whether each of the following accounts normally has a debit balance or a credit balance.

a. Unearned Revenue
b. Service Revenue
c. Dividends
d. Land
e. Accounts Receivable
f. Cash
g. Common Stock
h. Prepaid Rent
i. Supplies
j. Accounts Payable
k. Interest Revenue
l. Rent Expense

Exercise 3-4A *Applying debit/credit terminology to accounting events*

Required

a. In parallel columns, list the accounts that would be debited and credited for each of the following unrelated transactions:

  (1) Provided services on account.
  (2) Paid cash for operating expenses.
  (3) Acquired cash from the issue of common stock.
  (4) Purchased supplies on account.
  (5) Purchased land for cash.
  (6) Paid a cash dividend to the stockholders.
  (7) Provided services for cash.
  (8) Recognized accrued salaries at the end of the period.
  (9) Recognized accrued interest revenue.

b. Show how each transaction affects the financial statements by placing a + for increase, − for decrease, and NA for not affected under each component in a horizontal statements model like the one shown below. Also, in the Cash Flow column, use the letters OA to designate operating activity, IA for investing activity, and FA for financing activity. The first event is recorded as an example.

Assets	=	Liab.	+	Equity	Rev.	−	Exp.	=	Net Inc.	Cash Flow
+		NA		+	+		NA		+	NA

Exercise 3-5A *Debit/credit terminology*

Required

For each of the following independent events, identify the account that would be debited and the account that would be credited. The accounts for the first event are identified as an example.

Event	Account Debited	Account Credited
a	Cash	Common Stock

a. Received cash by issuing common stock.
b. Received cash for services to be performed in the future.
c. Provided services on account.
d. Paid accounts payable.
e. Paid cash in advance for one year's rent.
f. Paid cash for operating expenses.
g. Paid salaries payable.
h. Purchased supplies on account.
i. Paid cash dividends to the stockholders.
j. Recognized revenue for services completed; previously collected the cash in Event *b*.

k. Received cash in payment of accounts receivable.

l. Paid salaries expense.

m. Recognized expense for prepaid rent that had been used up by the end of the accounting period.

n. Recognized accrued interest revenue.

LO 1

Exercise 3-6A   *Identifying transaction type, its effect on the accounting equation, and whether the effect is recorded with a debit or credit*

Required

Identify whether each of the following transactions is an asset source (AS), asset use (AU), asset exchange (AE), or claims exchange (CE). Also explain how each event affects the accounting equation by placing a + for *increase,* − for *decrease,* and NA for *not affected* under each of the components of the accounting equation. Finally, indicate whether the effect requires a debit or credit entry. The first event is recorded as an example.

						Stockholders Equity		
Event	Type of Event	Assets	=	Liabilities	+	Common Stock	+	Retained Earnings
a	AS	+ Debit		NA		NA		+ Credit

a. Provided services on account.

b. Received cash in payment of accounts receivable.

c. Purchased land by paying cash.

d. Recognized revenue for services completed; cash collected previously.

e. Paid a cash dividend to the stockholders.

f. Paid cash in advance for one year's rent.

g. Received cash for services to be performed in the future.

h. Incurred other operating expenses on account.

i. Paid salaries payable.

j. Recognized expense for prepaid rent that had been used up by the end of the accounting period.

k. Provided services for cash.

l. Purchased supplies on account.

m. Recognized expense for supplies used during the period.

n. Recognized accrued interest revenue.

LO 1, 2

Exercise 3-7A   *Identifying increases and decreases in T-accounts*

Required

For each of the following T-accounts, indicate the side of the account that should be used to record an increase or decrease in the account balance.

Cash		**Accounts Payable**		**Common Stock**	
Debit	Credit	Debit	Credit	Debit	Credit

Accounts Receivable		**Salaries Payable**		**Dividends**	
Debit	Credit	Debit	Credit	Debit	Credit

Supplies				**Service Revenue**	
Debit	Credit			Debit	Credit

				Other Operating Expense	
				Debit	Credit

Exercise 3-8A   *T-accounts and the accounting equation*   LO 2

Required

Record each of the following Cummings Co. events in T-accounts and then explain how the event affects the accounting equation.

a. Received $20,000 cash by issuing common stock.
b. Purchased supplies for $900 cash.
c. Performed services on account for $7,000.
d. Paid cash for $4,000 of salaries expense.

Exercise 3-9A   *Recording receivables and identifying their effect on financial*   LO 2
                    statements

Wong Company performed services on account for $60,000 in 2011, its first year of operations. Wong collected $48,000 cash from accounts receivable during 2011 and the remaining $12,000 in cash during 2012.

Required

a. Record the 2011 transactions in T-accounts.
b. Record the 2011 transactions in a horizontal statements model like the following one:

Assets		=	Liab.	+	Equity	Rev.	−	Exp.	=	Net Inc.	Cash Flow
Cash	+ Accts. Rec.	=			Ret. Earn.						

c. Determine the amount of revenue Wong would report on the 2011 income statement.
d. Determine the amount of cash flow from operating activities Wong would report on the 2011 statement of cash flows.
e. Open a T-account for Retained Earnings, and close the 2011 Service Revenue account to the Retained Earnings account.
f. Record the 2012 cash collection in the appropriate T-accounts.
g. Record the 2012 transaction in a horizontal statements model like the one shown in Requirement *b*.
h. Assuming no other transactions occur in 2012, determine the amount of net income and the net cash flow from operating activities for 2012.

Exercise 3-10A   *Recording supplies and identifying their effect on financial statements*   LO 2

Kim Perz started and operated a small family consulting firm in 2011. The firm was affected by two events: (1) Perz provided $18,000 of services on account, and (2) she purchased $5,000 of supplies on account. There were $900 of supplies on hand as of December 31, 2011.

Required

a. Open T-accounts and record the two transactions in the accounts.
b. Record the required year-end adjusting entry to reflect the use of supplies.
c. Record the above transactions in a horizontal statements model like the following one.

Assets			=	Liab.	+	Equity	Rev.	−	Exp.	=	Net Inc.	Cash Flow
Accts. Rec.	+	Supplies	=	Accts. Pay.	+	Ret. Earn.						

d. Explain why the amounts of net income and net cash flow from operating activities differ.
e. Record and post the required closing entries, and prepare an after-closing trial balance.

LO 2

Exercise 3-11A   *Recording unearned revenue and identifying its effect on financial statements*

Zhen received a $60,000 cash advance on March 1, 2011, for legal services to be performed in the future. Services were to be provided for a one-year term beginning March 1, 2011.

Required

a. Record the March 1 cash receipt in T-accounts.

b. Record in T-accounts the adjustment required as of December 31, 2011.

c. Record the preceding transaction and related adjustment in a horizontal statements model like the following one:

Assets	=	Liab.	+	Equity	Rev.	−	Exp.	=	Net Inc.	Cash Flow

d. Determine the amount of net income on the 2011 income statement. What is the amount of net cash flow from operating activities for 2011?

e. What amount of unearned revenue would Zhen report on the December 31, 2011, balance sheet?

LO 2

Exercise 3-12A   *Using a T-account to determine cash flow from operating activities*

Koch Inc. began the accounting period with a $75,000 debit balance in its Accounts Receivable account. During the accounting period, Koch earned revenue on account of $320,000. The ending Accounts Receivable balance was $62,000.

Required

Based on this information alone, determine the amount of cash inflow from operating activities during the accounting period. (*Hint:* Use a T-account for Accounts Receivable. Enter the debits and credits for the given events, and solve for the missing amount.)

LO 2

Exercise 3-13A   *Using a T-account to determine cash flow from operating activities*

Cole Company began the accounting period with an $18,000 credit balance in its Accounts Payable account. During the accounting period, Cole incurred expenses on account of $54,000. The ending Accounts Payable balance was $24,000.

Required

Based on this information, determine the amount of cash outflow for expenses during the accounting period. (*Hint:* Use a T-account for Accounts Payable. Enter the debits and credits for the given events, and solve for the missing amount.)

LO 3

Exercise 3-14A   *Recording events in the general journal and the effect on financial statements*

Required

Record each of the following transactions in general journal form and then show the effect of the transaction in the horizontal statements model. The first transaction is shown as an example.

Account Title	Debit	Credit
Cash	8,000	
Unearned Revenue		8,000

Assets	=	Liab.	+	Equity	Rev.	−	Exp.	=	Net Inc.	Cash Flow
8,000	=	8,000	+	NA	NA	−	NA	=	NA	8,000 OA

a. Received $8,000 cash for services to be performed at a later date.
b. Purchased supplies for $1,200 cash.
c. Performed $25,000 worth of services on account.
d. Charged $1,500 on account for operating expense.
e. Collected $19,000 cash on accounts receivable.
f. Paid $900 on accounts payable.
g. Paid $4,800 cash in advance for an insurance policy.
h. Recorded the adjusting entry to recognize $3,600 of insurance expense.
i. Recorded the adjusting entry to recognize $300 of accrued interest revenue.

Exercise 3-15A *Determining the effect of errors on the trial balance*   LO 4

Required

Explain how each of the following posting errors affects a trial balance. State whether the trial balance will be out of balance because of the posting error, and indicate which side of the trial balance will have a higher amount after each independent entry is posted. If the posting error does not affect the equality of debits and credits in the trial balance, state that the error will not cause an inequality and explain why.

a. A $1,000 credit to Salaries Payable was not posted.
b. A $2,400 debit to Cash was posted as a $4,200 debit.
c. A $2,000 debit to Prepaid Rent was debited to Rent Expense.
d. The collection of $500 of accounts receivable was posted to Accounts Receivable twice.
e. A $2,000 credit to Accounts Payable was posted as a credit to Cash.

Exercise 3-16A *Recording prepaid items and identifying their effect on financial*   LO 3
statements

California Mining began operations by issuing common stock for $100,000. The company paid $90,000 cash in advance for a one-year contract to lease machinery for the business. The lease agreement was signed on March 1, 2011, and was effective immediately. California Mining received $115,000 of cash revenue in 2011.

Required

a. Record the March 1 cash payment in general journal format.
b. Record in general journal format the adjustment required as of December 31, 2011.
c. Record all 2011 events in a horizontal statements model like the following one:

Assets			=	Liab.	+	Equity	Rev.	−	Exp.	=	Net Inc.	Cash Flow
Cash	+	Prep. Rent	=			Ret. Earn.						

d. What amount of net income would California Mining report on the 2011 income statement? What is the amount of net cash flow from operating activities for 2011?
e. Determine the amount of prepaid rent California Mining would report on the December 31, 2011, balance sheet.

Exercise 3-17A *Recording accrued salaries and identifying their effect on financial*   LO 3
statements

On December 31, 2011, Red River Company had accrued salaries of $9,500.

Required

a. Record in general journal format the adjustment required as of December 31, 2011.

b. Record the above adjustment in a horizontal statements model like the following one:

Assets	=	Liab.	+	Equity	Rev.	−	Exp.	=	Net Inc.	Cash Flow
		Sal. Pay.	+	Ret. Earn.						

c. Determine the amount of net income Red River would report on the 2011 income statement, assuming that Red River received $25,000 of cash revenue. What is the amount of net cash flow from operating activities for 2011?

d. What amount of salaries payable would Red River report on the December 31, 2011, balance sheet?

LO 3

Exercise 3-18A   *Preparing closing entries*

The following financial information was taken from the books of Ritz Salon.

Account Balances as of December 31, 2011	
Accounts Receivable	$28,000
Accounts Payable	7,500
Advertising Expense	2,500
Cash	40,300
Common Stock	20,000
Dividends	5,000
Land	13,500
Prepaid Rent	3,200
Rent Expense	7,800
Retained Earnings 1/1/2011	19,400
Salaries Expense	32,000
Salaries Payable	11,800
Service Revenue	76,500
Supplies	400
Supplies Expense	2,500

Required

a. Prepare the journal entries necessary to close the temporary accounts December 31, 2011, for Ritz Salon.

b. What is the balance in the Retained Earnings account after the closing entries are posted?

LO 2, 3

Exercise 3-19A   *Recording transactions in general journal and T-accounts*

The following events apply to Pearson Service Co. for 2011, its first year of operation.

1. Received cash of $50,000 from the issue of common stock.
2. Performed $90,000 worth of services on account.
3. Paid $64,000 cash for salaries expense.
4. Purchased supplies for $12,000 on account.
5. Collected $78,000 of accounts receivable.
6. Paid $8,500 of the accounts payable.
7. Paid a $5,000 dividend to the stockholders.
8. Had $1,500 of supplies on hand at the end of the period.

Required

a. Record these events in general journal form.

b. Post the entries to T-accounts and determine the ending balance in each account.

c. Determine the amount of total assets at the end of 2011.

d. Determine the amount of net income for 2011.

Exercise 3-20A   *Preparing a trial balance*   LO 4

Required

On December 31, 2011, Chang Company had the following normal account balances in its general ledger. Use this information to prepare a trial balance.

Common Stock	$25,000
Salaries Expense	16,000
Office Supplies	1,800
Advertising Expense	2,500
Retained Earnings, 1/1/2011	14,200
Unearned Revenue	18,000
Accounts Receivable	6,500
Cash	60,000
Service Revenue	76,000
Dividends	5,000
Prepaid Insurance	6,400
Land	22,000
Rent Expense	15,000
Accounts Payable	2,000

Exercise 3-21A   *Recording events in the general journal, posting to T-accounts, and*   LO 2, 3, 4
preparing a trial balance

The following events apply to Complete Business Service in 2011, its first year of operations.

1. Received $30,000 cash from the issue of common stock.

2. Earned $25,000 of service revenue on account.

3. Incurred $10,000 of operating expenses on account.

4. Received $20,000 cash for performing services.

5. Paid $8,000 cash to purchase land.

6. Collected $22,000 of cash from accounts receivable.

7. Received a $6,000 cash advance for services to be provided in the future.

8. Purchased $900 of supplies on account.

9. Made a $7,500 payment on accounts payable.

10. Paid a $5,000 cash dividend to the stockholders.

11. Recognized $500 of supplies expense.

12. Recognized $5,000 of revenue for services provided to the customer in Event 7.

13. Recognized $900 of accrued interest revenue.

Required

a. Record the events in the general journal.

b. Post the events to T-accounts and determine the ending account balances.

c. Test the equality of the debit and credit balances of the T-accounts by preparing a trial balance.

LO 2, 3, 4

Exercise 3-22A *Recording events in the general journal, posting to T-accounts, and preparing closing entries*

At the beginning of 2011, Mitchell Cleaning Service had the following normal balances in its accounts:

Account	Balance
Cash	$30,000
Accounts Receivable	19,000
Accounts Payable	12,400
Common Stock	24,000
Retained Earnings	12,600

The following events apply to Mitchell for 2011.

1. Provided $65,000 of services on account.
2. Incurred $3,100 of operating expenses on account.
3. Collected $56,000 of accounts receivable.
4. Paid $36,000 cash for salaries expense.
5. Paid $15,000 cash as a partial payment on accounts payable.
6. Paid an $8,000 cash dividend to the stockholders.

Required

a. Record these events in a general journal.
b. Open T-accounts and post the beginning balances and the preceding transactions to the appropriate accounts. Determine the balance of each account.
c. Record the beginning balances and the events in a horizontal statements model such as the following one:

Assets		=	Liab.	+	Equity		Rev.	–	Exp.	=	Net Inc.	Cash Flow
	Accts.		Accts.		Common	Ret.						
Cash +	Rec.	=	Pay.	+	Stock	+ Earn.						

d. Record the closing entries in the general journal and post them to the T-accounts. What is the amount of net income for the year?
e. What is the amount of *change* in retained earnings for the year? Is the change in retained earnings different from the amount of net income? If so, why?

LO 5

Exercise 3-23A *Using ratio analysis to assess financial risk*

The following information was drawn from the balance sheets of two companies:

Company	Assets	=	Liabilities	+	Equity
East	$200,000		$ 84,000		$116,000
West	600,000		168,000		432,000

Required

a. Compute the debt to assets ratio to measure the level of financial risk of both companies.
b. Compare the two ratios computed in Requirement *a* to identify which company has the higher level of financial risk.

IFRS

Exercise 3-24A *IFRS and U.S. GAAP*

a. Describe some way that U.S. GAAP and IFRS are different.
b. How are U.S. GAAP and IFRS alike for reporting purposes?

PROBLEMS—SERIES A

All applicable Problems in Series A are available with McGraw-Hill's
Connect Accounting.

connect
|ACCOUNTING

Problem 3-25A *Identifying debit and credit balances*

LO 1

Required

CHECK FIGURES
a. Land: Debit
o. Accounts Payable: Credit

Indicate whether each of the following accounts normally has a debit or credit balance.

a. Land
b. Salaries Expense
c. Rent Expense
d. Common Stock
e. Cash
f. Salaries Payable
g. Accounts Receivable
h. Insurance Expense
i. Prepaid Insurance
j. Retained Earnings

k. Supplies Expense
l. Prepaid Rent
m. Service Revenue
n. Supplies
o. Accounts Payable
p. Unearned Revenue
q. Operating Expense
r. Dividends
s. Interest Revenue
t. Interest Receivable

Problem 3-26A *Transaction type and debit/credit terminology*

LO 1

The following events apply to Box Enterprises.

1. Acquired $30,000 cash from the issue of common stock.
2. Paid salaries to employees, $8,000 cash.
3. Collected $9,000 cash for services to be performed in the future.
4. Paid cash for utilities expense, $1,200.
5. Recognized $28,000 of service revenue on account.
6. Paid a $5,000 cash dividend to the stockholders.
7. Purchased $2,000 of supplies on account.
8. Received $18,000 cash for services rendered.
9. Paid cash to rent office space for the next 12 months, $7,800.
10. Paid cash of $9,200 for operating expenses.
11. Paid on accounts payable, $1,200.
12. Recognized $3,250 of rent expense related to cash paid in a prior transaction (see Event 9).
13. Recognized $6,000 of revenue for services performed for which cash had been previously collected (see Event 3).
14. Recognized $4,800 of accrued salaries expense.
15. Recognized $400 of accrued interest revenue.

Required

Identify each event as asset source (AS), asset use (AU), asset exchange (AE), or claims exchange (CE). Also identify the account to be debited and the account to be credited when the transaction is recorded. The first event is recorded as an example.

Event No.	Type of Event	Account Debited	Account Credited
1	AS	Cash	Common Stock

LO 2, 4

Problem 3-27A *Recording events in a statements model and T-accounts and preparing a trial balance*

The following accounting events apply to Parks Co. for the year 2011:

Asset Source Transactions

1. Began operations when the business acquired $20,000 cash from the issue of common stock.
2. Performed services and collected cash of $1,000.
3. Collected $4,500 of cash in advance for services to be provided over the next 12 months.
4. Provided $12,000 of services on account.
5. Purchased supplies of $420 on account.

Asset Exchange Transactions

6. Purchased $4,000 of land for cash.
7. Collected $8,500 of cash from accounts receivable.
8. Purchased $500 of supplies with cash.
9. Paid $3,600 in advance for one year's rent.

Asset Use Transactions

10. Paid $3,000 cash for salaries of employees.
11. Paid a cash dividend of $2,000 to the stockholders.
12. Paid $420 for supplies that had been purchased on account.

Claims Exchange Transactions

13. Placed an advertisement in the local newspaper for $150 and agreed to pay for the ad later.
14. Incurred utilities expense of $125 on account.

Adjusting Entries

15. Recognized $3,000 of revenue for performing services. The collection of cash for these services occurred in a prior transaction. (See Event 3.)
16. Recorded $900 of accrued salary expense at the end of 2011.
17. Recorded supplies expense. Had $120 of supplies on hand at the end of the accounting period.
18. Recognized that three months of prepaid rent had been used up during the accounting period.
19. Recognized $450 of accrued interest revenue.

Required

a. Record each of the preceding transactions in T-accounts and determine the balance of each account.
b. Prepare a before-closing trial balance.
c. Use a horizontal statements model to show how each event affects the balance sheet, income statement, and statement of cash flows. Indicate whether the event increases (+), decreases (−), or does not affect (NA) each element of the financial statements. Also, in the Cash Flow column, use the letters OA to designate operating activity, IA for investing activity, and FA for financing activity. The first event is recorded as an example.

Assets	=	Liab.	+	Equity	Rev.	−	Exp.	=	Net Inc.	Cash Flow
+		NA		+	NA		NA		NA	+ FA

Problem 3-28A *Effect of journal entries on financial statements*   LO 3

Event No.	Account Title	Debit	Credit
1	Cash	xxx	
	Common Stock		xxx
2	Cash	xxx	
	Unearned Revenue		xxx
3	Supplies	xxx	
	Accounts Payable		xxx
4	Accounts Receivable	xxx	
	Service Revenue		xxx
5	Cash	xxx	
	Accounts Receivable		xxx
6	Cash	xxx	
	Service Revenue		xxx
7	Salaries Expense	xxx	
	Cash		xxx
8	Dividends	xxx	
	Cash		xxx
9	Prepaid Rent	xxx	
	Cash		xxx
10	Property Tax Expense	xxx	
	Cash		xxx
11	Supplies Expense	xxx	
	Supplies		xxx
12	Rent Expense	xxx	
	Prepaid Rent		xxx
13	Unearned Revenue	xxx	
	Service Revenue		xxx

Required

The preceding 13 different accounting events are presented in general journal format. Use a horizontal statements model to show how each event affects the balance sheet, income statement, and statement of cash flows. Indicate whether the event increases (+), decreases (−), or does not affect (NA) each element of the financial statements. Also, in the Cash Flow column, use the letters OA to designate operating activity, IA for investing activity, and FA for financing activity. The first event is recorded as an example.

Assets	=	Liab.	+	Equity	Rev.	−	Exp.	=	Net Inc.	Cash Flow
+		NA		+	NA		NA		NA	+ FA

Problem 3-29A *Identifying accounting events from journal entries*   LO 3

Required

The following information is from the records of Swan Design. Write a brief explanation of the accounting event represented in each of the general journal entries.

Date	Account Titles	Debit	Credit
Jan. 1	Cash	12,500	
	Common Stock		12,500
Feb. 10	Supplies	1,550	
	Accounts Payable		1,550
Mar. 1	Cash	13,000	
	Unearned Revenue		13,000
Apr. 1	Prepaid Rent	10,200	
	Cash		10,200
20	Accounts Receivable	18,400	
	Service Revenue		18,400
June 15	Salaries Expense	6,100	
	Cash		6,100
30	Property Tax Expense	3,000	
	Cash		3,000
July 28	Cash	9,300	
	Service Revenue		9,300
Aug. 30	Dividends	3,000	
	Cash		3,000
Sept. 19	Cash	16,000	
	Accounts Receivable		16,000
Dec. 31	Supplies Expense	2,025	
	Supplies		2,025
31	Rent Expense	6,400	
	Prepaid Rent		6,400
31	Unearned Revenue	8,500	
	Service Revenue		8,500

LO 3

Problem 3-30A *Recording adjusting entries in general journal format*

Required

Each of the following independent events requires a year-end adjusting entry. Record each event and the related adjusting entry in general journal format. The first event is recorded as an example. Assume a December 31 closing date.

Date	Account Titles	Debit	Credit
Oct. 1	Prepaid Rent	9,600	
	Cash		9,600
Dec. 31	Rent Expense (9,600 × 3/12)	2,400	
	Prepaid Rent		2,400

a. Paid $9,600 cash in advance on October 1 for a one-year lease on office space.

b. Purchased $3,200 of supplies on account on June 15. At year end, $300 of supplies remained on hand.

c. Received a $9,600 cash advance on September 1 for a contract to provide services for one year.

d. Paid $3,600 cash in advance on May 1 for a one-year insurance policy.

Problem 3-31A *Effect of errors on the trial balance*

The following trial balance was prepared from the ledger accounts of Cook Inc.:

LO 4

CHECK FIGURE
Corrected cash balance: $8,200

COOK INC.
Trial Balance
May 31, 2011

Account Titles	Debit	Credit
Cash	$ 7,200	
Accounts Receivable	1,770	
Supplies	420	
Prepaid Insurance	2,400	
Land	5,000	
Accounts Payable		$ 1,500
Common Stock		1,800
Retained Earnings		7,390
Dividends	400	
Service Revenue		19,600
Rent Expense	3,600	
Salaries Expense	9,000	
Operating Expenses	2,500	
Totals	$32,290	$30,290

The accountant for Cook, Inc., made the following errors during May 2011.

1. The cash purchase of land for $3,000 was recorded as a $5,000 debit to Land and a $3,000 credit to Cash.
2. An $800 purchase of supplies on account was properly recorded as a debit to the Supplies account but was incorrectly recorded as a credit to the Cash account.
3. The company provided services valued at $8,600 to a customer on account. The accountant recorded the transaction in the proper accounts but in the incorrect amount of $6,800.
4. A $600 cash receipt from a customer on an account receivable was not recorded.
5. A $400 cash payment of an account payable was not recorded.
6. The May utility bill, which amounted to $550 on account, was not recorded.

Required

a. Identify the errors that would cause a difference in the total amounts of debits and credits that would appear in a trial balance. Indicate whether the Debit or Credit column would be larger as a result of the error.

b. Indicate whether each of the preceding errors would overstate, understate, or have no effect on the amount of total assets, liabilities, and equity. Your answer should take the following form:

Event No.	Assets	=	Liabilities	+	Stockholders' Equity
1	Overstate		No effect		No effect

c. Prepare a corrected trial balance.

Problem 3-32A *Comprehensive problem: single cycle*

LO 2, 3, 4

The following transactions pertain to Abbott Corporation for 2011.

Jan.	1	Began operations when the business acquired $50,000 cash from the issue of common stock.
Mar.	1	Paid rent for office space for two years, $16,800 cash.
Apr.	14	Purchased $800 of supplies on account.

CHECK FIGURES
d. Net Income: $12,900
Total Assets: $76,300

June 30   Received $24,000 cash in advance for services to be provided over the next year.
July   5   Paid $600 of the accounts payable from April 14.
Aug.   1   Billed a customer $9,600 for services provided during July.
           8   Completed a job and received $3,200 cash for services rendered.
Sept.   1   Paid employee salaries of $36,000 cash.
           9   Received $8,500 cash from accounts receivable.
Oct.   5   Billed customers $34,000 for services rendered on account.
Nov.   2   Paid a $1,000 cash dividend to the stockholders.
Dec. 31   Adjusted records to recognize the services provided on the contract of June 30.
          31   Recorded $2,200 of accrued salaries as of December 31.
          31   Recorded the rent expense for the year. (See March 1.)
          31   Physically counted supplies; $100 was on hand at the end of the period.

Required

a. Record the preceding transactions in the general journal.
b. Post the transactions to T-accounts and calculate the account balances.
c. Prepare a trial balance.
d. Prepare the income statement, statement of changes in stockholders' equity, balance sheet, and statement of cash flows.
e. Prepare the closing entries at December 31.
f. Prepare a trial balance after the closing entries are posted.

LO 2, 3, 4

CHECK FIGURES
b. Ending Cash Balance, 2011: $55,700
g. Net Income, 2012: $26,650

Problem 3-33A   *Two complete accounting cycles*

Pacific Machining experienced the following events during 2011.

1. Started operations by acquiring $50,000 of cash from the issue of common stock.
2. Paid $6,000 cash in advance for rent during the period from February 1, 2011, to February 1, 2012.
3. Received $4,800 cash in advance for services to be performed evenly over the period from September 1, 2011, to September 1, 2012.
4. Performed services for customers on account for $65,200.
5. Incurred operating expenses on account of $31,500.
6. Collected $56,900 cash from accounts receivable.
7. Paid $22,000 cash for salaries expense.
8. Paid $28,000 cash as a partial payment on accounts payable.

Adjusting Entries

9. Made the adjusting entry for the expired rent. (See Event 2.)
10. Recognized revenue for services performed in accordance with Event 3.
11. Recorded $2,100 of accrued salaries at the end of 2011.

Events for 2012

1. Paid $2,100 cash for the salaries accrued at the end of the previous year.
2. Performed services for cash, $40,500.
3. Paid $25,000 cash to purchase land.
4. Paid $5,400 cash in advance for rent during the period from February 1, 2012, to February 1, 2013.
5. Performed services for customers on account for $82,000.
6. Incurred operating expenses on account of $49,100.
7. Collected $76,300 cash from accounts receivable.
8. Paid $48,000 cash as a partial payment on accounts payable.
9. Paid $41,000 cash for salaries expense.
10. Paid a $5,000 cash dividend to the stockholders.

Adjusting Entries

11. Recognized revenue for services performed in accordance with Event 3 in 2011.

12. Made the adjusting entry for the expired rent. (*Hint:* Part of the rent was paid in 2011.)

13. Recorded $3,500 of accrued salaries at the end of 2012.

Required

a. Record the events and adjusting entries for 2011 in general journal form.

b. Post the events for 2011 to T-accounts.

c. Prepare a trial balance for 2011.

d. Prepare an income statement, statement of changes in stockholders' equity, balance sheet, and statement of cash flows for 2011.

e. Record the entries to close the 2011 temporary accounts to Retained Earnings in the general journal and post to the T-accounts.

f. Prepare a post-closing trial balance for December 31, 2011.

g. Repeat requirements *a* through *f* for 2012.

Problem 3-34A   *Using ratio analysis to make comparisons between companies*   **LO 5**

At the end of 2013 the following information is available for the Maine Company and the Iowa Company.

	Maine Co.	Iowa Co.
Total assets	$695,000	$151,000
Total liabilities	417,000	106,000
Stockholders' equity	278,000	45,000
Net income	41,000	10,000

Required

a. For each company, compute the debt to assets ratio and the return on equity ratio.

b. Determine what percentage of each company's assets were financed by the owners.

c. Which company has the greatest level of financial risk?

d. Based on profitability alone, which company performed better?

e. Do the above ratios support the concept of financial leverage? Explain.

EXERCISES—SERIES B

Exercise 3-1B   *Matching debit and credit terminology with accounts*   **LO 1**

Required

Complete the following table by indicating whether a debit or credit is used to increase or decrease the balance of the following accounts. The appropriate debit/credit terminology has been identified for the first account as an example.

Account Titles	Used to Increase This Account	Used to Decrease This Account
Accounts Receivable	Debit	Credit
Accounts Payable		
Common Stock		
Land		
Unearned Revenue		
Service Revenue		
Retained Earnings		
Insurance Expense		
Rent Expense		
Prepaid Rent		
Interest Revenue		

LO 1

Exercise 3-2B   *Debit/credit rules*

Matt, Allison, and Sarah, three accounting students, were discussing the rules of debits and credits. Matt says that debits increase account balances and credits decrease account balances. Allison says that Matt is wrong, that credits increase account balances and debits decrease account balances. Sarah interrupts and declares that they are both correct.

Required

Explain what Sarah meant and give examples of transactions where debits increase account balances, credits decrease account balances, credits increase account balances, and debits decrease account balances.

LO 1

Exercise 3-3B   *Matching debit and credit terminology with account titles*

Required

Indicate whether each of the following accounts normally has a debit balance or a credit balance.

a. Land

b. Dividends

c. Accounts Payable

d. Unearned Revenue

e. Consulting Revenue

f. Salaries Expense

g. Salaries Payable

h. Cash

i. Prepaid Insurance

j. Common Stock

k. Interest Revenue

l. Rent Expense

LO 1

Exercise 3-4B   *Applying debit/credit terminology to accounting events*

Required

a. In parallel columns, list the accounts that would be debited and credited for each of the following unrelated transactions:

(1) Provided services for cash.

(2) Paid cash for salaries expense.

(3) Paid in advance for two-year lease on office space.

(4) Acquired cash from the issue of common stock.

(5) Provided services on account.

(6) Purchased supplies for cash.

(7) Recognized expense for prepaid rent that had been used up by the end of the accounting period.

(8) Recorded accrued salaries at the end of the accounting period.

(9) Recognized accrued interest revenue.

b. Show how each transaction affects the financial statements by placing a + for increase, − for decrease, and NA for not affected under each component in a horizontal statements model like the one shown below. Also, in the Cash Flow column, use the letters OA to designate operating activity, IA for investing activity, and FA for financing activity. The first event is recorded as an example.

Assets	=	Liab.	+	Equity	Rev.	−	Exp.	=	Net Inc.	Cash Flow
+		NA		+	+		NA		+	+ OA

LO 1

Exercise 3-5B   *Debit/credit terminology*

Required

For each of the following independent events, identify the account that would be debited and the account that would be credited. The accounts for the first event are identified as an example.

Event	Account Debited	Account Credited
a	Cash	Common Stock

a. Received cash by issuing common stock.
b. Received cash for services to be performed in the future.
c. Paid salaries payable.
d. Provided services on account.
e. Paid cash for operating expenses.
f. Purchased supplies on account.
g. Recognized revenue for services completed. Cash had been collected in Event *b*.
h. Paid accounts payable.
i. Received cash in payment of accounts receivable.
j. Paid a cash dividend to the stockholders.
k. Recognized accrued salaries expense.
l. Recognized expense for supplies used during the period.
m. Performed services for cash.
n. Recognized accrued interest revenue.

Exercise 3-6B *Identifying transaction type, its effect on the accounting equation, and whether the effect is recorded with a debit or credit* LO 1

Required

Identify whether each of the following transactions is an asset source (AS), asset use (AU), asset exchange (AE), or claims exchange (CE). Also explain how each event affects the accounting equation by placing a + for *increase,* − for *decrease,* and NA for *not affected* under each of the components of the accounting equation. Finally, indicate whether the effect requires a debit or credit entry. The first event is recorded as an example.

Event	Type of Event	Assets	=	Liabilities	+	Common Stock	+	Retained Earnings
						Stockholders' Equity		
a	AE	+ Debit − Credit		NA		NA		NA

a. Purchased land with cash.
b. Provided services for cash.
c. Purchased supplies on account.
d. Paid accounts payable.
e. Acquired cash from the issue of common stock.
f. Received cash in payment of accounts receivable.
g. Paid cash in advance for one year of rent.
h. Paid salaries payable.
i. Received cash for services to be performed in the future.
j. Paid a cash dividend to the stockholders.
k. Recognized revenue for services completed for which cash had been collected previously.
l. Recognized expense for supplies used during the period.
m. Incurred other operating expenses on account.
n. Recognized accrued interest revenue.

Exercise 3-7B *Identifying increases and decreases in T-accounts* LO 1, 2

Required

For each of the following T-accounts, indicate the side of the account that should be used to record an increase or decrease in the financial statement element.

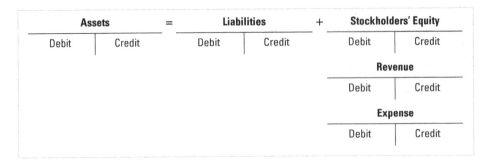

Assets		=	Liabilities		+	Stockholders' Equity	
Debit	Credit		Debit	Credit		Debit	Credit
						Revenue	
						Debit	Credit
						Expense	
						Debit	Credit

LO 2

Exercise 3-8B *T-accounts and the accounting equation*

Required

Record each of the following Lang Co. events in T-accounts, and then explain how the event affects the accounting equation.

a. Received $5,000 cash by issuing common stock.
b. Purchased supplies for $250 cash.
c. Purchased land for $10,000 cash.
d. Performed services for $800 cash.

LO 2

Exercise 3-9B *Recording receivables and identifying their effect on financial statements*

Boone Company performed services on account for $40,000 in 2011. Boone collected $25,000 cash from accounts receivable during 2011, and the remaining $15,000 was collected in cash during 2012.

Required

a. Record the 2011 transactions in T-accounts.
b. Record the 2011 transactions in a horizontal statements model like the following one:

Assets			= Liab. +	Equity	Rev.	− Exp.	= Net Inc.	Cash Flow
Cash	+	Accts. Rec. =		Ret. Earn.				

c. Determine the amount of revenue Boone would report on the 2011 income statement.
d. Determine the amount of cash flow from operating activities Boone would report on the 2011 statement of cash flows.
e. Open a T-account for Retained Earnings, and close the 2011 Service Revenue account to the Retained Earnings account.
f. Record the 2012 cash collection in the appropriate T-accounts.
g. Record the 2012 transaction in a horizontal statements model like the one shown in Requirement *b*.
h. Assuming no other transactions occur in 2012, determine the amount of net income and the net cash flow from operating activities for 2012.

LO 2

Exercise 3-10B *Recording supplies and identifying their effect on financial statements*

Wayne Dunn started and operated a small family architectural firm in 2011. The firm was affected by two events: (1) Dunn provided $25,000 of services on account, and (2) he purchased $6,000 of supplies on account. There were $500 of supplies on hand as of December 31, 2011.

Required

a. Open T-accounts and record the two transactions in the accounts.
b. Record the required year-end adjusting entry to reflect the use of supplies.

c. Record the preceding transactions in a horizontal statements model like the following one:

Assets			=	Liab.	+	Equity	Rev.	–	Exp.	=	Net Inc.	Cash Flow
Accts. Rec.	+	Supplies	=	Accts. Pay.	+	Ret. Earn.						

d. Explain why the amounts of net income and net cash flow from operating activities differ.

e. Record and post the required closing entries, and prepare an after-closing trial balance.

Exercise 3-11B *Recording unearned revenue and identifying its effect on financial statements*

LO 2

Margarete received a $60,000 cash advance payment on June 1, 2011, for consulting services to be performed in the future. Services were to be provided for a one-year term beginning June 1, 2011.

Required

a. Record the June 1 cash receipt in T-accounts.

b. Record in T-accounts the adjustment required as of December 31, 2011.

c. Record the preceding transaction and related adjustment in a horizontal statements model like the following one:

Assets	=	Liab.	+	Equity	Rev.	–	Exp.	=	Net Inc.	Cash Flow

d. Determine the amount of net income on the 2011 income statement. What is the amount of net cash flow from operating activities for 2011?

e. What amount of liabilities would Margarete report on the 2011 balance sheet?

Exercise 3-12B *Using a T-account to determine cash flow from operating activities*

LO 2

ABC began the accounting period with a $58,000 debit balance in its Accounts Receivable account. During the accounting period, ABC earned revenue on account of $126,000. The ending Accounts Receivable balance was $54,000.

Required

Based on this information alone, determine the amount of cash inflow from operating activities during the accounting period. (*Hint:* Use a T-account for Accounts Receivable. Enter the debits and credits for the given events, and solve for the missing amount.)

Exercise 3-13B *Using a T-account to determine cash flow from operating activities*

LO 2

The Dive Company began the accounting period with a $40,000 credit balance in its Accounts Payable account. During the accounting period, Dive incurred expenses on account of $95,000. The ending Accounts Payable balance was $28,000.

Required

Based on this information, determine the amount of cash outflow for expenses during the accounting period. (*Hint:* Use a T-account for Accounts Payable. Enter the debits and credits for the given events, and solve for the missing amount.)

Exercise 3-14B *Recording events in the general journal and effect on financial statements*

LO 3

Required

Record each of the following transactions in general journal form and then show the effect of the transaction in a horizontal statements model. The first transaction is shown as an example.

Account Title	Debit	Credit
Accounts Receivable	19,000	
Service Revenue		19,000

Assets	=	Liab.	+	Equity	Rev.	−	Exp.	=	Net Inc.	Cash Flow
19,000				19,000	19,000		NA		19,000	NA

a. Performed $19,000 of services on account.
b. Purchased land for $24,000 cash.
c. Purchased supplies for $530 cash.
d. Received $3,000 cash for services to be performed at a later date.
e. Collected $8,400 cash on accounts receivable.
f. Paid $2,300 cash in advance for an insurance policy.
g. Paid $1,200 on accounts payable.
h. Recorded the adjusting entry to recognize $800 of insurance expense.
i. Recorded the adjusting entry to recognize $600 accrued interest revenue.

LO 4

Exercise 3-15B   *Determining the effect of errors on the trial balance*

Required

Explain how each of the following posting errors affects a trial balance. State whether the trial balance will be out of balance because of the posting error, and indicate which side of the trial balance will have a higher amount after each independent entry is posted. If the posting error does not affect the equality of debits and credits in the trial balance, state that the error will not cause an inequality and explain why.

a. A $400 debit to Rent Expense was posted twice.
b. A $1,200 credit to Accounts Payable was not posted.
c. A $400 credit to Unearned Revenue was credited to Service Revenue.
d. A $200 debit to Cash was posted as a $2,000 debit.
e. A $520 debit to Office Supplies was debited to Office Supplies Expense.

LO 3

Exercise 3-16B   *Recording prepaid items and identifying their effect on financial statements*

The Far East Company began operations when it issued common stock for $50,000 cash. It paid $48,000 cash in advance for a one-year contract to lease delivery equipment for the business. It signed the lease agreement on March 1, 2011, which was effective immediately. Far East received $60,000 of cash revenue in 2011.

Required

a. Record the March 1 cash payment in general journal format.
b. Record in general journal format the adjustment required as of December 31, 2011.
c. Record all events in a horizontal statements model like the following one:

Assets			=	Liab.	+	Equity	Rev.	−	Exp.	=	Net Inc.	Cash Flow
Cash	+	Prep. Rent				Ret. Earn.						

d. What amount of net income will Far East report on the 2011 income statement? What is the amount of net cash flow from operating activities for 2011?
e. Determine the amount of prepaid rent Far East would report on the December 31, 2011, balance sheet.

Exercise 3-17B *Recording accrued salaries and identifying their effect on financial statements* LO 3

On December 31, 2011, IBC Company had accrued salaries of $9,600.

Required

a. Record in general journal format the adjustment required as of December 31, 2011.

b. Record the above adjustment in a horizontal statements model like the following one.

Assets	=	Liab.	+	Equity	Rev.	−	Exp.	=	Net Inc.	Cash Flow
		Sal. Pay.	+	Ret. Earn.						

c. Determine the amount of net income IBC would report on the 2011 income statement, assuming that IBC received $12,000 of cash revenue. What is the amount of net cash flow from operating activities for 2011?

d. What amount of salaries payable would IBC report on the December 31, 2011, balance sheet?

Exercise 3-18B *Preparing closing entries* LO 3

The following financial information was taken from the books of Better Shape Health Club, a small spa and health club.

Account Balances as of December 31, 2011	
Accounts Receivable	$16,150
Accounts Payable	5,500
Salaries Payable	2,150
Cash	20,725
Dividends	1,750
Operating Expense	31,550
Prepaid Rent	600
Rent Expense	4,200
Retained Earnings 1/1/2011	32,650
Salaries Expense	11,200
Service Revenue	48,400
Supplies	450
Supplies Expense	4,240
Common Stock	6,515
Unearned Revenue	8,050
Land	12,400

Required

a. Prepare the journal entries necessary to close the temporary accounts at December 31, 2011, the Better Shape Health Club.

b. What is the balance in the Retained Earnings account after the closing entries are posted?

Exercise 3-19B *Recording transactions in the general journal and T-accounts* LO 2, 3

The following events apply to Godwin Company for 2011, its first year of operation.

1. Received cash of $48,000 from the issue of common stock.
2. Performed $85,000 of services on account.
3. Incurred $8,000 of other operating expenses on account.
4. Paid $34,000 cash for salaries expense.
5. Collected $65,000 of accounts receivable.

6. Paid a $5,000 dividend to the stockholders.
7. Performed $9,200 of services for cash.
8. Paid $4,400 of the accounts payable.

Required

a. Record the preceding transactions in general journal form.
b. Post the entries to T-accounts and determine the ending balance in each account.
c. Determine the amount of total assets at the end of 2011.
d. Determine the amount of net income for 2011.

LO 4

Exercise 3-20B   *Preparing a trial balance*

Required

On December 31, 2011, Grey Company had the following normal account balances in its general ledger. Use this information to prepare a trial balance.

Land	$ 80,000
Unearned Revenue	52,000
Dividends	20,000
Prepaid Rent	19,200
Cash	58,000
Salaries Expense	50,000
Accounts Payable	12,000
Common Stock	80,000
Operating Expense	50,000
Office Supplies	10,000
Advertising Expense	4,000
Retained Earnings, 1/1/2011	18,000
Service Revenue	184,000
Accounts Receivable	54,800

LO 2, 3, 4

Exercise 3-21B   *Recording events in the general journal, posting to T-accounts, and preparing a trial balance*

The following events apply to Electronics Services Inc. in its first year of operation.

1. Acquired $80,000 cash from the issue of common stock.
2. Earned $56,000 of service revenue on account.
3. Incurred $30,400 of operating expenses on account.
4. Collected $52,800 cash from accounts receivable.
5. Made a $27,200 payment on accounts payable.
6. Paid a $4,000 cash dividend to the stockholders.
7. Received a $14,200 cash advance for services to be provided in the future.
8. Purchased $3,200 of supplies on account.
9. Recognized $4,800 of revenue for services provided to the customer in Event 7.
10. Recognized $2,400 of supplies expense.
11. Recorded $3,200 of accrued salaries expense.
12. Recognized $900 of accrued interest revenue.

Required

a. Record the events in T-accounts and determine the ending account balances.
b. Test the equality of the debit and credit balances of the T-accounts by preparing a trial balance.

Exercise 3-22B   *Recording events in the general journal, posting to T-accounts, and*   LO 2, 3, 4
preparing closing entries

At the beginning of 2011, Tim's Consulting had the following normal balances in its accounts:

Account	Balance
Cash	$13,000
Accounts Receivable	9,500
Accounts Payable	3,600
Common Stock	9,900
Retained Earnings	9,000

The following events apply to Tim's Consulting for 2011.

1. Provided $118,000 of services on account.
2. Incurred $11,980 of operating expenses on account.
3. Collected $124,000 of accounts receivable.
4. Paid $71,000 cash for salaries expense.
5. Paid $13,600 cash as a partial payment on accounts payable.
6. Paid an $11,000 cash dividend to the stockholders.

Required

a. Record these transactions in a general journal.

b. Open T-accounts, and post the beginning balances and the preceding transactions to the appropriate accounts.

c. Record the beginning balances and the transactions in a horizontal statements model such as the following one:

Assets		=	Liab.	+	Equity		Rev.	−	Exp.	=	Net Inc.	Cash Flow
	Accts.		Accts.		Common	Ret.						
Cash +	Rec.	=	Pay.	+	Stock	+ Earn.						

d. Record the closing entries in the general journal and post them to the T-accounts. What is the amount of net income for the year?

e. What is the amount of *change* in retained earnings for the year? Is the change in retained earnings different from the amount of net income? If so, why?

Exercise 3-23B   *Using ratio analysis to assess financial risk*   LO 5

The following information was drawn from the balance sheets of two companies.

Company	Assets	=	Liabilities	+	Equity
Terry's Tutoring	725,000		240,000		485,000
Lisa's Learning	340,000		74,800		265,200

Required

a. Compute the debt to assets ratio to measure the level of financial risk of both companies.

b. Compare the two ratios computed in Requirement *a* to identify which company has the higher level of financial risk.

Exercise 3-24B   *IFRS and U.S. GAAP*   IFRS

Using one of the websites referenced on page 143, define the IASB and describe its function.

PROBLEMS—SERIES B

LO 2

Problem 3-25B   *Identifying debit and credit balances*

Required

Indicate whether each of the following accounts normally has a debit or credit balance.

a. Common Stock
b. Retained Earnings
c. Land
d. Accounts Receivable
e. Insurance Expense
f. Cash
g. Dividends
h. Unearned Revenue
i. Operating Expense
j. Accounts Payable
k. Service Revenue

l. Supplies
m. Utilities Payable
n. Consulting Revenue
o. Supplies Expense
p. Salaries Expense
q. Salaries Payable
r. Land
s. Prepaid Insurance
t. Interest Revenue
u. Interest Receivable

LO 1, 2

Problem 3-26B   *Transaction type and debit/credit terminology*

The following events apply to Mask Enterprises.

1. Acquired $25,000 cash from the issue of common stock.
2. Paid salaries to employees, $1,750 cash.
3. Collected $8,100 cash for services to be performed in the future.
4. Paid cash for utilities expense, $402.
5. Recognized $22,500 of service revenue on account.
6. Paid a $1,250 cash dividend to the stockholders.
7. Purchased $1,600 of supplies on account.
8. Received $6,250 cash for services rendered.
9. Paid cash to rent office space for the next 12 months, $6,000.
10. Paid cash of $8,750 for other operating expenses.
11. Paid on account payable, $876.
12. Recognized $1,500 of rent expense. Cash had been paid in a prior transaction (see Event 9).
13. Recognized $2,500 of revenue for services performed. Cash had been previously collected (see Event 3).
14. Recognized $2,600 of accrued salaries expense.
15. Recognized $650 of accrued interest revenue.

Required

Identify each event as asset source (AS), asset use (AU), asset exchange (AE), or claims exchange (CE). Also identify the account that is to be debited and the account that is to be credited when the transaction is recorded. The first event is recorded as an example.

Event No.	Type of Event	Account Debited	Account Credited
1	AS	Cash	Common Stock

Problem 3-27B *Recording events in a statements model and T-accounts and preparing a trial balance*   **LO 2, 4**

The following accounting events apply to Ginger's Designs for the year 2011.

Asset Source Transactions

1. Began operations by acquiring $40,000 of cash from the issue of common stock.
2. Performed services and collected cash of $2,000.
3. Collected $12,000 of cash in advance for services to be provided over the next 12 months.
4. Provided $24,000 of services on account.
5. Purchased supplies of $3,000 on account.

Asset Exchange Transactions

6. Purchased $8,000 of land for cash.
7. Collected $14,000 of cash from accounts receivable.
8. Purchased $1,260 of supplies with cash.
9. Paid $4,800 for one year's rent in advance.

Asset Use Transactions

10. Paid $8,000 cash for salaries of employees.
11. Paid a cash dividend of $4,000 to the stockholders.
12. Paid off $1,260 of the accounts payable with cash.

Claims Exchange Transactions

13. Placed an advertisement in the local newspaper for $1,600 on account.
14. Incurred utility expense of $1,200 on account.

Adjusting Entries

15. Recognized $8,800 of revenue for performing services. The collection of cash for these services occurred in a prior transaction. (See Event 3.)
16. Recorded $3,000 of accrued salary expense at the end of 2011.
17. Recorded supplies expense. Had $1,200 of supplies on hand at the end of the accounting period.
18. Recognized four months' of expense for prepaid rent that had been used up during the accounting period.
19. Recognized $300 of accrued interest revenue.

Required

a. Record each of the preceding events in T-accounts
b. Prepare a before-closing trial balance.
c. Use a horizontal statements model to show how each event affects the balance sheet, income statement, and statement of cash flows. Indicate whether the event increases (+), decreases (−), or does not affect (NA) each element of the financial statements. Also, in the Cash Flow column, use the letters OA to designate operating activity, IA for investing activity, and FA for financing activity. The first event is recorded as an example.

Assets	=	Liab.	+	Equity	Rev.	−	Exp.	=	Net Inc.	Cash Flow
+		NA		+	NA		NA		NA	+ FA

LO 3

Problem 3-28B *Effect of journal entries on financial statements*

Event No.	Account Title	Debit	Credit
1	Cash Common Stock	xxx	 xxx
2	Prepaid Rent Cash	xxx	 xxx
3	Dividends Cash	xxx	 xxx
4	Utilities Expense Cash	xxx	 xxx
5	Accounts Receivable Service Revenue	xxx	 xxx
6	Salaries Expense Cash	xxx	 xxx
7	Cash Service Revenue	xxx	 xxx
8	Cash Unearned Revenue	xxx	 xxx
9	Supplies Accounts Payable	xxx	 xxx
10	Cash Accounts Receivable	xxx	 xxx
11	Rent Expense Prepaid Rent	xxx	 xxx
12	Supplies Expense Supplies	xxx	 xxx
13	Unearned Revenue Service Revenue	xxx	 xxx

Required

The preceding 13 different accounting events are presented in general journal format. Use a horizontal statements model to show how each event affects the balance sheet, income statement, and statement of cash flows. Indicate whether the event increases (+), decreases (−), or does not affect (NA) each element of the financial statements. Also, in the Cash Flow column, use the letters OA to designate operating activity, IA for investing activity, and FA for financing activity. The first event is recorded as an example.

Assets	=	Liab.	+	Equity	Rev.	−	Exp.	=	Net Inc.	Cash Flow
+		NA		+	NA		NA		NA	+ FA

LO 3

Problem 3-29B *Identifying accounting events from journal entries*

Required

The following information is from the records of attorney Steve Ray. Write a brief explanation of the accounting event represented in each of the general journal entries.

Date	Account Titles	Debit	Credit
Jan. 1	Cash	20,000	
	Common Stock		20,000
Feb. 10	Cash	4,000	
	Unearned Revenue		4,000
Mar. 5	Supplies	2,000	
	Cash		2,000
Apr. 30	Prepaid Rent	800	
	Cash		800
May 1	Accounts Receivable	24,000	
	Service Revenue		24,000
June 1	Salaries Expense	2,000	
	Cash		2,000
Aug. 5	Cash	12,000	
	Service Revenue		12,000
10	Dividends	1,000	
	Cash		1,000
Sept. 10	Cash	4,400	
	Accounts Receivable		4,400
Oct. 1	Property Tax Expense	3,000	
	Cash		3,000
Dec. 31	Supplies Expense	800	
	Supplies		800
31	Rent Expense	4,400	
	Prepaid Rent		4,400
31	Unearned Revenue	2,240	
	Service Revenue		2,240

Problem 3-30B *Recording adjusting entries in general journal format*

LO 3

Required

Each of the following independent events requires a year-end adjusting entry. Record each event and the related adjusting entry in general journal format. The first event is recorded as an example. Assume a December 31 closing date.

Event No.	Date	Account Titles	Debit	Credit
a	Sept. 1	Prepaid Rent	15,000	
		Cash		15,000
a	Dec. 31	Rent Expense (15,000 × 4/12)	5,000	
		Prepaid Rent		5,000

a. Paid $15,000 cash in advance on September 1 for a one-year lease on office space.

b. Purchased $2,000 of supplies on account on April 15. At year-end, $300 of supplies remained on hand.

c. Received a $3,600 cash advance on July 1 for a contract to provide services for one year.

d. Paid $5,100 cash in advance on February 1 for a one-year insurance policy.

Problem 3-31B *Effect of errors on the trial balance*

LO 4

The following trial balance was prepared from the ledger accounts of Kona Company.

KONA COMPANY
Trial Balance
April 30, 2011

Account Title	Debit	Credit
Cash	$ 41,500	
Accounts Receivable	40,000	
Supplies	2,400	
Prepaid Insurance	3,200	
Land		$ 10,000
Accounts Payable		8,500
Common Stock		96,000
Retained Earnings		56,720
Dividends	6,000	
Service Revenue		40,000
Rent Expense	7,200	
Salaries Expense	26,400	
Operating Expense	65,240	
Totals	$191,940	$211,220

When the trial balance failed to balance, the accountant reviewed the records and discovered the following errors:

1. The company received $470 as payment for services rendered. The credit to Service Revenue was recorded correctly, but the debit to Cash was recorded as $740.
2. A $430 receipt of cash that was received from a customer on accounts receivable was not recorded.
3. A $450 purchase of supplies on account was properly recorded as a debit to the Supplies account. However, the credit to Accounts Payable was not recorded.
4. Land valued at $10,000 was contributed to the business in exchange for common stock. The entry to record the transaction was recorded as a $10,000 credit to both the Land account and the Common Stock account.
5. A $200 rent payment was properly recorded as a credit to Cash. However, the Salaries Expense account was incorrectly debited for $200.

Required

Based on this information, prepare a corrected trial balance for Kona Company.

LO 2, 3, 4

Problem 3-32B *Comprehensive problem: single cycle*

The following transactions pertain to Sky Training Company for 2011.

Jan. 30 Established the business when it acquired $75,000 cash from the issue of common stock.
Feb.   1 Paid rent for office space for two years, $24,000 cash.
Apr. 10 Purchased $5,300 of supplies on account.
July   1 Received $50,000 cash in advance for services to be provided over the next year.
      20 Paid $1,800 of the accounts payable from April 10.
Aug. 15 Billed a customer $32,000 for services provided during August.
Sept. 15 Completed a job and received $19,000 cash for services rendered.
Oct.   1 Paid employee salaries of $20,000 cash.
      15 Received $25,000 cash from accounts receivable.
Nov. 16 Billed customers $37,000 for services rendered on account.
Dec.   1 Paid a dividend of $6,000 cash to the stockholders.
      31 Adjusted records to recognize the services provided on the contract of July 1.
      31 Recorded $4,500 of accrued salaries as of December 31.
      31 Recorded the rent expense for the year. (See February 1.)
      31 Physically counted supplies; $480 was on hand at the end of the period.

Required

a. Record the preceding transactions in the general journal.

b. Post the transactions to T-accounts and calculate the account balances.

c. Prepare a trial balance.

d. Prepare the income statement, statement of changes in stockholders' equity, balance sheet, and statement of cash flows.

e. Prepare the closing entries at December 31.

f. Prepare a trial balance after the closing entries are posted.

Problem 3-33B   *Two complete accounting cycles*   **LO 2, 3, 4**

Cummings Enterprises experienced the following events for 2011, the first year of operation.

1. Acquired $13,000 cash from the issue of common stock.
2. Paid $4,000 cash in advance for rent. The payment was for the period April 1, 2011, to March 31, 2012.
3. Performed services for customers on account for $27,000.
4. Incurred operating expenses on account of $13,500.
5. Collected $25,150 cash from accounts receivable.
6. Paid $8,500 cash for salary expense.
7. Paid $11,500 cash as a partial payment on accounts payable.

Adjusting Entries

8. Made the adjusting entry for the expired rent. (See Event 2.)
9. Recorded $900 of accrued salaries at the end of 2011.

Events for 2012

1. Paid $900 cash for the salaries accrued at the end of the prior accounting period.
2. Performed services for cash of $8,500.
3. Purchased $1,200 of supplies on account.
4. Paid $4,500 cash in advance for rent. The payment was for one year beginning April 1, 2012.
5. Performed services for customers on account for $42,000.
6. Incurred operating expense on account of $19,250.
7. Collected $40,500 cash from accounts receivable.
8. Paid $20,000 cash as a partial payment on accounts payable.
9. Paid $14,000 cash for salary expense.
10. Paid a $6,000 cash dividend to stockholders.

Adjusting Entries

11. Made the adjusting entry for the expired rent. (*Hint:* Part of the rent was paid in 2011.)
12. Recorded supplies expense. A physical count showed that $300 of supplies were still on hand.

Required

a. Record the events and adjusting entries for 2011 in general journal form.

b. Post the 2011 events to T-accounts.

c. Prepare a trial balance for 2011.

d. Prepare an income statement, statement of changes in stockholders' equity, balance sheet, and statement of cash flows for 2011.

e. Record the entries to close the 2011 temporary accounts to Retained Earnings in the general journal and post to the T-accounts.

f. Prepare a post-closing trial balance for December 31, 2011.

g. Repeat requirements *a* through *f* for 2012.

LO 5

Problem 3-34B *Using ratio analysis to make comparisons between companies*

At the end of 2012, the following information is available for City Cinema and Feature Flicks.

	City Cinema	Feature Flicks
Total assets	$219,000	$981,000
Total liabilities	136,000	529,000
Stockholders' equity	83,000	452,000
Net income	18,000	69,000

Required

a. For each company, compute the debt to assets ratio and the return on equity ratio.

b. Determine what percentage of each company's assets were financed by the owners.

c. Which company has the greatest level of financial risk?

d. Based on profitability alone, which company performed better?

e. Do the above ratios support the concept of financial leverage? Explain.

ANALYZE, THINK, COMMUNICATE

ATC 3-1   Business Applications Case   *Understanding real-world annual reports*

Required

Use the Target Corporation's annual report in Appendix B to answer the following questions.

a. What was Target's debt to assets ratio for 2008 and 2007?

b. What was Target's return on assets ratio for 2008 and 2007?

c. What was Target's return on equity ratio for 2008 and 2007?

d. Why was Target's return on equity ratio higher than its return on assets ratio for 2008 and 2007?

ATC 3-2   Group Assignment   *Financial statement analysis*

The beginning account balances for Mabry Company were as follows for 2011, 2012, and 2013:

	January 1		
	2011	2012	2013
Cash	$12,000	$19,000	$42,600
Accounts Receivable	6,000	10,000	6,000
Land	9,000	9,000	9,000
Prepaid Rent	0	1,000	1,400
Accounts Payable	12,300	11,300	15,300
Salaries Payable	0	0	2,100
Common Stock	10,000	10,000	10,000
Retained Earnings	4,700	17,700	31,600

Mabry Company experienced the following events for the accounting periods 2011, 2012, and 2013.

2011

1. Performed services for $36,000 on account.
2. Paid rent of $6,000 for the period March 1, 2011, to March 1, 2012.
3. Incurred operating expense of $18,000 on account.
4. Collected $32,000 of accounts receivable.
5. Paid $19,000 of accounts payable.
6. Recorded expired rent.

2012

1. Performed services on account of $48,000.
2. Paid rent of $8,400 for the period March 1, 2012, to March 1, 2013, and recorded the expired rent for the period January 1, 2012, to March 1, 2012.
3. Incurred operating expenses of $24,000 on account.
4. Collected $52,000 of accounts receivable.
5. Paid $20,000 of accounts payable.
6. Recorded expired rent.
7. Recorded accrued salaries of $2,100.

2013

1. Paid accrued salaries.
2. Performed services on account of $56,000.
3. Paid rent of $9,000 for the period March 1, 2013, to March 1, 2014, and recorded the expired rent for the period January 1, 2013, to March 1, 2013.
4. Incurred operating expenses of $32,000 on account.
5. Collected $55,000 of accounts receivable.
6. Paid $33,000 of accounts payable.
7. Sold land for $5,000; the land had a cost of $5,000.
8. Recorded expired rent.

Required

Divide the class into groups of four or five students. Organize the groups into three sections. Assign each section of groups the financial data for one of the preceding accounting periods.

Group Task

a. Prepare an income statement, balance sheet, and statement of cash flows. It may be helpful to open T-accounts and post transactions to these accounts before attempting to prepare the statements.

Class Discussion

b. Review the cash flows associated with the collection of receivables and the payment of payables. Comment on the company's collection and payment strategy.
c. Did net income increase or decrease between 2011 and 2012? What were the primary causes?
d. Did net income increase or decrease between 2012 and 2013? What were the primary causes?

ATC 3-3   Real-World Case   *Choice of fiscal year*

Consider the following brief descriptions of four companies from different industries. Michaels Stores claims to be the largest arts and crafts specialty retailer in North America. It operates over 1,000 retail stores. In 2008 Pulte Homes built new houses in 459 communities in 25 states. Toro Company manufactures and sells professional and residential lawn care products, such as irrigation systems. Vail Resorts, Inc. operates ski resorts in Colorado, including Breckenridge Mountain and Vail Mountain Resort, the largest in the United States.

The chapter explained that companies often close their books when business is slow. Each of these companies ends its fiscal year on a different date. The closing dates, listed chronologically, are:

February 2
July 31
October 31
December 31

Required

a. Try to determine which fiscal year-end matches which company. Write a brief explanation of the reason for your decisions.
b. Because many companies deliberately choose to prepare their financial statements at a slow time of year, try to identify problems this may present for someone trying to analyze the balance sheet for Toys R Us. Write a brief explanation of the issues you identify.

ATC 3-4   Business Applications Case   *Performing ratio analysis using real-world data*

The following data were taken from Yahoo, Inc.'s 2008 annual report. *All dollar amounts are in millions.*

	Fiscal Years Ending	
	December 31, 2008	**December 31, 2007**
Total assets	$13,689.8	$12,229.7
Total liabilities		
Stockholders' equity	11,250.9	9,532.8
Net income	424.3	660.0

Required

a. For each year, compute Yahoo's debt to assets ratio, return on assets ratio, and return on equity ratio. You will need to compute total liabilities.
b. Did the company's level of financial risk increase or decrease from 2007 to 2008?
c. In which year did the company appear to manage its assets most efficiently?
d. Do the above ratios support the concept of financial leverage? Explain.

ATC 3-5   Business Applications Case   *Performing ratio analysis using real-world data*

The following data were taken from the 2008 annual reports of Biogen Idec, Inc., and Genentech, Inc. Both companies are leaders in biotechnology. *All dollar amounts are in millions.*

	Biogen Idec	**Genentech**
	December 31, 2008	**December 31, 2008**
Total assets	$8,479	$21,787
Total liabilities	2,673	6,116
Stockholders' equity	5,806	15,671
Net income	783	3,427

Required

a. For each company, compute the debt to assets ratio, return on assets ratio, and return on equity ratio.

b. Which company has the greatest level of financial risk? Explain.

c. Which company appears to have managed its assets most efficiently? Explain.

d. Which company performed better from the perspective of the owners? Explain.

ATC 3-6 Writing Assignment *Effect of land sale on return on assets*

Toyo Company is holding land that cost $900,000 for future use. However, plans have changed and the company may not need the land in the foreseeable future. The president is concerned about the return on assets. Current net income is $425,000 and total assets are $3,500,000.

Required

a. Write a memo to the company president explaining the effect of disposing of the land, assuming that it has a current value of $1,500,000.

b. Write a memo to the company president explaining the effect of disposing of the land, assuming that it has a current value of $600,000.

ATC 3-7 Ethical Dilemma *Choice of brothers: ethics, risk, and accounting numbers in a medieval setting*

In the late 1400s, a wealthy land owner named Caster was trying to decide which of his twin sons, Rogan or Argon, to designate as the first heir to the family fortune. He decided to set up each son with a small farm consisting of 300 sheep and 20 acres of land. Each twin would be allowed to manage his property as he deemed appropriate. After a designated period, Caster would call his sons before him to account for their actions. The heir to the family fortune would be chosen on the basis of which son had produced a larger increase in wealth during the test period.

On the appointed day of reckoning, Argon boasted that he had 714 sheep under his control while Rogan had only 330. Furthermore, Argon stated that he had increased his land holdings to 27 acres. The seven-acre increase resulted from two transactions: first, on the day the contest started, Argon used 20 sheep to buy 10 additional acres; and second, he sold three of these acres for a total of 9 sheep on the day of reckoning. Also, Argon's flock had produced 75 newborn sheep during the period of accounting. He had been able to give his friends 50 sheep in return for the help that they had given him in building a fence, thereby increasing not only his own wealth but the wealth of his neighbors as well. Argon boasted that the fence was strong and would keep his herd safe from predatory creatures for five years (assume the fence had been used for one year during the contest period). Rogan countered that Argon was holding 400 sheep that belonged to another herder. Argon had borrowed these sheep on the day that the contest had started. Furthermore, Argon had agreed to return 424 sheep to the herder. The 24 additional sheep represented consideration for the use of the herder's flock. Argon had agreed to return the sheep immediately after the day of reckoning.

During the test period, Rogan's flock had produced 37 newborn sheep, but 2 sheep had gotten sick and died during the accounting period. Rogan had also lost 5 sheep to predatory creatures. He had no fence, and some of his sheep strayed from the herd, thereby exposing themselves to danger. Knowing that he was falling behind, Rogan had taken a wife in order to boost his productivity. His wife owned 170 sheep on the day they were married; her sheep had produced 16 newborn sheep since the date of her marriage to Rogan. Argon had not included the wife's sheep in his count of Rogan's herd. If his wife's sheep had been counted, Rogan's herd would contain 516 instead of 330 sheep suggested by Argon's count.

Argon charged that seven of Rogan's sheep were sick with symptoms similar to those exhibited by the two sheep that were now dead. Rogan interjected that he should not be held accountable for acts of nature such as illness. Furthermore, he contended that by isolating the sick sheep from the remainder of the herd, he had demonstrated prudent management practices that supported his case to be designated first heir.

Required

a. Prepare an income statement, balance sheet, statement of sheep flow (cash flow) for each twin, using contemporary (2009) accounting standards. Note that you have to decide whether to include the sheep owned by Rogan's wife when making his financial statements (what is the accounting entity?). (*Hint:* Use the number of sheep rather than the number of dollars as the common unit of measure.)

b. Refer to the statements you prepared in Requirement *a* to answer the following questions:

    (1) Which twin has more owner's equity at the end of the accounting period?

    (2) Which twin produced the higher net income during the accounting period?

    (3) Which son should be designated heir based on conventional accounting and reporting standards?

c. What is the difference in the value of the land of the twins if the land is valued at market value (that is, three sheep per acre) rather than historical cost (that is, two sheep per acre)?

d. Did Argon's decision to borrow sheep increase his profitability? Support your answer with appropriate financial data.

e. Was Argon's decision to build a fence financially prudent? Support your answer with appropriate financial data.

f. Assuming that the loan resulted in a financial benefit to Argon, identify some reasons that the shepherd who owned the sheep may have been willing to loan them to Argon.

g. Which twin is likely to take risks to improve profitability? What would be the financial condition of each twin if one-half of the sheep in both flocks died as a result of illness? How should such risk factors be reported in financial statements?

h. Should Rogan's decision to "marry for sheep" be considered from an ethical perspective, or should the decision be made solely on the basis of the bottom-line net income figure?

i. Prepare a report that recommends which twin should be designated heir to the family business. Include a set of financial statements that supports your recommendation. Since this is a managerial report that will not be distributed to the public, you are not bound by generally accepted accounting principles.

ATC 3-8   Research Assignment   *Investigating Nike's 10-K report*

Many companies must file financial reports with the SEC. Many of these reports are available electronically through the EDGAR database. EDGAR is an acronym for Electronic Data Gathering, Analysis, and Retrieval system, and it is accessible through the World Wide Web on the Internet. Instructions for using EDGAR are in Appendix A.

Using the most current 10-K available on EDGAR or on the company's Web site at www.nikebiz.com, answer the following questions about Nike Company.

a. In what year did Nike begin operations?

b. Other than the Nike brand, what business does Nike operate?

c. How many employees does Nike have?

d. Describe, in dollar amounts, Nike's accounting equation at the end of the most recent year.

e. Has Nike's performance been improving or deteriorating over the past three years? Explain your answer.

ATC 3-9   Spreadsheet Assignment   *Use of Excel*

Adams Company started operations on January 1, 2011. Six months later on June 30, 2011, the company decided to prepare financial statements. The company's accountant decided to problem solve for the adjusting journal entries and the final adjusted account balances by using an electronic spreadsheet. Once the spreadsheet is complete, she will record the adjusting entries in the general journal and post to the ledger. The accountant has started the following spreadsheet but wants you to finish it for her.

Required

a. On a blank spreadsheet, enter the following trial balance in Columns A through C. Also enter the headings for Columns E through I.

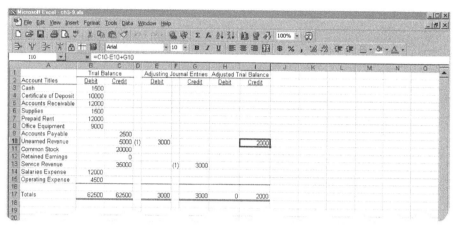

b. Each of the following events requires an adjusting journal entry. Instead of recording entries in general journal format, record the adjusting entries in the Debit and Credit columns under the heading Adjusting Journal Entries. Entry (1) has already been recorded as an example. Be sure to number your adjusting entries on the spreadsheet. It will be necessary to insert new accounts for the adjustments. Recall that the accounting period is for six months.

(1) Received a $5,000 cash advance on April 1 for a contract to provide five months of service.

(2) Had accrued salaries on June 30 amounting to $1,500.

(3) On January 1 invested in a one-year, $10,000 certificate of deposit that had a 5 percent interest rate.

(4) On January 1 paid $12,000 in advance for a one-year lease on office space.

(5) Received in the mail a utility bill dated June 30 for $150.

(6) Purchased $1,500 of supplies on January 1. As of June 30, $700 of supplies remained on hand.

(7) Paid $9,000 for office equipment on January 1. The equipment was expected to have a four-year useful life and a $1,000 salvage value. Depreciation is computed on a straight-line basis.

c. Develop formulas to sum both the Debit and Credit columns under the Adjusting Journal Entries heading.

d. Develop formulas to derive the adjusted balances for the adjusted trial balance. For example, the formula for the ending balance of Unearned Revenue is =C10−E10+G10. In other words, a credit balance minus debit entries plus credit entries equals the ending balance. Once an ending balance is formulated for one credit account, that formula can be copied to all other credit accounts; the same is true for debit accounts. Once an ending balance is formulated for a debit account, that formula can be copied to all other debit accounts.

e. Develop formulas to sum both the Debit and Credit columns under the Adjusted Trial Balance heading.

Spreadsheet Tips

1. Rows and columns can be inserted by positioning the mouse on the immediate row or column after the desired position. Click on the *right* mouse button. With the *left* mouse button, choose Insert and then either Entire Column or Entire Row. Use the same method to delete columns or rows.

2. Enter the sequential numbering of the adjusting entries as labels rather than values by positioning an apostrophe in front of each entry. The first adjusting entry should be labeled '(1).

ATC 3-10   Spreadsheet Assignment   *Mastery of Excel*

At the end of the accounting period, Adams Company's general ledger contained the following adjusted balances.

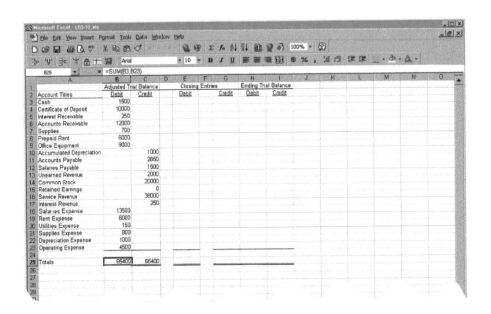

Required

1. Set up the preceding spreadsheet format. (The spreadsheet tips for ATC 3-9 also apply for this problem.)
2. Record the closing entries in the Closing Entries column of the spreadsheet.
3. Compute the Ending Trial Balance amounts.

COMPREHENSIVE PROBLEM

The trial balance of Pacilio Security Services Inc. as of January 1, 2013 had the following normal balances:

Cash	$8,900
Accounts Receivable	1,500
Supplies	65
Prepaid Rent	800
Land	4,000
Accounts Payable	1,050
Unearned Revenue	200
Salaries Payable	1,200
Notes Payable	2,000
Common Stock	8,000
Retained Earnings	2,815

During 2013, Pacilio Security Services experienced the following transactions:

1. Paid the salaries payable from 2012.
2. Paid the balance of $2,000 on the debt owed to the Small Business Government Agency. The loan is interest free.

3. Performed $32,000 of security services for numerous local events during the year; $21,000 was on account and $11,000 was for cash.

4. On May 1, paid $3,000 for 12 months' rent in advance.

5. Purchased supplies on account for $700.

6. Paid salaries expense for the year of $9,000.

7. Incurred other operating expenses on account, $4,200.

8. On October 1, 2013, a customer paid $1,200 for services to be provided over the next 12 months.

9. Collected $19,000 of accounts receivable during the year.

10. Paid $5,950 on accounts payable.

11. Paid $1,800 of advertising expenses for the year.

12. Paid a cash dividend to the shareholders of $4,650.

13. The market value of the land was determined to be $5,500 at December 31, 2013.

Adjustments

14. There was $120 of supplies on hand at the end of the year.

15. Recognized the expired rent.

16. Recognized the earned revenue from 2012 and transaction no. 8.

17. Accrued salaries were $1,000 at December 31, 2013.

Required

a. Record the above transactions in general journal form.

b. Post the transactions to T-accounts and determine the account balances.

c. Prepare a trial balance.

d. Prepare an income statement, statement of changes in stockholders' equity, balance sheet, and statement of cash flows for 2013.

e. Prepare the closing entries and post to the T-accounts.

f. Prepare a post-closing trial balance.

Accessing the EDGAR Database Through the Internet

Successful business managers need many different skills, including communication, interpersonal, computer, and analytical. Most business students become very aware of the data analysis skills used in accounting, but they may not be as aware of the importance of "data-finding" skills. There are many sources of accounting and financial data. The more sources you are able to use, the better.

One very important source of accounting information is the EDGAR database. Others are probably available at your school through the library or business school network. Your accounting instructor will be able to identify these for you and make suggestions regarding their use. By making the effort to learn to use electronic databases, you will enhance your abilities as a future manager and your marketability as a business graduate.

These instructions assume that you know how to access and use an Internet browser. Follow the instructions to retrieve data from the Securities and Exchange Commission's EDGAR database. Be aware that the SEC may have changed its interface since this appendix was written. Accordingly, be prepared for slight differences between the following instructions and what appears on your computer screen. Take comfort in the fact that changes are normally designed to simplify user access. If you encounter a conflict between the following instructions and the instructions provided in the SEC interface, remember that the SEC interface is more current and should take precedence over the following instructions.

1. To connect to EDGAR, type in the following address: **http://www.sec.gov/.**
2. After the SEC home page appears, under the heading **Filings & Forms (EDGAR),** click on **Search for Company Filings.**
3. From the screen that appears, click on **Companies & Other Filers.**
4. On the screen that appears, enter the name of the company whose file you wish to retrieve and click on the **Find Companies** button.
5. The following screen will present a list of companies that have the same, or similar, names to the one you entered. Identify the company you want and click on the CIK number beside it.
6. Enter the SEC form number that you want to retrieve in the window titled **Form Type** that appears in the upper right portion of the screen that appears. For example, if you want Form 10-K, which will usually be the case, enter **10-K,** and click on the **Retrieve Filings** button.
7. A list of the forms you requested will be presented, along with the date they were filed with the SEC. You may be given a choice of **[text]** or **[html]** file format. The **[text]** format will present one large file for the form you requested. The **[html]** format will probably present several separate files from which you must choose. These will be named Document 1 . . ., Document 2 . . ., etc. Usually, you should choose the file whose name ends in **10k.txt.** Form 10-K/A is an amended Form 10-K and it sometimes contains more timely information, but usually, the most recent Form 10-K will contain the information you need.
8. Once the 10-K has been retrieved, you can search it online or save it on your hard drive. If you want to save it, do so by using the **Save As** command from the pull-down menu at the top of the screen named **File.**
9. The financial statements are seldom located near the beginning of a company's 10-K, so it is necessary to scroll down the file until you find them. Typically, they are located about one-half to three-fourths of the way through the report.

APPENDIX B

Annual Report for The Topps Company, Inc.

This appendix contains a portion of the Form 10-K for the Topps Company that was filed with the Securities and Exchange Commission on May 10, 2006. The document included in this appendix is Topps' annual report, which was included *as a part* of its complete Form 10-K for the company's 2006 fiscal year.

This document is included for illustrative purposes, and it is intended to be used for educational purposes only. It should not be used for making investment decisions. Topps Company's complete Form 10-K may be obtained from the SEC's EDGAR website, using the procedures explained in Appendix A. The Form 10-K may also be found on the company's website at www.topps.com.

UNITED STATES SECURITIES AND EXCHANGE COMMISSION
Washington, D.C. 20549

FORM 10-K

(Mark One)

☑ ANNUAL REPORT PURSUANT TO SECTION 13 OR 15(d) OF THE SECURITIES EXCHANGE ACT OF 1934

For the fiscal year ended February 25, 2006

OR

☐ TRANSITION REPORT PURSUANT TO SECTION 13 OR 15(d) OF THE SECURITIES EXCHANGE ACT OF 1934

For the transition period from   to

Commission file number 0-15817

THE TOPPS COMPANY, INC.
(Exact name of registrant as specified in its charter)

Delaware	11-2849283
(State or other jurisdiction of incorporation or organization)	(I.R.S. Employer Identification No.)
One Whitehall Street, New York, NY	10004
(Address of principal executive offices)	(Zip Code)

(212) 376-0300
(Registrant's telephone number, including area code)

Securities registered pursuant to Section 12(b) of the Act:
Not Applicable

Securities registered pursuant to Section 12(g) of the Act:
Common Stock par value $.01
(Title of class)

Indicate by check mark if the registrant is a well-known seasoned issuer, as defined in Rule 405 of the Securities Act   Yes ☐   No ☑ .

Indicate by check mark if the registrant is not required to file reports pursuant to Section 13 or Section 15(d) of the Act. Yes ☐   No ☑ .

Indicate by check mark whether the registrant (1) has filed all reports required to be filed by Section 13 or 15(d) of the Securities Exchange Act of 1934 during the preceding 12 months (or for such shorter period that the registrant was required to file such reports), and (2) has been subject to such filing requirements for the past 90 days. Yes ☑   No ☐

Indicate by check mark if disclosure of delinquent filers pursuant to Item 405 of Regulation S-K is not contained herein, and will not be contained, to the best of registrant's knowledge, in definitive proxy or information statements incorporated by reference in Part III of this form 10-K or any amendment of this Form 10-K. ☐

Indicate by check mark whether the registrant is a large accelerated filer, an accelerated filer or a non-accelerated filer. See definition of "accelerated filer" and "large accelerated filer" in Rule 12b-2 of the Exchange Act.

Large accelerated filer ☐   Accelerated filer ☑   Non-accelerated filer ☐

Indicate by check mark whether the registrant is a shell company (as defined in Rule 12b-2 of the Act). Yes ☐   No ☑ .

The aggregate market value of Common Stock held by non-affiliates as of the last business day of the most recently completed fiscal second quarter was approximately $384,077,750.

The number of outstanding shares of Common Stock as of May 4, 2006 was 39,380,471.

Exhibit 13

Dear Stockholders,

Fiscal 2006 was a busy year for Topps as we made measurable progress on a number of key initiatives aimed at streamlining the business, strengthening our management team and fostering a culture of accountability to drive stockholder value. Although our financial results for the year were below expectations, we enter fiscal 2007 a stronger company, with a clear plan and confidence in our prospects for a more profitable year.

In February 2005, the board authorized the company to pursue, with the assistance of Lehman Brothers, a sale of the candy business believing such a step might provide value for the stockholders, in light of recent industry transactions at attractive multiples.

While the sale process evolved during the first half of fiscal '06, we held off restructuring the organization and implementing certain strategic initiatives, anticipating a successful transaction. That failed to occur, however, and the sale process was ultimately terminated in September 2005.

Since then, the nature and pace of activities, in line with recommendations stemming from a strategic study conducted by independent consultants, has been substantial. Here is a sampling of effected changes:

FISCAL 2006

Restructured The Business To Drive Operating Profitability: We restructured the business to focus on operating profit net of direct overhead rather than contributed margin at our two business units, Confectionery and Entertainment. Beginning in the first quarter of fiscal 2007, financial reporting will reflect this change and lead to more transparency, improved cost management and greater accountability. Now, 80% of our employees report to someone with direct P&L responsibility for a business unit as opposed to 20% before the change.

Created New Culture of Accountability: We redesigned the Company's incentive bonus plan to focus heavily on business unit results and track personal performance against specific, measurable goals identified at the outset of the fiscal year. Our new structure increases the visibility of performance by business unit down to its operating profit net of direct overhead, thus enhancing each individual's accountability.

Reduced Direct and Indirect Costs: With a tight focus on managing costs, we implemented an 8% reduction in U.S. headquarters headcount for annualized savings, net of strategic hires, of $2.5 million. We also reduced indirect costs during the year by freezing the pension plan, modifying our retiree medical plan and reducing certain non-medical insurance, litigation and consulting expenses which will generate an additional $2 million in savings for fiscal 2007.

Strengthened Leadership to Support New Initiatives: We made a number of key hires in a few important areas to support our current strategic initiatives. These include:

- Bazooka brand re-launch
- Improved sales through the hobby channel
- Sports marketing to kids
- New product development for candy
- Confectionery marketing and sales in Europe

1

Improved Efficiency: We progressed major systems upgrades and expect phase one of an enterprise resource planning (ERP) system to be operational this summer. The ERP system will link key areas of the business electronically and provide improved control of our purchasing, order entry, customer service, credit and shipping functions. In addition, we are now operational on a new comprehensive trade spending system to help manage this important business cost.

Achieved Structural Marketing Changes to Benefit Each of our Business Units:
In Entertainment, we successfully negotiated important changes in our agreements with sports card licensors that are already paying dividends. In Confectionery, we relocated Bazooka manufacturing to reduce costs and have re-launched the brand, complete with reformulated product, new packaging, line extensions and marketing programs.

FISCAL 2007

ENTERTAINMENT

We believe that progress made in fiscal '06 sets the stage for growth in fiscal '07 and beyond. We will focus on key priorities to create long term value for our stockholders, employees and distribution partners in fiscal 2007.

On the sports card side, having engineered an important change in the licensing structure of the category, our priorities include capturing additional market share and revenue, engaging more kids to collect our sports products and reducing costs.

With respect to market share, as one of the two licensees marketing Major League baseball cards (last year there were four), Topps will now offer 50% of all baseball card products. We intend to increase our category leadership position by garnering more than our "fair share" of dollars spent. For your information, the football card market witnessed a reduction in licensees from four to three last year and we increased both volume and share.

To generate further success, we have set up a specialized group within our sports department dedicated to developing new products at the medium and high price points for serious collectors. The first two products developed by this team, Topps "Triple Threads" and "Co-Signers Baseball" are both enjoying positive initial trade reception. Moreover, early sales of popularly priced Topps Baseball Series 1 already show considerable improvement over fiscal year 2006.

Among efforts to reconnect with kids, we have entered into agreements with video game publisher, 2KSports and the magazine, Sports Illustrated for Kids, both of which should help promote our products in these kids-focused sports venues. For instance, this year Topps Series 1 Baseball contains cards with special codes by which gamers can apply enhanced powers playing the 2K6 video game. In addition, SI for Kids and Topps have developed a Kids Card Club which is now featured monthly in the magazine and on SIKids.com.

We have also implemented marketing programs at virtually every Major League Baseball ballpark this summer, a first for Topps. Whether through our sponsorship of starting lineups where Topps cards will be featured all season long on in-stadium "Jumbotrons" or special card give-aways, Topps will be on the field, so to speak, not just in the stores. Moreover, we will be part of a $2 million plus industry TV campaign beginning in May, dedicated to showing kids how much fun card collecting truly can be.

Internationally, we intend to devote special efforts to the World Cup this year. We have created a number of World Cup-related collectible products that we will launch in targeted markets. Also, we have extended and expanded our English Premier League Football (Soccer) rights, which we believe will yield good results.

Turning to gaming, the market has been soft according to industry sources and we forecast a difficult year for WizKids. Under today's conditions, we believe there is a flight to quality and that the more critical mass one can sustain the better. Accordingly, for the time being we will focus more on our core properties and continue to be extra selective regarding new product introductions such as Horror Clix, planned for launch in the second half of fiscal '07.

Our Entertainment publishing unit will continue to focus on growing franchises and exploiting third party licenses as opportunities are perceived. The Company's own intellectual properties, Wacky Packages and Garbage Pail Kids, enjoy ongoing acceptance in the U.S. marketplace. Series 3 Wacky Packs are heading for a TV advertising test and sampling in select metro markets during the Spring. Later, the product will be packaged with bubble gum qualifying Wackys to appear on candy counters.

On the cost side, we are taking steps to manage operating expenses and grow margins in both the Entertainment and Confectionery businesses. These measures, combined with a planned reduction of obsolescence and returns as a percentage of sales, are expected to result in a further savings of over $2 million in fiscal 2007.

In sports cards, for instance, our initial focus is on pre-press costs which we anticipate reducing by at least 10% beginning in August. In Confectionery, we will apply the new Synectics trade funds management system and use a consultant to help identify means of reducing both operational complexity and costs at facilities manufacturing our confectionery products in Asia. We will also conduct internal reviews to reduce product component costs on a variety of SKU's.

CONFECTIONERY

The Confectionery business unit in fiscal 2007 is executing a number of strategic initiatives including:

- The re-launch of "new" Bazooka in the US
- Refreshing existing brands, and
- Introducing new products at home and abroad, an activity vital to long term growth.

Having relocated our manufacturing operation, Bazooka products will be more competitively priced and offered in a variety of formats and sku's.

Many activities are associated with product refreshment. Among them, our Baby Bottle Pop brand continues to show growth, most recently driven by a line extension called 2 ·D ·Max. Promotional programs with Nickelodeon and new advertising will be used in support of these initiatives. We will also introduce an addition to the Push Pop family this fall. Overseas, we are in our sixth year successfully marketing container candies featuring Pokemon characters.

On the new products front, we have added resources to this important activity and adopted the theme "Fewer, Bigger, Better." Through this process, we are developing a rather revolutionary new candy product for release in January 2007. Called "Vertigo," the product is aimed at tweens and teens, a different consumer segment than our traditional target, and we are excited about it.

CONCLUSION

In totality, the number of concrete activities underway to build stockholder value is unprecedented in our Company's history. Together with fellow employees throughout the Company, our senior leadership team is confident that we have the people, products and vision to see them through.

On behalf of the organization, we thank our stockholders, consumers, fans, collectors, licensors and suppliers for their loyal support.

Officers of the Topps Company, Inc.

(Signatures)

With profound sorrow, we record the passing of our esteemed board member and friend Stanley Tulchin. His vision, warmth and dedication will be well remembered by us all.

Appendix B

Table of Contents

602   Appendix B

Financial Highlights

| | Fiscal Year Ended | | |
	February 25, 2006	February 26, 2005 (a)	February 28, 2004 (a)
	(in thousands of dollars, except share data)		
Net sales	$ 293,838	$ 294,231	$ 294,917
Net income from continuing operations	3,946	11,268	13,628
Loss from discontinued operations — net of tax	(2,707)	(353)	(744)
Net income	1,239	10,915	12,884
Cash (used in) provided by operations	(6,543)	22,930	11,954
Working capital	127,713	139,910	134,099
Stockholders' equity	204,636	219,168	211,340
Per share items:			
Diluted net income — from continuing operations	$ 0.10	$ 0.27	$ 0.33
Diluted net income — after discontinued operations	$ 0.03	$ 0.26	$ 0.31
Cash dividend paid	$ 0.16	$ 0.16	$ 0.12
Weighted average diluted shares outstanding	41,163,000	41,327,000	41,515,000

(a)   As restated, see Note 2 to Notes to Consolidated Financial Statements

MANAGEMENT'S DISCUSSION AND ANALYSIS OF FINANCIAL CONDITION AND RESULTS OF OPERATIONS

This section provides an analysis of the Company's operating results, cash flow, critical accounting policies, and other matters. It includes or incorporates "forward-looking statements" as that term is defined by the U.S. federal securities laws. In particular, statements using words such as "may", "should", "intend", "estimate", "anticipate", "believe", "predict", "potential", or words of similar import generally involve forward-looking statements. We based these forward-looking statements on our current expectations and projections about future events, and, therefore, these statements are subject to numerous risks and uncertainties. Accordingly, actual results may differ materially from those expressed or implied by the forward-looking statements. We caution readers not to place undue reliance on these forward-looking statements, which speak only as of the date of this report.

The following Management's Discussion and Analysis ("MD&A") gives effect to the restatement discussed in Note 2 to the Consolidated Financial Statements.

CONSOLIDATED NET SALES

The Company has two reportable business segments, Confectionery and Entertainment. The following table sets forth, for the periods indicated, net sales by business segment:

	Fiscal Year Ended		
	February 25, 2006	February 26, 2005	February 28, 2004
	(in thousands of dollars)		
Confectionery	$144,261	$143,762	$147,188
Entertainment	149,577	150,469	147,729
Total	$293,838	$294,231	$294,917

Fiscal 2006 versus 2005*

In fiscal 2006, the Company's consolidated net sales decreased 0.1% to $293.8 million from $294.2 million in fiscal 2005. Weaker foreign currencies versus the prior year reduced fiscal 2006 sales by approximately $600,000. Excluding the impact of stronger foreign currencies, net sales increased by 0.1%.

Worldwide net sales of the Confectionery segment, which includes Ring Pop, Push Pop, Baby Bottle Pop, Juicy Drop Pop and Bazooka brand bubble gum, increased 0.3% to $144.3 million in 2006 from $143.8 million in 2005. Foreign exchange had virtually no impact on full year confectionery sales comparisons. Confectionery products accounted for 49% of the Company's net sales in each of 2006 and 2005.

In the U.S., fiscal 2006 confectionery sales reflected distribution gains and strong retail sales of Juicy Drop Pop, now in its third year. In addition, sales of Baby Bottle Pop increased, driven by a successful new media campaign and initial shipments of 2DMax, a new line extension, which will be officially launched in fiscal 2007.

Confectionery sales in overseas markets were influenced by the introduction of Mega Mouth Candy Spray and continued growth of Pokemon candy products, offset by lower year-on-year performance of core brands in select markets, principally the U.K. and Italy. International sales represented 28% of total confectionery sales in fiscal 2006 versus 31% in 2005.

---

* Unless otherwise indicated, all date references to 2006, 2005 and 2004 refer to the fiscal years ended February 25, 2006, February 26, 2005 and February 28, 2004, respectively.

Going forward, the Company intends to execute a number of strategic initiatives both in the U.S. and abroad aimed at improving the sales and operating profit of the Confectionery segment. Major initiatives include further establishing Topps as a leader in youth-oriented candy products, building the top line through the relaunch of Bazooka, a focus on innovation and the implementation of a disciplined new product process to fuel future growth, enhanced retail distribution and a renewed emphasis on system-wide cost reduction.

Net sales of the Entertainment segment, which includes cards, sticker album collections, Internet activities and strategy games, decreased 0.6% in fiscal 2006 to $149.6 million. Weaker foreign currencies versus the prior year served to reduce fiscal 2006 sales by $0.7 million. Entertainment products represented 51% of the Company's net sales in each of 2006 and 2005.

During the year, the Company reached an agreement on new terms with Major League Baseball and the Players' Association which addressed the industry's product proliferation issues. The deal reduces the number of industry participants from four to two, places a cap on the number of products in the marketplace and requires increased marketing commitments from industry participants targeted at bringing youth back into the market. The combined impact of a positive football season, and to a lesser extent, the new baseball agreement which took effect in January, drove year-over-year increases in sales of sports card products.

Net sales of non-sports products also increased during 2006, a function of successfully marketing products featuring WWE, Star Wars, Pokemon and Wacky Packages. These legacy licenses are a testament to the Company's ability to generate strong publishing sales even in periods of relative licensing inactivity.

Sales of European sports products were below fiscal 2005 levels which was in part a reflection of the absence of products associated with the European Football Championship, which occurs once every four years. In addition, sales of both the Premier League collection in the U.K. and Calcio in Italy were lower than in fiscal 2005. In fiscal 2007, the Company will be marketing products featuring the World Cup, another soccer tournament held every four years.

Finally, sales from WizKids, a developer and marketer of strategy games acquired in July 2003, increased on the strength of a new internally-created category, constructible strategy games, and specifically Pirates products. However, weakness in the gaming industry is expected to put pressure on 2007 sales, at least through the first half, causing the Company to place greater focus on core properties and be more selective in new offerings.

Fiscal 2005 versus 2004

In fiscal 2005, the Company's consolidated net sales decreased 0.2% to $294.2 million from $294.9 million in fiscal 2004. Stronger foreign currencies versus the prior year added $6.6 million to fiscal 2005 sales. Excluding the impact of stronger foreign currencies, net sales decreased 2.5%.

Worldwide net sales of the Confectionery segment decreased 2.3% to $143.8 million in 2005 from $147.2 million in 2004. Stronger foreign currencies provided a $2.7 million benefit to fiscal 2005 sales. Confectionery products accounted for 49% of the Company's net sales in 2005 and 50% in 2004.

Fiscal 2005 U.S. confectionery sales were impacted in part by industry trends such as consumer nutritional concerns and retail consolidation, particularly in the first nine months of the year. Incremental sales of chewy candy products and strong gains on Juicy Drop Pop contributed favorably to results. For the full year, declines in U.S. confectionery sales of 2.8% were in line with trends in the non-chocolate industry.

Net sales of international confectionery products were also down comparatively in fiscal 2005 due to strong 2004 performance of both Push Pop Flip N'Dip in Japan and Yu-Gi-Oh! candy products in Europe. International sales represented 31% of total confectionery sales in each of fiscal 2005 and fiscal 2004.

Net sales of the Entertainment segment increased 1.9% in fiscal 2005 to $150.5 million. Stronger foreign currencies provided a $3.9 million benefit to fiscal 2005 sales. Entertainment products represented 51% of the Company's net sales in 2005 and 50% in fiscal 2004.

Within the Entertainment segment, sales from WizKids increased $6 million to $22 million, reflecting a full year of ownership in fiscal 2005 versus a partial year in fiscal 2004. In late fiscal 2005, WizKids created a new product category, constructible strategy games, and launched two new products, Pirates and Football Flix. In addition, sales of European sports products increased in fiscal 2005, reflecting the inclusion of products featuring the European Football Championship held once every four years.

Net sales of U.S. sports products were below the prior year, a function of the absence of a NHL hockey season and continued industry softness in general. The Company believes that this downtrend is due largely to the proliferation of card and memorabilia products and significantly higher price points.

As anticipated, sales of Internet products were below year ago levels in fiscal 2005 as the Company reduced advertising support and explored new directions for this venture. As a result, Internet operations were virtually breakeven in fiscal 2005 versus a loss of almost $3 million in fiscal 2004.

Finally, fiscal 2005 sales of non-sports publishing products were impacted by the absence of strong licenses, particularly in the fourth quarter. However, during the year, WWE, Barbie, Pokemon and Yu-Gi-Oh! were solid contributors in Europe and Garbage Pail Kids performed well in the U.S.

RESULTS OF OPERATIONS

	Fiscal Year Ended					
	February 25, 2006		February 26, 2005		February 28, 2004	
Net sales	$293,838	100.0%	$294,231	100.0%	$294,917	100.0%
Cost of sales	198,054	67.4%	189,200	64.3%	191,213	64.8%
Gross profit	95,784	32.6%	105,031	35.7%	103,704	35.2%
Sales, general and administrative expenses	98,096	33.4%	92,350	31.4%	87,527	29.7%
(Loss) income from operations	(2,312)	(0.8%)	12,681	4.3%	16,177	5.5%

Fiscal 2006 versus 2005

Fiscal 2006 consolidated gross profit as a percentage of net sales was 32.6% versus 35.7% in 2005. Margins this year were negatively impacted by increases in returns provisions, reported as a net against gross sales. Higher returns resulted from a softer Italian entertainment market and WizKid's expansion into new products and markets. Increased royalty costs driven by the higher mix of royalty-bearing U.S. sports sales and an increase in the effective royalty rate on Premier League products due to lower sales, also put pressure on gross profit margins.

Selling, general & administrative expenses ("SG&A") increased as a percentage of net sales to 33.4% in 2006 from 31.4% in 2005. SG&A dollar spending increased to $98.1 million in 2006 from $92.4 million. The primary cause of higher 2006 SG&A is one-time costs associated with the implementation of strategic initiatives totaling $4.2 million. These include severance and pension costs of $3.7 million related to a corporate restructuring, $0.3 million in costs to move Bazooka production to a less expensive manufacturer and a one-time expense of $0.2 million related to the freeze of our pension plan. Additionally, higher 2006 overhead costs reflect the impact of inflation on salaries and health care costs as well as consulting fees incurred in relation to systems implementation, Sarbanes-Oxley and strategic planning initiatives. Fiscal 2006 overhead cost comparisons benefited from a $1.8 million WizKids' legal settlement net of legal fees and the absence of a $1.9 million fine paid to the European Commission in 2005.

Also within SG&A, full year advertising and marketing expenses of $26.8 million were $3.5 million above 2005 due to the reinstatement of historical levels of spending for the U.S. confectionery business, advertising support for WizKids' new product format and media for Wacky Packages in the U.S.

Net interest income increased slightly to $2.9 million in fiscal 2006 from $2.7 million in fiscal 2005, reflecting rising interest rates.

In fiscal 2006, the Company had a tax benefit versus an effective tax rate of 26.8% in fiscal 2005. The tax benefit was a function of a low earnings base combined with the reversal of tax reserves as a result of a successful IRS tax audit and the Company's tax planning initiatives.

The Company sold thePit.com Internet operations to a third party in January 2006. Accordingly, financial results for this operation have been reclassified and are reported as Loss from discontinued operations – net of tax. In fiscal 2006, this loss, including the asset write-off, totaled $2.7 million.

Net income in fiscal 2006 was $1.2 million, or $0.03 per diluted share, versus $10.9 million, or $0.26 per diluted share in 2005.

Fiscal 2005 versus 2004

Financial results for thePit.com Internet operations have been reclassified to the Discontinued Operations line. See Note 7 – Discontinued Operations – thePit.com.

Fiscal 2005 consolidated gross profit as a percentage of net sales was 35.7%, up from 35.2% in 2004. Fiscal 2005 margins were favorably impacted by lower obsolescence costs following abnormally high write-offs at WizKids and the domestic confectionery and European publishing businesses in fiscal 2004. Improved gross profit margins also reflected lower tooling and mold costs on WizKids and European confectionery products. Partially offsetting these improvements were higher autograph and relic costs on U.S. sports cards and an increase in effective royalties associated with England Premier League products.

Selling, general & administrative expenses increased as a percentage of net sales to 31.4% in 2005 from 29.7% in the prior year. SG&A dollar spending increased to $92.4 million in 2005 from $87.5 million. A $1.9 million fine paid to the European Commission and the full year of WizKids ownership versus a partial year in 2004, were the primary reasons for the dollar increase. Additionally, higher professional fees, in particular legal, Sarbanes-Oxley and consulting-related expenses, impacted fiscal 2005 SG&A. The Company estimates fees paid to third parties related to Sarbanes-Oxley Section 404 compliance were approximately $1.1 million in 2005.

Within SG&A, full year advertising and marketing expenses of $23.3 million were $0.5 million below 2004 due to reduced spending on U.S. confectionery and Internet products, partially offset by increased marketing activity overseas. U.S. confectionery advertising exceeded historical levels in the fourth quarter.

Net interest income increased slightly to $2.7 million in fiscal 2005 from $2.4 million in fiscal 2004, reflecting rising interest rates and higher average investment balances.

The fiscal 2005 effective tax rate was 26.8% versus 26.7% in fiscal 2004.

Net income in fiscal 2005 was $10.9 million, or $0.26 per diluted share, versus $12.9 million, or $0.31 per diluted share in 2004. Excluding the impact of the non-tax deductible European Commission fine, fiscal 2005 net income was $12.8 million, or $0.31 per diluted share.

Quarterly Comparisons

Management believes that quarter-to-quarter comparisons of sales and operating results are affected by a number of factors. The Company's sales of Confectionery products are generally stronger in the first two fiscal quarters of the year. However, sales can be significantly impacted by the introduction of new products and line extensions as well as by advertising and consumer and trade support programs.

In the Entertainment segment, sales of U.S. sports card products are sold throughout the year, spanning the three major sports seasons in which the Company currently participates, i.e. baseball, football, and basketball. The new baseball agreement condensed the period during which baseball products are sold causing certain products previously sold in the third quarter to be pushed to the fourth quarter of fiscal 2006. Topps Europe's sales generally of sports sticker album products are driven largely by shipments of Premier League Soccer products, with much of the sales activity occurring in the fourth fiscal quarter. Sales of non-sports cards, sticker albums and games tend to be impacted by the timing of product introductions and the property on which they are based, often peaking with the release of a movie or the rise in popularity of a particular licensed property.

The net result of the above factors is that quarterly results vary. See Note 22 of Notes to Consolidated Financial Statements.

Inflation

In the opinion of management, inflation has not had a material effect on the operations or financial results of the Company.

Liquidity and Capital Resources

Management believes that the Company has adequate means to meet its liquidity and capital resource needs over the foreseeable future as a result of the combination of cash on hand, anticipated cash from operations and credit line availability.

The Company entered into a credit agreement with Chase Manhattan Bank on September 14, 2004. The agreement provides for a $30.0 million unsecured facility to cover revolver and letter of credit needs and expires on September 13, 2007. With the exception of $0.6 million reserved for letters of credit, the $30.0 million credit line was available as of February 25, 2006. (See Note 11 – Long-Term Debt.)

The Company has presented its portfolio of auction rate securities as short-term investments. Year-over-year changes in the amounts of these securities are being shown under investing activities on the Consolidated Statement of Cash Flows.

As of February 25, 2006, the Company had $28.2 million in cash and cash equivalents and an additional $53.3 million in short-term investments, for a total of $81.4 million.

During fiscal 2006, the Company's net decrease in cash and cash equivalents was $8.3 million versus a decrease of $20.5 million in 2005. The net decrease in cash and cash equivalents and short-term investments combined was $25.0 million in fiscal 2006, versus an increase of $12.6 million in fiscal 2005.

Net cash used by operating activities in 2006 was $6.5 million versus cash generated by operating activities of $22.9 million in 2005. The fiscal 2006 cash use was primarily a function of the low level of net earnings as well as an increase in working capital resulting from a reduction in income taxes payable, higher inventories reflecting the acquisition of sports autographs and a build up of stock prior to a shift in Bazooka production and an increase in receivables driven by the strong sales and timing of U.S. sports card shipments.

Cash generated by investing activities in 2006 of $13.8 million largely reflects the net sale of $16.7 million of short-term investments. The Company also spent $2.9 million in capital expenditures, primarily for computer hardware and software related to the implementation of a the first phase of an ERP system, as well as for other IT-related investments in the U.S. and Europe. Fiscal 2007 capital spending is projected to be approximately $4 million, driven by investments in Ring Pop production equipment and computer software and hardware. Capital spending will be funded out of cash flow from operating activities.

Cash used in financing activities in 2006 of $12.5 million reflects $6.0 million of treasury stock purchases net of options exercised plus $6.5 million in dividend payments, versus $2.3 million in treasury stock purchases net of options exercised and $6.5 million in dividend payments in 2005. The increase in treasury stock purchases in 2006 is a result of the Company's 10b5-1 program, initiated mid-year, which provides for a minimum purchase of 500,000 shares a quarter, assuming the share price remains below a certain threshold.

Finally, the $3.1 million unfavorable effect of exchange rate changes on cash and cash equivalents, which is due to the impact of weaker currencies on foreign subsidiaries' cash balances when translated into U.S. dollars, was $4.1 million worse than in 2005. This change reflects a weakening of European currencies against the U.S. dollar in fiscal 2006, versus a strengthening in fiscal 2005.

In October 2001, the Company's Board of Directors authorized the repurchase of up to 5 million shares of Company common stock. During fiscal 2005, the Company purchased 444,400 shares at an average price of $9.25 per share. During the first half of fiscal 2006, the Company did not purchase any shares due to a strategic business review being performed by investment banking and consulting firms. In September 2005, the Company entered into a written trading plan that complies with Rule 10b5-1 under the Securities Exchange Act of 1934, as amended, which provides for the purchase of 500,000 shares for each of the next four quarters starting in the third quarter of fiscal 2006 at the prevailing market price, per share, subject to certain conditions. In addition, the Board of Directors increased the outstanding share authorization by 3,390,700 shares to 5 million shares. As of February 25, 2006, the Company had purchased 1,027,899 shares under this amended authorization, leaving 3,972,101 shares available for future purchases. See Note 15 - Capital Stock. The Company anticipates purchasing additional shares in the future to complete the authorization.

Contractual Obligations

Future minimum payments under existing key contractual obligations are as follows: (in thousands)

	Total	2007	2008	2009	2010	2011	Thereafter
Future payments under non-cancelable leases	$ 10,600	$ 2,579	$ 2,247	$ 2,128	$ 1,826	$1,284	$ 536
Purchase obligations	16,797	11,011	2,151	952	700	700	1,283
Future payments under royalty contracts	81,642	23,362	20,167	19,793	18,320	—	—
Total	$109,039	$36,952	$24,565	$22,873	$20,846	$1,984	$ 1,819

The Company anticipates making a payment of approximately $1.5 – 2.5 million in fiscal 2007 for the funding of its qualified pension plans.

Critical Accounting Policies

The preparation of financial statements in conformity with accounting principles generally accepted in the United States of America requires Topps management to make estimates and judgments that affect the reported amounts of revenue, expenses, assets, liabilities and the disclosure of contingent assets and liabilities. Actual results may differ from these estimates under different assumptions or conditions.

Note 1 to the Company's consolidated financial statements "Summary of Significant Accounting Policies" summarizes its significant accounting policies. Following is a summary of the critical policies and methods used.

Revenue Recognition: Revenue related to sales of the Company's products is generally recognized when products are shipped, the title and risk of loss has passed to the customer, the sales price is fixed or determinable and collectibility is reasonably assured. Sales made on a returnable basis are recorded net of a provision for estimated returns. These estimates are revised, as necessary, to reflect actual experience and market conditions.

Returns Provisions: In determining the provision for returns, the Company performs an in-depth review of wholesale and retail inventory levels, trends in product sell-through by sales channel, and other factors. The provision for returns was $29.8 million in 2006, $22.0 million in 2005 and $17.4 million in 2004, which equates to 10.2%, 7.5% and 5.9% of net sales, respectively. The recent increase in returns provisions is largely the result of a softer Italian entertainment market in fiscal 2006, unusually high returns of products associated with the European Football championship in fiscal 2005 and WizKids' expansion into new products and markets. An increase or decrease in the provision for returns by 1% of sales would decrease or increase operating income by approximately $3.0 million.

Goodwill and Intangible Assets: Management evaluates the recoverability of finite-lived intangible assets under the provisions of Statement of Financial Accounting Standards No. 144 *Accounting for the Impairment or Disposal of Long-lived Assets* ("SFAS 144") based on projected undiscounted cash flows. The recoverability of goodwill is evaluated in accordance with SFAS No. 142 *Goodwill and Other Intangible Assets* ("SFAS 142") and is based on a comparison of the fair value of a reporting unit with its carrying amount. Both the market approach (use of multiples from comparable companies) and the income approach (present value of future income streams) are used in determining the fair value of a reporting unit. The Company performs its annual test of impairment of goodwill as of the first day of its fourth quarter.

Intangible Assets: Intangible assets include trademarks and the value of sports, entertainment and proprietary product rights. Amortization is by the straight-line method over estimated lives of up to fifteen years. Management evaluates the recoverability of finite-lived intangible assets under the provisions of Statement of Financial Accounting Standards No. 144 *Accounting for the Impairment or Disposal of Long-lived Assets* ("SFAS 144") based on the projected undiscounted cash flows attributable to the individual assets, among other methods.

Accruals for Obsolete Inventory: The Company's accrual for obsolete inventory reflects the cost of items in inventory not anticipated to be sold or anticipated to be sold at less than cost. This accrual may be deemed necessary as a result of discontinued items and packaging or a reduction in forecasted sales. The provision for obsolete inventory was $5.4 million in fiscal 2006, $4.9 million in fiscal 2005 and $7.5 million in fiscal 2004, which equates to 1.8%, 1.7% and 2.5% of net sales, respectively. An increase or decrease in the provision for obsolescence by 1% of sales would decrease or increase operating income by approximately $3.0 million.

Income Taxes: Deferred tax assets and liabilities represent the tax effects of temporary book-tax differences which will become payable or refundable in future periods. The Company has accrued tax reserves for probable exposures and, as a result, any assessments resulting from current tax audits should not have a material adverse effect on the Company's consolidated net income.

Disclosures About Market Risk

There is no material risk to financial results due to market risk. The Company's exposure to market risk is largely related to the impact of mark-to-market changes in foreign currency rates on forward contracts. As of February 25, 2006, the Company had $21.0 million in forward contracts which were entered into for the purpose of reducing the impact of changes in foreign currency rates associated with firm and forecasted receipts and disbursements.

The Company's primary exchange rate exposure is with the Euro against the British pound, the Japanese yen and the U.S. dollar. At maturity, the proceeds or outlays from the foreign exchange contracts offset a corresponding additional or reduced outlay in the underlying currency. The recognition of mark-to-market gains and losses on these contracts accelerates the gains and losses that would otherwise be recognized when the contracts mature and generally does not result in an incremental impact on earnings or cash flows. The Company has no long-term debt and does not engage in any commodity-related derivative transactions.

New Accounting Pronouncements

In 2004, the Financial Accounting Standards Board ("FASB") issued FASB Statement No. 151, *Inventory Costs,* to clarify the accounting for abnormal amounts of idle facility expense, freight, handling costs, and wasted material (spoilage). This statement is effective for annual periods beginning after June 15, 2005 and requires that those items be recognized as current period charges regardless of whether they meet the criterion of "so abnormal" as defined by Accounting Research Bulletin No. 43. The provisions of this Statement are effective for inventory costs incurred during fiscal years beginning after June 15, 2005. The Company will adopt this Statement on February 26, 2006 and expects that the adoption will not have a material effect on the Company's consolidated financial statements.

In 2004, the FASB issued Statement No. 123 (revised 2004), *Share-Based Payments* ("SFAS 123R"). This Statement requires that the cost resulting from all share-based payment transactions be recognized in the financial statements and establishes fair value as the measurement objective in accounting for all share-based payment arrangements. The Company will adopt SFAS 123R using the modified prospective basis on February 26, 2006. The adoption of this Statement is expected to result in compensation expense of approximately $200,000 in fiscal 2007 (unaudited) related to unvested options outstanding at February 25, 2006. The estimate of future stock-based compensation expense is affected by the Company's stock price, the number of stock-based awards that may be granted in fiscal 2007, fluctuation in the Company's valuation assumptions and the related tax effect.

In 2004, the FASB issued FSP No. 109-2, *Accounting and Disclosure Guidance for the Foreign Earnings Repatriation Provision with the American Job Creation Act of 2004.* FSP No. 109-2 provides guidance for reporting and disclosing certain foreign earnings that are repatriated, as defined by the Act, which was signed into law on October 22, 2004. The Act would have allowed the Company to deduct 85% of certain qualifying foreign earnings available for repatriation to the United States during the fiscal years ended 2005 and 2006. The Company evaluated the potential impact of repatriating earnings and decided not to do so under the provisions of the Act.

In 2004, the FASB issued SFAS No. 153, *Exchanges of Non-monetary Assets*, which eliminates the exception for non-monetary exchanges of similar productive assets and replaces it with a general exception for exchanges of non-monetary assets that do not have commercial substance. SFAS No. 153 will be effective for non-monetary asset exchanges occurring in fiscal periods beginning after June 15, 2005. The Company is currently evaluating the impact of adopting this standard in its future financial statements.

In 2005, FASB Interpretation No. 47, *Accounting for Conditional Asset Retirement Obligations*, an interpretation of FASB Statement No. 143, *Accounting for Asset Retirement Obligations* required that an entity recognize the fair value of a liability for a conditional asset retirement obligation in the period in which it is incurred if a reasonable estimate of fair value can be made. An asset retirement obligation would be reasonably estimable if (a) it is evident that the fair value of the obligation is embodied in the acquisition price of the asset, (b) an active market exists for the transfer of the obligation, or (c) sufficient information exists to apply to an expected present value technique. FASB Interpretation No. 47 became effective for companies with fiscal years ending after December 15, 2005. The adoption of this statement did not have an impact on the Company's consolidated financial statements.

The Topps Company, Inc. and Subsidiaries
Consolidated Statements of Operations
(in thousands of dollars, except per share and share data)

	Fiscal Year Ended		
	February 25, 2006	February 26, 2005 (As restated, see Note 2)	February 28, 2004 (As restated, see Note 2)
Net sales	$ 293,838	$ 294,231	$ 294,917
Cost of sales	198,054	189,200	191,213
Gross profit on sales	95,784	105,031	103,704
Selling, general and administrative expenses	98,096	92,350	87,527
(Loss) income from operations	(2,312)	12,681	16,177
Interest income, net	2,912	2,706	2,426
Income before benefit (provision) for income taxes	600	15,387	18,603
Benefit (provision) for income taxes	3,346	(4,119)	(4,975)
Net income from continuing operations	3,946	11,268	13,628
Loss from discontinued operations — net of tax	2,707	353	744
Net income	$ 1,239	$ 10,915	$ 12,884
Basic net income per share:			
- From continuing operations	$ 0.10	$ 0.28	$ 0.34
- From discontinued operations	$ (0.07)	$ (0.01)	$ (0.02)
Basic net income per share	$ 0.03	$ 0.27	$ 0.32
Diluted net income per share:			
- From continuing operations	$ 0.10	$ 0.27	$ 0.33
- From discontinued operations	(0.07)	$ (0.01)	$ (0.02)
Diluted net income per share	$ 0.03	$ 0.26	$ 0.31
Weighted average shares outstanding			
- basic	40,349,000	40,471,000	40,604,000
- diluted	41,163,000	41,327,000	41,515,000

See Notes to Consolidated Financial Statements

15

The Topps Company, Inc. and Subsidiaries
Consolidated Balance Sheets
(in thousands of dollars, except per share and share data)

	February 25, 2006	February 26, 2005 (As restated, see Note 2)
ASSETS		
Current assets:		
Cash and cash equivalents	$ 28,174	$ 36,442
Short-term investments	53,269	69,955
Accounts receivable, net	31,180	27,851
Inventories	36,781	32,936
Income tax receivable	1,407	338
Deferred tax assets	5,687	5,380
Prepaid expenses and other current assets	11,134	14,541
Total current assets	167,632	187,443
Property, plant and equipment, net	11,028	11,968
Goodwill	63,405	67,566
Intangible assets, net	6,424	8,544
Deferred tax assets	6,334	3,022
Other assets	13,815	11,847
Total assets	$268,638	$ 290,390
LIABILITIES AND STOCKHOLDERS' EQUITY		
Current liabilities:		
Accounts payable	$ 11,263	$ 12,658
Accrued expenses and other liabilities	25,345	27,485
Income taxes payable	3,311	7,390
Total current liabilities	39,919	47,533
Accrued pension obligation	24,083	23,689
Total liabilities	64,002	71,222
Stockholders' equity:		
Preferred stock, par value $.01 per share authorized 10,000,000 shares, none issued	—	—
Common stock, par value $.01 per share, authorized 100,000,000 shares; issued 49,244,000 shares as of February 25, 2006 and February 26, 2005	492	492
Additional paid-in capital	28,644	28,293
Treasury stock, 9,539,000 shares and 8,790,000 shares as of February 25, 2006 and February 26, 2005, respectively	(91,376)	(85,060)
Retained earnings	269,954	275,205
Minimum pension liability adjustment	(5,551)	(5,824)
Cumulative foreign currency adjustment	2,473	6,062
Total stockholders' equity	204,636	219,168
Total liabilities and stockholders' equity	$268,638	$ 290,390

See Notes to Consolidated Financial Statements

16

The Topps Company, Inc. and Subsidiaries
Consolidated Statements of Cash Flows
(in thousands of dollars)

	Fiscal Year Ended		
	February 25, 2006	February 26, 2005 (As restated, see Note 2)	February 28, 2004 (As restated, see Note 2)
Cash flows (used in) provided by operating activities:			
Net income from continuing operations	$ 3,946	$ 11,268	$ 13,628
Adjustments to reconcile net income to cash flows:			
Depreciation and amortization	5,829	5,833	5,768
Deferred taxes	(3,749)	2,261	1,523
Net effect of changes in:			
Accounts receivable	(3,335)	2,258	(2,538)
Inventories	(4,086)	84	501
Income tax receivable/payable	(5,153)	585	(2,256)
Prepaid expense and other current assets	3,376	(2,847)	(1,048)
Payables and other current liabilities	(3,068)	2,329	(7,083)
All other	445	781	3,737
Cash (used in) provided by operating activities – continuing operations	(5,795)	22,552	12,232
Cash (used in) provided by operating activities – discontinued operations	(748)	378	(278)
Cash (used in) provided by operating activities – total	(6,543)	22,930	11,954
Cash flows from investing activities:			
Purchase of business	—	—	(28,650)
Purchase of short-term investments	(291,567)	(155,487)	(49,953)
Sale of short-term investments	308,253	122,410	41,650
Purchases of property, plant and equipment	(2,885)	(2,625)	(2,720)
Cash provided by (used in) investing activities – continuing operations	13,801	(35,702)	(39,673)
Cash provided by (used in) investing activities – discontinued operations	—	(9)	(122)
Cash provided by (used in) investing activities – total	13,801	(35,711)	(39,795)
Cash flows from financing activities:			
Dividends paid	(6,490)	(6,477)	(4,868)
Exercise of stock options	1,831	1,814	1,770
Purchase of treasury stock	(7,796)	(4,123)	(2,781)
Cash used in financing activities – continuing operations	(12,455)	(8,786)	(5,879)
Effect of exchange rate changes on cash and cash equivalents	(3,071)	1,050	4,995
Net decrease in cash and cash equivalents	(8,268)	(20,517)	(28,725)
Cash and cash equivalents at beginning of year	36,442	56,959	85,684
Cash and cash equivalents at end of year	$ 28,174	$ 36,442	$ 56,959

17

614   Appendix B

| | Fiscal Year Ended | | |
	February 25, 2006	February 26, 2005 (As restated, see Note 2)	February 28, 2004 (As restated, see Note 2)
Supplemental disclosures of cash flow information:			
Interest paid	$ 107	$ 258	$ 322
Income taxes paid	$ 2,082	$ 3,883	$ 6,398

See Notes to Consolidated Financial Statements

The Topps Company, Inc. and Subsidiaries
Consolidated Statements of Stockholders' Equity and Comprehensive Income
(in thousands of dollars)

	Total	Common Stock	Additional Paid-in Capital	Treasury Stock	Retained Earnings	Accumulated Other Comprehensive (Loss) Income
Balance at March 1, 2003 as originally reported	$196,768	$ 492	$ 27,344	$(80,791)	$262,877	$ (13,154)
Effect of restatement (see Note 2)	(126)				(126)	
Stockholders' equity as of March 1, 2003 (As restated, see Note 2)	196,642	492	27,344	(80,791)	262,751	(13,154)
Net income (As restated, see Note 2)	12,884	—	—	—	12,884	—
Translation adjustment	6,823	—	—	—	—	6,823
Minimum pension liability, net of tax	870	—	—	—	—	870
Total comprehensive income (As restated, see Note 2)	20,577	—	—	—	12,884	7,693
Cash dividends	(4,868)	—	—	—	(4,868)	—
Purchase of treasury stock	(2,781)	—	—	(2,781)	—	—
Exercise of employee stock options	1,770	—	485	1,285	—	—
Stockholders' equity as of February 28, 2004 (As restated, see Note 2)	211,340	492	27,829	(82,287)	270,767	(5,461)
Net income (As restated, see Note 2)	10,915	—	—	—	10,915	—
Translation adjustment	1,864	—	—	—	—	1,864
Minimum pension liability, net of tax	3,835	—	—	—	—	3,835
Total comprehensive income (As restated, see Note 2)	16,614	—	—	—	10,915	5,699
Cash dividends	(6,477)	—	—	—	(6,477)	—
Purchase of treasury stock	(4,123)	—	—	(4,123)	—	—
Exercise of employee stock options	1,814	—	464	1,350	—	—
Stockholders' equity as of February 26, 2005 (As restated, see Note 2)	219,168	492	28,293	(85,060)	275,205	238
Net income	1,239	—	—	—	1,239	—
Translation adjustment	(3,589)	—	—	—	—	(3,589)
Minimum pension liability, net of tax	273	—	—	—	—	273
Total comprehensive income	(2,077)	—	—	—	1,239	(3,316)
Cash dividends	(6,490)	—	—	—	(6,490)	—
Purchase of treasury stock	(7,796)	—	—	(7,796)	—	—
Exercise of employee stock options	1,831	—	351	1,480	—	—
Stockholders' equity as of February 25, 2006	$204,636	$ 492	$ 28,644	$(91,376)	$269,954	$ (3,078)

See Notes to Consolidated Financial Statements

NOTE 1 – SUMMARY OF SIGNIFICANT ACCOUNTING POLICIES

Principles of Consolidation: The consolidated financial statements include the accounts of The Topps Company, Inc. and its subsidiaries (the "Company"). All intercompany items and transactions have been eliminated in consolidation.

The Company and its subsidiaries operate and report financial results on a fiscal year of 52 or 53 weeks which ends on the Saturday closest to the end of February. Fiscal 2004, fiscal 2005 and fiscal 2006 were all comprised of 52 weeks.

Foreign Currency Translation: The financial statements of subsidiaries outside the United States, except those subsidiaries located in highly inflationary economies or where costs are primarily U.S. dollar-based, are generally measured using the local currency as the functional currency. Assets and liabilities of these subsidiaries are translated at the rates of exchange as of the balance sheet date, with the resultant translation adjustments included in accumulated other comprehensive income. Income and expense items are translated at the average exchange rate for the month. Gains and losses from foreign currency transactions of these subsidiaries are included in net income. The Company has no foreign subsidiaries operating in highly inflationary economies or where inventory costs are U.S. dollar-based for which the financial statements are measured using the U.S. dollar as the functional currency.

Derivative Financial Instruments: From time to time, the Company enters into contracts that are intended and effective as hedges of foreign currency risks associated with the anticipated purchase of confectionery inventories from foreign suppliers. It also enters into contracts in order to hedge risks associated with the collection of receivables from certain foreign countries. The Company does not hold or issue derivative financial instruments for trading purposes.

Cash Equivalents: The Company considers investments in highly liquid debt instruments with a maturity of three months or less to be cash equivalents.

Short-term investments: Investments in auction rate instruments as well as bank certificates of deposit and other debt investments with maturities in excess of three months and subject to an early withdrawal penalty are reported as short-term investments.

Inventories: Inventories are stated at lower of cost or market. Cost is determined on the first-in, first-out basis.

Property, Plant and Equipment ("PP&E"): PP&E is stated at cost. Depreciation is computed using the straight-line method based on estimated useful lives of twenty-five years for buildings, three to twelve years for machinery, equipment and software, and the remaining lease period for leasehold improvements. Expenditures for new property, plant or equipment that substantially extend the useful life of an asset are capitalized. Ordinary repair and maintenance costs are expensed as incurred. In accordance with Statement of Financial Accounting Standards ("SFAS") No. 144, *Accounting for the Impairment or Disposal of Long-Lived Assets* ("SFAS 144"), the Company periodically evaluates the carrying value of its PP&E for circumstances which may indicate impairment.

Goodwill and Intangible Assets: Management evaluates the recoverability of finite-lived intangible assets under the provisions of SFAS 144 based on projected undiscounted cash flows. The recoverability of goodwill is evaluated in accordance with SFAS No. 142 *Goodwill and Other Intangible Assets* ("SFAS 142") and is based on a comparison of the fair value of a reporting unit with its carrying amount. Both the market approach (use of multiples from comparable companies) and the income approach (present value of future income streams) are used in determining the fair value of a reporting unit. The Company performs its annual test of impairment of goodwill as of the first day of its fourth quarter.

Revenue Recognition: The Company recognizes revenue when the following criteria are met: the products are shipped, the title and risk of loss has passed to the customer, the sales price is fixed or determinable and collectibility is reasonably assured. Sales made on a returnable basis are recorded net of a provision for estimated returns. These estimates are revised, as necessary, to reflect actual experience and market conditions. In fiscal 2006, approximately 68% of the

Company's sales were made on a returnable basis, and the returns expense for the years ended February 25, 2006, February 26, 2005 and February 28, 2004 were $29.8 million, $22.0 million and $17.4 million, respectively.

Estimates: The preparation of financial statements in conformity with generally accepted accounting principles requires management to make estimates which affect the reporting of assets and liabilities as of the dates of the financial statements and revenues and expenses during the reporting period. These estimates primarily relate to the provision for sales returns, allowance for doubtful accounts and inventory obsolescence. In each case, prior to booking an accounting entry, the Company does an in-depth review of available information including wholesale and retail inventory levels and product sell-through in the case of returns, receivables aging and account credit-worthiness for the allowance for doubtful accounts and component and finished goods inventory levels and product sell-through for obsolescence. Actual results could differ from these estimates.

Income Taxes: The Company provides for deferred income taxes resulting from temporary differences between the valuation of assets and liabilities in the financial statements and the carrying amounts for tax purposes. Such differences are measured using the tax rates and laws in effect for the years in which the differences are expected to reverse.

Employee Stock Options: The Company accounts for stock-based employee compensation based on the intrinsic value of stock options granted in accordance with the provisions of APB 25, *Accounting for Stock Issued to Employees.* The pro forma effect, had the Company accounted for stock-based employee compensation based on the fair value of stock options granted in accordance with SFAS 123, *Accounting for Stock-Based Compensation,* is shown below:

	As Reported	Stock-based Employee Compensation	Pro forma
	(In thousands of dollars, except share data)		
2006			
Net income	$ 1,239	$ (312)	$ 927
Earnings per share			
Basic	$ 0.03		$ 0.02
Diluted	$ 0.03		$ 0.02
2005			
Net income	$10,915	$ (1,054)	$ 9,861
Earnings per share			
Basic	$ 0.27		$ 0.24
Diluted	$ 0.26		$ 0.24
2004			
Net income	$12,884	$ (1,247)	$11,637
Earnings per share			
Basic	$ 0.32		$ 0.29
Diluted	$ 0.31		$ 0.28

618   Appendix B

Options typically vest within a three-year period. In determining the preceding pro forma amounts under SFAS 123, the fair value of each option grant is estimated as of the date of grant using the Black-Scholes option pricing model. Following are the key assumptions: $0.16 per share dividend on fiscal 2006, 2005 and 2004 options; risk free interest rate, estimated volatility and expected life as follows: fiscal 2006 options — 4.4%, 29% and 5.8 years, respectively; 2005 options — 4.4%, 32% and 5.8 years, respectively; fiscal 2004 options — 4.4%, 38% and 6.5 years, respectively. Changes in assumptions used could have a material effect upon the pro-forma results.

Advertising and Marketing Expenses: Advertising and marketing expenses (which encompass media spending, customer promotions and research) included in selling, general and administrative expenses amounted to $26,772,000 in fiscal 2006, $23,253,000 in fiscal 2005 and $23,820,000 in fiscal 2004. Advertising and marketing expenses are recognized as incurred. Costs relating to future periods are classified as prepaid.

Reclassifications: Certain items in the prior years' financial statements have been reclassified to conform with current year's presentation.

Research and Development Expenses: Research and development costs are included in selling, general and administrative expenses and are recognized as incurred.

New Accounting Pronouncements

In 2004, the Financial Accounting Standards Board ("FASB") issued FASB Statement No. 151, *Inventory Costs,* to clarify the accounting for abnormal amounts of idle facility expense, freight, handling costs, and wasted material (spoilage). This statement is effective for annual periods beginning after June 15, 2005 and requires that those items be recognized as current period charges regardless of whether they meet the criterion of "so abnormal" as defined by Accounting Research Bulletin No. 43. The provisions of this Statement are effective for inventory costs incurred during fiscal years beginning after June 15, 2005. The Company will adopt this Statement on February 26, 2006 and expects that the adoption will not have a material effect on the Company's consolidated financial statements.

In 2004, the FASB issued Statement No. 123 (revised 2004), *Share-Based Payments* ("SFAS 123R"). This Statement requires that the cost resulting from all share-based payment transactions be recognized in the financial statements and establishes fair value as the measurement objective in accounting for all share-based payment arrangements. The Company will adopt SFAS 123R using the modified prospective basis on February 26, 2006. The adoption of this Statement is expected to result in compensation expense of approximately $200,000 in fiscal 2007 (unaudited) related to unvested options outstanding at February 25, 2006. The estimate of future stock-based compensation expense is affected by the Company's stock price, the number of stock-based awards that may be granted in fiscal 2007, fluctuation in the Company's valuation assumptions and the related tax effect.

In 2004, the FASB issued FSP No. 109-2, *Accounting and Disclosure Guidance for the Foreign Earnings Repatriation Provision with the American Job Creation Act of 2004.* FSP No. 109-2 provides guidance for reporting and disclosing certain foreign earnings that are repatriated, as defined by the Act, which was signed into law on October 22, 2004. The Act would have allowed the Company to deduct 85% of certain qualifying foreign earnings available for repatriation to the United States during the fiscal years ended 2005 and 2006. The Company evaluated the potential impact of repatriating earnings and decided not to do so under the provisions of the Act.

In 2004, the FASB issued SFAS No. 153, *Exchanges of Non-monetary Assets*, which eliminates the exception for non-monetary exchanges of similar productive assets and replaces it with a general exception for exchanges of non-monetary assets that do not have commercial substance. SFAS No. 153 will be effective for non-monetary asset exchanges occurring in fiscal periods beginning after June 15, 2005. The Company is currently evaluating the impact of adopting this standard in its future financial statements.

22

In 2005, FASB Interpretation No. 47, *Accounting for Conditional Asset Retirement Obligations*, an interpretation of FASB Statement No. 143, *Accounting for Asset Retirement Obligations* required that an entity recognize the fair value of a liability for a conditional asset retirement obligation in the period in which it is incurred if a reasonable estimate of fair value can be made. An asset retirement obligation would be reasonably estimable if (a) it is evident that the fair value of the obligation is embodied in the acquisition price of the asset, (b) an active market exists for the transfer of the obligation, or (c) sufficient information exists to apply to an expected present value technique. FASB Interpretation No. 47 became effective for companies with fiscal years ending after December 15, 2005. The adoption of this statement did not have an impact on the Company's consolidated financial statements.

NOTE 2 – RESTATEMENT OF CONSOLIDATED FINANCIAL STATEMENTS

Subsequent to the issuance of the consolidated financial statements for the year ended February 26, 2005, the Company determined (i) that upon performing a full property, plant and equipment analysis and implementation of a new fixed asset tracking system various assets that had been abandoned, sold or impaired, were still being depreciated at their original cost values, as well as that errors had been made in the calculation related to the depreciation of certain assets, and (ii) that there were errors in the prior years' state tax provision raised by the Company while preparing its 2006 tax provision primarily related to a deferred state tax over-accrual in 2004 that was not properly reversed in 2005. As a result, the Company has restated the accompanying fiscal 2005 and 2004 consolidated financial statements.

The impact of the restatement on the Company's beginning retained earnings as of March 1, 2003 was a reduction of $126,000.

The significant impacts of the restatement on the consolidated financial statements are as follows (in thousands, except per share amounts):

	As of February 26, 2005	
	As Previously Reported	As Restated
	(In thousands)	
Consolidated Balance Sheet:		
Deferred tax assets	$ 3,616	$ 5,380
Total current assets	185,679	187,443
Property, plant and equipment, net	12,553	11,968
Deferred tax assets	4,222	3,022
Total assets	290,411	290,390
Retained earnings	275,226	275,205
Total stockholders' equity	$ 219,189	$219,168

	Fiscal Year Ended February 26, 2005			
		Effect of		
	As Previously Reported	Discontinued Operations (1)	Restatement	As Restated
		(In thousands, except per share amounts)		
Consolidated Statement of Operations:				
Selling, general and administrative expenses	$ 93,237	(735)	(152)	$ 92,350
Income from operations	11,967	562	152	12,681
Income before provision for income taxes	14,673	562	152	15,387
Provision for income taxes	3,674	209	236	4,119
Net income	10,999	—	(84)	10,915
Net income per share — basic	0.27	—	—	0.27
Net income per share — diluted	$ 0.27	—	(0.01)	$ 0.26

	Fiscal Year Ended February 28, 2004			
		Effect of		
	As Previously Reported	Discontinued Operations (1)	Restatement	As Restated
		(In thousands, except per share amounts)		
Selling, general and administrative expenses	$ 89,302	(1,454)	(321)	$ 87,527
Income from operations	14,595	1,261	321	16,177
Income before provision for income taxes	17,021	1,261	321	18,603
Provision for income taxes	4,326	517	132	4,975
Net income	12,695	—	189	12,884
Net income per share — basic	0.31	—	0.01	0.32
Net income per share — diluted	$ 0.31	—	—	$ 0.31

(1) See Note 7 for a complete discussion of the discontinued operation.

The restatement did not impact the total amounts presented in the consolidated statements of cash flows for net cash (used in) provided by operating activities, net cash provided by (used in) investing activities or net cash provided by financing activities, although it did impact certain components of cash flows from operating activities.

NOTE 3 – EARNINGS PER SHARE

Earnings per share ("EPS") is computed in accordance with SFAS No. 128 "*Earnings Per Share*". Basic EPS is computed using weighted average shares outstanding. Diluted EPS is computed using weighted average shares outstanding plus additional shares issued as if in-the-money options were exercised (utilizing the treasury stock method).

The following table represents the computation of weighted average diluted shares outstanding:

| | Fiscal Year Ended | | |
	February 25, 2006	February 26, 2005	February 28, 2004
Weighted average shares outstanding:			
Basic	40,349,000	40,471,000	40,604,000
Dilutive stock options	814,000	856,000	911,000
Diluted	41,163,000	41,327,000	41,515,000

In the above calculation, the impact of out-of-the-money options, (i.e. where the exercise price exceeds current market price) was not included as their inclusion would have had an antidilutive effect. These incremental shares totaled approximately 1,198,000 in 2006, 824,000 in 2005 and 1,070,000 in 2004.

NOTE 4 – ACCOUNTS RECEIVABLE

	February 25, 2006	February 26, 2005
	(in thousands of dollars)	
Gross receivables	$ 55,244	$ 51,265
Reserve for estimated returns	(21,181)	(20,824)
Other reserves	(2,883)	(2,590)
Net receivables	$ 31,180	$ 27,851

Other reserves consist of allowances for discounts, doubtful accounts and customer deductions for marketing promotion programs.

NOTE 5 — INVENTORIES

	February 25, 2006	February 26, 2005
	(in thousands of dollars)	
Raw materials	$10,123	$ 7,468
Work in process	4,623	3,703
Finished product	22,035	21,765
Total inventory	$36,781	$32,936

NOTE 6 — PROPERTY, PLANT AND EQUIPMENT, NET

	February 25, 2006	February 26, 2005
	(in thousands of dollars)	
Land	$ 42	$ 42
Buildings and improvements	2,606	2,722
Machinery, equipment and software	27,782	28,384
Total PP&E	30,430	31,148
Accumulated depreciation	(19,402)	(19,180)
Net PP&E	$ 11,028	$ 11,968

NOTE 7 – DISCONTINUED OPERATIONS — thePit.com

In August 2001, the Company acquired all the outstanding common stock of thePit.com, Inc., which operated a sports card exchange, for a net cash purchase price of $5.7 million. The acquisition was accounted for using the purchase method of accounting and resulted in recognizing $0.8 million in intangible assets and $4.1 million in goodwill. The Company included this subsidiary in the Entertainment segment of its business. The Company was unable to operate the subsidiary profitably and in January 2006 sold the subsidiary for $360,000, with scheduled payments to be made over four years.

Per Statement of Accounting Standards No. 144 *Accounting for the Impairment of Long-Lived Assets*, the net book value of the assets of thePit.com, Inc., which consisted primarily of the $4.1 million goodwill from the acquisition as well as smaller amounts of inventory and unamortized intangibles, was written down $2,432,000 net of tax to $360,000, which is the fair value of the assets based on the expected proceeds from the sale of the subsidiary.

The $2,432,000 write-down of the assets to fair value and, additionally, the $275,000 loss from operations net of tax of thePit.com, Inc. for fiscal 2006, which total $2,707,000, are being reported as Loss from discontinued operations – net of tax on a separate line on the Consolidated Statements of Operations.

Revenue for thePit.com for fiscal 2006, 2005, and 2004 was $987,000, $1,634,000 and $2,421,000, respectively, and pre-tax loss for thePit.com for fiscal 2006, 2005 and 2004 was $295,000, $468,000 and $1,167,000, respectively. The purchaser has paid the Company $30,000 of the $360,000 sales price as of February 25, 2006. The remaining $330,000 is reported in Prepaid expenses and other current assets and Other assets on the Consolidated Balance Sheet as of February 25, 2006. The Company has restated its Consolidated Statements of Cash Flows for the years ended February 26, 2005 and February 28, 2004 to reflect this discontinued operation.

NOTE 8 – GOODWILL AND INTANGIBLE ASSETS

Goodwill and Intangible Assets represent amounts paid for the purchase of businesses in excess of the fair value of the acquired assets. Intangible assets consist principally of licenses and contracts, intellectual property, and software; amortization is by the straight-line method over estimated lives of up to fifteen years. Goodwill represents the purchase price less the fair value of acquired assets and less the appraised value of the intangible assets. Goodwill is not amortized.

Licenses and contracts consist primarily of licensing rights to produce sticker albums featuring Premier League soccer players obtained as a part of the Merlin Publishing Group acquisition in July 1995. Intellectual property refers to rights including trademarks and copyrights related to branded products obtained as part of the July 2003 acquisition of Wizkids, LLC. Software and other consists of proprietary software developed by thePit.com for fiscal 2005. In connection with the disposal of thePit.com during fiscal 2006 (see Note 7), $0.1 million of intangible assets and $4.2 million of goodwill were written off in the third quarter of fiscal 2006.

Intangible assets consisted of the following as of February 25, 2006 and February 26, 2005:

	February 25, 2006		
	Gross Carrying Value	Accumulated Amortization	Net
	(in thousands of dollars)		
Licenses and contracts	$ 21,569	$ (18,611)	$2,958
Intellectual property	18,784	(15,318)	3,466
Software and other	2,482	(2,482)	—
Total intangibles	$ 42,835	$ (36,411)	$6,424

	February 26, 2005		
	Gross Carrying Value	Accumulated Amortization	Net
	(in thousands of dollars)		
Licenses and contracts	$ 21,569	$ (17,942)	$3,627
Intellectual property	18,784	(14,284)	4,500
Software and other	2,953	(2,811)	142
FAS 132 pension	275	—	275
Total intangibles	$ 43,581	$ (35,037)	$8,544

Useful lives of the Company's intangible assets have been established based on the intended use of such assets and their estimated period of future benefit, which are reviewed periodically. Useful lives are as follows:

Category	Useful Life	Weighted Average Remaining Useful Life
Licenses and contracts	15 years	4.4 years
Intellectual property	6 years	3.4 years

27

The weighted average remaining useful life for the Company's intangible assets in aggregate is 3.8 years. Over the next five years the Company expects the annual amortization of intangible assets to be as follows:

Fiscal Year	Amount
	(in thousands)
2007	$ 1,703
2008	$ 1,703
2009	$ 1,703
2010	$ 1,036
2011	$ 279

Following the write-down of the goodwill associated with thePit.com, Inc., reported goodwill was reduced from $67,566,000 as of February 26, 2005 to $63,405,000 as of February 25, 2006. Goodwill is broken out by business segment as follows:

	February 25, 2006	February 26, 2005
	(amounts in thousands)	
Confectionery	$ 7,699	$ 7,699
Entertainment	55,706	59,867
Total goodwill	$63,405	$67,566

Intangible assets and goodwill for the reporting units are tested for impairment on an annual basis and between annual tests in certain circumstances. The impairment test is conducted at the reporting unit level by comparing the reporting unit's carrying amount, including intangible assets and goodwill, to the fair value of the reporting unit. If the carrying amount of the reporting unit exceeds its fair value, a second step is performed to measure the amount of impairment, if any. Further, in the event that the carrying amount of the Company as a whole is greater than its market capitalization, there is a potential that some or all of its intangible assets and goodwill would be considered impaired. There can be no assurances given that future impairment tests of goodwill will not result in an impairment.

NOTE 9 — DEPRECIATION AND AMORTIZATION

	Fiscal Year Ended		
	February 25, 2006	February 26, 2005	February 28, 2004
	(in thousands of dollars)		
Depreciation expense	$ 3,542	$ 3,375	$ 3,312
Amortization of:			
Intangible assets	1,703	1,797	1,881
Compensation & other	500	570	452
Deferred financing fees	84	91	123
Total depreciation and amortization	$ 5,829	$ 5,833	$ 5,768

NOTE 10 — ACCRUED EXPENSES AND OTHER LIABILITIES

	Fiscal Year Ended	
	February 25, 2006	February 26, 2005
	(in thousands of dollars)	
Royalties	$ 6,864	$ 5,400
Advertising and marketing expenses	3,659	5,079
Employee compensation	2,938	4,031
Deferred revenue	828	1,555
Inventory in transit	1,647	1,363
Deferred rent expense	1,031	1,123
Other	8,378	8,934
Total accrued expenses and other liabilities	$25,345	$27,485

NOTE 11 — LONG-TERM DEBT

On September 14, 2004, the Company entered into a new credit agreement with JPMorgan Chase Bank. The agreement provides for a $30.0 million unsecured facility to cover revolver and letter of credit needs and expires on September 13, 2007. Interest rates are variable and a function of market rates and the Company's EBITDA. The credit agreement contains restrictions and prohibitions of a nature generally found in loan agreements of this type and requires the Company, among other things, to comply with certain financial covenants, limits the Company's ability to sell or acquire assets or borrow additional money and places certain restrictions on the purchase of Company shares and the payment of dividends. The Company cannot pay dividends and purchase the Company's shares where the total cash outlay exceeds $30 million in three consecutive quarters or $50 million over the term of the credit agreement.

The credit agreement may be terminated by the Company at any point over the three-year term (provided the Company repays all outstanding amounts thereunder) without penalty. With the exception of $0.6 million currently reserved for letters of credit, the $30.0 million credit line was available as of February 25, 2006.

NOTE 12 — INCOME TAXES

The Company provides for deferred income taxes resulting from temporary differences between the valuation of assets and liabilities in the financial statements and the carrying amounts for tax purposes. Such differences are measured using the enacted tax rates and laws that will be in effect when the differences are expected to reverse.

Total Benefit (provision) for income taxes for each year is as follows:

	Fiscal Year Ended		
	February 25, 2006	February 26, 2005	February 28, 2004
	(in thousands of dollars)		
Continuing operations	$ 3,346	$(4,119)	$(4,975)
Discontinued operations	1,865	209	517
Total	$ 5,211	$(3,910)	$(4,458)

U.S. and foreign continuing operations contributed to income (loss) before provision for income taxes as follows :

	Fiscal Year Ended		
	February 25, 2006	February 26, 2005	February 28, 2004
	(in thousands of dollars)		
United States	$ (106)	$12,364	$ 9,163
Europe	1,325	4,049	10,941
Canada	(1,011)	(1,282)	(996)
Latin America	392	256	(505)
Total	$ 600	$15,387	$18,603

Benefit (provision) for income taxes consists of:

	Fiscal Year Ended		
	February 25, 2006	February 26, 2005	February 28, 2004
	(in thousands of dollars)		
Current income tax benefit (provision):			
Federal	$1,074	$ 124	$ 19
Foreign	501	(1,031)	(2,771)
State and local	(532)	(1,081)	(186)
Total current	$1,043	$(1,988)	$(2,938)
Deferred income tax benefit (provision):			
Federal	$1,737	$(1,880)	$(1,454)
Foreign	(101)	(41)	(373)
State and local	667	(210)	(210)
Total deferred	$2,303	$(2,131)	$(2,037)
Total benefit (provision) for income taxes	$3,346	$(4,119)	$(4,975)

The total benefit (provision) for income taxes from continuing operations is less than the amount computed by applying the statutory federal income tax rate to income before benefit (provision) for income taxes. This difference is largely due to the fiscal 2006 reversal of certain tax reserves related to tax audits resolved in the current year and the impact of lower tax rates in foreign countries as shown below:

	Fiscal Year Ended		
	February 25, 2006	February 26, 2005	February 28, 2004
	(in thousands of dollars)		
Computed expected tax provision	$ (210)	$ (5,385)	$ (6,511)
Decrease (increase) in taxes resulting from:			
Effect of foreign operations	292	2,282	967
State and local taxes, net of federal tax effect	87	(917)	(308)
European Commission fine	—	(578)	—
Tax-exempt interest income	489	285	208
Reversal of reserve for tax exposure items	2,536	—	—
R & D tax credits	—	210	310
Meals and entertainment disallowance	(41)	(43)	(24)
Merchandise contributions	111	111	174
Medicare Part D prescription subsidy	84	—	—
Other items, net	(2)	(84)	209
Benefit (provision) for income taxes	$ 3,346	$ (4,119)	$ (4,975)

U.S. income taxes have not been provided on undistributed earnings of foreign subsidiaries as the Company considers such earnings to be permanently reinvested in the businesses. As of February 25, 2006, the cumulative amount of unremitted earnings from foreign subsidiaries that is expected to be permanently reinvested was approximately $21 million. These undistributed foreign earnings could become subject to U.S. income tax if remitted, or deemed remitted, as a dividend. Management has determined that the U.S. income tax liability on these unremitted earnings should not be material, although it is dependent on circumstances existing at the time of the remittance.

The Company is currently under audit by New York State, Pennsylvania, and Ontario, Canada. Taxing authorities periodically challenge positions taken by the Company on its tax returns. On the basis of present information, it is the opinion of the Company's management that the Company has appropriately accrued tax reserves for probable exposures and, as a result, any assessments resulting from current tax audits should not have a materially adverse effect on the Company's consolidated financial statements. To the extent the Company were to prevail in matters for which accrued tax reserves have been established or be required to pay amounts in excess of such reserves, the Company's consolidated financial statements in a given period could be materially impacted. During fiscal 2006, the Company completed certain taxing authority audits which resulted in the reversal of $2.5 million of tax reserves.

The components of current deferred income tax assets and liabilities are as follows:

	February 25, 2006	February 26, 2005
	(in thousands of dollars)	
Deferred income tax assets:		
Pension	$ 1,137	$ 4,047
Inventory	3,192	3,034
Postretirement benefits	3,395	1,969
Foreign tax credits	2,533	1,399
Estimated losses on sales returns	2,578	2,442
Rent	423	463
Other	277	581
Capital loss	1,632	—
Total deferred income tax assets	$15,167	$13,935
Deferred income tax liabilities:		
Depreciation	(2,853)	(3,042)
Package design	—	(1,204)
Prepaid expenses	(293)	(1,287)
Total deferred income tax liabilities	(3,146)	(5,533)
Net deferred	$12,021	$ 8,402

Prior to fiscal 2005, the Company had not recorded a deferred income tax asset relating to its minimum pension obligation (which is included within accumulated other comprehensive income). As of February 25, 2006, the deferred income tax asset relating to the minimum pension obligation is $3.8 million. At the end of fiscal 2005, the deferred income tax asset relating to the minimum pension obligation was $4.0 million. Amounts relating to prior periods were not considered material.

The deferred tax assets and liabilities reflected in the previous table are included on the Company's balance sheets as net current deferred tax assets of $5.7 million and $5.4 million in fiscal 2006 and fiscal 2005, respectively, and as net long term deferred tax assets of $6.3 million and $3.0 million in fiscal 2006 and fiscal 2005, respectively.

As of February 25, 2006, the Company had foreign tax credits of approximately $2.5 million available for use that will expire beginning in fiscal 2009 through fiscal 2016. The Company also had a capital loss of approximately $4.0 million that will expire in fiscal 2011.

NOTE 13 — EMPLOYEE BENEFIT PLANS

The Company maintains qualified and non-qualified defined benefit pensions in the U.S. and Ireland as well as a postretirement healthcare plan in the U.S. for all eligible non-union personnel (the "Plans"). The Company also contributes to a multi-employer defined pension plan for its union employees. The Company's policy is to fund the domestic plans in accordance with the limits defined by the Employee Retirement Income Security Act of 1971 and U.S. income tax regulations. The Ireland plan is funded in accordance with local regulations.

In addition, the Company sponsors a defined contribution plan, which qualifies under Sections 401(a) and 401(k) of the Internal Revenue Code (the "401(k) Plan"). While all non-union employees are eligible to participate in the 401(k) Plan, participation is optional.

Effective April 1, 2006, the Company froze all future benefit accruals under its U.S. qualified defined pension plan and initiated an employer match on 401(k) contributions. In addition, beginning in fiscal 2007, the Company will make non-elective transitional 401(k) contributions with respect to certain employees. As a result of these changes, the Company anticipates a reduction in the amount and volatility of its pension expense and cash contributions. Neither the employee contributions nor matching contributions are invested in the Company's securities.

The Company's investment strategy with respect to its defined benefit plans is to achieve positive return, after adjusting for inflation, and to maximize the long-term total return within prudent levels of risk through a combination of income and capital appreciation. Risk to capital is minimized through the diversification of investments across and within various asset categories. The Company intends to fund its defined benefit plan obligations with the need for future contributions based on changes in the value of plan assets and movements in interest rates. The Company contributed a total of $3.7 million in funding to its pension plans in fiscal 2006 and estimates fiscal 2007 contributions at approximately $1.5 – $2.5 million.

The asset allocation for the Company's U.S. qualified pension plan at the end of 2006 and 2005 and the projection for 2007 are as follows:

| | Percentage of Plan Assets | | |
	2007	2006	2005
Asset Category			
Equity Securities	62%	65%	54%
Debt Securities	38%	35%	40%
Cash	—%	—%	6%

The fair value of plan assets for these plans is $30,260,000 and $29,751,000 as of February 25, 2006 and February 26, 2005, respectively. The expected long-term rate of return on these plan assets was 8.0% in both fiscal 2006 and fiscal 2005. The expected long-term rate of return is estimated using a variety of factors including long-term historical returns, the targeted allocation of plan assets and expectations regarding future market returns for both equity and debt securities. The measurement date for all Topps plans is February 25, 2006.

The following tables summarize benefit costs, benefit obligations, plan assets and the funded status of the Company's U.S. and Ireland pension plans and U.S. postretirement healthcare benefit plan:

	Pension		Postretirement Healthcare	
	February 25,2006	February 26,2005	February 25,2006	February 26,2005
	(in thousands of dollars)			
Change In Benefit Obligation				
Benefit obligation at beginning of year	$ 45,191	$ 39,709	$ 10,569	$ 10,755
Service cost	1,703	1,419	394	305
Interest cost	2,516	2,414	615	568
Benefits paid	(1,779)	(1,462)	(674)	(619)
Actuarial (gains) / losses	1,627	2,786	1,143	(440)
Participants' contributions	28	19	—	—
Foreign currency impact	(574)	306	—	—
Plan amendments	386	—	(1,729)	—
Curtailments	(4,639)	—	—	—
Settlements	(3,520)	—	—	—
Special termination benefits	573	—	309	—
Benefit obligation at end of year	$ 41,512	$ 45,191	$ 10,627	$ 10,569
Change in Plan Assets				
Fair value of plan assets at beginning of year	$ 29,751	$ 25,551	$ —	$ —
Actual return on plan assets	2,571	1,722	—	—
Employer contributions	3,718	3,666	674	619
Benefits paid	(5,299)	(1,462)	(674)	(619)
Participants' contributions	28	19	—	—
Foreign currency impact	(509)	255	—	—
Fair value of plan assets at end of year	$ 30,260	$ 29,751	$ —	$ —

Below are the assumptions for the pension and postretirement healthcare plans as of the end of the fiscal year:

	Pension Plan		Postretirement Healthcare Plan	
	2006	2005	2006	2005
Discount rate	5.7%	5.6%	5.7%	5.6%
Rate of compensation increase	N/A	4.0%	N/A	N/A
Healthcare cost trend on covered charges	N/A	N/A	10.0%, grading to to 5.0% in 2011	10.0%, grading to to 5.0% in 2010

The discount rate and rate of compensation increase for the Ireland Pension Plan are 4.5% and 3.25%, respectively at year end 2006 and at year end 2005.

	Pension		Postretirement Healthcare	
	February 25, 2006	February 26, 2005	February 25, 2006	February 26, 2005
	(in thousands of dollars)			
Funded status				
Funded status at year end	$(11,253)	$(15,440)	$(10,628)	$(10,568)
Unrecognized actuarial losses	9,058	14,599	2,824	1,789
Unamortized prior service cost	360	276	(1,728)	—
Unrecognized initial transition obligation / (asset)	(611)	(744)	1,701	1,900
Accrued benefit cost	$ (2,446)	$ (1,309)	$ (7,831)	$ (6,879)

The total accumulated benefit obligation for all pension plans was $40,747,000 at the end of fiscal 2006 and $40,592,000 at the end of fiscal 2005.

Amounts recognized in the consolidated balance sheets are as follows:

	Pension		Postretirement Healthcare	
	February 25, 2006	February 26, 2005	February 25, 2006	February 26, 2005
	(in thousands of dollars)			
Prepaid benefit cost	$ 4,602	$ 5,353	$ —	$ —
Accrued benefit liability	(16,252)	(16,808)	(7,831)	(6,879)
Intangible asset	—	275	—	—
Accumulated other comprehensive income	9,204	9,871	—	—
Net amount recognized in the consolidated balance sheets	$ (2,446)	$ (1,309)	$(7,831)	$(6,879)

At the end of fiscal 2006 and 2005, the projected benefit obligation, the accumulated benefit obligation and the fair value of pension assets for pension plans with a projected benefit obligation in excess of plan assets and for pension plans with an accumulated benefit obligation in excess of plan assets were as follows:

	Projected Benefit Obligation Exceeds the Fair Value of Plan Assets		Accumulated Benefit Obligation Exceeds the Fair Value of Plan Assets	
	February 25, 2006	February 26, 2005	February 25, 2006	February 26, 2005
	(in thousands of dollars)			
Projected benefit obligation	$36,761	$45,191	$36,761	$40,081
Accumulated benefit obligation	36,761	40,591	36,761	36,429
Fair value of plan assets	$24,943	$29,751	$24,943	$24,851

35

The postretirement medical plan has no assets, and the premiums are paid on an on-going basis. The accumulated postretirement benefit obligation at the end of fiscal 2006 and 2005 was $10,627,000 and $10,568,000, respectively.

The weighted-average assumptions used to calculate net periodic benefit costs are as follows:

	U.S. Pension Plan			Postretirement Healthcare Plan		
	2006	2005	2004	2006	2005	2004
Discount rate	5.6%	6.0%	6.3%	5.6%	6.0%	6.3%
Expected return on plan assets	8.0%	8.0%	8.0%	N/A	N/A	N/A
Rate of compensation increase	4.0%	4.0%	4.5%	N/A	N/A	N/A
Healthcare cost trend on covered charges	N/A	N/A	N/A	10.0%, decreasing to 5.0% in 2010	10.0%, decreasing to 5.0% in 2009	10.0%, decreasing to 5.0% in 2008

The discount rate and rate of compensation increase for the Ireland Pension Plan are 4.5% and 3.3% respectively for 2006, 5.3% and 3.3%, respectively, for 2005 and 5.5% and 3.8%, respectively, for 2004. The expected return on assets for the Ireland Pension Plan was 6.75% for 2006, 7.25% for 2005, and 7.25% for 2004.

The components of net periodic benefit costs are as follows:

	Pension Fiscal Years Ended			Postretirement Healthcare Fiscal Years Ended		
	February 25,2006	February 26,2005	February 28,2004	February 25,2006	February 26,2005	February 28,2004
			(in thousands of dollars)			
Service cost	$ 1,703	$ 1,419	$ 1,384	$ 394	$ 304	$ 283
Interest cost	2,516	2,414	2,390	615	568	602
Expected return on plan assets	(2,239)	(2,096)	(1,451)	—	—	—
Amortization of:						
Initial transition obligation (asset)	(62)	(59)	(51)	199	199	199
Prior service cost	81	132	131	—	—	—
Actuarial losses	1,011	808	1,117	109	—	47
Curtailments, settlements, and special termination benefits	1,842	—	—	309	—	336
Net periodic benefit cost	$ 4,852	$ 2,618	$ 3,520	$1,626	$1,071	$1,467

Prior service cost changes are amortized on a straight-line basis over the average remaining service period for employees active on the date of an amendment. Gains and losses are amortized on a straight-line basis over the average remaining service period of employees active on the valuation date.

Expected employer contributions are between $1,500,000 and $2,500,000 for both the qualified plan and the Ireland plan during the fiscal year ending March 3, 2007.

Expected benefit payments are as follows:

Fiscal year ending	Pension	Postretirement	Federal Subsidy
2007	$ 2,491,000	$ 688,000	$ 83,000
2008	$ 2,960,000	$ 749,000	$ 89,000
2009	$ 3,366,000	$ 820,000	$ 96,000
2010	$ 3,192,000	$ 885,000	$102,000
2011	$ 2,917,000	$ 931,000	$108,000
2012-2016	$14,179,000	$4,499,000	$524,000

The above table includes benefits expected to be paid from Company assets.

Assumed health care cost trend rates have a significant effect on the amounts reported for health care plans. A one percentage point change in assumed health care cost trend rates would have the following effect:

	One Percentage Point	
	Increase	Decrease
	(in thousands of dollars)	
On total service and interest cost component	$ 163	$ (133)
On postretirement benefit obligation	$1,251	$(1,059)

NOTE 14 — STOCK OPTION PLAN

The Company has Stock Option Plans that provide for the granting of non-qualified stock options, incentive stock options and stock appreciation rights (SARs) to employees, non-employee directors and consultants within the meaning of Section 422A of the Internal Revenue Code. Options are granted with an exercise price equal to the closing market price of the stock on the grant date, generally vest within three years and expire ten years after the grant date.

The following table summarizes information about the Stock Option Plans.

	February 25, 2006		February 26, 2005		February 28, 2004	
Stock Options	Shares	Wtd. Avg. Exercise Price	Shares	Wtd. Avg. Exercise Price	Shares	Wtd. Avg. Exercise Price
Outstanding at beginning of year	3,762,919	$7.22	3,800,407	$6.90	3,756,977	$6.73
Granted	60,000	$7.74	262,000	$9.34	890,000	$8.52
Exercised	(261,886)	$5.06	(270,550)	$4.55	(234,680)	$4.85
Forfeited	(146,823)	$9.34	(28,938)	$9.50	(611,890)	$9.01
Outstanding at end of year	3,414,210	$7.30	3,762,919	$7.22	3,800,407	$6.90
Options exercisable at end of year	2,956,624	$7.08	2,973,416	$6.80	2,973,323	$6.44
Weighted average fair value of options granted during the year	$ 2.25		$ 2.99		$ 2.70	

In 2006, of the 146,823 stock options forfeited, 130,498 were unvested options which were lost when employees were terminated from the Company. The remaining 16,325 "forfeited" options were the result of the expiration of options in the normal course. In 2005, the shares forfeited represent those cancelled due to termination of employment; none expired during the year. In 2004, of the 611,890 stock options forfeited, 90,390 were unvested options which were lost when employees were terminated from the Company. The remaining 521,500 "forfeited" options were the result of the expiration of options in the normal course.

Summarized information about stock options outstanding and exercisable at February 25, 2006 is as follows:

	Options Outstanding			Options Exercisable	
Exercise — Price Range	Outstanding as of February 25, 2006	Weighted Average Remaining Contractual Life	Weighted Average Exercise Price	Exercisable as of February 25, 2006	Weighted Average Exercise Price
$1.76-$3.53	673,150	1.9	$ 2.64	673,150	$ 2.64
$3.54-$5.29	416,250	3.0	$ 4.45	416,250	$ 4.45
$5.30-$7.05	96,500	3.3	$ 6.96	96,500	$ 6.96
$7.06-$8.81	1,029,583	6.9	$ 8.27	746,665	$ 8.24
$8.82-$10.57	973,977	6.1	$ 9.84	799,309	$ 9.94
$10.58-$12.34	224,750	4.9	$11.23	224,750	$11.23
	3,414,210	5.0	$ 7.30	2,956,624	$ 7.08

NOTE 15 — CAPITAL STOCK

In October 1999, the Company's Board of Directors authorized the repurchase of up to 5 million shares of the Company's common stock. In October 2001, the Company completed purchases against this authorization and the Company's Board of Directors authorized the repurchase of up to another 5 million shares of the Company's common stock. During fiscal 2004, the Company repurchased 318,800 shares at an average price of $8.69 per share. During fiscal 2005, the Company purchased 444,400 shares at an average price of $9.25 per share.

During the first six months of fiscal 2006, the Company did not purchase any shares due to a strategic business review being performed by investment banking and consulting firms. In September 2005, the Company entered into a written trading plan that complies with Rule 10b5-1 under the Securities and Exchange Act of 1934, as amended, which provides for the purchase of up to 500,000 shares for each of the next four quarters starting in the third quarter of fiscal 2006 at the prevailing market price, per share, subject to certain conditions. In addition, the Board of Directors increased the outstanding share authorization by 3,390,700 shares to 5 million shares. As of February 25, 2006, the Company had purchased 1,027,899 shares under this amended authorization, leaving 3,972,101 shares available for future purchases.

NOTE 16 — DIVIDENDS

On June 26, 2003, the Board of Directors of the Company initiated a regular quarterly cash dividend of $0.04 per share. Four quarterly payments totaling $0.16 per share or $6.5 million were made in fiscal 2006 and 2005, and in 2004, three quarterly payments totaling $0.12 per share, or $4.9 million, were made.

NOTE 17 – LEGAL PROCEEDINGS

In November 2000, the Commission of the European Communities (the "Commission") began an investigation into whether Topps Europe's past distribution arrangements for the sale of Pokemon products complied with European law (the "EU investigation"). On June 17, 2003, the Commission filed a Statement of Objections against The Topps Company, Inc. and its European subsidiaries, therein coming to a preliminary conclusion that these entities infringed Article 81 of the EC treaty during 2000 by preventing parallel trade between member states of the European Union. A hearing in front of the European Commission Tribunal took place on October 23, 2003, and on May 27, 2004, the Commission found The Topps Company, Inc. and its European subsidiaries jointly and severally liable for infringement of Article 81(1) of the EC treaty. The Commission imposed a total fine of 1.6 million euros ($1.9 million) which was recorded as an expense and paid during fiscal 2005.

In another matter, on November 19, 2001 Media Technologies, Inc. sued the Company and nine other manufacturers of trading cards (the "Defendants") in the Federal District Court for the Central District of California for their sales of all types of "relic" cards that contain an authentic piece of equipment, i.e., a piece of sporting equipment or jersey. Plaintiffs alleged infringement of U.S. Patent Nos. 5,803,501 and 6,142,532. On May 23, 2005 the Company entered into a settlement agreement in which it paid Media Technologies, Inc. a sum of $2,000,000 which is being amortized over the term of the contract. Media Technologies Inc. agreed to dismiss all claims against the Company and to issue a license to the Company to distribute relic cards for seven years. The Company further agreed that under certain conditions which may arise in the future, it would make additional payments to Media Technologies, Inc. as part of the ongoing license.

In another matter, in September of 1999, the Company filed a lawsuit against Cadbury Stani S.A.I.C. ("Stani"), a corporation organized and existing under the laws of Argentina, in federal court in the Southern District of New York. The case centers on the licensing relationship the parties had since 1957 in which the Company had granted Stani the exclusive right to manufacture and distribute gum using the Bazooka brand and related formulas and technologies in Argentina, Bolivia, Chile, Paraguay and Uruguay. In particular, at issue is a 1980 Licensing Agreement (the "Agreement") between the parties and a 1985 Amendment to that Agreement. In its September 17, 2003 Fourth Amended complaint, the Company alleges that Stani continued to use the Company's proprietary and specialized knowledge and experience, and its trade secrets, regarding the production of gum after the Agreement's expiration in April 1996, that it unlawfully disclosed this information to Cadbury Schweppes PLC ("Schweppes") which purchased Stani in 1993 and that it deliberately concealed its use and disclosure from the Company. The Company has filed claims for breach of contract, misappropriation of trade secrets and fraudulent inducement to enter into the 1985 Amendment. The Company is seeking to recover disgorgement of Stani's profits, certain lost royalties and punitive damages, interest and costs. It is also seeking a permanent injunction against Stani's future use and dissemination of the Company's proprietary information and trade secrets. In the Fourth Amended Complaint, the Company demanded damages in excess of $250 million. The Fourth Amended Complaint also initially contained claims against Schweppes, which the parties agreed to dismiss on February 4, 2003.

On December 17, 2003, Stani moved for partial summary judgment and to limit the Company's possible damages. In its August 2, 2005 decision, the Court denied Stani's summary judgment motion, in part, and ruled that (i) the Company's claims were not barred by the statute of limitations; and (ii) disgorgement of profits and punitive damages are available remedies on the Company's misappropriation of trade secrets claims. The Court granted Stani's summary judgment motion, in part, and ruled that (i) disgorgement of profits and punitive damages are not available remedies on the Company's breach of contract and fraudulent inducement claims; and (ii) Stani was not estopped from claiming the 1985 Amendment altered the 1980 Agreement.

On February 9, 2006, the Court adjourned the trial which had been scheduled for March 13, 2006 and ruled it would consider a new motion by Stani for partial summary judgment which argues that the Agreement permitted Stani to use the Company's information and trade secrets after the Agreement's expiration in 1996. Oral argument was held on March 15, 2006 and the parties await a decision. If the Company ultimately prevails in this litigation, it could have a material impact on the Company's consolidated financial statements.

In another matter, on December 12, 2003, WizKids, Inc. ("Wizkids") and Jordan Weisman filed a complaint in Washington state court for professional malpractice, breach of fiduciary duty and disgorgement of fees against the law firm Michael, Best & Friedrich, LLP ("MB&F), and Timothy Kelley, one of its partners, based on their submission of a PCT patent application for WizKids' combat dial that alleged to have prejudiced WizKids' United States patent rights by failing to designate the United States as one of the member states for subsequent conversion to a national application. In a settlement reached on October 31, 2005, defendants agreed to pay Wizkids $2,950,000. The Company received the $2,950,000 ($1,833,000 net of legal fees) in the third quarter of fiscal 2006 and has recorded it as a reduction to SG&A.

The Company is a party in several other civil actions which are routine and incidental to its business. In management's opinion, after consultation with legal counsel, these other actions will not have a material adverse effect on the Company's financial condition or results of operations.

NOTE 18 — SEGMENT AND GEOGRAPHIC INFORMATION

Following is the breakdown of industry segments as required by SFAS 131, *Disclosures About Segments of an Enterprise and Related Information.* The Company has two reportable business segments: Confectionery and Entertainment.

The Confectionery segment consists of a variety of candy products including Ring Pop, Push Pop, Baby Bottle Pop, Juicy Drop Pop, the Bazooka bubble gum line and, from time to time, confectionery products based on licensed characters, such as Pokémon and Yu-Gi-Oh!

The Entertainment segment primarily consists of cards and sticker album products featuring sports and non-sports subjects. Trading cards feature players from Major League Baseball, the National Basketball Association, the National Football League as well as characters from popular films, television shows and other entertainment properties. Sticker album products feature players from the English Premier League and characters from entertainment properties such as Pokémon and Yu-Gi-Oh! This segment also includes products from WizKids, a designer and marketer of strategy games acquired in July 2003.

The Company's chief decision-maker regularly evaluates the performance of each segment based upon its contributed margin, which is profit after cost of goods, product development, advertising and promotional costs and obsolescence, but before general and administrative expenses and manufacturing overhead, depreciation and amortization, other income (expense), net interest and income taxes. Beginning in fiscal 2007, segment performance will be evaluated based on contributed margin after direct overhead.

The majority of the Company's assets are shared across both segments, and the Company's chief decision-maker does not evaluate the performance of each segment utilizing asset-based measures. Therefore, the Company does not include a breakdown of assets or depreciation and amortization by segment.

BUSINESS SEGMENTS

	Fiscal Year Ended		
	February 25, 2006	February 26, 2005	February 28, 2004
	(in thousands of dollars)		
NET SALES:			
Candy	$ 134,117	$ 133,214	$ 134,637
Gum	10,144	10,548	12,551
Total Confectionery	144,261	143,762	147,188
Sports	95,376	105,384	107,308
Non-sports	54,201	45,085	40,421
Total Entertainment	149,577	150,469	147,729
Total Net Sales	$ 293,838	$ 294,231	$ 294,917
CONTRIBUTED MARGIN:			
Confectionery	$ 43,842	$ 46,781	$ 45,734
Entertainment	34,983	44,950	42,355
Total Contributed margin	$ 78,825	$ 91,731	$ 88,089
Reconciliation of contributed margin to income before (provision) for income taxes:			
Total contributed margin	$ 78,825	$ 91,731	$ 88,089
Unallocated general and administrative expenses and manufacturing overhead	(76,383)	(73,217)	(66,237)
Depreciation and amortization	(4,754)	(5,833)	(5,675)
(Loss) income from operations	(2,312)	12,681	16,177
Interest income, net	2,912	2,706	2,426
Income before benefit (provision) for income taxes	$ 600	$ 15,387	$ 18,603

Net sales to unaffiliated customers and (Loss) income from operations are based on the location of the ultimate customer (Loss) income from operations is defined as contributed margin less unallocated general and administrative expenses and manufacturing overhead and depreciation and amortization. Certain foreign markets are in part supported from the U.S. and Europe; however, the full cost of this support has not been allocated to them. Identifiable assets are those assets located in each geographic area.

McLane Distribution Services, Inc. ("McLane") accounted for approximately 13% and 12% of consolidated net sales in fiscal 2006 and fiscal 2005, respectively. McLane purchases primarily confectionery products from the Company and distributes them to Wal-Mart, Sam's Club, Southland Corp., and convenience stores in the U.S. The loss of this customer could have a material adverse effect on the Company's results of operations and future plans. The sales to McLane are recorded in the Company's Confectionary segment.

GEOGRAPHIC AREAS

	Fiscal Year Ended		
	February 25, 2006	February 26, 2005	February 28, 2004
		(in thousands of dollars)	
Net Sales:			
United States	$207,834	$ 197,998	$201,181
Europe	61,350	70,252	65,135
Canada, Latin America and Asia	24,654	25,981	28,601
Total Net Sales	$293,838	$ 294,231	$294,917
Income from Operations:			
United States	$ (5,336)	$ 7,029	$ 2,992
Europe	(843)	795	9,535
Canada, Latin America and Asia	3,867	4,857	3,650
Total (Loss) Income from Operations	$ (2,312)	$ 12,681	$ 16,177

	As of February 25, 2006	As of February 26, 2005
Identifiable Assets:		
United States	$ 217,495	$ 236,974
Europe	44,781	47,623
Canada, Latin America and Asia	6,362	5,793
Total Identifiable Assets	$ 268,638	$ 290,390

NOTE 19 – ACQUISITION OF WIZKIDS, LLC

On July 9, 2003, the Company acquired Wizkids, LLC ("WizKids"), a designer and marketer of collectible strategy games, for a cash purchase price of approximately $28.4 million. The intent of the acquisition was to enhance and accelerate the expansion of the Company's entertainment business. The acquisition was accounted for using the purchase method of accounting. The financial statements of WizKids have been consolidated into the financial statements of the Company subsequent to the date of acquisition. The allocation of the purchase price is reflected in the financial statements contained herein.

The total consideration paid by the Company to WizKids' shareholders was comprised of $29,500,000 in cash, net of a working capital adjustment of $1,123,500. The purchase price also reflected a $1,326,130 payment to a third party for associated licenses and legal, accounting, and investment banking fees of $679,075. The purchase price was determined based on discounted cash flow projections, which reflected expected synergies with the Company. The purchase price includes a $6.2 million allocation for intellectual property rights associated with the WizKids product line, which is being amortized over an estimated useful life of 6 years. There were no contingent payments with the purchase price.

Contemporaneous with the acquisition, the Company entered into an employment agreement with Jordan Weisman, the majority shareholder and founder of WizKids, for a forty-eight month period following the closing. As part of this employment agreement, $2 million of the consideration paid to Mr. Weisman as a shareholder is being accounted for as deferred compensation and is being amortized over four years. If Mr. Weisman does not remain a WizKids employee for the full four years of the agreement, he will be required to pay the Company the unamortized balance of his deferred compensation. As an additional part of his employment agreement, Mr. Weisman is entitled to contingent payments during the forty-eight months subsequent to the closing equal to 2% of WizKids' annual net revenue in excess of $35 million, assuming that certain operating margin targets are met. In addition, Mr. Weisman was granted 165,000 options to acquire the Company's common stock, which were granted at fair market value on the date of grant and vest over a four-year period.

The following table sets forth the components of the purchase price:

Total consideration	$29,500,000
Less: Working capital adjustment	(1,123,500)
Deferred compensation agreement	(2,000,000)
Plus: Purchase of license	1,326,130
Transaction costs	679,075
Total purchase price	$28,381,705

The following table provides the fair value of the acquired assets and liabilities assumed based upon WizKids' July 9, 2003 balance sheet:

Current assets	$ 8,201,851
Property and equipment	564,743
Other assets	115,000
Liabilities assumed, current	(5,426,072)
Fair value of net assets acquired	3,455,522
Intangible assets	6,200,000
Goodwill	18,726,183
Total estimated fair value of net assets acquired and goodwill	$28,381,705

The final purchase price differs slightly from the amount shown for Purchase of business in the Consolidated Statement of Cash Flows as of February 28, 2004 which reflects estimated transaction costs.

The goodwill of $18.7 million is included in the Entertainment business segment and is deductible for tax purposes over a fifteen-year period.

The impact of including WizKids in the consolidated statements of operations on a pro forma basis as if the acquisition had occurred on March 3, 2002, is as follows:

	Fiscal Year Ended February 28, 2004 (restated) (amounts in thousands, except share data)
Net sales	$310,726
Income from operations	14,374
Net income	$ 11,773
Net income per share — basic	$ 0.29
— diluted	$ 0.28

NOTE 20 — FAIR VALUE OF FINANCIAL INSTRUMENTS

The carrying value of cash, accounts receivable, accounts payable and accrued liabilities approximates fair value due to their short-term nature.

The Company enters into foreign currency forward contracts to hedge its foreign currency exposure. As of February 25, 2006, the Company had outstanding foreign currency forward contracts, which will mature at various dates during fiscal 2007, in the amount of $20,973,000, as compared to $26,563,000 as of February 26, 2005. Over 62% of the contracts will mature within six months.

The fair value of these forward contracts is the amount the Company would receive or pay to terminate them. The approximate pre-tax benefit or cost to the Company to terminate these agreements as of February 25, 2006 and February 26, 2005 would have been $363,000 and $49,000 respectively. The Company may be exposed to credit losses in the event of non-performance by counterparties to these instruments. Management believes, however, the risk of incurring such losses is remote as the contracts are entered into with major financial institutions.

NOTE 21 – OFF-BALANCE SHEET ARRANGEMENTS

The Company does not have any off-balance sheet arrangements that have, or are reasonably likely to have, a current or future effect on our financial condition, changes in financial condition, revenue or expenses, results of operations, liquidity, capital expenditures or capital resources that is expected to be material.

NOTE 22— QUARTERLY RESULTS OF OPERATIONS (Unaudited)

(in thousands of dollars, except share data)

	Quarter Ended						
	May 28, 2005		Agust 27, 2005		November 26,2005		February 25, 2006
	As Previously Reported (a)	As Restated (b)	As Previously Reported (a)	As Restated (b)	As Previously Reported (a)	As Restated (b)	As reported
Net sales	$78,866	$78,584	$75,277	$74,936	$72,808	$72,808	$67,510
Gross profit on sales	27,674	27,644	28,420	28,376	21,306	21,306	18,458
Income (loss) from continuing operations	397	507	3,285	3,378	(1,300)	(1,300)	(4,897)
(Loss) gain from discontinued operations — net of tax	—	(65)	—	(53)	(3,691)	(3,691)	1,102
Net income (loss)	897	897	4,837	4,837	(3,662)	(3,662)	(833)
Basic net income (loss) per share							
- From continuing operations	$ 0.02	$ 0.02	$ 0.12	$ 0.12	$ —	$ —	$ (0.05)
- After discontinued operations	$ —	$ 0.02	$ —	$ 0.12	$ (0.09)	$ (0.09)	$ (0.02)
Diluted net income (loss) per share							
- From continuing operations	$ 0.02	$ 0.02	$ 0.12	$ 0.12	$ —	$ —	$ (0.05)
- After discontinued operations	$ —	$ 0.02	$ —	$ 0.12	$ (0.09)	$ (0.09)	$ (0.02)

642   Appendix B

	May 29, 2004		August 28, 2004		November 27, 2004		February 26, 2005	
	As Previously Reported (a)	As Restated (b)	As Previously Reported (a)	As Restated (b)	As Previously Reported (a)	As Restated (b)	As Previously Reported (a)	As Restated (b)
Net sales	$ 88,089	$ 87,592	$ 68,781	$ 68,405	$ 70,278	$ 70,278	$ 68,345	$ 67,956
Gross profit on sales	33,799	33,738	26,280	26,192	23,621	23,621	21,459	21,480
Income (loss) from continuing operations	5,639	5,804	4,812	4,964	3,367	3,405	(1,712)	(1,492)
(Loss) gain from discontinued operations— net of tax	—	(76)	—	(66)	(82)	(82)	—	(129)
Net income (loss)	4,102	4,125	3,655	3,677	2,791	2,814	451	299
Basic net income (loss) per share								
- From continuing operations	$ 0.10	$ 0.10	$ 0.09	$ 0.09	$ 0.07	$ 0.07	$ 0.01	$ 0.01
- After discontinued operations	$ —	$ 0.10	$ —	$ 0.09	$ 0.07	$ 0.07	$ 0.01	$ 0.01
Diluted net income (loss) per share								
- From continuing operations	$ 0.10	$ 0.10	$ 0.09	$ 0.09	$ 0.07	$ 0.07	$ 0.01	$ 0.01
- After discontinued operations	$ —	$ 0.10	$ —	$ 0.09	$ 0.07	$ 0.07	$ 0.01	$ 0.01

(a) As previously reported amounts have been reclassified to give effect to the discontinued operations as discussed in Note 7.

(b) See Note 2.

NOTE 23- COMMITMENTS

Future minimum payments under non-cancelable leases are as follows: (in thousands)

Fiscal Year	Amount
2007	$ 2,579
2008	2,247
2009	2,128
2010	1,826
2011	1,284
Thereafter	536
	$10,600

The Company anticipates making payments of approximately $1.5 – $2.5 million in fiscal 2007 for the funding of its qualified pension plans.

Historically, lease expense under the Company's contracts was $3,075,000 (2006), $3,141,000 (2005) and $2,752,000 (2004).

Historically, the total royalty expense under the Company's sports and entertainment licensing contracts was $25,117,000 (2006), $24,916,000 (2005), and $23,912,000 (2004).

NOTE 24- RESTRUCTURING CHARGE

On September 29, 2005, a restructuring program was announced which separates the Confectionery and Entertainment businesses to the extent practical and streamlines the organizational structure through headcount reductions. In connection with the headcount reductions, the Company incurred charges of approximately $3.7 million; $1.3 million for termination costs in each of the third and fourth quarters of fiscal 2006 and $1.1 million for pension settlement costs. These charges are reflected in selling, general and administrative expenses in the Consolidated Statements of Operations for the year ended February 25, 2006. The table below reconciles the activity to the liability related to the restructuring from November 26, 2005 through February 25, 2006 (in thousands):

	November 26, 2005	Payments	Additions	February 25, 2006
Termination costs	$ 1,100	$(1,420)	$ 1,300	$ 980
Pension settlement	—	—	1,050	1,050
	$ 1,100	$(1,420)	$ 2,350	$ 2,030

Management's Report on Internal Control Over Financial Reporting

Management of The Topps Company, Inc. (the "Company") is responsible for establishing and maintaining adequate internal control over financial reporting. The Company's internal control over financial reporting is designed to provide reasonable assurance to the Company's management and to the Board of Directors regarding the preparation and presentation of financial statements in accordance with accounting principles generally accepted in the United States of America.

Internal control over financial reporting, no matter how well designed, has inherent limitations. Therefore, even those internal controls determined to be effective can provide only reasonable assurance with respect to financial statement preparation and presentation.

Management assessed the effectiveness of the internal control over financial reporting as of February 25, 2006. In making this assessment, it used the criteria set forth by the Committee of Sponsoring Organizations of the Treadway Commission (COSO) in *Internal Control — Integrated Framework*. Based on this assessment and those criteria, we believe that, as of February 25, 2006, the Company's internal control over financial reporting was effective.

Deloitte & Touche LLP, the Company's independent registered public accounting firm, has issued an attestation report on management's assessment of the Company's internal control over financial reporting, and its report is included herein.

The Topps Company, Inc.
New York, NY
May 9, 2006

REPORT OF INDEPENDENT REGISTERED PUBLIC ACCOUNTING FIRM

To the Board of Directors and Stockholders of
The Topps Company, Inc.

We have audited the accompanying consolidated balance sheets of The Topps Company, Inc. and its subsidiaries (the "Company") as of February 25, 2006 and February 26, 2005, and the related consolidated statements of operations, stockholders' equity and comprehensive income and cash flows for each of the three fiscal years in the period ended February 25, 2006. These consolidated financial statements are the responsibility of the Company's management. Our responsibility is to express an opinion on these financial statements based on our audits.

We conducted our audits in accordance with the standards of the Public Company Accounting Oversight Board (United States). Those standards require that we plan and perform the audit to obtain reasonable assurance about whether the financial statements are free of material misstatement. An audit includes examining, on a test basis, evidence supporting the amounts and disclosures in the financial statements. An audit also includes assessing the accounting principles used and significant estimates made by management, as well as evaluating the overall financial statement presentation. We believe that our audits provide a reasonable basis for our opinion.

In our opinion, such consolidated financial statements present fairly, in all material respects, the financial position of the Company and its subsidiaries as of February 25, 2006 and February 26, 2005, and the results of their operations and their cash flows for each of the three fiscal years in the period ended February 25, 2006, in conformity with accounting principles generally accepted in the United States of America.

As discussed in Note 2 to the Consolidated Financial Statements, the accompanying consolidated financial statements for fiscal 2005 and 2004 have been restated.

We have also audited, in accordance with the standards of the Public Company Accounting Oversight Board (United States), the effectiveness of the Company's internal control over financial reporting as of February 25, 2006, based on the criteria established in *Internal Control—Integrated Framework* issued by the Committee of Sponsoring Organizations of the Treadway Commission and our report dated May 9, 2006 expressed an unqualified opinion on management's assessment of the effectiveness of the Company's internal control over financial reporting and an unqualified opinion on the effectiveness of the Company's internal control over financial reporting.

New York, New York
May 9, 2006

REPORT OF INDEPENDENT REGISTERED PUBLIC ACCOUNTING FIRM

To the Board of Directors and Stockholders of The Topps Company, Inc.:

We have audited management's assessment, included in the accompanying Management's Report on Internal Control Over Financial Reporting, that The Topps Company, Inc. and its subsidiaries (the "Company") maintained effective internal control over financial reporting as of February 25, 2006, based on criteria established in *Internal Control—Integrated Framework* issued by the Committee of Sponsoring Organizations of the Treadway Commission. The Company's management is responsible for maintaining effective internal control over financial reporting and for its assessment of the effectiveness of internal control over financial reporting. Our responsibility is to express an opinion on management's assessment and an opinion on the effectiveness of the Company's internal control over financial reporting based on our audit.

We conducted our audit in accordance with the standards of the Public Company Accounting Oversight Board (United States) ("PCAOB"). Those standards require that we plan and perform the audit to obtain reasonable assurance about whether effective internal control over financial reporting was maintained in all material respects. Our audit included obtaining an understanding of internal control over financial reporting, evaluating management's assessment, testing and evaluating the design and operating effectiveness of internal control, and performing such other procedures as we considered necessary in the circumstances. We believe that our audit provides a reasonable basis for our opinions.

A company's internal control over financial reporting is a process designed by, or under the supervision of, the company's principal executive and principal financial officers, or persons performing similar functions, and effected by the company's board of directors, management, and other personnel to provide reasonable assurance regarding the reliability of financial reporting and the preparation of financial statements for external purposes in accordance with generally accepted accounting principles. A company's internal control over financial reporting includes those policies and procedures that (1) pertain to the maintenance of records that, in reasonable detail, accurately and fairly reflect the transactions and dispositions of the assets of the company; (2) provide reasonable assurance that transactions are recorded as necessary to permit preparation of financial statements in accordance with generally accepted accounting principles, and that receipts and expenditures of the company are being made only in accordance with authorizations of management and directors of the company; and (3) provide reasonable assurance regarding prevention or timely detection of unauthorized acquisition, use, or disposition of the company's assets that could have a material effect on the financial statements.

Because of the inherent limitations of internal control over financial reporting, including the possibility of collusion or improper management override of controls, material misstatements due to error or fraud may not be prevented or detected on a timely basis. Also, projections of any evaluation of the effectiveness of the internal control over financial reporting to future periods are subject to the risk that the controls may become inadequate because of changes in conditions, or that the degree of compliance with the policies or procedures may deteriorate.

In our opinion, management's assessment that the Company and its subsidiaries maintained effective internal control over financial reporting as of February 25, 2006, is fairly stated, in all material respects, based on the criteria established in *Internal Control—Integrated Framework* issued by the Committee of Sponsoring Organizations of Treadway Commission. Also in our opinion, the Company and its subsidiaries maintained, in all material respects, effective internal control over financial reporting as of February 25, 2006, based on the criteria established in *Internal Control—Integrated Framework* issued by the Committee of Sponsoring Organizations of Treadway Commission.

We have also audited, in accordance with the standards of the PCAOB, the Company's consolidated financial statements as of and for the year ended February 25, 2006 and our report dated May 9, 2006 expressed an unqualified opinion on those consolidated financial statements.

As discussed in Note 2 to the Consolidated Financial Statements, the accompanying Consolidated Financial Statements for fiscal 2005 and 2004 have been restated.

New York, New York
May 9, 2006

Market and Dividend Information

The Company's common stock is traded on the Nasdaq National Market under the symbol *TOPP*. The following table sets forth, for the periods indicated, the high and low stock price for the common stock as reported on the Nasdaq National Market as well as cash dividends per share paid by the Company. As of February 25, 2006, there were approximately 4,200 shareholders of record.

| | Fiscal year ended February 25, 2006 | | | Fiscal year ended February 26, 2005 | | |
| | Stock Price | | Dividends | Stock Price | | Dividends |
	High	Low	Paid	High	Low	Paid
First quarter	$ 9.55	$ 8.47	$ 0.04	$ 9.76	$ 8.40	$ 0.04
Second quarter	$ 10.94	$ 8.97	$ 0.04	$ 10.09	$ 8.82	$ 0.04
Third quarter	$ 10.26	$ 7.11	$ 0.04	$ 10.55	$ 9.23	$ 0.04
Fourth quarter	$ 8.22	$ 6.99	$ 0.04	$ 10.00	$ 9.38	$ 0.04

Selected Consolidated Financial Data

	2006	2005 (1)	2004 (1)	2003 (1)	2002 (1)
			(in thousands of dollars, except share data, unaudited)		
OPERATING DATA:					
Net sales	$ 293,838	$ 294,231	$ 294,917	$ 284,649	$ 296,053
Gross profit on sales	95,784	105,031	103,704	101,684	113,717
Selling, general and administrative expenses	98,096	92,350	87,527	78,801	79,240
(Loss) income from operations	(2,312)	12,681	16,177	22,883	38,403
Interest income, net	2,912	2,706	2,426	2,515	4,892
Loss from discontinued operations — net of tax	(2,707)	(353)	(744)	(1,736)	(1,614)
Net income	$ 1,239	$ 10,915	$ 12,884	$ 16,936	$ 28,462
Basic net income per share					
From continuing operations	$ 0.10	$ 0.28	$ 0.34	$ 0.45	$ 0.70
From discontiinued operations	(0.07)	(0.01)	(0.02)	(0.04)	(0.04)
Basic net income per share	$ 0.03	$ 0.27	$ 0.32	$ 0.41	$ 0.66
Diluted net income per share					
From continuing operations	$ 0.10	$ 0.27	$ 0.33	$ 0.44	$ 0.68
From discontiinued operations	(0.07)	(0.01)	(0.02)	(0.04)	(0.04)
Diluted net income per share	$ 0.03	$ 0.26	$ 0.31	$ 0.40	$ 0.64
Dividends per share	$ 0.16	$ 0.16	$ 0.12	$ —	$ —
Wtd. avg. shares outstanding — basic	40,349,000	40,471,000	40,604,000	41,353,000	43,073,000
Wtd. avg. shares outstanding — diluted	41,163,000	41,327,000	41,515,000	42,065,000	44,276,000
BALANCE SHEET DATA:					
Cash and equivalents	$ 28,174	$ 36,442	$ 56,959	$ 85,684	$ 98,007
Short-term investments	53,269	69,955	36,878	28,575	23,050
Working capital	127,713	139,910	134,099	142,416	137,504
Net property, plant and equipment	11,028	11,968	13,049	13,548	13,102
Total assets	268,638	290,390	275,526	262,875	257,561
Long-term debt	—	—	—	—	—
Stockholders' equity	$ 204,636	$ 219,168	$ 211,340	$ 196,642	$ 193,665

(1) See description of restatement at Note 2 to the Consolidated Financial Statements.

BOARD OF DIRECTORS

Arthur T. Shorin*
Chairman and Chief Executive Officer

Allan A. Feder
Independent Business Consultant

Stephen D. Greenberg
Managing Director
Allen & Company, LLC

Ann Kirschner
President
Comma International

David Mauer
Chief Executive Officer
E&B Giftware, LLC

Edward D. Miller*
Former President and CEO
AXA Financial, Inc.

Jack H. Nusbaum
Partner and Chairman
Willkie Farr & Gallagher, LLP

Richard Tarlow
Chairman
Roberts & Tarlow

_____

*Nominated to stand for re-election to the Company's Board of Directors at the 2006 Annual Meeting of Stockholders.

OFFICERS

Arthur T. Shorin
Chairman and Chief Executive Officer

Scott Silverstein
President and Chief Operating Officer

John Budd
Vice President – Confectionary Marketing

John Buscaglia
Vice President – Entertainment Sales

Michael P. Clancy
Vice President — International and
Managing Director, Topps International Limited

Ira Friedman
Vice President – Publishing and
New Product Development

Warren Friss
Vice President — General
Manager Entertainment

Catherine K. Jessup
Vice President — Chief
Financial Officer and Treasurer

Michael K. Murray
Vice President — Confectionery Sales

William G. O'Connor
Vice President — Administration

Christopher Rodman
Vice President – Topps Europe

SUBSIDIARIES

Topps Argentina SRL
Managing Director -
Juan P. Georgalos

Topps Europe Limited
Managing Director -
Christopher Rodman

Topps Canada, Inc.
General Manager -
Paul Cherrie

Topps Italia SRL
Managing Director -
Furio Cicogna

Topps International Limited
Managing Director -
Michael P. Clancy

WizKids, Inc.
President -
Jordan Weisman

Topps UK Limited
Managing Director -
Martin Tilney

Topps Finance, Inc.

Topps Enterprises, Inc.

CORPORATE INFORMATION

Annual Meeting
Thursday, July 28, 2006
10:30 A.M.
JPMorgan Chase & Co.
270 Park Avenue
New York, NY 10022

Investor Relations
Brod & Schaffer, LLC
230 Park Avenue, Suite 1831
New York, NY 10169
212-750-5800

Corporate Counsel
Willkie Farr & Gallagher,
LLP
787 Seventh Avenue
New York, NY 10019

Independent Auditors
Deloitte & Touche LLP
Two World Financial Center
New York, NY 10281

Registrar and Transfer Agent
American Stock Transfer & Trust Company
59 Maiden Lane
New York, NY 10038
877-777-0800 ext 6820

54

Online Supplements

Connect Plus for Fundamental Financial Accounting Concepts, Seventh Edition

McGraw-Hill Connect™ is a web-based assignment and assessment platform that gives students the means to better connect with their coursework, with their instructors, and with the important concepts that they will need to know for success now and in the future. With Connect, instructors can deliver assignments, quizzes and tests easily online. Students can practice important skills at their own pace and on their own schedule.

GETTING STARTED:

To get started in Connect, you will need the following:

1. Your instructor's unique Connect URL

    Sample of Connect URL
    http://www.mcgrawhillconnect.com/class/instructorname_section_name

2. Connect Access Code

    Using a Print Book? Your access code will appear at the back of the book. Reference your Table of Contents for an exact page number.

    Using an eBook? Once you have purchased your Create eBook, you will automatically have access to Connect. Simply go to your instructor's unique URL and sign in using the username and password you established when accessing your Create eBook.

REGISTRATION AND SIGN IN:

- Go to www.mcgrawhillcreate.com/shop.
- Search for the ISBN and select your book.
- Enter your access code.
- Click on **Sign In** or **Register Now**.
- Enter your email address.
    TIP: If you already have a McGraw-Hill account, you will be asked for your password and will not be required to create a new account.
- Go to your instructor's unique site.
- Sign in using your username and password
- You are now ready to use Connect.

Need Help?
Contact us online: www.mcgrawhillconnect.com/support
Give us a call: 1-800-331-5094

How to access the Online Supplements that accompany your McGraw-Hill Create™ book:

1. Go to https://create.mcgraw-hill.com/shop/
2. Search for the following ISBN: 9780697810380
3. Enter the access code listed below
4. Follow directions to either "Sign in" or "Register"

Note: Access Code is for one use only. If you did not purchase this book new, then the access code below is no longer valid.

Access Code: | **E6GU-HPV9-WWGH-T4KM-GPPY** |

List of **Online Supplements** included in this book:

Connect Plus for Fundamental Financial Accounting Concepts, Seventh Edition

Instructions: To access this product, follow the four simple steps outlined above. Then go to your instructors UNIQUE CONNECT URL. Sign In using the username and password you just created. You will then have access to Connect Plus

http://www.mcgrawhillconnect.com/class/instructorname_section_name